D1238439

1905 in St. Petersburg

Studies of the Harriman Institute, Columbia University

1905

IN

ST. PETERSBURG

LABOR, SOCIETY,
AND REVOLUTION

GERALD D. SURH

1989

STANFORD UNIVERSITY PRESS

STANFORD, CALIFORNIA

Stanford University Press, Stanford, California

© 1989 by the Board of Trustees of the Leland Stanford Junior University

Printed in the United States of America

CIP data appear at the end of the book

Published with the assistance of North Carolina State University

Founded as the Russian Institute in 1946, the W. Averell Harriman Institute
for Advanced Study of the Soviet Union is the oldest research institution
of its kind in the United States. The book series *Studies of the Harriman Institute*,
begun in 1953, helps bring to a wider audience some of the work conducted under
its auspices by professors, degree candidates and visiting fellows. The faculty
of the Institute, without necessarily agreeing with the conclusions reached in these
books, believes their publication will contribute to both scholarship and a greater
public understanding of the Soviet Union.

TO MY MOTHER

Acknowledgments

This book owes its existence to the help of many people, and it is my pleasure to acknowledge the debt. Above all, Reginald E. Zelnik has rendered invaluable aid as friend, critic, and counselor as well as my dissertation supervisor and the most careful reader of the last version of the manuscript. His comments have always been distinguished by their temperate, balanced tone and by the unique insight into my work that his own mastery of Russian labor and urban social history has given him. Reggie's unstinting generosity in all of these capacities is well known by his students and colleagues, and I have been fortunate to count myself among them. Laura Engelstein has also read the manuscript at various stages, and I have greatly benefited from her incisive observations and judicious advice. Leopold H. Haimson and the participants in his seminar on Russian labor history at the Harriman Institute, Columbia University, made it possible for me to compare my work with that of some of the leading contributors to the field, and Leo himself has offered encouragement, advice, and support at every turn.

Several others should be singled out from a much longer list of those who eased and facilitated my work. (As with those just mentioned, none of them bears any responsibility for the book's ideas or conclusions, for which I alone am accountable.) In the Soviet Union scholarly counsel and encouragement were generously offered me by Boris V. Anan'ich, Valerii I. Bovykin, Rafail Sh. Ganelin, and Ura A. Shuster of the Institute of History of the USSR Academy of Sciences. My work in the magnificent research facilities of the USSR was aided immeasurably by the administration and staff of the three archives and three principal libraries I used: the Central State Archive of the

October Revolution (TsGAOR) and the Lenin State Library in Moscow; and the Central State Historical Archive (TsGIA), the Leningrad State Historical Archive (LGIA), the Library of the Academy of Sciences, and the Saltykov-Shchedrin Public Library in Leningrad. I am especially grateful for the kindness and professional skills of Ludmilla E. Selivanova of the Main Archival Administration, Lidiia A. Nikulina and Elena A. Suntsova of LGIA, and the reading room supervisor at TsGAOR whom I knew only as Nina Vasil'evna. In the United States, I wish to thank the Slavic specialists and other personnel at the libraries of the University of California, Berkeley; the Hoover Institution; Columbia University; the University of North Carolina, Chapel Hill; Duke University; and North Carolina State University, Raleigh. Particular thanks are due to the Interlibrary Loan staffs at the first and last of the libraries just named for years of prompt and cheerful assistance; to Hilja Kukk and Marina Tinkoff Utechin (formerly) of the Hoover Library for valuable aid and advice; to Jonathan Sanders (formerly) of the Harriman Institute for his generous assistance; to Dennis Draughon and Dana Kletter, who, in turn, made the maps and the index; and to Peter Kahn and the staff of Stanford University Press, who are responsible for the appearance of the book.

Among the institutions whose support made the completion of this book possible, I would like to thank the International Research and Exchanges Board and its predecessor, the Inter-University Committee on Travel Grants, which made it possible for me to work in the libraries and archives of the USSR; the Center for Slavic and East European Studies of the University of California, Berkeley, for aid long ago rendered but still appreciated; the College of Humanities and Social Sciences, North Carolina State University, for generous research support and timely leaves; and the W. Averell Harriman Institute for Advanced Study of the Soviet Union, Columbia University, where a year as a Senior Fellow provided me with invaluable support and stimulation.

For their friendship and moral support through the many years of the book's gestation, no less gratitude is due to Elena Balashova, Emma Gee, Rose Glickman, Eileen Grampp, Yuji Ichioka, Nicholas Riasanovsky, Kit-Bing Surh, Tom Surh, and Elaine Zelnik. The greatest debt of gratitude is owed my wife, Nelia Berko, who has sacrificed much of her leisure and enjoyment in making my work on the book a part of her life and who has lovingly taken on many of my cares as her own.

G. D. S.

Contents

———◆•◆———

Tables

Preface

The subject of this book is workers in revolution. My intention has been to illuminate the double meaning of the term "revolution" by treating both the manner in which workers acted to change the conditions around them and the process by which they changed their own views and attitudes. The emphasis here is on what was attempted and expressed rather than on what was attained, as the latter would not become clear until a later revolution. Yet, looking back from the early years of the Soviet regime, the 1905 Revolution may be said to have carried the country the greatest part of the way toward the decisive break of 1917. It had mobilized a massive opposition to continued Tsarist rule and made revolution a compelling practical possibility for the first time. It had shattered the belief that the economic and cultural modernization of the country could continue without a significant transformation of the Tsarist regime. The certainty and security of the government's continued monopoly of power was henceforth openly contested and decisively undermined.

Throughout the revolutionary period, the workers of St. Petersburg played an extremely important role, quite out of proportion to their numbers. If in 1905, as in 1917, the capital of the Russian Empire also became the capital of the Russian Revolution, this was due above all to the concentration in the city of the most militant and politically sophisticated labor movement and the most radical and politicized intelligentsia. In 1905 St. Petersburg workers first emerged as a mass labor movement, displaying remarkable political ingenuity and revealing themselves to be the most forceful collective voice in the rising chorus of opposition and revolt. St. Petersburg's long history of underground labor organizing and its substantial background of industrial militancy bore fruit in 1905, when the city led the Empire in the magnitude of strike activity[1] and in organizational initiative and innovation. Practically every category of wage earner eventually took part in the Petersburg strikes, demonstrations, and organizations that began to emerge in January and continued to grow until the application of violent government repression in December.

This book is deliberately and self-consciously revisionist. The interpretation I have given these events has been significantly shaped by a desire to ask questions and explore problems conspicuously absent from Soviet accounts of the prerevolutionary labor movement, which have generally failed or refused to evaluate the political development of the labor movement apart from its relationship to the Social Democratic Party, particularly the Bolshevik faction. At its best, this approach has resulted in accurate and informative monographic work, which nevertheless lacks any conceptualization or inquiry that would contradict or alter Leninist canons.[2] At its worst, it has made the labor movement a branch of Party history, exhibiting a determination to affirm the leadership of the Bolshevik Party among workers at all times, irrespective of the factual record.[3]

This is not to deny that the Social Democratic Party played a major role in the labor movement of 1905. I hope to demonstrate that in the course of that year workers did, on the whole, move significantly closer to the revolutionary parties, particularly to the Social Democrats. The problem with Soviet assertions to this effect is less with their

1. In 1905 some 23 percent of all strikers recorded in the Empire resided in Petersburg province, which was dominated by the capital city. (This figure includes repeat strikers, the number of whom amounted to 4.75 times the number of individual workers who struck at least once in St. Petersburg province. Excluding repeat strikers, St. Petersburg province still accounted for 13.3 percent of workers who struck in the Empire. *Stachki 1905*, Appendix, pp. 2, 5, 103–4. (For the full form of the abbreviation *Stachki 1905*, and of all other abbreviations used in the footnotes, see the list at the start of the Bibliography.)

2. Although Lenin was an acute political observer, whose writings are indispensable to historians of the Russian revolution and labor movement, the codification of his views and their transformation into a litmus test for historiographical orthodoxy within the Soviet historical profession has led to distortion and dullness in Soviet historiography of the period.

3. Generally, rigidly orthodox work was most characteristic of the period of Stalin's dictatorship, while informative but limited work has been more frequent in recent decades. Interesting and professionally valuable labor histories and source materials were published in the 1920's, however, and this study has benefited greatly from the works of that period.

accuracy as such than with the way they are normally demonstrated, i.e., with a narrow investigative scope that avoids complexity and contradictory evidence. An obvious and glaring example of this is the practical exclusion from consideration of the role of Mensheviks and Socialist Revolutionaries in the labor movement, a bias unmitigated by an occasional veiled mention of Mensheviks under the rubric "Social Democrats." This has led to significant distortions of the historical record. In St. Petersburg, for example, the Mensheviks recruited more members in 1905 and exercised greater influence among workers than Bolsheviks; yet, from reading Soviet works one would have no way of ever knowing this, let alone evaluating its meaning. Equally as important for labor history, one cannot gain from Soviet writings a very concrete idea of the historical specificity of workers' lives and consciousness. In Soviet practice, the mentality of actual workers is normally eclipsed by exclusive emphasis on the consciousness ascribed to workers in Marxist theory. The result is a portrait of workers that lacks the specifics of time, place, and culture—the proletariat as a faceless sociological entity. This often brings about the dominance of theory over observed reality, of ascribed over actual consciousness, and renders unnecessary the more authentic historical task of exploring and determining their interrelationship.[4]

In seeking to reconstruct the larger social and political context in which the rapid transformation of the political views of Petersburg workers took place, I have been particularly attentive to the sources and processes of transformation internal to the working class. To this end I have focused much of my attention on the forms of worker autonomy and initiative inside the factory and the shop. Both the urge and the opportunity to press forcefully for an improvement in their working and living conditions came upon Russian workers rapidly and suddenly in 1905, but because of the lagging social and economic development of Imperial Russia, they were in a sense institutionally unprepared. They lacked leaders, organizations, a public press, and those social networks among labor organizers and politicians that facilitated the earliest steps in industrial labor organization in the West. As a result, the massive upheaval of 1905 organized itself with whatever came to hand, throwing into sharp relief the workers' most essential assumptions and beliefs about their collective identity

4. For a discussion of "ascribed" and "actual" consciousness, see Eric Hobsbawm, *Workers: Worlds of Labor* (New York, 1984), pp. 16–17, and Georg Lukacs, *History and Class Consciousness. Studies in Marxist Dialectics*, trans. R. Livingstone (London, 1971), p. 51.

and about the political views and allies appropriate to it. What emerged now were the boundaries and outlines of a new self-awareness that had dimly appeared in earlier strikes and protests, but which in 1905 assumed a definite and unmistakable shape—and nowhere more clearly than in St. Petersburg.

I have also made a special effort to bring to light the interplay between workers and members of the liberal and democratic intelligentsia,[5] people whose role in the revolution and especially in mobilizing workers has been neglected or assumed to be relatively unimportant. Even in Western literature, the politicization of workers in 1905 has been attributed almost exclusively to the organizing activities of the revolutionary parties.[6] Yet an account of the 1905 Revolution and of worker politicization cannot neglect the unique sense of unity workers shared with the liberal intelligentsia as well as with the revolutionary parties. The most interesting part of this—and the most elusive—is the influence the liberal movement had upon the formation of political views and practices among workers. This influence seems to have been greater than the liberals were able to use to their own political advantage, as the mixed record of their actual contact with workers will show, and it may even have been greater than they themselves realized. Nevertheless, I have tried to specify its strengths and dynamics as a feature of the 1905 Revolution not present in later upheavals and not normally assessed.

Apart from all these questions of interpretation, the workers of St. Petersburg constitute a subject of consuming interest, and their story is worth telling for its own sake. As one of the most important locations of militant labor and antigovernment politics throughout the early twentieth century, St. Petersburg usually figures prominently in general accounts of the Russian Revolution. Yet its revolutionary role is rarely assessed in the light of the city's historic and geographic uniqueness.[7] I have tried to do that here, even though such concerns

5. For brevity, "liberals and democrats" will normally be referred to simply as "liberals." The meaning of this terminology will be clarified in Chapter 3.

6. E.g., J. L. H. Keep, *The Rise of Social Democracy in Russia* or Harcave, *First Blood. The Russian Revolution of 1905*. Some more recent works that have begun to break new ground and to restore some of the original complexity to accounts of 1905 include Engelstein, *Moscow, 1905*; Bushnell, *Mutiny amid Repression*, and Robert Edelman, *Proletarian Peasants. The Revolution of 1905 in Russia's Southwest* (Ithaca, N.Y., 1987). A new work on a more general plane, which still manages to bring more sophistication to this problem, is Abraham Ascher, *The Revolution of 1905. Russia in Disarray* (Stanford, Calif., 1988).

7. The great exception to this is Zelnik, *Labor and Society in Tsarist Russia*, which, though set in the 1860's, constitutes a valuable model for local labor studies in later pe-

are eventually crowded off the canvas by the rush of revolutionary events. My intention has been to write about labor in a specific locale, and my findings are meant to apply only to St. Petersburg's workers, even though I have at times not resisted suggesting a wider relevance when that has seemed appropriate.[8]

---

riods as well. Cf. Smith, *Red Petrograd*, and David Mandel, *The Petrograd Workers and the Fall of the Old Regime. From the February Revolution to the July Days, 1917* (New York, 1983) and *The Petrograd Workers and the Soviet Seizure of Power. From the July Days 1917 to July 1918* (New York, 1984), which place somewhat more emphasis on the features of the labor force than on location and context.

8. Valuable local studies of the 1905 Revolution are slowly beginning to appear. See e.g., Engelstein, *Moscow, 1905*; Robert Weinberg, "Social Democracy and Workers in Odessa. Ethnic and Political Considerations," *The Carl Beck Papers in Russian and East European Studies*, No. 504 (Pittsburgh, 1986); Kathleen Prevo, "Voronezh in 1905: Workers and Politics in a Provincial City," *Russian History*, 12, no. 1 (Spring 1985), pp. 48–70; and Rex A. Wade and Scott J. Seregny, *Politics and Society in Provincial Russia: Saratov, 1590–1917* (forthcoming, 1989).

Map 1 St. Petersburg in 1905 (see key below)

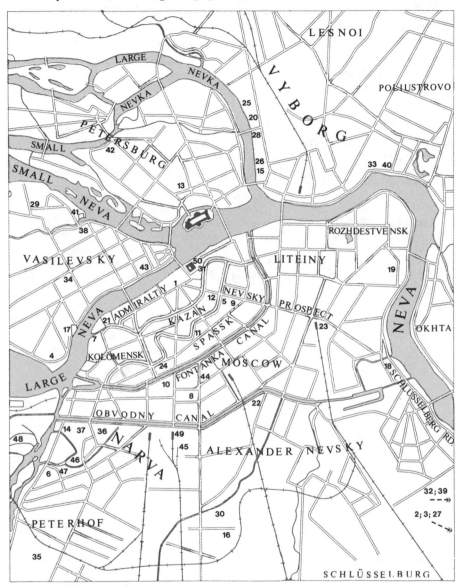

Key to Map 1: Factories and Points of Interest

1. Aleksandrovsk Garden
2. Aleksandrovsk Machine Works
3. Atlas Iron & Copper Foundry & Machine Plant
4. Baltic Shipyards
5. City Duma
6. Ekaterinhof Spinnery
7. Franco-Russian Machine Building Works
8. Free Economic Society
9. Gostinyi Dvor
10. Government Stationers
11. Haymarket (*Sennoi rynok*)
12. Kazan Cathedral and Square
13. Kirchner Bindery
14. L. L. König Spinnery
15. Lessner Machine Works
16. Mechanized Shoe Factory
17. Nail Plant
18. Nevsky Shipbuilding and Machine Works
19. Nevsky Spinnery
20. Nevsky Thread Factory ("Nevka")
21. New Admiralty Shipyards
22. New Spinnery
23. Nikolaev Railroad Station
24. Nikol'skii Market
25. Nikol'sk Weaving Factory

Map 2 City District and Subdistrict Boundaries

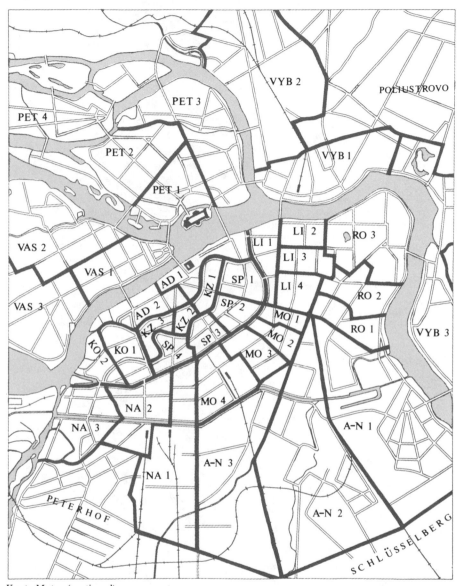

Key to Map 1 (continued)

26. Nobel' Plant
27. Obukhov Steel Mill
28. Old Sampson Spinning and Weaving Factory
29. Osipov Leather Works
30. Ozoling Machine Plant
31. Palace Square
32. Paul Factory
33. Phoenix Machine Construction Works
34. Possel' Horseshoe Works
35. Putilov Plant or Works
36. Russian-American Rubber Factory
37. Russian Spinnery
38. Siemens & Halske Electric Works

39. Spassk & Petrovsk Cotton Mills
40. St. Petersburg Metal Works
41. St. Petersburg Pipe Plant
42. St. Petersburg Rolling & Wire Mill
43. St. Petersburg University
44. Technological Institute
45. Train Car Construction Plant
46. Triumphal Arch (Narva Gates)
47. Triumphal Spinnery
48. Voronin, Liutsh & Cheshire Weaving Factory
49. Warsaw Railroad Station
50. Winter Palace

1905 in St. Petersburg

CHAPTER ONE

The City and the Workers

———◆•◆———

St. Petersburg is probably better remembered for the elegance of its imperial past than for the suffering and triumphs of its workers. The glitter of the court, the stunning architectural ensemble of the city, the presence of foreign embassies and merchants, and an artistic and cultural life of world stature all but concealed from the eyes of the privileged the increasingly squalid reality in which the great bulk of *peterburzhtsy* were immersed. If Russia's backwardness was symbolized by the peasant and the village, in contrast to which the monarchy, the gentry, and educated society defined themselves, then St. Petersburg was the leading symbol of culture and civilization as opposed to the "dark masses." Those who sought education and high culture came to Petersburg, and those who came there for other reasons were shaped anew by the city's conspicuous involvement in science, the arts, publishing, commerce, and higher learning. The very appearance of St. Petersburg was a forceful statement of its high purpose. The stately elegance of the city's center and riverfront, the generous proportions of its public spaces, the restrained, sculpted delicacy of its stone and ironwork bespoke a dignity and refinement that locked visitor and settler alike in a spiritual embrace that both elevated and transformed.

Yet the city was from its inception a site of intense labor exploitation, worsened by severe climatic conditions and the frequent onset of disease. In the very construction of the city between 1703 and 1721, thousands of workmen, mostly conscripts and forced laborers, perished from the poor rations and severe conditions.[1] The imperial

1. L. N. Semenov, "Masterovye i rabotnye liudi v pervye desiatiletiia sushchestvovaniia Peterburga," *Istoriia rabochikh Leningrada* (L., 1972), vol. 1, pp. 26–28, 31–32, 36, 44. V. Mavrodin, *Osnovanie Peterburga* (2d ed., L., 1983), pp. 83–85.

capital was built on the lowest point of the Neva River delta, and flooding has been a regular, if not annual, occurrence. The mean January temperature of the city was measured in 1914 at −9.3 degrees C. (+16 F.), and it has been estimated that only 36 days per year are completely clear, and only six without wind. Epidemics of cholera, typhus, diphtheria, and scarlet fever visited the city regularly until well after the establishment of Soviet power.[2]

Peter I, the city's founder, gave a decisive start to Petersburg's importance as an industrial center by making it the prime location of state or state-chartered factories producing war matériel—ships, weapons, munitions, and uniforms—as well as building materials, luxury goods, and paper.[3] Petersburg's position as Russia's chief entrepôt for European commerce, ideas, and cultural influence shaped and sustained this industrial preeminence. The city's dominance of foreign trade peaked in 1825, but even in the 1860's a quarter of Russia's exports and three-eighths of its imports passed through the capital's port.[4] The leading merchants and entrepreneurs of the capital thus developed a dependence on both a foreign trading presence and government protection against foreign competition that set them apart from their colleagues elsewhere in Russia. Yet, Alfred Rieber writes, this dependence on the government also "nourished a passivity toward state authority equal to that displayed by their provincial brethren," oriented toward a domestic market. As a result of both their passivity and their separateness of interest, "the St. Petersburg merchants failed to emerge as the champions of a strongly self-conscious Russian bourgeoisie."[5]

2. N. S. Dorovatovskii, "Geograficheskii i klimaticheskii ocherk Peterburga," in *Peterburg i ego zhizn'*, pp. 7–10, 12–13. Karl Baedeker, *Russland. . . . Handbuch für Reisende* (7th ed., Leipzig, 1912), p. 99. Bater, *St. Petersburg. Industrialization and Change*, pp. 344–47. This chapter is much indebted to Bater's weighty and informative study.

3. A. E. Suknovalov, "Ekonomicheskaia zhizn' Peterburga do 60–kh godov XVIII veka," in *Ocherki istorii Leningrada*, vol. 1, pp. 72–77. Iatsunskii, "Rol' Peterburga v promyshlennom razvitii dorevoliutsionnoi Rossii." For a concise and thoughtful discussion of industry and labor in St. Petersburg before the 1860's, see Zelnik, *Labor and Society in Tsarist Russia. The Factory Workers of St. Petersburg, 1855–1870*, chap. 2. This chapter has benefited greatly from Zelnik's masterful and pioneering study of the capital's workers, which is also a thoroughgoing account of government policy toward factory industry and the urban lower classes in the mid-nineteenth century.

4. Bater, *St. Petersburg*, p. 298.

5. Rieber, *Merchants and Entrepreneurs in Imperial Russia*, pp. 21–22. See also Bater, *St. Petersburg*, pp. 369–70. For a more nuanced view of both the St. Petersburg entrepreneurs and how they compared with those of Moscow, see Bater, *St. Petersburg*, pp. 250–55, and Victoria A. P. King, "The Emergence of the St. Petersburg Indus-

The close proximity of the court and government attracted foreign, as well as Russian, residents and investors, helping to make Petersburg a banking and commercial center from the time of Catherine II. Yet in Petersburg, as in Russia as a whole, commercial and industrial life were always overshadowed by the life of the court and the bureaucracy. The municipal authority was a gift of the autocracy rather than the institutionalized assertion of real indigenous urban power and influence, and its weakness contributed to the failure of the Petersburg merchantry and, later, capitalist bourgeoisie to develop as a strong and influential class. This dominance of local urban society by the state played out on a smaller and more intensive scale the central drama of Russian history as a whole.

The unusually large European presence in the capital made for a cosmopolitanism and openness to Westerners that has remained part of the city's identity ever since, and this attitude facilitated absorption of the latest technical, scientific, and cultural developments from abroad. Petersburg emerged as a cotton textile center as early as the 1830's, aided by imported machinery, foreign technicians, and American raw cotton. The growth of this industry promoted the application of machinery and the use of hired wage labor in St. Petersburg to a much greater extent than in any other Russian city, and at a time when serfdom was still the dominant system of labor. Seaborne access to foreign coal and iron ore, as well as to foreign technicians, entrepreneurs, and skilled workers, made possible the development of metal-processing and machine-building industries in Petersburg well before the construction of an internal transportation network gave the city access to Russia's richest indigenous stores of these resources.[6]

From the beginning, the city developed a large working population whose character took shape along the fault line that divided the cultures of the country and the city. Together with the high concentration of hired wage labor, there also existed in Petersburg, in the pre-Reform period, a great many laborers working under various forms of compulsion—possessional serfs working in factories owned by nobles, military conscripts and state peasants working in the govern-

---

trialist Community, 1870 to 1905: The Origins and Early Years of the St. Petersburg Society of Manufacturers" (Ph.D. diss., U.C. Berkeley, 1982), pp. 112–19.

6. Tugan-Baranovskii, *Russkaia Fabrika*, pp. 69–74. William L. Blackwell, *The Beginnings of Russian Industrialization, 1800–1860* (Princeton, N.J., 1968), pp. 46–47, 68. Stolpianskii, *Zhizn' i byt peterburgskoi fabriki za 210 let ee sushchestvovaniia 1704–1914 gg.*, pp. 133–47.

ment-owned plants, and skilled workers imported under contract. In the wake of the Serf Emancipation, thousands were freed in a number of special decrees affecting the great shipyards of the Naval Ministry, the armaments and explosives works, and other large-scale state enterprises. These industrial serfs were transformed into wage laborers, but as their actual situations often did not change very much, it is not surprising that "the survivals of serfdom told in their [moral and material] condition for a long time yet," as even a Soviet historian notes.[7]

This legacy survived in the factories of the early twentieth century, state and private. It took the form of management paternalism and favoritism, integrated living and working arrangements, and an expectation of obedience to the workshop master or factory management so strict and unquestioning that infractions were treated as violations not only of the labor contract, but of the very law of the land. It could be said that, like the former serfs themselves, the Russian workers did not complete their liberation until 1905.

In addition to the powerful legacies of serfdom in industrial Petersburg, the city always had a sizable contingent of foreign and non-Russian workers, beginning with the first skilled artisans brought by Peter I to build the city and staff his state factories. From that time on, skilled and specialized workers from Western and Central Europe were a small but permanent presence. Far more numerous were the ethnic Germans, Poles, Finns, Jews, and Estonians from among the subject nationalities of the Russian Empire.[8] The presence of a significant minority of non-Russians introduced into the factories a kind of familiarity with strangers that could temper the often strong distrust of outsiders characteristic of the isolated villagers of the preindustrial countryside, and this gave Petersburg workers their own kind of cosmopolitanism.[9]

7. I. A. Baklanova, "Formirovanie i polozhenie promyshlennogo proletariata. Rabochee dvizhenie (60-e gody–nachalo 90-kh godov)," *Istoriia rabochikh Leningrada*, vol. 1, p. 127. See also Zelnik, *Labor and Society*, pp. 259–63. The less skilled workers at the Government Stationers in the pre-Reform period were drawn from serfs, soldiers' sons, pupils from the orphans' home, and ex-soldiers. LGIA, Fond 1458, opis' 2, delo 888, listok 19 ob.

8. In 1900, 85.8 percent of the city's population was Russian, Belorussian, or Ukrainian. Of the remainder, the five groups mentioned constituted 11.1 percent. ("Jews" were and are considered a nationality in Russia.) Iukhneva, *Etnicheskii sostav i etnosotsial'naia struktura naseleniia Peterburga*, p. 24.

9. See, for example, Aleksei Buzinov's sharply drawn sketch of the Germans who worked at his plant. Buzinov described the source of enmity between the German and

From the mid-nineteenth century on, however, the radical separation of St. Petersburg and peasant Russia began to be bridged in a manner already familiar in the West. In the post-Emancipation era, the Russian intelligentsia actively took up the cause of the country's neglected and benighted majority. In the 1860's and 1870's the students of St. Petersburg, responding to both the promise and the disappointments of the Reform era, organized projects of popular education and revolutionary conspiracy that sought to lead the newly emancipated serfs to both enlightenment and revolt. This Populist movement was paralleled in educated society as a whole by an unconcealed, if often ambivalent, sympathy for the young revolutionaries and by a new political sensibility apparent in the committed realism and utilitarianism in art that took such a powerful hold of educated Russia until the end of the old regime.

Modernization and industrialization under government sponsorship during the second half of the nineteenth century created serious dilemmas that eventually made a popular revolution possible and even likely. St. Petersburg, home of the largest and most politically attuned factory population and of some of the most prominent revolutionary organizations and leaders, became the locale where these contradictions developed most clearly and sharply. Populist agitation among students in the 1860's developed during the ensuing decades into an increasingly sophisticated movement, which eventually produced groups of professional revolutionaries drawn from university students and other offspring of the new urban, industrial, secular society growing up in the interstices of the most poorly governed, brutal, and oppressive military monarchy in Europe. Despite their need to work underground, these revolutionaries had nonetheless succeeded, by the 1880's, in organizing a more or less continuous series of groups or "circles" of educated leaders among industrial workers in Petersburg.[10]

In these same decades a liberal reform movement took shape among educated professionals, whose numbers were now significantly

---

Russian workers, but also acknowledged the Germans' enterprising ways and group cohesiveness. *Za nevskoi zastavoi. Zapiski rabochego*, pp. 27–28.

10. Zelnik, *Labor and Society*, chaps. 6, 9; Zelnik, "Populists and Workers. The First Encounter between Populist Students and Industrial Workers in St. Petersburg, 1871–74." Pearl, "Revolutionaries and Workers: A Study of Revolutionary Propaganda Among Russian Workers, 1880–1892." Nikitin, *Pervye rabochie soiuzy i sotsialdemokraticheskie organizatsii v Rossii (70–80 gg. XIX veka)*. McKinsey, "From City Workers to Peasantry: The Beginning of the Russian Movement 'To the People'."

augmented as a result of Russia's modernization. They mixed with the more progressive and better-educated members of the landed gentry to form a new, moderate and progressive political elite, which played a role out of proportion to its actual strength, owing to Russia's hitherto small and weak middle class. But in the last six decades of the Old Regime this weakness was not as apparent as it would be later, and the gentry-intelligentsia elite of culture and the free professions, combining between them both traditional and modern forms of authority, constituted for many not only the most highly visible leadership of the anti-Tsarist opposition, but the harbinger of bourgeois class rule as well.

Finally, in the two decades before 1900, the factory workers of St. Petersburg grew into the largest and most highly politicized industrial labor force in the country, unmatched in its immersion in urban values, toughened by its proximity to and frequent encounters with the repressive organs of the state, and schooled by long exposure to revolutionary ideas and organization. The potential for explosive and sustained revolt that these conditions contained would not become fully known, to the wider world or to the workers themselves, until 1905, when the labor movement proved to be the decisive part of the revolutionary alliance because it alone was capable of translating into action the revolutionary strategies of the intelligentsia. The liberal and socialist intelligentsia consequently remained limited in its ability to effect change until it linked up with the labor movement. But the labor movement would not have taken on such large proportions in national politics in so short a time had it not reached an awareness of its own strength within or in association with a movement of political opposition largely created by the intelligentsia.

WORKERS AND THE WORKING CLASS

A problem arises when one tries to define "the working class" as a historical concept, as opposed to a simple catalog of occupations. When historians speak of a working class, they most often have in mind working people acting in pursuit of their own interest. But the concept of class interest invariably involves judgments of value. Since historians cannot avoid this problem, their usual response has been to study the ways in which the workers, through their actions, have defined their own class interests. When this self-definition takes place over an extended period, as it has in the case of most European countries, then it must be treated as a process, and it is relatively difficult at any point along the way to specify just which groups have developed a self-consciousness about their interests and which have not.[11]

In the case of Russian workers, it is somewhat easier to specify just when a working class may be said to have arisen; although a process of gradual development had been under way for decades, workers made such a large leap in 1905 that many years of progress under non-revolutionary conditions were telescoped into a single year. Before 1905, workers' awareness of their collective strength as a factor in national political life was uneven at best and undeveloped overall. After 1905, however, Russian workers' sense of their power, in all but the sleepiest locales and trades, was an established fact. Earlier, the relative newness and rootlessness of Russian workers conspired with the government's repression of the labor movement to deprive most of them of the means to act together or of even an awareness of common aims. The breach of state authority in 1905 made possible an explosion of strikes and protests greater than any seen before or since in Russia, an upheaval that finally forced the government's hand and educated an entire generation of workers in the ways state and society conspired to insure their deprivation and their obedience. At the same time, the existence of fully developed liberal and socialist opposition movements and parties drew this outpouring of proletarian energy in a direction that gave a high political profile to the workers' dramatic self-definition of their class interest.

In setting out a definition of the Russian working class, therefore, the experience of 1905 is a ready guide. What this experience shows for St. Petersburg is that the factory proletariat was on the whole more active than other categories of workers and usually set the example and led the way for them; but the scope of the labor movement included practically every category of worker, seeking improvement in trade or shop or office and very often in the country's political arrangements as well. Indeed, the hallmark of the labor movement in Petersburg and in Russia in 1905 was the general strike of October, in which virtually every category of worker and citizen took part, a strike that came not as a flash of anger, but as the culmination of over a year of oppositional agitation. Hence, although some would prefer to confine the working class to factory workers alone, the study of their self-definition as a class calls for as all-inclusive a formula as possible.

In existing sources and literature on Russian labor, two types of definitions have been put forth, a larger and a smaller variant. The

11. Thompson, *The Making of the English Working Class*. The treatment of workers in this book illustrates the point.

smaller variant seeks to confine itself to factory workers, although even here disagreements arise.[12] In 1905 the Factory Inspectorate found only 149,811 workers in the factories of St. Petersburg province.[13] Since many more workers were mobilized and active in the strikes and demonstrations of 1905, it is clear that this figure considerably understates the breadth and variety of the working class that will concern us here.[14] It is nevertheless true that, on the whole, factory workers generally, and especially certain leading trades and skilled categories among them, may be said to have played a vanguard role in the labor movement in 1905 and throughout the revolutionary era. Their larger numbers, greater concentration, and even the enforced discipline of the factory regimen gave them the means to wage sometimes successful struggles with their employers that other categories of workers lacked. They developed a solidarity and momentum of their own that found special expression in some of the signal events and organizations of 1905; their strikes and militancy served as a spur to the entire opposition movement. Labor activism and the development of working-class consciousness in 1905 were certainly not confined to factory workers, but they constituted the working class's cohesive and influential core.

The larger variant is usually constructed from national and urban census data, which by their completeness make possible a much more precise tabulation of occupations and promote the formulation of broader definitions. Students of the St. Petersburg population are

12. This definition relies directly or indirectly on the Factory Inspectorate's twelve categories of factory labor: five categories of textiles, metal and machinery, printing and paper, food, and the manufacture of products from wood, minerals, animals, and chemicals. The Factory Inspectorate recorded a number of key features of working-class life, including strikes and wages, and its systematically compiled data are also often our sole source of information, providing an indispensable resource in all studies of Russian labor, including this one. This makes it all the more important to bear in mind these data's shortcomings: they normally omitted workers in state factories, those in workshops having fewer than 16 workers, and those in factories subject to the excise tax, such as breweries and distilleries. Their totals therefore do not represent a wholly satisfying count of even factory workers. The omission of state factories is particularly significant for St. Petersburg, where about 36,000 workers were employed in them around 1905.

13. *Svod otchetov fabrichnykh inspektorov za 1905 g.*, (Spb., 1908), pp. 44–45.

14. Some authors have sought to overcome the omissions of the Inspectorate's data by supplementing them with data from other sources. See, for example, Pogozhev, *Uchet, chislennost' i sostav rabochikh v Rossii*, and, more satisfactorily, Semanov, *Peterburgskie rabochie nakanune pervoi russkoi revoliutsii*, chap. 1, which, by a circuitous but learned route, arrived at the estimate of 250,000–260,000 factory workers in 1905.

blessed with the existence of city censuses for 1869, 1881, 1890, 1900, and 1910. In analyzing the occupational makeup of the population, these censuses employed the rubric "Workers," along with three others, "Proprietors," "Administration" (white-collar personnel), and "Loners" (*odinochki*, or self-employed workers and tradesmen). Moreover, the city censuses also enumerated the family dependents for each of these categories and even the servants (*prisluga*) attached to households headed by persons in the four categories.[15] According to the 1900 St. Petersburg census, there were 442,353 "workers" in the city and suburbs.[16] This figure included 251,678 people classified as factory workers and 190,675 classified as non-factory workers, including workers in construction, transportation, service trades, public

15. The *odinochka* has never been clearly defined in the censuses, but the term seems to have designated an isolated, self-employed person. Gogol's tailor, Petrovich, who made the new overcoat for Akaki Akakievich, working out of his own apartment and dealing directly with his customers, was clearly an *odinochka*. Indeed, 25 percent of the 69,234 *odinochki* appearing in the 1900 city census were classified as part of a group called "Clothing and Shoes," so the lone tailor or cobbler was a fairly typical representative of the group. Bernshtein-Kogan, *Chislennost'*, pp. 15–19, 90–94, 106. *Peterburg, 1881*, tom 1, chast' 2, p. 6. *Peterburg, 1900*, vyp. 2, pp. 68–69, 92. Otherwise, loners were rare among factory workers, and most of the rest were to be found in service and commercial trades and among unskilled day laborers (28 percent, the largest single group of loners). Their class position would have been ambiguous at best, since some were proprietors rather than workers.

In 1900, 99,079 *prisluga* were counted in St. Petersburg, of whom 90,128 were women. The vast majority were probably employed as domestics, yet a certain number seem to have been employed in industrial enterprises, probably smaller shops in which patriarchal arrangements still prevailed and the modern worker had not yet become distinct from the domestic servant and nonfamily household dependent. Bernshtein-Kogan, *Chislennost'*, p. 1. *Peterburg, 1900*, vyp. 2, pp. 87, 89, 91, 93, 99, 101, 105.

I have excluded *odinochki* and *prisluga* from the figures for the "working class," but this exclusion should not imply firm and unambiguous boundaries to our understanding of the working class; on the contrary, it is a reminder of the impossibility of establishing such boundaries. The omission of *prisluga* affects one other important index of labor demography in Petersburg: the percentage of women in the work force. As noted above, women made up 15–17 percent of workers around 1900. This proportion held true not only for factory workers or the more inclusive definitions of the class drawn from the city censuses (the larger and smaller variants) in Petersburg, but also for the percentage of women workers commonly given for the Empire as a whole in these years (14–18 percent). *Peterburg, 1900*, vyp. 2, p. 218; Bernshtein-Kogan, *Chislennost'*, p. 32; Kutsentov, "Naselenie Peterburga," pp. 176, 188; Semanov, *Peterburgskie rabochie*, p. 25. But if *prisluga* are added, women constituted some 32 percent of the resulting composite work force. Rashin, *Formirovanie*, p. 243; Glickman, *Russian Factory Women*, pp. 60–61.

16. *Peterburg, 1900*, vyp. 2, p. 90.

utilities, and commerce. These 442,353 workers lived with another
198,399 family members, making a population bloc that might be
considered a "working class" of 640,752 people, or 45 percent of St.
Petersburg's population in 1900.

The labor movement that arose in 1905 overflowed the boundaries
set by factory occupation. In the course of the year workers of every
imaginable occupation mobilized to advance or defend their working
and living situations, albeit with widely varying degrees of thorough-
ness and success. Hence, as a representation of the *types* rather than
the exact number of workers in the city who actually evinced an
awareness of their industrial and political subjugation by their willingness to struggle against it, the figure of 442,353 will be used in the
tables here whenever possible, with due allowance for the crudeness
and necessary imprecision of such a figure.[17]

MIGRATION AND URBANIZATION

This mass of industrial workers and other working people of St.
Petersburg represented the largest such concentration in urban Russia. More importantly, the Petersburg working class was growing
faster than that of any other urban area: by 82 percent from 1881 to
1900, compared to 51 percent for Moscow in a similar period.[18] Along
with the greatest number of workers, therefore, Petersburg also contained the largest concentration of *new* workers.

Workers were drawn principally from two estates or *sosloviia*, the
peasantry and the petty bourgeoisie (*meshchanstvo*). The latter numbered 275,122 in 1900, or 19.1 percent of the urban population,

17. Unfortunately, it will not be possible to discuss this larger working class in a balanced fashion, for when it comes to sources, far more information is available about
factory workers than others. The larger variant is, however, used in Bernshtein-Kogan's
critical and well-informed study *Chislennost', sostav i polozhenie peterburgskikh rabochikh.
Opyt statisticheskago issledovaniia*, although Kogan omits unskilled day laborers, while I
have included them. Although precise numbers will be used in the text and in tables,
the precision is, as stated, illusory. One small example of this: Occupational Group 18
of the 1900 St. Petersburg census listed 29,703 industrial workers (6.7 percent) whose
exact occupations were *unknown*. Finally, changes in working-class composition between 1900 and 1905 are difficult to gauge, since the data are incomplete. Except where
otherwise noted, no demographic novelties seem to have appeared, and the major
trends under way in the 1890's are assumed to have continued into the first half-decade
of the twentieth century.

18. Rashin, *Formirovanie*, pp. 113, 114. Moscow province contained more workers
than St. Petersburg province, but the city of Moscow had fewer workers than the capital city.

TABLE 1
Workers and Peasants in the St. Petersburg Population, 1869–1914

Year	Total population	Workers		Peasants	
		No.	Pct.	No.	Pct.
1869	718,000	–	–	207,000	31.0%
1881	928,000	243,300	26.2%	389,900	42.0
1900	1,439,600	442,300	30.7	908,800	63.1
1910	1,905,600	504,000	26.4	1,310,400	68.8
1914	2,217,500	654,700[a]	29.5	–	–

[a] 1913 figure.

SOURCES: Rashin, *Formirovanie*, pp. 113, 354, 437, 513; Rashin, *Naselenie Rossii za 100 let*, p. 129. Kutsentov, "Naselenie Peterburga," p. 178; Kruze and Kutsentov, "Naselenie Peterburga," pp. 113–14; Bernshtein-Kogan, *Chislennost'*, p. 72.

NOTE: The total population figure for 1869 includes 50,000 suburban residents, as estimated by Bater in *St. Petersburg* (p. 160, n. 8); however, the 1869 figure for peasants excludes the suburban population. All the 1890 figures exclude the suburbs and have been omitted.

which represented a rise of less than 3 percent since 1862. However, a much larger part of the *meshchane* than of peasants was born in Petersburg (over one-half in 1910). They were more urbanized and better represented among the skilled occupations, although their exact percentage in the working class can only be estimated. One study indicates that their proportions among factory workers was somewhat below that in the population as a whole.[19]

By contrast, the peasant population of the city increased by 518,000 between 1881 and 1900; and from 1900 to 1910 it grew by another 401,600. During this three-decade period the proportion of peasants in the city's population rose from 42 to 63 to 69 percent (see Table 1), and this made the peasantry, together with the *meshchanstvo*, the only registered estate to increase its share of the population in these years.

Most of this population expansion was due to migration to the capital from other provinces. During the decade 1900–1910 the excess of births over deaths in the whole city came to only 85,834, and there would have been even fewer in the late nineteenth century, as the population base for births was smaller, and the birthrate began to exceed the death rate only in 1885. The attraction of the capital's industry in the two decades before 1900 greatly increased the peasant

19. Kutsentov, "Naselenie Peterburga," pp. 178–79, where the 1900 figure is described as "petty bourgeois and artisans" (*meshchane i tsekhovye*). A comparable group made up only 16.75 percent of skilled workers at the Baltic Shipyard in 1901, and its proportion of unskilled workers would have been even smaller. Blek, ed., "Usloviia truda rabochikh na peterburgskikh zavodakh po dannym 1901 goda," p. 80.

population of the city, which was the terminus of one of Russia's most popular and frequently taken treks in search of work. In 1900, over two-thirds of St. Petersburg's population was born outside the city, and over 80 percent of its workers.[20]

This large and accelerating peasant migration was fundamental to the formation of the Petersburg working class. It argues for the presence of a large number of peasant workers who, if not new to city life altogether, were certainly new to St. Petersburg—a heterogeneous, unintegrated, disunified population, docile according to some, volatile according to others. All of these features could probably be attributed to Petersburg's workers in the 1905 era, but the impact of peasant migration on the overall nature of working-class politics and consciousness is a subject of considerable intricacy and controversy. It would be wise, therefore, to proceed with more than the usual caution from the known to the unknown, bearing in mind that the topic of rural-urban migration and the transformation of peasants into workers in Russia, despite its fundamental importance, has been far from adequately studied.[21]

Table 2 shows that in 1900, nearly four-fifths of persons registered in the peasant *soslovie* were born outside the city (79.1 percent). Of the remaining fifth born in the city (190,376), over half were probably under 16 years of age.[22] Nevertheless, the existence of some 95,000 city-born adult "peasants" is a clear reminder that the estate or *soslovie* of a person's official registration often had little to do with his or her actual social identity. The peasant estate living in Petersburg in fact

20. Bater, *St. Petersburg*, pp. 309–12. A total of 983,714 persons, or 68 percent of Petersburg's population of 1,439,613 in 1900, was born outside the city. Kutsentov, "Naselenie Peterburga," p. 175, or *Peterburg, 1900*, vyp. 1, pp. 32–33. The last figure given in the text is drawn from the 1897 national census, and lumps workers with domestics (*prisluga*). As a result, it may be slightly inflated for workers alone. Rashin, *Formirovanie*, p. 356. Cf. Table 2, below.

21. Barbara A. Anderson, *Internal Migration During Modernization in Late Nineteenth-Century Russia* (Princeton, 1980). On rural-urban migration in Russia as a whole, see Von Laue, "Russian Labor Between Field and Factory, 1892–1903"; and Zelnik, "The Peasant and the Factory." Some thoughtful and cogent remarks on migration to Petersburg may be found in Shuster, *Peterburgskie rabochie, 1905–1907 gg.*, pp. 17–32. Critical comment on the state of the problem in Soviet historiography and elsewhere may be found in Zelnik, "Russian Workers and the Revolutionary Movement," pp. 216–22.

22. Children were normally registered in the place of their parents' registration, so that only those born of parents registered in Petersburg province would themselves be registered there. No figure on the number of peasants under 16 is available, but 53.5 percent of the general population born in Petersburg was under 16. *Peterburg, 1900*, vyp. 1, p. 32.

TABLE 2

Peasant Residents of St. Petersburg in 1900, by Province of Registration and Birth

	Registered		Born outside city	
Province	No.	Pct.	No.	Pct.
Tver	172,349	19.0%	138,602	15.3%
Iaroslav	114,384	12.6	92,188	10.1
St. Petersburg	88,013	9.7	55,888	6.1
Novgorod	73,555	8.1	58,812	6.5
Pskov	61,943	6.8	52,676	5.8
Riazan	42,555	4.7	35,350	3.9
Smolensk	39,007	4.3	30,667	3.4
Vitebsk	37,841	4.2	30,625	3.4
Kostroma	37,074	4.1	30,215	3.3
Moscow	22,070	2.4	15,449	1.6
Subtotal	688,791	75.8%	540,472	59.5%
All provinces	908,786	100.0%	718,410	79.1%

SOURCE: *Peterburg, 1900*, vyp. 1, pp. 168–69, 172–73.

contained an entire world of urban types, ranging from those fresh from the country to those who had lost all connections and sense of identity with rural life. But it also embraced fairly recent arrivals whose families, occupations, and/or surroundings facilitated a rapid assimilation to city ways, as well as long-term residents and even natives whose restricted environments encouraged the preservation of rustic attitudes and a certain caution toward the greater urban world surrounding them. Most skilled artisans and factory workers and a few prosperous merchants and successful tradesmen were in fact registered peasants. But far more numerous among the urban peasants were the degraded craftsmen, unskilled workers, domestics, small peddlers, tramps, beggars, and other impoverished residents of the capital. Hence, though most workers—factory and otherwise—were peasants (80–90 percent) the peasant *soslovie* in the city included social strata more varied than would be covered by even the broader definition of "workers" discussed above.[23]

Seventy-nine percent of all peasants in the capital in 1900 were born outside the city, and 73 percent outside the province of St. Petersburg altogether. That is, almost three-quarters of the city's peasants had migrated to the city from another province. Almost all

23. Given these proportions, it is not very surprising that, although there were many more domestics, small tradesmen, and self-employed types than workers in the peasant *soslovie*, yet, with respect to *proportions of natives and migrants*, the category of workers in Petersburg matched that of peasants. Rashin, *Formirovanie*, p. 358.

of these peasants had their legal residences elsewhere. Only 3.5 percent of the city's peasants were *registered* in the city (out of 21 percent born there), because birth in the city did not normally confer registration in it.

One salient feature of the trek to Petersburg was the fact that the bulk of the migrants came from quite distant locales, and this affected their relationship to their peasant heritage and their attitudes toward the city. James Bater even points to an increase in distances traveled by Petersburg migrants between 1869 and 1910.[24] Of those born outside the city, only 26.8 percent came from either Petersburg province or the first tier of provinces directly adjacent (Novgorod, Pskov, Olonets, Lifland, Estland), which means that nearly three-quarters came from places two or more provinces distant (or 57.9 percent of *all* peasant residents of the capital). Since even the straight-line distance from St. Petersburg to the nearest point in the second tier (Tver province) was 200 miles, frequent visits home for most Petersburg factory workers would therefore not have been likely. The expansion of the railroad system and the lowering of fares did promote migration to the city, but whether it increased the frequency of movement back to the village is a separate question. In the same years when rail travel was becoming easier, the village was growing poorer and the city more attractive to surplus rural labor. Even seasonal workers normally made the trip only once a year, and most settled factory workers apparently avoided doing it more often than that.[25]

The direct influence of the village on migrants to Petersburg and on their surroundings would therefore have been weaker, and the impact of the city more constant and unrelieved, than on migrants to factory sites located in the same county, district, or even province. This is not to say that the greater distance from village origins in itself made Petersburg migrants more receptive to city ways, but the process of transition from farm to factory for the Petersburg peasant-worker certainly differed significantly from that of short-distance migrants. In many industrial areas isolated from urban influences, hiring local labor was favored because of the belief that local labor was more docile than that which came from afar. In those areas, frequent trips home, seasonal migration to and from the factory, and close ties to agriculture were possible and prevalent. These circumstances produced the kind of peasant-worker so often attributed to the Russian

24. Bater, *St. Petersburg*, pp. 304–6.
25. Evidence for this is only indirect. See note 29 below on the low incidence of seasonality among Petersburg factory workers.

labor force as a whole. The dominant situation among Petersburg's workers was obviously quite different. The capital's great need for labor far outpaced available local supplies, and the presence of long-distance migrants had constituted one of the city's distinguishing features for some time.[26]

Petersburg also experienced annual waves of seasonal migration in addition to the steady and increasing settlement of new people. In the 1900 census, 156,617 persons born outside the city were listed as either settling in that year or being in the city as "temporary migrants" (*vremenno-priezzhie*). Since an average 46,000 persons settled in the city each year in the 1890's, we can estimate that 110,000 temporary migrants were in St. Petersburg at the time of the 1900 census, some 89,000 of them registered peasants.[27] These would have been winter migrants, as the census was taken in December. Slightly fewer migrants arrived in the city for the summer season.[28]

Relatively few of these seasonal migrants would have been factory workers. Petersburg workers did not normally leave their jobs in the course of the year. In fact, Petersburg's factory population contained the highest percentage of year-round (*postoiannye*) workers in the Empire.[29] Rather than factory work, these annual migrants performed

26. Shuster, *Peterburgskie rabochie*, pp. 26–27. Prokopovich, *K rabochemu voprosu v Rossii*, pp. 70–72. The point has been stressed because sustained and frequent contact with the village has too often been taken as typical of all Russian workers. In addition, the process of peasant assimilation to urban ways is hardly ever given the attention it deserves. For a contrasting view of peasant-worker adjustment to urban life, see Johnson, *Peasant and Proletarian. The Working Class of Moscow in the Late Nineteenth Century*.

27. *Peterburg, 1900*, vyp. 1, pp. 32–33, 169. The estimates were arrived at by taking the numbers of new residents (whether all persons or just peasants) born outside the city, 1891–99, and dividing by 9 to yield the average annual number of settlers. This figure was then subtracted from the settlers and temporary migrants for 1900.

28. One study found about 42,000 summer migrants each year in 1888 and 1889, but around 1900 a British observer estimated their numbers at about 100,000. Bernshtein-Kogan, *Chislennost'*, pp. 24–26. George Dobson, *St. Petersburg* (London, 1910), p. 126.

29. Rashin, *Formirovanie*, p. 565, citing Pogozhev, *Uchet, chislennosti*, p. 101, showed that the Petersburg industrial *okrug* (the northwest sector of the Empire) had the highest percentage of year-round workers, 89 percent in 1886–93. The percentage for the city of Petersburg would have been even higher once the migratory workers in rural factories in the *okrug* were subtracted. That this figure did not diminish in the 1890's is indicated by the fact that only 5 percent of a group of Petersburg cotton workers studied in 1901 (1,200–1,300 workers) left for field work, although 65 percent of them owned land. Leontief, *Die Baumwollindustrie in St. Petersburg*, pp. 62–63. In most areas, seasonal migration was quite common in the cotton textile industry. See also Bernshtein-Kogan, *Chislennost'*, pp. 24–27.

other categories of labor around the city. The summer migrants came for work in construction, transportation, gardening, and a great variety of other crafts and trades that could be pursued only in fair weather. At the end of the 1880's one writer found more than 150 kinds of workers among summer migrants from Iaroslav province alone, including mess boys, horse dealers, bakers, used-book sellers, greengrocers, waiters, kvass brewers, footmen, and ragpickers.[30] Fall and winter migrants probably included a large number of domestics (*prisluga*) and service workers, come to the city to meet the needs of the middle and upper classes returning from summer absences.

In addition to the time of the year these seasonals came and went, they may be further distinguished by their intentions in migrating. Most of those just mentioned pursued regular trades and came to the city to practice them, fully intending to return to established homes elsewhere, or at least to leave the city once the season ended. But the influx of seasonal migrants also included those in search of a better position than the one they left behind, and therefore prepared to settle in the city if that proved feasible. These were not always sharply distinguishable from the first group. Those among them in possession of skills naturally stood a better chance of finding work. But many also came without a particular skill and without contacts in the city, hoping perhaps to acquire both, but constituting in the meantime a sizable, uprooted, needy, often desperate and even dangerous element. How did these migrants live until they found labor and lodgings? Many, having failed to find work, would leave the city with the beginning of cold weather, thereby becoming involuntary seasonal migrants. Others remained in the city, apparently merging with various subpopulations of beggars, prostitutes, the unemployed, and criminals. Whatever the case, these marginal or failed labor migrants formed a part of the "lumpenproletarian" underbelly to the great body of working-class Petersburg, a group that nonetheless had a significant impact on both educated society's fearful image of the lower classes and the workers' image of themselves.[31]

This marginal element is also associated with those who performed factory labor as unskilled and day laborers (*chernorabochie* and *poden-*

30. Bakhtiarov, *Briukho Peterburga. Obshchestvenno-fiziologicheskie ocherki*, p. 220.
31. There is a fairly extensive literature on this marginal, subproletarian population of Petersburg, reaching back into the 1860's and 1870's, of which two distillations by A. Bakhtiarov may be cited at this point: *Proletariat i ulichnye tipy Peterburga. Bytovye ocherki*, and *Otpetye liudi. Ocherki iz zhizni pogibshikh liudei*. Discussion of this population of the ruined and the lost will be resumed below.

shchiki), two practically synonymous categories of workers normally paid and often also hired on a daily basis. Such temporary workers were not part of the factory complement as recorded in the census, nor were they listed under the industry they worked in. In 1900 the census reported 43,045 such workers in the city, and a large number of these apparently not only worked in factories as unskilled labor, but also sometimes even worked in skilled positions, despite their designation, temporary status, and normally low pay.[32] These day and unskilled laborers had with them 16,313 family dependents,[33] which indicates they were nearly as settled and established a part of the working class as other workers, notwithstanding their presumed temporary status.

The implication of all this for the survival of rural ways among workers is mixed and complex. Because of the great distance of most Petersburg workers from their place of origin and/or registered domicile, the majority of the factory, service, temporary, and other workers were year-round residents. For such workers, even the ownership of village land or an allotment share was often of little economic or social significance since the land was worked by others.[34] Moreover, many factories and branches of industry harbored fairly high concentrations of urban and urbanized elements. The large contingents of skilled and literate workers in printing and metalworking establishments, for instance, made for work forces with one-third or more seasoned citydwellers.[35]

32. Shuster, *Peterburgskie rabochie*, pp. 33–34.

33. *Peterburg, 1900*, vyp. 2, pp. 74–77, 142–45. This made for a ratio of family members to workers among the unskilled and day laborers (counting *odinochki*) of 37.9 percent; the same ratio for the entire working class, as defined by the census, was 44.9 percent. The difference could easily be accounted for by the lower wages among the unskilled workers.

34. Shuster, *Peterburgskie rabochie*, p. 29.

35. The figure of a third has been estimated by taking the Baltic Shipyard as an example of such a concentration of skilled labor, although higher concentrations existed in the city. In 1901, 19.4 percent of the Baltic workers were of *meshchane*, artisan, gentry, and *raznochintsy* origins (Blek, "Usloviia truda," p. 80). It is assumed that these workers were predominantly, if not totally, urbanized. Of the remaining 80.6 percent peasants at Baltic, some had undoubtedly been born in the city and were urban in their basic identity. We can estimate this population using the 14.7 percent figure for the proportion of the over-16 general population born in the city, which yields 11.8 percent. Adding these city-born peasants to the nonpeasant, urbanized elements, we can estimate that some 31.2 percent of the Baltic Shipyard consisted of more-or-less urbanized workers. The attraction of better pay and conditions and the requirement of skill and literacy in some of the Baltic jobs probably drew an even higher percentage of

Yet there was clearly another side to this. Among factory workers in most other industries, among the working class conceived more broadly, and among all Petersburg workers in the course of their lives outside the workplace, the impact of the village in Petersburg was unmistakable, extensive, and ever-present. Seasonal migration brought over 100,000 predominantly rural visitors to the city twice each year. Those who plied regular trades and left at the season's end brought a possibly picturesque, but also jarring and unavoidable rural presence to the city. Those who came in search of permanent work, because they blended with and swelled the numbers of the criminal and socially marginal underworld, added an unsavory and dangerous flavor to migration and to the city's peasant presence. Both elements brought a village ambience to lower-class and factory neighborhoods, or reinforced that which was already there, regularly reenacting the origins of many of those already settled.

But even apart from seasonal migration, a large part of the regular work force consisted by 1900 of villagers who had arrived only a few years earlier. This was due to the phenomenal demographic expansion during the industrial boom of the 1890's, when the city's working population increased by two-thirds.[36] In other words, almost two out of five workers in 1900 had migrated to the city within the last decade.

In addition, a number of other features of working-class life in Petersburg enhanced the impression of the nearness of village life. The annual renewal of residency registration required the approval of the village authorities, involving for many a trip to the village. Many workers, even those who rarely or never returned, continued to send money to their villages long after their departures. Workers sometimes returned to the village to marry, and many more left wives and families behind.[37] Collective living arrangements in the city—artels and communal apartments—often grouped *zemliaki* (workers from the same district or village), and these networks of common ac-

---

urbanized workers to the yards than this estimate shows. On the other hand, other metalworking and machine-construction plants harbored higher proportions of skilled, and therefore predominantly urbanized, workers than the Baltic, and printers and certain artisanal trades also had large proportions of urbanized workers.

36. The worker population of the city proper grew by 145,286 during the boom decade, an increase of 65.3 percent. This figure reflects increases only in the city districts because the 1890 census excluded the suburbs from consideration. The rate of suburban settlement among workers would at least have kept pace with that of the city in the 1890's and probably even surpassed it.

37. Shuster, *Peterburgskie rabochie*, pp. 30–31.

quaintances and roots served to preserve and vivify village memories. The presence of some unskilled and/or temporary labor in all factories injected varying amounts of rural culture directly into the industrial world. Moreover, even if workers minimized their exposure to peasant ways in the factories, they could not do the same in their lives outside the factory. The milieu in which factory workers moved, be it in the city center or in factory settlements on the outskirts, was stamped with peasant life. In lodging, eating, drinking, and worship, the predominantly peasant workers encountered powerful reminders of their own country origins, whether recent or distant.

Yet to conceive of the migrants' identities as a simple tension between the two poles of village and city would be to oversimplify the situation considerably. Compared to migrants in more thoroughly urbanized countries, where workers lived at a greater distance from their village past, most migrants to Petersburg, whatever the geographic distance, made much longer journeys in historic time and suffered more abrupt transitions. Compared to Russian migrants who worked in nearby rural factories and visited their villages frequently, those who traveled to the imperial capital crossed a much greater social and historical space. The journey from the traditional Russian village to the industrial city proved to be so drastic a change, and the migrants so ill-prepared for it, that continuity with village ways could not help but be seriously affected.

Most rural migrants to cities encountered a strong sense of their inferiority in the eyes of the citydwellers, and they have typically banded together as much for self-protection and mutual assurance as from a sense of affinity. Yet the diversity of the Russian migrants to Petersburg, as well as the poverty and degradation of so much of the village life they left behind, seem to have led most migrants to break with the brutality of rural Russia even if they did not embrace city ways wholeheartedly.[38] Eugen Weber, speaking of peasant migrants to nineteenth-century Paris, notes that migrants from the same regions clustered in "tight, homogeneous" communities, speaking their own patois or a special jargon peculiar to their urban ghetto.[39] There is no evidence of a comparable phenomenon among rural migrants to Petersburg, although Table 2 shows that the city harbored sufficient

38. Again, this adjustment to urban life is intended to contrast with that described among Moscow workers in the late nineteenth century by Johnson in *Peasant and Proletarian*.

39. Eugen Weber, *Peasants into Frenchmen. The Modernization of Rural France, 1870–1914* (Stanford, Calif., 1976), p. 282.

numbers of *zemliaki* to support such subcultures. Judging by the admittedly sparse existing evidence, peasant collectivism in the capital seems not to have gone beyond consumer artels, collective living arrangements, and pockets of *zemliaki* in parts of some Petersburg factories. The resulting lack of a strong cultural cohesiveness of their own to cushion the shock of the city would have led some to leave the city, but among the many who remained, it weakened further their resistance to change. For some, this lack of rootedness in the city seems to have hastened their personal, psychological, and social disintegration; for others, it spurred the search for alternative forms of group solidarity and support.

But the village origins of so many Petersburg workers around the turn of the century became inextricably combined with a number of other circumstances they encountered once they arrived in the capital, and these need to be reviewed in order to assess the impact of migration.

CONDITIONS OF WORK IN THE CAPITAL

Occupations and Working Conditions

The Petersburg city census of 1900 showed that the greatest industry of the city was metalworking and machine production, which accounted for some 80,000 workers, or about 18 percent of the total of 442,353 (see Table 3). This was followed by general commerce, clothing, transportation, construction, woodworking, and textiles, with about 7 to 11 percent each. Metalworking was also the fastest-growing major industry in the city during the two decades before 1900.[40] Its rate of expansion was nearly twice that of any other major industry; slightly more than one out of every four persons entering the Petersburg factory work force in these years became a metalworker. Of the remaining industries, clothing, transportation, and printing doubled their work forces in these years; the construction trades and the paper, resin, and hide industries nearly doubled. The textile industry grew by 74 percent, but this did not keep pace with the growth rate for the entire work force. The slowest growth was recorded in food manufacture and service industries (commerce and the hotel trade).

A measure of the relatively great weight of Petersburg's metal-

40. Unskilled and day labor showed a rapid rate of growth, but it did not constitute a branch of industry, and a significant part of these workers would have been employed in metal and machine plants.

TABLE 3

Size and Growth of the St. Petersburg Work Force, 1881–1900

Industry	No. of workers		Percent increase
	1881	1900	
1. Metalworking	19,390	60,146	+210.1%
2. Machinery	12,071	19,710	+63.3
3. Chemicals	753	4,550	+504.2
4. Fats, Oils, etc.	841	1,875	+122.9
5. Paper, Resin, Hides	9,666	18,073	+86.9
6. Textiles	17,030	29,680	+74.2
7. Woodworking	13,012	33,101	+77.5
8. Food, Tobacco	16,759	23,030	+37.4
9. Clothing, Shoes	22,731	45,458	+100.0
10. Baths, Laundries	4,050	8,795	+94.6
11. Construction	18,490	34,422	+86.1
12. Printing	7,491	15,387	+105.4
13. General Commerce	38,703	47,400	+22.4
14. Transportation	21,148	43,794	+107.9
15. Hotels, Inns	16,923	18,829	+11.2
16. Unskilled and Day Labor	16,982	49,009	+188.6
Totals	236,040	443,259	+87.8%

SOURCES: 1–15, Bernshtein-Kogan, *Chislennost'*, p. 74; 16, *Peterburg, 1900*, vyp. 2, pp. 74, 76, 142, 144, and *Peterburg, 1881*, Tom 1, chast' 2, p. 307, Appendix, p. 4.

working industry may be found in the fact that it was proportionately twice the size of Moscow's and half again as large as the Empire's. On the other hand, textiles was the leading industry of Moscow, where its relative weight was twice that found in Petersburg.[41]

The growth of the "unskilled and day laborer" category is a measure of the increase of the "industrial reserve army" in the capital, and illustrates the capacity of the city and of its increasingly mechanized industrial plant to absorb large numbers of untrained work hands. In a related sense, the growth of this category is a rough measure of the growth of the city's impoverished "lower depths."[42]

Size of Enterprise

Petersburg's industrial enterprises were larger overall and in almost every branch of industry than those of European Russia as a

41. The figures for this comparison were drawn from Bernshtein-Kogan, *Chislennost'*, p. 74. Semanov, *Peterburgskie rabochie*, p. 25. *Perepis' Moskvy 1902 goda*, part 1, vyp. 2, pp. 116–59, as summarized in Engelstein, *Moscow, 1905*, Table 3, p. 26.

42. The category "unskilled and day labor" in Table 3 was calculated by combining two types of "persons whose industrial occupation was not precisely indicated": "day laborers" and "factory and plant workers" (items XV, b. and g., in the 1881 census, and

TABLE 4

*Percent Distribution of Workers by Size of Enterprise
in St. Petersburg and the Empire*

	Size of enterprise				
	Fewer than 50 workers	50–99 workers	100–499 workers	500–999 workers	1,000 and more workers
St. Petersburg	6.7%	8.1%	31.8%	15.5%	37.9%
Empire[a]	14.1	9.8	28.5	16.4	31.2

[a]"Empire" includes St. Petersburg province and European Russia.

SOURCE: Semanov, *Peterburgskie rabochie*, p. 37 (drawn from reports of the Factory Inspectorate, 1901–5).

whole. According to data of the Factory Inspectorate (on which Table 4 is based), well over half of Petersburg's workers were employed in factories with 500 or more workers, while nearly two in five worked in plants with 1,000 and more. The smallest group of Petersburg workers and the greatest difference between Petersburg and Empire proportions occurred among the very smallest enterprises. When we recall that the data omit state-owned enterprises, which were mostly very large and heavily concentrated in Petersburg, it should be clear that the actual difference between Petersburg and the rest of the Empire at both ends of the scale was even greater than that shown in Table 4.

The average size of enterprises was increasing everywhere in Russia in the years before 1900, although the trend toward concentration was more consistent and substantial in the capital. For instance, the average number of workers per enterprise in the Empire's metal factories rose by 65 percent between 1881 and 1900; in Petersburg, the increase for the same period was 286 percent. In those years Petersburg's cotton enterprises grew by 21 percent, while those of the Empire remained the same size.[43] The average Petersburg factory in almost every branch of industry was significantly larger than the average Russian factory (see Table 5). The averages conceal an important fact about Petersburg's industrial composition: the greatest number of enterprises employing 1,000 or more workers were the metal process-

---

XVIII, 162 and 164, in the 1900 census). The latter category may have included some skilled workers; it numbered about 4,400 in 1881 and about 6,000 in 1900. In addition, the 1900 figure included 19,578 loners (*odinochki*) listed as "unskilled" and "day laborers" (a similar category was not given in the 1881 census).

43. Bernshtein-Kogan, *Chislennost'*, p. 100.

TABLE 5
Enterprise Size by Industry in St. Petersburg and the Empire

Industry	SPb. enterprises		SPb. workers		Workers in one enterprise	
	No.	Pct.	No.	Pct.	SPb.	Empire
Metalworking[a]	154	29.7%	76,130	50.9%	494	139
Cotton	34	6.6	24,748	16.5	727	528
Wool	4	0.7	2,284	1.5	571	151
Food, tobacco	57	11.0	13,241	8.8	232	54
Printing, paper	109	21.0	10,912	7.3	100	70
All others	160	30.9	22,386	15.0	–	–
Totals/averages	518		149,701		289	104

[a] Figures adjusted by the addition of 8 state enterprises with 28,400 workers.
SOURCE: Bernshtein-Kogan, *Chislennost'*, p. 97.

ing, machine, and shipbuilding plants grouped under "metalworking." But the branch average was lowered by the great number of small and middle-sized metal plants in the city. By contrast, there were fewer cotton and wool textile factories with over 1,000 workers, but proportionately even fewer small and medium enterprises in these branches, so their average factory size was higher than that in the metal industry.

Wages

Wages in Petersburg contrasted sharply with those paid throughout Russia generally. By one calculation, the average daily wage of the city's factory workers in 1900 was 39 percent higher than that of workers in European Russia as a whole (see Table 6). Every category of factory worker but one earned more in St. Petersburg.

The lowest-paid factory workers in both Petersburg and the Empire were those in the textile industry, where extensive mechanization had created large numbers of unskilled and semiskilled positions that did not command a high wage because the workers filling them could be so easily replaced. In addition, women and children were more widely employed in textiles than elsewhere, and they were always paid considerably less than adult men. A study of cotton workers in Petersburg around 1900, for instance, found that men earned an average of 23.5 rubles per month compared to 18 rubles among women.[44]

The highest-paid group was metalworkers, who were widely admired and respected by most other workers because of their relatively

44. Leontief, *Die Baumwollindustrie in St. Petersburg und ihre Arbeiter*, p. 74.

TABLE 6
Wages and Days Worked in St. Petersburg and the Empire

Industry	Annual wages[a]		Days worked/yr.		Daily wages[a]	
	SPb.	Empire	SPb.	Empire	SPb.	Empire
Cotton	236	171	296	256	0.79	0.66
Wool	209	170	311	266	0.67	0.63
Silk	273	176	286	256	0.95	0.68
Linen, hemp, jute	148	139	288	247	0.51	0.56
Mixed fibers	243	223	287	284	0.84	0.78
Printing, paper	312	217	295	279	1.05	0.77
Woodworking	331	215	271	211	1.22	1.01
Metalworking	408	341	272	261	1.49	1.30
Mineral products	273	204	248	232	1.10	0.87
Animal products	284	197	284	251	1.00	0.78
Food, tobacco	258	182	293	239	0.88	0.76
Chemicals	277	252	291	276	0.95	0.91
Averages	314	213	282	264	1.11	0.80

[a] In rubles.
SOURCE: Bernshtein-Kogan, *Chislennost'*, p. 111 (from V. E. Varzar, *Statisticheskie svedeniia o fabrikakh ne oblozhennykh aktsizom za 1900 g.* [Spb., 1903]).

privileged position. Employment as a skilled metalworker was the kind of work young and ambitious workers sought, the kind of trade solicitous working-class parents hoped their sons would enter. The leadership role assumed by metalworkers in the strike movement of 1905 and later was due in part to their position at the top of the pay and prestige scales of industrial labor in Russia. However, wide wage differentials existed within the industry: iron and steel foundry workers, for instance, earned about 37 rubles per month in 1900, whereas those employed at shipbuilding and repair yards averaged only 22 rubles. At the other end of the scale, skilled metalworkers could earn considerably more.[45]

The wages of non−factory workers are more difficult to determine

45. V. E. Varzar, *Statisticheskie svedeniia o fabrikakh i zavodakh ne oblozhennykh aktsizom, za 1900 g.* (Spb., 1903), the wage tables from which were reproduced in Bernshtein-Kogan, *Chislennost'*, pp. 182−86. These figures were based on different kinds of *factories* within each branch of industry; in many cases they conceal further wage differentials, based on actual *occupation* and skill level. Thirty-seven rubles per month would come to 444 rubles per year. Another estimate of wages at 17 of the largest metal plants in the capital found the average annual wage in 1901 for skilled, unskilled, and apprentices to come to 431 rubles. For skilled alone, the annual wage in the same year was 624 rubles, ranging from 402 at one plant to 950 and 980 at two others. Bulkin, *Na zare profdvizheniia. Istoriia Peterburgskogo soiuza metallistov 1906−1914*, table facing p. 52. See also Kir'ianov, *Zhiznennyi uroven' rabochikh Rossii (konets XIX−nachalo XX v.)*, pp. 113−15.

since they have never been systematically compiled and published, but they ranged normally somewhat below those of factory workers. Whereas a skilled tailor in a first-rate shop might earn 60 rubles per month, the vast bulk of clothing workers made only 10–20 rubles, in addition to a meager food allowance and the right to sleep in the shop of the owner or subcontractor. Construction workers in Petersburg earned between 1.3 and 1.9 rubles per day in 1903, depending on their trade and the contractor. In addition, construction work was seasonal, as indeed were parts of the clothing trades and some forms of transportation work, so actual monthly earnings on a year-round basis were considerably lower.[46] Government employees outside the high-priority armaments works were no better paid. Postal officials, for instance, began at 25 rubles per month and might, after fifteen years, advance to 50, but guards and messengers earned only 10–23 rubles, and mail carriers, 12–33 rubles.[47]

The great majority of Petersburg's non–factory workers thus seem to have been paid rather less than the 314 rubles per year (or 26 per month) received by the average factory worker (Table 6). But even factory workers did not actually take home all their wages, due to fines and other involuntary payments such as contributions to the church collected in the factory.

The inadequacy of these wages for most workers in Petersburg may be judged by estimates of their living expenses. A study of the budget needs of workers and their families, conducted by the War Ministry at its enterprises between 1902 and 1905, indicated that most workers had a hard time making ends meet. Taking current prices for food, clothing, housing, and other expenses, the study concluded that single male workers in Petersburg required 21 rubles per month and male supporters of families of four required 51 rubles. (Women workers were deemed to require less, 17 and 34 rubles, respectively.) Commenting on the study, one analyst noted that the estimates for all expenses other than food were unrealistically low. Living expenses in Petersburg were the highest in the Empire, a fact that offset the generally higher wages paid there.[48]

46. Gruzdev, *Trud i bor'ba shveinikov v Peterburge 1905–1916 gg. Istoricheskii ocherk*, pp. 2, 16–19. Semanov, *Peterburgskie rabochie*, pp. 77–78. Others have reported considerably lower wages for construction workers—for example, *Sbornik materialov po istorii Soiuza stroitelei. 1906 6/V 1926*, pp. 52–53. Cf. Kir'ianov, *Zhiznennyi uroven'*, pp. 116–18.

47. Bazilevich, *Ocherki po istorii professional'nogo dvizheniia rabotnikov*, p. 22.

48. N. M. Lisovskii, *Rabochie v voennom vedomstve* (Spb., 1906), analyzed and summarized by Semanov, *Peterburgskie rabochie*, pp. 78–87.

Hours and Days Worked; Turnover

The length of the workday in Petersburg was excessive, as it was everywhere in Russia. Varying conditions of work and the dearth of statistical data make it impossible to compare Petersburg directly with other areas, but average workdays in the capital around 1895 ranged from 10½ to 14 hours, depending on the industry and the enterprise. In general, the shortest hours prevailed in the metal industry, and the longest in textiles and brickmaking.[49]

After 1897, when the government limited the factory workday throughout Russia to 11½ hours, most industries adjusted their working hours to conform. But even then the workday continued to vary by industry, plant, and the economic conditions prevailing from year to year. Industries whose productive processes required constant attendance, such as chemical plants, foundries, and public utilities, remained tied to longer work schedules (two shifts of 12 hours each continued to be the prevailing practice in these occupations rather than three of 8 hours each). Certain categories of workers, like oilers and steam plant operators, were required to arrive early, depart late, or both. Finally, overtime work was an ever-present option of employers for lengthening the workday at the expense of the employees (except for a brief period in 1897–98 when it was regulated by law). Mandatory overtime paid time-and-a-half, but voluntary overtime was to pay whatever employer and worker agreed upon. Since less skilled workers normally had no bargaining power in these situations, the employers' wage offers usually prevailed, and such "voluntary" overtime became simply a way of extending the workday at the behest of management.[50]

After 1900 the amount of overtime in Petersburg metal plants increased to such an extent that by 1902 metalworkers had to work on the average an extra hour every day. With the beginning of the Russo-Japanese War in 1904, additional weapons contracts in the Petersburg area added further to the need for overtime work in the metal industry. In cotton textiles during the same period, many plants responded to the economic downturn that gripped the Russian economy after 1899 by reducing the number of workdays. These two trends tem-

49. Semanov, *Peterburgskie rabochie*, p. 89. See Kutsentov, "Peterburgskii proletariat v 90-kh godakh XIX veka (Chislennost', sostav i ekonomicheskoe polozhenie rabochikh)," pp. 29–31.

50. Semanov, *Peterburgskie rabochie*, p. 98. Kutsentov, "Peterburgskii proletariat," pp. 30–31.

porarily reversed the usual positions of cotton workers and metal-workers with respect to hours worked. In 1902, cotton workers in the capital worked an average of 10.6 hours per day, and metalworkers, 11.4 hours.[51]

The greater intensity of labor in Petersburg is even more apparent when we consider the number of days worked per year. In almost every branch of production the workers of the capital put in from 11 to 60 days more per year than workers in the Empire as a whole (see Table 6). All the industries of the city operated on a year-round basis, whereas in rural areas work was often either seasonal, as in wood-working, or adjusted to the needs of a work force with agricultural responsibilities, as was often the case in the textile industry. In pre-dominantly urban industries like printing, or in more recently estab-lished ones like metalworking and chemicals, where work routines could be expected to be more highly organized and rationalized, the differences were not pronounced. On the whole, however, Peters-burg's more intensive work schedule (together with much else) sharp-ened the contrast with rural ways and increased for peasant migrants the pain and difficulty of making the transition to urban, indus-trial life.

The rate of turnover within the factory work force of Petersburg seems to have been quite high, although it cannot be established with great precision. In 1900, 64 percent of the city's cotton workers had worked at the same factory for five years or less; in 1906, a similar proportion of the Baltic Shipyard's work force (65 percent) had been employed there for a comparable length of time. Although some of this volatility may be attributed to the influx of new workers, most of it was due to the replacement of departed workers. In the textile indus-try as a whole, for instance, only slightly more than 11 percent of the work force in 1900 could be accounted for by overall growth in the previous five years; something like 50 percent of the city's cotton workers in 1900 were replacements for workers who had vacated their positions in the previous five years.[52] A great many of these were probably cotton workers who had simply changed jobs within the city.

In the better-paid trades of the metal industry turnover should not have been as high and probably traditionally had not been. But here too the situation had changed by about 1900. The figure given above

51. *Sverkhurochnye raboty v promyshlennykh zavedeniiakh Peterburgskogo fabrichnogo okruga za 1902 g.* (Spb., 1904), pp. 18–19, cited in Semanov, *Peterburgskie rabochie*, p. 97; see also pp. 93, 99.

52. Estimated from figures in Table 3, above.

for turnover at the Baltic Shipyards applied to 1906, and it was thus inevitably swelled by the unprecedented dismissals, departures, and lockouts of the previous year. The overall trend in the metal industries in these years was expansion at a much more rapid rate than textiles, so that the addition of new workers in metal plants made up a larger part of labor turnover than in the textile industry.

This is not to deny that the Petersburg metal industry was severely affected by the depression of 1899–1904, for many plants were forced to reduce production significantly. In 1902, for instance, the Putilov Plant cut its work force by 2,797 workers, or 23 percent. New government armaments orders resulting from the outbreak of war with Japan in 1904 allowed the Putilov and other metal and machine plants to expand once more. Thus, although the depression and the new government contracts affected different Petersburg metal and machine plants differently, their overall effect would not only have sustained but even exacerbated a high turnover rate in the Petersburg metal industry in the period just before 1905.[53]

Smaller enterprises and less skilled workers seem to have experienced higher turnover rates. A survey of 5,720 Petersburg metalworkers in 1908 showed that factories with over 1,000 workers employed 47 percent of their workers five years or less, whereas the comparable figure for factories with 200 or fewer workers was 77 percent. In isolated cases, large factories could display extraordinary stability: in 1899 over 93 percent of the work force at Moscow's huge Ramenskaia Cotton Factory (5,000 workers) had been employed there for five or more years, and 72 percent for ten or more.[54] Nevertheless, unskilled and semiskilled workers were normally more volatile because they were more easily replaced, and in some cases they were more footloose as well. Data from the Baltic Shipyards cited earlier show that between 80 and 100 percent of the apprentices, riveters, unskilled workers, and assistants had worked at the plant for five years or less; yet only 40 percent of assemblers, 41 percent of the ma-

53. Rashin, *Formirovanie*, pp. 502, 503. Iakovlev, *Ekonomicheskie krizisy v Rossii*, p. 272. A fairly high turnover rate, by the way, was characteristic of other industrial centers as well. As many as 56 percent of the workers of Vladimir province had been employed in the same factory for five years or less in 1897, and at one linen factory in Kostroma province, 50 percent of the men and 44 percent of the women had worked there for the same length of time. Rashin, *Formirovanie*, pp. 500, 502.

54. This figure seems to have been unusually low: as recently as 1881 about 35 percent of Moscow's textile workers as a whole had worked in one factory for six years or less. Rashin, *Formirovanie*, pp. 496, 499, 504–5.

chinists and firemen, and 54 percent of the machine operators were in this category.[55]

The causes of high labor turnover in Russia are harder to specify than the structural correlates, but they are surely related to specific historical and cultural features of Russian working-class life. The lack of organization, and therefore protection, at the workplace meant, among other things, that the inevitable disputes between workers and foremen or managers were more frequently resolved in Russia by resignation or dismissal. From the worker's viewpoint, the one sure and legal redress to an intolerable situation at work was departure and a new position elsewhere. Like Russian peasants before the advent of serfdom, industrial workers escaped from onerous conditions by migrating to the service of another master. The lack of job security itself made for a lack of job loyalty and longevity.

In some trades, the habit of movement from job to job had, by the early twentieth century, assumed the form of an ingrained custom. For instance, around 1900, two-thirds of Moscow's compositors (the most skilled and highly paid trade in printing) changed jobs every year, and fewer than 1 percent remained with the same employer longer than three years. As a feature of the trade itself, the same wandering tradition applied to Petersburg compositors. This was due in part to the existence of a surplus of compositors and to the organization of work, but it was also associated with a *style* of work that made a virtue of regular vacations and of migration to warmer places. This *Wanderlust* was not confined to compositors, but has been attributed to skilled metalworkers as well, so it may be said that there were migrant habits among skilled and unskilled workers alike which combined material necessity with the dignity of an accepted tradition.[56]

Hence, turnover in the capital's work force was rapid and disruptive. A large part of it was due to the overall expansion of industry, to movement *within* the city, and, among unskilled workers, to seasonal migration. With the replacement of one-half to two-thirds of the work force every five years, management-worker relations were always in some state of disruption and turbulence. This condition was consistent with the dynamism of Petersburg's industry and the city's place as Russia's commercial, political, industrial, and cultural capital. At the level of immediate, individual experience, this dynamism translated into an ambience of greater restlessness and nervousness among

55. *Ibid.*, p. 503.
56. *ILSRPP*, pp. 33–34. Semenov-Bulkin, *Soiuz metallistov i departament politsii*, p. 62.

workers, a feeling of greater distance from management, and perhaps a greater openness to the risk of losing jobs whose permanence
was in any case fairly uncertain.

Sex Ratios, Age, Literacy, and Family Situation

The percentage of women in Petersburg's work force around 1900
varied between 15 and 17 percent. In the capital city and in the country as a whole, women were concentrated in certain industries and
were absent, or nearly so, from others (see Table 7). Significant concentrations of women were found in the textile, paper and hides, food
and tobacco, clothing, and bath and laundry industries; in all other
trades they were present in only small proportions and modest numbers. Custom, prejudice, and vested male interest vied with the willingness of employers to use cheaper female labor in accounting for this
distribution. The near absence of women in such strenuous locales as
metal factories, sawmills, and brickyards was probably due only in
part to the physical demands of the work there, for there were large
numbers of women in the textile industry, which involved extremely
taxing physical labor.

The number of women in the Petersburg work force was increasing, rising from 49,600 in 1881 to 73,724 in 1900, a gain of 48.6 percent.[57] The proportion of women in the city's work force also grew,
from 14.4 percent in 1881 to 16.7 percent in 1900 and 20.3 percent in
1910.[58] Those industries which already had high concentrations of
women grew the most, such as textiles and clothing. Only the pres-
sures of the First World War brought the hiring of significant numbers of women in traditional bastions of male dominance such as
metal and machine work.

Although the use of child labor in these years was generally declining, it remained sizable in a few industries. Girls under 15 constituted
27.1 percent of the workers in clothing production, and boys of the
same age, 18.9 percent. Twenty percent of workers in commerce were
boys under 15, as were 12.4 percent of those in the tavern trade. All
other trades employed children of this age group in proportions
ranging below 10 percent, mostly under 5 percent.[59]

St. Petersburg was nevertheless becoming an increasingly younger

57. The male work force increased by 98.2 percent in the same period.
58. *Peterburg, 1881*, Chast 2, vyp. 1, p. 309. Rashin, *Formirovanie*, pp. 244, 247. Bernshtein-Kogan, *Chislennost'*, p. 76. For women workers in Petersburg and Russia generally, see Glickman, *Russian Factory Women. Workplace and Society, 1880–1914*.
59. Bernshtein-Kogan, *Chislennost'*, pp. 43, 70, 51.

TABLE 7
Proportions of Male and Female Workers in St. Petersburg, 1881–1900

Industry	Male 1881	Male 1900	Female 1881	Female 1900
Metalworking	99.7%	99.2%	0.3%	0.8%
Machinery	99.2	97.3	0.8	2.7
Chemicals	84.6	61.5	15.4	38.5
Fats, Oils, etc.	84.0	89.2	16.0	10.8
Paper, Resin, Hides	78.7	71.2	21.3	28.8
Textiles	57.5	44.4	42.5	55.6
Woodworking	98.2	98.7	1.8	1.3
Food, Tobacco	70.2	66.7	29.8	33.3
Clothing, Shoes	73.0	55.2	37.0	44.8
Baths, Laundries	51.4	34.0	48.6	66.0
Construction	99.3	99.8	0.7	0.2
Printing	96.9	92.7	3.1	7.3
General Commerce	98.0	93.6	2.0	6.4
Transportation	99.4	99.7	0.6	0.3
Hotels, Inns	90.5	86.3	9.5	13.7
All groups	87.2%	83.5%	12.8%	16.5%

SOURCE: Bernshtein-Kogan, *Chislennost'*, p. 77.

TABLE 8
Age Structure of the St. Petersburg Population

Age groups	1890 No.	1890 Pct.	1900 No.	1900 Pct.
0–15	211,542	22.2%	288,730	23.1%
16–30	363,733	38.1	496,594	39.8
31–45	224,613	23.5	283,965	22.8
46–60	108,862	11.4	125,907	10.1
61 and older	45,650	4.8	52,926	4.2
Total	954,400[a]	100.0%	1,248,122[a]	100.0%

[a] Excludes suburbs.
SOURCES: *Peterburg, 1890*, Vyp. 1, pp. 20–23; *Peterburg, 1900*, Vyp. 1, pp. 125–29.

city around 1900, as Table 8 indicates. This shift was due to the predominance of births over deaths, which began in the mid-1880's, and to the prevalence of young people among migrants to the city. This increasing youthfulness was consequently most pronounced among peasants and workers, and it had important consequences for the literacy and family situations among them, as will soon become clear.

Literacy in Petersburg was higher than in the Empire, both for workers and for the general population, although a sharp difference existed everywhere between men and women and among different

TABLE 9

Literacy Rates in St. Petersburg and the Empire, by Age and Sex, 1897

	Age group				
	10–14	15–19	20–39	40–59	60+
Male					
Workers, St. Petersburg	88%	83%	71%	59%	54%
Workers, Empire	77	78	55	42	34
Whole Empire	45	46	34	30	20
Female					
Workers, St. Petersburg	72	66	34	35	15
Workers, Empire	51	43	25	13	15
Whole Empire	21	22	18	12	10

SOURCE: Bernshtein-Kogan, *Chislennost'*, p. 66.

age groups (see Tables 8 and 9). When both sexes are taken together, the literacy of workers and the general population of the capital was practically identical (69.1 and 69.2 percent, respectively) because of the much lower proportion of women among workers. St. Petersburg's high literacy rate reflected the higher concentration of skilled labor and the higher educational standards of the capital, and the lower rate for women marked the denial of skilled work and education to them.

The distribution of literacy rates among the industries of the city was very much what we might expect: very high in printing and all commercial trades (roughly 80–90 percent); high in trades where skilled workers predominated, such as woodworking, metalworking, and food (70–80 percent); somewhat below average in most of the others, except very low in textiles and animal products (35–45 percent). Almost invariably in all industries and age groups, male workers were more highly literate than female; the one exception was that younger workers were more likely to be literate than older ones. Hence, the higher literacy of women than of men workers in the clothing industry is explained by the high proportion of *younger* women in it. These same relations and proportions applied to the industries of the Empire as a whole, though almost always at lower magnitudes.[60]

The most striking aspect of literacy in this period is that it was rising particularly among the peasant part of the population, as Table 10 clearly shows. That this increase in literacy took place in the decade

60. A detailed breakdown of the literacy rates of Petersburg workers by age and industry may be found in Bernshtein-Kogan, *Chislennost'*, p. 70. See also Semanov, *Peterburgskie rabochie*, pp. 52–56. The source for both these accounts was *Chislennost' i sostav rabochikh v Rossii na osnovanii dannykh pervoi vseobshchei perepisi naseleniia* (Spb., 1906), vol. 2, pp. 16–25.

TABLE 10
The Growth of Literacy in St. Petersburg, 1890–1900

	Percent literate	
	1890	1900
Entire city[a]	64.8%	70.5%
Men	74.4	79.7
Women	53.5	59.3
Peasants	51.0	60.8
Men	65.1	74.0
Women	28.2	40.0
Nonpeasants	80.3	86.1
Men	88.5	91.9
Women	73.5	81.3

[a]Excludes suburbs.
SOURCES: *Peterburg, 1890*, Ch. 1, Vyp. 1, pp. 43, 84; *Peterburg, 1900*, Vyp. 1, pp. 43, 136, 168.

of the city's most rapid growth is all the more remarkable because of the high proportion of rural migrants in that period. The city not only kept pace with the influx of far less literate peasant migrants, but made progress against it.

This overall increase was due to a higher literacy rate among provincial migrants to big cities and probably also to increased participation in formal schooling in the capital itself.[61] Certainly, a higher proportion of every age group in 1900 had had some formal schooling, or was enrolled in school, than in 1890. For instance, in 1890 some 61.3 percent of males aged 16 to 20 were receiving or had received some schooling; in 1900 the comparable figure was 78 percent.

The literacy of workers was thus increasing in the decade of their most rapid growth, enabling them better to review and reflect on the conditions of their existence than ever before. The fact that the great bulk of this increased literacy was concentrated among the younger workers made for a more explosive situation than might have been the case had it been more evenly distributed among the entire range of age groups. It meant that greater access to the literate and secular culture of the capital, and therefore greater interest in it, was disproportionately concentrated among an age group with less to lose, more impatient for change, and always more willing to challenge authority than the working class (or any population) as a whole. The increasing number of contacts between workers and revolutionary in-

61. Anderson, *Internal Migration*, pp. 100, 102, 104. Ben Eklof, *Russian Peasant Schools. Officialdom, Village Culture, and Popular Pedagogy, 1861–1914* (Berkeley, Calif., 1986), pp. 124–25.

TABLE 11
Marriage Rates in St. Petersburg and the Empire, 1897

	Married	
	Men	Women
Workers, St. Petersburg	46.8%	33.3%
All St. Petersburg	49.5	41.3
Workers, Empire	54.2	36.6
Whole Empire	64.3	64.0

SOURCE: Bernshtein-Kogan, *Chislennost'*, p. 59.

tellectuals in the 1890's was one sign of the working-class political culture being shaped by the new literacy. Within the factory, the shop, and the work group, youthful literacy also reinforced the generational rivalries always present to some degree between younger and older workers, marking it now with more sharply differing cultural and political orientations, with different attitudes toward educated society, toward authority, and toward each other.

Petersburg workers tended to be single or to live apart from their families. Marriage rates among the city's workers were lower than those among residents of the Empire or the city as a whole (Table 11). These figures are hardly surprising, given the low wages of most workers and the high cost of living in Petersburg. In addition, the working population was younger than the general population, and younger people earned less and married less.

A high percentage of St. Petersburg's workers lived apart from their families. Though this is not surprising for single workers, fully 81 percent of married workers also lived on their own.[62] For social strata still oriented to family and community, this was surely one of the most important conditions affecting workers, although its exact results have not been and perhaps cannot be adequately studied. At the very least it indicates the virtual negation of the family as a nurturing and stabilizing influence in the lives of the city's working class. It also represents another likely link between Petersburg workers and their rural roots, since a great many of the absent families would have been left behind in the village.

Summary

This survey of labor demography and working conditions in St. Petersburg has highlighted certain key characteristics and processes that may be briefly recapitulated and summarized.

62. Bernshtein-Kogan, *Chislennost'*, p. 53.

Petersburg workers were employed in bigger enterprises and for more days of the year, on average, than workers in the rest of the country. The greater intensity and impersonality of factory life created by these conditions meant that much of the Petersburg working environment was at the farthest remove from working conditions in the countryside and was even more demanding than that of most other industrial centers. These conditions probably contributed more than they took away from the radicalization of the capital's work force. Whereas large year-round factories occasioned greater fatigue and disunity among workers, this was offset by a greater need to find close and comfortable social relations lacking at the workplace and by the unavoidable tendency to view the managements of large firms as a distant and alien authority, having little in common with their workers.

The Petersburg work force expanded more rapidly than that of Moscow and probably any other urban industrial center in Russia during the two decades before 1900. This was due mostly to the rapid and heavy inflow of peasant settlers and migrants, who staffed the city's industrial reserve army and sharpened competition for available work, especially in unskilled categories. But these settlers and the much greater number of migrant seasonal laborers also apparently brought to the city information about labor conditions in other parts of the country and a willingness to change jobs frequently. The distress and ambition of these wandering laborers blended with the footloose traditions of Russian workers generally, including some of the skilled and urbanized elements, to produce a milieu of mobility and impermanence which was reflected in the presence of large numbers of idle and underemployed hands in the city and in the high turnover rates among Petersburg workers. The uprootedness inherent in this vast mobility and expansion was considerably enhanced by the lower marriage rate among Petersburg workers and by the astonishingly high percentage of all workers who lived apart from their families (86 percent).

Despite the vast inflow and outflow of seasonal migrants, they did not on the whole take factory work, and factory workers did not return to the countryside seasonally or regularly. Year-round work was universally the rule in Petersburg factories, and new factory hands normally ceased to migrate and became settlers. Despite the unavoidable presence of rural hands and habits in the city, the stereotype of the peasant-worker frequently attributed to Russian labor as a whole applies far less to Petersburg factories than it does to those in more remote parts where workers actually departed on a regular basis to engage in field work. In Petersburg, migration helped shape the working class far more by the disruption, turmoil and uprootedness it contributed to the urban ambience as a whole than by the supposed conservatism and rootedness of the peasant-worker.

Petersburg also distinguished itself from most other industrial areas of the Empire by its high proportions of skilled workers. They were concentrated in the city's principal industry, metalworking and machine building (roughly 20 percent of the larger, and 40 percent of the smaller variant of the working class; see Tables 3 and 6), but were also found in printing and to a lesser degree in woodworking, leather, and other industries. Altogether, they provided the capital with a large group of highly literate, well-paid, proud, and enterprising workers, the natural leaders and enthusiastic supporters of organized labor protest everywhere.

The skilled workers gave the city's working class as a whole more rapid and direct access to the culture and politics of the capital than workers in other areas. The better-informed, often more committed members of the group were the principal conduit by which news of the faltering autocratic regime and of the city's lively intellectual life reached the factories and industrial suburbs. They supplied the most articulate and outspoken critics (and sometimes, defenders) of the regime among workers; they provided most of the recruits to revolutionary circles and study groups. Skilled workers were often the spokesmen and drafters of demands during strikes and other breaches of factory discipline; and they were chosen, more often than not, leaders and deputies to represent fellow workers before employers and society. The consciousness and style of these urbanized, literate elements contrasted sharply with those of the large numbers of countrified workers who streamed into Petersburg in these years. The interaction of these two groups made for both conflict and mutual suspicion as well as, at crucial moments, cooperative, concerted action against employers and the public authorities; it provided the yeast to the political ferment widely noted among Petersburg factory workers.

CITY CENTER AND PERIPHERY

In order to restore a concrete sense of reality to this portrait of the workers of Petersburg, let us return to the city's physical setting and social geography. We may begin by posing a question, then attempt to answer it by examining two significantly diverse working-class districts of the city. The question is, in what ways did the social and geographic organization of the city set the framework for the pattern of strikes and protests that would soon unfold among its workers? This question begins an inquiry into the markedly greater militancy (as demonstrated in strike and protest activity) of workers in outlying districts and suburbs, and the slower mobilization of workers in the central districts, who by and large followed the lead and example of those from the suburbs.[63] In subsequent chapters this question will be addressed in terms of enterprise size, skill and literacy levels, and political traditions among the factory population. For the moment, however, we can prepare ourselves for these approaches by raising related questions about urban social relations and their cultural context.

What the visitor to St. Petersburg around 1900 would have noticed was not only the labor unrest, but the more obvious fact that the entire city as a social, political, and even biological system was coming unraveled. In the context of this all-encompassing process, the great labor upheaval of 1905 may be viewed as both a part of the disintegration and a reaction to it. As we have seen, the capital city was in the throes of an immense population explosion, which put great pressure on every public service and civic amenity, from housing to police protection. Attendant problems of pollution of the water supply, sewage disposal, and public ignorance increased the death rate from infectious diseases, so that St. Petersburg was known around 1900 as the most unhealthy and dangerous of major European capitals, as well as of Russian cities. An underfinanced, undervalued, and compromised city government failed to address these problems on a scale equal to their magnitude. Overcrowding and unemployment produced a growing homeless population and a rising rate of crime and vice. After about 1900 a new form of wanton public violence and mockery, immediately dubbed "hooliganism," appeared in the city for the first time. In addition to this, liberal, socialist, and student protest, centered in Petersburg, was on the rise, political assassinations were becoming increasingly common, and the local labor force had been penetrated by revolutionary organizations and ideas to a greater degree than any other industrial area in the country.[64] Given the urgency of these many dimensions of deprivation and anxiety, it is imperative to situate the working population within the wider urban context of which it was but one part.

63. For the fullest picture of the social geography of industrial Petersburg, see Bater, *St. Petersburg*. A summary of some of Bater's more important investigations and conclusions may be found in his "Between Old and New: St. Petersburg in the Late Imperial Era."

64. Bater, *St. Petersburg*, chap. 6, especially pp. 335–52, 380–82.

The two districts to be considered are those of Spassk and Schlüsselburg (*Shlissel'burg*; see Map). In size and population they are comparable units, but administratively and terminologically, Spassk was a
proper city district (*chast'*, one of 12 such units in Petersburg, also
called "boroughs"), and it was further subdivided into four subdistricts (*uchastki*, sometimes also called "wards" or "precincts"),[65] each
an administrative and police subdivision. Schlüsselburg, on the other
hand, despite its size, was designated only a subdistrict or precinct. It
was also a suburb (*prigorod*), one of four such areas contiguous to the
outermost districts of the city proper.[66]

These districts were representative of a division of the city between
a center, clustered about the Winter Palace and the Admiralty, and a
wide periphery of open fields, woods, cemeteries, and factory settlements. The center was densely populated, with many four-story or
taller buildings arranged along straight boulevards and wandering canals (as well as in the somewhat irregular grids of streets they defined). Three wide straight avenues radiated southward and eastward
from the Admiralty, of which the most famous was Nevsky Prospect,
the prime artery of retail commerce and the most celebrated and
prestigious boulevard in the city. The center was the site of the government's and the court's chief institutions and showcases—the ministries, departments, and palaces, as well as the theaters, cathedrals, and
museums. Although it was bounded roughly by the Fontanka Canal
on the left bank, the "center" could be said to extend across the Neva
to the University Embankment and "Strel'ka" of Vasilevsky Island,
where St. Petersburg University, the Academy of Sciences, and the
Stock Exchange were located.

Between the center and the semirustic periphery lay a sort of near
periphery of districts, roughly between the Fontanka and the Obvod-
nyi canals on the left bank, and in an area extending one to two kilometers beyond the river on the right. In these areas factories and
workshops could be found along with the multistoried, predominantly stone dwellings characteristic of the center; the population was
heterogeneous here and the commercial life lively. In the far periphery, by contrast—i.e., the southern halves of the Narva and Alexan-

65. The precincts of a district will be indicated here with roman numerals (Spassk I,
Spassk II, etc.).

66. The four suburbs regularly listed in the censuses were Peterhof, Schlüsselburg,
Lesnoi, and Poliustrovo. Sometimes police records list other suburban *uchastki*, e.g., Aleksandrovsk. In 1900 at least two precincts of districts also had their own names, indicating that they too had once been named suburbs: Vasilevsky III was called "Suvorov-
skii," and Vyborg III, "Okhtenskii," or simply "Okhta."

der Nevsky districts, the distant precincts of the northern districts, and the suburbs like Schlüsselburg—workers from large factories often lived in factory barracks or wooden houses and apartments, in disorderly, uncomfortable, and unsanitary conditions. These outer districts and suburbs enjoyed more open space, but they lacked many of the already inadequate services of the city proper, basic items such as sewage disposal, paved roads, and a clean water supply.[67]

Whereas the center may be said to have been dominated by the state, its institutions, and its servants—the gentry, the bureaucracy, and the intelligentsia—the periphery of outlying districts and suburbs was left to the poor and the working classes. Such was the unwritten sociospatial code of imperial Petersburg, the arrangements set and maintained by its rulers and probably based on the supposedly more ordered standards of pre-Reform days. Although reality in 1900 corresponded less than ever to this arrangement, the feeling that the center was state and gentry territory survived among the authorities and older residents, albeit only semiconsciously. Acting on this code—or against it—may be seen in the importance attached by the authorities to keeping demonstrating workers off Nevsky Prospect or away from the Winter Palace, and in the increasing popularity among workers, from about 1901 onward, of penetrating to the city center to plead their cause. It may be seen in the importance attached by the press and the public to the appearance of "hooligans" on Nevsky Prospect—again shortly after 1900, when they began to harass and annoy "respectable" citizens—though similar events had taken place in the poorer parts of town for some time before, and continued to take place.[68]

To be sure, the center was never free of workers and poor people, because Petersburg was segregated vertically as well as horizontally, with poor and working people in the upper floors and basements, businesses on the ground floor, and wealthier people in the favored first-floor locations. What made Petersburg stand out among European capitals was that such vertical segregation continued after the

67. This general ecology is confirmed by Bater, *St. Petersburg*, esp. chaps. 4 and 6, as well as by memoirs and descriptions of the city. Detailed and measured descriptions may often be found, apart from the censuses, in the writings of medical inspectors, especially Eremeev, *Gorod S.-Peterburg s tochki zreniia meditsinskoi politsii. Sostavlenno po rasporiazheniiu S.-Peterburgskogo Gradonachal'nika general-maiora N.V. Kleigel'sa vrachami Peterburgskoi stolichnoi politsii*; Nikol'skii, "Shlissel'burgskii prigorodnyi uchastok v sanitarnom otnoshenii"; and the articles of Dr. M. I. Pokrovskaia.

68. Neuberger, "Crime and Culture: Hooliganism in St. Petersburg, 1900–1914," pp. 59, 62–68, 79–82.

TABLE 12
Social Composition of St. Petersburg in 1900, by District

	Total population		District/suburb population of:			
District/suburb	No.	Pct.[a]	Workers	Pct.	Peasants	Pct.
Admiralty	40,272	2.8%	5,745	14.3%	23,429	58.2%
Kazan	56,483	3.9	12,667	22.4	27,949	49.5
Spassk	112,773	7.8	39,624	35.1	76,883	68.2
Kolomensk	71,431	5.0	18,648	26.1	39,913	55.9
Narva	121,909	8.5	43,265	35.5	80,668	66.2
Moscow	154,658	10.7	42,095	27.6	93,139	60.2
Al.-Nevsky	124,931	8.7	53,871	43.1	94,994	76.0
Rozhdestvensk	105,361	7.3	31,690	30.1	64,800	61.5
Liteiny	114,022	7.9	19,245	16.9	59,164	51.9
Vasilevsky	131,087	9.1	39,165	29.9	78,027	59.5
Petersburg	119,625	8.3	30,199	25.2	66,488	55.6
Vyborg	95,570	6.6	31,402	32.9	60,010	62.8
City total/Ave.	1,248,212	86.7%	367,616	29.5%	765,464	61.3%
Peterhof	68,889	4.7%	29,740	43.2%	54,845	79.6%
Schlüsselburg	78,714	5.5	33,979	43.2	60,879	77.3
Poliustrovsk	21,544	1.5	6,797	31.5	14,953	69.4
Lesnoi	22,334	1.6	4,212	18.9	12,645	56.6
Suburb total/Ave.	191,491	13.3%	74,737	39.0%	143,322	74.8%
Grand total/ Combined ave.	1,439,613	100.0%	442,353	30.7%	908,786	63.1%

[a] Percentage of total population of city and suburbs. Other percentages refer to proportions of the district or suburb for which they are given.

advent of mass public transportation, when the working population might have been displaced to the suburbs.[69] Part of the good life in the center, after all, was to have domestics and service workers conveniently close, and living at close quarters dictated a fairly strict code of deference and obedience. The understanding that the center was the domain of the privileged classes was therefore inseparable from a heightened sense of place and of subordination, especially harshly felt by lower-class persons, permanent and temporary, who happened to be in the center of Petersburg. Indeed, much of the stifling psychological oppression made famous by some of Gogol's and Dostoevsky's Petersburg characters was probably related to the need for order and decorum at the heart of the Empire felt by the government authorities and the gentry alike.

69. Bater, *St. Petersburg*, pp. 318–21, 379–80. While stressing the tenacity of vertical segregation, Bater also believes the city was simultaneously horizontally segregated (pp. 373–79).

TABLE 12 (*continued*)

District/suburb	District/suburb population of:		District/suburb proportion of:		
	Migrants	Pct.	Petty bourgeoisie[b]	Nobility	Honorary citizens[c]
Admiralty	5,348	13.3%	16.9%	11.4%	4.9%
Kazan	4,197	7.4	23.4	10.4	4.9
Spassk	11,662	10.3	17.8	5.8	2.7
Kolomensk	7,224	10.1	21.7	11.4	4.3
Narva	13,238	10.9	19.8	6.4	3.3
Moscow	18,670	12.1	19.7	10.0	4.2
Al.-Nevsky	16.258	13.0	16.0	2.3	1.6
Rozhdestvensk	11,615	11.0	19.3	9.0	3.7
Liteiny	11,449	10.0	19.7	16.7	4.6
Vasilevsky	14,349	10.9	19.1	9.6	4.0
Petersburg	12,626	10.6	20.2	11.9	4.5
Vyborg	9,503	9.9	20.6	6.0	2.4
City total/Ave.	137,117	11.0%	19.4%	8.9%	3.6%
Peterhof	8,259	12.0%	15.5	1.6	1.0
Schlüsselburg	7,719	9.8	16.8	1.6	1.2
Poliustrovsk	2,025	9.4	20.3	3.4	2.1
Lesnoi	1,497	6.7	21.9	9.0	4.6
Suburb total/Ave.	19,500	10.2%	17.3%	2.7%	1.6%
Grand total/ Combined ave.	156,617	10.9%	19.1%	8.1%	3.4%

[b] "Meshchanstvo i tsekhovye i ikh sem'i," one of the four largest sosloviia in the city (the others were the peasantry, the nobility, and honorary citizens).

[c] "Pochetnye grazhdane," a soslovie containing, like the nobility, both hereditary and lifetime categories.

SOURCE: *Peterburg, 1900*, vyp. 1, pp. 17, 23, 32–33, 44, 45; vyp. 2, p. 17.

Though the need for social order and deference lingered on, industrialization had in fact transformed the inner anatomy of the city. By 1900, there were large numbers of workers, peasants, and migrants in every district (see Table 12). Spassk and Liteiny districts in the city center contained more peasants than Peterhof suburb and more migrants than either Peterhof or Schlüsselburg. The predominance of peasant settlement in the central districts of the city dated at least to the 1860's, and the cumulative result of it is apparent in the very large numbers of peasants in Spassk and the three districts directly to the south, Narva, Moscow, and Alexander-Nevsky.[70] This pattern of settlement is perfectly in keeping with the fact that most of the seasonal migrants came not to work in factories, but to perform services and engage in petty trades that were carried on in the center. While some of them eventually found their way into higher paying work of the industrial economy, approaches to it were more obscure

70. *Ibid.*, pp. 165–66.

and forbidding to the newcomer than the open bustle of the city center, and the desire to settle close to this visible opportunity rather than in a distant industrial suburb requires little explanation.

The Spassk district was Petersburg's oldest and largest trading center, and it still contained the largest wholesale and retail markets of the city, ranging from *Gostinyi Dvor*, fronting on Nevsky Prospect in the first precinct, to the Nikol'skii Market in the fourth. Between them, in the heart of Spassk III was the Sennoi or Haymarket, the fourth-largest market in the city and specializing in foodstuffs. At the *Obzhornyi riad* in the Nikol'skii Market the poor could eat a meal for as little as 5 kopecks. A labor exchange for temporary workers and domestics was also located at the market, where cooks, carpenters, and gardeners, fresh from the country, could be seen waiting for work.[71] Well before the mid-nineteenth century these markets attracted not only the peasant traders, peddlers, haulers, and clerks that worked directly in and around the markets, but also skilled artisans and their assistants who produced goods for them, especially shoes and clothing, but many other items as well. The markets, the inexpensive food and housing in the area, and the Nikol'skii labor exchange also attracted large numbers of unskilled and day laborers to Spassk district.

With this type of economic structure, Spassk III and the precincts around it became home not only to a sizable working population, but to large numbers of transients as well—those in search of work, the newly unemployed, the newly arrived. But the market area was also home to a population of chronically unemployed or underemployed, fallen, and criminal elements: alcoholics, "former people," beggars, vagrants, prostitutes, petty thieves, and those without passports. They inhabited such unsavory and degraded areas as the Viazemskii slums, a set of buildings close by the Haymarket dating back at least to the 1840's, which embraced not only the fallen and criminal elements but the working poor as well.[72] The density of this population, combined with poverty and the rigorous Petersburg climate, took its toll on public health: as early as the 1860's Spassk III was stigmatized as the most disease-ridden area of the city.[73]

71. *Ocherki istorii Leningrada*, vol. 1, pp. 502–3; vol. 2, pp. 147–56; vol. 3, pp. 74–78. Bater, *St. Petersburg*, p. 265. Eremeev, *Gorod S.-Peterburg*, pp. 369–406. Bakhtiarov, *Proletariat i ulichnye tipy Peterburga*, pp. 171–72.

72. *Ocherki istorii Leningrada*, vol. 2, p. 795. Sveshnikov, *Peterburgskie Viazemskie trushchoby i ikh obitateli. Original'nyi ocherk s natury*. The area appeared in some of Dostoevsky's Petersburg novels and in V. V. Krestovskii, *Peterburgskie trushchoby* (SPb., 1889). On beggars in Petersburg, see Bakhtiarov, *Briukho Peterburga*, pp. 282–303, and *Otpetye liudi*.

73. Bater, *St. Petersburg*, pp. 192, 344–45. Zelnik, *Labor and Society*, pp. 242, 246.

The working population of Spassk III and most of the precincts surrounding it shared the same social, physical, and moral environment with the other denizens of the Haymarket. Not only were wages lower than those earned by factory workers, as we have seen, but living and working conditions were cramped, meager, and oppressive as well. Consider the conditions police medical inspectors found among the three kinds of working arrangements for cobblers in Spassk district in the 1890's. In the best case, a master cobbler producing for his own retail shop, which faced a street from a first- or second-floor location, worked with two or three journeymen and a "boy" or two, presumably apprentices, in the back of the shop. These businesses were deemed to be satisfactorily operated, and only the apprentices slept in the shop. A second type of cobbling arrangement did not have its own store, but produced for the mass market in a third- or fourth-floor apartment of several rooms, rented by a master cobbler and filled with as many as 25 to 30 workers. The effect was a sleep-in sweatshop, and, given the nature of the market around 1900, this kind of shoe-making would have been much more common than the first type described. Each worker rented a corner of a room from the master where he both worked and slept, usually on the floor amidst cobbling equipment. The workers received piece rates, probably worked excessively long hours, and normally drank a lot. The "boys" in these shops suffered beatings from the drunken workers, a familiar story among apprentices in small shops of all kinds. The third type was an *odinochka* arrangement—a solitary cobbler working on his own account, or at most with a relative. If he let an apartment, he might rent out rooms or corners like the cobbler contractor in the second case, but each renter worked on his own, thereby avoiding the city's licensing fee and spatial strictures. However, the inspector clearly felt that many working situations that claimed *odinochka* status were only deceptive fronts, put up only to avoid the fees and regulations and presumably concealing arrangements like those of the second case.[74]

The cramped working conditions and close personal supervision, the long hours and low wages evident in all these cobbling arrangements were likely to have discouraged and retarded the organization of protest among such workers, although the raw material of anger and indignation was likely to have been present in abundance.

The southern periphery, including the southernmost regions of the Narva and Alexander-Nevsky districts as well as the suburbs of

74. Eremeev, *Gorod S.-Peterburg*, pp. 417–19.

Schlüsselburg and Peterhof, had more in common with Spassk III
than it had with most other central districts. Peasants predominated in
the population, and gentry and honorary citizens were rare. The
working community also included many transients, and a large population of seasonal migrants and recent arrivals was always present
around 1900. Population *density* was not as great, but the *crowding* may
have been quite comparable to that of Spassk III, which had one of
the city's highest crowding rates. (Density [*gustota*] measured the
number of square *sazhens* per person, while crowding [*skuchennost'*]
measured the number of persons per room.) The density and crowding figures were 2.5 and 2.6, respectively, for Spassk III in 1890. A
direct comparison with Schlüsselburg is not possible because the suburbs were not included in the 1890 census. However, we do know that
housing was in short supply in the suburb and that overcrowding was
common.[75] Alexander-Nevsky III was similar in many respects, including the presence of a large factory population, and its density and
crowding figures for 1890 were 36.0 and 2.7, showing that though
workers of the periphery might enjoy more outdoor space, they could
be just as cramped indoors.[76]

Yet it is the differences in these two working-class districts that
should be stressed in this comparison. Most striking, of course, was
the relative isolation of the Schlüsselburg Road workers, who lived in
factory villages and settlements 1 to 10 kilometers south of Nevsky
Prospect along the river. Despite the completion of a horse tramline
to the settlements on the road in 1878, there was no regular movement to and from the city that would result from city workers residing
in the suburbs. Neither Schlüsselburg nor any of the outlying districts
became "dormitory suburbs." Commuting on the horse tram was
simply not practical, since a round trip could take several hours.[77]
This left suburban workers more isolated than if there had been a
large volume of daily contact with the city. Nor were urban institutions and urban ways very extensively reproduced in the suburb. Of
444 businesses in the suburb in 1899, all were concerned with the sale
of articles or services of direct consumption—cafes, drinking establishments, baths, stores for food and other items. The banks, hospitals, theaters, museums, libraries, institutes, and large markets of the

75. Nikol'skii, "Shlissel'burgskii," p. 1143.
76. Eremeev, *Gorod S.-Peterburg*, pp. 306, 267, 520, 523. Cf. Maps 58 and 65 in Bater,
St. Petersburg, pp. 319, 349, which clearly show that in the late nineteenth century density
decreased toward the outskirts of town, but crowding increased (except for Spassk III).
77. Bater, *St. Petersburg*, pp. 271, 320, 332.

center of the city were conspicuously absent in the suburbs. Even schools, provided by the zemstvo or the factories, were in short supply; in 1901, they were so overcrowded that as many applicants were admitted as were turned away.[78]

From all descriptions, the settlements along the road bore a closer resemblance to rural villages than they did to the central city, even its plebeian districts. The buildings were predominantly one- and two-story wooden structures, many of them built for rental to workers and so cheaply and poorly put together that even residents with fuel to burn froze in the winter. Practically all the streets were unpaved except for the Schlüsselburg Road itself, and even it was pitted with craters and potholes. Sidewalks were rare, and rains and thaws made streets impassable, producing mud and pools of standing water. Piles of trash and refuse were to be found in almost every yard and often blocked side streets. Finally, a stench pervaded every house, even the better ones, a result of poorly made latrine facilities.[79]

The factories, usually multistoried buildings of brick and stone, were the true temples and palaces of the Schlüsselburg Road, dominating the skyline above the shabby wooden houses and dominating the lives of the bulk of the suburb's residents. Some of the largest and most important industrial establishments in the city were located here: the Nevsky Shipbuilding and Machine Works (6,000 workers), the Obukhov Steel Works (6,000), the Spassk and Petrovsk Mills (formerly Maxwell Mills; 5,700 workers), the Paul Factory (cotton textiles) (2,000), the Aleksandrovsk Machine Works and Nikolaev Railroad Shops (3,000), and the Thornton Woolen Goods Factory (1,000). There was a time when the industrial wonders of the Schlüsselburg Road attracted curious strollers, but in 1900 the area was not even mentioned in guidebooks, and many of the factories maintained their offices in the center of town.[80]

Hence, workers dominated the Schlüsselburg suburb not because they made a particular effort to do so but because of an absence of competitors. And what set the Schlüsselburg workers apart from the workers of Spassk district was the fact that so many worked in very large factories, industrial communities answerable to a single manage-

78. Nikol'skii, "Shlissel'burgskii," pp. 1151, 1155.

79. *Ibid.*, pp. 1138, 1142. N. Paialin, *Nevskaia zastava* (L., 1938), pp. 12–13.

80. Paialin, "Shlissel'burgskii trakt (Nevskaia zastava)," p. 53, quoting *Severnaia pchela*, Dec. 4, 1839. Baedeker, *Russland* (cited in n. 2). *S.-Peterburg. Putevoditel' po stolitse s istoriko-statisticheskim ocherkom i opisaniem eia dostoprimechatel'nostei i uchrezhdenii* (SPb., 1903). *Spisok 1903*.

rial authority. In periods of protest this authority could become the focus of anger and indignation in a manner not possible among workers in smaller factories and workshops. The Schlüsselburg workers also lived in larger residential groups, either factory barracks or other rented housing that averaged 50 inhabitants, but could amount to hundreds.[81] Although some of these houses were organized as artels of *zemliaki* or of members of the same shop or section, their large size made possible the formation of supportive communities off the job. The homogeneity of these factory subcommunities was strengthened by the relative lack of contact with migrant workers. Although seasonal migrants did settle in the suburbs, their numbers and proportions were no greater than in central city districts, and in some cases were less (See Table 12). Some of these seasonals found factory work, but largely as unskilled labor in sawmills, brickyards, and other suburban industries. A great many of them lived in their own artels as well, so their contact with the year-round factory labor force was somewhat less frequent than it would have been in the center of the city.[82]

All of this points to the existence of a core group of workers that worked and lived in the Schlüsselburg suburb on a regular basis. This group apparently married and raised families more frequently and regularly than workers in the city districts. First of all, a significantly higher proportion of suburban residents were married than city residents.[83] We have seen that marriage rate alone does not establish family position, since so many married workers in Petersburg lived apart from their families, but the city census reported the numbers of dependents living with such separate population categories as "workers," and these have been compared in Table 13. What we find is a significantly higher ratio of family members ("dependents") to workers in the suburbs than in the city proper. If one considers the separate trades shown, it is clear that there was a greater difference between trades than between city and suburb in the same trades. However, among metal- and machine workers, there is also a notable difference between city and suburban residents. As might be expected, workers in better-paid trades were more likely to have families. It has been pointed out that, although better-paid workers were less likely to be married than the less well off, a much higher proportion of them actually lived with their families in the city.[84] The somewhat larger core

81. Nikol'skii, "Shlissel'burgskii," p. 1141.

82. *Ibid.*, pp. 1145, 1147–49. Eremeev, *Gorod S.-Peterburg*, pp. 588–89.

83. The figures were 40.1 and 57.1 percent, respectively. *Peterburg, 1900*, vyp. 1, pp. 31–33.

84. Bernshtein-Kogan, *Chislennost'*, p. 55.

TABLE 13
Ratios of Dependents to Workers in Selected Industries

Industry	City	Suburbs	No. of workers	Wages[a]
Metalworking	73.3	108.4	60,146	408
Machine prod.	62.8	82.3	19,690	–
Printing	68.0	79.5	15,387	312
Animal prods.	41.3	42.2	10,270	284
Textiles	28.7	34.0	29,780	235
Food	20.8	19.4	23,030	258
Clothing/Shoe	16.1	18.7	45,458	–
All workers	39.9	69.1	442,353	314

[a] In rubles, from Table 6 above.
SOURCE: *Peterburg, 1900*, vyp. 2, pp. 38–92, 106–61.

of family people among suburban workers, especially among the metalworkers, helped solidify the community in many ways that the collective living arrangements could facilitate but not guarantee.[85]

Descriptions of people's nonworking lives in the factory villages of the Schlüsselburg Road indicate that the residents spent most of their free time within the local community. This pattern was probably based on habit and the lack of sufficient time and money to visit the city in search of diversion, rather than on the range of amusements available locally. On the contrary, the worker memoirists complain of the stultifying surroundings and the lack of stimulation. On weekdays, the streets were deserted, with only unattended children visible, but on Sundays they filled up. In good weather the skilled workers put on their better clothes and took to the fresh air; young people strolled by the river with accordians; the taverns overflowed. The merriment ended early on work nights, however, and this may have been enforced by local ordinances closing taverns early. Reminders of village life were everywhere on hand, from the stoop culture of the idle workers to the fistfights, more or less organized, from which emerged the heroes of the shop floor and factory washrooms. Drunkenness was as common in the suburbs as in the city, but the extremes of debauchery possible in Spassk district seem not to have been present. Young men with money enough for a binge (*gul'nia*) apparently went into the city to drink, dance, and visit brothels in areas like the Ligovka slums; there was no other place for dancing in the winter,

85. One example of this was the network of support to workers in times of great need. When Aleksei Buzinov's father suddenly died from a work accident, his friend offered the mother advice on how 12-year-old Aleksei could land work in the same plant, then took him on as his own apprentice. Buzinov, *Za nevskoi zastavoi. Zapiski rabochego*, pp. 13–14.

a memoirist noted, "and to dance in a sober condition would be shameful."[86]

A kind of "blue collar" ethic seems to have prevailed in the factory villages; workers were hardworking if not always sober, parochial, straitlaced, and conventional. Traditional peasant mores usually prevailed: God, Tsar, and the male-dominated, patriarchal family reigned supreme, although atheism and revolutionary ideas were not without their attraction and often not as incompatible with this cultural setting as might appear. More than one worker memoirist, recounting his conversion to revolution, has confessed to his own earlier religious faith.[87]

Views of education and the intelligentsia also differed in the two areas of the city being compared. Worker residents of the city center simply encountered the intelligentsia more frequently and in a greater variety of guises and venues and therefore had a more complex and realistic view of the group. They probably associated them more with the glamour and inaccessibility of educated society generally and would not normally have thought that they had anything to do with workers. Workers of the factory suburbs, by contrast, would normally not have encountered members of educated society on a daily basis at all, unless it were the factory's engineers. When they did encounter them, it was more likely to be in some kind of public service role, as teachers, physicians, lecturers, or performers. Smallish groups of workers had contact with revolutionary agitators and propaganda circle leaders, and a larger group encountered teachers at evening schools for workers such as the Smolensk Sunday Evening Adult School in the Schlüsselburg suburb, where Nadezhda Krupskaia once taught. Because of this, the workers of the suburbs were more likely to think of the intelligentsia in a positive light, as the source of enlightenment, and even to harbor expectations about the intelligentsia's proclaimed role as apostles of liberation.[88]

All of this suggests an outlook among the workers of the factory suburbs that contrasted in interesting ways with that of workers in the small trades, workshops, and seasonal outdoor work of the center.

86. *Ibid.*, p. 26. Bakhtiarov, *Proletariat i ulichnye tipy*, pp. 107–9. Lunev and Shilov, *Nevskii raion*. Buiko, *Put' rabochego. Zapiski starogo bol'shevika*, pp. 15–16. Buiko wrote about the Peterhof suburb, but the subculture of the factory village was quite similar.

87. E.g., Buiko, *Put' rabochego*, pp. 15, 17, tells of his own religiosity and of the forbidding presence of a forceful and outspoken atheist worker, who offended older workers but fascinated the younger ones. See also Shapovalov, *Na puti k marksizmu (Po doroge k marksizmu)*, chaps. 1–3, pp. 21–32.

88. See Krupskaia's recollection of the devotion of her Schlüsselburg workers to their teachers in *Memories of Lenin*, pp. 7–8.

The former were undoubtedly more naive, less knowledgeable and worldly, less conversant with urban ways than the latter, but by the same token they preserved some of the moral innocence of the provincial and breathed freer for being removed from the domination of gentry and bourgeois elements and from the need constantly to defer to social superiors. They may even have harbored less rancor and bitterness against the privileged classes per se than those who faced on a daily basis the indignity of the need to pay deference to them. To be sure, workers of the suburbs faced factory owners and foremen on a daily basis, but in the villagelike setting of the factory settlements, this authority was more easily associated with the factory alone, and factory authority was not reinforced outside the workplace in the dress, demeanor, and language of streets and squares full of urban strangers, in thousands of words and gestures and customs.

For workers and peasants in Tsarist Russia, not to be intimately acquainted with urban culture meant not to be as dominated by the class system and government surveillance which it made so sharply apparent. The absence of civil liberties had its effect on workers as well. It meant that Russian craft guilds, invented by Peter I and not by medieval artisans, never afforded skilled workers social or juridical shelter from state domination and did not foster a sense of autonomy and independence.[89] In Russia, urban workers faced the power of their employers and the state with little or no institutional protection, and those most directly exposed to this power, the lower classes of the central districts, were the most poorly placed to initiate activity against it.

This initiative came instead from the workers of the periphery, who began and led the greatest and most disruptive strikes in 1905, strikes that from the outset went beyond factory issues to link up with the older opposition movement and its demands for a new political order. The factory suburbs seem to have nurtured the development of a kind of peasant-worker who had left behind not only village life but the rural habits of abject subordination to the rule of the *barin* as well, yet who at the same time had not been reintegrated into the subservient position prescribed for the lower classes in the city center. This is not to suggest that the workers of the center were so broken in

89. Walkin, *The Rise of Democracy in Pre–Revolutionary Russia. Political and Social Institutions under the Last Three Czars*, pp. 14–15; Bonnell, *Roots of Rebellion. Workers' Politics and Organizations in St. Petersburg and Moscow, 1900–1914*, p. 102. For an account of the guilds' organization and nineteenth-century fate, see Zelnik, *Labor and Society*, pp. 11–15, 120–25, 231–32; and Pazhitnov, *Problema remeslennykh tsekhov v zakonodatel'stve russkogo absoliutizma*, chaps. 3, 4.

spirit that they would refrain from striking or would prove incapable of producing their own leaders. It is more a matter of the prevailing pattern, of which kinds of workers were more self-assured in the release of aggression and resentment, which were better positioned to give their anger effective, organized expression, and which could best root visions of a broader political liberation in their own experience.

CHAPTER TWO

Strike Movements and the Rising Political Tide, 1896-1904

The motive force of the 1905 Revolution was supplied by the mass strike movement of Russia's urban and industrial workers. In the year 1905 alone, the country witnessed over 13,000 strikes involving some 2.7 million strikers, about seven times as many as occurred in the entire preceding decade. In addition, 33 percent of the factories and 60 percent of the workers struck, compared to fewer than 1 percent of the factories and 3 percent of the workers in the period from 1895 to 1904.[1]

This vast strike movement was the most distinctive feature of the revolution in 1905, and workers were the most important single social group responsible for bringing about the political reforms granted by the Tsarist regime in response to the disorders. Their mass strikes supplied most of the force behind the revolutionary alliance against the autocracy, an alliance that ranged from peasant to professional. The rapid adoption of the slogans of radical democracy by the strikers inspired the educated opposition at every turn, encouraging it to believe that the alliance was more solid than it in fact proved to be. After October 17, the government's promise of civil liberties and an elected legislature mollified much of the opposition, and most of the liberals abandoned militant unity for orderly electoral campaigning as separate parties. The strikers, meanwhile, focused on their still unsatisfied political and workplace demands and, where they did not escalate to armed revolts, they rallied to the authority of the newly created cen-

1. *Stachki 1905*, p. 13. The actual magnitudes were even greater than are indicated by Varzar's Factory Inspectorate data, for the reasons given in Chapter 1.

ters of revolutionary power, the soviets of workers' deputies. This abrupt "desertion" of the labor movement by the political bourgeoisie became a distinctive and formative feature in Russia's development when compared with that of the West, where industrial workers were typically led by radical bourgeois politicians and adopted their values before the emergence of their own class parties and ideologies. In Russia, by contrast, socialist beliefs and organizations were fully developed before liberal ones, and they enjoyed a practical monopoly over working-class politics, even though they were severely hindered by the police. By the end of 1905, this politically awakened working class, feeling deserted by its erstwhile liberal allies, became unusually suggestible and open to the more angry and intransigent opposition of the revolutionaries. The commitment of Russian workers to socialism was not a necessary or natural certainty, but a politically contingent, gradual, and ragged process that developed its characteristic forms in 1905 but was still under way in 1917.

Petersburg workers played the leading role in these events. They provided nearly a quarter of all strikers and organized most of the influential unions and the most important soviet. The demography and structure of the Petersburg proletariat predisposed it to play a vitally important role in the Russian workers' first bid for political power. How it came to play that role is another and more complex matter. This chapter will seek the sources of Petersburg's labor militancy in the history of the factory population in the decade or so before 1905. This ten-year period was given shape by two great "strike movements," in 1896 and 1901, which were seminal events not only for Petersburg but for the development of Russian workers as a whole. These were the first examples of clusters of strikes occurring beyond a single district or neighborhood which, by their timing and nature, influenced one another, even if no central leadership or organizational guidance was present. Prior to 1896, strikes in Petersburg had been discrete occurrences, confined to individual factories or, at most, the factories of one or two districts, and never approaching a situation that might be described as citywide.[2] The 1896 and 1901 strike movements represented two clear-cut cases of concerted working-class unity and self-activity as well as two stages or variants in the history of the interpenetration of revolutionary socialist activity and factory struggle.

2. The word "strike" will be used to refer either to work stoppages in single enterprises or, more loosely, to what is being described here as "strike movements."

THE STRIKE MOVEMENT OF 1896

Although the first strike movement in St. Petersburg might actually be considered to date from the end of 1895, when strikes at the Thornton and Lebedev textile factories and the Laferm Tobacco Factory signaled that a new militancy was afoot in the capital, the 1896 strikes of cotton textile workers are better remembered for their suddenness, scale, and interfactory solidarity. During three weeks in May and June, some 16,000 workers in 19 cotton spinning and weaving factories stopped work. Most of the factories raised demands for a shorter workday and payment for two days out of a three-day factory closing to celebrate the coronation of Nicholas II. The common demands gave the impression of a unified and concerted effort, and although that may have been exaggerated, there were several new developments in the 1896 strike.

For the first time, revolutionary agitators and organizers played an important part in strengthening and broadening the strike. The "Union of Struggle for the Liberation of the Working Class," a new organization of Marxist intellectuals, successfully joined its efforts to those of large numbers of workers already in a fight with their employers. This vindicated the new technique of agitation, advocated by Lenin and others and applied by the Union in Petersburg for the first time in the 1896 strike. Strikers and revolutionaries confirmed to each other that they could work together to promote mutual interests, and this opened a new era of underground activity among industrial workers, in which contacts became much more frequent and widespread.[3]

In addition, the strike put Petersburg cotton workers in the front ranks of the Russian proletariat; it inspired a number of other strikes among textile workers elsewhere; and it led to a second textile strike in the capital in January 1897, which resulted in the law of June 2, 1897, establishing an 11½-hour workday throughout Russia. Though this was by no means Russia's first labor law, it was one of the first pieces of legislation won by the mass activity of workers themselves.[4]

These achievements were all the more remarkable because textile

3. Wildman, *The Making of a Workers' Revolution. Russian Social Democracy, 1891–1903*, esp. chap. 3.
4. Sh., "K istorii peterburgskoi stachki tekstil'shchikov v 1896 g." Suslova, "Peterburgskie stachki 1895–1896 godov i ikh vliianie na razvitie massovogo rabochego dvizheniia," pp. 77–81.

workers were among the lowest paid, most exploited, and least educated parts of the Petersburg proletariat. The average Petersburg textile worker was paid 231 rubles in 1900, or less than 20 rubles per month. This put the textile worker at the bottom of a list of the major branches of factory industry in the city (metalworkers, at the top, averaged 407.5 rubles in the same year).[5] What the worker actually took home was considerably reduced by fines imposed to enforce labor discipline and to compensate for spoiled goods. Judging from lists of grievances and strike demands, such fines made up a sizable portion of the cotton and textile workers' wages.

Petersburg cotton workers spent from 12½ to 14 hours in the factory in 1894 and 1895, which was above the average for Petersburg factory industry as a whole, and one of the longest workdays for a single branch of industry.[6] During that long workday spinners, for instance, walked an average of 8.3 miles in front of machines that demanded their constant attention. This noisy and monotonous work was performed at high temperatures and humidities, purposely maintained in spinneries for the sake of the product but to the detriment of the producers' health. The result of these conditions, a government report observed,

> can be visually confirmed by [the workers'] outer appearance—emaciated, haggard, worn out, with sunken chests; they give the impression of sick people, just released from the hospital. The striking workers spoke a bitter truth to the [factory] inspectors, who had referred to the fact that they had no appetite: "We are not," the workers said calmly, "those fitters and turners of the machine plants; they finish work at the plant, come home, and eat a bowl of kasha straight away; but we come home after dragging ourselves around the factory all day long completely separated from [the thought of] food, we have no appetite."[7]

The intensity of work in the cotton factories of St. Petersburg was particularly high, the result of more efficient machinery and harsh and exacting management policy. While Russia as a whole averaged 16.6 workers per 1,000 spindles, Petersburg averaged only 8.1. (Spinning predominated over weaving, dyeing, and printing factories in

5. Semanov, *Peterburgskie rabochie*, p. 61. The figure given there for all textile workers is very close to the average wage of cotton workers in the same period: see Leontief, *Die Baumwollindustrie in St. Petersburg und ihre Arbeiter*, p. 74.

6. Semanov, *Peterburgskie rabochie*, p. 89.

7. From a discussion in the Finance Ministry's Department of Trade and Manufacturing dealing with the conditions underlying the 1896 cotton strike. *RDR*, vol. 4, pt. 1, pp. 232–33.

the capital, although a number of factories combined two or more of these functions.) Output per worker in Petersburg spinneries was 46 percent above the Russian average, which compared favorably with the productivity of West European spinneries (except those of England).[8] Yet the comparison is spurious because Petersburg spinners worked longer hours for less pay than their European counterparts. Petersburg cotton workers also worked more days out of the year than workers in most other industries and areas of the Empire.[9]

The low wages and poor working conditions meant that the cotton industry recruited from the less skilled and more disadvantaged elements of the city and elsewhere. Women, who made up about half the work force of the textile industry, and newly arrived, unskilled peasants, both male and female, predominated. This is amply reflected in the literacy rate among textile workers, about 40 percent around 1900. Workers of the textile industry ranked with those of the animal products industry as the least lettered sectors of the city's work force. By contrast, literacy among metalworkers was about 73 percent.[10] Why this politically disadvantaged, superexploited occupation became the first to engage in a citywide strike will be discussed presently. Let us first learn how it came about.

The strike began as a walkout by the spinning assistants (*podruchnye*) at the Russian Spinnery (Rossiiskaia Bumagopriadil'nia) in the Narva district on May 23, 1896. One hundred spinners (out of 700 workers at the factory) demanded pay for the two recent holidays and compensation for an extra 20 minutes they had been forced to work each day since 1887. Although the hasty appearance of Factory Inspector F. I. Rykovskii led them to return to work that day, they tried (unsuccessfully) to close the entire factory on the following day, and they remained on strike until May 27. The management finally promised to compensate them for the extra work time for the past year.[11]

Inspired by the assistants' example, and perhaps encouraged by

8. Leontief, *Die Baumwollindustrie*, pp. 24–25.

9. Petersburg cotton workers put in 296 days per year around 1900, cotton workers elsewhere 256, and metalworkers in the capital 272. The only workers in the capital who were expected to serve more days than cotton workers were woolen workers. Bernshtein-Kogan, *Chislennost'*, p. 111.

10. *Ibid.*, pp. 35, 70. The figures for textile workers apply to both sexes of the 20–39 age group; literacy among older workers was lower in all industries. The figure for the metal industry applies to male workers of the same age group; women made up a very small part of metalworkers in this period, about 1–2 percent.

11. *Spisok 1903*, p. 35, whose data stem from 1901. Sh., "K istorii , . . 1896 g.," pp. 95–96. *RDR*, vol. 4, pt. 1, p. 255.

their partial success, 100 spinners at the same factory demanded a shorter workday on the morning of the 28th and went on strike when they were refused. They were joined by most of the other spinners, and the entire plant struck till June 5. Meanwhile, word of the assistants' initiative had reached at least two other spinneries in the same district, the Ekaterinhof and the L. L. König. A similar pattern unfolded there, beginning on May 27. Preceded by the spinning assistants, a generally younger and more daring element, the workers demanded shorter workdays and compensation for the two holidays. The König mill remained in operation that day, but the Ekaterinhof spinners joined their assistants in striking for a shorter workday. On the 28th, both spinneries were on strike, and they remained idle for the next seven or eight days.[12]

Two features of these first strikes that would characterize the entire 1896 strike movement were the unevenness of strike sentiment and the interdependence of the factories in initiating and sustaining the will to strike. At all three mills, smaller groups took the initiative, others followed, and still others wanted to continue to work and had to be threatened and cajoled into joining the strike. This pattern was characteristic to some degree of all Russian strikes and perhaps of all strikes everywhere. But the absence of unions or workshop organizations and the low levels of literacy and political awareness among textile workers of this period bring these features to the fore. The lack of unity and organizational definition within each factory was compensated for by a sense of interdependence among factories, and, remarkably, the more active strikers sensed this need from the very beginning and acted decisively to meet it.

As early as May 27, and with certainty by the 28th, groups of strikers went around to neighboring cotton factories to persuade their workers to join the strike. The Ekaterinhof Park, close to the striking factories, served as a staging ground and meeting place for this strike-building activity. The strike agitators met with almost immediate success at the Mitrofaniev Spinnery, where 60 spinners and assistants led a walkout of the 675 workers. At the smaller Triumphal Spinnery in the neighboring Peterhof suburb, workers responded more slowly, partly owing to the intervention of the factory inspector, but they did strike on May 29. The Voronin, Liutsh, & Cheshire Weaving Factory on Rezvyi Island stopped work for a while, but later resumed.[13]

12. *RDR*, vol. 4, pt. 1, pp. 255–57.
13. *Ibid.*, pp. 257–58. Sh., "K istorii . . . 1896 g.," p. 97.

The strike was also spread by other, more informal means. Some of the textile workers lived amid other workers, including those from other textile factories, even if at some distance from their places of work. Unmarried workers in Petersburg and other industrial areas often lived in collective board and lodging arrangements called *arteli* (sing., *artel'*) and often composed of persons from the same province and district and/or from the same factory. The *artel'*, however, was only a formalized variant of a more widespread and general preference for reproducing in the city the extended family and collective arrangements familiar to most of the village population. This situation made for relatively rapid communication of news about the strikes and served as a conduit for the strike fever.[14] This was how word of the strikes probably first spread to other districts of the city. Some workers at the factories still operating were therefore prepared for the visits of the roving agitators calling them out to strike. Such was the case at the New Spinnery when on May 30

> twelve assistants of the spinning department, voluntarily stopping work, went out of the factory building to the gates. They were joined by workers [from other plants], and this crowd began to shout in front of the factory windows, demanding a work stoppage. But these shouts did not achieve their aim, and work in the factory continued. Then this same crowd went to the neighboring Kozhevnikov Factory, which has 510 workers, including 230 women, and called for a strike there, whereupon all the workers simultaneously stopped work.[15]

Willingness to strike frequently outstripped the existence of a precise and common idea of what the strike was about or the ability to raise concrete demands. For example, striking Kozhevnikov workers presented no demands for three days, and other factories failed to formulate any demands of their own whatsoever. Such occurrences were open to misinterpretation. Government reports frequently maintained (and this continued right through 1905) that whole factories sometimes struck against their will, in response to threats of violence by agitators from without the factory. Certainly threats, coercion, and

14. *RDR*, pp. 233–34. On *arteli*, see Eremeev, ed., *Gorod S.-Peterburg s tochki zreniia meditsinskoi politsii*, pp. 314–19, 588–93. The absence of mention of artels among textile workers in this district-by-district survey of the city indicates that they may not have been very common among them by the late nineteenth century. For other living arrangements among textile workers, see Mikhailov, *Iz zhizni rabochego. Vospominaniia chlena Soveta Rabochikh Deputatov. 1905 g.*, p. 9; and Bakhtiarov, *Proletariat i ulichnye tipy Peterburga. Bytovye ocherki*, pp. 107–9.

15. *RDR*, vol. 4, pt. 1, p. 258.

violence were applied by strikers to persuade reluctant workers. It is
also true that when telling an investigating policeman or factory inspector that they were striking because of outside coercion, workers
were sometimes protecting themselves from reprisal. In the absence
of unions and legally guaranteed rights, most workers found it difficult to assume an out-and-out adversary posture toward managers
and foremen to whom they were beholden for their jobs and whom
they would have to face on the morrow of the strike bereft of the unity
and solidarity of purpose that the strike had generated.

The failure to raise strike demands was often easily explained. The
illegality of labor organization in Russia forced workers to strike first,
then deliberate. With interruptions and harrassment from the police
and management, formulating a list of demands that had the support
of the strikers could take several days. The remarkable and less easily
explained aspect of this was the almost universal readiness of workers
during strike movements to walk out first and find the reasons afterward or to strike without raising demands or without an immediate
material gain in mind. Cotton workers were the first to do this in large
numbers, but the practice was soon characteristic of Petersburg workers as a whole. In 1905 the practice was attributed to the superheated
political atmosphere, and even the Factory Inspectorate, keeper of
the most systematic strike statistics, in that year began to classify sympathy strikes that did not raise separate demands as "political" rather
than "economic." This categorization was probably chosen without intending to make a theoretical statement, but simply because it was
logical to view sympathy strikes without demands as not economic; yet
the strikes had to be tabulated somewhere, so they became "political"
by default, and the political category came to mean not only having a
clearcut political motive, but "intangible or unknown cause" as well.

The "political" and "economic" categories used by the Factory Inspectorate should not be confused with attributions of actual motives
and results. In the case of labeling strikes without demands "political"
the name happens to coincide with the process in that half-conscious
efforts to join with others to alter relations of power can be regarded
as "political," even though economic motives might actually have been
involved. But then, using this definition, all strikes, including those
whose intended motive and external features were unmistakably "economic," could also be regarded as "political," as could strike movements
generated in the absence of a political atmosphere, such as those of
1896. In addition, the effect of strikes on the social order was always
more political than it need have been due to the Tsarist regime's low

tolerance of urban disorder. For all these reasons the textile strikes of 1896, whose participants' actual consciousness probably ought to be described as "economic," were in fact quite "political."

By May 30 the strike had spread beyond the neighborhood of its origins—the Narva district and the southwestern part of the city—as factories in the Alexander-Nevsky and Rozhdestvensk districts (to the southeast and northeast, respectively) stopped work. On June 1, it spread even farther to the southeast when the large Spassk & Petrov spinning and weaving complex (2,740 workers) and the Paul (Pal') Factory (2,220 workers) struck. During the week of June 3, cotton workers were still beginning strikes in the Vyborg and Petersburg districts, while those in the Narva district were ending theirs.[16] The initial pattern of the strike reproduced itself in the later phases: strikes at several factories of the same district on the same day or within a day or two of each other; demands for shorter hours and pay for the two holidays, sometimes accompanied by demands for higher wages and a reduction of fines; the initial example often set by younger workers with less to lose, especially spinners' assistants; and participation by bands of roving agitators. Another feature should be added to this list: the strikes were remarkably peaceful. To be sure, on one occasion at the Nevsky Spinnery, several policemen were injured when they interfered with strikers barring the factory gates to strikebreakers, and on another occasion, at the Old Sampson Spinning and Weaving Factory, strikers broke windows, beat up some women who refused to quit work, greeted the City Governor, who came by to talk them out of striking, with "mockery and insolence," and had to be dispersed by soldiers and gendarmes.[17] These incidents, however, stood out as exceptions in what were generally peaceful and orderly strikes. This self-restraint was hailed by revolutionaries, at the time of the strike and later, as an advance over the quick resort to violence that had characterized earlier expressions of worker discontent. But this near lack of violence was probably due more to the caution of the police and to the disunity and weak leadership of the strike than to strike discipline or the absence of hostility toward the authorities among cotton workers.

Beyond agitational activity, the presentation of demands, and the barring of strikebreakers at some factories—all of which occurred in and around the premises of the workplace—there seems to have been little strike activity and organizing. Overt labor organizing was illegal,

16. *Ibid.*, pp. 259–62.
17. *Ibid.*, pp. 260–61. Sh., "K istorii . . . 1896 g.," p. 98.

after all, and the strikers were carefully watched by the authorities. Once the attention of the police was aroused during the first few days of a strike, it became even more difficult than normal to hold meetings. Certainly, many small groups met and discussed the strike informally, both on the job and off. Yet it is not surprising that the few known attempts to provide guidance and leadership for the strike as a whole emanated from revolutionaries, and that the cotton workers themselves failed to develop their own, self-sustaining leadership and strategy.

At the initiative of the Union of Struggle, a meeting of two or three representatives from each striking factory was called for June 2 at the Putilov Embankment. It is not clear how many representatives showed up, and the Union of Struggle members seemed more interested in gathering information about the strike and distributing leaflets than in developing a strike leadership among the workers. Apparently, the attendance of workers was neither sizable nor representative, and a second meeting was called at the same place for the next day, at which the revolutionaries promised to distribute strike support money that had been collected abroad. About 300 workers appeared, but the revolutionary intellectuals failed to show up with the money, and one of the Social Democratic workers delivered a speech instead.[18] A participant in these events and later a leading writer-editor for *Rabochaia mysl'*, K. M. Takhtarev, has mentioned other meetings of workers during the strike: "Worker meetings and gatherings took place continually. The most heated one occurred on [one of] the first days of June at the Volkov Cemetery. The [politically] conscious workers wanted to explain the importance of this unprecedented strike," but the fate of this meeting was not determined by them. "Because of the harassment of spies and police, the meeting lasted a very short time, and only about a hundred workers attended."[19]

It seems remarkable that the Union of Struggle had as much impact as it did, given the difficulties of public meetings, the suspicion with which most workers viewed revolutionaries, and the Union's own internal weaknesses. The Union's activity in this period was confined chiefly to printing and distributing leaflets that contained timely and accurate references to conditions in specific factories, but that refrained from overt revolutionary sloganry. The Union also solicited

18. *RDR*, vol. 4, pt. 1, pp. 332–33.

19. Takhtarev's failure to describe any of the other meetings he claimed took place "continually" may mean that they were smaller, less heated, less political, or more informal. Takhtarev, *Rabochee dvizhenie v Peterburge (1893–1901 gg.)*, p. 63.

and distributed funds to support the strikers, but the amount was far from adequate. The leaflets, as well as simple pamphlets written for workers, were aimed only at helping workers to recognize the need to struggle on their own behalf, and they were read, discussed, and referred to frequently in the course of the 1896 textile strikes.[20] In some cases, Union of Struggle leaflets helped bring returning workers out on strike again.[21] More workers surely knew about the Union of Struggle and had a favorable opinion of it after the 1896 strikes than before, and these facts mark an advance in political awareness and sophistication among Petersburg workers.

On balance, however, it is more reasonable to stress the self-activity of the cotton workers and the relative lack of leadership than to claim, as Social Democrats did at the time, that the Union of Struggle *led* the strike.[22] The Union of Struggle had few cadres inside the cotton factories, and there is no evidence that those that existed played a direct leadership role in the strike. The worker who was charged with calling the June 2 meeting, for instance, was not even a cotton worker, but a metalworker from the shops of the Petersburg-Warsaw Railroad.[23] On the other hand, leaders of Social Democratic propaganda circles at the Spassk & Petrov and the Paul cotton mills, workers with ties to the Union of Struggle, seem to have engaged principally in the formulation and distribution of leaflets during the strike. If they and their circles were also engaged in leading the strikes at their factories, there is no record of this.[24] The activists of the Union of Struggle, new to the strategy of mass agitation and very much aware of their weaknesses and of the generally low tolerance of revolutionary agitators among workers, sensibly confined themselves to a support role and did not try to substitute themselves for the inadequate worker leadership.

At the factory level, of course, there were individual workers who came to the fore, just as there were those who hung back, but they remain a shadowy and indistinct group whose aims, intentions, and composition are unclear. It appears that they did not go beyond directing and encouraging crowds of workers and sometimes formulat-

20. Wildman has carefully and convincingly shown this in *The Making of a Workers' Revolution*, chap. 3.

21. Takhtarev, *Rabochee dvizhenie*, p. 66.

22. See, for example, the hyperbolic account of the Union's role in the strike in *Listok 'Rabotnika'*, no. 1 (Nov. 1896), reprinted in *RDR*, vol. 4, pt. 1, p. 302.

23. *Ibid.*, pp. 332, 896.

24. Kochergin, "90-e gody na fabrike 'Rabochii' (b. Maksvel')," p. 110.

ing and presenting demands to the management. The police were usually quite determined to identify the leaders in a strike situation, hoping to exert control over the situation by arresting and punishing the "instigators" and "ringleaders." Yet a memorandum on the strike by the procurator of the Petersburg Judicial Court, A. E. Kichin, could name only 16 workers who stood out from the crowd at various factories, usually only in superficial ways. Some were heard to threaten the management, some stood out by the "sharpness and rudeness" of their statements to the crowd, others were only "noticed." In only one case was a worker named who presented the strikers' demands to the management.[25]

At most of the striking factories, the spinners' assistants played a key role in initiating the walkouts. Often they were the first to strike and sometimes the only workers on strike for the first day or so. This is understandable, in that assistants had the least to risk by striking. They were less likely to be heads of families, earned less (even though they performed much the same work as spinners), and changed jobs more frequently.[26] In addition, the assistants were younger (15 to 25) than the other workers, and therefore more likely to be literate and susceptible to revolutionary propaganda. In most cases the assistants brought along the other workers by the force of their example, a reflection of the strength of the others' desire to strike. Although the spinneries' inability to function without the assistants' labor undoubtedly gave them additional influence, one need not accept the claim of some spinners that it was the assistants' withdrawal that prevented them from working. Indeed, had they wished to do so spinners could have kept their part of the factory in operation even after their assistants had left, as happened in at least one recorded instance.[27]

The chief circumstance limiting the leadership potential of the assistants, and therefore limiting the potential of the textile strikes altogether, was the assistants' low status within the factory order. Their youthfulness and low wages meant that they lacked any elements of

25. *RDR*, vol. 4, pt. 1, pp. 253–64. Kichin's list is incomplete since 56 "chief leaders and organizers" from among the strikers were eventually convicted and exiled (*Ibid.*, n. 64, p. 841). Nevertheless, it gives an idea of the difficulty of identifying the strike's leaders.

26. One government report mentioned that only 50 percent of the assistants were permanent, the remainder constituting an "itinerant element." *Ibid.*, p. 234.

27. *Ibid.*, p. 256. Sh., "K istorii . . . 1896 g.," p. 96. Spinners as a unified group, by creating a bottleneck, were able to shut down those factories which combined spinning with functions that depended on a constant output of thread, such as weaving and dyeing. *RDR*, vol. 4, pt. 1, p. 255.

natural authority within the work force. That a sustained and citywide strike could function with only their example and limited guidance attests to the depth and breadth of strike sentiment among the other workers.[28]

Hence, the city, district, and factory leadership of the strike was uneven, inadequate, and unsure of itself overall. In several cases the intervention of the factory inspector persuaded striking workers to resume work. In others, strikers stood up to the threats and blandishments of the authorities with aggressiveness and political savvy. There seemed to be no middle ground, and throughout the strike each side viewed the unconditional surrender of its opponents as the principal means of resolving the conflict. Certainly the Factory Inspectorate and owners did not propose negotiations, although early in the strike some of the latter tried to mollify their strikers with small concessions. Finance Minister Witte and Factory Inspector Rykovskii firmly opposed concessions, thinking that they would only encourage more factories to strike in the hope of gaining something.[29] On the other hand, there is no evidence that the strikers ever proposed a compromise either.

Yet the textile strikers did not take the political offensive. They displayed a political awareness of their position in the sense that they understood that they could not trust the police and the government, yet they did not see their strike effort as directed against the authorities. An illustration of this occurred at the Spassk & Petrov complex on the first day of the strike there. Soon after the workers walked out, two factory inspectors arrived and proposed that the strikers elect five persons to explain their demands. "The elections began, but voices were heard [saying] that elections were completely unnecessary. Let the inspector himself come out and talk with everyone. Both inspectors departed."[30] Given the cynicism of the factory inspectors in calling for negotiations when a "no concessions" policy was in effect, the workers' response was wise and tactically astute; they categorically rejected an attempt to create the appearance of compromise that would be used to gain the resumption of work. At other factories, deputies and representatives were elected, although similar "voices"

28. Actually, spinning assistants' wages of 80–90 kopecks per day placed them in the middle ranks of cotton workers, among whom, one study found, 57 percent of the women and 34 percent of the men earned less. Leontief, *Die Baumwollindustrie*, pp. 75–77.

29. Sh., "K istorii . . . 1896 g.," pp. 95, 100–101.

30. Takhtarev, *Rabochee dvizhenie*, pp. 65–66.

were probably heard there as well. Yet, portentous though the 1896 strikes were of the overtly political labor movement of a few years later, the textile workers did not distill the meaning of their protest into demands for systemic changes, either in the factory or in the state. None of the strikers' demands went beyond those already mentioned—a shorter workday with no loss of pay, payment for the two holidays, and other demands confined to working conditions.[31]

Yet the strike had obvious political content: it brought to the surface resentment and anger against state authority, and it educated workers to the unfailing support the government rendered the factory owners when their power was really threatened. Because of this, the failure of the strikers to formulate political demands does not mean that the phrase "economic strike" adequately describes the whole experience. Thousands of workers risked their livelihoods in a fight which arrayed the Factory Inspectorate, the City Governor, and the police against them, all of whom they normally feared and obeyed. The awareness of their own power led the workers of one striking factory to institute a 10½-hour day at their own initiative. Although it lasted only a couple of days, this early adumbration of the eight-hour day campaigns of 1905 shows that this kind of direct-action tactic was not specific to revolutionary conditions, but was one of the options built in to militant strikes in the polarized and unyielding conditions of prerevolutionary Russia.[32]

The fight for a shorter workday among cotton workers did not end on June 15, with the return to work of the last strikers. On January 2, 1897, Spassk & Petrov workers began a second strike, and they were soon joined by workers from other textile factories. Although the second strike was not as long or as widespread as the first, it moved the authorities to announce a reduction of the maximum length of the workday to 11½ hours, beginning April 16. (The promise was made good in the Law of June 2, 1897.) No advance in leadership and organization among the workers was evident in the second strike, and the role of the Union of Struggle was less extensive than in 1896. Nevertheless, the workers' militancy did not entirely end with the announcement of a shorter workday. Several factories struck on the very day the government made the announcement, and many factories de-

31. The only surviving lists of demands are those drawn up in Union of Struggle leaflets. See, e.g., *RDR*, vol. 4, pt. 1, pp. 205–68. The failure to raise even minimal political demands stemmed not only from the cotton workers, but from their political mentors as well.

32. Sh., "K istorii . . . 1896 g.," p. 99.

manded the *immediate* introduction of a regulated workday as well as other concessions.[33]

Despite the setbacks, the inadequate organization, and the lack of a clear understanding of the full political meaning and consequences of their actions, the striking workers had opened a new chapter in the urban politics of Tsarist Russia. The conditions that gave rise to their strikes existed elsewhere, and it was only a matter of time until the conflict in the Petersburg cotton industry reproduced itself, on a greater or lesser scale, in other factories, industries, and cities.

1896 AND 1901: FROM TEXTILE WORKERS TO METALWORKERS

One of the characteristic, and usually unexplained, features of the textile strikes is their failure to spread immediately to other industries. Strike support funds were collected in Petersburg and even in other provinces, and discontent was expressed at other plants in the city during the strikes. But, despite extensive leafleting by the Union of Struggle at many of the larger metal and machine plants and despite the dominance of metalworkers in the revolutionary circles, only one other plant in another industry struck along with the cotton workers.[34]

The exceptional case illustrates an important difference between workers in the metal and machine trades and those in the textile industry and most other industries. On June 8, 1896, 3,000 workers of the Aleksandrovsk Machine Works (Aleksandrovskii Mekhanicheskii Zavod) in the Schlüsselburg suburb refused to start work until they were paid overdue back wages and compensation for the same holidays for which the textile workers were demanding payment. The police were immediately called, but instead of taking a hard line, as was being done in the case of the cotton workers, the chief of police arranged for both demands to be met. In addition, the strikers were promised that three unpopular foremen would be dismissed and that the workday on Saturdays would end at 2 P.M.[35]

33. Suslova, "Peterburgskie stachki," pp. 77–78.

34. Korol'chuk and Sokolova, *Khronika revoliutsionnogo rabochego dvizheniia v Peterburge*, pp. 218, 221, 222. Small parts of some other plants did strike during the next round of textile strikes, in January 1897. Suslova, "Peterburgskie stachki," p. 78. For unrest in factories outside textiles, see Shotman, *Zapiski starogo bol'shevika*, pp. 23–24, and n. 36 below.

35. *RDR*, vol. 4, pt. 1, pp. 247–49, 252. A second group of metalworker strikers

The police chief was clearly interested in mollifying the Aleksandrovsk workers before their discontent ignited the numerous other metalworkers in the area, but he was also responding to a fact of industrial life: skilled metalworkers were harder to replace and much more in demand in St. Petersburg than semiskilled textile workers, and they were almost always better treated as a result. They worked shorter hours, received higher wages, and often enjoyed milder treatment from managements anxious to avoid disorders and to preserve industrial peace. One reason for the relative passivity of the metalworkers during the textile strikes is that most of them already worked 11 hours or less per day. In addition, workers in state-owned plants, which included many of the city's biggest metal plants, were paid for the three holidays, so the grievance precipitating the textile workers' strike did not affect them (the Aleksandrovsk Works was an exception in this regard). This is not to idealize the situation of metalworkers, only to point out that they were relatively better off. Along with other workers, they certainly faced authoritarian practices from their managements, arbitrariness from their foremen, and instability in employment and wages.

The scarcity of skilled metalworkers was heightened by the expansion of the metalworking and machine-building industries in the 1890's, noted in the previous chapter (see Table 3). That decade witnessed relatively little unrest in Petersburg's metal and machine plants, and certainly nothing even approaching the 1896 textile strike. The few strikes and protests that took place tended to be short-lived, usually involved only a small part of the plant, and had no important consequences. For instance, in December 1894, workers at the Nevsky Ship and Machine Works wrecked the company store, blocked traffic, and broke windows in passing trolleys and in the company offices to express their outrage over a delay in the arrival of the payroll. No demands were made, no discussions were held, and when the payroll finally arrived the disorders ceased. At the Putilov Works, 100 workers of the Locomotive Machine Shop struck briefly in June 1896 for an 8-hour day and other demands, but they were not joined by fellow workers despite the example of the cotton workers and months of agitation at the plant over pay cuts.[36]

---

from the Putilov Works, also inspired by the textile workers, has not been mentioned here due to their small number.

36. *RDR*, vol. 3, pt. 2, pp. 542–43; vol. 4, pt. 1, pp. 26–27, 251–53, 841 (n. 63).

TABLE 14
*Percent Distribution of Strikers Within Industries
over the Decade 1895–1904*

Year	Russia			Petersburg		
	Cotton	Metal	All	Cotton	Metal	All
1895	9.9%	1.9%	7.2%	2.4%	0.2%	5.5%
1896	11.7	2.0	6.8	27.9	7.6	17.4
1897	24.9	2.7	13.9	17.3	12.3	13.5
1898	13.3	6.1	10.0	18.8	15.9	16.5
1899	8.3	16.8	13.3	0.2	4.5	2.0
1900	7.1	7.7	6.8	0.0	0.3	0.1
1901	4.0	13.3	7.5	9.0	49.8	21.9
1902	8.2	10.8	8.5	2.0	0.2	1.2
1903	10.2	26.4	20.1	21.2	6.1	20.2
1904	2.0	12.3	5.8	1.2	3.0	1.6
Total no.	185,101	116,973	431,254	66,615	40,890	124,385
Total pct.	42.9%	27.1%	100.0%	53.6%	32.9%	100.0%

SOURCES: Russia—*Stachki 1895–1904*, p. 17; *Stachki 1905*, p. 17 and Appendix, p. 2.
Petersburg—estimated from "Khronika", in *RDR*, vol. 4, pt. 2, pp. 736–826, and from *Rabochee
dvizhenie v Rossii v 1901–1904 gg.*, pp. 383–537.

Nevertheless, there is reason to believe that the dissatisfaction of metalworkers was mounting by the end of the decade. The industrial slump that struck Russian factories in 1899 and the new political initiatives by the Social Democrats among factory workers after 1896 contributed to this growing discontent and helped precipitate its expression in the strikes of 1901 and later. Both these topics will be discussed later in the chapter, but in order to comprehend these changes in the broadest possible context, we shall begin by examining the nature of work and work-generated social patterns in Petersburg's two major industries.

One of the most obvious changes in this period was a shift in the leading industry engaged in strikes from cotton textiles to metal and machinery, both in Petersburg and in the country as a whole (see Table 14). In both Petersburg and the Russian Empire, these two industries accounted for the great bulk of strikers (86.5 and 70.0 percent, respectively). Cotton textile workers clearly predominated, contributing 185,101 strikers during the decade, or over two-fifths of all 431,254 strikers in Russia, and over half of those in Petersburg (66,615 of 124,385). The shift from textiles to metals shows up most dramatically in the figures for Russia, where the balance between the two halves of the decade shifted from 70-30 to 30-70. In Petersburg the shift was less dramatic, mainly because the number of metalworker strikers fell off sharply after 1901, while the number of textile strikers, declining after 1898, suddenly jumped again in 1903. Yet despite the predominance of textile strikers for the decade as a whole, the trend of change is clear from the fact that in 1905, 55 percent of Petersburg strikers worked in the metal industry and 18 percent in cotton textiles.[37]

What can explain the fact that skilled, highly paid, and highly literate metalworkers were relatively quiescent in the 1890's, when workers with similar advantages were in the forefront of labor militancy in other countries? It takes more than severe exploitation to account for labor militancy; having the *means* of protest, rather than the best cause for it, is usually a surer guide in explaining which groups protest most effectively, if not first or most frequently. And why, by the same token, did the cotton workers, who stood at the opposite end of the pay, literacy, skill, and prestige scales, strike first, in greater numbers, and with greater collective solidarity in the citywide upheavals of 1896 and 1897?

These questions have not been posed in the past, seemingly because once the leadership of metalworkers in the labor movement became unmistakably manifest to all in 1905, their higher consciousness, literacy, and social status among workers seemed a sufficient explanation for the ascendancy of "advanced" metalworkers over "backward" workers generally.[38] However, for most of the period preceding 1905, the very opposite of this formula was nearer the truth, and that situation does demand an answer. In 1905 and later, other workers did not

37. These figures should be corrected to allow for the fact that metalworkers constituted 43 percent and cotton workers only 13 percent of the city's work force in 1905. If one divides the percent of strikers by the percent of workers, one receives the *strike propensity*, a measure of strike intensity of various components of the working class that corrects for their varying proportions within it. The strike propensity of cotton textile workers in 1905 was 1.39; that of metalworkers, 1.28. However, if one corrects for the predominance of large factories among cotton mill workers by counting strikers at only the larger metal plants, the propensity of metalworkers is higher than that of any other industry. The sources for these calculations consist of those publications listed in Table 14 and my own data compiled from diverse published and unpublished sources, hereafter referred to as the City File. Extensive use of the notion of strike propensity is made by Engelstein in "Moscow in the 1905 Revolution: A Study in Class Conflict and Political Organization," and by Shorter and Tilly, *Strikes in France 1830–1968*. The wider use of propensity calculations in this study has been hampered by the absence of precise data on numbers of strikes and workers.

38. The counterposing of "advanced" metalworkers to "backward" textile and other workers is a stock formula in most Soviet textbooks, and the view is shared or repeated by some Western authors as well.

follow metalworkers blindly, but had their own reasons for striking, and textile workers in particular continued to strike at very high rates. Workers certainly underwent profound and important changes in 1905, but their behavior, far from being totally determined by the developments of that year, was rooted in the activity of protest and resistance of earlier years.

The volatility of the kinds of workers in textile mills has sometimes been cited as a reason for their early strike activity in the absence of politically conscious leadership. One eminent Soviet historian has addressed this problem in the following manner: "the prevalence among textile workers of semipeasant and peasant elements and of submissive and downtrodden, although easily inflamed, masses of women and teenagers [*podrostki*] led to a situation in which the unbearable conditions of life raised the whole mass of them to struggle, not only its politically conscious part."[39]

Despite the somewhat simplistic correlation of "downtrodden masses" with the propensity to revolt, this passage expresses an important truth in its recognition that volatility was as much a part of "backward" or peasant workers as was submissiveness. Yet the argument is too broad to offer an adequate explanation of textile worker behavior: there were large enough concentrations of peasant (or semipeasant) workers in the metal industry for its workers to have become "easily inflamed," yet on the whole they did not. Clothing workers included disproportionately large shares of underpaid and otherwise exploited women and youths, yet they did not revolt. Women tobacco workers in Petersburg, by contrast, struck on several occasions in the mid-1890's. Yet neither tobacco workers nor metalworkers nor any others organized a citywide strike or dominated all strikes before 1901 as did textile workers. More than oppression and the capacity to become "easily inflamed" stood behind the leading role of textile workers in strike activity.

And yet, textile workers seemed particularly ill-placed to develop their own leaders. Though the spinning assistants served as the instigators of the 1896 strikes, we have seen that they stood at the middle or even the bottom of the wage, authority, and length-of-service hierarchies in their factories. The weak leadership of the textile strikes would seem to have been due in large part to the lack of correspondence between strike initiative and authority conferred by the work

39. Pankratova, ed., *Ocherki istorii proletariata SSSR. Proletariat tsarskoi Rossii*, p. 114. See also Shapovalov, *Na puti k marksizmu (Po doroge k marksizmu)*.

process. The spinning assistants took the initiative but lacked this authority, while those enjoying the authority—if such an element existed at all among textile workers—were not prominent among the strike's leaders.

It is certainly unlikely that strike leadership was exercised by cotton mill foremen (*mastera*), who seem to have been totally identified with the management and whose relationships with workers, especially in spinneries, were unmediated either by participation in their work or by the presence of intermediate layers of skilled workers. To add to the polarization of workers and management, foremen were often foreigners who sometimes did not even speak Russian. Foremen at the large mills were the captains and colonels of the industrial army, commanding battalions of unskilled or semiskilled men, women, and children, organized into huge departments (*otdeleniia*). To these already impersonal and regimented conditions must be added an inescapable fact of life in large textile mills: between the foremen and their workers stood the machines of Russia's largest mass-production industry, insuring, by their deafening noise, their regular and continuous rhythm, and their need for the constant attention of the operators, the near elimination of those networks of personal relations with fellow workers so familiar in fields and workshops and so essential to the development of a consciousness of self and community in the workplace. Cotton workers were thus hard put to generate labor leaders from their own ranks, and the formlessness of the 1896 strikes reflected this. They were highly atomized and weakly differentiated among themselves because cotton mills created fairly flat hierarchies of skill and pay, with even the highest-paid workers barely earning a subsistence wage at the best of times.[40]

The polarization of workers and management and the absence of worker leaders generated by the work process meant that a dispute in any part of a cotton mill tended to bring workers immediately up against the management, with little chance that a foreman could play a mediating role since the nature of the work kept him at a distance

40. Leontief, *Die Baumwollindustrie*, pp. 74–78. I have found no direct evidence of the nature of textile mill organization, even in the *fondy* of the mills themselves in the Leningrad City Historical Archive (LGIA). The sketch of conditions in large cotton mills presented in this and the next paragraph is drawn from Leontief; Bakhtiarov, *Proletariat i ulichnye tipy*, pp. 106–29; "Dnevnik upravliaiushchego Nevskoi Nitochnoi Fabrikoi K.I. Monkera za 1905–1907 gody"; and, above all, a number of the documents in *RDR*, vols. 3 and 4. Monker's diary shows that the most common sources of strikes and discontent in 1905 were smaller, more specialized groups like the dyers or sizers rather than the large departments of spinners.

from the workers and invested him with little authority once the fairness of management practice or policy was called into question. The
diary of K. I. Monker, Assistant Director of the Nevsky Thread Factory in 1905, shows that a large number of workshop disputes were
appealed directly to the top level of management.[41] This placed foremen in a difficult position and probably led them to defend management policy more quickly and to rely more on their formal authority
than on personal persuasiveness in dealing with workers' complaints.
In addition, the universally low wages and lack of variety in the work
had a homogenizing effect on cotton workers so that "an injury to
one" was more easily perceived as "an injury to all." These circumstances created a brittle situation in cotton mills, and the volatility of
cotton workers owed at least as much to this as to "peasant rebel-
liousness." The endemic tension between textile workers and foremen
expressed itself in frequent demands during strikes for the dismissal
of specific foremen.

The situation of metalworkers contrasted strikingly with that of
textile workers. The average size of Petersburg's metal shops and
plants was smaller than that of cotton mills, although there were more
very large enterprises (over 2,000 workers) in the metal than the textile industry. Even in the metalworking giants, however, work was less
dominated by the machine than in textile mills; more handwork and
job control by the workers were clearly in evidence.[42] The organization of work in metal plants also differed. Medium and large plants
were conglomerations of shops (*masterskie*), each responsible for one
product or process in the plant's output. For instance, the Obukhov
Steel Mill, which specialized in naval ordnance, was divided into shops
for smelting steel and pig iron, casting copper, hammering, pressing,
rolling, and toolmaking; there were also divisions for making optical
instruments, mines, guns, and high-velocity shells, plus twenty other

41. "Dnevnik . . . Monkera."
42. In 1904, cotton mills in Petersburg averaged 696 workers and metal plants 346.
*Statistika neschastnykh sluchaev s rabochimi v promyshlennykh zavedeniiakh podchinennykh
nadzoru fabrichnoi inspektsii za 1904 god*, pp. 16–21; Bulkin, *Na zare profdvizheniia. Istoriia
Peterburgskogo soiuza metallistov 1906–1914*, table facing p. 52. On mechanization, my
generalization is based on photographs, memoirs, and descriptions of metal work by
contemporaries, e.g., Bakhtiarov, *Proletariat i ulichnye tipy Peterburga*, pp. 129–44. A
calculation showing that cotton mills averaged 1.42 h.p. per worker (compared with
0.90 h.p. per worker in metal plants) illustrates but cannot prove the broader point,
especially because larger metal plants, by this standard, were more highly mechanized
yet: 11 plants with 500 or more workers averaged 1.73 h.p. per worker. *Spisok fabrik i
zavodov Rossii za 1910 g.*

shops, offices, and service functions. Each part of the plant consisted of workers with the appropriate skills, together with their assistants and apprentices, and each shop ranged in size from a handful of workers to several hundred. Mass production techniques in machine building had not been much developed even in more advanced countries, so much of the work was done by hand, employing fairly simple tools. Close identification with the product and pride of craftsmanship were characteristic of the skilled workers in this field. The interdependent and cooperative nature of machine building and foundry work fostered an *esprit de corps* among the skilled men reminiscent of that of the preindustrial workshop.[43]

This pride in the mastery of a skill probably accounted for a large part of shop and factory patriotism noted among Russian workers generally, but actually most characteristic of metalworkers. "Workers would consider themselves, and would be considered by others, as 'putilovtsy,' if they worked at the colossal Putilov Works; as 'obukhovtsy,' if they worked at the Obukhov Steel Works; or as 'semyannikovtsy,' if they worked at the Semyannikov Works—the old name for the Nevskii Shipbuilding Company."[44] Shop membership also gave rise to fierce loyalties, and this "shopism" or "shop orientation" was most pronounced in the same metal plants that manifested the strongest factory patriotism. The coexistence of these two foci of loyalty bore witness to an apparently contradictory but fundamental truth about the metalworker community: they were more coherent and better organized and acted more effectively than other workers, both on the shop floor and at the factory level. Where the balance between shop-oriented divisiveness and all-factory unity would fall in any given period depended on circumstances outside the area of structure and organization.

The uplifting force of the mastery of skilled work in metal plants was admirably described by the *putilovets* A. M. Buiko:

43. Informative firsthand reportage on life and labor in Petersburg's large metal plants is available in Timofeev, *Chem zhivet zavodskii rabochii*, which appeared earlier as articles: "Zavodskie budni (Iz zapisok rabochego)," *Russkoe bogatstvo*, nos. 8 and 9 (1903), and "Ocherki zavodskoi zhizni," *ibid.*, nos. 9 and 10 (1905). Selections from this memoir have been translated in Victoria Bonnell, ed., *The Russian Worker. Life and Labor Under the Tsarist Regime* (Berkeley, Calif., 1983), pp. 73–112. On the close cooperation required in two types of metal work, see the sketches of *"Liteishchiki"* and *"Kuznetsy"* in Bakhtiarov, *Proletariat i ulichnye tipy*, pp. 129–44.

44. Smith, "Craft Consciousness, Class Consciousness: Petrograd, 1917," pp. 34–35, is a sound summary statement of a phenomenon as characteristic of Petrograd workers in 1917 as of Petersburg workers in 1900.

In those days it was felt that if a worker did not master his trade, did not become a good craftsman, then he was not a proper fellow. This point of view had its roots in the days of *kustarshchina*, when old craftsmen regarded unskilled workers as a casual element in their midst. . . . If a young man began a conversation with an older skilled fitter or turner he would be told: "Learn first how to hold a hammer and use a chisel and a knife, then you can begin to argue like a man who has something to teach others."

Fulfillment of the expectations of the heavily masculine metalworker tradition could have an energizing and exhilarating effect on a young man's personal development: "I was totally taken with interest in work at the plant and in the comrades around [me], I felt myself cheerful and confident. A link with an immense human collective began to awaken in me an inquisitiveness, an interest in various problems of work life, to call forth a desire to learn and to understand phenomena of the milieu surrounding me."[45]

The steep gradation of skills, which of necessity characterized metal work, became the framework upon which was superimposed a hierarchy of management and control. At the gigantic Putilov Plant (over 12,000 workers in 1901), shops were subordinated to larger "divisions" (*otdely*), e.g., for metallurgy, machines, railroad cars, locomotives, and so forth. The organization of the division and shop illustrates the manner in which skill and managerial hierarchies paralleled one another: (1) division manager; (2) his assistant (*pomoshchnik*); (3) the head of a shop; (4) his assistant; (5) masters or foremen (*mastera*); (6) their assistants; (7) the senior worker (a fitter); (8) skilled workers (*masterovye*); (9) assistants (*podruchnye*); (10) apprentices; (11) unskilled workers; (12) engineers, harness makers, sweepers.[46]

The word *master* means both "foreman" and "master," in the sense of a master craftsman, and this ambiguity embodies the history of skilled work after the rise of factory industry in Russia and elsewhere. In textile mills, the *master* had evolved into a supervisor of machinery and machine operators; but in metal shops, he remained to a greater degree a master of his skill, involved directly in the work process together with subordinates, and therefore accorded an authority in his

45. Buiko, *Put' rabochego. Zapiski starogo bol'shevika*, pp. 13–14, partly translated by Smith in "Craft Consciousness," p. 42.
46. Stolpianskii, *Zhizn' i byt peterburgskoi fabriki za 210 let ee sushchestvovaniia 1704–1914 gg.*, pp. 161–62, 166. Timofeev, *Chem zhivet*, pp. 4–5. A more detailed breakdown of the state-owned, mainly metal and munitions plants in Petersburg may be found in the LGIA, fond 2075, op. 5, delo one, ll. 1–8.

managerial functions based on this superior skill and direct involvement that the textile foreman lacked. To be sure, metalworking *mastera* also took advantage of their authority and earned the resentment of the workers under them, although the selectiveness of human memory has meant that we hear much more frequently about this side of the foremen/masters than we do about their mediation between managerial authority and the work process. In the schema outlined above, the masters were separated from the heads of shops, and it is not clear whether these heads (*nachal'niki*) were senior masters who rose to managerial posts or engineers and administrative functionaries. However, even in the latter case, it is likely that the Putilov masters themselves shared much of the responsibility for the work actually performed in the shops and had to transmit management policy to their subordinates. The same would have applied even more in smaller metal plants, where it is clear *mastera* actually headed shops.[47]

Unskilled workers, assistants, and apprentices also had a place within the elaborate hierarchy of the shop, albeit on the lowest rungs, yet their working conditions would have been less depersonalized and alienated than those of cotton mill workers. Of course, they were less stable than the skilled workers, coming and going more frequently, and were the more obviously exploited and discontented, as well as the more supine, element of metal plants, the "backward and volatile" part. But their volatility did not break the surface as soon or as frequently as that of textile workers because they made up a smaller part of metal plants than did the same element in textile mills, and because they normally had to move at the pace of the skilled workers.[48] In organizing a protest or strike, both skilled and unskilled workers had to overcome the shop structure of the plants, which isolated one group of workers from another, both spatially and in terms of social cohesiveness. The unevenness of conditions from one shop to another also meant that unrest, even when it materialized, could be contained within one work team or shop of the plant.

Status distinctions, especially between skilled and unskilled, but also among different skills and specialties, between those of urban and rural origins (and culture), and even among those with different grades and qualities of training and apprenticeship, also helped to divide metalworkers against themselves. Though the average wages of

47. Timofeev, *Chem zhivet*, p. 11, maintains that workers sometimes rose to head even divisions, a position normally filled by trained engineers. Worker-*mastera* would therefore, in this view, have been the norm at the shop level, even in the largest plants.

48. *Ibid.*, pp. 11–12.

metalworkers were higher than those in other industries, a break-down by skill level reveals a great deal about the stratification of metal plants. The study of workers' budgets cited earlier pegged monthly subsistence expenses for a single male worker in Petersburg at 21 rubles. In 1904 skilled workers at 15 large metal plants in Peters-burg earned an average of 54.5 rubles, unskilled workers 19.2 rubles, and apprentices 10.4 rubles.[49] The poverty line ran right through the middle of the metal shops.

These conditions—the greater psychological authority of metal foremen, the isolation and cohesiveness of shops, and the stratification of the workers along various lines—kept the metalworkers at first from playing the leading role in the strike movement that they later assumed. Yet some of the very same conditions underlay the politiciza-tion and rapid strike mobilization of metal workers in large plants in 1901 and 1905. Shop cohesiveness and loyalty, the subordination of newer, less skilled workers to masters and skilled workers who en-joyed an authority based partly on their participation in the work, and the greater autonomy of the work teams and parties within shops—these features of the large metal plants later came to strengthen the ability of their workers to mobilize and organize themselves. The presence of leaders and supervisors of the work process meant that there were individuals on hand able and ready to assume leadership positions in the course of worker-management disputes; lines of au-thority and deference established in the work process transferred more easily into organized resistance than where no such hierarchy existed. The prevalence of handwork in small groups enhanced the metalworkers' ability to communicate with one another on the job. Networks of personal relations in work parties and shops invested this communication with firmer bonds of trust than was possible in other factories and other industries. Even the loyalty and *esprit de corps* of the shop served to unify strike sentiment and opinion within it and to ameliorate the sense of rivalry often prevailing between and among shops. Revolutionary workers had an immediate and familiar audi-ence for their ideas; once strike and protest sentiment became gen-eral, such workers could exercise an influence far out of proportion to their numbers, often unifying a whole shop behind their politi-cal aims. Political and strike militancy took an uneven hold in metal plants; some shops were usually much more ready for action than others. Although intershop rivalries sometimes coincided with, and

49. Semanov, *Peterburgskie rabochie nakanune*, p. 85, citing N. M. Lisovskii, *Rabochie v voennom vedomstve* (SPb., 1906). Bulkin, *Na zare profdvizheniia*, table facing p. 52.

thereby reinforced, pro- and antistrike sentiment, in 1901 and later the more militant shops were very often able to bring out on strike the more divided and less motivated ones with varying mixtures of persuasion and force.

But what occurred in the world of the metalworkers to politicize them and to reverse the management's apparent advantage in shop structure and conflict resolution? The impact of the economic crisis after 1899 and of intensified organizing efforts by political revolutionaries will be considered below. Here we will restrict ourselves to the theme of work and factory organization. However, the limitations of the evidence compel us to move at this point into the realm of informed speculation. We shall proceed by eliminating what we know is not true, then by suggesting what might be true.

The growing militancy of metalworkers was a worldwide trend in the years under consideration.[50] Yet many of the conditions explaining this shift among metalworkers in other countries and periods did not apply to Petersburg. Let us consider, for example, scientific management policies. Soon after 1905 and partly in response to its mass protests, metal plant owners and managers led the country in adopting rationalization schemes, and this change may have played a major role in precipitating the second great period of labor unrest in Petersburg, from 1912 to July 1914.[51] But the rapid assimilation of Taylorist and related *ideas* in Russia, though begun before 1905 in response to shifts in the metal industry and the economy, did not result in their practical *application* until later; worker militancy in 1905 could not have been a response to the rise of scientific management.[52]

Nor is there evidence before 1905 of a major increase in the rate of mechanization, the replacement of skilled handwork by a number of simpler machine operations performed by cheaper, less-skilled workers.[53] Even where such a process was under way, in the larger metal plants, it was not a major source of discontent in this period, judging by strike demands. On the contrary, contemporaries still distinguished metal plants (*zavody*) from the less-skilled work of the mechanized fac-

50. See E. J. Hobsbawm, "Custom, Wages & Workload in Nineteenth Century Industry," in his *Labouring Men*, p. 424.

51. Heather Hogan makes a compelling argument for this view in "Industrial Rationalization and the Roots of Labor Militance in the St. Petersburg Metalworking Industry, 1901–1914," and in greater detail in "Labor and Management in Conflict: The St. Petersburg Metal Working Industry, 1900–1914."

52. This may be discerned in Hogan, "Industrial Rationalization," pp. 166–77, even though she stresses the importance of the causes predating 1905.

53. As David Brody found to be true in the U.S. metal industry; see his *Steelworkers in America. The Non-Union Era*, pp. 31–32, 85–86.

tories (*fabriki*) precisely because of the limited amount of "labor specialization" in the former.[54] Heather Hogan points out that the universalism of production characteristic of the Petersburg metal industry (due to the diversity of market demands in Russia) retarded the development of specialization and assembly-line arrangements.[55]

If anything, in fact, it is the continuing legacy of organizational and technical backwardness in Petersburg metal plants that must be stressed. This began with the very physical layout and equipping of plants, which expanded so enormously in the 1890's.

> In the 1890's, many of the metalworking plants that had been founded decades earlier for rails and diverse metallurgical products shifted their production to rolling stock, trying to take advantage of the new market for these goods. Old plant and auxiliary services were rarely reconstructed; rather, new equipment and new shops sprang up in haphazard fashion in the rush to capitalize on lucrative government contracts. Equipment was bought with an eye to profitable orders, with little attention to future markets and future needs. Plant layout was chaotic, electrical and mechanical power limited, connecting track between shops inadequate and poorly laid out, and as new machinery was added, floor plan was ignored and shops became congested. The work force was significantly expanded as well and was the principal factor in the increased output of these plants in the 1890's.[56]

Significant changes in the structure of managerial authority also came to the metal plants only after 1905. The use of trained engineers both in the shops and at the highest levels of management and planning was increased as part of the broader innovations in plant equipment and managerial technique adopted by metal industrialists following the 1905 Revolution. But before 1905, despite Count Witte's successes at improving and expanding the education of engineers in Russia in the 1890's, the numbers actually entering the factories remained limited owing to the overall industrial contraction after 1899; indeed, the full benefits of Witte's efforts were not felt in Russia until after 1907 or even later.[57]

It would seem, then, that the great expansion of the industry's work force in the 1890's was carried out within existing organizational

54. Timofeev, *Chem zhivet*, p. 63.
55. Hogan, "Labor and Management," pp. 108–9.
56. *Ibid.*, pp. 105–6. See also Mitel'man, Glebov, and Ul'ianskii, *Istoriia Putilovskogo zavoda. 1801–1917*, pp. 44–45.
57. Hogan, "Labor and Management," pp. 118–19, and Harley Balzer, "Educating Engineers: Economic Politics and Technical Training in Tsarist Russia" (Ph.D. diss., Univ. of Pennsylvania, 1980), chap. 5, and pp. 407, 411.

arrangements.[58] Some of the expansion took the form of new plants, but most of it entailed the growth of existing enterprises. The work force of the city's 16 largest firms, all of which existed in 1890, grew from 22,000 to 47,000 workers in the period 1891–1901. The net growth of 25,000 constituted over 50 percent of the city's total increase in metalworkers in the 1890's (about 48,000).[59] Both the metals work force as a whole and that of the largest plants had more than doubled in a decade. The influx of hundreds of new workers every year must have placed a great strain on existing shop relations, sharpening the tension along already existing fault lines: between skilled and unskilled, young and old, seasoned and inexperienced, urbanized and countrified.

The new, younger workers would have been significantly more literate than older workers and those already in place, given the growth of literacy in the 1890's. This was particularly true of the skilled workers and apprentices, and this younger, skilled, literate contingent would have stemmed disproportionately from the city. Some of them would have been conversant with the short history of labor struggles and socialist propaganda in Petersburg, just developing at the turn of the century, and many of them were surely sympathetic to the urban values underlying that history: survival and self-advancement through the cultivation of social relations among "strangers," i.e., those outside one's primary community; acknowledgment of the power of money, knowledge, science, and technology; skepticism (at least) about the natural and supernatural forces that ruled the village; and a somewhat disenchanted view of the autocracy from living in close proximity to it and its servants. The appearance of this generation in the factories hastened the breakdown of older ways, challenging the established patterns of deference and status so apparent in the stability of relations in metal shops.[60]

The influx of younger workers would have made for closer rela-

58. As noted earlier, scientific management ideas and plans were *discussed* prior to 1905, but one is hard put to find evidence of their application. See, for example, the account of the 1901 reforms of Baltic Shipyard director Ratnik in *Arkhiv istorii truda v Rossii*, no. 2, pp. 70–85, analyzed by Heather Hogan in "The Origins of the Scientific Management Movement in Russia" (unpublished paper, Jan. 1983). Also see Hogan, "Labor and Management," pp. 81–82.

59. Bulkin, *Na zare profdvizheniia*, table facing p. 52. The figures for the total 1900 and 1890 metalworker population, 79,856 and 31,963, respectively, were drawn from *Peterburg, 1900*, vyp. 2, and estimated from the 1881 and 1890 city censuses, since the 1890 census lacks data for the suburbs.

60. Workers' memoirs often relate the thirst of the younger workers in this period for knowledge and political involvement. It should be remembered that these writers

tions between factory managers and at least some of the older workers, because the latter would have both filled most of the new senior positions necessarily created by the expansion and been increasingly dependent on management to protect whatever seniority rights they enjoyed on the shop floor. Moreover, older workers often held religious and paternalistic views that would have made them less sympathetic to socialist propaganda and probably also to open protest.

This generational polarization was surely not invariable, nor was it the only development among metalworkers underlying their increased militancy after 1900. Indeed, older radical or skeptical workers often served as role models and teachers to curious newcomers to the metal shops, and the new militancy also relied on the survival of traditional elements of the artisanal shop such as hierarchies of knowledge and experience paralleling hierarchies of skill.[61] Though loyalty to separate shops continued, the numbers of newcomers and the suddenness of their arrival probably softened the usual shop exclusiveness by exceeding the ability of the shop structure to absorb and integrate them. This meant that the search for new communal ties, for *Gemeinschaft*—pursued by all newcomers to large, impersonal organizations—was left to follow other paths that could transcend shop exclusiveness. For example, the foundry worker Aleksei Buzinov told of the pain of discovering that the low regard in which "hot metal" workers like himself were held by "cold metal" workers like machinists and fitters was actually warranted. With obvious exaggeration, he claimed that "next to the most experienced foundryman, even a poor fitter seemed an educated, thinking man." Buzinov was denied a request to transfer out of the foundry to learn a cold metal trade, but he took to socializing with young workers from the cold shops.[62]

Yet, whatever the contributions of older workers or the restrictions

---

were themselves advocates of learning and political commitment, and they brought that special perspective to their experiences and memories. See, for example, the recollections of the Petersburg metalworkers A. M. Buiko (*Put' rabochego*, p. 20) and A. V. Shotman (*Zapiski starogo bol'shevika*, pp. 33–34). Interesting qualifications to the picture described there are provided by Aleksei Buzinov in *Za Nevskoi Zastavoi. Zapiski rabochego*, pp. 18–19, 22.

61. E.g., Buiko, *Put' rabochego*, p. 17; Buzinov, *Za Nevskoi Zastavoi*, pp. 29–30; Onufriev, *Za Nevskoi Zastavoi (Vospominaniia starogo bol'shevika)*, pp. 11–12.

62. *Za Nevskoi Zastavoi*, p. 21. The passage is translated and cited in Smith, *Red Petrograd*, pp. 29–30. The term "socialist" is used deliberately here and throughout the book to include Socialist Revolutionaries and other neo-Populists along with SDs when the context suggests that the involvement or participation probably went beyond the SDs, but evidence for it was not available.

of existing shop structures, something fundamental in the composition of the work force changed in the course of the 1890's and began to destabilize worker-management relations in the largest plants as never before. Evidence presented earlier points to the rapid expansion of the industry and the failure of its managers to modify the physical and administrative structure of their plants to accommodate the expansion of personnel and productive capacity. The crucial element in this expansion would seem to have been the recruitment of large numbers of young, urban-bred and -oriented, skilled, and literate workers. These new workers brought to the metal plants a much larger number of potential strike and protest leaders and seeded the shops with potential supporters and instigators. They also accounted for the growing popularity among workers of socialist-sponsored, overtly political activities such as demonstrations and May 1st meetings, noticeable after 1900. Although these newcomers had predecessors in the shops with whom they now combined forces, politicized metalworkers before the late 1890's were so few and far between that their typical experience at work was one of intense isolation. The impasse in socialist labor organizing known as the *kruzhkovshchina* had in part been based on this isolation. The relative handfuls of politicized workers clung to the propaganda circles (*kruzhki*) and to intelligentsia tutelage rather than educating and leading their still unconverted fellow workers because their sense of isolation was reinforced by the ethic of self-improvement they typically absorbed from their educations in the circles. But now, the great expansion of the 1890's was providing the social base for a shift from propaganda to agitation, from the slow training of a few leaders to the rapid "conquest of the masses" and the formation of a party rooted in the working class.

THE POLITICS OF ECONOMISM

One of the distinguishing features of Petersburg workers in the 1890's and early 1900's was their capacity to respond to events outside the factory milieu. Russian workers have played a more critical role in the political transformation of their nation than the workers of any other European country. Though the reasons for this are many and complex, one of the factors that cannot be ignored is the systematic effort of professional revolutionaries to organize, educate, and mobilize the Russian workers. The facts that Russia had a small but highly advanced revolutionary movement long before it had a politicized class of industrial workers, and that the first political steps by the fledgling working class were taken in close association with dedicated underground workers equipped with sophisticated revolutionary ideas, were of the greatest importance in the development of the Russian labor movement.

Although revolutionaries had made contact with workers in Petersburg on a small scale since the 1870's, this process of joint oppositional activity took decisive shape between the two strike movements of 1896 and 1901. The repercussions of the 1896–97 strikes were significant and far-reaching. The organization of a citywide strike by cotton workers, practically on their own initiative, and the achievement of legislative regulation of the length of the workday enlivened labor activity in all major industrial centers in the years that followed. Most revolutionaries felt that the strikes had confirmed and vindicated their efforts, and that the method of mass agitation was the key to success. The years immediately following witnessed a great expansion of the type of agitational work that the Union of Struggle had performed in 1895 and 1896: the concentration on local, in-factory grievances, with strike demands based on them and political issues raised carefully and concretely; and the limitation of the organization's role to leaflet publication, without trying at the outset to lead strikes or recruit large numbers of workers. In roughly this form, socialist organizations spread to areas where they had never existed earlier, and thousands of workers were exposed to a socialist presence and agitation for the first time.[63]

In Petersburg and elsewhere, the period after the 1896 strike is associated with the rise to prominence of the journal called *Workers' Thought* (*Rabochaia mysl'*) and of a certain number of small groups of underground workers (*praktiki*) whose activities were condemned by radical émigré socialists as seeking to limit the socialist movement to the scope and pace set by the workers themselves. This phenomenon, later called "Economism" because of the presumed economic, as opposed to political, thrust implied by giving the workers their own head, is known to us largely from Lenin's merciless attack on it in his work *What Is to Be Done?*. In this attack, Lenin misunderstood or misrepresented the origins and aims of the great bulk of the activity labeled "Economism," and the strong impression of the period he has left behind has distorted its actual social history.

Lenin's chief concern was to warn against the establishment in the

63. Wildman, *The Making of a Workers' Revolution*, pp. 78–88, convincingly shows that political issues were raised more frequently and boldly in areas outside Petersburg and toward the end of the period 1896–1901.

Russian party of those Revisionist views that were then dividing the German Social Democrats, views that rejected both the necessity and the ethical desirability of proletarian revolution in favor of a socialist movement devoted to democratic reform. He saw the Revisionist danger in Russia as embodied not so much in the views of conscious Revisionists as in the much more widespread tendency among underground socialists to be guided by the democratically expressed wishes of the workers they led, and he was at pains to stress the indispensable role of the party and the intelligentsia in shaping and leading the revolutionary movement. Lenin wrote that "the history of all countries shows that the working class, exclusively by its own effort, is able to develop only trade union consciousness," and that "class political consciousness can be brought to the workers *only from without*, that is, only from outside the economic struggle, from outside the sphere of relations between workers and employers."[64]

Given his political aims and the conditions of the period, these were timely and reasonable concerns: the newness of the party as an organized force, the disunity among its leaders and underground groups alike, and the existence of at least a few intellectual leaders in Russia committed to Revisionism did make for a danger that a rival center of labor leadership might eventually develop, even though the groups he attacked hardly presented such a danger at the time. Moreover, for all the advances workers were to make in self-reliance, organization, and political understanding in 1905, developments in that year also partially bore out Lenin's sense of the malleability of the mass labor movement and his fear of its willingness to follow nonsocialist leadership. Nevertheless, the image he created of the labor movement and its intelligentsia allies hardly did justice to all the parties involved.

Allan Wildman has shed considerable light on the issues at stake in the campaign against Economism by studying the actual activities, disputes, and problems of the key underground groups and *praktiki*. He shows that the great bulk of the underground groups avoided both Revisionism and the teachings of *Rabochaia mysl'*. In fact, most of the groups were inspired by the success of the Union of Struggle in 1896 and sought to apply the same approach as the Union, based on the pamphlet *On Agitation*: the tactical use of economic issues, to which inexperienced workers could be expected to respond, in order to

64. *What Is to Be Done?*, as translated and reprinted in Robert C. Tucker, ed., *The Lenin Anthology* (New York, 1975), pp. 24, 50. Emphasis in the original. On Revisionism, see Peter Gay, *The Dilemma of Democratic Socialism. Eduard Bernstein's Challenge to Marx* (New York, 1952).

draw them into a confrontation with their employers, which itself would teach them the need for political struggle.[65] After a few years even the *Rabochaia mysl'* group and other leaders who were previously convinced Revisionists had abandoned their views to such a degree that "by 1901, when *Iskra* launched its attack on Economism, there was not a trace of this dangerous heresy in the Social Democratic movement," and Revisionist politics in Russia was lodged henceforth among the liberal democrats.[66]

Wildman shows that the desire to see workers in control of their own organizations and policies was a very powerful sentiment that became entwined with the politics of Economism, but that it operated among all the groups, Economist or not. The passion took a variety of forms; it could result in a crude "workerist" urge simply to exclude intellectuals from the labor movement, or it could take the form of including intellectuals, but guarding against their turning the workers from their chosen path. It is noteworthy that those who feared the excessive influence of the intelligentsia often viewed the problem from contrasting perspectives: some defined the workers' interests as tied to concrete economic gains, whereas others stressed the goal of proletarian revolution. In short, intelligentsia influence was condemned, by turns, as irresponsibly adventuristic or as excessively compromising.[67]

What emerges is that workers did not confine their protests to economic or material concerns. This was indisputably established in 1905, but even beginning in this earlier period, Russian workers raised political protests and linked economic and political issues with an often surprising lack of hesitation. What are the origins of this openness to politics? Certainly the teachings of the revolutionaries played some part in linking narrower working conditions with broader political concerns. In addition, political oppositionism was growing

65. Wildman, *The Making of a Workers' Revolution*, p. 191. *Ob agitatsii* (Geneva, 1896), a selection from which is translated in Harding, ed., *Marxism in Russia. Key Documents, 1879–1906*, pp. 192–205. Also, see Wildman, *The Making of a Workers' Revolution*, pp. 45–50.

66. Wildman, *The Making of a Workers' Revolution*, p. 144. Schwarz, *The Russian Revolution of 1905*, pp. 315–19. Also, see Chapter 3 below.

67. Wildman, *The Making of a Workers' Revolution*, chap. 4, pp. 123, 127–28, 194–95. "Workerism" is a translation of the French "*ouvrierisme*," which has been succinctly defined as a "system that considers the workers as alone qualified to direct a popular movement" (*Grand Larousse de la langue française en sept volumes* [Paris, 1976], vol. 5, p. 3382). As an assertion of the belief that workers can and should direct their own affairs, *ouvrierisme* can—though it need not—lead to the exclusion of nonworkers even if they share the workers' beliefs.

throughout Russian society in the decade or so before 1905, and ever newer groups were discovering their protest voices. But what were the circumstances that predisposed workers to heed the promptings of the revolutionaries, who were, after all, still distrusted by most workers and whose advice could have been rejected? In part, the answer must be sought in the very character of repressive political regimes like Russia's, where workers were not allowed to step out of line in "civil society" without almost immediately provoking the coercive power of the state. Even when planning a peaceful strike, for example, workers instinctively watched out for the imminent police charge. This condition necessitated the development of a far more politically charged conception of factory struggle among workers than in countries where the bias of the political authorities in favor of property and capital was more subtly and complexly concealed.

This combination of factors was played out in a strike that broke out at the Spassk & Petrov Cotton Mills (formerly the Maxwell Mills) in December of 1898. Maxwell workers had participated in the textile strike of 1896 and had also been the first to strike again in January of 1897. In February 1898 they struck once again, and successfully, to restore holidays abolished by the law of June 2, 1897. Throughout 1898 additional discontent developed over reduced piece rates and increased fines. In December an underground circle associated with Rabochee Znamia, one of two or three socialist groups represented at Spassk & Petrov, issued a leaflet containing exclusively economic demands and calling for a strike. After reading and discussing the leaflet, workers went out on December 14. Despite the peaceful bearing of the workers, police surrounded the strike area and closed down restaurants and other local businesses to inconvenience the workers. They arrested strikers and beat the workers they encountered on the streets with Cossack whips (*nagaiki*) in an attempt to intimidate and punish them. On the next day a factory spy was beaten by workers, and on December 16 members of the Rabochee Znamia circle and of another socialist group were arrested. In all, some 200 workers and 16 intellectuals were rounded up in the first three days. On the night of December 16 eight policemen in search of the workers responsible for beating the spy came to the door of the workers' barracks and demanded admission. They were greeted by a hail of logs, furniture, and hot water, thrown from the windows above. An hour later, reinforced by 50 mounted police and a group of Cossacks, the police stormed the barracks, arresting and beating its inhabitants. Some of the workers resisted, others were surprised in their sleep as the police rampaged from floor to floor and room to room. Everyone in their way was beaten, including a pregnant woman who gave premature birth as a result. Forty-three workers were arrested, of whom 15 were later put on trial. It was reported that Hubbard, the factory owner, paid each policeman six rubles for the night's work.[68]

The role of Rabochee Znamia in precipitating the Maxwell strike marked an advance over the situation of 1896 and 1897. This time the initiative came from an organized socialist group within the factory, acting with confidence that the other workers would be responsive to a strike call. Equally significant was the fact that a group of workers that met with the Factory Inspector during the strike, after witnessing the public arrest and beatings of strikers, raised a demand for the right to strike and freedom of assembly. *Rabochee delo*, one of the journals favoring a gradual approach on political issues, found in this occurrence a vindication of its strategy, claiming that it was the first time that Petersburg workers had "put forth political demands *in large numbers and completely independently.*"[69] The journal also claimed that the same political demands had appeared as a list of grievances "compiled by the workers themselves" prior to drafting the strike leaflet, but that they had been omitted from the leaflet "completely by accident," an omission that had left the workers "very upset."[70]

Here, indeed, was an example (assuming the accuracy of the report) of the way in which workers were discovering the interrelationship between economic and political issues on their own, learning the implications of struggles over narrower, in-factory grievances for the broader concerns of freedom and civil liberties, exactly as the authors of *On Agitation* had anticipated. Some of the workers had even drafted the political demands before the strike began and asked the party workers to include them, rather than the other way around, as was more typical. The bulk of the strikers reaffirmed the demands after witnessing the arrests and the other one-sided, antistrike actions of government officials. Intimidation of this sort had certainly been used against workers before, but now there was a new element: large numbers of workers were prepared to resist with physical force, as was dramatically demonstrated by the workers' defiance of the police and Cossacks who attacked their barracks.

Although political consciousness in the Maxwell strike was not yet

68. *Rabochee delo*, Apr. 1899, reprinted in *RDR*, vol. 4, pt. 2, pp. 43–47. Kochergin, "90-e gody na fabrike 'Rabochii' (b. Maksvel')," pp. 184–209. Korol'chuk and Sokolova, *Khronika revoliutsionnogo rabochego dvizheniia v Peterburge. Tom 1 (1870–1904 gg.)*, pp. 251–52, 259–61.

69. *RDR*, vol. 4, pt. 2, p. 44. Emphasis in the original.

70. *Ibid.*, p. 43.

as well developed as it would become even among textile workers in 1905 and later, a significant step forward had been taken. A dispute over factory issues overflowed its boundaries due to the introduction of state coercion, first because the state failed to see its interest in confining the dispute to the factory, and second because workers began to assert themselves against state authority as a direct extension of their conflict with factory authority. The Maxwell workers moved from the more or less passive resistance of 1896 and 1897 to active resistance as a result of the awareness of the power of a concerted and unified labor movement possible only since the earlier strikes, and as a result of the attention organized revolutionaries had devoted to their strikes since then.

A new working class, lacking any tradition of compromise or negotiation with the factory authority, was forced to choose between the acceptance of insulting and intolerable working conditions and the perpetration of what the government had defined as criminal activity. The development of a labor movement in these circumstances entailed the acceptance and routinization by a growing number of workers of rebellious behavior, the linkage of a new sense of entitlement to protest unjust conditions with the need to defy constituted authority. The government, in its shortsightedness, was schooling them to lessons that would work to its immense detriment. By the turn of the century, Petersburg workers had clearly begun to accept the notion that fighting and defying the police was a normal part of the routine of striking. In so doing, they moved a step or two closer to repudiating imperial authority altogether.

Thus, at the very moment when revolutionaries of the *Iskra* camp were sharpening the distinction between an "economic" and a "political" path for workers, between trade-unionism and socialism, the clash of the government's rigid view of public order with the dictates of industrial life was fusing economic and political struggle in the consciousness of the new working class then coming to birth. In the gap between the still unformed political attitudes of most striking workers and the strategies of the few consciously Revisionist leaders among the intelligentsia fell a great, uncharted field of potential development. To suggest that workers on their own would of necessity develop along Economist, trade-unionist lines was premature at best, and at worst overreliant on West European examples and insufficiently attentive to the specific circumstances of Russian workers. Lenin's struggle against Economism is more meaningfully construed as an effort to impose control and organization on a chaotic and elemental reality, to achieve the ascendency of the revolutionary party's "consciousness" over the "spontaneity" of the working masses.[71] For, in Lenin's eyes, even the most highly politicized strikes and confrontations would amount to little in the overall revolutionary struggle unless the still isolated and disunified labor movement shared a common strategy, common aims, and a common leadership. So the thrust of Lenin's attack was not only against the reformism of certain groups and figures, but also against the "workerism" of those socialists who felt that the undertaking by workers of any kind of activity on their own behalf was itself "revolutionary."

This reconstruction of the campaign against Economism is compatible with the view that the new Russian working class was developing a precocious willingness to battle state authority in the same gesture, so to speak, with which it confronted its employers. At this stage of its development, the political potential of this tendency was still malleable and ambiguous; it was capable of taking either reformist or revolutionary form, depending on the reception it met with and the forces that arose to shape it. The imperial authorities cultivated such a narrow and easily aroused sense of public order, particularly acute in the capital city, that they were unable or unwilling to distinguish between a reformist and a revolutionary labor movement. This rigid stance was now being mirrored in the attitudes of workers, who increasingly fought with the Tsarist police, but did so for the time being to resist their employers rather than to threaten the state order. Nevertheless, these militant, sometimes violent explosions of labor unrest could be seen as aimed as much at the overthrow of autocracy as at trade unions and the right to strike, chiefly because the government made a demand for one tantamount to a demand for the other, and its perceptions determined the uses to which political power was put. The government's continued brittleness about labor's challenge to public order and its rigidity and obtuseness in meeting this challenge were far more significant than the influence of revolutionaries in encouraging them to interpret the meaning of their actions in terms of political extremism.

THE 1901 STRIKES

The first major strike in the history of the gigantic Obukhov Steel Mill arose in response to the threat of dismissal of several scores of

71. Haimson, *The Russian Marxists and the Origins of Bolshevism*, pp. 132–38.

workers who had walked out to honor May Day, the international workingmen's holiday, in 1901. This situation could have arisen at only a handful of Petersburg's larger metal plants, and it marks the Obukhov Mill as one of the establishments where socialist agitation and underground circle work had begun to make some headway. But these were developments of fairly recent origin, and the greater part of the plant's history had been dominated by conservative values.

The innovative weapons producer P. M. Obukhov had established the plant in 1863 about seven kilometers upriver from the city in the village of Aleksandrovskoe. Obukhov had acquired the land from the government and in exchange had agreed to equip military fortifications and produce armored naval vessels. Because of this agreement specialists and other factory personnel were sometimes hired directly from the ranks of the army and navy. In 1883 the Naval Ministry purchased the plant and assumed control. Over the years a stratum of privileged, conservative workers, leavened by army and navy personnel, took shape at the factory. The management effectively screened new workers by encouraging this group to favor their friends, relatives, and *zemliaki* in hiring. To insure their loyalty, these "old-timers" (*starozhily*) were permitted to occupy the best of the government housing, adjacent to the plant. On the job, their power and influence were unmatched by any other group: they controlled whole shops, especially in the hot metal trades, and the pursuit of their self-interest underpinned a stable and conservative regime in labor relations at the plant.[72]

The old-timers always exercised some influence at the Obukhov Mill, but they probably held unchallenged sway until the late 1890's, when the influx of younger workers and the penetration of socialist ideas and organizations began to alter the balance of forces. The work force at the plant grew from about 1,560 in 1891 to 3,700 in 1901. This growth probably increased the tension between generations of workers and upset the earlier equilibrium within and among the shops of the Obukhov Plant, as was apparently the case in the Petersburg metalworking industry as a whole. As early as 1896 a socialist circle headed by Vasilii Poliakov was operating among the Obukhov workers, although the strength of its following is not known. By 1901, a number of circles existed, including several socialist groups, a populist group, and even a liberal group. Membership numbered about 100 members, including participants from two neighboring factories.

72. Stolpianskii, *Zhizn' i byt*, pp. 167–69. Rozanov, *Obukhovtsy*, pp. 79, 99. Shotman, *Zapiski*, pp. 32–33.

There also seem to have been a number of unaffiliated workers who were skilled, educated, well-read, and known in the plant to defend workers against the management. These worker-intellectuals were particularly strong in those shops requiring a high degree of skill and literacy (e.g., the design and pattern-making shops), and they were known to serve as conduits into the underground groups for younger workers, even though they themselves may not have been members.

Another such conduit was the evening schools, aimed at helping workers improve their skills, where young workers also came into contact with worker-intellectuals and factory dissidents, as well as socialist intellectuals who often served as teachers. "Even at the mathematics lectures," recalled a former Obukhov worker, "the lecturer told us about the Populists, Alexander II and III, Nicholas, Khodynka, and the strikes of the Ivanovo-Voznesensk workers. Sometimes we learned that in place of a certain woman teacher someone else would come because they had arrested her."[73]

The spring of 1901 witnessed the rapid rise of the political temperature in Petersburg. In February, Minister of Education Nikolai Bogolepov was assassinated by a revolutionary terrorist. In March, a similar, but unsuccessful, attempt was made on the life of Konstantin Pobedonostsev, the Tsar's close adviser and the gray eminence of Russian reaction. On March 4, a protest demonstration of students, intellectuals, and a handful of workers in Kazan Square was violently dispersed by the police.[74] An April 7 leaflet issued by the Union of Struggle called on workers to demonstrate on Nevsky Prospect on April 22, the first Sunday after the Western May 1 (April 18, Old Style). On the appointed day, some 3,000 workers from different parts of the city, including about 60–70 from the Obukhov Mill, gathered on Nevsky Prospect in preparation for a march up the city's busiest and most stylish avenue, carrying red flags and singing revolutionary songs. The demonstration was attacked and dispersed by Cossacks, but the leaders called on workers to return nine days later, on the Russian May 1. In the interim, the participants returned to their factory districts with antigovernment feelings aroused.[75]

73. Sulimov, "Vospominaniia obukhovtsa (1900–1903 gg.)," pp. 145–47. Wildman, *The Making of a Workers' Revolution*, pp. 119–20. Rozanov, "'Obukhovskaia oborona' (Iz istorii Obukhovskogo zavoda–1901 g.)," pp. 70–71.

74. Valk, "Obshchestvennoe dvizhenie v Peterburge v 90-kh i nachala 900-kh godov," pp. 204–8.

75. Chaadaeva, ed., *Pervoe maia v tsarskoi Rossii. 1890–1916 gg. Sbornik dokumentov*, pp. 46–47. Rozanov, "Obukhovskaia oborona," pp. 75–77. Korol'chuk and Sokolova, *Khronika*, pp. 283–86.

In the Vyborg district, at the other end of the city from the Obukhov Mill, 6,000 workers from fifteen factories went out on strike May 1 and 2. The authorities were prepared, and the district was saturated with police from the morning of May 1. Across the river, the authorities again frustrated the second attempt to march on Nevsky Prospect by arranging a military review for the same day and effectively filling the avenue with soldiers. On May 1 the strikers were predominantly peaceful, though a small clash between strikers and police did occur. But on the next day the Vyborg strikers came out into the streets with red flags, intending both to build the strike by agitating in front of other factories and to march across the river for yet another attempt to demonstrate on Nevsky Prospect. The mounted and foot police went into action, repeatedly blocking the line of march and forcing the demonstrators onto the side streets between two large boulevards. In the midst of this an impromptu meeting was held on a streetcorner at which orators summoned workers to "fight for freedom, against the tyranny of Tsar and capital."[76] The workers responded to the police by barricading themselves behind fences and in the upper stories of the houses along the streets and hurling stones, bricks, and metal objects at the police. The fight apparently began when some of the textile strikers began throwing stones at the windows of the Lessner Machine, Foundry, and Boiler Works, in an ultimately successful attempt to bring its workers out on strike. Two companies of army troops were called from their nearby barracks to aid the police, and the authorities, thus reinforced, won the day. Over 200 arrests were made, and a statement by the City Governor posted on the factories ordered the workers to end their strike by May 3. But the next day, another 300 workers were arrested for disobeying the order, the strike continued, and for the first time a factory in the Vasilevsky district struck. On May 4, a smaller contingent of Vyborg workers renewed plans to demonstrate in the city and again clashed with the police, this time near a bridge leading to the Petersburg district, where yet another factory had gone on strike, and more arrests were made. Most of those arrested since May 2 was released on May 7, when work resumed at all factories.[77]

At the center of the Vyborg district strike were the workers of the

76. Taimi, *Stranitsy perezhitogo*, p. 34.
77. "Rabochee dvizhenie na zavodakh Peterburga v mae 1901 g.," pp. 52–54. *Rabochee dvizhenie v Rossii v 1901–1904 gg.*, pp. 23–25. Iukhneva, "Nakanune Obukhovskoi oborony (Pervomaiskaia stachka v Peterburge v 1901 godu)." "Khronika," in *Rabochee dvizhenie v 1901–1904 gg.*, pp. 383–88. Korol'chuk and Sokolova, *Khronika*, pp. 286–89.

Nikol'sk (or Cheshire) Weaving Factory (1,200 workers), where a May 1 demonstration of some kind had been discussed since mid-April, and where 500 workers on the night shift preceding May 1 walked off the job, raising demands for an eight-hour day, higher piece rates to compensate for the shorter hours, and construction of a factory school and hospital. The eight-hour demand clearly reflected the presence of socialist influence, as did the determination to demonstrate on May 1. Although we can be certain of only one socialist who worked at the factory during the strike,[78] the Social Democrats had a particularly strong presence in the district.[79] Even so, the Nikol'sk workers were divided, and some of them had to be coerced into striking. The police reports mention no leaders or deputies, and the only arrests seem to have been connected with the street fighting and refusal to return to work. Still, the eight-hour-day demand (one of its first appearances among textile workers), the revolutionary songs and red flags, and the attempts to repeat the May 1 demonstrations in the city show that cotton workers had begun to acquire a political awareness they had clearly lacked in the strikes of 1896 and 1897. Nine of the 15 striking factories on the Vyborg Side were cotton textile firms, and three-fourths of the strikers were cotton workers. The small number of workers still trying to demonstrate on May 4 were from the Nikol'sk Factory. The other four striking factories were small and medium-size metal plants, which struck only on May 2 and seemed to be following the lead of the Nikol'sk weavers, although nothing is known about their strikes.

Word of the Vyborg district strike and fighting apparently reached Obukhov workers only on May 4. By that time, a strike was already brewing among them, and the news probably only sharpened their own determination. The plant's revolutionaries had tried to call a strike on May 1 but were only partly successful. Two whole shops and an indefinite number of other workers from around the plant—one source claims as many as one-third of the workers—refused to work but did not leave the premises, instead loafing around arguing and smoking. After the lunch break, some of them did leave the plant. Next day, the management posted a list of ten names of those who were to be dismissed for failure to appear the day before. In a show of solidarity and defiance, 72 other workers from the same shops asked to be dismissed along with their comrades. The management selected

78. Ivanov, "Maiskaia zabastovka 1901 goda na fabrike Cheshera (Vospominaniia)," pp. 255–56.
79. Iukhneva, "Nakanune," p. 57.

16 additional names and posted a composite list of 26. Rumors flew among the workers that this was only the first installment of a list that would eventually total in the hundreds. This rumor only increased the alarm already felt a week earlier, when it was said that the management was planning to dismiss all workers over 50, as had been done at another plant of the Naval Ministry (the Izhorsk Works in Kolpino).[80]

The rumor of these dismissals is the only hint in the sources that the industrial crisis under way in Russia since 1899 may have affected the readiness of the Obukhov workers to strike in 1901. Existing information on the crisis's impact on the Petersburg labor movement is incomplete and contradictory, although the particular mix of industries in the capital seems to have cushioned the blow.[81] It is therefore impossible to say whether, for instance, economic hardship at the Obukhov Plant contributed more to the strike itself or more to the relative inactivity following the strike among metalworkers at the plant and in Petersburg generally.

In a remarkable show of unity, the leaders of the various underground circles called a joint meeting at which a strike was decided upon and a set of demands drafted. On Saturday, May 5, about 30 of these self-appointed leaders called a strike for the following Monday, May 7. Apparently, sufficient anger and alarm had been aroused among Obukhov workers that the proposal—whose initiators included some of the plant's respected militants—met a receptive response from many workers. The rest of May 5 and the next day, a Sunday, were filled with dozens of meetings, small and large, indoors and out (although concealed). Plans were made to protect liquor stores from vandalism, thereby avoiding drunkenness among the strikers. The following strike demands were drafted:[82]

1. No one should be dismissed for celebrating May Day.
2. Add May 1 to the schedule of plant holidays.
3. Introduce an eight-hour day.
4. Recognize the elected deputies from the workers.
5. Dismiss the assistant plant director, Colonel Ivanov.
6. Dismiss the foremen and apprentices not wanted by the workers in the lock-and-gunsight and mine shops.
7. Treat workers politely.

---

80. Rozanov, "Obukhovskaia oborona," p. 77.

81. Iakovlev, *Ekonomicheskie krizisy v Rossii*, p. 272. See Appendix 1 for a discussion of the crisis of 1899–1904 and St. Petersburg.

82. Rozanov, *Obukhovtsy*, pp. 99, 101–4; Rozanov, "Obukhovskaia oborona," pp. 79–80.

   8. Raise wage rates.
   9. Abolish overtime work.
  10. Abolish all fines.
  11. Install tanks for drinking water.
  12. Install washup facilities.

On the morning of May 7, a gathering of several hundred workers in the factory yard elected two delegates to carry the demands to the management. A group of moderate workers dissented, but the show of unity was impressive enough to force factory director Vlas'ev to appear briefly before the workers to show them he was on his way to deliver their demands to the Naval Ministry. Though most of the workers then began to work, the strike leaders were prepared for this. Workers from the gun carriage shop appeared in the yard, led by a fiery young worker, Nikolai Iunikov. They marched through the shops of the plant, closing them down by force and by persuasion. Armed with tools and pieces of metal, they burst into the shops still at work and shut off the machinery. Those who resisted were forcibly ejected. Opposition was fiercest in the shops dominated by the old-timers, where workers hid behind and fought around the machinery. The strikers allowed nothing to stand in their way. When a policeman tried to prevent a group of them from leaving the plant, he was disarmed, knocked out, and thrown in a ditch. Later, other policemen were beaten and even stabbed by angry workers. Through their violence and disruptiveness, as much as through the readiness of many workers to strike and the need of others to use the threat of violence as a pretext for a walkout, the strikers succeeded in shutting down a sizable part of the plant.[83]

Next, the strikers went to the neighboring paper factory, many of whose women workers then joined them in the street. The more or less self-appointed strike leaders put their heads together at this point to work out a plan for responding to the imminent arrival of the police. Led by the nonparty militant Anatolii Gavrilov, a former student in a military gymnasium, the Obukhov "defenders" gathered at a railroad crossing on the road leading into the village from the city. Cobblestones and other projectiles were carefully cached, and workers were stationed in the upstairs windows of nearby buildings. As the mounted police rode in from the city, the strikers cleverly lowered

83. Chaadaeva, ed., *Pervoe maia*, pp. 49–50. Rozanov, *Obukhovtsy*, pp. 106–12. Rozanov claimed they closed the whole plant after about two hours of forceful persuasion in the shops. Yet a participant recalled in his memoirs that after the morning gathering he resumed work and was disturbed again only at 4 P.M. Sulimov, "Vospominaniia," pp. 149–50.

the railroad crossing barrier, forcing the horsemen to bunch up at the crossing. When the barrier was raised and the policemen began slowly to proceed, the workers rained stones and missiles on them and then closed the barrier again. Surprised, the police suffered a number of casualties and lost this first skirmish. Their captain, Palibin, was wounded, and he and several of his policemen had to be hospitalized for treatment.

Unfortunately for the strikers, the authorities called in armed sailors and later also infantry to assist the police in rounding up strikers and assaulting an apartment house where many of them had taken refuge. Firearms were used, and seven persons eventually died in the fighting. Contrary to what was said at the time, a few of the strikers were also armed, although they were no match for police assisted by armed troops.[84] Once the apartment house was taken, the police and troops raged through it till late that night, beating inhabitants, wrecking furnishings, and arresting large numbers of suspects. Although most of the initial 300 detainees were released, the arrests continued, and 400 more workers were rounded up over the next two days. The confusion was so great, however, that many of the actual leaders were able to hide out and escape arrest. On May 8, the plant remained closed under police guard. It reopened on May 11, after the management had granted some of the strikers' demands and agreed to negotiate over others.

One of the demands agreed to was the election of deputies from the various shops of the plant, and the first election was held on the very day the plant reopened. Deputies were granted immunity from retaliation and the right to meet, both with their constituents and as a body. Despite the election of only two Social Democratic workers and the presence of a number of older and nonrevolutionary workers among the 29 chosen on May 11, the deputies approved a list of 14 strike demands which, like the first list, included the release of arrested workers, the establishment of May 1 as a recognized holiday, an eight-hour working day, and higher wages.[85]

One week after the Obukhov workers battled the police, Director Vlas'ev reported to the deputies that the Naval Ministry had granted

84. Rozanov, *Obukhovtsy*, pp. 112–22. Gavrilov, a declassed *dvorianin* who became a skilled worker after being expelled from his gymnasium for striking a professor, has not always been given credit for his leadership of the "Obukhov Defense." His account of the events of May 7 describes the workers' heroism and the violent revenge they wreaked on individual policemen with a relish and a vividness undimmed by the passage of 25 years: "Vospominaniia starogo obukhovtsa."

85. Rozanov, *Obukhovtsy*, pp. 122–32.

all the demands except the four just mentioned. Despite the rejection of the most important demands, this appeared to the workers as a great victory. They had won a number of concessions, forcing the management to adopt fairer policies on fines, dismissals, and passes, to agree not to change piece-work rates before the end of a contract, and to abolish unpaid overtime work. In addition, Lt. Col. Ivanov, Vlas'ev's hated assistant, was to be dismissed. Because they had fought for these demands and because the legitimization of their own representatives in the factory was itself a gigantic advance and promised further improvements, the workers were deservedly proud of these concessions. Moreover, in the ensuing weeks more of the arrested workers were released, and wage rates were raised.[86]

However, this advantageous situation for the workers did not last very long, and Vlas'ev and the Naval Ministry probably did not intend it to do so. In June, Vlas'ev placed restrictions on who could be elected as deputies and where they were to meet. On July 2, he restored Ivanov to his former position. The deputies immediately demanded to know the reason for this action, and when Vlas'ev and the ministry stood firm, they called a demonstration in the factory yard. Vlas'ev broke it up with a detachment of sailors, but he could not prevent 300 workers from walking out on July 6. On the next day the entire plant was on strike again. This time the strike was better organized, since it was led by the deputies, who now functioned both as shop stewards and as a central strike authority. They stipulated that *all* the original demands must be met before the workers would return. On July 8, when Vlas'ev declared a lockout, fighting between workers and police erupted again in the village. Searches and arrests resumed for several days. On July 14, Vlas'ev stripped the deputies of their powers, declaring that in the future he alone would decide when new elections could be held. Work at the plant resumed on July 17 after Vlas'ev made a concession by again dismissing Ivanov.[87]

The Obukhov workers now retired from battle in defeat, despite the *élan* with which they had entered the strike movement two months earlier and their early successes against the management. They ended up with a shadow of what they had originally won because they had lost the means to prevent the retraction of the concessions, i.e., their deputies. Revolutionary politics at the plant regressed to the stage of agitation and propaganda, which inched forward slowly and clandestinely through the day-to-day work of persuasion and conversion.

86. *Ibid.*, pp. 133, 139.
87. *Ibid.*, pp. 139–45.

Although from time to time the plant's radicals joined their counterparts from other factories in public demonstrations, the Obukhov
workers did not turn out in force again until 1905.[88]

The "Obukhov Defense" of May 7 made a great impression on the
workers of other Petersburg metal plants and catalyzed strikes and
protests at several of them. The Aleksandrovsk Steel Mill (1,770 workers) struck for one day along with the neighboring Obukhov Plant.
Orators went around to several other factories on May 8 to tell of the
previous day's events and ask for support. One plant stopped work
in protest, and workers at the Putilov Works and the Nevsky Ship
and Machine Works actually set out to help the Obukhov workers,
clashing with police sent to guard their neighborhoods.[89] Strikes later
broke out at Nevsky Ship (5,000 workers), the Aleksandrovsk Machine Works (4,000 workers [not to be confused with the steel mill]),
and the Baltic Shipyards (4,560 workers). The Aleksandrovsk workers won some concessions, but the strikes at the other two plants
ended with the temporary dismissal of all the workers. Violence by
strikers against the property and sometimes the personnel of these
plants did take place, and the police were summoned to all of the
strikes, but nothing like the pitched battle at the Obukhov Mill and
the Vyborg district now recurred.[90]

Taken together, these strikes were much larger than those in the
Vyborg district and were more comparable, in numbers of strikers, to
the textile strike of 1896. The four large metalworker strikes (including the Obukhov) shared a number of common features. In all cases,
strike sentiment was concentrated in one or two shops, from which it
spread to the other shops by a combination of sympathy, persuasion,
and force. In three of the four cases, workers elected deputies to
present and argue for their demands. At the Nevsky Works, the deputies went first to the management to secure a guarantee of their own
immunity and the right to meet with the workers to draw up a list of
grievances. In all cases, the strikers seemed to feel at home on the
plant's premises. They held meetings there and ranged about, agitating among other workers. At the Baltic Shipyard, striking workers
gathered at the plant day after day to guard against strikebreaking,
although the practice also served to renew the solidarity and commitment of the strikers.[91] Except in the Obukhov case, information about
the leadership of these strikes is sparse, but the election of deputies

88. Sulimov, "Vospominaniia," pp. 152–64.
89. *Rabochee delo*, no. 10 (Sept. 1901), pp. 94, 100.
90. *Ibid.*, pp. 100–101. "Rabochee dvizhenie . . . v mae 1901," pp. 58–61.
91. In this respect, striking metalworkers were no different from other workers,

indicates at least that an acknowledged leadership existed. Finally, the individual metal strikes were longer and more tenacious than the textile strikes in either 1896 or 1901 (three of the four plants struck a second time over unmet demands from the first strike), an outcome probably due most of all to the better financial situation of the metalworkers.[92]

In most of these features, the 1901 metalworker strikes present a clear contrast with those of 1896 and 1897. The most notable new development was the presence at the Obukhov Plant of a variety of political circles. We know that similar groups operated at the Nikol'sk Weaving Factory, and they were probably active at the other metal plants, and possibly at other large textile mills, especially those of the Vyborg and Schlüsselberg districts. Although small in numbers, these groups had begun to put metalworkers in touch with the revolutionary underground in one of its largest and most active centers. Most of the Obukhov workers did not respond to the revolutionaries' call to strike on May Day, but the protection from dismissal of those who did strike proved to be an effective wedge in opening a much greater part of the work force to a whole set of other grievances, large and small. Politically committed workers seem to have played a leading part in the preparations for the May 7 strike, although the list of demands indicates that they were joined by more moderate elements. The Obukhov workers thus had a set of leaders before the strike began, and the demand for the recognition of elected deputies was intended to legitimize and institutionalize this arrangement, not to call it into existence. The openness and authority that the deputies exercised was partly attributable to this preparation and organization, but partly also to the higher literacy, the networks of shop relations flowing from the organization of work, and the high incidence of skilled work among metalworkers.

Revolutionary organizers had apparently also made greater headway among textile workers since 1896, in the Vyborg district at any rate. Yet they clearly did not meet with the same response as they did among metalworkers. Though it is true that textile workers led the Vyborg Side strike, and that the Nikol'sk weavers showed greater tenacity and militancy than did workers from neighboring metal plants, there is no evidence in the Vyborg Side strikes of advanced prepa-

---

who often returned each day to the struck factory to prevent strikebreaking. Iukhneva, "Nakanune," p. 59.

92. *Ibid.* Iukhneva, "Iz istorii stachechnogo dvizheniia peterburgskikh rabochikh posle Obukhovskoi Oborony (stachka rabochikh Nevskoi Zastavy v mae 1901 goda)."

ration among the workers, of elected deputies, or of efforts to press demands by coming to grips with managements afterward. The differences in the performances of the strikers in the two industries were probably due less to the strength of the revolutionary presence or to variations in the anger and willingness to fight of individual workers than to their organizing capacities, including their capacities to respond to the new and increasingly politicized factory milieu in Petersburg after 1896.

After 1900 the political development of the working class in Russia as a whole became increasingly and more rapidly linked with that of other groups and classes. The "Obukhov Defense" was one local indication of this fact, combining socialist leadership with mass action of the factory population, encouraging solidarity across the city and across industrial lines, and even being preceded by worker support of a student and intelligentsia demonstration. This political ferment was due to the more rapid emergence of forces antagonistic to the government, including the outbreak of massive strikes in south Russia in 1902, 1903, and 1904; the growth of Social Democratic organizations and the spread of their influence during the first years of the new century; and the rapid rise of an increasingly well-organized demand for political participation by liberal *zemstvo* and intelligentsia activists. Student demonstrations, the renewal of large-scale peasant riots in 1902, and the founding of the neopopulist Socialist Revolutionary Party in 1900 contributed to this process and to an anxious sense of expectation in these years.

These developments took different concrete shape in different parts of the country. In St. Petersburg the liberal intelligentsia played a more prominent oppositionist role after 1901 than it did in most other parts of the country, and the Social Democrats a less prominent one. The capital's workers, although relatively more conversant with revolutionary politics than workers in most other towns from many years of exposure to socialist agitation, were mobilized immediately before 1905 by a legal labor organization and by the dramatic public opposition of the liberal intelligentsia.

In order, therefore, to keep pace with the unfolding of labor politics, we must move from the factory district and view the situation from the wider angle of the city as a whole, and we must treat not only the politics of immediately perceived grievances, but those of constitutional reform and civic participation as well.

CHAPTER THREE

1904

———————◆•◆◆◆———————

In 1904 the liberation movement came to life. From 1905 St. Petersburg became the acknowledged center of the Russian Revolution, yet its role in the awakening of 1904 was possibly even more seminal and initiatory. Already in January 1904, the founding congress of the Union of Liberation, a loose coalition of zemstvo and intelligentsia liberals, and two professional congresses, held in Petersburg, marked a new stage in the maturation and growing momentum of the zemstvo and intelligentsia opposition throughout the country. These meetings were transformed from private into public events, demonstrating that the mobilization of the opposition was accelerating even before war and other dramatic external events intervened to spur ever wider circles of the educated public to open commitment.

The outbreak of the Russo-Japanese War in February at first set the process back, both by calling forth a patriotic enthusiasm among the broad public and by convincing even many of the liberal leaders to temper their opposition with concessions to the popular mood and efforts in the national defense. Despite some early lapses, most liberals remained quite skeptical of the importance of the war and of the regime's motives in it. With the first defeat at the Yalu in April of 1904, followed by further reverses in May and early June, the public was reminded of the regime's incompetence and indifference to public opinion. With each ensuing defeat the war became an engine of discontent, accelerating the consolidation of support for the entire political opposition, but especially the liberals, who were most effective in mobilizing urban opinion. They had, since April, linked their call for constitutional reform to a demand for the immediate conclusion of peace. Some zemstvo leaders even viewed the defeat of Tsarist arms as related to reform, in that an unvictorious regime would have to rely more than ever on support from Society.[1]

Then, on July 15, Minister of the Interior Pleve was killed by an SR assassin, E. S. Sozonov. The barely concealed relief, not to say joy, in liberal circles at the demise of this archenemy of political reform was heightened by the already existing oppositionist mood and by some small concessions to antiwar, oppositionist sentiment, ostensibly marking the christening of the *tsarevich* (August 11).

In the hope of reconciling educated society with the regime, the Tsar appointed as Pleve's successor Prince P. D. Sviatopolk-Mirskii, a man of humane and moderate views (August 25). This reputation seemed to be vindicated when the new minister announced a program of reforms that included increased religious tolerance, a promise of broader zemstvo autonomy, a redefinition of political crime to exclude nonviolent opposition, and an extension of press rights. It seemed to many as if the era of reaction initiated in 1881 might be drawing to a close, largely because these initiatives from the top coincided with a conscious and growing opposition of educated society and of the Russian population generally.

The mood thus engendered by these concessions can be compared only with the explosion of civic euphoria that ensued upon Alexander II's announcement of the imminence of peasant emancipation in the late 1850's. In the fall of 1904, as in the earlier period, new liberal journals and newspapers were founded, and the entire press took advantage of the temporarily relaxed censorship to criticize the government and the conduct of the war openly and to print accounts of the now expanding number of public meetings and discussions. Only in 1904, nearly 50 years later, the enthusiasm and impatience of patriotic Russians for reform resonated through an urban population

1. Pavlovich, "Vneshnaia politika i russko-iaponskaia voina," pp. 18–26. Galai, "The Impact of the War on the Russian Liberals in 1904–5," pp. 85–109. *Krizis samoderzhaviia v Rossii, 1895–1917*, pp. 152, 160.

On the liberals in 1904 more generally, see Chermenskii, *Burzhuaziia i tsarizm v pervoi russkoi revoliutsii*, chap. 1; Emmons, *The Formation of Political Parties and the First National Elections in Russia*, pp. 22–36, 92–96; Fischer, *Russian Liberalism. From Gentry to Intelligentsia*, chap. 5; Galai, *The Liberation Movement in Russia, 1900–1905*, pp. 196–238; D. I. Shakhovskoi, "Soiuz Osvobozhdeniia," *Zarnitsy*, no. 2, pt. 2 (1909); Shatsillo, *Russkii liberalizm nakanune revoliutsii 1905–1907 gg.*; "Formirovanie programmy zemskogo liberalizma i ee bankrotstvo nakanune pervoi russkoi revoliutsii (1901–1904 gg.)," *Istoricheskie zapiski*, no. 97 (1976), pp. 74–98; and "O sostave russkogo liberalizma nakanune revoliutsii 1905–1907 godov," *Istoriia SSSR*, no. 1 (1980), pp. 62–74.

whose numbers, complexity, and modernity were far more advanced. Although still a small part of a predominantly rural society, this urban minority—industrial, professional, and commercial—was far more capable of supplanting the ancient autocratic system than a half century earlier, and the imminence of a genuine revolution was consequently far greater. Hence, both the optimism of urban society and the autocracy's fearful paralysis and sense of crisis had more basis in reality in 1904 and 1905 than ever before.

To the disappointment of this new reform-minded public, the promise of Mirskii's program resulted in the timid imperial *ukaz* of December 12, 1904, which addressed many of the opposition's demands, but in language hedged in with vagueness, qualifications, and small concessions. Thus, the zemstvos were promised broadened participation, but not greater autonomy and larger budgets; the exceptional laws in effect in Petersburg and other areas of the Empire were to be reviewed and their application limited "as much as possible"; restrictions of the rights of non-Russians and tribal peoples of the Empire (*inorodtsy* and *urozhentsy*) were to be reviewed and only those retained "that serve the vital interests of the State and definitely benefit the Russian people"; and "unnecessary" limitations on press freedom were to be removed. The *ukaz* also promised to enforce laws already in effect on religious tolerance and an independent judiciary, and it promised to institute "state insurance" for workers. Most importantly, it gave no indication of when and how these reforms would be implimented, and Mirskii's proposal that elected representatives from the zemstvos and town dumas be added to the State Council was dropped from the final draft.[2] By mid-December the mobilization of public protest was so far advanced that this faint-hearted promise of reforms served mainly to spur it on to more determined struggle.

From the late summer on, the discussion of imminent reform, growing antiwar sentiment, and the initiatives of zemstvo and professional groups combined to draw more of urban society into oppositionist politics and more of those already active further to the left. This culminated, for St. Petersburg and for the nation, in the First Congress of Zemstvo Activists, held in early November, and in the campaign of political banquets and meetings that followed, events

2. *Pravitel'stvennyi vestnik*, Dec. 14, 1904. Reprinted in *Sputnik izbiratelia na 1906 god. Osvoboditel'noe dvizhenie i sovremennyia ego formy*, pp. 235–37; and (in English) in Harcave, *First Blood. The Russian Revolution of 1905*, pp. 282–85. Accounts of the discussion of the *ukaz* within the government appear in *Krizis samoderzhaviia*, pp. 158–67, and in Verner, "Nicholas II and the Role of the Autocrat," chap. 4, pp. 7–50.

that immediately preceded the outbreak of revolution in early 1905. Throughout this period the regime's unrelieved string of defeats in the war with Japan and the Tsar's decision to seek an accommodation with public opinion through minimal concessions played the greatest role in the politicization and radicalization of urban society. However, the readiness of certain parts of the professional intelligentsia to take advantage of these events *even before* the outbreak of the war deserves perhaps more emphasis than it has received in most of the existing literature.

The longer-standing opposition of zemstvo and intelligentsia activists, employing the gentlemanly and "parliamentary" methods of journal articles, discussion circles, and congress resolutions gave way, for the first time in January 1904, to bold, impatient, and boisterous public demonstrations, swelled by elements of an urban crowd, and linking occupational issues, the needs of other social groups, and broad political reforms in their pronouncements and closing statements. This transformation of the oppositionists' political style was illustrated most clearly in St. Petersburg, although it reflected a mood that represented much of the rest of urban and professional Russia.

In late December 1903 and the first days of the new year, some 600 elementary school teachers' delegates and a large but indeterminate number of other educators attended the Third Congress of Activists in Technical and Professional Education, held at St. Petersburg University. Congress organizers, including the Liberationists G. A. Falbork and V. I. Charnolusskii, distributed admission tickets to students and workers, and total attendance at the congress reached 3,000. Apparently emboldened and encouraged by the presence of a more general public and the agitational activity of local revolutionaries, several speakers made speeches on the need for freedom of speech and press, universal education without government interference, and the right to assemble and unionize. At a session devoted to workers' education, reportedly the largest and the liveliest of the congress, additional demands for an eight-hour workday and the abolition of religious and national discrimination were made. Other speakers mentioned the need for a constitution. Discussions of the need to improve the working conditions and status of teachers (already well-known to the delegates from debates at the previous year's congress in Moscow) led in this political environment to demands for freedom to organize as a profession. These events proved to be too much for the ever watchful police, who closed the congress on the night of

January 4. Several of the more outspoken political orators were arrested and exiled.[3]

That same night, it so happened, the Ninth Congress of the Pirogov Society of Physicians was just getting started at the Military-
Medical Academy, and many of the participants in the educators' congress simply transferred their new-found enthusiasm for combining
professional and political issues to the new location. Along with the
2,136 physicians in attendance, these newly mobilized supporters
of vociferous and public opposition swelled the congress sessions on
separate topics to several hundred, and for the next week the Pirogov
congress reverberated with often heated political debate, denunciations of government repression, and demands for civil and constitutional rights.

The physicians adopted the metaphor of ministering to the Russian body politic, and the theme of the destruction of the Russian
social fabric by the harsh policies of the government was carried
through several sessions. The physicians linked together a widely assumed government complicity in the pogroms of 1903 with its promo-
tion of alcoholism through its lucrative liquor monopoly and with its
flagrant neglect of sanitary conditions in the housing of factory workers. At the closing session on January 11, attended by a mixed crowd
of over 2,000, the congress's organizers, already fearing for the continued legal existence of the Society due to the plethora of political
speechmaking, closed the congress without allowing a final reading of
the resolutions from its separate sessions. Angry participants shouted
insults at the congress officials, while others stood on chairs to make
speeches. A military band, apparently called in for just such a contin-
gency, drowned them out with march music, while the enraged public
hurled chairs at the musicians and illegal literature was distributed
among the audience. Some 600 to 700 of those remaining assembled
in an adjoining room, where the veterinarian K. V. Rodionov managed
to call for a united front of Society to employ all means of struggle
against the autocracy before the police arrived to clear the hall.[4]

3. Scott J. Seregny, "Professional and Political Activism: The Russian Teachers'
Movement, 1864–1908" (Ph.D. diss., University of Michigan, 1982), pp. 387–89. Sanders, "The Union of Unions: Political, Economic, Civil, and Human Rights Organizations in the 1905 Revolution," chap. 2, pp. 48–49. Galai, *The Liberation Movement*,
p. 188.

4. Sanders, "The Union of Unions," chap. 2, pp. 50–52. Nancy M. Friedan, *Russian Physicians in an Era of Reform and Revolution, 1856–1905* (Princeton, N.J., 1981),
pp. 242–61.

These meetings were remarkable for a number of reasons. First, they brought many students and a number of workers out in support of gatherings that had previously been confined to members of a given profession—an exclusivity which, in the government's eyes, guaranteed their right to associate at all. Members of the intelligentsia had, of course, supported and even attended student demonstrations in previous years, as had small numbers of workers and other urban elements. But the events of January 1904 represented a new phenomenon, which would be replayed with greater frequency and intensity over the next two years. It seems to have occurred at the behest of the professionals themselves, who found it more important at this juncture to speak to a general audience and to voice broad political demands than to safeguard their organizations' continued immunity from police interference. One of the doctor-orators even noted that the political demands had to be made at professional congresses due to the illegality of public political life, adding that "all congresses in their own way are Russian parliaments, where the most urgent needs of the nation can be addressed."[5]

Second, the presence of the clients of the teachers and the doctors, especially the workers, added an urgent and dramatic new meaning to the tradition of community service in their professions. Both organizations had long concerned themselves with the health and cultural development of the common people, of course. But now, pleading their cases before their clients had the effect of transforming the subordination implicit in the relationship of professionals and nonprofessionals into a political alliance among equal parties, based on a mutual recognition of needs in the face of a common enemy. The zemstvo doctors and teachers, the factory physicians, the instructors at evening schools for workers and among the poverty-stricken lower classes were familiar enough with the needs of the common people. But the January congresses also exposed the occupational needs of the professionals themselves to a public audience for the first time, laying the basis for a common political initiative and transcending the social gap normally dividing *intelligentsiia* from *narod*.

Finally, the newness of protest that emerged in January 1904 was not due alone to the mixing of the urban public with educated specialists; it also represented a new phase in the ongoing relationship of the urban professionals with the government. Hitherto, both physicians and teachers had campaigned for improvements in the way the

5. Sanders, "The Union of Unions," chap. 2, p. 51.

government regulated their performance of professional responsibilities, but they had done so through the channels approved by the government, namely through written recommendations and petitions. In January 1904, both teachers and physicians found the usual ineffectiveness of these channels and methods no longer acceptable, and they acted dramatically on this conclusion by violating the exclusiveness and narrow professional agendas required by the government and by generalizing their occupational grievances into civic concerns of the wider urban public. By thus moving beyond petitions to public political debate and protest, the professionals took the first step in spreading open opposition to the government beyond the revolutionary parties and small groups of students and workers, "legitimizing" it among the ranks of educated society and transforming the professional conventions into "Russian parliaments."[6]

Under the cover of these tumultuous events in the capital, the First or Founding Congress of the Union of Liberation took place from January 2 to 5. Delegates from 22 towns of the Empire adopted "Union of Liberation" (*Soiuz osvobozhdeniia*) as the official name of the organization, indicating thereby not a political party, but a loose alliance of diverse liberal elements committed to drawing in more followers in approximate agreement with the views expressed in the journal *Liberation*. The congress also chose a directing Council composed of five zemstvo and five intelligentsia members.[7] The care in creating this parity undoubtedly reflected the concern of a basically intelligentsia organization that the zemstvo element continue to feel that it had free access.[8]

A similar concern was reflected in the discussion of the Union's program. An objection by certain populist democrats to the support of private ownership, which appeared in an earlier draft, was overridden by the majority, but rightist objections to stands in favor of national self-determination and to "the defense of the interests of the

6. Seregny, "The Russian Teachers' Movement" (cited in n. 3 above), pp. 389–90. Friedan, *Russian Physicians* (cited in n. 4 above), pp. 244–46.

7. The composition of the Council soon tilted significantly in favor of the intelligentsia as new members were co-opted in the months that followed; for details, see Shatsillo, "Novoe o 'Soiuze Osvobozhdeniia,'" pp. 141–44. The very distinction between zemstvo and intelligentsia types may also be questioned, as have Sanders (in "The Union of Unions," chap. 2, pp. 60–61) and Freeze (in "A National Liberation Movement and the Shift in Russian Liberalism, 1901–1903"). Fuller accounts of the founding congress of the Union of Liberation are available in most of the works cited in n. 1 above.

8. Galai, *The Liberation Movement*, pp. 191–92.

toiling masses" were also voted down. As with the professional congresses, the Union's program expressed its common link among its diverse components and made its bid for the allegiance of yet other social groups by means of general political formulas, a democratic, constitutional regime elected according to "four-tail" suffrage (suffrage that was universal, equal, direct, and secret). No detailed social or economic program was worked out at this time for fear of arousing antagonisms prematurely, and the program itself would not even be published before the fall of 1904.[9]

The most important political task of these liberal and professional organizations, already acknowledged and addressed in early 1904, was the wider mobilization of all social forces in the Empire and their formation into a united, antiautocratic opposition. Although the revolutionary parties were organized and active for many years before the liberals took their first organizational steps in 1904, the liberals were nevertheless far more effective in forming a national opposition. This was due to the public prominence of their intelligentsia and zemstvo leaders, and to their relatively easy access to the public means of communication. Their task was also facilitated by the limitations of their goals: "opposition" still meant for most of those involved the rapid reform of the existing *political* arrangements, but not a precipitous transformation of the *social* order. Most of the rhetoric of unity and political alliance heard among liberals from January 1904 onward assumed that the mass movement was still largely slumbering and was intended to aid in the mobilization of educated society and to express the universality of their own politics rather than to create a genuinely unified and all-inclusive movement.[10] Ironically, their rhetoric nevertheless aided in awakening other social elements such as urban workers to their own needs and grievances, and therefore in mobilizing the constituencies of their chief political rivals in the revolutionary parties.

FATHER GAPON AND THE ASSEMBLY OF RUSSIAN WORKERS

Although in 1904 the emergence of the liberal elite and the discredit of government authority drew the bulk of public attention in

9. *Ibid.*, pp. 189–90. The program and organizational statutes have been published by K. F. Shatsillo, "Obzor dokumental'nykh materialov kruzhka 'Beseda' i 'Soiuza Osvobozhdeniia' vo fonde D. I. Shakhovskogo," *Arkheograficheskii ezhegodnik za 1974* (Moscow, 1975), pp. 294–96; and by Emmons, "The Statutes of the Union of Liberation."
10. Emmons, *The Formation of Political Parties*, p. 30.

the capital and in the country as a whole, the year also witnessed the formation and growth of the first mass organization of labor in the history of Petersburg workers: The Assembly of Russian Mill and Factory Workers of St. Petersburg (*Sobranie russkikh fabrichno-zavodskikh rabochikh g. Peterburga*), which later organized the icon-bearing procession to the Winter Palace resulting in the massacre of Bloody Sunday, January 9, 1905. The seminal importance of that event in the history of Russian labor and revolution, as well as the pivotal role of the Assembly in the mobilization and organization of Petersburg labor, makes the reconstruction of its origins of central importance in this account, although they were known to relatively few persons at the time.[11]

The Assembly was the last significant variant of a series of labor organizations initiated and directed by the Tsarist police official Sergei Zubatov in an attempt to disarm the appeal of the revolutionary parties by satisfying workers' economic and cultural needs while encouraging their more conservative political inclinations. As such, the Assembly shared features with similar organizations in Moscow, Minsk, Vilna, and Odessa. All the Zubatov organizations were aimed at factory workers, and all attracted large followings within a short time; they all included former revolutionary workers and/or intellectuals in their organizing nuclei; and, except in Minsk, they all involved themselves in industrial strikes on the side of the workers and, as a result, were all closed or severely restricted by the government shortly afterward.

Nothing was more indicative of the eagerness of Russian workers around 1900 for the formation of class organizations than the popularity that greeted the Zubatovist unions and the rapidity with which they were adapted to industrial struggle. On several successive occasions the police unions were taken over by the tumultuous activity of a new and rapidly growing proletariat struggling for recognition and better conditions, and Zubatovists ended by providing the organization and leadership for several massive strikes. While leading the workers away from the influence of the revolutionaries, they were

11. See my "Petersburg's First Mass Labor Organization: The Assembly of Russian Workers and Father Gapon," on which much of this chapter is based. The most detailed and accurate account of Gapon and the Assembly is Sablinsky, *The Road to Bloody Sunday. Father Gapon and the St. Petersburg Massacre of 1905*. See also Gurevich, *Deviatoe ianvaria*; Ainzaft, *Zubatovshchina i gaponovshchina*; Shilov, "K dokumental`noi istorii 'Petitsii' 9-go ianvaria 1905 goda"; Shuster, *Peterburgskie rabochie v 1905–1907 gg.*, pp. 59–95; and the dissertation version of Sablinsky, "The Road to Bloody Sunday. Father Gapon, His Labor Organization, and the Massacre of Bloody Sunday."

drawn by the workers into their labor struggles, technically "economist" and limited in aims, but by their scale, aggressiveness, and social
repercussions far more threatening to the authorities than anything
yet organized by the revolutionary parties.[12]

Georgii Gapon, a former seminary student and priest in Petersburg's working-class quarter, fell heir to the legacy of Zubatovism.[13]
In the end, he subverted the movement more thoroughly and consciously than any of his predecessors by turning a government union
not only against the employers, but against the government and the
established order as well. He clearly did not intend this outcome from
the start, and it became possible and even necessary only through the
complex interaction of Gapon, a group of radical workers assisting
him, and the mass of Petersburg workers, now increasingly ready for
militant protest and struggle, largely due to the abrupt shift in the political mood after mid-1904.

There is little in Gapon's background that permits a very definite
characterization of his political views and nothing that foretold his
catalytic role in the development of the labor movement. He came
from a respected peasant family of moderate means (*seredniak*, or
small *kulak*) in the Ukraine, and although he studied for the priesthood, he showed doubts about his calling at an early date, even inter-
rupting his schooling to work as a zemstvo statistician for a short time.
Plans to attend a university were frustrated by bad conduct marks at
the seminary. As he explained it, these were due to his failure to attend classes and to an adolescent brush with Tolstoyan views on the
superiority of the inner spirit of religion over its outward forms. Although he did become a priest, he retained some of his youthful re-
belliousness and remained critical of the incompetence, venality, and
corruption of the Orthodox church and priesthood. These things
seemed to him all the less tolerable in light of the church's high calling
and the poverty and suffering of ordinary people. This idealism may
nevertheless have found a satisfying outlet in his priestly duties after
he took up his first parish in his native Poltava province. But the early

12. Schneiderman, *Sergei Zubatov and Revolutionary Marxism: The Struggle for the
Working Class in Tsarist Russia.* References to much of the Soviet and prerevolutionary
literature on the subject may be found in the bibliography of this work.

13. An older, predominantly Soviet literature of the Stalin and post–Stalin period
gives overriding importance to Gapon's police connections and to the vague, if persistent, suggestion that his primary motive was that of an *agent provocateur.* See, e.g.,
A. M. Pankratova, ed., *Ocherki istorii SSSR. Pervaia russkaia burzhuazno-demokraticheskaia
revoliutsiia 1905–1907 gg.* (Moscow, 1955). This view will not be explicitly rebutted
here, and interested readers are referred to the works cited in n. 11.

death of his beloved first wife apparently again destabilized his career, sharpening his discontent with existing alternatives and propelling him to seek a more challenging situation.

While still a priest, Gapon displayed the ability to attract a following and considerable talent as an orator. These qualities were possibly also linked to his success, through his charm and apparent sincerity, at influencing important personages to aid him. (He later used all these abilities to considerable advantage in the cause of labor.) He was able, for example, in a personal interview with K. P. Pobedonostsev, to win the right to matriculate in the St. Petersburg Theological Academy, despite his somewhat checkered career. But he found much to criticize among his teachers and fellow students, and, after absenting himself from the Academy for a year, simultaneously resumed his studies and took work as a priest, choosing parishes that put him in touch with the lower classes of the capital. There he developed ambitious self-help projects for the rehabilitation of the city's outcasts, seeking (without success) to win acceptance for them in philanthropic and government circles. In this work he made his first contacts with industrial workers, "going among them at their work on the Baltic wharves and entering into conversations with them. They got to trust me, and some of them confessed to having become infected with political ideas. I did not at that time think that political change was necessary. I told them that by some industrial organization they might reach better results for their own elevation than by entering into conflict with the Government."[14]

Gapon's interest in the city's lower classes and his organization of self-help projects came to the attention of the authorities late in 1902, and he was brought to meet Zubatov, just then attempting to establish one of his unions in the capital. The police official was impressed by the priest's abilities and demeanor and tried to entice him into joining the effort. Gapon demurred, although he befriended Zubatov, consulted with him on a regular basis, and borrowed from him otherwise illegal literature on the labor movement. He also began visiting the workers' social club and tearoom established by Zubatov's assistants in Petersburg. This first Zubatovist experiment never became popular

14. Gapon, *The Story of My Life*, p. 62. Gapon's memoirs, source for much of the biographical material given here, were first published in English in *The Strand Magazine*, vol. 30, nos. 175–79 (July–Nov. 1905), and only later translated into Russian as *Istoriia moei zhizni*. See especially the carefully and informatively annotated edition of A. A. Shilov. A more detailed account of Gapon's life and career up to this point may be found in Sablinsky, *The Road to Bloody Sunday*, pp. 34–48.

with workers, and it was closed within a year. On his visits, Gapon befriended some of the workers and began to form a small circle of his
own adherents.[15]

Gapon was aware, thanks to his close contacts with workers, that
the experiment's lack of success was due to its close ties with the police
and the fear and disapproval this aroused among Petersburg workers.
This reaction resulted not only from the prior example of the Moscow
organization, but from the more pronounced awareness of police
presence among the workers of the capital and from the stronger tradition of antigovernment opposition among the Petersburg population as a whole. Accordingly, Gapon and his coterie of workers began
to plan another organization that would avoid this pitfall by downplaying police supervision and by involving its members more intimately
in its functioning. As a protégé of Zubatov, Gapon was able to secure
permission to put his ideas into effect, and the first meeting of the St.
Petersburg Assembly of Russian Factory and Mill Workers was held in
August 1903, the same month Zubatov himself was dismissed for dis-
loyalty to Pleve.[16]

This group was only an organizing nucleus with no official standing, and Gapon's first task was to justify its existence to the government, which had already seen two other such experiments end in
disaster. In a memorandum written in October 1903 he criticized previous Zubatovist organizations for making use of police, paid agents,
and non-Russians to lead Russian workers, and he outlined a plan for
the new organization that would avoid undue police supervision and
make use instead of self-supporting workers, especially more "consciously developed persons, who are dedicated to the [Zubatovist]
idea, and understand it."[17] Thus, Gapon implicitly promised a better
performance if his organization were allowed greater autonomy from
police supervision. In a single stroke he both offered the authorities an alternative to the now discredited police unions and justified a
plan that would give him and his worker colleagues greater freedom
of action.

15. This organization was called the St. Petersburg Mutual Aid Society of Workers in Machine Industries, a conscious parallel to the Moscow branch. Zubatov,
"Zubatovshchina," p. 169. Schneiderman, *Sergei Zubatov*, pp. 173–81. Sviatlovskii, *Professional'noe dvizhenie v Rossii*, pp. 68–70. Varnashev, "Ot nachala do kontsa s gaponovskoi organizatsiei (Vospominaniia)," pp. 179–89 (hereafter cited as Varnashev,
"Vospominaniia").

16. Schneiderman, *Sergei Zubatov*, pp. 350–54. Korelin, "Russkii 'politseiskii sotsializm' (Zubatovshchina)," pp. 57–58.

17. Kobiakov, "Gapon i okhrannoe otdelenie do 1905 goda," pp. 33–45.

The statutes Gapon drafted for the new organization, despite their recognition of the need to respect the government's ultimate authority, did embody his ideas on organizational autonomy and worker independence and therefore differed significantly from the statutes of earlier Zubatovist organizations. Essentially, Gapon centralized supervision of the organization in his own hands, as its "Representative," a figure charged with overall responsibility and authority in the Assembly. This made it possible to keep the police out of the day-to-day functioning of the Assembly, whereas in the Moscow organization, for instance, they had been more intimately and regularly involved. The statutes, unlike those in Moscow, also provided a clear definition of membership, financial independence by means of dues, and a considerable degree of self-government by the workers' own chosen officers, organized into a Governing Board, Audit Committee, and other bodies. Even financial responsibility for the physical premises of the Assembly was assumed by a body of charter members, the Circle of Responsible Persons, which expanded by co-optation and from which all officers were to be chosen. Finally, the government's responsible supervisory agent was not the police, as in Moscow, but the St. Petersburg City Governor, who exercised a veto over electees to the Governing Board, approved the choice of the Representative, and reviewed all directives given by the general meetings to the Assembly's officers.[18]

The success of the enterprise thus projected was further assured by several more specific circumstances. The authorities necessarily relied on Gapon's probity and caution, as well as on the information he himself gave them, for an intimate knowledge of what was actually going on in the organization. Gapon established a personal relationship with the key mediator in this relationship, the St. Petersburg City Governor, who from February 1904 was General I. A. Fullon, a soft-hearted old soldier who viewed the Assembly favorably and trusted Gapon implicitly, consistently reassuring the police and the Interior

18. A translation of the Assembly's statutes may be found in Sablinsky, *The Road to Bloody Sunday*, pp. 323–43. A complete Russian text is available only in Soviet archives (*ibid.*, pp. 400–401), but a selection is printed in Kats and Milonov, *1905 god. Professional'noe dvizhenie*, pp. 90–95. The Moscow Zubatov organization's statutes are published in *Katorga i ssylka*, no. 14 (1925), pp. 113–14; *Byloe*, no. 14 (1912), pp. 89–91; Grigor'evskii, *Politseiskii sotsializm v Rossii (Zubatovshchina)*, pp. 20–23; a translation and summary of them appear in Pospielovsky, *Russian Police Trade-Unionism. Experiment or Provocation?*, pp. 165–69. For a more detailed discussion of the statutes, see Surh, "Petersburg's First Mass Labor Organization," pp. 249–53.

Ministry of the Assembly's reliability and lawfulness right up to the eve of January 9.[19]

Like Moscow's Zubatov organization, the Assembly organized a program of concerts and lectures as well as cooperative and self-improvement projects. Unlike the Moscow organization, however, the Petersburg Assembly did not seek to intervene in labor disputes. The statutes did not provide for this, and Gapon confined himself to informal intervention on behalf of individual workers in trouble with their employers, using his influence as a priest and semiofficial trustee of the government to help settle particular problems. Although 1904 witnessed relatively few strikes in St. Petersburg, growing opposition to the war and the increasing activism of the government's intelligentsia critics necessitated even greater caution than usual. Moreover, previous Zubatovist organizations had had a way of catalyzing strike activity, so that the Assembly's noninvolvement was the result of a conscious decision to desist from it. Prior to the Putilov Plant strike of January 1905, which immediately preceded the January general strike and the procession to the Winter Palace, the Assembly appeared to most participants and observers simply as a self-help and self-improvement society. During most of its existence it was outwardly a better embodiment of the Zubatovist idea, less of an incipient labor union, and less interested in becoming one, than the earlier Zubatovist organizations had been.[20]

Gapon had bigger plans in mind. He wanted the Assembly to grow into a gigantic organization with branches in other cities and to become a nationwide force for labor reform in Russia. He knew that premature involvement in industrial conflict would hinder that aim, and he resolved to proceed cautiously and quietly for the time being. In other words, he intended in the long run to use his Zubatovist cover to form an independent workers' movement whose exact political identity was unclear, except that it would not be part of the established revolutionary parties, but not a buttress of the autocracy either.[21] Gapon claimed in his memoirs to have lost faith in the Zubatovist ideal as early as mid-1903 and to have conceived at that time of using his position to further the aims described here. This is partly confirmed by an independent witness and acquaintance of Gapon, who reported being told of such far-reaching plans sometime prior to the approval of the statutes, possibly as early as Gapon

19. *NPRR*, p. 99. Sablinsky, *The Road to Bloody Sunday*, pp. 91, 97.
20. Gapon, *The Story of My Life*, pp. 118–19.
21. *Ibid.*, pp. 94, 99, 103–4.

claimed.[22] Although it is quite likely that Gapon held such ideas as early as he claimed, they took concrete shape more gradually, less dramatically, somewhat later, and with altogether more ambivalence than he admitted, as will become clear below. As to the claim that he lost faith in the Zubatovist ideal, this undoubtedly meant at most that he became more indifferent to supplanting the revolutionary parties, not that he opposed the autocracy. On the contrary, it is clear that until January 9, Gapon fully expected that the Tsar could and would approve independent labor organizing in Russia.

The chief problem in doing this was controlling his worker assistants, whose very sincerity and earnestness might lead them to intervene in protests and factory disputes and so embroil the Assembly with the authorities before it was strong enough to account for itself. Fortunately for his plans, Gapon began with a rather conservative group, many of them remnants of the first Zubatovist organization in Petersburg, including its monarchist founders, M. A. Ushakov and V. I. Pikunov. The group became a nucleus of leaders once the Assembly expanded throughout the city. They were described as consisting of family men, over thirty years old, who were "comparatively well-off materially. . . . None of them had any special fondness for politics, and [they] were proponents of a peaceful trade union movement." That is to say, they did not think workers had to fight for political rights in order to attain even trade-unionist goals, but trusted in the "benevolent attitude of the authorities toward labor."[23]

The feature that most of these men shared was a certain naive trust in Gapon. More significantly, they came from that stratum of skilled workers, predominantly in the metal and machine trades, which produced most of the natural worker leaders of all political stripes. As noted earlier, these workers were better paid, better educated, and therefore better read than other workers, and largely for these reasons commanded the respect and allegiance of workers less well off. More knowledgeable, respected, and public-spirited though these men may have been, however, they were at the same time politically quite inexperienced. To be sure, a handful of them, like Ushakov and

22. Pavlov, "Iz vospominanii o 'Rabochem soiuze' i sviashchennike Gapone," p. 34.

23. Varnashev, "Vospominaniia," pp. 190, 193–94. Cf. Schwarz, *The Russian Revolution of 1905. The Workers' Movement and the Formation of Bolshevism and Menshevism*, p. 282, where this same passage is cited as evidence of the essential character of the worker leadership of the Assembly throughout its existence, rather than its make-up in early 1904, as it was intended. Schwarz fails to explain how this same group later demanded a political demonstration and supported the organization of a strike.

Pikunov, were confirmed monarchists and conservatives, while others
had been exposed to the influence of the revolutionary parties. But
these constituted a small minority.

Even in St. Petersburg, whose proletariat was acquiring a reputation as the most advanced in Russia, it was possible before 1905 to
find men like the machinist Nikolai Varnashev, a 16-year veteran of
Petersburg metal plants, who claimed to have "read most of the Russian classics," yet who knew nothing about labor problems or politics.
He later wrote: "In 1906 every little boy declined the names of the
parties with no difficulty, [but] I well recall a time in 1902 when I myself asked that words like 'esdek' [SD] and 'eser' [SR] and others be
deciphered for me." He recalls never having seen or even heard of
party leaflets, let alone the parties themselves or their ideas, even
though he worked in some of the city's larger plants, where political
intrigues and propaganda were more frequently encountered.[24] Men
like Varnashev, valued for their skills, better educated and more
highly paid, felt themselves to one degree or another different from
and superior to ordinary workers. The transformation of this sense of
status into a consciousness of responsibility to the class as a whole was
revealed with remarkable clarity by Varnashev when he described
meeting the organizers of the first Zubatovist organization in Petersburg: he regretted he had not heard earlier "of these energetic and
intelligent innovators, who ennobled the title of 'worker' [*rabochii*],
which sometimes jarred me and [which] I disguised with the more
pleasant-sounding word—'mechanic' [*mekhanik*]. Be that as it may, I
resolve[d] to support this worthy initiative with everything I had."[25]

This remarkable admission reveals how Zubatovists, almost universally vilified by revolutionaries as traitors to the labor movement, were
viewed by naive but otherwise accomplished, well-intentioned workers.
More important still, it indicates that even the government unions,
whatever their political intentions, could call into question subjective
status distinctions among workers, stressing their common fate and
thereby promoting incipient class consciousness. Varnashev took an
active part in both the Mutual Aid Society and the Assembly, becoming one of Gapon's most trusted and important assistants.

Those other educated workers and would-be leaders who, like

24. Varnashev, "Vospominaniia," pp. 177–78.
25. *Ibid.*, p. 180. In 1903, the metalworker memoirist Timofeev pointed out the
melding of earlier status distinctions in the fairly recent adoption of the term "rabochii"
to describe both skilled and unskilled alike. Timofeev, *Chem zhivet zavodskii rabochii*,
pp. 5–6, or "Zavodskie budni (Iz zapisok rabochego)," p. 32.

Varnashev, gravitated to the Assembly found in Gapon not so much an object of faith as an admirable complement to their own views and aspirations. Gapon's appeal to workers has been attributed to the similarity of his political development to that of the average educated worker, and there is great validity to the claim.[26] But to leave it at that is to tell only half the story. His assistants understood the need to organize workers to help themselves but often did not have very much faith in the ability of ordinary workers to accomplish this.[27] As an educated cleric Gapon was able to speak and to write the language of the authorities and of the intelligentsia, lending to the workers' cause the dignity of a functional *intelligent* as well as the sanctity of his priest's robes. At the same time, he could talk to workers not only in their own language, but also without conveying the feeling that he was speaking down to them, and this ability surely made him the envy of many party intellectuals. Although apparently not an accomplished orator, Gapon possessed a certain richness of feeling and expression that more than compensated for his technical shortcomings, infusing his pronouncements with conviction and inspiring trust (even when adequate grounds for it did not exist).[28]

This bond of trust, always so important to the unity and cohesion of the Assembly, was probably cemented for most of Gapon's followers by his own political inexperience and naive belief in the government's potential for self-reform. Although he had read a great deal of revolutionary literature and became more open to an oppositionist stance in the course of 1904, he never really overcame his faith in the government and distrust of the Left, and he remained a man whose basic interest was in the moral and material uplift of society's victims. To the depth of his being, therefore, he represented the ambivalences characteristic of many Russian workers at the moment of their political awakening. Gapon's vision did not really transcend that moment, and as events developed rapidly beyond that point, he was left stranded; but while it lasted, he was the leader of the hour, seemingly possessed of superhuman powers.

26. S. Somov, "Iz istorii sotsialdemokraticheskogo dvizheniia v Peterburge v 1905 godu," p. 38.

27. For example, when Varnashev first told his friend Nikolai Stepanov about the Mutual Aid Society, the latter said he "did not believe that workers could produce anything sensible." Later, however, Stepanov joined the Assembly and became an officer of one of its locals. Varnashev, "Vospominaniia," pp. 180, 190.

28. On Gapon's language and demeanor, see Somov, "Iz istorii," pp. 37–39; and Pavlov, "Iz vospominanii," pp. 30–38, 40.

CONSENSUS AND CONFLICT
IN THE ASSEMBLY

Most of Petersburg's influential worker leaders who were members or ex-members of revolutionary parties avoided Gapon's organization because the parties viewed it as an emanation of the government itself, aimed at subverting the labor movement. Gapon realized this boycott of the Assembly would prove an obstacle to recruiting members, especially among the better-educated and more radical workers, who were more inclined to share the revolutionaries' assessment of Zubatovism or were more sensitive to the opinions of informed persons. He also realized that he needed the help of leaders with some experience in labor politics and organizing if the Assembly was to become the mass organization that he envisioned. Gapon therefore cultivated the interest of a group of independent Social Democrats who, weary of the party's impotence, secrecy, and domination by intellectuals, looked to the Assembly as a means of reaching large numbers of hitherto unpoliticized workers. This group cautiously held aloof during the early months of the Assembly's existence while Gapon was occupied with drafting the Assembly's statutes and establishing his credibility with the authorities. By the end of 1903 he felt confident enough to expel from the Assembly the only serious rivals and threats to his leadership, the orthodox Zubatovists Ushakov and Pikunov. Gapon had begun to shape a group of worker assistants whose primary loyalty would be to him. By eliminating the monarchists he also reassured the leftists and paved the way for their full and active participation in the Assembly.[29]

Almost from the earliest days of his contacts with industrial workers in the capital, Gapon was acquainted with one particular group of them that distinguished itself from the rest by its developed political experience and knowledge. The head of the group was the lithographer Aleksei Karelin, a self-educated worker-intellectual and native of St. Petersburg, a former participant in the Brusnev Circle of the early 1890's who, in 1903, still considered himself a revolutionary Social Democrat. Gapon took Karelin into the small circle of workers with whom he discussed forming the organization that later became the Assembly.[30] Karelin's prestige among workers as a self-educated

29. Karelin, "Deviatoe ianvaria i Gapon. Vospominaniia" (hereafter "Vospominaniia"), pp. 106–7. Sviatlovskii, *Professional'noe dvizhenie*, pp. 89–90. Pavlov, "Iz vospominanii," pp. 25–28, 38.
30. Karelin, "Vospominaniia," p. 106. *Pervaia russkaia revoliutsiia v Peterburge 1905 g.*, vol. 1, pp. 141–42.

political activist who had suffered arrest and exile, his large number of acquaintances and contacts in the work force of the capital, and his willingness to take part in Gapon's self-help schemes more than compensated for the risk of associating with him. At a minimum, Karelin's friendship would pave the way to recruiting Assembly members in the Vasilevsky Island district of the city, where he and his group were most active and influential. More important than that was the moral respectability these revolutionary workers lent to an organization tainted with the suspicion of police connections, the reassurance their presence would give to ordinary, nonrevolutionary workers who were also suspicious of police unions.[31]

The labor historian V. V. Sviatlovskii, himself a participant in the early circle movement in St. Petersburg and a friend of Karelin, described the group's members as "eagles, . . . that is, people dissatisfied with the party but more or less [politically] conscious, having been in a party and left it, and always an important and influential group among the Petersburg proletariat."[32] We do not know very much about the exact political views of the Karelin group, but its attitude toward the Social Democratic party was very positive.

Karelin described his group as including "real Social Democrats, that is, people who either were party workers or are now prepared to become the same, but who disagree on tactical details which are sometimes of considerable importance. Therefore, not only will we refrain from interfering with the activity of the parties but, on the contrary, [we] will try as far as possible to help them." The reason the group did not work within the party was due in part to its inability to reach the greatest numbers of workers, although Karelin put a positive construction on this problem: "Our activity will be concentrated among those circles of workers to which access will be difficult for party activists or to which they have no access whatsoever—namely, the masses with the lowest [political] consciousness."[33]

The group caucused outside the Assembly in meetings held at Karelin's apartment.[34] Its members, all of whom participated in the Assembly's ruling circle, were thus able to concert their efforts and keep alive a sense of their loyalty to a revolutionary tradition and outlook. This was the only group of Assembly leaders, as far as is known, which maintained a political identity separate from the Assembly itself while playing a leading role in it, and it bears testimony, among

31. Sviatlovskii, *Professional'noe dvizhenie*, p. 90.
32. *Ibid.*
33. Pavlov, "Iz vospominanii," p. 27.
34. *Pervaia russkaia revoliutsiia*, vol. 1, pp. 139, 140.

other things, to the depth of Social Democratic penetration of the Petersburg work force. Karelin and his group, themselves the products of a long tradition of circle work, both Populist and Social Democratic, had internalized the latter's wider political aims so well that they were able to break from intelligentsia tutelage, to raise their own critique of party policies, and to pursue an independent policy in their own circle—all in the name of what they thought of as a broader Social Democratic strategy.[35]

Karelin served as treasurer of the Assembly and occupied a leading position in its ruling group. Vera Karelina, whose record of circle work and arrests paralleled that of her husband, was a very remarkable person in her own right and a leading spokesman for the group within the Assembly. Pavlov described her as "warmer, kinder, and more sensitive" than her husband, yet pointed out that "she alone boldly and openly contested Gapon's authority and always forced him to agree with her viewpoint and, consequently, to subordinate himself to the opinion of the staff members." She provided a rallying point for the opposition, and Gapon acknowledged her frankness and sincerity by confiding in her as in no other staff member.[36] As in the days of her circle work, Karelina also took a special interest in women workers, and she organized seven regional sections for them under the auspices of the Assembly. Gapon encouraged this work partly as a way of nurturing progressive ideas within the Assembly, and partly as a way of reaching a large and important part of the city's work force. It was also well understood that male workers would be that much more encouraged to participate if their wives and sisters were drawn into the Assembly's life.[37]

35. S. Ainzaft characterized the Karelin group as composed of local variants of a type of skilled worker, trained in the Social Democratic circle movement but not making the turn to mass agitation and underground work in the second half of the 1890's. Instead, he gravitated toward legal, moderate groups such as Khar'kov's Mutual Aid Society for Persons in Artisanal Labor, with which Ainzaft implicitly compares the Assembly: *Zubatovshchina i gaponovshchina*, pp. 115–18. As with Schwarz's characterization of the Karelinists as captives of an apolitical, conservative worker elite (see n. 23 above), this view ignores the actual role they played in the Assembly as well as their own professed motives for working with Gapon, which were explicitly *political* ones. Also, as argued above, the Assembly was not chartered to redress industrial conflicts, and did not seek to do so until the end of its existence. To be sure, the Assembly harbored workers of the type Schwarz and Ainzaft had in mind, but they were clearly not coterminous with the Karelin group and offered, on the whole, no concerted, conscious alternative or opposition to its influence.

36. Pavlov, "Iz vospominanii," pp. 25, 51–52.

37. Karelin, "Vospominaniia," p. 108. V. A. Ianov's testimony, *KL*, no. 1 (1922), p. 316. Sviatlovskii, *Professional'noe dvizhenie*, pp. 81–83. Karelina, "Rabotnitsy v Gapo-

Ivan Kharitonov and Gerasim Usanov, two other members of the Karelin group were, like Karelin, printers and sons of poor Petersburg workers. Usanov became secretary of the Vasilevsky Island branch of the Assembly and Kharitonov president of the Kolomensk branch. Stepan Sergeev was a metalworker from Saratov who came to Petersburg in 1903 and immediately joined Karelin's group, then the Assembly, in which he also served as a branch officer. All three were later elected deputies to the St. Petersburg Soviet of Workers' Deputies in 1905, as were both Karelins.[38]

In addition to these regular members of the Karelin group, a number of nonparty but radically inclined leaders joined forces with them on specific issues and with varying degrees of frequency to form what has been called "the Opposition." These included Nikolai Varnashev, president of the original Vyborg branch; the weaver Ivan Vasil'ev, president of the Governing Board; the upholsterer V. Smirnov; Nikolai Petrov, president of the Neva branch; and Vladimir Inozemtsev, president of the Narva branch, whom Varnashev later described as a "very remarkable man, and all-round clear mind," with a special ability for winning over the crowd by his rough and ready manner of speaking, giving the impression of a man "telling the unvarnished truth." There were a number of others whose names have not survived.[39]

From the viewpoint of the Karelin group, Gapon's experiment offered a rare opportunity to reach the immense number of workers not previously exposed to political propaganda. They were, of course, very much aware of the stigma of police associations that surrounded Gapon and the Assembly. They therefore proceeded very slowly and cautiously during the early months of the new organization's existence. As we have seen, this suited Gapon's own aims of reassuring the authorities of his reliability and winning recognition for the Assembly. They attended meetings, including Responsible Circle meetings, but held aloof, refusing to take an active and leading role in Assembly affairs. The expulsion of Ushakov and Pikunov encouraged them, but they still held back, as if waiting for assurances of Gapon's trustworthiness. Once Gapon felt more secure about his own and the Assembly's autonomy, he moved to break the stalemate.

---

novskikh obshchestvakh," pp. 25–26. On Karelina herself, see Karelina, "Na zare rabochego dvizheniia"; *Pervaia russkaia revoliutsiia*, vol. 1, p. 142; Gurevich, *Deviatoe ianvaria*, n. 6, pp. 75–76; and Glickman, *Russian Factory Women*, pp. 173–80, 184–86.

38. *Pervaia russkaia revoliutsiia*, vol. 1, pp. 138–44.

39. Varnashev, "Vospominaniia," pp. 194, 199.

In March 1904 he called a highly secret meeting at his apartment, inviting four Assembly leaders whose trust he sought—Varnashev, Vasil'ev, Karelin, and Dmitrii Kuzin, a Menshevik worker not associated with the Karelin group. Gapon showed them a document he had written listing the demands later incorporated in the petition of January 9. He suggested that it be adopted as the secret program of the Assembly. Those present seem to have been pleased with the program for, although a lengthy discussion ensued, it was not modified.[40] They decided to keep the program to themselves, "and to conduct future work only under the aegis of this program, not revealing it all at once, but gradually, on every convenient occasion, instilling it into the consciousness of the assembled workers." For all the agreement, however, the occasion was also marked by a lingering distrust of Gapon. Realizing perhaps that the very secrecy of the program and the Assembly's need to maintain a façade of legality put their political lives in the priest's hands, the worker leaders made him swear an oath to uphold the program, and they threatened to take his life if he betrayed it.[41]

The resulting "Secret Program" or "Program of the Five," as it is sometimes called, was not distinctive in its individual demands, but taken together made up a unique combination (see Table 15). The political part of the program contained elements of the liberal and moderate democratic agendas that emerged in 1904 and 1905: civil liberties, ministerial responsibility, equality before the law. But it did not call for the overthrow of autocracy or even demand an elected legislature, though ministerial responsibility implied the existence of some kind of representative body. Hence, it lacked the key political demand of the Union of Liberation, a constituent assembly elected in accordance with the "four-tail" formula. At the same time, its economic and social demands were matched only by the programs of the revolution-

40. Karelin, "Vospominaniia," p. 107. Varnashev claimed that those present were not surprised by the program since they had forced Gapon to write it ("Vospominaniia," p. 198). He probably meant that they had asked for an expression of his political views rather than that they had proposed the points of the program. All other sources attribute its authorship to Gapon alone. The list of demands seems to have been the same as that later reprinted as one version of the January 9 Petition in *Vpered*, no. 4 (18 Jan. 1905); *Osvobozhdenie*, no. 65 (27 Jan. 1905), pp. 241–42; *NPRR*, pp. 30–31; Shilov, "K dokumental'noi istorii 'Petitsii'," p. 21. (This version is reproduced in this chapter.) Shilov's 1925 meeting with two of the participants in the March meeting confirmed and clarified what they had stated in their memoirs—Varnashev, "It was the petition of January 9th, 1905" ("Vospominaniia," p. 198); Karelin, it contained "the basic demands of his petition" ("Vospominaniia," p. 107).

41. Shilov, "K dokumental'noi istorii 'Petitsii'," p. 21. Sviatlovskii, *Professional'noe dvizhenie*, pp. 90–91.

TABLE 15
The Assembly's Secret Program

I. Measures to Eliminate Ignorance of, and Arbitrariness Toward, the Russian People:

1. Freedom and inviolability of person; freedom of speech, press, assembly, and freedom of conscience in matters of worship.
2. Universal and compulsory education, financed by the state.
3. Responsibility of the ministers before the people and guarantees that the government will abide by the law.
4. Equality of all before the law without exception.
5. Immediate pardon of those who suffered for their convictions.

II. Measures to Eliminate the Poverty of the People:

1. Abolition of indirect taxation and the introduction of direct, progressive income taxes.
2. Abolition of the land redemption tax, [establishment of] cheap credit, and the gradual transfer of land to the people.

III. Measures to Eliminate the Oppression of Labor by Capital:

1. Protection of labor by law.
2. Freedom of cooperative associations and professional labor unions.
3. An eight-hour workday and regulation of overtime work.
4. Freedom of struggle for labor against capital.
5. Participation of representatives of the working class in drafting of legislation for the state insurance of workers.
6. Normal wages [minimum wage].

SOURCE: Sablinsky, *The Road to Bloody Sunday*, p. 103 (citing Varnashev, "Vospominaniia," p. 198; Karelin, "Vospominaniia," p. 107; and Shilov, "K . . . istorii 'Petitsii,'" p. 21).

ary parties, and therefore more radical than anything the Union would put forth publicly before its third congress in March 1905: a progressive income tax, freedom to strike and unionize, the eight-hour day, state workers' insurance, the transfer of land to the people.[42] These demands clearly presupposed a more radical regime than that implied by the demands and omissions of the political part of the program.

Was it a sign of Gapon's political naïveté or of his guile that he wrote such a political incongruity into his program? It is not incon-

42. For the Social Democrats' 1903 program, see *Vtoroi s"ezd RSDRP. Iiul'–avgust 1903 goda. Protokoly*, pp. 418–24. In English, see *Resolutions and Decisions of the Communist Party of the Soviet Union. Volume I: The Russian Social Democratic Labour Party. 1898–October 1917*, ed. R. C. Elwood (Toronto, 1974), pp. 39–45. For the Liberationists' March 1905 program, see *Osvobozhdenie*, no. 69–70 (May 7, 1905), pp. 305–6.

ceivable that for Gapon it was both. On the one hand, he was by his own word confident that constitutional rights could be granted by the Tsar, whom he imagined "to be very kind-hearted and noble."[43] At the same time, it is possible that he had formed the habit from his tutelage by Zubatov of believing that many of the changes in industrial life held forth by the socialists could be achieved by enlightened autocratic initiative. On the other hand, the immediate aim of the program was not to give the Assembly a public political identity, but to win the allegiance of two socialists (Karelin and Kuzin) and to assure the other two of his freedom from police connections without appearing to be a revolutionary. To all four, above all, he was concerned to manifest a certain long-term insight into the needs of the working class. For these purposes, the formula of radical class demands implying revolutionary change without an explicit call for a political overturn filled the bill perfectly.

By confiding his program to the four men and winning their qualified support, Gapon gave his organization, publicly suspected of counterrevolutionary collaboration with the government, a semihidden, private kind of integrity. It became a small political conspiracy in conservative disguise, a kind of Trojan horse of labor radicals in the Tsarist camp. These men represented various political views and degrees of development, but all were inclined toward organizing a broad and independent workers' movement. The March agreement made it possible for them to link service to that cause with personal loyalty to Gapon. This loyalty was important to Gapon's self-esteem and therefore to his effectiveness as the Assembly's leader, and it was important to the internal stability of the Assembly's ruling group. Commitment to the secret program lent a selfless, idealistic quality to the work of the leaders, who could feel they were building something of greater moment than what the organization's Statutes permitted and described. In the long run, of course, this was an unstable arrangement since these leaders would one day collect on the moral debt Gapon had contracted with them, and he would be obliged to make public the program. But in the short run it worked out quite successfully.

Karelin and his faction were at least partially reassured about Gapon's motives. They did not give up their political identity and even led the only group vocally and consistently critical of Gapon's leadership, but they did so perforce as a loyal opposition which accepted the organization's outward aims and their own ultimate powerlessness. All the same, they were an effective opposition and soon took on the

43. Gapon, *The Story of My Life*, p. 135.

kind of leading role in the Assembly to which their knowledge, prestige, and experience suited them. Despite their formal subordination to Gapon's leadership, the Karelinists' active participation had a decisive effect on the further development of both the Assembly and Gapon. Most Assembly members, including many leaders, were apolitical or prepolitical in their views and feelings, holding unexamined and traditional beliefs and prejudices that certainly amounted programmatically to something rather more moderate than the Secret Program. At the same time, these very workers, as the experience of Moscow and Odessa had shown, would rally to the defense of fellow workers in fights with their employers. The revolutionary potential in the Assembly consisted not in the members' professed views, but in their capacity for social action. The Assembly was a working-class organization and would function as one in a crisis, even if its members did not yet understand or accept the full political meaning of that fact.

The Karelin group clearly understood the militancy latent in the Assembly. As independent socialists they suffered ostracism from the ranks of Social Democracy and were accused of Zubatovism from all sides. Karelin had to "break with the intelligentsia and the party" when he finally committed himself to Gapon's organization, and all members of the Karelin group were undoubtedly placed in a comparable position. Yet the group remained committed to drawing workers into a more or less revolutionary political posture, rather than giving way to the pursuit of economic gains, as might be expected from Social Democratic "deserters" to Zubatovism. When Karelin told Pavlov that his group took its task to be building bridges between the least conscious workers and party organizations, he was describing a project in political education.[44]

This educational work necessarily involved some departure from the full Social Democratic program if the Karelin group were to communicate meaningfully with Assembly members. Instead, they used the Secret Program to structure and orient the group's agitational work. Karelin seems to have found it well suited to discussions with politically unschooled workers, remarking that it was "broader and better" than that of the Social Democrats.[45] As might be expected of worker militants who had received their own political education in propaganda circles, the group invested its political work in the Assembly with the spirit of enlightenment and self-improvement. "On Sundays after the lecture [Karelin wrote] we entered into conversations

44. Karelin, "Vospominaniia," p. 109. Pavlov, "Iz vospominanii," pp. 27–28.
45. Karelin, "Vospominaniia," pp. 107–10.

with the workers, advising them what they should read. In every section there were good libraries which were taken away to the Okhranka after the Ninth [of January]. So we did a very good job cleaning up the workers' thinking."[46] These conversations must have kept to a fairly fundamental level because of the danger of denunciation, but they became bolder and more overtly political as the year wore on, especially after the relaxation of press censorship in August 1904. The active instigation and propagation of even the most fundamental forms of working-class consciousness were to have an effect that outstripped all expectations.

The influence of the Karelin group on the more active Assembly members, those who sat on the Secret Committee and the central Responsible Circle (and to a lesser extent, its counterparts in the separate branches), was probably even greater than on the general membership. In smaller, more exclusive meetings they could speak more openly and bring the weight of their experience and knowledge to bear with greater effect. Varnashev recalled their impact with admiration:

> Their general self-education was worthy of esteem for, politics aside, they had completely enlightened convictions on all questions of life and society, which along with their unsullied civic integrity, made them an unshakable authority among workers on the job. . . .
>
>   These were the people who were fully aware of their actions, and their original entry into the organization, I am forced to admit, came from the desire to criticize it and its activities and to create an opposition to Gapon. . . . Without trying to guess what the future destiny of the Assembly would have been had there been no Karelin group, the fact of *their entry* into the organization *must be acknowledged* as an event of *decisive importance,* both for the Assembly and for Gapon.[47]

The most important member of the inner circle to come under the influence of the Karelin group was Gapon himself. Although he was the unquestioned leader of the Assembly to whom all, even the Left oppositionists had ultimately to defer, he relied equally on them. Gapon hid this fact from public view, and perhaps from himself as well, but more disinterested observers have pointed it out.[48] Gapon did not have the knowledge or experience to direct the political propaganda work with the same authority and self-assurance as the Karelin group. Moreover, his role as the outwardly loyal, apolitical, and idealistic servant of labor precluded too active a part in the Assembly's surreptitious political life. More important than any of this, however, was

46. *Ibid.,* p. 110.
47. Varnashev, "Vospominaniia," p. 195.

the effect the oppositionists had upon Gapon's own erratic and unstable political convictions. Varnashev speaks of Gapon's "gradual move to the left" under the influence of the Karelinists, and this should be understood to mean his increasing consistency with the March program and a lessening of backsliding and vacillation rather than the complete abandonment of old and the acceptance of new views. The presence of the Karelin group supplied the ruling circle with an intellectual and moral vitality that would otherwise have been missing, kept its political life and its too malleable leader on an even keel, and brought the membership to an increasingly political conception of itself.

THE EXPANSION AND DIFFUSION OF LIBERAL OPPOSITIONISM

Beyond the confines of the Assembly a political storm of unprecedented proportions was brewing in the second half of 1904, an upheaval that would soon infect its members and disrupt the tenuous basis of its own existence. As noted earlier, the relaxation of restrictions on public life introduced by the ministry of Sviatopolk-Mirskii gave rise to a rebirth of civic-minded activity on the part of Russia's political elites—leaders of the zemstvo and noble assemblies and of urban professionals. These liberal and democratic elites had been somewhat divided and less active since the outbreak of war in February, but now, reacting to the regime's failures in the Far East, they went on the offensive again and within a short time enlivened every corner of the country with their hopes and plans. Throughout urban Russia, public political discussion surfaced in the form of new newspapers and journals, public meetings, petitions to the throne and to agencies of the government, all reflecting an earnest and forceful determination that the autocracy should henceforth heed the voices of educated society by modifying its monopoly of power and political authority. The Union of Liberation took the lead, targeting precisely these urban and provincial leaders for a focused campaign of constitutionalist agitation and mobilization.[49]

The groups and strata of society best-placed to take advantage of the new conditions of freedom were those which sought to expand civic life as an end in itself. In the short run, the rural and urban lib-

48. Especially Pavlov, "Iz vospominanii," pp. 40–42; but Varnashev also clearly implies this: "Vospominaniia," pp. 194–95.
49. See the references in the second paragraph of n. 1, above.

eral elites already organized for legal activity and in motion before Mirskii's liberalization drew the greatest benefit from the new conditions. The revolutionary parties benefited less because both their programs and their daily modus operandi, by and large, depended on profounder modifications of the status quo. Even so, a large part of the revolutionary camp proved willing to take advantage of the new legal opportunities, as will be seen presently.

The organization that made the most of the situation was the Union of Liberation. It alone both projected a vision that called for the active participation of all elements of Russian society in building a new social and political order and worked to implement it. Expanding upon the kinds of semipublic protests that occurred around the time of its first congress in January 1904, members of the Union of Liberation, preparing for their second congress in October, set an agenda of political tasks intended to press the struggle against the autocracy on to a new stage. They resolved:

1. To take the most active part in the coming congress of zemstvo and municipal leaders and make every effort to steer it toward stating constitutional demands openly.

2. November 20 being the fortieth anniversary of the Judicial Statutes, to have our members organize banquets on that day in Petersburg, Moscow, and as many other cities as possible, at which must be adopted constitutional and democratic resolutions much more decisive in tone than could be expected from a congress of zemstvo and municipal leaders.

3. Through our zemstvo members, to raise at as many of the coming *uezd* and province conventions as possible the question of introducing a constitutional order in Russia and of the need to convoke to this end representatives of the people on a broad democratic basis.

4. To begin to agitate for the formation of unions of lawyers, engineers, professors, writers, and others in the liberal professions for having them organize conventions and elect permanent bureaus; and for having these bureaus among themselves as well as with the bureaus of zemstvo and municipal leaders into a single union of unions.[50]

---

50. I. P. Belokonskii, "K istorii zemskogo dvizheniia v Rossii," *Istoricheksii Sbornik* (Spb., 1907), p. 29, as paraphrased in Schwarz, *The Russian Revolution of 1905*, pp. 33–34. There is a dispute between historian-participants Belokonskii and Shakhovskoi over whether the fourth point of the agenda was officially adopted or only discussed. The point is more or less academic, since the Liberationists did take measures to implement it in the fall of 1904. See Sanders, "The Union of Unions," ch. 3, pp. 18–20.

The Liberationists' strategy was at once to draw the ongoing moderate and constitutionalist agitation of the zemstvo elements to the left, while expanding the protest of professional and civic groups to encompass urban educated society as a whole. The strategy outlined in these resolutions met with extraordinary success. Rarely before in Russian history had the organizing plans of the opposition so perfectly expressed the mood of its constituents and given rise to such fulsome and enthusiastic support. On November 6 through 9 delegates to the First Zemstvo Congress, stirred by the same mood that swelled Liberationist ambitions, called in their program statement not for the usual consultative assembly, nor for the addition of zemstvo notables to the State Council, but for an elected legislature with specific powers over the government.[51] Somehow, the idea that Russia's landed notables could rise to the occasion and demand constitutional reform for the first time seemed to dissolve whatever political inhibitions remained among large parts of the moderate and middle strata of educated society, with the result that the floodgates of public protest by these elements were opened.

Beginning in mid-November and lasting most of the next two months, some 38 banquets and 42 public meetings throughout European Russia and the Caucasus delivered a deluge of political rhetoric and demands that transformed the civic life of autocratic Russia and set the stage for the next and most volatile phase of the liberation movement, the Revolution of 1905.[52] The resemblance of the banquet

51. Galai, *The Liberation Movement in Russia*, pp. 225–31.

52. The count of banquets and meetings is that of Emmons, "Russia's Banquet Campaign," pp. 49, 69, 84–86. Some writers are inclined to insist that the 1905 Revolution began with the events just described, rather than with the events of January 9, 1905, the most commonly assigned beginning; in other words, the First Revolution was begun by Russia's liberal and democratic landowners and intelligentsia rather than by her workers. E.g., Galai, "The Role of the Union of Unions in the Revolution of 1905," pp. 516–17. What is the point of insisting that one part of society or another started the revolution when it is quite plain that interaction and mutual encouragement between educated society and the labor movement had been under way since the 1870's? In place of utter certainty on this point, therefore, two observations may be offered: first, the events at the end of 1904 were an absolute prerequisite and organically related to those that culminated in the workers' demonstration of January 9th, as will be shown presently. The revolt of labor had begun long before the fall of 1904, but the form it took in 1905 in the capital was significantly shaped by the preceding revolt of the intelligentsia and zemstvo liberals. Second, whatever the portent and potential of the protests of educated society at the end of 1904, the revolution still involved only a very small minority of the Russian population, and therefore its impact on the government remained seriously restricted. The liberation movement did not become a mass phenomenon, even in urban Russia, until after January 9.

campaign to that of 1847 and 1848 in France was deliberately intended by the organizers, but the practice of doing political business
over a meal also had solid Russian roots among the intelligentsia and
public men prior to 1904. Although a handful of these thinly disguised political demonstrations adopted the Liberationist demand for
a constituent assembly elected according to the "four-tail" suffrage,
the overwhelming majority of them reiterated some variant of the
First Zemstvo Congress's program calling for civil liberties and an
elected legislature with specific powers over the government.[53]

This represented not only a move to the left for many of the participants but, more importantly, the mobilization of sympathetic but hitherto inactive elements. The Liberationists, whose efforts stood behind
most, if not all, of these gatherings, were justly pleased with the results of the campaign despite the fact that their more radical program
demands were seldom adopted. A large part of educated society had
moved within a very short time from near political inertness to a position that could be described as constitutionalist or protoconstitu-
tionalist. Many of the proceedings were carried in the new or newly
revitalized liberal newspapers—*Nasha zhizn', Nashi dni, Rus', Russkaia
gazeta, Syn otechestva*—and their dispatches were sometimes reprinted
by the moderate and conservative press, so that the liberals' unification movement acquired as a result national and societywide renown.

The Liberationists intended to exploit the opportunity while it
lasted and to push to the limit the political and organizational possi-
bilities now in the offing. Many of the banquets and meetings consisted principally of the members of a single profession—lawyers,
physicians, engineers, writers—and this made it possible to begin to
implement the fourth point of the October agenda, the organization
of unions along professional lines. Members of the Union of Liberation's Council actively promoted the idea, and several professional
groups took the occasion of their political gatherings to discuss the
need for more permanent professional organization. Where such organization already existed, the professionals were encouraged to turn
their activities in a more overtly political direction and to expand their
membership on this basis. Thus, the first steps in the formation of
some of the member organizations of the Union of Unions, officially
founded only in the spring of 1905, were taken at the banquet of engineers (December 5), at the banquet of physicians (December 18),
and at a meeting of professors (December 20), all held in St. Petersburg. It is likely that yet other professional groups discussed the possi-

53. Emmons, "Russia's Banquet Campaign," pp. 50, 55–57, 69–71.

bility of new and more political organizations at this time, although the movement was not yet as developed as it would be in the spring of 1905.[54]

Agitation for the formation of professional and political unions in late 1904 and the first half of 1905 contributed greatly to welding the intelligentsia, numerically weak and traditionally riven by disagreements, into a political entity of some force and effectiveness. The idea recommended itself in part because it was based on existing organizations and traditions, albeit not of long standing. Professional associations like the Moscow Society of Jurisprudence (founded 1863) and the Pirogov Society of Russian Doctors (1885) formed the basis of political mobilization of those groups in 1904 and 1905 and served as respected precedents for other professionals.

Along with such hitherto purely professional organizations, a smaller and more exclusive tradition of open defense of human and political rights had been established by the first, short-lived Writers' Union (*Soiuz vzaimopomoshchi russkikh pisatelei*, 1896–1901), whose Petersburg branch, by its outspoken criticism of the government, continuously laid its legal existence on the line. It eventually provoked the authorities to end its legal existence by openly condemning the government's violence against the student demonstration of March 4, 1901, in which the writers also participated. Many of those most active in that first "professional-political" union became leaders of the Petersburg branch of the Union of Liberation (the so-called "Big Group"), and it was they above all who revived the older idea of a union of intelligentsia and Society in a new guise combining professional associations with the kind of public, semilegal, oppositionist pressure group that the Writers' Union had been.[55]

Serious attention was thus already being paid during the banquet campaign to the organization of the urban professional intelligentsia, but in the fall of 1904 those Liberationists who sought to draw together the intelligentsia still looked with at least equal interest to their zemstvo allies. The strategy rested on the Liberationists' recognition of the fact that the *zemtsy*, potentially more influential, were less easily mobilized than the urban professionals. The Liberationists therefore did not rest their efforts after the encouraging resolutions passed by the Third Zemstvo Congress, but carried their constitutionalist agitation into the provinces, to the annual meetings of zemstvo boards,

54. Sanders, "The Union of Unions," ch. 3, pp. 21–22, 47–62.
55. *Ibid.*, ch. 2, pp. 6–16, 33. A. V. Ushakov, *Revoliutsionnoe dvizhenie demokraticheskoi intelligentsia v Rossii 1895–1904*, pp. 69–75. Freeze, "A National Liberation Movement," p. 85.

which sat in December and January. The mobilization of the intelligentsia evident in the banquets and meetings was simultaneously aimed at liberal landowners, larger numbers of whom were willing to make common cause with the urban professionals than at any time in the past.

The Union of Liberation itself stood further to the left than most zemstvo constitutionalists and a great many urban professionals as well. This fact was only gradually revealed, and its full meaning would not emerge as public knowledge until the publication of the Union's complete program in March 1905. But in the fall of 1904 the Liberationists were already reaffirming and strengthening their ties with the Left by taking an active part in the Conference of Oppositional and Revolutionary Parties of the Russian Empire, which met in Paris in September and October. This undertaking committed the Union to the replacement of the autocracy with a democratic regime, elected according to the "four-tail" formula; to national self-determination for the various peoples of the Empire; and to a policy of "no enemies on the Left." Its commitment to unity on the Left was underscored by the fact that all the other participants in the Paris Conference were representatives of groups more radical than the Liberationists: SRs and six other revolutionary and oppositionist parties from among the non-Russian nationalities. Fully reaffirming this policy, the Union's October congress voted to incorporate the positions of the Paris Conference in the Union's program and to publish it for the first time.[56]

These actions were taken simultaneously with the Union's approval at the same October congress of the four-point tactical plan, outlined above, which incorporated a balance of attention to both moderate and radical wings of the opposition movement. Thus, even while the exciting developments of the fall of 1904 were carrying prevailing sentiment in the Union of Liberation to the left, the strategy of organizing a fairly broad liberal-democratic front against the regime was reaffirmed. The Liberationists clearly expected that the regime would continue to falter, that the opposition would continue to grow in strength, and that the single task of the moment was therefore to minimize differences among the constituent elements of the opposition for the sake of bringing to bear the combined strength of Russian society on a single point, the defeat of the autocracy.

In the vocabulary of the period, the projected united front would

56. *Listok Osvobozhdeniia*, no. 17 (Nov. 19, 1904). Galai, *The Liberation Movement*, pp. 214–23. The Russian Social Democrats were conspicuous by their (intentional) absence from this conference, although representatives of the small Latvian SD party attended.

form a sort of *Vorparlament*, a standing committee of the united opposition that would design the popular regime to replace the autocracy, much like the Frankfurt Parliament of 1848, to which the Liberationists explicitly alluded. It is a measure of the overweening self-assurance of the Liberationists in the appropriateness and suitability of their leadership—their ranks, it is true, contained the most eminent and cultivated intelligentsia and zemstvo figures of the time—that they cast themselves in the role of the chief organizers of this vast enterprise. In this sense, the entire Liberationist effort to make a political break with the Old Regime rested on prestige and status distinctions that were very much a part of Old Regime society.[57] Their only rivals for this leadership role were the Social Democrats, who had avoided the Paris Conference and were preserving their autonomy and freedom of action, even though the Mensheviks were on the whole more willing than the Bolsheviks to contemplate limited modes of cooperation with the democratic wing of the intelligentsia.

This supreme self-confidence, even superiority, together with the need to form an alliance of convenience with all other oppositionist forces, led the Liberationists to assume diverse positions toward their allies on the left and toward the working class. The more moderate and cautious among them had always opposed and would continue to oppose, even in 1905, close support of labor by the liberal movement. For instance, at the first congress of the Union of Liberation in January 1904, some of the *zemtsy* had raised objections to the commitment in the Union's credo "to defend the interests of the laboring masses" because the phrase "could be taken as recognition of socialism and could alienate those elements who 'did not believe in socialism.'"[58] But the center and left of the Union, which included the most active and influential among the leaders, favored the adoption of specific social programs affecting workers and peasants, measures that would be added to the Union's program only at their third congress in March 1905. Prior to that time, the Union leadership's desire to appeal to a broad spectrum of educated opinion was probably the main reason why the phrase on the "laboring masses" was neither removed nor given more specific content.

Meanwhile, toward the end of the banquet period, an informal but

57. Belokonskii, "K istorii zemskogo dvizheniia" (cited in n. 50), p. 29. Shakhovskoi, "Soiuz Osvobozhdeniia" (cited in n. 1), p. 132. Sanders, "The Union of Unions," ch. 3, pp. 19–21. Freeze, "A National Liberation Movement," pp. 85–87. *Osvobozhdenie*, no. 58 (Oct. 14, 1904), p. 129.

58. Sanders, "The Union of Unions," ch. 2, p. 55, citing Shakhovskoi, "Soiuz Osvobozhdeniia," pp. 111–12. Emmons, "The Statutes of the Union of Liberation," p. 83.

authoritative Liberationist policy toward labor and socialism was articulated for the first time in an article by Petr Struve, editor of the Union's chief organ, *Osvobozhdenie* (*Liberation*), and one of its chief strategists. Explicitly addressing himself to the Social Democrats and noting their internal disagreements over the role of input by actual workers into SD policy at the local level (the "Economist" controversy), he stressed the need for the cultural development (i.e., education, literacy) of Russian workers as a prerequisite to their political mobilization. "Only cultural work, 'legal' and 'unpolitical' forms, can create a sufficiently solid and sufficiently broad basis for [any] movement of the working class that would deserve the name *revolutionary*. . . ."[59] He then stated the intention of the Liberationists to engage in precisely this kind of work, although he disclaimed any intention to do battle with the Social Democrats for the allegiance of the workers. Instead, he proposed that the two organizations cooperate at the local level in forming trade unions for workers, which, though formally unpolitical, would nonetheless fight for the right to strike and, he felt, would eventually produce recruits for the Social Democrats. Comparing the present period in Russia to the period of the Anti-Socialist Law in the German Empire (1878–90), Struve urged the Russian Social Democrats to assume the role of their German fellow Marxists who "with incredible difficulties, applying large doses of caution and opportunism, gradually, step by step . . . reconstituted a workers' trade union organization." This urging to embrace reformism openly was perhaps sincerely intended, but the contemptuous reaction of revolutionaries to the claim that real revolution demanded that they become trade unionists and opportunists can well be imagined and was probably not lessened by the personal acquaintance some of them had with the author—on the contrary. One can only conclude, first, that Struve assumed that an apparently open door to the revolutionary Left was a prerequisite for the recruitment of unaffiliated intelligentsia radicals to Liberation and, second, that he expected that liberal initiative, factional divisiveness and weakness among the revolutionaries, and the relative inactivity of workers and peasants, characteristic of 1904, would continue indefinitely.

But he was also combining his own sense of what *should* be with what existed. Replying to the charge that this view of the labor movement was not going to produce any great political results, Struve

59. "Nasushchnaia zadacha vremeni," *Osvobozhdenie*, no. 63 (Jan. 7, 1905), pp. 221–22.

stated some of his fundamental assumptions about the political potential of workers in the coming antiautocratic revolution:

> The political education of the masses is a very difficult task, and this
> difficulty should be looked right in the eye. The Russian worker is cul-
> turally backward, downtrodden [*zabit*], and (here we have in mind,
> above all, Petersburg and Moscow workers) still insufficiently prepared
> for organized social and political struggle. That is why "mobilizing" him
> politically will not be easy; for such mobilization a solid foundation is
> required.

Writing in an issue of his journal dated two days before Bloody
Sunday, Struve revealed an inability to conceive of workers mobilizing themselves irrespective of their cultural or political "preparedness." Yet he went on to raise the question of the place of labor in a
revolution:

> Let's even say that a constitutional overturn arises in the very near fu-
> ture. In a constitutional Russia as well the problem of trade unions of
> workers will have immense cultural and political significance. If Ger-
> man Social Democracy represents in the country such a great cultural
> fact, this is precisely because it is supported by a solid and harmonious
> and growing trade union organization of workers.[60]

In this formulation of the labor question, Struve managed to have
the best of both the backwardness of workers, as he saw them, and the
potential rivalry of the Liberationists and the Social Democrats. He
appeared to be not party-bound, but concerned with the presumed
long-term best interests of workers, and he apparently included the
Social Democrats as partners of the Liberationists in taking the first
necessary steps in the formation of a modern labor movement. He
even allowed that the Social Democrats would benefit in the long run
by gaining seasoned and politically educated worker recruits. In fact,
however, Struve's formulation of the problem was highly unrealis-
tic, assuming as it did that the Russian SDs, having so recently condemned the Economists, would themselves become reformists. But to
imply that the Liberationists sought and would achieve no gain from
the trade-unionization of the labor movement, as Struve did, was
simply insincere: under a free and open political system the all-class
party of democracy would stand to win at least as many recruits
among workers as the socialists.

It seems apparent that the Liberationists' policy on labor was di-

60. *Ibid.*

rected primarily toward neither the workers nor the socialists, but toward the democratic, nonsocialist elements of the intelligentsia and of
educated society generally that the Union of Liberation in late 1904
took to be its most immediate constituency. Struve's views placed the
intelligentsia, as the guardians and arbiters of education and culture,
in a position that made it and its values indispensable to the development of a labor movement. His outwardly non-antagonistic, seemingly cooperative approach to the Social Democrats was probably
meant less as a step toward making joint initiatives with them a practical reality than as a way to appeal to the broad sympathy felt for the
revolutionaries among the democratic intelligentsia. *Liberation*'s editor
was concerned more with taking a position that sounded reasonable
to the democratic intelligentsia, less with the feasibility of actual joint
cooperation on the basis of a reformist platform, the unacceptability
of which to the Social Democrats he surely realized. Finally Struve's
tone of paternalistic tutelage toward workers signaled that he was addressing readers whom this tone would not offend, i.e., the usual
members and followers of the Union of Liberation, not workers and
socialists. These considerations provide an insight into the thinking of
liberals and democrats about labor that may help to balance the many
outpourings of rhetoric and sentiment for unity on the left and support of the popular cause that began in 1904 and lasted throughout 1905.

    While entertaining these considerations on the level of program
and strategy, liberals also confronted workers and socialists publicly at
a number of the banquets and meetings organized by the Union of
Liberation. In the spirit of the January congresses, the workers attended as tribunes of the people, in order to urge more democratic
resolutions on the intellectuals and landowners and notables present.
Although their actual impact on the positions adopted was more limited than was once thought,[61] the appearance of workers impressed on
the leaders of society's middle strata, from whom they were normally
quite isolated, that the fourth estate of working men and women was
also awakening to the political music of the period. However, in all
known cases these groups of workers appear to have been organized

    61. This is the finding of Emmons, "Russia's Banquet Campaign," pp. 55–63,
against the claims of Cherevanin, "Dvizhenie intelligentsii," pp. 149–63. Emmons examined a larger number of meetings and banquets more carefully than did Cherevanin
and concluded that the pressure of the workers and their allies succeeded in radicaliz-
ing banquet resolutions in only two or three cases.

by the Social Democrats or to have attended as parts of larger leftist delegations that included students and other lower-status intelligentsia, and this led to some interesting dynamics at the meetings.[62]

Of the four banquets known to have been held in Petersburg, workers attended two, making no appearance at the first, marking the 40th anniversary of the Judicial Reform (November 20), or at that of the engineers (December 5). At a banquet of writers and journalists of the capital on December 14, however, upwards of 30 or 40 workers attended in the company of Social Democratic intellectuals and delivered a number of speeches, the import of which was that the wording of a resolution under discussion should be changed from the diffuse demand for "freely elected representatives of all the people" to a harder-edged version calling for "a universal, equal, direct, and secret election law." A vote easily passed the second variant, so there seems to be little doubt about the prevailing sentiment at the banquet, yet a few of the writers raised serious objections to the intervention of the uninvited guests. Some speakers called the socialists "crazy little kids" (*sumashedshie mal'chishki*) for whom everything had to be stated clearly and exactly. A further socialist attempt to win approval of voting rights for women apparently failed to carry. Clearly, the influence of the workers and socialists sharpened a division of opinion that already existed within the meeting, polarized it, and may have alienated the moderates present whom the more softly worded variant of the resolution was probably intended to mollify. The fact that the "four-tailer" demand raised by the Social Democrats was wholly in line with the Liberationists' own program only emphasized the actual divisions within the latter's own constituency at a time when many liberals insisted on agreement and unity.[63]

62. Emmons, "Russia's Banquet Campaign," pp. 58–60. For an account of Bolshevik and Menshevik disagreement on the attitude the Social Democrats should assume toward the banquet campaign and the Liberationist offensive of fall 1904 generally, see Schwarz, *The Russian Revolution of 1905*, pp. 36–51. The Mensheviks claimed to favor participation as a means of furthering the political education of workers by demonstrating to them that the "bourgeois" banqueters would refuse their just demands. Lenin at first opposed worker demonstrations at the liberal banquets in favor of direct protest against the institutions of the state, but he later changed his mind: Lenin, "O khoroshikh demonstratsiiakh proletariev i plokhikh rassuzhdeniiakh nekotorykh intelligentov," *Vpered*, no. 1 (Dec. 22, 1904), translated and reprinted in *Collected Works* (M., 1962), vol. 8, pp. 29–34.

63. *Iskra*, no. 82 (Jan. 1, 1905), p. 4. For the program of the Union of Liberation in 1904 see *Listok Osvobozhdeniia*, no. 17 (Nov. 19, 1904) and Emmons, "The Statutes," p. 81.

An even sharper confrontation between Social Democratic workers and liberal banqueters, again divided among themselves, occurred at a gathering of physicians in a Petersburg restaurant on December 18. On this occasion some 50 workers were nearly refused admission by the banquet organizers, but the 300 to 400 doctors present overruled their leaders, and the workers were admitted. Once the meeting began the banquet president attempted to win approval, without debate, of a resolution that apparently called for a constituent assembly elected according to the "four-tail" formula. But he was again overruled by those present, and the floor was opened to a series of speeches and proposals for modifying the resolution. A major point at issue seems to have been whether the resolution should confine itself to political demands such as that proposed or whether it should elaborate social and economic demands as well. The workers spoke in favor of including a demand for the right to strike, again contributing to divisions of opinion already existing among the doctors themselves. The doctors, voting alone, defeated this proposal, but passionate disagreement and speechmaking continued to the point of a *skandal*, and the banquet president closed the meeting amid expressions of resentment and frustration from the departing doctors. The workers then attempted to continue the meeting as a workers' banquet, but the owner of the restaurant ended all further banqueting by threatening to call the police.[64]

The appearance of these workers at banquets of the liberal intelligentsia was a sign of the times, indicating that in late 1904 those workers most prepared to knock at the doors of the new hothouses of free speech, so far only vouchsafed the privileged and semiprivileged orders, were associated with the Social Democratic party. The only other workers in Petersburg organized in such numbers at this time were members of Gapon's Assembly, and there is no evidence of their having approached the liberal banquets and meetings.[65]

The opposition to worker and socialist participation in the liberal banquets of St. Petersburg, aside from simple class prejudice, is most

64. Mandel'berg, *Iz perezhitogo*, pp. 44–45. *Iskra*, no. 83, p. 3. *Osvobozhdenie*, no. 63 (Jan. 7, 1905), pp. 226–27.

65. The Socialist Revolutionaries could possibly have mounted worker demonstrations had they chosen, since there is evidence that the organization had working-class members in Petersburg and other cities in this period; the numbers of such members, however, remain uncertain. See Melancon, "The Socialist Revolutionaries from 1902 to 1907"; and Hildermeier, *Die Sozialrevolutionäre Partei Russlands*, pp. 111–12.

easily explained by the disruption it caused to the established agenda and the danger it posed of provoking police intervention. This would account especially for the attitude of the banquet organizers and presidents.

It could also have been due to a principled objection, by the more moderate and conservative participants, to associating the liberal movement with socialism. The Petersburg banquets were noticeably more radical than those in most of the rest of the country. Of the six banquets that called for both constituent assembly and "four-tail" suffrage, four were held in the capital.[66] Finally, some may have shared Struve's view of the Social Democrats as direct rivals to the Liberationists for leadership of the rising national opposition movement and sought, on these grounds, to oppose what could be viewed as brazen political party crashing.[67]

What is noteworthy is that a majority of the Petersburg banqueters, and probably a considerable portion of participants in other locales, were prepared to tolerate the presence of both socialists and workers and on certain issues vote with them against both the right and the guardians of the meetings' orderliness. This sympathy constituted a continuation and enlargement of the public manifestations by workers and liberal intelligentsia elements witnessed in Petersburg in January 1904, and it foreshadowed the much more substantial worker-intelligentsia alliance of 1905. But what did it signify, if anything, about intelligentsia attitudes toward workers at this juncture, i.e., *before* workers had joined the opposition en masse?

An unequivocal answer is not possible, as the workers appeared in a double guise, as workers and as socialists. What is clear is that none of the objections mentioned above was sufficient to prevent a predominantly positive reception from being accorded the "crashers." The stated policies of the Liberationists gave encouragement both to those who would be inclined to view the Social Democrats as allies and to those who saw them as rivals. Had not the Union of Liberation's second congress adopted a stance of "no enemies on the left"? Simul-

66. Emmons, "Russia's Banquet Campaign," p. 61.

67. Not every banquet cast the socialists in the role of outsiders knocking at the gates, however. In Saratov, for instance, a banquet on December 17 was jointly organized among SDs, SRs, and Liberationists, but it stood out as an exceptional occurrence. SD and worker agitation at the liberal banquets probably met with some resistance in most of the thirteen cases. Emmons, "Russia's Banquet Campaign," pp. 61, 62. Sanders, "Lessons from the Periphery: Saratov 1905," pp. 233–35.

taneously, Struve had been encouraging his readers to make an independent approach to both workers and peasants, irrespective of the attitude of the socialists.[68] Consequently, even those who might still have been inclined to view the Social Democrats as "enemies" could have had a good political reason to make the workers feel welcome at an intelligentsia function.

Yet it is likely that another consideration, less political, more immediate and irresistible, was at play in those euphoric and emotionally charged banquets. This was the powerful sense, called forth by the mere appearance of the workers, of being in the presence of the real victims of Tsarist oppression, people whose suffering and deprivation gave concrete and authentic meaning to the high-flown and abstract, albeit earnestly felt, demands and slogans of their banquet resolutions. This "martyrs' aura" was probably as much a result of the intelligentsia's psychological ambivalence about its own moral and political position as it was a feature of the workers' demeanor. An inordinate sympathy toward the more dramatically deprived victims of every oppressive system is probably always felt to some degree by progressive members of the system's middle strata, i.e., by those who both suffer and to some degree benefit from the system. In Russia, this passion had had a long and distinguished history by the early twentieth century, reaching back at least to the 1860's and the rise of the *raznochintsy* intelligentsia, so that to be an educated Russian meant to share intelligentsia values and to acknowledge, if not fully accept, its self-proclaimed mission of uplifting the *narod* and supplanting the autocracy with a more humane political system.[69]

Hence the dictates of a humane education as well as of a professional identity were suffused with an imperative to social and political action that had peculiarly Russian roots. The militancy of the physicians and educators in January had by the fall of 1904 grown into a passionate cause for all of educated Russia. Although the social structure of urban Russia had been significantly altered since the 1860's, the political structure of autocracy had not been. As a result, the lim-

68. "Komitet Ministrov i komitet reform," and "Nasushchnaia zadacha vremeni," *Osvobozhdenie*, no. 63 (Jan. 7, 1905), pp. 219, 221.

69. See, e.g., Haimson, *The Russian Marxists and the Origins of Bolshevism*, ch. 1; Malia, "What Is the Intelligentsia?"; Pollard, "The Russian Intelligentsia: The Mind of Russia"; Confino, "On Intellectuals and Intellectual Traditions in 18th and 19th Century Russia"; Riasanovsky, "Notes on the Emergence and Nature of the Russian Intelligentsia." Precisely how far back one should seek the beginnings of the intelligentsia is one of the problems debated in this literature. See also Raeff, *The Origins of the Russian Intelligentsia. The 18th Century Nobility*.

ited scope of personal rights, the narrow compass of individual dignity, and with it the impulse to desperate and extravagant visions of change had survived to inform political attitudes forty years later. Such, in broad perspective, was the reason why the measured and dignified proceedings of writers' and physicians' banquets in St. Petersburg were disrupted, not just by socialists and workers from outside these professions, but by many of their own members, rushing to close the gap and to acknowledge their unity of purpose with "the people." Such a striving for cross-class unity was to become institutionalized in the Union of Unions and to continue as the central political aim of the left Liberationists throughout 1905.

INTO THE ABYSS: THE ASSEMBLY JOINS THE OPPOSITION

The government's liberalization measures and the mobilization of the zemstvo and intelligentsia opposition that ensued also reached into the ranks of the Assembly of Russian Workers, affecting its development and its members' perception of events. By the summer of 1904, the organization's rate of growth began to accelerate noticeably. When Gapon left Petersburg on a trip to the south, two locals of the Assembly were officially in operation (in the Vyborg and Narva districts) and permission for a third, on Vasilevsky Island, was being sought. By the end of October there were nine sections throughout the city and suburbs, and by November eleven, with 7,000 members.[70]

Thanks to the preparations of the Assembly's Secret Committee, the politicized minority of the organization was ready for the new developments. When Sviatopolk-Mirskii's "Springtime" began, Karelin recalls, the group abandoned lectures as vehicles for propaganda work and began discussing only newspapers. Some of the staff, probably under Karelin's leadership, proposed that the Assembly present a petition of its own to the government, much as the zemstvo activists were doing, but Gapon refused.[71] This initiative opened a debate in the Assembly that would lead, with the addition of unforeseen and fortuitous events, to the historic role the Assembly would play on January 9, 1905. That the Karelinists should present the idea to the other leaders as a gesture paralleling those of the *zemtsy* indicates that they were playing on what they took to be a shared understanding

70. Gapon, *The Story of My Life*, p. 130.
71. Karelin, "Vospominaniia," p. 110.

that the zemstvo men were making protest acceptable, if not respectable. By portraying the proposed worker petition as adherence to activity already undertaken by recognized elites, the Karelinists sought to disarm it of the apprehension that previously apolitical workers would have felt at the prospect of such a new and unfamiliar initiative. This strategem sheds indirect light on the political, or perhaps protopolitical, assumptions of some of Gapon's nonsocialist worker assistants; its efficacy in mobilizing the Assembly for a political demonstration, or at least in disarming objections to one, also links the political debut of a mass labor movement in Petersburg with the liberal ferment of 1904.

Gapon was not unalterably opposed to the idea of a petition, but he wanted to proceed at his own pace and in keeping with his own evaluation of the situation. In partial response to the Oppositionists, he agreed to consult with representatives of the political intelligentsia. Sometime in early November, probably following the Third Zemstvo Congress that created such a stir in Petersburg, Gapon and the four worker leaders who had been a party to the "Program of the Five" met with the writers and left Liberationists S. N. Prokopovich, E. D. Kuskova, and V. Ia. Bogucharskii at Gapon's apartment.[72]

In arranging this meeting, Gapon was probably seeking an outside opinion on the kind of action the Karelinists were pressing on him as well as on the contents of the March program, which he showed to the Liberationist visitors. The latter reinforced the plans for some kind of public action or demonstration by the Assembly in the spirit of those being carried out by the intelligentsia and zemstvo activists, and they found the March Program comparable to the resolutions of those same groups. Gapon seems to have been both reassured by these opinions and determined not to be rushed into action; he intended first to "broaden his activities" and to await the advent of some momentous external event such as the fall of Port Arthur.[73]

72. *Ibid.* Gurevich, *Deviatoe ianvaria*, pp. 13–14. Belokonskii, "K istorii zemskogo dvizheniia," (cited in n. 50), p. 30. Sviatlovskii, *Professional'noe dvizhenie*, pp. 84–85. Karelin claimed that two women he does not identify accompanied the three Liberationists, and others may have been present or have consulted with Gapon at another time: Shatsillo, *Russkii liberalizm*, p. 316. Note, in Gapon's memoirs, the strong impression produced by the zemstvo congress on him and on the Assembly: *The Story of My Life*, p. 134.

73. Gurevich, *Deviatoe ianvaria*, pp. 13–14, quotes one of the Liberationist participants, but no direct attribution is made. I have nevertheless preferred this version of what transpired because Gurevich copied it directly from the participants at the time of the meeting and because of her uniquely thorough and scrupulous research on the topic (see *ibid.*, pp. 5–8). Karelin gave a somewhat different version of the meeting

Perhaps the most remarkable single aspect of this encounter is that Gapon entrusted these liberal intellectuals with such potentially damaging information about his plans and intentions. As far as is known, they were the first group outside of the Secret Committee itself to be told, and this is a significant comment on Gapon's political instincts. It indicates not only that he found these democratic intellectuals more trustworthy than members of the revolutionary parties, whose advice he sought only much later, but also more trustworthy than all of his own workers and assistants in the Assembly outside those four to whom he had confided his program in March. There is no evidence that Gapon was acquainted with these representatives of the democratic intelligentsia prior to the meeting, and his confidence in them would seem to signify not so much personal trust in them as a vote of confidence in a newly emergent political activism seeking substantial reform by peaceful and public means, with which the projected political debut of the Assembly might safely associate itself.[74]

On the Liberationists' side, this contact can be read merely as an act of several individuals sharing the same political outlook and not as an expression of their organization's official attitude toward the labor movement. Indeed, in his overtures to the Social Democrats, Struve had even condemned the government's Zubatovist projects, attributing their failure to the refusal of the intelligentsia to cooperate with them.[75] Yet the Liberationist policy toward labor was at this point still sufficiently fluid to encompass the kind of contact and advice Prokopovich and the others gave Gapon and to have made this advice quite compatible with their overall strategy of drawing into the opposition as many social groups as possible. In fact, the aim of a nationwide labor organization, independent of the revolutionary Left and dedicated to the protection and improvement of the lives of working people on and off the job, which Gapon professed to have stood for, coincided completely with the broader perspective on labor developed by Struve

---

("Vospominaniia," p. 110), claiming that Prokopovich made a long speech and ended by recommending adoption of the Social Democratic program by the Assembly, but that, when shown the Program of the Five, felt "that it was a better program, broader." While most of this is reconcilable with Gurevich's version, it seems unlikely that a left Liberationist would have called the March Program, politically more moderate and less demanding than that passed even by the Third Zemstvo Congress and most of the banquets (not to mention the SD program), "better and broader," except perhaps as a patronizing gesture.

74. Shatsillo, *Russkii liberalizm*, pp. 315–17, notes the likelihood that the liberal petitions inspired that of the Assembly.

75. "Nasushchnaia zadacha vremeni," *Osvobozhdenie*, no. 63 (Jan. 7, 1905), p. 221.

in the very same article in which he condemned Zubatovism. Thus, although Prokopovich and his companions may have differed with Struve in some particulars, they had, by accident or instinct, come to the correct address. Their project and Gapon's belonged to the same overall conception of Russia's political future.

In the short run, the Liberationists' advice helped to further the idea that the Assembly's workers should sooner or later present in a political arena some statement of their needs, and that the statement should probably be based on the March Program. In the meantime, seeking to hurry Gapon into action, the Opposition began to implement its strategy among Assembly members. "Beginning in November," wrote Karelin, "an unseen agitation was conducted: '[Let's] present [something of] our own, from the ranks.' . . . We surreptitiously drove in the idea of presenting a petition at every meeting in every section." [76]

This agitation for an Assembly petition was necessarily moderate, aiming only at support of the liberal campaign already under way, and it was presented in a manner that did not seem to challenge conventional beliefs among workers:

> Propaganda and agitation were conducted around two propositions: the first was that it was impossible any longer to live as we did, [and that] the *Tsar needed* the help of a *popular representative body* because corrupt ministers surrounded and betrayed him; the second was that the workers should join their voice to that of all the estates of Russia, even if [only] in the form of another resolution, but in such a way that the government would be unable to "silence" this resolution and quietly shelve it. [77]

This agitation apparently found a deep response among Assembly workers, and the Secret Committee was encouraged in its tentative plans to organize some kind of petition presentation and/or demonstration. Gapon accordingly agreed to seek the approval of a wider group of Assembly leaders. For this purpose a special meeting was called at Gapon's apartment on November 28, 1904. Two or three representatives from each section were invited, making a group of about 35 in all.

> Each person present was asked to sense the seriousness of the step being taken, to weigh his resources and readiness to take responsibility for the consequences, and, in cases of disagreement, to leave the meet-

76. Karelin, "Vospominaniia," p. 110.
77. Varnashev, "Vospominaniia," p. 200.

ing quietly, giving his word of honor to remain silent. That was the precise aim of this meeting, called by Gapon. I state this categorically [wrote Varnashev] for Gapon asked the author of these lines to open the meeting. "Invest your thoughts, your feelings in this," he said at the time, and now, 18 years later, I remember the tone, the facial expression, with which it was said. This was the only time I saw Gapon uncertain, as if seeking support outside himself.[78]

Despite Gapon's trepidations, the proposal that the Assembly take a political position in the current crisis was met with hearty approval, and a fierce debate arose over the means and methods. The meeting's consensus favored some kind of demonstration that would not simply mark the Assembly's agreement with other oppositionist groups, but would set it apart and attract nationwide attention to the cause of the independent labor organization.[79]

Gapon was both favorable to the idea of a petition presentation and still extremely cautious about endangering the existence of the Assembly. This ambivalence caused indecisive behavior. At one point he spoke of awaiting a widely recognized occasion customarily marked by petitions to the government, such as the anniversary of the Peasant Emancipation (February 19); at another, he felt a labor strike should be organized in place of a political demonstration. Karelin and his supporters read this inconstancy with distrust, regarding it as a stall, and they therefore pressed for an *immediate* political demonstration. In his awkward middle position Gapon appeared at times to support a political demonstration, if delayed; at others, he appeared to oppose a demonstration but to favor submitting a petition to the authorities; at still others, he seemed to oppose both demonstration and petition. Thus, at a series of special meetings of the Assembly's officers over the next month he temporized and vacillated, thereby reviving suspicions of his motives and aggravating the divisions in the Assembly. Because of his great prestige and influence with most of the Assembly's officers, his vacillations caused confusion and consternation in the group, and opinion shifted back and forth from meeting to meeting.

At one point, Gapon invited one of the Assembly's lecturers, the lawyer I. M. Finkel', to meet with the Responsible Circle and argue for a petition demonstration. Finkel' attended three meetings in mid-December, where he strongly recommended that labor join its voice to that of the other estates and classes lest its needs be forgotten in a future distribution of reforms, maintaining that the risk of arrest was

78. *Ibid.*, p. 201.
79. *Ibid.*, pp. 201–2.

worth taking for the sake of accomplishing something for the entire
working class.[80] This was the second instance of liberal intelligentsia
figures being given access to the Assembly's leadership by Gapon. In
this case, Gapon chose a spokesman known for his commitment to
piecemeal change and close attention to workers' needs. Finkel' should
also have been less objectionable than a complete outsider as he had
already appeared at Assembly meetings as a lecturer, and his presence could have been more easily explained should there have been a
leak to the authorities. Yet it also seems likely that Gapon was using
Finkel' to express sentiments and to advocate actions that his position
as the Assembly's Representative prevented him from doing himself.

However, the lawyer's appearance had the effect of precipitating a
protest among a small group of Assembly leaders. Although the protesters objected to the presence of outsiders at the meetings of the Responsible Circle and their participation in the voting—a violation of
Assembly Statutes—it also made reference to another issue, namely
"why [the petition under discussion] had to be submitted as if in support of the petitions of other estates, whose demands were set forth
there, and what their essence and importance were." The protest was
written by Vladimir Inozemtsev and Vladimir Ianov of the Putilov (or
Narva) local and signed by three other officers from another local.
Gapon received the protest and later promised Ianov to read and support it at the next meeting.[81]

The emergence of the Ianov-Inozemtsev faction signified the existence of a group of worker leaders who adhered to Gapon's earlier
and more cautious version of the Assembly, and who had remained
more or less immune to the radicalization and politicization sweeping
Russian society in late 1904. Unfortunately, very little evidence of this
group's position survives, though judging from Ianov's words it seems
to have stood for a narrow, almost corporatist workerism: the Assembly was to concern itself exclusively with "creating better conditions,"
was to avoid politics, even in the form of Gapon's cautious approach,
as well as advice from outsiders, especially intellectuals. This trend of
opinion was probably always present in the Assembly, but its ad-

80. Ianov's testimony, *KL*, no. 1 (1922), pp. 314–15. Sablinsky, *The Road to Bloody
Sunday*, pp. 129, 136–37. Finkel' was an ex-socialist from Moscow who had undergone
arrest and exile and who, by 1904, had become some variety of reformist socialist and
spokesman for "workers' petty, private needs." Kolokol'nikov and Rapoport, *1905–
1907 gg. v professional'nom dvizhenii. I i II vserossiiskie konferentsii professional'nykh soiuzov*,
pp. 16–17.

81. Ianov's testimony, *KL*, no. 1 (1922), pp. 308, 314–15. Gapon apparently never
had to make good on this promise, as the entire petition project was overtaken by other
events at the end of December.

herents had less cause before December to separate themselves from Gapon. Their brand of conservative workerism was probably present to a degree in every working class of the day, and in Russia it pervaded the organizing nuclei of real Zubatovist unions—e.g., those in Moscow and the Ushakov unions in St. Petersburg.

Though the group of Assembly leaders who shared Ianov's sentiments emerged rather late in the day, it may have existed informally all along. Unfortunately, it is impossible to say how large or unified or influential it was. The advent of the Putilov Plant crisis, moreover, soon diverted the attention of the Ianov-Inozemtsev group from the matter of the petition, as it did that of the entire Assembly. Ianov continued an active participation in Assembly affairs despite his misgivings, and Inozemtsev fell into line with the defense of the embattled organization, recalling later that "I went along with everyone else, without asking myself why. My calm attitude to events when I had stood up against revolutionary [*sic*] influence on workers was lost to me, and I acted almost unconsciously."[82]

In his explanation of the protest, Ianov made it clear that he was aware of the shift of positions that Gapon had taken over the past year. He complained that the priest "at this time departed from the path which he had followed earlier in his relations with workers. Earlier, so it seemed to me, he concerned himself exclusively with creating better conditions for the individual development of each worker and was extremely attentive to the workers. . . . Now Gapon, seeing that the majority of worker representatives was unsympathetic to the petition, nonetheless held to another opinion."[83] There is probably no more cogent a statement both of the fact that Gapon had once been perceived as an apolitical "friend of labor" and of the fact that he was now becoming an advocate of a political role for the labor movement. The conversion of this impressionable and ambitious figure through the efforts of his radical assistants and the irresistible opportunities created by the events around him was to prove decisive for the development of labor in Petersburg and Russia.

At the same time, along with Gapon, the Assembly itself had changed since earlier in the year. In the spring there had still been some doubt about the viability of the whole enterprise; now, in December, with over 7,000 registered members in nine or ten branches, it seemed only a matter of time until the Assembly became the representative and spokesman for all Petersburg workers. In the spring one

82. Inozemtsev's testimony, *KL*, no. 1 (1922), p. 309.
83. Ianov's testimony, *ibid.*, pp. 315–16.

made promises and struck agreements in order to insure the acceptance of the Assembly among the hitherto unorganized and justifiably suspicious masses of workers; now, when there was something in hand to risk losing, one had to give more thought to its continuing acceptance and approval by the government and the influential ranks of society. Gapon took a very possessive attitude toward the Assembly, a fact clearly reflected in the language of his memoirs, where he continually spoke of "my workers," "my assistants," and "my Secret Committee," and attributed every major idea and accomplishment to himself alone. Therefore, it is understandable and believable that he resisted the drive under way in December 1904 that would risk and endanger "his" whole gigantic and promising organization. "Although you have the majority," he was wont to say after a vote against him, "I did not want this and will not allow it because this is all my creation. I am a practical man and know more than you, while you are all dreamers. . . ." "I know better than you," he said on another occasion, referring this time to the issue of the petition. "I am thinking of how not to come out of this worse off."[84]

In other words, Gapon realized that a demonstration with general political demands must be reserved as the last act of the Assembly, its own trump card, after which the game would be up. As events showed, he was willing to play that card at the proper moment, but during most of December he did not think the time had arrived. As a "practical man" he must also have worried about losing by too sudden a leap into political life a great part of the thousands of relatively new members, most of whom more likely thought of the Assembly as a haven from the hardships of their social and industrial lives than as an instrument for confronting their causes. Although most Assembly members would thus probably have supported Gapon had they been privy to the debate, he could rally only about half the Responsible Circle to his side. This situation affected him powerfully since his authority was most seriously threatened among those whose support he relied on the most. In addition, he was still distrusted by some members, and the position he was now taking heightened suspicions that he was, after all, only doing the work of the police, an imputation to which he was extremely sensitive.[85] He was thus not passive in his opposition to presenting a petition, but actively sought a reconciliation of the division among his closest associates.

The opportunity to unite the Assembly that finally appeared, al-

84. Petrov, "Zapiski o Gapone," pp. 36, 42.
85. Pavlov, "Iz vospominanii," pp. 85–86. Petrov, "Zapiski o Gapone," pp. 37–38.

though immensely consequential in the end, was deceptively routine and ordinary at first. In early December a worker in the woodworking shop of the Putilov Plant was dismissed for incompetence. At first the event attracted no particular notice since it was a fairly common occurrence. However, because the man, Sergunin, was a member of the Assembly, its representatives made inquiries in an attempt to get his job back. Grounds for dismissal probably existed, and the injustices really lay in the absence of any legal or financial protection, a condition Sergunin shared with practically all Russian workers. Gapon was preoccupied with the debate over the petition and did not personally attend to the problem for at least two weeks. By that time a pattern was beginning to emerge. Three more workers from the same shop, Subbotin, Fedorov, and Ukolov, were either dismissed or threatened with dismissal, and the three were also Assembly members. The man responsible for the firings, the shop foreman Tetiavkin, was a member of Ushakov's Society of St. Petersburg Machine Workers, revived in October as a counterweight to the Assembly.[86] It was beginning to seem as if some kind of campaign against Gapon's organization were under way in which a rival government union was in collusion with the Putilov Plant management.

Whether or not all these circumstances were known to Gapon, he initially approached the matter in a conciliatory spirit. He was accustomed to using his government mandate and his personal influence as a priest to help workers threatened by managers and foremen. This time he went to see his friend E. E. Johanson [Ioganson], the grievances manager at the Putilov Plant. There he discovered the true scope and seriousness of the situation. "As Gapon told it to me [Pavlov reported], Mr. Johanson openly declared that there was nothing he could do since this was the business of the management, which wanted to stop the rapid growth of the Assembly's Narva section; Mr. Johanson approved of this action, believing that if the section's growth was not halted the whole Putilov Plant, inside of a month, would be members of the Assembly. They had a fairly lengthy conversation, but when they parted, they were no longer friends."[87]

Here was clear confirmation that the Putilov management *did* intend the dismissals as part of a campaign against the Assembly's influence among workers, and that more was at stake than the jobs of the threatened men. "If we abandoned them to their fate," Gapon wrote,

86. Romanov, "K kharakteristike Gapona (nekotorye dannye o zabastovke na Putilovskom zavode v 1905 g.)," pp. 42–43.

87. Pavlov, "Iz vospominanii," p. 81.

"the authority of the society would be shaken, possibly fatally, and similar arbitrary action would be encouraged; while, on the other hand, if we succeeded in obtaining their reinstatement, our prestige in the eyes of the laboring population would be tremendously increased."[88] The realism of this observation was supported by the fast-spreading rumor among the city's factory workers that the firings were aimed at the Assembly, and in the bated curiosity with which all workers, members or not, must have anticipated the clash of two giants, the outcome of which, it was increasingly felt, involved all workers.

Within days of Gapon's interview with Johanson, news of the fall of Port Arthur reached the Russian capital. The imperial regime suffered yet another blow to its faltering prestige, appearing even more corrupt, incompetent, and ridiculous in the eyes of critics and well-wishers alike. The shock of the event was even greater than it might otherwise have been, because the press had not prepared the public for the gradually approaching defeat, but had stressed Japanese losses and the impregnability of the fortress.[89]

Practically overnight, therefore, the entire situation confronting the Assembly changed. It was no longer a question of whether to present a petition or organize a demonstration; whether it should be this month or next; or whether a strike should be organized simultaneously or substituted for the demonstration. The Putilov administration and the watchful expectations of thousands of workers were forcing the Assembly to take a stand; like it or not, the Assembly would have to assert and defend itself. The authority of the government had simultaneously reached an all-time low, and this opened the way to go even as far as presenting political demands if necessary. Sometime during the fourth week of December, this became clear to Gapon and the other Assembly leaders, and they called an extraordinary meeting to plan a response to the firings for Monday, December 27.

This meeting is not usually accorded the importance it is due in the course of events that led to the general strike and the demonstration of January 9. Its chief accomplishment, according to most accounts, was to focus the rumors and apprehension about the firings into a discussion that concluded by drawing up a list of demands and appointing three delegations to present them over the next few days to the City Governor, the Chief Factory Inspector, and the director of the

88. Gapon, *The Story of My Life*, p. 143.
89. Pavlovich, "Vneshnaia politika," p. 27.

Putilov Plant.[90] Since the dismissals also threatened the Assembly, other plans and contingencies were discussed, including not only a possible strike at the Putilov Plant, but the desirability of a general strike as well should the delegations not meet with success. A meeting was set for the coming Sunday, January 2, to consider the need for a strike at the Putilov Plant on the following day. The firmness and self-assurance of the delegations during the intervening week, which we shall discuss presently, confirm the contention that strong sanctions for noncompliance were planned in advance.

Equally as important as the tactics considered was the political rapprochement that took place on December 27 among the Assembly leaders. They realized that the organization could not defend itself or wage an effective strike if it remained internally divided. Consequently, the meeting would have to inform other branches of the threat to the organization and determine whether and to what degree its members were willing to support the relatively conservative Narva branch (the Putilov Plant's district). The meeting was held at the Vasilevsky rather than the Narva branch, probably in order to insure that it would not be dominated by Putilov workers and to give those from other branches easier access, especially supporters of the Karelin group, who were most numerous in the Vasilevsky and other nearby districts. As a counterbalance, Gapon proposed that Vladimir Inozemtsev, a leader of the Narva branch and a Putilov worker, chair the meeting. This was vigorously opposed by proponents of a petition demonstration and of friendly relations with the revolutionary intelligentsia, since Inozemtsev had opposed both. After a long fight, Gapon's recommendation carried the day, although the leftists went on to make their presence felt by stressing the need to organize a general strike.[91]

Gapon further contributed to reconciling the leftist and moderate factions by finally agreeing, earlier on the 27th, to the principle of a political demonstration. This was accomplished at a smaller meeting, held at Gapon's apartment, of the same select group that had been debating the question of a political demonstration since November 28. The priest began by voicing the tougher variant of his shifting position and once more opposed a political demonstration. Speakers on both sides of the question were heard. When a vote was taken, apparently without Gapon's participation, the meeting was fairly evenly divided. Then Karelin rose and said: "'Comrades! They call us Zuba-

90. E.g., Nevskii, *Rabochee dvizhenie v ianvarskie dni 1905 goda*, pp. 65–66.
91. Inozemtsev's testimony, *KL*, no. 1 (1922), pp. 308–9.

tovists. But the Zubatovists vindicated themselves by the movement they [brought about] in Odessa [the 1903 general strike] and we will vindicate ourselves by presenting a petition.' It was as if my words were the last drop. Gapon said, 'If you want to break the stake, well, break it!' and voted for the demonstration. That decided the matter since the majority voted with Gapon."[92]

The Assembly's top leaders were thus more united at the larger meeting that evening than they otherwise would have been. However, Gapon's reversal was less of a surrender than it appeared, for the meeting did not organize a political demonstration but a limited and more specific defense of the harassed Putilov workers. Rather than the broad political demands of the Secret Program, or even middle-range demands aimed at reforming the factory order, the delegations prudently asked only that the four dismissed men be rehired, that the malevolent foreman Tetiavkin be dismissed, and that the City Governor and Factory Inspector try to prevent similar things from happening again. The meeting's resolution did vaguely urge that "labor's abnormal position" in relation to arbitrary foremen and management practices be acknowledged, and it darkly threatened that "the Assembly does not guarantee the further peaceful course of life among Petersburg workers" should its demands not be satisfied.[93] But the political demonstration was, in effect, put off to a later time. The fact that the Assembly was taking a firm stand and was preparing to back up its demands with a general strike seems to have mollified the leftists, while the cautious and limited demands must have reassured at least some of the moderates and conservatives from the Narva branch and elsewhere. At the same time, the Narva representatives were forced to consider bolder actions by the storm brewing in their own district and the growing agitation of their constituents. After December 27 events moved very rapidly, and there was no further disagreement in the leadership as all drew together in the escalating struggle with the Putilov management.

92. Karelin, "Vospominaniia," p. 111; *Petrogradskaia pravda*, Jan. 22, 1922, p. 1. There is conflicting evidence both on the dates of these meetings and on whether the discussion and vote on a political demonstration took place at the general meeting or at a separate, more select meeting. In preferring two meetings to one and December 27 to December 28, I have followed Gurevich, *Deviatoe ianvaria*, n. 18, pp. 81–82, whose reasoning and review of the evidence seem persuasive. Shuster also follows Gurevich (*Peterburgskie rabochie*, pp. 70–71); but compare Sablinsky, *The Road to Bloody Sunday*, pp. 148–50.

93. The demands of the December 27 meeting appeared in the St. Petersburg daily *Rus'*, Dec. 29, 1904, p. 3; in the SR organ *Revoliutsionnaia Rossiia*, 1905, no. 60, p. 17; in Gapon, *The Story of My Life*, p. 144; and in Nevskii, *Rabochee dvizhenie*, p. 66.

The political reconciliation and solidarity established on December 27 reflected itself in the militant tone of the Assembly's delegations to Chief Factory Inspector Chizhov, Putilov Director Smirnov, and City Governor Fullon, carried out over the next several days. For instance, when Smirnov rebuffed a delegation headed by Ivan Vasil'ev on December 29, the delegation warned him that the "incident might end very badly for the plant" and that the delegation "could not guarantee tranquility among the workers" if the Assembly's demands were not met.[94] In his interview with Chizhov, also on December 29, Gapon was even more aggressive. He told the Chief Factory Inspector to break off his relations with the new Ushakov union and to transfer his support to the Assembly "or to bear in mind that everything will be unleashed against [him]: the courts, the press, and the hostility of 6,000 workers. "To my question [Chizhov's] whether this hostility of the workers meant that I could be killed, he answered—Yes. The hostility of the workers was also extended to [factory] inspector V. P. Litvinov-Falinskii and to the head of the Industry Department, N. P. Langovoi, as the latter had conversed with Father Gapon in an unfriendly manner during the past year."[95]

It is noteworthy that Gapon concentrated his efforts not on the situation of the dismissed workers but on the threat to the Assembly underlying the events at the Putilov Plant. This was the cause that brought the Assembly leaders together in the first place and led them to assume an adversary posture. A common commitment to the organization was all that ever bound them together, and it was now to prove sufficient to keep them firmly on "the road to Bloody Sunday." Gapon's threats to Chizhov made it clear that he was now not going to settle the dispute over the dismissals without also obtaining reassurances from higher circles on the continuing legitimacy and acceptability of Assembly activities. As it turned out, neither the Putilov management nor the government ever made it necessary for him to choose between one and the other, an offer they could have forced by offering to rehire the workers while withholding approval of the Assembly.

Gapon's strident tone can thus be explained by his suspicion that all his work and dreams were now seriously threatened by forces that could snuff them out definitively. The newspapers were now carrying full accounts of the Putilov dispute, and one of them gave credence to

94. *Putilovets v trekh russkikh revoliutsiiakh. Sbornik materialov po istorii Putilovskogo zavoda*, ed. S. B. Okun' (M.-L., 1933), pp. 51–53.
95. Romanov, "K kharakteristike Gapona," pp. 42–43.

Gapon's worst fears by suggesting that the dismissals were part of a campaign to combat the Assembly's influence, planned at a meeting of St. Petersburg industrialists.[96] Gapon's claim to have the whole Assembly behind him contained an element of boastful exaggeration, since he could not know at this point just how strong his support would be among the Assembly's rank and file. This uncertainty also must have lent his and the other leaders' conduct of the delegations a degree of desperation and shrillness.

The tactics of the Assembly's leaders did not move their opponents in the desired direction but, on the contrary, stiffened their resistance and led them to open communications with one another. Whether or not their opposition to the Assembly's demands were part of a campaign planned in advance, it soon became part of a collective effort to back the organization down. Chizhov's reply to Gapon's threats was that he would support only those worker organizations that observed the limits of their statutes and that the Assembly was overstepping its limits by directing "its members along the road of struggle with capital."[97] Smirnov likewise regarded the immediate dispute as secondary in importance to the recognition of the Assembly's authority in the affair, which his acceptance of the delegation would signify. Both men therefore treated the delegations rudely and asked the dismissed workers to appear before them without Assembly representatives. City Governor Fullon, the third official to be visited by a delegation, seemed not to understand completely what was at stake, spoke to Gapon privately, and promised to do what he could. Later he turned against the Assembly but was too late to be effective, and his overall bungling earned his dismissal on January 11.

In denying the legitimacy of the organization representing the dismissed workers, these officials were playing a role familiar in modern history when employers and their political allies have confronted the first organized struggles of industrial workers. In this case, both the Putilov management and the Tsarist government were hampered by poor information about the Assembly and by their decision to act against it too late in the game and with insufficient force. The Assembly continued to function and none of its leaders was arrested until after January 9. The failure of the Putilov management and the government to offer a quick settlement allowed them to make political capital out of the dispute. Although the dismissed men all appeared

96. *Rus'*, no. 379 (Dec. 29, 1904).
97. Romanov, "K kharakteristike Gapona," p. 44.

before both Chizhov and Smirnov during the week of December 27 (unaccompanied, as ordered), no resolution of their grievances was proposed until the following week when a strike at Putilov and other plants was already under way and when the stakes were, as a consequence, higher. Management and government alike remained self-contentedly imprisoned by their slow and cumbersome bureaucratic procedures and by their illusions as to the essential servility of the Russian worker. Once they felt the situation had escaped their control, they reacted on January 9 with unmeasured haste, force, and, eventually, violence.

The mass meeting of January 2, held at the Narva branch and attended by about 6,000 workers, easily and enthusiastically voted a strike at the Putilov Plant for Monday, January 3. Many of those in attendance had probably heard the results of the previous week's negotiations and made up their minds. Strike support was voted immediately after the delegations read their reports.[98] The meeting was small compared to those that would gather within a few days in this and other factory districts of the city and was probably composed of workers who were already committed to the Assembly, the cause of the dismissed workers, or both.

Over the next two days the Putilov strikers, led by the woodworking shop, closed down the huge engineering works, idling 12,600 workers. By Friday, January 7, upwards of 105,000 Petersburg workers from 382 enterprises were on strike.[99] During the week before Bloody Sunday, the Assembly's activities linked up with the less visible forces that were quietly transforming the workers of St. Petersburg, that "molecular process" which underlay those outbursts of proletarian energy so characteristic of Tsarist Russia's declining years. Worker support of the Assembly was so strong and determined that Gapon was able to revive plans to present a petition with political demands and to mount the largest political demonstration ever seen in St. Petersburg.

98. *NPRR*, pp. 3–5.
99. *Ibid.*, p. 223.

CHAPTER FOUR

The January Strike

For most people the events of January 1905 in St. Petersburg struck suddenly and without warning. The Assembly of Russian Workers remained unknown to most residents of the city, and even revolutionaries, who generally knew about it, for the most part misjudged it, failing to grasp the political significance of its widespread popularity among workers until the January strike overtook them. Official Petersburg viewed it as a harmless set of tearooms and social clubs, and oppositionist Petersburg as a repellent and dangerous experiment in police unionism. Practically no one outside Gapon's inner circle realized the Assembly's potential for mass political mobilization, and even some intimates had scoffed at the priest's grandiose plans.

Not surprisingly, therefore, many contemporaries and historians have regarded working-class activity in January (and to some degree throughout 1905) as "spontaneous." This characterization is, of course, partly accurate if taken to describe activity that was relatively autonomous, self-initiated, and without external prompting. But the term has also been used to describe activity thought to be undertaken out of transient enthusiasms and misguided motives rather than as a result of a conscious and consistent political outlook. Social Democratic and, later, Soviet authors in particular have too often simplistically contrasted the "spontaneity" of most workers with the "consciousness" of the party and its Marxist viewpoint. This has led to a neglect of the historical and dialectical development of working-class politics. "Conscious" views are contrasted with "unconscious" ones, as if people cannot behave in a revolutionary manner unless they possess the "correct" understanding of the situation, as if motives and outcomes are never mixed, as if historical actors never behave effectively on the basis of faulty views or step falsely while acting with the clearest understanding.

In fact, working-class militancy in January and later was the result of many levels and kinds of motivations and consciousness, continually interacting with historical and social circumstances, including but not limited to the influence of revolutionary parties and of the Assembly. A central aim of this and the following chapters will be to analyze the development of the conscious activity of workers in 1905 in the light of this fuller set of circumstances.

THE JANUARY DAYS

Once Gapon had decided that a fight to the finish to preserve his organization would have to be waged, and once a semblance of unity among his closest assistants had been established, their efforts to save the Assembly became virtually indistinguishable from building the strike at the Putilov Works into the greatest display of labor solidarity ever seen in the capital city. Gapon's immense popularity among rank-and-file workers, his tactical shrewdness, and his flair for the dramatic gesture were now pitted against the ignorance and inflexibility of factory managements and the police. The Tsarist regime was unprepared to meet such an open, bold, and determined challenge to its authority. It blundered, then reacted in a paroxysm of butchery, creating for the Russian opposition its first martyrs and the first great cause of the year. The massacre of Bloody Sunday electrified the nation and initiated the events later called the Revolution of 1905.

Although the history of the Assembly is inseparable from the events of January, the beginning of the strike on January 3 and 4 transformed one factory's dispute into a citywide event, and the defense of the Putilov workers became a mass movement. At this juncture the history of the Assembly intersected older but well-remembered patterns and traditions of strike activity in the capital. It is appropriate, therefore, to step back and examine the wider field of forces with which the Assembly had cast its fate.

At the Putilov Works, the issue at first was the rights of the Assembly and the four men dismissed from the woodworking shop. That was the first shop to strike, and it led the way in closing down the rest of the plant on Monday, January 3. That day, Gapon read a more elaborate set of demands, which included establishment of a permanent body of elected shop representatives to oversee rates and investi-

January Strikers in St. Petersburg, 1905

Day	No. of striking factories	No. of strikers
January 3	1	12,600
January 5	6	26,000
January 7	382	105,000
January 8	456	111,000
January 10	625	125,000

SOURCE: R-v, "Ianvarskaia zabastovka 1905 g. v Peterburge."

gate grievances and strike pay. On January 4 this list was further extended to include the eight-hour day, abolition of overtime work, and free medical care.[1] The struggle over the legality and rights of the Assembly had become translated into the language of a full-blown industrial conflict, embodying the entire range of "economic" demands then current. Just such a list of demands was circulated among the branches of the Assembly and offered to workers in other plants as a model for their own petitions and lists, should they decide to strike in sympathy with the Putilov workers. Many workers chose to do that during the next several days, and the Putilov demands were widely imitated.

So many Petersburg workers were on strike on the eve of January 9 that the strike was in fact general, as most authors have conceded. The figures shown above, drawn from a report of Chief Factory Inspector Chizhov, are not complete, since they omit state-owned and smaller enterprises, as noted in earlier discussions of the Inspectorate's statistics. Still, they are impressive enough. Never before had even 100,000 workers struck in the capital at the same time, and perhaps even more significant, this all-but-general strike was formed in less than a week. One of the important questions to ask about the January Days, therefore, is how this immense strike took shape, and what the process of its formation both reflected and modified in the practices and consciousness of Petersburg workers.

On January 4, the second day of the Putilov strike, while Gapon was reworking the demands and arranging to head a delegation of workers to meet with Putilov Director S. I. Smirnov, groups of Putilov strikers visited several other Petersburg factories, seeking to bring their workers out on strike. At the large Franco-Russian Machine Building Works in the Kolomensk district, their efforts met with suc-

1. Sablinsky, *The Road to Bloody Sunday*, pp. 160–63. *NPRR*, pp. 5–7.

cess. On Wednesday, January 5, the Nevsky Ship and Machine Works on the Schlüsselburg Road struck after a second day of efforts to close it by Assembly supporters who worked at the plant. In addition, three cotton textile factories struck, two in the Rozhdestvensk district and one in the Peterhof suburb, near the Putilov Works. All or most of these factories had their own reasons for striking, and while some of them were urged to strike by Putilov workers, the encouragement had the effect of bringing them around to their own needs. This may be judged by the fact that most of these strikes raised their own demands, although in one case they were modeled on those of the Putilov workers.[2]

The tabulation above shows that the point of significant change came on January 7, when striking factories were suddenly numbered in the hundreds and the number of strikers surpassed 100,000. It is this point in the development of the January strike that requires careful examination, since it was then that the greatest bulk of strikers came out. After January 9, pain and anger at that day's events must be added to the reasons for workers' willingness to stay out, although the numbers on strike stabilized, and around the 13th strikers began to resume work in large numbers.

But what happened on January 6? It was a religious holiday, the Epiphany, a day off for Petersburg workers, and it was marked by the arrival of the imperial family from Tsarskoe Selo to participate in the traditional, solemn ceremony surrounding the Tsar's "blessing of the waters" on the banks of the Neva. The event was marred by the accidental discharge of a live round by careless artillerists during a military salute. This inspired rumors of an assassination plot since the round struck near the Tsar, wounding a policeman. Some historians have been distracted by this occurrence, and all have failed to stress the fundamental material reason for the day's actual impact on the development of the general strike: that it was a holiday for the workers of the capital.[3] There seems to be little doubt that the work of strike instigators on January 7 was facilitated by the fact that workers had

2. R-v, "Ianvarskaia zabastovka 1905 g. v Peterburge," pp. 32–33. *NPRR*, pp. 8, 13. Mitel'man et al., *Istoriia Putilovskogo zavoda*, p. 185. Paialin, *Zavod imeni Lenina 1857–1918*, p. 113.

3. E.g., see Harcave, *First Blood. The Russian Revolution of 1905*, pp. 78–79; or *Ocherki istorii SSSR. Pervaia russkaia burzhuazno-demokraticheskaia revoliutsiia 1905–1907 gg.*, p. 78. Some have even overlooked the fact that January 6 was a holiday and describe workers as going on strike that day: Mitel'man et al., *Istoriia Putilovskogo zavoda*, p. 189; or Nevskii, *Rabochee dvizhenie v ianvarskie dni 1905 goda*, p. 75. Sablinsky mentions that it was a holiday from work and notes that workers were therefore free to

had a free day on January 6 and had only two days left until their normal day of rest on Sunday. Moreover, the Epiphany was the last holiday of the Christmas season (or Twelfth Day), and it is likely that the
absentee rate for the entire week of January 3 was higher than normal
throughout the city. Holidays were an occasion for extraordinary
drinking binges for many Russian peasants and workers, as well as
time to relax and be with family and friends. Anti-industrial sentiment peaked in such periods, when leisure and enjoyment sharpened
awareness of the pain and indignity of the factory routine. Mass activity inevitably has many faces, and to conceive of a strike as, in part,
a *progul*, an escape from work for the sake of more pleasurable pur-
suits, does not alter its serious purpose or the sacrifice and determination it also involved.

The strike continued to build. On the evening of the 5th Gapon
and a delegation of Putilov workers had been rebuffed by the plant's
board of directors with whom they had met to discuss strike demands.
This proved to be the last straw for the earnest (if aggressive) nego-
tiators. In response they abandoned negotiations and turned all their
energies toward building a general strike in the city and toward presenting to a high government official a petition on workers' needs.[4]
The moment had arrived to unveil the Program of the Five and to
turn the strike in an overtly political direction. A series of continuous
meetings began at the Assembly branches to discuss the petition.
Workers took the occasion to pour out all the misery and bitterness of
their factory lives before their assembled fellow workers. The coinci-
dence of this petition discussion with the January 6 holiday definitely
helped to attract supporters both of the strike and of the march to the
Winter Palace, since communication among workers was mainly oral,
and many workers flocked to the meetings in the Assembly branches
at precisely the time when the Assembly decided to address itself to
wider circles of workers. On January 6, as Gapon was redrafting the
Program of the Five, the idea seemed to occur to him of delivering the
petition to the Tsar himself rather than to a minister, as was originally
intended, and to combine this with an assemblage of workers in a

---

spend more time around the section meetings of the Assembly, but he attaches greater
significance to the gunnery accident: *The Road to Bloody Sunday*, pp. 168, 198–99.

4. Gapon did approach Justice Minister Murav'ev on Friday, January 7, but not with
the aim of settling the strike. Instead, he hoped the minister would persuade the Tsar
to receive the delegation now set to march to the Winter Palace. The attempt failed
utterly, as did Gapon's effort to reach Interior Minister Sviatopolk-Mirskii on the same
day. Sablinsky, *The Road to Bloody Sunday*, pp. 203–4.

public place. This was a stroke of genius, as the immediate popularity of the plan began to make apparent when it was announced at Assembly meetings that night.[5]

News of the proposed procession also reached government circles on the 6th. The response, planned by the Tsar and the country's top ministers and dignitaries, was incomplete, contradictory, and uncoordinated. Though perhaps understandable owing to the novelty of the situation, the clumsy response that resulted would cause the death and suffering of hundreds of people and would furnish dramatic and irresistible proof of the regime's unfitness to rule. On January 7, the day the strike reached citywide proportions, the Tsar stated his intention to declare martial law (*voennoe polozhenie*), and the Commander of the Guard, Prince Vasil'chikov, took charge of security arrangements. At a meeting that evening, Interior Minister Mirskii, Finance Minister Kokovtsov, Justice Minister N. V. Murav'ev, and top city, police, and military officials authorized a plan for a strong police and army presence in the capital, including reinforcements to be sent from other cities of the Northwest. The purpose of the troops was left ambiguous: some understood that they were to block the march and gathering at the Winter Palace; others, that they would only preserve the peace in case of disorders.[6]

At another meeting the following day the military commanders agreed that the marchers not only ought to be prevented from assembling in Palace Square, they ought to be stopped long before they came near it. The conferees reaffirmed decisions taken at the previous meeting neither to arrest Gapon and his followers nor to declare martial law, the formal institution of which the Tsar had apparently left to his ministers; Kokovtsov believed the latter measure would adversely affect Russian financial credit abroad. Later that evening, Mirskii received Nicholas's compliance with the ministers' recommendation; yet the capital was already an armed camp, under the control of eight generals, each in charge of a different district. If Mirskii, Kokovtsov, and others refused to institute martial law lest it harm Russia's foreign credit, they certainly must have believed that their

5. *Ibid.*, pp. 166–71. Varnashev, "Vospominaniia," p. 204. The text of the January 9th petition may be found in *NPRR*, pp. 28–31, and in Sablinsky, *The Road to Bloody Sunday*, pp. 344–49.

6. Semanov, *Krovavoe voskresen'e*, p. 66. Ganelin, "Kanun 'Krovavogo Voskresen'ia' (Tsarskie vlasti 6–8 ianvaria 1905 goda)," pp. 33–36. A briefer version of these developments by the same author appears in *Krizis samoderzhaviia v Rossii, 1895–1917*, pp. 173–75.

order to mass police and troops in the capital would avoid the greater scandal of a breakdown of public order. Though the troop commanders were apparently not trained or briefed to make a measured response to the demonstrators, Russia's highest officials seemed not to suspect that the inadequately prepared military men might themselves initiate the violence that the ministers hoped to avoid.

In addition, no one informed Gapon directly of the government's expectations about the procession. Gapon himself had tried without success to reach Mirskii on January 7, and the next day he finally resorted to sending him a letter explaining the Assembly's plans and peaceful intentions. On January 8 an ambiguous government notice was posted forbidding gatherings and processions, threatening military force not against these occurrences, but against "massive disorder." Most participants, not intending to be disorderly, were clearly justified in believing they would be safe from harm.

Hence, the government had taken a number of measures to prepare for the procession, yet it had left some rather obvious gaps unattended. The Tsar planned not to receive the petition and was not even present in the Winter Palace, having returned to his residence in Tsarskoe Selo after January 6. Yet no one thought of calming the worker petitioners by providing a substitute to accept the petition in his place, the topic was apparently never even raised at either of the ministers' meetings, and the standard that normally flew in front of the Winter Palace announcing the presence of the imperial family was left in place. Finally, despite the reinforcement of the military garrison, and although the top police officials were aware of the preparations, the city police precincts were never ordered to take any special measures on January 9.[7]

No one at the top of the government was aware of the unprecedented upsurge of feeling taking place among Petersburg's workers. The numbers and the mood of the workers who attended Assembly meetings were certainly one of the most important and impressive developments of the dramatic week preceding January 9, to both insiders and outsiders alike. Once the organization became identified with the Putilov strike, thousands of new members joined and several times as many flocked to the branch meetings, now held daily, to hear the news and the inspired oratory. A tense and excited atmosphere, at

7. Ganelin, "Kanun," pp. 36–41. Although this article is based on the most complete assemblage of the information bearing on the government's preparations for the Assembly's procession, neither it nor the standard Western account clarifies all points. Cf. Sablinsky, *The Road to Bloody Sunday*, pp. 206–9.

once both solemn and energetic, prevailed at these meetings. Even at the Nevsky (Schlüsselburg) branch, where attitudes were normally tempered by the presence of numerous well-read and critical metal-workers, astonishing and unprecedented scenes were witnessed. "Even now I still remember," wrote the Menshevik organizer S. I. Somov, "the enormous impression which this meeting produced on me and my comrades."

> A kind of mystical, religious ecstasy reigned the whole time at the meet-ing; thousands of people stood side by side for hours in the dreadful heat and closeness and thirstily devoured the artless, strikingly power-ful, simple, and passionate speeches of their exhausted worker orators. The whole time the content of the speeches was meager, the [same] phrases being repeated in many ways: "our patience has come to an end," "our suffering has gone beyond all measure," "better death than this life," "impossible to flay three skins from a man," and so forth. But they were all pronounced with such marvelous, touching sincerity, flowed so much from the very depths of an exhausted human soul, that the same phrase, pronounced for the hundredth time, brought tears to the eyes, compelled [one] to feel it deeply, and instilled the firm cer-tainty that it was really necessary to resolve to do something in order to give vent to this worker bitterness and dissatisfaction, which had over-flowed its limits.[8]

As the week progressed, the size of these crowds increased and the mood became more elevated. Once Gapon and the other leaders broke off negotiations, they had more time to speak at Assembly meetings, and Gapon would make the rounds from branch to branch, lending his impressive authority and oratory to the growing excite-ment. After January 6, attention focused on the petition, drafts of which were read and reread, explained, and debated at the meetings. The most careful contemporary student of the Gaponist movement at its climax recorded some of the mood and flavor of Assembly meet-ings on January 7 and 8:

> Ever new crowds flowed to the locals. In the evening near the locals a sea of human heads could be seen beneath the light of the streetlamps, dimly flickering into the distance. On the streets, in separate groups, one heard conversations about the war, its burdensome consequences for the people, and about the general strike. Now and then some prob-lem connected with the petition and being discussed inside the hall of the branch was brought out onto the street. Orators mounted any kind

8. Somov, "Iz istorii sotsialdemokraticheskogo dvizheniia," p. 33.

of improvised tribune, like an overturned box, and spoke to the crowd. At several branches the petition was read to the people from an open window of the Assembly, and the people listened to it reverentially, "as if in church." Despite the frost, many stood without hats. Inadequately understood passages of the petition were interpreted and reinterpreted, and each separate point was again and again put to the vote. The crowd expressed its sympathy with shouts and a hum of voices carrying far away. Sometimes it repeated the orator's last words, as a sign of sympathy, picking them up as a choir follows up its leader. . . . "What is it to live this way, is it not better for us to go to the grave?" said the orator, concluding his speech, and the crowd answered him: "Better to the grave, to the grave." . . . "When the reading of the petition was finished," wrote one eyewitness from Vasilevsky Island, "the [branch] president posed a question to the workers: 'And what, comrades, if the Ruler will not receive us and does not want to read our petition—how shall we answer this?' Then, exactly [as] from a single breast a mighty, shattering cry exploded: 'Then we have no Tsar!'—and like an echo, repeated from all corners: 'No Tsar. . . . No Tsar.'"[9]

The apocalyptic tone of the last meetings was undoubtedly set by the possibility of violence during the petition demonstration, which Gapon discussed more or less openly, and by the posing of ultimate questions to the ultimate authority (Will he accept our petition? Do we have a Tsar, a Savior?). The traditional cast of the feelings, thoughts, and manner with which most workers experienced these events contrasted, however, with the thoroughly pragmatic measures taken to spread the strike and build the January 9 demonstration. The mass branch meetings themselves probably did more to further these aims than any other single activity; inspirational oratory, discussions of the issues in smaller groups, and the mere coming together of thousands of workers demonstrated the strength and solidarity of the movement and allayed the misgivings of more cautious participants. Those workers already on strike at the Putilov Works and elsewhere visited neighboring workers in other firms and by a combination of persuasion, raillery, and threats succeeded in most cases in turning out the other workers.

So great was the excitement, so thoroughgoing the activation of Petersburg workers, that some Social Democrats, despite the rigid opposition of both factions to Gapon and his politics, were drawn into the vortex.[10] Those among them capable of suspending disbelief at

9. Gurevich, "Narodnoe dvizhenie v Peterburge 9–go ianvaria 1905 g.," p. 204.
10. "While the regular Social Democratic organizations maintained their hostile attitude toward Gapon and his Assembly, local party circles and scattered individuals

the gigantic and enthusiastic following the priest had gathered, those who succeeded in catching hold of the rapidly unfolding events of the days following January 3, were able to speak at the Assembly's meetings and, when they adapted their speeches to the prevailing mood, even found favorable receptions. Some of the Mensheviks followed up this success by aiding workers to organize their strikes. Somov wrote:

> Thus, along with the general, public assemblies, began a series of semi-conspiratorial meetings of the maturer workers of each plant and factory, meetings at which Social Democrats helped the workers formulate lists with special plant and factory demands. I had to be at several of these meetings, and their characteristic feature appeared to be a "search for justice" (*poiski spravedlivosti*) penetrating all the demands, a common striving to be done with the impossible conditions that had been created. In working out the demands, workers were concerned not only with future improvements, they also sought to take revenge for all their previous, longstanding offences and abuses. Thus, they demanded that bonuses abolished decades before be paid workers for all the years between, and that compensation be made for lower wage rates in effect for many years. At one meeting a worker even proposed that I write into the list the demand that upon the introduction of the eight-hour day the workers be compensated for the unpaid extra two-three hours of work in the course of the last several years. And it occurred to me that in all these demands the workers were guided not so much by considerations of a material nature, as by a purely moral striving to structure everything "in a fair manner" (*po spravedlivomu*) and to force the owners to atone for their past sins.
>
> These meetings, in which 50–100 workers normally took part, also promoted the growth of workers' sympathy toward Social Democracy, but, of course, the main thing was that the Social Democratic orators had subordinated themselves to the mood of the crowd and adapted their speeches to it.[11]

The efforts of this apparently small number of meetings can be taken as representative of what much larger numbers of workers would have felt and demanded had time and circumstances permitted the drafting of demands at all or even most factories. As it was, most

---

were drawn by the excitement of the spontaneous upheaval." Sablinsky, *The Road to Bloody Sunday*, pp. 178–79. This summation of the general situation is not at variance with the more detailed discussions of the Bolshevik V. I. Nevskii in "Peterburgskaia sotsial-demokraticheskaia organizatsiia v ianvare 1905 goda," or that of the Menshevik Somov in "Iz istorii," pp. 22–23.

11. Somov, "Iz istorii," pp. 34–35.

of the worker participants in the January movement seemed to be totally captivated by the desire that the moral debt they bore be redressed by the *Tsar batiushka* himself. So powerful was the feeling that
the Tsar *should* respond favorably to their supplications that it over-
whelmed and enfeebled any desire or need to think calmly about
whether or not he *would*. A kind of holy madness had taken hold of
proletarian Petersburg, and it seems to have captivated most of the
Assembly leadership, including Gapon, as well. The response of the
city's workers to the appeals of the Assembly and the Putilov strikers,
the bearing witness in the packed and stuffy meetings to years and
decades of suffering, had created a paroxysm of moral fervor, and
the projection of this energy into a direct confrontation with the Tsar
himself had by January 8 created an irresistible force of colossal
proportions.

    Some have taken this force as the expression of a traditional, naive,
and popular faith in the goodness of the Tsar (and far more have
worried about it being so taken). Even a brief consideration of its
genesis, however, points to other factors that, taken together, suggest
a different emphasis. Judging by the accounts of witnesses, the subject
of the discussions at Assembly meetings that week was not the Tsar
and his good deeds, but the injustices of factory life and the burdens
of the wageworker's existence. For some of the speakers, and for a
great many of the listeners as well, this experience had the effect of
breaking a lifetime's silence. Willingness to experience the regret and
pain attendant upon these revelations depended upon the illusion
that such injustices would not be allowed to continue once they were
known. In this respect, faith in the Tsar was the necessary condition
for revealing to themselves the truth about their lives, the indispensable harmonizing principle without which the workers' deprivations
and suffering would have had no meaning. The depth of this feeling
would seem to explain the extreme conclusions the workers spon-
taneously drew when the possibility of rejection by the Tsar was
raised: both "we have no Tsar" and the wish for death (expressed in
different ways at several branch meetings) marked the desolation and
emptiness felt at the possibility of their suffering going unheeded.
Likewise, the tenacity with which participants clung to the profoundly
improbable belief that the Tsar would appear on Palace Square and
receive their petition was less a measure of their naïveté than an overwhelming profession of faith in a world in which victims are succored
and injustice redressed. Whatever the vintage of the political theory
involved, the January 9 demonstration was a cry for freedom and jus-

tice, and the feelings accompanying it were firmly grounded in the real-life experience of workers.

On January 9 the guns of the Tsar's troops laid to rest the illusion that justice could be had for the asking and announced to the world a new era of social and political struggle in Russia. The military commanders ordered the violent dispersal of the demonstrators, which resulted in the death or injury of about 1,000 participants and bystanders.[12] This number hardly conveys the shock, anger, and disbelief felt by participants and observers alike at the shameless butchery of Bloody Sunday; nor does it measure adequately the steep plunge taken by the regime's already faltering political stock immediately afterward.

The events of January 9 will not be recounted here in any detail, since this has been competently done in several other places,[13] except to observe that the workers' determination to demonstrate for their petition was undaunted by the appearance of troops and an official warning to stay off the streets posted on January 8, and it did not desert them on the morning of the 9th.

Fairly early that Sunday, Assembly members and supporters gathered at several points throughout the city, preparing to converge in columns on the Winter Palace; one group marched from the distant suburb of Kolpino; all braved the frost of the wintry morning. Almost all the columns were met by armed troops, who either drove them back or dispersed them.

Led by Father Gapon, the marchers from the Narva branch and the Putilov Works met a troop concentration guarding a short bridge over the Tarakanovka River, on the line of march and in the vicinity of the Triumphal Arch. A warning volley was fired at 200 paces, then a second, both over the heads of the marchers; the crowd did not stop or hesitate, but *continued to march forward*. In fact, before the third and

12. This estimate is from Nevskii, *Rabochee dvizhenie v ianvarskie dni*, pp. 123–25. He found that plausible estimates of casualties ranged from 600 to 1,500, including 150 to 500 killed. Figures on January 9 casualties fluctuated wildly because of the shock and confusion occasioned by the events and because many dead and wounded were removed to private homes for fear of criminal charges, and therefore failed to appear in hospital and cemetery estimates. Nevskii maintained that *most* of the victims were overlooked in this manner. For an account of the range and reasoning of the estimates, see Sablinsky, *The Road to Bloody Sunday*, pp. 261–68.

13. E.g., Gurevich, "Narodnoe dvizhenie," pp. 210–22; selections from "Doklad komissii, izbrannoi obshchim sobraniem prisiazhnykh poverennykh 16 ianvaria 1905 g., po povodu sobytii 9–11 ianvaria," in *NPRR*, pp. 105–24; Nevskii, *Rabochee dvizhenie v ianvarskie dni*, pp. 101–28; Sablinsky, *The Road to Bloody Sunday*, pp. 229–71.

lethal volley, the people in the front ranks began to *run* toward the soldiers. This foolhardiness, if such it was, was stopped by the third and seven subsequent volleys. Perhaps those in front hoped that by running they could get past the readied rifles before they fired again; perhaps they only panicked. That they could have approached so close to guns loaded and pointed at them, however, does attest—for some of their number at least—to colossal stubbornness and reckless courage. Large numbers of this and every other march column that was dispersed at the first point of contact with troops continued determinedly on toward Palace Square in smaller groups, moving through side streets and across the frozen Neva.

The confrontation on the Petersburg Side gives a little more insight into the quality of this determination.

> As the soldiers stood with their rifles poised, a police officer approached the crowd and ordered the marchers to halt. He repeated the order three times, warning that the troops would open fire if the crowd refused to stop. Some of the workers began to argue with him, saying they were unarmed and meant no harm. A few unbuttoned their coats to show no arms were hidden and, baring their chests, shouted: "Then shoot, if you want to."
>
> According to the testimonies of survivors, the crowd halted at the police officer's command, and several of the march leaders fell on their knees before him, opening their coats and turning out their pockets to show they were unarmed. The officer walked over to one of them and took a piece of paper from his hands, probably a copy of the petition. Meanwhile a bugle call sounded. The crowd apparently thought the police officer moved aside, out of the line of fire, to let them pass. Those who were talking with him followed, still pleading, and the crowd surged after them. Just then the first volley was fired.[14]

Not all the columns were fired upon, and one of them, from Vasilevsky Island, prevented from crossing to the city center at all, was bottled up in its water-bound district.

It appears that the demonstrators' courage to push up to the armed soldiers, to challenge them, and to continue on their way even after parts of the march had been shot up stemmed from a feeling of innocence and righteousness about the cause and purpose of the march. Only after a considerable number had reached the Palace Square, some bloodied and disheveled from their first encounter, and were again shot at and sabred did this determination give way to anger and

14. Sablinsky, *The Road to Bloody Sunday*, pp. 242, 246–47.

violence against the soldiers. This kind of reaction was particularly sharp and consequential in Palace Square and the surrounding area and on Vasilevsky Island, where the marchers' anger had been provoked in a somewhat different manner, as will be described below.

THE INTELLIGENTSIA RESPONSE

By the end of the day of January 9, the Petersburg labor movement had entered an entirely new epoch of its history, even if most of its participants were not yet fully aware of this. The liberation movement among the intelligentsia and zemstvo notables, on the other hand, did not keep pace. Until the end of December they had constituted the only visible and vocal opposition in the country, and the rate of change they anticipated was linked to their own plans and expectations: for January they had projected a wider penetration of the provinces with banquets and political initiatives at the zemstvo meetings and the continued, expanded organization of professional unions beyond the small beginnings already made. One month later, they found themselves on a crowded stage, with much of the government's attention refocused on the labor movement, and they faced the prospect of being swept into a much more rapid and uncontrollable assault on the established order. The professionals and *zemtsy* met the activization of the labor movement with a mixed response. Although many of them were ambivalent or undecided, the democratic-liberal side of the opposition was on the whole positively inclined toward the new developments, while the liberal-constitutionalist side was resoundingly indifferent, many of them even preferring a reform scenario confined to a legalistic and gentlemanly arrangement among elites.

The former group was particularly prominent in Petersburg, where the venerable flame of the intelligentsia's commitment to the popular cause still burned brightest. Even here, or particularly here, however, the intelligentsia failed to establish firm ties with the Assembly and the January strike movement. This was due above all to the stigma both revolutionaries and liberals attached to Gapon's movement. Even in Petersburg, that is, the city with the longest and most impressive record of worker-intelligentsia interaction, the first truly mass labor movement was greeted by the great majority of the progressive educated stratum as a government conspiracy that had duped its followers and threatened to derail the revolutionary and liberation movements. Although this attitude was in part attributable to the atmosphere of fear and suspicion created by government repression, it was also due to a widespread assumption that the great majority of workers, even Petersburg workers, were gullible, politically naive, and in need of guidance and leadership from the educated elite. Lenin's famous dictum about workers left to their own devices was but the Bolshevik version of a broader belief shared, mutatis mutandis, by most of the Russian intelligentsia.

The small group of left Liberationists that had met with the Assembly's inner circle in December apparently understood enough about the organization's actual potential to have approached it in a different spirit. This was confirmed by the fact that at least one of their number, Vladimir Ia. Bogucharskii, and probably Sergei N. Prokopovich as well, again lent his political and editing advice to Gapon in preparing the petition to the Tsar, immediately prior to January 9.[15]

As plans for the petition march took shape, however, these same advisers, along with their colleagues and peers among the writers and other professionals who led the Union of Liberation in Petersburg, became alarmed at the possibility of bloodshed on January 9. A group of four representatives, led by Bogucharskii, met with Gapon on the afternoon of January 8 to dissuade him from going through with the procession. At the same meeting they also raised anew the suspicion that he was acting the part of provocateur, questioning him about the freedom of action he was enjoying and about his apparent indifference to the clear prospect of violence.[16] Whether or not the writers were reassured on this score, they failed signally to alter his plans.

At the offices of the liberal daily *Nasha zhizn'* on Nevsky Prospect, the informal headquarters of this group, the writers and professionals sat up all evening and into the night discussing what they might do to prevent all but certain tragedy on the streets of the capital the following day. This sense of responsibility was self-imposed, and is explained in part by the powerful intelligentsia ethic the group self-consciously embodied. Their numbers included the most prominent and civic-minded of Petersburg's democratic intellectuals, in previous years the core of the Writers' Union, now the leaders of the Union of Liberation in the capital. If there were an executive committee of Russia's "Republic of Letters," it was surely this group.

Having failed to dissuade Gapon from the march, the members of

15. Sanders, "The Union of Unions," ch. 3, p. 65 and n. 240. Sablinsky, *The Road to Bloody Sunday*, pp. 170, 187–88.

16. Sanders, "The Union of Unions," ch. 3, pp. 66–67, where this meeting is described for the first time. Sanders' account is based on the unpublished memoirs of a participant, V. V. Khizhniakov.

the group decided to try to obtain assurances of restraint from the government. Around 11:00 P.M. they elected a group they called the "Deputies of Literature and Scholarship" to visit some of the influential personages of the capital to win support for the slogan "The demonstration will be peaceful, the troops must be restrained." The "deputies" consisted of N. F. Annenskii, K. K. Arsen'ev, I. V. Gessen, Maxim Gorky, N. I. Kareev, E. I. Kedrin, V. A. Miakotin, A. V. Peshekhonov, and V. I. Semevskii—all writers, scholars, or lawyers. Despite this impressive roster, the "deputies" were turned away without satisfaction from late-night visits to both Interior Minister Sviatopolk-Mirskii and Committee of Ministers President Witte. Powerless to affect events yet certain of disaster on the following day, the "deputies" broke up to return home in the early hours of January 9.[17]

The events of January 9 probably disturbed many of these leaders and their intelligentsia constituents more than they realized. At a large public meeting held at the Free Economic Society on the evening of the massacre, a kind of formless, hysterical confusion reigned. Several witnesses testified to the distraught and helpless feeling, undoubtedly a heavily guilt-ridden one, that haunted educated society in the wake of the massacre. In this setting of shocked indignation at the actions of the authorities and heightened sympathy for the victims, applause and cries of support greeted each report and comment on the day's events. Then Gorky read a denunciation of the Tsar and a call to revolution from Gapon, whom he claimed to be elsewhere. In actuality, the priest spoke at the meeting immediately after Gorky, though clean-shaven and disguised as a worker. Thus costumed, he appealed to the audience for arms and money for the freedom struggle, simultaneously denouncing the intelligentsia for empty talk and no action. This speech provoked wild enthusiasm among the listeners. Soon after his hasty departure, his identity was revealed, and a new hero of educated society was born: Gapon became the embodiment of the indignant rebellion of innocence wronged.[18]

In 24 hours the priest had been transformed from shady suspect in a government provocation into the tribune of the popular revolution. This rapid change of image reveals more about the labile sensibilities not only of persons in the grips of the day's distressing events, but of those whose fundamental political expectations have been suddenly disrupted as well. The workers' revolution that burst upon Russia in January 1905 threatened to transform not only the state and indus-

17. *Ibid.*, pp. 67–70. Gurevich, *Deviatoe ianvaria*, pp. 35–37.
18. Sablinsky, *The Road to Bloody Sunday*, pp. 268–71.

trial order against which it was ostensibly directed, but also the aims and expectations of the erstwhile revolutionaries of the banquet halls and zemstvo assemblies.

THE STRUCTURE OF PROTEST

A unique angle of vision on the January events is offered by a record of arrests for a variety of "disorders" throughout the city from January 7 through January 19. These reports include the numbers arrested, the nature of the violations, their location, and other information.[19] An examination of this record, summarized in Table 16, provides us with an insight into the larger urban context of the popular movement preceding and following Bloody Sunday not afforded by the sequence of events in Gapon's Assembly or in the strike movement. It shows that the January Days witnessed a widespread breakdown of public order that affected not only the working-class districts and the political intelligentsia, but the commercial districts and classes and the criminal and lower-class elements all over the city as well.

The tabulated data show that the largest numbers of arrests for disorderly conduct and looting occurred in the Vasilevsky district. Since most of them took place on January 9 and 10 in the first precinct of the district (Vasilevsky I), they were occasioned by the lengthy and intensive confrontations between the Assembly marchers and the police and army troops. Not content simply to block the march into the city center, the forces of order had pressed into Vasilevsky I to disperse the crowd. Although some of the marchers did obey the order to disperse, smaller groups barricaded the side streets and offered fierce resistance, resorting not only to stones and other missiles but to firearms as well. The crowds were forced to retreat before the better armed and organized soldiery as it swept through the district, but they built new strongpoints and continued through the afternoon and into the evening to resist and harass the authorities.

Meanwhile, once this fighting began, public order swiftly broke down. Stores were looted, and the police station in Vasilevsky II was raided and destroyed. As a result, the fury of the frightened soldiers and police was fully engaged, and they indulged themselves in brutal

19. LGIA, fond 569 (Kantseliariia S.-Peterburgskogo Gradonachal'nika), op. 18., d. 204, ll. 1–110, entitled "Nariad politseiskim protokolam o besporiadkakh 10–25 ianvaria 1905 g." (The dates given in the title are inaccurate.) For the purpose of this analysis, the completeness of these data will be assumed, although no claim or proof of this exists within the document itself.

TABLE 16
Arrests for Disorder in St. Petersburg, January 7–19, 1905,
by District and Type of Violation

District	Dis	S/I	L/R	N/C	Agn	Prp	Ref	Clo	Pol	Sra	Wpn	Vag
Admiralty	11	19	–	11	–	–	–	–	–	–	–	–
Kazan	–	18	–	–	–	–	–	–	–	–	–	–
Spassk	17	53	5	8	4	6	4	–	–	–	–	–
Narva	–	11	–	4	1	–	–	–	–	–	–	–
Moscow	30	2	6	–	–	–	–	6	1	3	–	–
A.-Nevsky	–	9	–	–	4	7	–	–	1	2	4	–
Rozhdest.	–	7	–	–	6	1	–	–	–	–	–	–
Liteiny	5	–	–	–	1	–	–	–	1	–	–	–
Vasilev.	152	2	91	13	5	1	–	–	6	–	1	4
Petersb.	–	4	17	–	2	5	8	2	–	–	–	–
Vyborg	–	7	–	–	1	1	–	2	–	2	–	–
Suburbs	–	5	–	15	–	–	–	–	–	–	–	–
Totals	215	137	137	51	24	21	12	10	9	7	5	4

Key: Dis = Disorder (*besporiadok*); S/I = strike instigation; L/R = looting or robbery; N/C = no cause given; Agn = agitation; Prp = destruction of property; Ref = refusal to obey police order; Clo = closing shops, or attempt; Pol = clash with police or troops; Sra = strike-related activity; Wpn = possession of a weapon; Vag = vagrancy.
SOURCE: LGIA, Fond 569, op. 18, d. 204.

excesses. Innocent bystanders were pursued, arrested, and in some cases beaten mercilessly. The occupation of the district and, with it, the resistance and arrest of residents continued for three days after the 9th. As late as January 12, fourteen looters and six disorderly persons were arrested.[20]

What seems to have happened on Vasilevsky Island, and in other districts on a lesser scale, was the unleashing of anger and resentment among some of the city's most deprived lower-class elements. Although the workers of Gapon's movement initiated the conflict with the authorities, the breakdown of order and the overreaction of the police and soldiers soon involved a much wider circle of urban types, especially those groups whose numbers and social genesis represented the breakdown of early industrial society—petty criminals, beggars, hooligans, and the unemployed. Such explosive power is always present to some degree among the "dangerous classes" of modern cities, but the social underbelly of the capital had swelled immensely in the industrial expansion of recent years and had quickly soured in the conditions of relative neglect encountered. As was ar-

20. See the lawyers' inquiry made into the events of January 9: *NPRR*, pp. 118–24. The viewpoint of the authorities is conveyed in the reports of the police and troop commanders on January 9–12, also in *NPRR*, pp. 50–61, 66–78.

gued earlier, Petersburg's "lumpenproletariat" was intimately related to the proletariat proper in genesis, life-style, and outlook, and yet was separate from it as well.

The sudden rise and rapid growth of hooliganism in Petersburg and other cities after the turn of the century was one clear marker of the rising level of disorder in the Empire.[21] It should be placed next to the peasant riots of 1902, the revival of anti-Semitic pogroms in 1903, the increasing labor unrest, and the growing opposition of the educated classes as a sign of organic breakdown in the social order and of the growing inability of the autocracy to govern the country. In the present instance, the labor protest led by Gapon triggered armed invasion and violent resistance in the Vasilevsky district, which both distracted the police sufficiently to tempt looters and released much bottled-up anger against not only the police, but that which they had presumably been sent to preserve, property and orderly conduct. The arrest report is not specific about the identity of those arrested, giving only their estate or occupation: of 40 persons arrested for disorder and looting in Vasilevsky II from January 10 to 12, 28 of them, or 70 percent, were registered peasants and the remaining twelve included five townsmen (*meshchane*), two artisans (*remeslenniki*), one apprentice, one sexton, one university student, one German citizen, and one unspecified.[22] This information does not make possible the telling distinctions between employed or unemployed, migrant or long-term resident, factory or non-factory labor, Assembly participant or bystander. Undoubtedly, some of the disorderly, if not the looters, were factory workers. The arrests probably brought in individuals whose manner and motives could have been described as "hooligan," although persons so described were also observed on January 11 aiding the police in stopping trams and beating the student passengers.[23]

This open and protracted fight against the organs and representatives of the state presented the government with a challenge never before encountered and opened a new chapter in Petersburg's history of popular resistance.[24] Fights with the police and massive arrests had

21. On hooliganism and the breakdown of social and political order, see Neuberger, "Crime and Culture: Hooliganism in St. Petersburg, 1900–1914," esp. pp. 31–32, 47, 68–69.

22. LGIA, "Nariad politseiskim protokolam," ll. 64–65 ob. Four of the arrests were for unspecified violations, and one was for insulting a policeman.

23. *NPRR*, p. 122. On both the difficulty of and the need for distinguishing hooligans from workers, who apparently both joined them and fought them, see Neuberger, "Crime and Culture," esp. ch. 1.

24. The wider field of action opened in 1905 and the specifically urban context of much popular resistance are two key conditions of labor and other crowd violence not

occurred earlier, in 1898 and 1901, but at individual factories and factory neighborhoods over several hours, never throughout an entire district for three or four days. In addition, judging by the number of arrests for looting and robbery, petty criminal activity was unleashed on a large scale. In this regard, the decay of the social circumstances of the city's lower classes combined with the erosion of the regime's political authority to produce a double explosion, and for a brief moment in one quarter of the city, the specter of a true revolutionary upheaval was glimpsed. Though shooting, robberies, and violent clashes with the police did occur in other districts, the intensity of the events on Vasilevsky Island were simply not duplicated elsewhere. This leads one to suspect that the fiercer resistance in the Vasilevsky district was triggered by the authorities' *pursuit* of the marchers back into the district, after they were blocked from proceeding to Palace Square. This tactic was not applied in any other district on that day, and it seems to have precipitated a *defense* by the Vasilevsky workers of their own territory similar to those worker defenses against invading police and troops witnessed in 1898 and 1901.

For all the violence and disorder on Vasilevsky Island, however, the troops and police may actually have exercised *more* control over the situation there than they did on Palace Square, the rendezvous point for all the march columns. By the early afternoon of January 9, thousands of workers had gathered in the square and in the surrounding streets and public spaces, where they awaited Gapon and the presentation of the petition to the Tsar. (Unbeknownst to most of them, Gapon's column had been shot up and scattered, though the participants were not turned back, and the priest himself was already in hiding.) In seeking to disperse the crowd, one of the military units opened fire, provoking an angry and violent response that brought attacks on uniformed figures and shop windows in the area. Most important, the crowd still refused to disperse. More shooting by the troops and more attacks on soldiers, officers, and policemen followed. Soon the entire

---

assessed in the pioneering essay by Daniel R. Brower, "Labor Violence in Russia in the Late Nineteenth Century," pp. 417–31, with responses by Robert E. Johnson, Ronald G. Suny, and Diane Koenker, *ibid.*, pp. 432–53. The discussion developed there raises fruitful insights and criticisms in support of the present study's attempt to discuss violence in the context, and as an attribute, of the broader struggle of workers against their employers and state power, and not as a separate category of action in which "labor violence" forms one variety or moment. In particular, Johnson's insistence on establishing the exact motives and meaning of violence within a phenomenon which "had many faces" and Koenker's stress on the reactive nature of much working-class violence and on establishing the identity of its perpetrators parallel the methodological preferences applied here.

area around Palace Square, the Aleksandrovsk Garden, and the upper part of Nevsky Prospect down to Kazan Cathedral became a boiling caldron, and far more casualties were suffered here in a shorter amount of time than across the river in the Vasilevsky district. The relatively small number of arrests for disorder, looting, and other riot-related offences reported in the table above (in the relevant Admiralty, Kazan, and Spassk districts)[25] should not mislead one about the great violence of the events that occurred there. On the contrary, the very absence of such arrests bears silent but eloquent witness to the very brutal form of crowd control applied by the authorities in the Palace Square battle on January 9. Here they simply shot and killed many more people in a much more confined space and over a shorter period than on Vasilevsky Island. At first the crowd retaliated wherever it could, but it dispersed to its districts of origin fairly rapidly, and arrests were not possible or necessary. By nightfall, Palace Square and its environs were quite peaceful, in contrast with the continuing state of lawlessness in the Vasilevsky district. The territorial issue did not arise in the Palace Square melee because practically the entire crowd resided in other districts and came as visitors to a public space. Participants reacted angrily from shock and a sense of violated dignity, but they fled once the scale of the bloodshed had become apparent.[26]

But what accounted for the relatively large number of arrests of strike instigators in the *center* of the city, i.e., in the Admiralty, Kazan, and especially the Spassk districts? Why should arrests for strike instigation be higher, and those for looting and robbery lower, in the districts filled with retail businesses and small workshops (as well as the slums and large criminal element of Spassk III), while in a district like Vasilevsky, full of factory workers, the number of arrests for robbery and disorder was higher while that for strike instigation was negligible? The low number of strike arrests is not difficult to account for. Most factory workers were already on strike by January 7, and most of the arrests for disorder and looting, as we have seen, stemmed from the events of January 9.

What happened in the city center during these days is another matter. All but eight of the 90 arrests for strike instigation in the three central districts mentioned occurred on January 7 and 8, indicating

25. The eleven arrests for disorderliness in the Admiralty district were made on January 10.

26. Sablinsky, *The Road to Bloody Sunday*, pp. 247–53. Shuster, *Peterburgskie rabochie*, pp. 90–92.

(1) that many workers in these districts were still in the process of going on strike, and (2) that some kind of concerted effort may have been under way to bring the artisans and workers in the small work-shops typical of these districts into the general strike. Who were these instigators, and whom were they instigating? Information about them is uneven and incomplete, but there are a few clues. In the case of the 19 strike instigators arrested in the Admiralty district on January 8 the police record states that they included four printers, four jewelers, and ten goldsmiths agitating at *other shops in the same trades.* It is not clear whether the activity of these craftsmen was typical of those arrested for strike instigation, but this glimpse of what a part of them were up to supports the very plausible supposition that self-motivated, skilled craftsmen would take advantage of the general strike situation in the city to draw together the workers of their own trades.

In the Spassk district, where 39 percent of the strike instigation arrests were made, a more complex situation may have obtained. The home addresses for 41 of the arrestees in Spassk III were reported, and this list shows that these "strike instigators" came from all over the city, but about three-quarters (31) lived in Spassk or in districts directly adjacent to it. Unfortunately, this does not reveal whether the arrestees were Spassk workers who resided in nearby districts or strangers from other districts come to instigate strikes among the Spassk workers. Even less does it indicate whether these were workers in the same trade and therefore fellow artisans, as in the Admiralty district, or whether they were factory workers applying their technique of roving agitation to the artisan element. We do know that bands of such agitators were active in spreading the strike, stemming especially from the Narva district directly to the south and west of Spassk III, where many Putilov workers lived. These were precisely the workers who were most active in the roving agitation in January. It is highly likely that these Narva workers figured heavily among the strike instigators active in Spassk, because nearly two-thirds of them resided in the Moscow or Narva districts.

If these same data are examined for the distribution of *types* of arrests over the thirteen days they cover (Table 17), a kind of overview of the development of the January disorders emerges that enriches the district data already presented. Aside from the bunching up of arrests for disorderliness and looting on January 9 and 10, another fairly obvious pattern is the sustained nature of strike-related arrests, mainly for "strike instigation" but also for "agitation" and "strike-related activity" (see the table below). Other causes of arrest seemed to

TABLE 17
Arrests for Disorder in St. Petersburg, January 7–19, 1905,
by Date and Type of Violation

Date	Dis	S/I	L/R	N/C	Agn	Prp	Ref	Clo	Pol	Sra	Wpn	Vag
7th	–	25	–	6	–	–	–	–	–	–	–	–
8th	–	58	–	–	–	–	–	–	–	–	–	–
9th	97	–	47	2	5	–	–	4	1	–	1	–
10th	93	5	12	4	2	13	4	4	–	–	1	–
11th	10	2	4	7	–	–	–	2	2	2	2	–
12th	6	8	14	5	2	–	–	–	–	–	1	–
13th	–	7	–	–	3	–	–	–	–	–	–	–
14th	5	12	3	4	1	5	–	–	1	3	–	–
15th	–	3	4	–	1	2	8	–	3	1	–	4
16th	1	3	3	–	4	–	–	–	–	–	–	–
17th	–	5	–	–	4	–	–	–	–	1	–	–
18th	–	3	4	–	–	–	–	–	–	–	–	–
19th	–	5	1	6	–	–	–	–	–	–	–	–
No date	3	1	27	17	2	1	–	–	2	–	–	–

Key: Dis = Disorder (*besporiadok*); S/I = strike instigation; L/R = looting or robbery; N/C = no cause given; Agn = agitation; Prp = destruction of property; Ref = refusal to obey police order; Clo = closing shops, or attempt; Pol = clash with police or troops; Sra = strike-related activity; Wpn = possession of a weapon; Vag = vagrancy.
SOURCE: LGIA, Fond 569, op. 18, d. 204.

peak around January 9 and 10, then fall to a lower level or disappear, but arrests for strike activity continue through January 19. This well illustrates the sustained kind of disruptiveness that strikes produced in January 1905 and for many months afterward. Arrests for looting would seem to have been another continuing disruption, but several arrests per day for robbery would probably be normal for a city as full of poverty and unemployment as Petersburg. In addition, beginning on January 14, a number of persons on Vasilevsky Island began coming forward to return to the police goods that had been stolen during the earlier disorders, indicating that the looting of January 9 and after had reached a kind of cyclic conclusion.[27]

The regular arrest of from two to twelve strike instigators per day well into the second week after Bloody Sunday raises the question of whether this indicated the advent of a new pattern of strike behavior to which the police were simply responding, or a greater effort on the part of the authorities to stamp out strike activity, possibly even at the expense of neglecting other kinds of challenges to public order. A special concern with strike activity certainly did not begin in 1905,[28]

27. LGIA, "Nariad politseiskim protokolam," ll. 66–71.
28. One hundred sixty additional positions of police inspector (*politseiskie nadzirateli*) specifically assigned to reinforce the police in the factory districts of the capital, to-

although it was considerably enhanced by more urgent demands emanating from factory owners for special measures to protect their property from masses of angry and mobilized workers. In addition, strikes continued to flare up in the two weeks after Bloody Sunday, a wholly predictable result of raised expectations, unmet demands, and ongoing factory disputes from the first strike, a process that will be discussed below.

Whether the impetus to repress the strikes stemmed from fearful perceptions on the part of the government and the factory owners or from a new and real danger, however, it would soon become clear that something new *was* afoot among workers, and that the government's continued insistence that the maintenance of public order excluded the pursuit by workers of just treatment and a reasonable wage was making for a more explosive situation. By insisting on this standard of order, the regime was empowering workers to discredit it whenever they moved against their employers; by placing itself athwart the workers' path to more equitable working conditions, the autocracy elevated strikes to the level of political protest, no matter what the subjective motivations of the strikers might be, and as a result energized and vindicated the mutual attraction increasingly felt between the workers and large parts of the antigovernment opposition.

Finally, it is important to raise the broader question of what the whole set of data shows about the arrestees and the urban population generally as opposed to what it shows about police priorities. For instance, the clustering of looters and the disorderly in Vasilevsky and strike instigators in Spassk might be due to the presence of more police in the Vasilevsky district and thus a higher incidence of contact and consequent arrest of looters; hence it is possible that as much or more actual theft took place in Spassk district, but because the priorities were to prevent strikes first, the looters active there were simply not arrested. This ambiguity cannot be removed entirely because we do not know what emergency measures were in effect for the police in the January 9 period.

This much can be said, however: first, the *normal* distribution of police in St. Petersburg found Spassk district apparently better policed than Vasilevsky; the number of residents per policeman was 527

gether with supporting staff and equipment, were mandated in an act of the State Council on February 1, 1899. It was understood that heated and lighted quarters were to be provided by the appropriate factory and mill owners. S.—*Peterburgskaia stolichnaia politsiia i Gradonachal'stvo. Kratkii istoricheskii ocherk*, pp. 248–49.

and 943, respectively. If, however, one compares the same ratios for plebeian Spassk III (population 55,199) with proletarian Vasilevsky II (50,292), the ratios in the two subdistricts are much closer: 1,004 and 1,118, respectively. Hence, as might be expected, the generally wealthier, more commercial, and more densely populated Spassk district was normally more heavily policed than Vasilevsky, although the high-crime (but also poverty-ridden and working-class) subdistrict of Spassk III was relatively underpoliced.[29]

Second, troop strength from January 9 through 11 in the two districts gave Vasilevsky (whose population numbered 131,087 in 1900) 100 percent more infantry and about 10 percent more cavalry than were assigned to the Spassk, Kazan, and Liteiny districts combined (population 283,278). Even after some shifts over the three days, Vasilevsky still ended up with about 45 percent more troops in each category.[30] Additional police may have been shifted to Vasilevsky as well. It appears, therefore, that the authorities anticipated that the factory workers of Vasilevsky posed a greater potential threat to order than the artisans and denizens of the Haymarket; and that possibly the dignity and prestige of the state and the imperial presence were in greater danger than the material wealth of the city's commercial center.

On January 7 and 8, as police and army units were being massed and readied all over the city in anticipation of the march, they had nothing in particular to do for the time being. As a result, many areas were overpoliced on those days, and that probably accounts for the large number of strike instigation arrests on the eve of the disorders, i.e., before there were any disorderly persons and looters to arrest. Then on January 9 itself the police and troops in the three central districts probably concentrated their efforts on guarding the posh businesses on Nevsky Prospect and adjacent streets and were likely drawn into the fighting on upper Nevsky, so that police and military presence in Spassk III and neighboring subdistricts may have been even lower than normal on Bloody Sunday and possibly for a while afterward as well. There could easily have been considerable theft and vandalism in the city center during these days that simply went unnoticed and unreported.

It may be well at this point to balance these considerations, based on

29. The figures for this calculation are drawn from I. Vysotskii, *Alfavitnyi sbornik rasporiazhenii po S.-Peterburgskomu gradonachal'stvu i politsii, izvlechennykh iz prikazov za vremia s 1902 g. po 10 iiulia 1904 g.* (SPb., 1904), pp. 155–56; and *Peterburg, 1900*, vyp. 1.

30. *NPRR*, pp. 127–29, 137–39, 144–47.

imputed intentions, with others based on the strikers' stated aims—i.e., to turn from interpreting behavior to elaborating written evidence.

STRIKE DEMANDS

The Putilov strikers' demands were not only the first ones to be raised in January, they played a guiding role as a model for many other workers' demands as the strike expanded.[31] They were developed over two days, January 3 and 4, and were authored in each case by Gapon himself in consultation with the Putilov strikers, with whom he was then in close contact. On January 3 he read the following demands to a gathering of Putilov strikers:

1. Dismiss Foreman Tetiavkin and rehire two workers, Sergunin and Subbotin.
2. The foremen, with the voluntary agreement of workers' shop representatives, are to work out binding [piecework] rates on new items and to review all existing rates in a similar manner.
3. A permanent commission of workers' representatives must be established at the Putilov Works to examine, jointly with management, all grievances of individual workers. No worker is to be dismissed without this commission's approval.
4. No one is to suffer on account of the strike.
5. Workers are to be excused for their absence during the strike and are to be paid, it is suggested, according to average wage rates.

Sometime before a meeting with Putilov Director Smirnov the following day, six more demands were added:

6. An eight-hour workday.
7. Institute three shifts of work.
8. A pay raise for unskilled workers: from the present 60 kopecks to 1 ruble for men; from the present 40 to 75 kopecks for women, per day.
9. Abolish overtime work.
10. Improve the sanitation unit at the plant.
11. Grant free medical care by plant doctors for sick workers.[32]

---

31. This insight deserves all the revelatory force of the wheel's rediscovery, since it has been pointed out by other students of Petersburg labor, e.g., Pankratova, *Fabzav-komy Rossii v bor'be za sotsialisticheskuiu fabriku*, pp. 99–100, or Prokopovich, *K rabochemu voprosu v Rossii*, p. 165.

32. *NPRR*, pp. 6 (n. 2), 7, 12. Another version of the Putilov workers' extended list, otherwise identical, omits the point on three-shift work and adds demands for double pay for unavoidable overtime work, construction of child-care facilities, and plant re-

Leaving aside the first point, which applied only to the Putilov situation, these demands may be grouped under five rubrics: (1) length and structure of the workday, including items 6, 7, and 9; (2) wages, including items 2, 5, and 8; (3) worker control and representation, including items 2, 3, and 4; (4) sanitation and medical care, items 10 and 11; and (5) amnesty and strike pay, items 4 and 5.

The striking workers of at least seven other large metal and machine plants in the Petersburg area put forth demands encompassing these same five rubrics. They were the workers of the Franco-Russian, Izhorsk, and Aleksandrovsk Machine plants, the Baltic Shipyard, the Sestroretsk Armaments Works, the Pipe Plant, and shops of the Petersburg-Warsaw Railroad.[33] The close similarity of the demands at these firms to each other and to those of the *putilovtsy* was quite evident. Strikers at all of the plants demanded an eight-hour day, and most of them wanted overtime abolished or compensated at a higher rate. Almost all asked for a minimum wage for unskilled workers of 1 ruble per day. All lists included the establishment of permanent commissions of workers' deputies to rule on grievances and dismissals, and all but one demanded joint consultation on piece rates as well. Even the wording of the last two demands is strikingly similar in most of the lists examined. Finally, all demanded immunity from punishment for striking and some form of compensation for the days lost. Of course, strikers at each of the plants raised other demands, not mentioned in the Putilov list but specific to their separate workplaces and even to separate shops. But there was enough similarity and uniformity among them all to leave little doubt that they had access to

---

sponsibility for defective production. *Ibid.*, p. 12. That version emanated from the Ministry of Justice and suggests the existence of several variants of the demands. The list was probably copied and recopied for the purpose of circulating it around the city, in the process of which small departures from the original could have crept in. I have followed Sablinsky in preferring the variant sent by the Okhrana to the Department of Police. Cf. Sablinsky, *The Road to Bloody Sunday*, pp. 160–63.

33. *Peterburgskie bol'sheviki v period pod''ema pervoi russkoi revoliutsii 1905–1907 gg. Sbornik dokumentov i materialov*, pp. 140–41, 144–46, 164–69. LGIA, F. 1173, op. 1, d. 7205, ll. 1–2. L'vovich, "Trebovaniia rabochikh Baltiiskogo i drugikh morskikh zavodov v ianvarskie dni 1905 goda," pp. 86–87. Only the Izhorsk list omitted the fourth and fifth, the Pipe Plant the fifth, and the Sestroretsk plant the fourth types of demands; all the rest put forth demands in each of the five categories. The discussion that follows is based on the lists from these six plants (plus that of the Putilov workers), but much of what is said probably also applied to other strikers known to have raised demands, but whose actual lists were unavailable for examination, especially those from other large metal plants such as the Obukhov Works, the New Admiralty Shipyard, and the St. Petersburg Metal Works.

and substantially drew on the Putilov list. The activity of the Assembly was thus of fundamental importance, not only in spreading the Putilov strike, but in giving it shape and substance as well.

The Putilov demands were also significantly embellished and expanded in the lists of the other large metal plants, adding new dimensions to the complexion of the January strike. The additions can be grouped in three categories. One was the general demand for *politer treatment of workers* by management personnel and foremen. This kind of demand appeared in all but one of the lists examined, and distinguished itself by its simple directness and disarming pathos. The Izhorsk workers, for instance, demanded "Unconditionally polite treatment by the plant management of all workers without exception and the abolition of the use of '*ty*' with workers, who are insulted by it." ("*Ty*" is the familiar form of "you" and was reserved in public discourse for children and social inferiors like serfs and domestics.) Baltic Shipyard workers stated that "Foremen, subforemen, young foremen, and the whole management in general must without fail treat workers like people and not like an object (*veshch'*) and not use unpleasant and unnecessary words (*lishnie slova*) as is [now] done." Sometimes, medical personnel were singled out for separate mention, as when the Sestroretsk workers demanded "that the plant doctor treat workers humanely and politely." Because doctors reflected the prejudices of society outside the factory, it is clear that the workers were concerned with a social class problem as well as with the language and customs of the management hierarchy.[34]

Another demand added to the Putilov list by the strikers at other plants was *immunity from dismissal for elected deputies*. This one was confined to the plants of the Naval Ministry and the Franco-Russian Machine works, the latter located in close proximity to three of the Ministry's establishments, the Baltic, New Admiralty, and Galernyi Island Shipyards. (The Ministry also ran the Izhorsk and Obukhov works and several powder and munitions plants in and around Petersburg.) The demand may have been limited to naval enterprises because of experience with elected deputies at both the Obukhov and Baltic plants during the strikes in May and June 1901; but its appearance at just these plants may also have been due to the circulation of personnel, and therefore of information and strategies, among these same enterprises. The naval plant strikers may also have helped to spread the idea of elected deputies and the demand for their immunity

---

34. *Peterburgskie bol'sheviki*, p. 165.

to other strikers through the Assembly's branch meetings and other informal networks. As mentioned, immunity for deputies was demanded by Franco-Russian workers early in the strike, and by Putilov Plant strikers in a revised set of demands dated February 6.[35]

A third type of demand raised in the Assembly's petition but put forth by only one of the plants whose demands have been examined was the *call for a new political order* aimed not at the management but at the Tsarist state. Heading a list of 35 demands drawn up by workers of the Aleksandrovsk Machine Works and dated January 12 were the following points:[36]

1. In order to elaborate laws on popular participation in administering the country, a constituent assembly must be created immediately from representatives of all estates and religions, and elected by universal, direct, equal, and secret ballot.
2. Complete freedom of speech, freedom of press, freedom of assemblies, unions and strikes.
3. Inviolability of the person and home of every person.
4. Complete amnesty for all convicted of political and religious [violations].

All these points were contained in the Assembly's January 9 petition to the Tsar, for which workers had evinced overwhelming support at the meetings preceding Bloody Sunday. Their appearance among the Aleksandrovsk workers' demands was therefore somewhat redundant, and this circumstance may account for their absence in the other lists under examination. Nevertheless, when the head of the main locomotive shops at Aleksandrovsk spoke to a crowd of about 1,000 workers on January 12, he found they had not heard the demands and proceeded to read them aloud. When he read the first point on a constituent assembly, the workers "all replied: 'No, it was

---

35. *Ibid.*, pp. 140, 176. L'vovich argued that the similarity in demands among large metal plants in January stemmed from the existence of some kind of mutual ties "of revolutionary and leadership circles, which imbibed attitudes and organizational literary materials from common sources." "Trebovaniia rabochikh," p. 92. This vague formulation suggests that the leaflets and organizational work of the revolutionary parties shaped the demands of the January strikers in Petersburg. Though they certainly played a role in generalizing demands, L'vovich's failure to mention the example of the Putilov strike and the network of Assembly locals creates an erroneous imbalance of emphasis. In January 1905 the role of avowed revolutionaries in organizing and shaping the strike was subordinate in every respect to that of the Assembly and of the workers themselves.

36. *Peterburgskie bol'sheviki*, pp. 167–69.

not read to us and we don't want it.'" They also rejected the point on freedom of speech, press, and assembly: "We think it not necessary."[37] The incident demonstrated once again the unevenness of consciousness even at metal plants and serves as a reminder that demands normally originated with groups of more active and politically conscious workers, who did not always have the opportunity to consult with the workers for whom they purported to speak.

On balance, the absence of general political demands in these lists, taken together with the support of the Assembly's petition, indicates that in January workers were on the whole content to allow Gapon and his organization to voice their collective political needs and that they had not on the whole begun to raise general political demands as causes of strikes in separate factories. As the year progressed and the message of political leaders found wider acceptance in the factories, this situation would change. Yet, even in January, the absence of general political demands at the factory level did not indicate that the strikes were either "spontaneous" (in the pejorative sense defined earlier) or purely "economic" in inspiration.

The demands of the large metal plants in the first wave of January strikes, for all their concern with the details of the workday, wage rates, and conditions of work, nevertheless expressed both a deep discontent at the pain and powerlessness of factory life and a radical thrust aimed at the immediate redress of that condition. Between demands for a constituent assembly, on the one hand, and for tea water and washup facilities, on the other, all the lists put forth a middle range of demands which best expressed the intolerability of factory conditions and the workers' impatience with them. Above all, the demands for an eight-hour day and for elected deputies to represent workers before management captured much of the meaning of the strike movement in 1905 for the majority of strikers from the beginning till the end of the year. Lesser demands varied with the factory and the conditions of work and the state of the struggle. Overt political demands were appended to lists of demands with increasing frequency after January, but they became a general phenomenon and provided the focus for a citywide effort only in the fall. The eight-hour day and elected deputies who would function as real leaders and spokesmen were demands that seemed relevant to the immediate perceived needs of large numbers of workers and yet pointed to a new

37. Krugliakov, "Zabastovka sredi zheleznodorozhnikov v nachale 1905 goda v Peterburge," p. 61.

factory order incorporating justice and control for workers in the life of the factory. They were not exactly socialist demands, but they aimed well beyond the capitalism of early twentieth-century Russia. The popularity of these two demands throughout the revolutionary year expressed the determination of workers to wage a protracted struggle to make decisive changes in the conditions of employment, not just to win a concession here or there. The fact that these two demands could be directly implemented by the workers themselves, by simply electing deputies and refusing to work more than eight hours, increased the power of their appeal and enhanced their importance as the foci of struggle. These two issues, more than any others, served as a prism through which was refracted both more specific grievances and wider political demands because they raised, at base, questions of control of the workplace and, by extension, of workers' power in society. In this respect, they were eminently "political."[38]

Although these generalizations have been drawn from only seven lists of demands (two of which were from plants outside Petersburg, but under its political sway), there is good reason to believe that strikers who generated demands at 41 other plants[39] also took the Putilov list as a model for their own petitions. The larger metal plants, whose demands have been examined, were on the whole better placed to generate demands, considering their previous experience, internal organization, and success in holding meetings and electing deputies. If they nevertheless found it convenient and in keeping with their own needs to adopt many of the Putilov demands as their own, then strikers at other plants would have been even more dependent on the Putilov list as a model for their own demands. Although this cannot be conclusively demonstrated (given the absence of demand lists from these other plants), evidence and circumstances to be discussed below would seem to bear it out.

But what of the strikers who raised no demands at all? Many of them seem to have struck in response to the appeals of other strikers,

38. Gareth Stedman Jones describes a similarly consistent, radical stratum of demands for control of the work process and an eight-hour day (i.e., neither "trade unionist" nor yet "socialist" either) arising among Oldham cotton workers in the 1850's, indicating that such demands could and did originate in the absence of prompting by socialists. "Class Struggle and the Industrial Revolution," pp. 45–62. Although the appearance of these demands among workers in early-twentieth-century Russia probably owed something to socialist teachings, the case of Oldham shows that they also probably owed a great deal to workers' factory experience independently of socialist influence.

39. This figure is calculated from R-v, "Ianvarskaia zabastovka," pp. 25–44, which gives the most detailed breakdown of strikes in Petersburg for any month in 1905.

examples of which were given earlier in the discussion of roving agitation. Their silence, together with their willingness to strike in support of other workers (threats of violence aside), have been regarded as indications of the "spontaneity" of the January strikes, a term that suggests unconscious motivation and that frequently has been used as a substitute for an explanation of their behavior. Yet two general circumstances were present that made the strikes without demands more than responses to threats or expressions of an abstractly "spontaneous" labor revolt. One was the strike agitation carried on by the Assembly, with its lists of demands and extensive network of district branches. The approach of strike agitators was preceded, in all but the most isolated workshops, by knowledge of the worker priest and his organization, even when Assembly supporters or sympathizers were themselves not present. From January 4 onward, Assembly agitators made it clear that the Putilov demands could be applied, with some modifications, to all Petersburg workers. From the evening of January 5, these demands were expanded and generalized yet further, and the text of the January 9 Petition was made known to ever growing numbers of workers as of January 6. It is highly likely, therefore, that many of those who struck on January 7 felt that demands were already being raised in their name by the Assembly and that their major responsibility was to stop work in support of the demands. In the absence of in-plant strike leadership and guidance, that is, many workers apparently looked directly to their Assembly locals.

The other unifying factor underlying the apparent spontaneity of January 7 was the prestige and authority of the Putilov strikers and, even more, that of other industrial giants in the immediate neighborhood or district of most potential strikers. On January 15, Chief Factory Inspector Chizhov reported that all strikers on the Vyborg Side were likely to return to work within a few days because of the imminent return of workers at the St. Petersburg Metal Plant, which "gives the tone" to that district.[40] Although he did not point this out, it is apparent from strike patterns in January and later that almost every district had at least one large plant which "gave the tone" to the rest of the district: on Vasilevsky Island it was the Baltic Shipyard; in Kolomensk the Franco-Russian Works and the Admiralty's two gigantic shipyards; in Narva the Rechkin Train Car Construction Works and a number of smaller cotton textile factories (where the 1896 strike originated); on the Schlüsselburg Road (*Za nevskoi zastavoi*) the

40. *NPRR*, p. 159.

Obukhov, Nevsky, and Aleksandrovsk Machine plants, as well as the Paul and Maxwell textile giants.[41] Smaller factories and workshops fell under the sway of these giants not only because of the higher wages, skill levels, and usually more enlightened outlook the workers of the large plants often possessed, but because the sheer weight of their numbers changed the conditions of struggle in the district when they struck. The attention of the authorities and the police was drawn to the large plants, facilitating agitation and strikes at the smaller places, and generating an atmosphere of hope that districtwide strike solidarity might make the difference between victory (or at least some significant concessions) and defeat. The silence of the January strikers who raised no demands of their own may thus be said to have been broken in the heated and tumultuous meetings of the Assembly during the week preceding January 9 and in the demands and demonstrations of the more populous and better-organized plants and factories.

From another angle, the role of force and the threat of force are mentioned with disturbing regularity in strike reports written by the authorities. The use of force cannot be denied, but neither can it be documented with sufficient accuracy to gauge its overall importance. It is a reminder that a significant portion of the work force could be, in some circumstances, fairly docile and tractable. The question is whether this quality was of great or small importance in accounting for the near unanimity of the January strikes. Once again, lack of information prevents us from drawing definite conclusions, but there is at hand a very suggestive, if solitary, example of what may have occurred in some of the cases when strikes were reported as responses to the threat of force.

To the Plant Manager of the Atlas
Iron and Copper Foundry and Machine Plant
Mr. Aleksandr Fedorovich German

> [From] Workers of the Atlas
> Iron and Copper Foundry and
> Machine Plant

Petition

We have the honor most humbly to beg you and to petition you, Mr. Plant Manager Aleksandr Fedorovich German, in a matter wherein we the workers of your plant Atlas turn to you with the most humble request that pay be issued us for the idle time beginning January 7 of this

41. Paialin, *Zavod imeni Lenina*, pp. 122–23.

year from 9:00 o'clock in the morning and ending January 14. [We] resumed at 1:30 in the afternoon of January 14 the usual work as is ever our lot and beg you most humbly Mr. Plant Manager Aleksandr Fedorovich German to give an order which is in your power on the issuance of pay to us for six and one-quarter [*sic*] days in an amount you think fit in view of the fact that we did not leave the plant voluntarily, but [that] instigators and rioters from other plants drove us out, [that] we have worked peacefully in your plant [and that] we never had any kind of disorders [and] were always peaceful [MS torn] we also must humbly beg you, our plant manager Aleksandr Fedorovich German, [torn] shortening of the workday [torn] half hour, that is, from [torn] o'clock in the morning and ending 6:30 o'clock in the evening with a break for lunch of 1½ hours, so [torn] again beg you, Aleksandr Fedorovich [torn] worker of your Iron and Copper foundry and machine plant, Atlas all shops [*sic*] beginning [with] the foundry, pattern-making, trimming, machine, the forge and the economizer shop and unskilled workers also beg you Mr. Plant Manager Aleksandr Fedorovich German not to leave this petition without follow-up and to declare to us by [written] notice or you yourself tell us by word of mouth—since payday will be on January 29 of this year [torn] that, by an order which you have the power to issue, the office of your plant can count those days which we missed during the disorders in all factories and plants from January 7th to the 14th [torn] of this year.

[Unsigned] 1905, the 24th of January
Atlas Plant[42]

The peculiar combination of servility and aggressiveness in this petition should probably be taken as simple naïveté, since it is likely to have been the first such effort of its authors. The servile tone[43] may be exaggerated as a result of the workers' apparently weakened bargaining position and the nature of the request, but the claim that they were *forced* to strike for six days is almost certainly a fabrication. Yet the authors of the petition were not satisfied to flatter and deceive for the sake of their back pay alone, but added the much weightier demand for a shorter workday. The contradictory character of the resulting petition expressed well the consciousness of workers who had been overtaken by the need, the urge, and the opportunity to take a stand against their employers for the first time, but who did so with

42. TsGIA, fond 150, op. 1, d. 646, l. 6. An effort has been made to preserve in translation the stilted syntax of the original, but the misspellings could not be reproduced.

43. Servility is to be distinguished from polite form. For an example of the latter in a workers' petition which is by no means servile, see, e.g., the Obukhov workers' letter to the plant director of January 10 in *NPRR*, p. 134.

modes of address and moral reflexes formed by the degrading and oppressive conditions of a quasi-feudal agrarian order.

In other words, whether or not some outside coercive force was in fact brought to bear on the Atlas workers on January 7, somewhere along the line (if not from the very beginning) they had decided to make a virtue of necessity and to seek to win some gains from their employer. Force and the threat of force were not only compatible with the perception of positive reasons for striking; they could even serve as a bargaining point once the strikers returned to work and had to face a victorious employer. The ploy used by the Atlas strikers was probably not uncommon among other January strikers who reportedly struck as a result of external force, and it indicates simply that the struggle in the factories could and did take many forms. Although the petition involved a servile posture and an appeal to an image of industrial workers that was rapidly becoming obsolete, it can also be read as embodying a realistic, adversarial view of modern industrial relations, concealed by a mask of Schweikian cunning.

The outcome of the January strike at Atlas is not known, but its workers went on to strike on five other occasions during 1905. As a medium-size plant[44] (225 workers) in the Schlüsselburg suburb, it was one of the smaller enterprises under the sway of the Nevsky Works and other large centers of strike ferment. Atlas workers eventually elected their own deputies and participated in the eight-hour-day campaign in November, which indicated a significant development of political consciousness from the humble petition of the January Days.

One of the factors contributing to the continuation of strikes, and therefore to continuing political turmoil among workers, was the attitude of employers. Although the practice of institutionalized bargaining and negotiation barely existed in Russian industry, and although it was not entirely in the power of employers to end the strikes, a more flexible attitude on their part could have helped end strikes with greater dispatch or, in some cases, could have avoided them altogether. How did the Petersburg factory owners respond to the January strike and to the storm of demands that arose in its course?

On the whole, they maintained a firm and united stand against all but the most unimportant demands and appealed to the government for legislative and investigative solutions that they felt were beyond their authority and competence to institute. This was evident in a se-

44. The terms "small" and "medium" will be used to refer to factories with 100 or fewer and 101–500 workers, respectively. Those with 501 or more will be called "large," and occasionally those with more than 2,000 will be set off with the term "giant."

ries of conferences held by several combinations of industrialists in January and February and from references to measures adopted at individual factories. From January 8 to 18 representatives of the St. Petersburg Society to Assist in the Improvement of Factory and Mill Industries[45] met to coordinate their strategies in response to their rebellious workers. The conference produced the following concessions:

1. Striking workers would not be fined for absenteeism.
2. The identities of instigators and strike leaders would not be sought and punitive measures would not be applied to them.
3. The Society would collect and distribute money to the families of the January 9th victims at the rate of 20 kopecks per worker.
4. In applying the above measures, no distinction would be made between those who struck independently and those who were forced to strike.

Demands for an eight-hour day, for worker participation in setting wages and in internal plant administration, and for the abolition of fines for absenteeism and strike participation were not acted upon, but were all referred to the Finance Ministry for legislative action. No demands were to be satisfied before work resumed, and no pay would be issued workers for the period of the strike. Instead, individual owners were to give grants of aid to workers in cases of extreme need.[46]

St. Petersburg's largest and most influential association of industrialists could thus bring itself to grant only one of the Putilov workers' original demands (amnesty for strikers); otherwise it in effect adopted the policy of no concessions instituted by Putilov Director Smirnov during the early days of the strike. Although these guidelines had no binding power and were probably not strictly followed in all cases, especially by the smaller owners, the urgency of the moment and the sponsorship of most of the city's biggest industrialists must have invested them with considerable authority.[47]

45. This is Sablinsky's cumbersome but correct translation of "S.-Peterburgskoe obshchestvo dlia sodeistviia uluchsheniiu i razvitiiu fabrichno-zavodskoi promyshlennosti." It is also often called the "Obshchestvo (or Sobranie) zavodchikov i fabrikantov," and it will be referred to here simply as "the Society."

46. L'vovich, "Trebovaniia rabochikh," p. 89.

47. Concessions at several factories were reported in Bolshevik leaflets on January 13 and 15. Since the aim of the leaflets was to inspire workers to continue striking, the authenticity of the reports is open to question. Most of them concerned shortening of the workday, and all other evidence indicates extreme reluctance to give way on that demand at this point. In one case the information was even attributed to rumor. *NPRR*, pp. 151–52, 160–61.

About one week later, between January 26 and 29, another series of conferences of Petersburg industrialists was held, this time bringing together only the owners of metal and machine plants. It seems to have been an ad hoc group rather than an organized body, and its unique feature was to have united the directors and managers of both private and state-owned enterprises. As in the case of the Society, this group also postponed action on the length of the workday pending a general legislative enactment. Unlike the Society, however, the metal industrialists' conferences gathered data on the workday from among the 69 plants represented and formulated guidelines on its regulation, apparently aimed at influencing any legislation that might result from the January strikes. The participants resolved that regulation of the length of the workday must be tied to the question of holidays, and that the workweek should not fall below 57 hours (five 10-hour days, and a 7-hour day on Saturdays). The metal industrialists seemed to believe that Russian workers put in fewer hours per year than their West European counterparts due to the numerous additional holidays celebrated in Russia.[48]

The metal industrialists also went further than the Society had toward responding to the separate demands raised by their strikers, thereby seeming to adopt a more conciliatory attitude. In response to the demand for a one-ruble minimum for (male) unskilled work, a norm of 80 kopecks was set. Neither overtime work nor the system of fines was abolished, but time-and-a-half payment for overtime work was established, and a uniform set of rates for fines at relatively moderate amounts was adopted. On some points the conferees responded by asserting that existing conditions at metal plants already met the demands: searches of workers leaving the plant had already been abolished at most plants, but managements were to retain the right to reinstitute them; sanitary conditions at metal plants were already superior to those prevailing in other industries; arrangements for medical care were in force at many plants, but metal plant owners would contribute to hospital funds and petition the Finance Ministry to incorporate health care in a comprehensive system of state insurance. Finally, wage raises and strike pay for apprentices were rejected, although it was noted that most plants were giving hardship grants averaging about three days of shop pay (the guaranteed minimum paid piece-rate workers).

48. L'vovich, "Trebovaniia rabochikh," pp. 90–92. L'vovich's calculations argue that Russians probably worked even more hours in the year despite the additional holidays. *Ibid.*, p. 90, n. 3.

The metal industrialists therefore displayed much more of a conciliatory attitude than the members of the Society, but the scale of the concessions they envisioned was still quite far removed from what workers were demanding. They amounted to more of a standardization and restatement of the status quo in the Petersburg metal industry, which generally enjoyed somewhat better conditions than other industries, rather than an admission that significant changes were in order. The 80-kopeck norm for unskilled work, for instance, amounted to an increase of only a few kopecks at most plants.[49] More importantly, no mention was made about granting demands that would enable workers to resist the possible retraction of the "concessions" at a later date, once the strikes had subsided. For instance, nothing is reported to have been said with respect to the election of workers' deputies and their participation in setting wages and handling grievances and dismissals, although the demand was widespread at metal plants.

A formula combining small, revocable concessions with inflexibility toward weightier demands was also adopted at a third series of conferences held within the Naval Ministry from mid-January to early February. The Ministry's responses to demands raised by workers at its shipyards and armaments plants were fairly similar to those of the metal industrialists. The conferences gave ground on some more easily conceded points, such as the time and manner of pay distribution, polite treatment of workers, and plant responsibility for damaged production, but it also specifically denied immunity of workers' deputies from dismissal.[50]

The resolutions of the first two of these conference series contained a view of the strikers' motives that may account in part for the fairly meager responses to the demands. In giving reasons for refusing strike pay, both employer groups described the strikes as a "popular disturbance" (*narodnoe volnenie*) violating the law governing hiring practices. A letter sent by the Society to the Finance Ministry on January 27 elaborated on this view:

> It is not possible to expect a lasting calm even from the complete satisfaction of all the workers' demands since the labor movement did not arise from the workers' general awareness of economic adversity, but

49. Bulkin, *Na zare*, table facing p. 52, which shows the average wage of unskilled workers at 17 large Petersburg metal plants in 1904 to have been 77 kopecks, with the range from 65 k. to 1 ruble, 10 k.

50. L'vovich, "Trebovaniia rabochikh," pp. 92–93.

was provoked and is sustained by the surrounding milieu. It is impossible to isolate workers, and to calm them by concessions will also be impossible as long as the surrounding milieu is in ferment. The government is aware of the widely developed dissatisfaction in all strata of Russian society—the press, social organizations, zemstvo and municipal self-government, [institutions of higher learning, and not only in the person of the student youth, but also in that of the professors] . . .

Joining the very ferment it had referred to, the Society ended its letter by calling for "more profound reforms of a kind affecting the whole state" (*reformy obshchegosudarstvennogo kharaktera*).[51] The passage quoted went on to protest the seeming ease with which the workers' strikes and demonstrations were achieving "everything possible and even, perhaps, more than possible under the existing regime," and the fact that "rude demonstrations were listened to more attentively than statements in line with accepted standards."

This statement is remarkable for a variety of reasons. Emanating from an employers' group commonly regarded as one of the most cautious and loyal in the country, its call for political reform is an indication of how deeply even conservative circles had been affected by the recent events. Almost as striking, the employers seemed clearly to understand that the disorder in the factories and the streets involved more than workers' stated demands. The prominence of political motives among Petersburg strikers and some of the reasons for this have already been suggested, and the further development of the Russian labor movement in 1905 would confirm the accuracy of the observation. But how did the normally pro-government Society come to play such an unexpected and unaccustomed role in favoring reform and adopting such a penetrating view of the labor movement?

Actually, both the advocacy of reform and the insight into the political nature of labor protest resulted less from a change of heart or thinking than from the employers' defense of their interests against both the government and the workers in the altered circumstances following January 9. With talk of concessions and labor commissions in the air, the employers had reason to fear that the government would seek the causes of worker discontent in factory working conditions rather than in Russia's political structure. That being the case, it followed that the government would probably try to mollify the workers and end the strikes by a new spate of labor legislation. The passage cited above was part of a longer memo to the government opposing

51. TsGIA, Fond 150, op. 1, d. 646, ll. 80–81.

new measures regulating working conditions (*normirovka uslovii raboty*). The employers had noted their energetic efforts in negotiating and granting smaller economic concessions to their workers. When it came to the more significant concessions demanded in the recent strikes, however, the employers argued that the government, not they, ought to be called upon to make them—hence the formula: political, not social, reforms; better free speech and assembly than an eight-hour-day law and regulated overtime work.

The essentially defensive nature of the employers' political posture was borne out by their stance in the labor commissions of 1905, especially the Kokovtsov Commission, where they appeared as narrow advocates of their own interests rather than as broad political reformers.[52] Moreover, their continued opposition to significant labor reforms such as a shortened workday proved to be a major source of continuing friction with their employees, and the eight-hour day came to head the demand list of practically every strike in 1905. That demand and the one for elected and empowered workers' deputies had genuine roots in the labor movement rather than in the broader liberation movement, and there can be little doubt that labor protest would have been significantly reduced in 1905 had they been granted universally and at a fairly early point.

At the same time, such an empowerment of workers would have been incongruent with an unreconstructed political order, so there was a real point and a critical edge to the employers' call for reform of the state order. Even if the employers had permitted deputies in their factories, they would not have been able to function in a state that still forbade free association, assembly, and speech. The employers' willingness to defend their interests by pointing out the prior need for political reform aligned them with the other segments of society demanding such reform. However, it is important to recall that the employers were not leading the way but responding to a situation which suddenly threatened their control of their businesses, and that, had the workers not joined the opposition, the St. Petersburg employers group would probably not have taken a position at all.

But this is to anticipate developments somewhat, for a second wave of strikes in the capital soon demonstrated to employers the autonomy as well as the tenacity of the new workers' movement and persuaded some of them at least to depart from the hardline resolutions jointly agreed upon in January.

52. Romanov, ed., *Rabochii vopros v Komissii Kokovtsova.*

FROM JANUARY TO FEBRUARY

By the last week of January most workers had ended their strikes and returned to their factories with little to show save a few minor concessions. The tense peace in the city's plants and workshops barely concealed the angry resignation with which work was resumed. This was revealed in a new wave of strikes that began in the same week and lasted through most of February. This second strike wave grew out of the first but differed from it in that it was less unified and more fragmented. It represented, in fact, a new stage in the strike movement, setting patterns and modes of struggle that remained characteristic of working-class activity in the capital throughout most of the remainder of the year.

The February strikes demonstrated once again the superior capacity of the large plants for sustained strike activity and tactical inventiveness. The week of January 24 began with a walkout by 500 workers from the Obukhov boiler shop, although they returned when their demand for higher wages was immediately met. A "general ferment" was observed at Obukhov, and demands were presented by locomotive machine-shop workers at Nevsky Ship, with talk of a strike to follow. In the Narva district the Train Car Construction workers struck on the same day (January 24), and the Voronin weavers on nearby Rezvyi Island followed suit. Across town, Cartridge Plant workers in the Liteiny district struck for higher wages and the dismissal of several foremen; but when the first demand was met, they immediately resumed work.[53] Next day at the Putilov Works, where resentment was still running high over the dismissal of 200 workers for participation in the January events, about 1,000 members of the cannon shop left work after eight hours, thus underlining their demand for a shorter workday by direct action. Over the next week, three more metal plants in separate parts of the city adopted the same tactic. This indicated that the Putilov workers were not alone in experiencing both continuing strike fever and strong back-to-work sentiment. The tactic was admirably suited to reconciling these conflicting tendencies because it preserved the unity of the whole work force while granting each part some of what it wanted. On January 26 seven other shops joined the cannon shop workers in stopping work early, while other strikes across the city continued and the Petersburg-Warsaw Railroad shops struck anew. Next day the latter resumed

53. *NPRR*, pp. 179–81. Mitel'man et al., *Istoriia Putilovskogo zavoda*, pp. 197–98.

work, while Putilov Director Smirnov granted some of his workers' demands and refused others. In response, the whole Putilov Plant struck again shortly after reporting for work on the morning of January 28, led this time by the machine-shop workers.[54]

The chief causes of this renewed strike activity were unmet demands from the strikes begun three weeks earlier as well as the continuing hopefulness and anger aroused by that earlier experience. Only now the pattern of striking was less unified and continuous, more fragmented and intermittent. In the large plants, the unevenness of strike sentiment became more noticeable, and strikes of only part of the work force more common. Strikes thus resumed almost immediately after the great upsurge of January, but they did not recapture the citywide coordination of the earlier strike, and they lacked a unifying focus beyond the issues of the separate factories. Yet it was hardly the return to normal the authorities were seeking, even for those who remained at work.

Meanwhile, some of the older patterns recurred. Once the *putilovtsy* struck, they went in crowds to seek support at neighboring factories. On January 28, workers from sixteen other plants in the Peterhof and Narva districts, many of them also still rankling over unmet demands from earlier in the month, struck at the instigation of the Putilov workers. Train Car Construction workers, on strike since January 24, marched—over 1,000 strong—to join forces with the *putilovtsy* and to aid in shutting down other factories. One of the demonstrations that resulted on the 28th was reported to have numbered 5,000. Some of these crowds of strikers were driven away by troops and police, and others were rebuffed by the workers they approached.[55]

Resistance to the appeals of strikers by non-striking workers was now much more frequent than earlier in January. The first signs of resistance began at the end of the first strike, a result of the unevenness of the desire and ability to continue that struggle. On January 14 a small group of Putilov workers tried to prevent the resumption of work at a small bindery and a medium-size metal plant on Vasilevsky Island; here the appearance of the police sufficed to disperse the demonstrators. The next day similar disputes erupted within the Paul and Maxwell cotton mills in the Schlüsselburg district and at the Kreiton Shipyard in the Okhta. The increase in such clashes indicated that strike sentiment was coming alive again in the midst of a mood

54. *NPRR*, pp. 180, 181, 185, 187–89.
55. *Ibid.*, pp. 184–89, 706.

predominantly favoring continuation of work. The Putilov strikers who visited the large Mechanized Shoe Factory (*Fabrika mekhanicheskogo proizvodstva obuvi*) on the 28th were met with "swearing and mockery" by the workers, who then asked the management to release them early that day to avoid beatings by the angry *putilovtsy* who, they assumed, would be waiting for them outside the factory gates. On January 31 about 80 workers of the Obukhov Works' projectile shop burst into the hammer shop shouting "Quit work!," but the hammer workers threw them out and continued working; the rejected strikers themselves returned to their shop and resumed work. Many similar conflicts never broke the surface or found expression in police strike reports, although the numerous references in late January and early February to "discontent" (*brozhenie*) at factories that did not immediately strike probably stemmed from discussions and agitation among workers around just such conflicts.[56] This "discontent" and these open clashes were the logical concomitants of the self-initiated eight-hour days and the stop-and-start striking of the period.

A noticeable rise in the level of violence was also characteristic of this period. A "powerful discontent" at the shops of the Petersburg-Warsaw Railroad observed on January 25 resulted in the beating of an unpopular foreman, who later refused to name his assailants for fear of further reprisals. The night before, Petr Enbert, one of the shop workers chosen to visit Tsar Nicholas on January 19 to receive his "forgiveness" for the disorders of Bloody Sunday, was also beaten by his unappreciative fellow workers. This response among railroad shop workers to the deputation to the Tsar was quite typical of the reaction of most Petersburg workers to the anachronistic notion that the workers rather than the Tsar himself required forgiveness and reflected a widespread feeling that the handpicked deputies certainly did not represent them.[57] The Putilov strikers also vented their wrath by breaking windows in some of the shops before walking out on January 28. The next day the police reported considerable anger among workers against Director Smirnov and the rumor, "not without foundation," that they wanted to kill him.[58]

In the midst of this unrest the most common demand was for payment for the days lost during the earlier strike. Surprisingly, this and

56. *Ibid.*, pp. 156–57, 160, 161, 185, 189.

57. *Novoe vremia*, Jan. 20, 1905. Schwarz, *The Russian Revolution of 1905*, pp. 78–82. Kol'tsov, "Rabochie v 1905–1907 gg.," p. 195. Verner, "Nicholas II," ch. 5, esp. pp. 18–20.

58. *NPRR*, pp. 180, 186, 188.

other demands were now more frequently satisfied than they were immediately after the first strike—indicating that the employers' guidelines discussed earlier were partly aimed at countering what the conferees viewed as a dangerous trend. Workers of the Bush and Tis Woolen Spinnery, one of the Narva district factories that struck in solidarity with the Putilov workers on January 28, even won a 10-percent pay raise and a one-hour reduction of the workday.[59] This conciliatory attitude on the part of some employers was not lost on other workers, and it undoubtedly contributed to the continuing pattern of short strikes for limited aims.

Simultaneously, however, some employers initiated a new tactic of mass dismissals followed by rehiring (immediate or delayed) during which "troublemakers" would be weeded out. This practice had not been unknown in previous years, but it now was applied more liberally, foreshadowing the lockouts of the summer and fall. Mass dismissals or management shutdowns were applied to workers at the Putilov Works on Janaury 28; at the Train Car Construction Plant on the 29th; at the Franco-Russian Works on February 1; and at the Ekaterinhof Cotton Spinnery sometime before February 10. In January, Obukhov Plant Director Vlas'ev had threatened a similar measure, adding that he would send the reservists among the workers to serve in the army. By mid-February he had apparently made good on at least the first part of the threat: a Justice Ministry communication reported on Feburary 15 that the Obukhov and Franco-Russian plants, the Nevsky Ship and Machine Works, the Russian-American Rubber Factory, and the New Cotton Spinnery had been closed by their respective managements, and that the dismissed workers would soon be rehired.[60]

The application of mass dismissals clearly signaled the frustration and desperation overtaking many employers, who now perceived that the strike movement—that "anarchistic strikism," as a prominent Bolshevik called it at the time[61]—would simply not go away. Employers and many others outside the working-class milieu apparently ex-

59. *Ibid.*, p. 194.

60. *Ibid.*, pp. 187, 188, 192–93, 194, 200, 203.

61. The Social Democrats suffered their own form of frustration at the seemingly aimless strike fever. A. Bogdanov told the Bolshevik Third Party Congress in April: "The elementally discontented attitude [too] easily goes beyond purposeful forms and is very unpurposeful. After the revolutionary weeks of January in Petersburg such an anarchistic strikism (*stachkizm*) developed that at many factories it was enough for someone of the workers to cry: 'Boys, drop your work!' and a strike began. . . . In their agita-

pected peaceful conditions to return after the great movement of January 9, which they viewed as the temporary result of the extraordinary massacre of Bloody Sunday and the excitement stirred by the Assembly's dramatic defense of the Putilov workers. Besides, the tactic of mass dismissals was used only at very large factories (the Ekaterinhof Spinnery was the smallest, with 800 workers),[62] indicating that only the better-endowed enterprises could afford to resort to it. Smaller, poorer factories had to adopt other expedients, including concessions.

The harshness of the large factory owners was matched by that of the government. General D. F. Trepov, the capital's newly appointed governor-general, clearly did not intend to relax the reinforced surveillance of the workers, whatever his long-term reform plans may have been. Indeed, on January 28 he placed a ban on the printing of news about the labor movement abroad and in areas outside the capital, pointing out that "at the present time the strike movement has begun anew among workers in the plants and factories of St. Petersburg, and in the capital's newspaper articles and notices on the labor problem bearing an incendiary and polemical character continue to appear." But that measure was only the tip of the iceberg. On the same day a memorandum from the chief of the Okhrana in Petersburg, M. I. Gurovich, informed the Director of the Police Department that

> . . . on the orders of the Governor-General, special measures will be taken beginning tomorrow for the preservation of peace and order in the capital: troop units will be stationed at striking factories, as well as at those factories where the workers' attitude seems doubtful, for the prevention of possible attempts to damage the machinery; troop units, which will remain in [their] barracks in complete readiness to intervene at the first request, will be at the disposal of the police chiefs; orders are to be issued to arrest, for the purpose of exile from the capital, the more prominent co-workers of the priest Gapon, observed inciting workers to strike, a list of which persons will be presented to Your Excellency subsequently; and, finally, at the order of the Investigative Police, all those

---

tion and propaganda Social Democrats must fight against all such anarchistic forms of struggle." *Tretii s"ezd RSDRP. Aprel'–mai 1905 goda. Protokoly,* pp. 109–10; cited in Shuster, *Peterburgskie rabochie,* p. 98.

62. For some reason, the spinnery's productivity (and probably also its profits) was extraordinarily high. In 1901 it employed 1,260 workers and produced goods worth nearly 4 million rubles, compared to, say, the New Spinnery, which employed half again as many workers that year but produced only about 2.5 million rubles worth of thread. *Spisok fabrik i zavodov evropeiskoi Rossii,* pp. 34–35.

without passports and living in the capital without personal visas will be arrested tomorrow night.[63]

Of course, no one was more aware of these measures than the workers themselves, whether of "doubtful attitude" or not. Their usual indignant reactiveness to police interference in factory disputes would be exacerbated, and the likelihood of strikes would thereby be heightened more than ever, all by order of the St. Petersburg governor-general.

63. *NPRR*, pp. 185–86.

CHAPTER FIVE

The Workers' Movement in February

The response of the government to the events of January provided the framework for the development of the Petersburg labor movement in February and beyond. After January 9, the government remained stalemated by an indecisive yet willful monarch whose moral stamina and intellectual abilities were unequal to the enormous challenges at hand, a situation that was exacerbated by disorderly lines of authority among various government agencies and personalities. Accordingly, in seeking to recover its prestige and authority after Bloody Sunday and to "restore order"—a process in which there was no shortage of wise and informed counsel—the government again adopted a set of policies toward the labor movement that promoted rather than prevented disorder and revolution.

Although the government's disastrous performance on January 9 was the responsibility of a number of officials, and although it resulted from both long-term, systemic incapacities of the autocracy and short-term mistakes and oversights, the government placed the immediate blame at the door of Petersburg City Governor Fullon and Interior Minister Sviatopolk-Mirskii, both of whose resignations were accepted within a week of the massacre. St. Petersburg was made a governor-generalship, increasing the powers of Fullon's successor. For this post, the Tsar chose Dmitrii F. Trepov, the hard-line former Moscow police chief and a member of Nicholas's favored inner circle called the "Horse Guard Party." To aid him in "restoring order" in the capital, Trepov was given extraordinary powers under a martial law regime declared two days after his appointment. In fact if not in law, Trepov now became the virtual dictator of St. Petersburg.[1]

Together with this firm posture, both Nicholas and his closest advisers felt some kind of conciliatory statement was in order, explaining the government's understanding of the tragedy and how it would respond. From the beginning, Nicholas was primarily interested in reasserting his personal authority with his people, reassuring them of his ongoing paternal concern for them, and clearing the good name of his august office in the eyes of his subjects. His most influential ministers agreed with this and were even more solicitous of the need to repair whatever damage may have been done to the myth of the "little father Tsar," encouraging him to separate his good intentions from those of his bungling ministers, who were to take the blame for the massacre. They felt in addition that the Tsar should take decisive action to restore order before the autocracy's reputation in the eyes of foreign governments and money markets suffered any further damage.

But the planning discussions of the Tsar's statement also became the occasion for an outpouring of concern about what needed to be done to avoid the recurrence of similar disasters. A number of his advisers thought the Tsar should address the people's needs and just grievances by introducing fundamental reforms. Talk of some kind of *zemskii sobor* or popular representative body was renewed, now even by such eminent personages as Grand Duke Peter, the Tsar's brother-in-law. Finance Minister Kokovtsov viewed the entire Gapon episode as the result of the clash of capital and labor and believed quite plausibly that the Tsar should address the question of the workers' needs by better enforcement of existing laws and by support of the new labor legislation his ministry was preparing. Others, including Agriculture Minister A. S. Ermolov, stressed that the massacre highlighted the tangled and conflicting jurisdictions within the bureaucracy; they argued that a more unified and centralized government should be created through a restructuring of the highest organs of rule. Nicholas appeared to agree with both Kokovtsov and Ermolov on the need for reforms and on the need to refurbish the paternalistic ideology of the autocracy. And yet he was soon acting in a manner that not only contradicted these views, but that actually demonstrated the force of the

1. *Krizis samoderzhaviia v Rossii, 1895–1917*, pp. 174–75. Smolin, "Pervaia russkaia revoliutsiia v Peterburge," p. 273.

argument that the government was too disunited to speak with a single voice.[2]

Before the discussions of the issues bearing on the Tsar's public statement had concluded, Nicholas had 34 carefully chosen factory workers brought to him at Tsarskoe Selo. There, on January 19, he lectured them on the need to obey their masters and on the criminality of the January 9 demonstration, while promising an improvement for workers in the vague and noncommital terms that were the hallmark of his public statements. He warned them that if similar "disorders" were repeated, he would again order his soldiers to shoot. Instead of reassuring even this small group of his concern for his people, he unfeelingly brought out another aspect of his paternal role by actually expressing *his forgiveness* of his loving subjects for the contrition they must feel for the January 9 disorders. Although it is debatable whether any statement by the Tsar at this time could have tempered the grief and anger felt by so many Petersburg workers, this clumsy and insensitive gesture only succeeded in convincing most observers of the Tsar's continuing lack of concern for his subjects' welfare. Nicholas possessed neither the genuine feelings nor the political artistry needed to dispel the actual truth of the matter.[3]

The inspirer of the January 19 audience was General Trepov, who had lost no time in moving to the center of decision-making in the government, taking advantage of his closeness to the Tsar to circumvent the process of discussion among the ministers. On January 18, while the need for some kind of investigative body on the January 9 events was still under discussion, it was Trepov again who proposed to the Tsar the appointment of a commission to study the causes of worker dissatisfaction, comprising representatives of government, industry, and labor. The proposal was made in full knowledge and in deliberate contravention of the labor reforms then being prepared by the Finance Ministry. Trepov explained this as an effort to bring a broader and more comprehensive perspective to bear on the question of labor reforms, but the old rivalry between the Finance Ministry and Interior Ministry, of which Trepov was a product, was quite appar-

2. My account of the plans and debates of the government following January 9 summarizes the more nuanced and detailed analysis by Verner, "Nicholas II and the Role of the Autocrat," ch. 5, pp. 1–18.

3. *Ibid.*, pp. 19–20. *Novoe vremia*, Jan. 20, 1905. Schwarz, *The Russian Revolution of 1905*, pp. 78–82. Kol'tsov, "Rabochie v 1905–1907," p. 195. G. M. Derenkovskii et al., *Revoliutsiia 1905–1907 godov v Rossii* (M., 1975), p. 60.

ent.[4] Kokovtsov made this clear in his own "most humble report" to the Tsar the next day, in which he argued that the interference of the Interior Ministry in labor relations during the past quarter century (which included the multiple Zubatovshchina fiascoes) had increased labor militancy and impeded the simple redress of material grievances to which the Finance Ministry's reforms were addressed.[5]

Nicholas again appeared to agree with Kokovtsov's defense of his ministry's competence in the area of labor reform and with the need to free labor relations of interference from the Interior Ministry and the police. Nevertheless, on January 28, the day the Committee of Ministers was due to discuss Kokovtsov's report on labor reform, the Tsar commended to Witte as if it were his own Trepov's idea of a special commission on the needs of labor, headed by a respected figure from the State Council, and consisting of representatives of government, industry, and labor. He asked Witte to discuss the proposal with the ministers along with Kokovtsov's memorandum, which was not to be published. Here again was evidence of the initiative of Trepov, who had visited the Tsar the night before to urge him to support his plans over Kokovtsov's.[6] The Tsar followed up his request to Witte by issuing an Imperial Order (*vysochaishee povelenie*), establishing the investigative commission originally sought by Trepov and placing it under the chairmanship of Senator N. V. Shidlovskii. A report of the Committee of Ministers' meetings of January 28 and 31 leaves the clear impression that most of the ministers favored and supported Kokovtsov's January 19 memorandum, but that they then bowed to the Tsar's will by calling for both the Shidlovskii Commission *and* Kokovtsov's work to go forward, covering the nakedness of the compromise by praising the quality of the information on workers' needs that would be gathered from both employer and worker representatives and calling for the closest possible cooperation between the two projects.[7]

The Shidlovskii Commission was to confine itself to the workers

4. Verner, "Nicholas II," ch. 5, pp. 20–22. To my knowledge, Verner is the first to have clearly linked the origins of what became the Shidlovskii Commission to Trepov, although suggestions of the link have been made before. His documentation comes from two of the General's "most humble reports" (*vsepoddanneishie doklady*) to the Tsar, dated January 18 and 27: TsGAOR, fond 543, op. 1, delo 510, ll. 3–5.

5. Romanov, ed., *Rabochii vopros v komissii V. N. Kokovtsova v 1905 g.*, pp. 1–18.

6. Verner, "Nicholas II," ch. 5, pp. 22–23.

7. Romanov, ed., *Rabochii vopros*, pp. 18–34. Cf. Verner, "Nicholas II," ch. 5, p. 24.

and employers of St. Petersburg.[8] This was an obvious choice insofar as St. Petersburg was the place where workers' needs had been most recently and forcefully expressed, but it was a poor one if the government hoped to find a docile and cooperative work force that was ready to play along with its plans.

THE SHIDLOVSKII COMMISSION ELECTIONS

Soon after the announcement of the Commission and well before the election rules had been published, workers began to act on the news. As early as February 1 workers at one of the Cheshire cotton mills presented Senator Shidlovskii with a petition requesting their own system of elections, which included the following points:

1. Reopening the eleven locals of the Assembly closed by the government on January 10.
2. Election of deputies to take place in the locals, with representation on the basis of one deputy from every factory with less than 500 workers; two from those with more than 500; one additional deputy for every 1,000 workers at factories with 2,000 or more workers; and one deputy from each local.
3. The right to free elections and to elect nonworkers as well as workers to the Commission.

The petition went on to state that only under these conditions would those elected be considered "spokesmen for the needs of the whole working class, and only then could an agreement be reached that would bring peace and order into the relations existing between workers and entrepreneurs." They threatened to refuse participation in the Commission if a system of elections favorable to employers and bureaucrats were adopted, and they observed that such an arrangement would only bring greater unrest to the ranks of workers.[9]

Over the next several days—that is, before official election procedures were announced on February 7—workers at factories in almost every part of the city submitted similar petitions to Shidlovskii. They came from large and small enterprises, representing principally the

8. Schwarz, *The Russian Revolution of 1905*, pp. 86–88, gives the most comprehensive and balanced account of the Shidlovskii Commission campaign (pp. 75–128). See also Kol'tsov, "Rabochie 1905–1907," pp. 195–200; Shuster, *Peterburgskie rabochie*, pp. 96–112; Nevskii, "Vybory v komissiiu senatora Shidlovskogo (1905 g.)"; Perazich, "Tekstil'shchiki v komissii Shidlovskogo"; Kniazeva and Inozemtsev, "K istorii rabochikh vyborov v Komissiiu Shidlovskogo" [documents].

9. Kniazeva and Inozemtsev, "K istorii rabochikh vyborov," pp. 192–93.

metal and cotton textile industries; all demanded free elections and the reopening of the eleven locals; and all made some kind of threat, veiled or open, should the "requests" not be met. Some added demands for the immunity of the deputies from prosecution, for publication of the Commission's proceedings, and for the release of all comrades arrested since January 1, 1905. Many of the petitions expressed a concern that workers be accorded the freedom to discuss the Commission's work at their own meetings and that small factories as well as large be represented. The style in which the petitions were written also varied, some being supplicatory and indirect, others more blunt and businesslike, sounding much like the list of demands that had emerged during the January strike. The Train Car Construction workers' petitions, for instance, dispensed with the form of address "Your Excellency" used in the Cheshire petition, demanded not just the opening but the "immediate opening" of the 11 locals, and contained all the additions just mentioned plus the most explicit breakdown of the kinds of freedom of expression required for the effective functioning of the Commission.[10]

The ubiquity of the demand for the reopening of the 11 locals was a dramatic statement of the hope, trust, and affection that so many Petersburg workers had invested in the Assembly. It is difficult to establish the precise range of feelings toward the Assembly among workers at this time, but there can be no doubt that for most they were strong, vital, and positive. It is significant that all the petitions insisted that the *locals* be reopened rather than that the Assembly be reconstituted or Gapon returned to lead it. Only two petitions even mentioned the Assembly (none mentioned Gapon), and then erroneously, calling it the "Union of Factory and Plant Workers"; the others referred simply to the "eleven locals" (*otdely*). The petitioners apparently expected the Shidlovskii deputies to function as a leadership for which the locals would serve as points of contact, where the rank and

10. *Ibid.*, pp. 193–94. Aside from the Cheshire and Train Car workers' petitions there are petitions from seven other factories and three other groupings of workers in TsGIA, fond 1205, op. XVI t., 1905, delo 1, ll. 47, 133–43, 148. The factories involved were the Franco-Russian Works, the Putilov Works, the Leont'ev Textile Printing Factory, the Kozhevnikov Wadding and Weaving Factory, the Aleksandrovsk Machine Works (and shops of the Nikolaev Railroad), the Ozoling Wrought Iron and Metal Plant, and the Baltic Shipyard. This list is not necessarily exhaustive, since workers at other enterprises may have drafted similar petitions that did not find their way to this particular *fond*. Some of the petitions were published in the St. Petersburg newspapers at the time. That of the Putilov workers appears in Okun', ed., *Putilovets v trekh revoliutsiiakh*, pp. 100–101.

file could hear news of the deliberations in the Commission, hold discussions, and instruct the deputies. When this is considered along with the concern for the "constant exchange of ideas between representatives and workers" frequently mentioned in the petitions, one catches a glimpse of the formation of a fresh and radical vision of workers' democracy, framed by the experience of the Assembly and invested with a sense of self-reliance drawn from the ongoing strike movement and the newly deepened distrust of the government. Petersburg workers were not only organizing but reaching out toward new organizational forms, of which the Soviet of Workers' Deputies would later prove to be the most developed and popular embodiment.

The promptness with which these petitions appeared, as well as the uniformity of the demands, was due in part to the efforts of two Petersburg lawyers of left Liberationist views, Emmanuil Margulies and Georgii Stepanovich Nosar'. Although their advice to the worker petitioners was similar and was given at about the same time, and although it seems likely that they knew one another, it is not known whether they worked together. Nosar' soon took a leading role in the Shidlovskii campaign and will be discussed at greater length below. Margulies's story is somewhat briefer and simpler. He was arrested on the night of February 3 with copies of the Cheshire petition in his possession. Police agents reported that he had met in his office with nine workers on February 1, encouraging them to agitate for the reopening of the 11 locals and for permission to elect deputies from the intelligentsia as well as from workers. Margulies's efforts have been portrayed in Soviet accounts as *the* inspiration for the demand to reopen the locals, as if his advice did not also meet with a groundswell of enthusiasm from the workers themselves.[11]

In truth, the exact extent of Margulies' influence is not known. Did he himself suggest the demand for the reopening of the locals, or did he only write up what the workers requested, adding perhaps the point on the inclusion of nonworkers? The police documents on the subject note that he told the nine workers about the presentation of

11. For example, Kniazeva and Inozemtsev, "K istorii rabochikh vyborov," p. 193, note; Mitel'man et al., *Istoriia Putilovskogo zavoda*, p. 205; TsGAOR, fond 124, op. 43, d. 1741, 1905, l. 1; and Perazich, "Tekstil'shchiki," p. 54. One variation in Soviet writings on the subject has been simply to ignore the demand for the reopening of the locals, e.g., Nevskii, "Vybory v komissiiu," pp. 84–85, and Smolin, "Pervaia russkaia revoliutsiia," pp. 275–78. Cf. Schwarz, who mentions Margulies as a "guiding hand," but does not lose sight of the fact that the popularity of the demand also showed "how much the workers felt the need for organized unity." *The Revolution of 1905*, pp. 91, 123.

both demands by a delegation of four workers from the Petersburg district on the same day (probably referring to the Cheshire workers' petition), but they do not state who originated which demands and do not describe the nature of Margulies's relations with the four delegates. But even if Margulies or Nosar' (who was close to the Cheshire workers) or some other *intelligent* had authored all the demands, they clearly expressed sentiments that already enjoyed widespread sympathy and support among workers.[12]

The bulk of the energy and inspiration for the petition campaign originated with the workers themselves. It was certainly workers who distributed the demands among other factories after Margulies was arrested on February 3 (petitions continued to appear through the 6th). The variations in the wording of different factories' petitions indicates that they were rewritten, and even rethought, at each petitioning factory. The fact that five of the nine workers who met with Margulies came from the Putilov Works suggests that the extensive contacts formed during the January strike by Putilov workers were being used to distribute the petition among the city's factories. In addition, one of the petitions emanated from "Deputies of the 6th Section, Assembly of Factory and Plant Workers," apparently a core of members from the old Kolomensk branch that had maintained a clandestine existence.[13] This shows that the survival of interest in the Assembly even took organized form, and it raises the possibility that the organization's network of interbranch acquaintances and relations was used to build the campaign of critical enthusiasm with which workers greeted the Shidlovskii Commission.

And enthusiastic it was. The Petersburg Menshevik organizer S. I. Somov (I. A. Peskin) wrote that "the Shidlovskii Commission elicited great excitement among workers, and at the time workers animatedly discussed problems connected with it everywhere—at home, at work, in taverns, in the street—eagerly attended mass meetings, joined circles, attended the legal meetings of various unions, and everywhere asked insistent questions about their tactics in this Commission."[14] At a number of factories deputy elections were held prior to publication of

12. Kniazeva and Inozemtsev, "K istorii rabochikh vyborov," pp. 179–80. Okun', ed., *Putilovets*, pp. 98–100. Putilov workers requested elected deputies from their shop foremen apparently earlier in the same day Margulies met with the nine workers. LGIA, fond 2075, op. 6, d. 101, l. 6.

13. TsGIA, fond 1205, op. XVI t., 1905, delo 1, l. 137.

14. Somov, "Iz istorii," p. 45, as cited and translated in Schwarz, *The Revolution of 1905*, note, pp. 97–99.

the election rules, a practice encouraged by some employers and even, in one case, by the police. "On January 31 the police proposed to the large number of workers gathered in front of the Putilov Works to elect deputies, then and there, to take part in the special commission," while at the Paul cotton mill, where several days later the workers halted work in order to elect deputies, the management offered them a meeting place in the factory. Premature elections were also held at the Sampson Spinning and Weaving Factory on the Vyborg Side, the Neva Thread Factory in Rozhdestvensk district, the Russian-American Rubber Factory in the Narva district, and at several plants in the Schlüsselburg district.[15]

At many of the same factories seized by enthusiasm at the prospect of a new citywide labor organization, and at many others which have not left written evidence of such interest, strikes continued during the first three weeks of February. They followed the pattern already described: short, sharp outbreaks, sometimes recurring after a few days, sometimes involving only part of the work force, and everywhere raising more limited demands than earlier.[16]

What was the relationship of the reviving strike movement to the Shidlovskii campaign? Generally speaking, they fed and enlarged each other by promising to link the felt need to correct abuses and injustices of the workplace with the election of deputies, thereby empowering workers to better control their work lives. Those on strike or recently returned from one were more likely to welcome the elections and vice versa. Workers of the Paul Textile Mills and the Baltic Shipyard struck briefly in connection with election procedures. Those on strike at the Russian-American Rubber Factory in early February petitioned Shidlovskii directly to intervene with the management on their behalf to help them win their demands, which they listed in the petition;[17] later they joined other workers in taking a more militant stand toward the Commission. The promise of legal factory representation was particularly important among cotton textile workers, whose long-standing need and willingness to strike were frustrated by their limited opportunities to organize at the factory level. Simultane-

---

15. Schwarz, *The Revolution of 1905*, p. 89 (quoted from *Russkie vedomosti*, Feb. 1, 1905). Perazich, "Tekstil'shchiki," p. 45. Shuster, *Peterburgskie rabochie*, p. 102.

16. Further documentation and description may be found in *NPRR*, pp. 189–209; Shuster, *Peterburgskie rabochie*, pp. 96–97; and Perazich, "Tekstil'shchiki," note, pp. 46–47.

17. *NPRR*, p. 196. Kniazeva and Inozemtsev, "K istorii rabochikh vyborov," pp. 191–92.

ously with their premature petitions to the Commission, a rash of strikes broke out among them. Between February 4 and 8, eleven mills were struck.[18]

Hence not only did workers not moderate their strike fever in response to the announcement of the Commission, as the government hoped they would; in fact, their strike fever increased. At the larger machine and metal plants, the strike movement linked to unmet demands from the January Days was still the dominant concern. At Nevsky Ship and Machine Works, Director Ivan Hippius averted a strike on February 4 after a walkout in the steam engine shop by negotiating with the plant's deputies for two hours. The deputies took the extreme position that their key "economic" demands—an eight-hour day and worker participation in setting wage rates—were inseparable from their political demands: freedom of speech, press, assembly, and unionization, personal immunity, and equality before the law. Unless the latter were satisfied, there would be no end to strikes! Hippius replied that it was not in his power to grant the political demands, but that the workers had reason to hope that they would be taken up by the forthcoming Shidlovskii Commission. After Hippius promised to communicate with the Finance Minister on the deputies' behalf, work at the plant resumed. But the next day, workers from the same steam engine shop stopped work again and, defying the appeals of both Hippius and their own deputies, left the plant. The only reason that the Director could discern for the walkout was expressed by one of the departing workers, who said that they were striking in support of the Putilov workers, who were gaining their political rights. On Monday, February 7, after workers in all the shops had met with their deputies, a walkout of the whole plant took place, this time in agreement with the deputies. The frustrated Hippius concluded that "our workers were under the influence of some foreign element, and that their own decisions were not voluntary, but dictated to them by some kind of outside leaders."[19]

One of the most interesting aspects of this episode was that the rank-and-file workers were more intransigent and less willing to postpone strikes and entrust demands to the deliberations of the Commission than were their deputies. At some of the large metal plants, therefore, it was possible to attribute much of the continuing strike ferment to a kind of mass insurgency. Somov noted a similar phe-

18. Perazich, "Tekstil'shchiki," p. 46.
19. Kniazeva and Inozemtsev, "K istorii rabochikh vyborov," pp. 182–85.

nomenon among the Putilov workers in February. There, too, shop deputies had been elected in January and, in the course of negotiations with management, had won a number of important concessions; "but the factory masses [through their] strikes constantly drove their representatives to new demands," and kept the plant in perpetual turmoil.[20]

The struggle at the Putilov Plant was still, in many ways, at the heart of the Petersburg strike movement, having been linked in the public mind with the tragedy and pathos of Bloody Sunday. And while the movement among the *putilovtsy* incorporated some of the features of strikes mentioned earlier, it was also, by virtue of its greater intensity and tenacity, a partial exception. Beginning January 28, Putilov workers struck for one week; then on February 6 they voted to submit a new list of demands, but to return to work while awaiting a reply. The demands included most of those first raised on January 3 and 4 but added many new ones, mostly of a detailed "economic" nature. Director Smirnov announced his reply on February 10, granting half of the list of 22 demands, compromising or temporizing on seven, and refusing four. The demands he turned down were the eight-hour day, payment for strike time, payment of allowances for length of service, and either abolition of overtime (or payment of double wages for it). Although some may have considered this an acceptable offer, a reasonable first step in a much longer struggle, the bulk of the workers rejected the proffered compromise and struck again on February 11. The message of the mass insurgency seemed to be "all or nothing."[21]

An interesting feature of Smirnov's offer was his willingness to accept the demand for immunity of workers' deputies, a place to meet, and participation of their representatives in the plant's accident compensation commission. In addition, even before the strike had begun on January 28, Smirnov had agreed to accept the participation of workers' deputies in setting certain wage rates in the plant, a point he reiterated in his February 10 reply.[22] Hence, even when the manager of a major plant was willing to make significant concessions of both substance and principle, it proved insufficient to stop a strike. It was not as if the *putilovsty* were uninterested in legitimizing their own deputies. They had been among those workers who had petitioned Shidlovskii to base elections on the reopening of the 11 locals, and

20. Somov, "Iz istorii," p. 46.

21. *NPRR*, pp. 196–201.

22. *Ibid.*, p. 181. The demands and Smirnov's reply are also published in Okun', ed., *Putilovets*, pp. 91–96.

on February 6 had held a premature election of deputies to the Commission. The same deputies had even presented Smirnov the latest set of demands.

Why then did the strikers turn down Smirnov's offer, which would have strengthened the legitimate authority of their own deputies in management decision-making? No clear-cut answer suggests itself. Undoubtedly, some workers felt that the eight-hour day and the various wage demands Smirnov refused to satisfy were important enough to warrant continuation of the strike. Quite possibly, his concession on deputies was seen by the workers as nothing more than compliance with the spirit of the Shidlovskii Commission (even though the offer went beyond that) and not as the full measure of justice they felt the situation required. As ever in Russian labor relations, there was no guarantee that today's concession might not be retracted tomorrow. Most of all, the refusal of the offer expressed the workers' continuing anger at and distrust of the management. Whatever hope they might have taken in the Shidlovskii Commission, they seemed to feel that they had an older and more urgent score to settle.

For most Petersburg workers, then, the Shidlovskii campaign did not suspend or moderate the strike movement, but heated up the atmosphere and helped them to recover their fighting mettle. On February 13 elections were held in hundreds of plants and factories, posing directly to the majority of industrial workers for the first time the question of worker leadership and focusing their attention on the debate about the Commission in general and the February 18 electors' meeting in particular.

Election procedures were not as orderly or regulated as the election rules specified. Some factories voted on February 12th, some after the 13th. Workers at some larger metal plants proposed that deputies they had already elected during strikes become their Shidlovskii electors. Though the rules permitted women workers to take part in elections, they were not to be chosen as electors; nevertheless, women electors were chosen at some factories. Foremen (*mastera*) and their assistants and apprentices, along with management personnel, were not eligible to become electors; nevertheless, some of the former were elected and later had to be disqualified. The rules requiring at least one year of service at the factory and a minimum age of 25 for electors were likewise violated.[23]

23. Schwarz, *The Revolution of 1905*, pp. 93–94. Perazich, "Tekstil'shchiki," pp. 48–50. Shuster, *Peterburgskie rabochie*, p. 102. TsGIA, fond 1205, op. XVI, d. 2, ll. 150–51. Kniazeva and Inozemtsev, "K istorii rabochikh vyborov," pp. 168–71. Later, a group of women published a protest against the exclusion of women as electors, claiming that

These details reveal how eagerly the workers adopted the spirit if not the letter of factory representation, how ready they were to do something for themselves and in their own manner. In some cases factories and groups of workers excluded by the official rules petitioned to be included in the elections and in the Commission.[24] In other cases, however, workers failed to hold elections or held them among only part of the work force.[25] Many workers assumed that the electors would probably be arrested, and they accepted or refused the responsibility of serving accordingly. Almost every election meeting at the Putilov Works is reported to have ended with the words, "We solemnly promise our representatives to look after their families." In another vein, one of the elector candidates at the Paul textile factory, Zaitsev, withdrew with the plea, "I do not want to betray my workers."[26]

The spirit of boycott expressed by Zaitsev was the instinctive response of a small group of politically experienced workers long present in Petersburg. To those workers and intellectuals who viewed the labor movement as aimed at the overthrow of autocracy and the establishment of socialism, the Shidlovskii Commission seemed like another Assembly, i.e., an attempt to turn workers from their revolutionary destiny, a "Commission of Government Hocus-Pocus," as *Vpered* called it. Solomon Schwarz has shown that both the Bolshevik and Menshevik factions initially reacted to the Commission by favoring a boycott. Before they took a public position, however, each group had recognized the need to participate in the elections, to use them as a "platform for agitation," in the Menshevik phrase, but to refuse participation in the Commission itself until certain demands were met.

"when your Commission was announced, our hearts beat with hope." Internal evidence indicates that the authors were bourgeois moderates rather than women workers or revolutionaries. *Ibid.*, p. 195. A complete list of the 417 electors eventually chosen by the workers is available in TsGIA, fond 1205, op. XVI, d. 2. This list, giving names, trades, and factories of the electors and grouped in nine industrial categories, will be referred to here as the "Shidlovskii File." A discussion of the composition of the electors may be found in Surh, "Petersburg Workers in 1905," pp. 331–35.

24. See the petition from silk weavers at six shops, none of which had more than the requisite 100 workers: TsGIA, fond 1205, op. XVI t., 1905, delo 1, l. 133; and the requests of workers at the Sestroretsk Armaments Plant (outside the city) for inclusion in the Commission elections, the refusal of which occasioned a strike: *NPRR*, pp. 201–3.

25. TsGIA, fond 1205, op. XVI, d. 2, ll. 62, 143, 144, 150–51, 172. Shuster, *Peterburgskie rabochie*, p. 102. Among the factories failing or refusing to hold elections were the Aleksandrovsk Machine Works, the Ekval Machine Works, the Kersten Knitting Factory, and the Kibbel' Lithography and Box Factory.

26. Mitel'man et al., *Istoriia Putilovskogo zavoda*, p. 206. Perazich, "Tekstil'shchiki," pp. 49–50. Piskarev, "Vospominaniia chlena Peterburgskogo soveta rabochikh deputatov 1905 g.," p. 102.

The Social Democrats, realistically recognizing their lack of a sizable following among workers, wisely tailored their position to parallel closely that taken by the workers themselves in their earliest petition to Shidlovskii.[27]

The tactic proved a notable success for both the socialists and the workers. Both Bolsheviks and Mensheviks flooded the factories with their leaflets, and because the election rules forbade the presence of police, factory inspectors, or management personnel at the electoral meetings, both factions sent scores of agitators to address the meetings. This represented the first *mass* exposure of the Petersburg proletariat to socialists, and it advanced the fortunes of the revolutionaries considerably. Once the two Social Democratic factions joined the campaign, their activity was very similar, and workers could not tell them apart. But because the tactics of the party agitators paralleled those of non-party leaders, more workers found it easier to agree with what was said by the former and to allay their fears of the revolutionaries, while the agitators were able to draw the wider lessons of the Shidlovskii campaign and to acquaint the workers with a revolutionary viewpoint. At a number of factories the police intervened at meetings to arrest revolutionary speakers, giving participants a direct political lesson about the impossibility of genuinely inviolable meetings in the absence of more widely guaranteed freedoms, and in some cases workers fought the police to protect their speakers from arrest.[28]

27. "Komissiia gosudarstvennykh fokusov," *Vpered*, no. 8, Feb. 15, 1905, in *NPRR*, pp. 204–6. Schwarz, *The Revolution of 1905*, pp. 97–98, 104. Schwarz's generally excellent account of the Shidlovskii Commission episode is not evenhanded in its assessment of the initial reactions of the two SD factions to the Commission. Although he shows that they both began by favoring the boycott, then subsequently adapted themselves to the enthusiasm prevailing among workers, he claims that the Mensheviks did so out of attention to political realities and faithfulness to principle, while the Bolsheviks' Petersburg Committee gave up the idea of proclaiming outright boycott "only because it was forced to."

Without going into the differences between Bolsheviks and Mensheviks or the reasons for the greater success and popularity of the latter in Petersburg in 1905, the fundamental political fact for most active Petersburg workers was their refusal or inability to accept or comprehend the differences between the two factions. Among many such examples, see the protest of a Petersburg "Group of Metal Plant Workers" against the split in the party, and a similar appeal for unity from workers at a Narva district Bolshevik meeting in, respectively, *Vpered*, no. 14, Apr. 12, 1905, and *Proletarii*, no. 8, July 17, 1905.

In fairness to Schwarz, it should be noted that he was concerned with setting straight a record that has been systematically distorted by Bolshevik and Soviet historians, who have not been as scrupulous as Schwarz in thoroughly documenting accusations against their old rivals or even fully describing their ideas.

28. Perazich, "Tekstil'shchiki," p. 49. Schwarz, *The Revolution of 1905*, pp. 109, 111, 112. Shuster, *Peterburgskie rabochie*, p. 104. Nevskii, "Vybory v komissiiu Shidlovskogo,"

Workers also gained from the collaboration of the socialists. A large group of organized and articulate allies was acquired, providing them with a network of trained speakers who both sympathized with the upsurge of sentiment for democratic labor organization and understood the political pitfalls of placing faith in the government's good intentions. Worker morale also benefitted from the reinforcement educated activists lent to the meaningfulness of their strike activity. The socialists' broad political interpretation of the workers' anger and suspicion toward government and employers provided not only understanding, but also reassurance and reaffirmation that their actions were supported by educated persons.

Events came to a rapid conclusion during the week of February 14. The meeting of electors to choose the deputies to the Commission was scheduled for Friday, February 18. At the threat of boycott by the electors, Shidlovskii gave permission for preliminary meetings (on February 16 and 17), where deputies would be able to meet and discuss their demands.[29] Seven of the nine branches of industry into which the electors were divided met on February 16 in the Countess Panina House; the metalworkers met separately at Nobel House, and the ninth group (explosives workers) did not show up. The seven-branch meeting, under the chairmanship of the lawyer Georgii Nosar' (who had gained admission by assuming the identity of the textile elector Petr A. Khrustalev) began by expelling the police and right-wing press from the meeting. Then it proceeded to work out a set of demands closely paralleling the fuller versions of the petitions first sent to Shidlovskii by factories and other worker groups during the week of January 31. The major points of their Declaration were as follows:

1. In order to have a place freely to discuss workers' needs and to communicate with deputies, the "first and principal demand is the *immediate opening of the 11 plant and factory locals.*"
2. All the deputies must be present at general sessions of the Commission and not be called in small groups for questioning; that deputies enjoy complete freedom of speech in the Commission; and that Commission sessions be public, i.e., that accounts of them be published in the press without censorship.

---

pp. 87–88. For evidence of the quantity and quality of Social Democratic contacts with factory workers in this period, see *Peterburgskie Bol'sheviki v period pod"ema*, pp. 181–87; and Somov, "Iz istorii," pp. 45–52.

29. Perazich, "Tekstil'shchiki," p. 53, assigns the initiative in winning the preliminary meetings to metalworkers and, indirectly, to the Bolsheviks. No evidence for this assertion is cited, however, and none has been found elsewhere.

3. The deputies are to enjoy complete freedom of opinion and not be held accountable for their statements to the Commission. No confidence in the immunity of deputies from imprisonment until the release of all comrades arrested since January 1 for defending worker interests. [A list of such persons was appended.]

4. An additional election is to be held for workers in small shops, presently excluded from the Commission, on the basis of one representative from each factory local.

5. Unless a *"positive answer . . . to all our stated demands"* is received by 12 noon, February 18, 1905, *"we refuse to elect deputies."*[30]

The seven-branch meeting thus confined its demands to the functioning of the Commission itself and did not explicitly link its fate to wider social and political questions, although the need for societywide civil liberties was implicit in the declaration. A partial correction was added the next day by the metal and explosives workers (who had apparently met in the meantime). They stated their support for the seven-branch Declaration, adding demands for the personal inviolability of *all* workers in discussing their needs and for the inviolability of workers' homes. A strike was also threatened for February 19 in the event of an unfavorable answer.[31]

The metalworkers' electors were the most receptive to broader political demands and took the most militant approach to the Commis-

30. Perazich, "Tekstil'shchiki," pp. 53–55, claims that the basis of the "Declaration" was formed by Bolshevik and Menshevik "demands of public and legal guarantees," to which the demand for the reopening of the eleven locals was added from the earlier workers' petitions. However, the claim does not stand up to a careful comparison of the Declaration with the earlier petitions, which also asked for public guarantees. Social Democratic leaflets, on the other hand, only underlined and recapitulated these earlier demands and added general economic and political demands. For the text of the Declaration: Kniazeva and Inozemtsev, "K istorii rabochikh vyborov," pp. 196–97; Schwarz, *The Revolution of 1905*, pp. 114–15; and *Peterburgskie bol'sheviki v period pod"ema*, pp. 187–88. For the Social Democratic leaflets, see the last cited work, pp. 177–81, and *1905 god v Peterburge*, vol. I, *Sotsialdemokraticheskie listovki*, pp. 84–87, 101–20. One Menshevik leaflet even called for the reopening of the eleven Assembly locals: *ibid.*, p. 101.

31. Kniazeva and Inozemtsev, "K istorii rabochikh vyborov," pp. 197–98. A description of the meetings of February 16 and 17 by the Okhrana is printed on pp. 198–99, but see also Schwarz, *The Revolution of 1905*, pp. 112–20, which is more complete and accurate. A draft of the metalworker group's separate resolution reveals a strong and exclusive concern with political rights. However, sharp disagreements over this exclusivity apparently occurred at both the seven-branch and the metalworkers' meetings, and a majority at the former reportedly even opposed it. LGIA, fond 2075, op. 6, d. 101, ll. 9–11.

sion. They not only pressed for the February 17 meeting of all the electors, they also broadened the demands of the seven-branch Declaration to include immunity for all workers and added the threat of a strike. Their own group meeting on the 16th witnessed stormy political speeches on the position of workers, the war, and the autocracy. All political factions had their say—constitutional monarchists, moderates, and revolutionaries. The Liberationist worker Ivan Makeev presided over the meeting, which passed a Bolshevik resolution on the Commission and probably heard another, broader political manifesto authored by the Mensheviks. The result of all this activity was not so very different from that of the seven-branch meeting, judging by the actual resolutions passed and the action taken, but the mood of the metalworkers' meeting was altogether more political, more *engagé*.[32] Not surprisingly, the greater energy and political appetite of the metalworkers was communicated to the other deputies on February 17 and helped to strengthen their resolve.

On February 18 the electors once again came to the Countess Panina House, where they found Shidlovskii's reply to their declarations posted on the locked doors. He granted freedom of speech and opinion in statements made to the Commission, conceded the right of all workers' deputies to be present at its sessions, and promised to provide for discussion of the needs of workers at small enterprises. But he found that the other demands were beyond the competence of the Commission and therefore required no answer from him. The electors then went to their separate branch meetings, where seven of the nine branches, as promised, refused to elect deputies. Except for Shidlovskii's final report and the Tsar's cancellation of the Commission on February 20, the experiment was at an end.[33]

When the angry electors returned to their factories with the news of Shidlovskii's reply, the strike movement quickly reached a high for the month on February 19 and 21. Both the police and the revolutionaries estimated that a majority of Petersburg workers struck on those

32. Nikolaev, "Iz revoliutsionnogo proshlogo Nevskogo sudostroitel'nogo i mekhanicheskogo zavoda," pp. 71–72. Schwarz, *The Revolution of 1905*, p. 116. The Bolshevik resolution was a minimal variant of the faction's position, confined to issues posed by the Commission itself, and very close to the kinds of guarantees demanded by the seven-branch Declaration. The highly political ambience of the meeting makes it likely that the Menshevik manifesto, or the sentiments expressed in it, was heard there, although it seems not to have been passed as a resolution. Schwarz, *The Revolution of 1905*, p. 118, n. 78. The manifesto itself appeared in *Iskra*, no. 94 (Mar. 25, 1905), and in Somov, "Iz istorii sotsialdemokraticheskogo dvizheniia," pp. 51–55.

33. *NPRR*, p. 211. Somov, "Iz istorii," p. 55.

Dates	Number of workers on strike	Number of enterprises struck
February 17	22,191	14
February 18	35,643	33
February 19	52,862	91
February 20 (Sunday)	–	–
February 21	47,542	53
February 22	40,215	34
February 23	35,096	23
Total man-days lost	233,549	

days; but the actual count, shown in my tabulation, did not quite bear out the claim, even if one allows for the likelihood that these figures err on the low side.[34]

Still, even these figures show that more workers struck on those two days than at any time since the January Days, more than would strike again until October, although a comparable level was briefly approached in July. During the six working days listed, over one-third of the man-days lost in February (601,980) were accounted for.

The figures also show that strikes were more evenly distributed in February than in January, the February 19th figure representing more of a further swelling of a strike movement already under way than a dramatic peak. They reflect the stop-and-start pattern of strikes during the previous three weeks, which found some plants out of phase at the climax of the Shidlovskii campaign on February 18 and 19. For instance, the 13,000 workers of the Putilov Works went out only on February 21, having apparently expended most of their strike energies and resources before the stormy week of February 14. Moreover, the February strikes remained by and large an affair of the factory workers, entailing practically no participation by artisans or white-collar workers, most of whom were excluded from the Shidlovskii elections. Printing workers were still involved in their own wage rates struggle, so their attention was divided during the Shidlovskii campaign, although the wage rates deputies did issue a call to a one-day printers' strike on February 19 in connection with the Commission.[35]

The political aspirations of workers in February were almost totally absorbed by the Shidlovskii campaign and the issues surrounding

34. *NPRR*, pp. 214–19, 734–35 (from TsGIAM [not TsGAOR], fond DT i M [fabr. insp.], 1905 g., d. 64, ll. 10–14).

35. *ILSRPP*, p. 113.

it. Although the disastrous battle of Mukden was under way at the height of the campaign, no public notice of events in the Far East was taken by Petersburg workers. The Socialist Revolutionaries issued a leaflet calling for a strike and worker meetings on February 18 to mark the fortieth day since Bloody Sunday, while the authorities expected the anniversary of the peasant emancipation on February 19 to be marked by disorders among workers.[36] Again, workers did not publicly mark these dates, which fell at the height of the Shidlovskii struggle, although knowledge of them may have helped to swell the ranks of the strikers.

FACTORY DEPUTIES AND ORGANIZATION

The greatest benefit drawn by the labor movement from the upheaval over the Shidlovskii Commission was to be found not in the strikes that followed the Commission's collapse but in the encouragement the events gave to labor organization. By attempting to harness the popularity of worker representation to the cause of civil and industrial peace, the government both admitted the "legitimacy" of the elected representatives and provided the framework and occasion for workers to seize and redefine the moment with their own working-class brand of democracy. Viewing their needs within this framework, the workers extracted what was living and progressive from the memory of the Assembly and turned the movement into a weapon to further their unity and organization, undermining the aims of the government commission in the process. The militancy of the electors in the meetings of February 16–18 flowed from anger and frustration generated by the strike movement, which was in turn refueled by the gains made in the Shidlovskii campaign, foremost among them being the election of factory deputies.

The practice of electing factory deputies was almost as old as strikes among factory workers and was always connected with them. During a strike at the New Spinnery in Petersburg in January 1879, for instance, workers demanded that their elected representatives be permitted to oversee the work of the damage inspectors to prevent cheating and extortion (a standing grievance in textile mills was unjustified fines and charges levied on workers for damaged goods). In addition, the strikers chose deputies to carry out functions connected with the strike itself.[37] This early example of the election of representatives

36. TsGAOR, os. otd., 1905, d. 4, ch. 1, t. III, l. 81. "Dnevnik upravliaiushchego Nevskoi Nitochnoi Fabrikoi K.I. Monkera za 1905–1906 gody," p. 208.

37. *RDR*, vol. 2, pt. 2, pp. 306–7.

envisioned two functions for them—to share authority in the production process as a guarantee against abuses, and to provide strike leadership—although the functions were not necessarily to be carried out by the same body.

As a rule, however, employers were very reluctant to grant workers any share of authority on a permanent basis. Nevertheless, during strikes, they themselves often had occasion to call for elected spokesmen from the strikers. This was done, for instance, during the Morozov strike of 1885 in Orekhovo-Zuevo, and again in 1895 during another textile strike in Ivanovo-Voznesensk.[38] In both cases the deputies were either fired or arrested after the strike, so that the reluctance of the Petersburg textile strikers of 1896 to choose spokespersons at the request of their employers was perhaps understandable and well advised. The Petersburg metal strikers in 1901 chose deputies as strike leaders, although without prompting from the factory managements. In the case of the Obukhov strikers, it will be recalled, the deputies held authority in the plant for about two months, overseeing the fulfillment of demands, and they were removed only after a second strike went down to defeat.

Partly as a result of the 1901 strikes, the government passed its first piece of legislation regulating worker representation at private factories, the Law on *Starosty* (leaders or elders; sing. *starosta*) of June 10, 1903.[39] It provided for the selection by employers of *starosty* from among several candidates chosen by the workers. The *starosty* were to function not as labor representatives but as go-betweens, transmitting workers' grievances to the management and reporting back "instructions" and "statements" to the workers. The time, place, and manner of elections and of meetings between *starosty* and workers were left to the management to specify. No guarantees of immunity of the *starosty* from retaliation by either the employer or the police were given. The absence of immunity and the employers' intimate control over the elections help explain most workers' indifference to or outright rejection of the law. It had almost no practical relevance to the development of the labor movement and the long-established practice of bringing forth leaders during strikes. Although it is customary to mention the law as constituting a sort of vague background to the rise of factory committees,[40] its only relevance here is to show that the gov-

38. Anweiler, *The Soviets*, p. 24.

39. *Ibid.*, p. 25. Ozerov, *Politika po rabochemu voprosu v Rossii za poslednie gody*, pp. 260–72. *Polnoe sobranie zakonov Rossiiskoi imperii. Sobranie tret'e*, XXXIII (1) (SPb., 1903), pp. 734–35.

40. For example, Anweiler, *The Soviets*, pp. 25–26; Ward, "Wild Socialism in Rus-

ernment now recognized the importance of worker representation but that it was incapable of supporting it effectively. Its awkward efforts to do so only strengthened the case of those who argued that workers must look to themselves, not the government or their employers, for solutions.

These earlier patterns were repeated in 1905: worker leadership emerged from the dynamics of the strike movement; in some cases, employers encouraged the emergence or ratified the legitimacy of such leaders; the government attempted to co-opt this leadership by legalizing and regulating it; the workers responded with distrust and new demands of their own, whereupon the government arrested the leaders and dismissed them from work. In January deputies emerged at almost all of the city's larger metal plants, as well as the Izhorsk and Sestroretsk plants outside the city, at some of the textile mills, and at some printing shops (in connection with the printers' Wage Rates Commission, discussed in Chapter 6, below). On January 3, the first day of the Putilov strike, Director Smirnov requested that the workers choose deputies with whom he could talk; the Franco-Russian plant director made a similar request of his workers the next day. Soon enough, the large metal plants were swamped with deputies and demands, including guarantees of immunity for deputies and a permanent share of authority in plant decisions affecting wage rates, dismissals, and grievances. At the Obukhov Works, where experience with elected deputies dated from 1901, Director Vlas'ev tried to beat a retreat from these far-reaching demands to the conditions of the 1903 law by insisting on choosing deputies from the workers' candidates and on treating them as go-betweens acting as individuals rather than as a body with overarching authority.[41]

All of this preceded the establishment of the Shidlovskii Commission, of course; once it was announced, the petitions and premature elections that immediately followed showed that the example of the larger metal plants in the January strike and earlier had begun to inspire workers at smaller plants and in other industries. The Commission provided the legal cover for them to go ahead with what they al-

sia," p. 134; Pankratova, *Fabzavkomy*, p. 21, where a line of development is traced combining the "mining associations of 1863, the *starosty* of 1903, the workers' associations of 1905, and the trade societies of 4 March 1906" as the "stages of a single path along which bureaucratic, legislative regulation of relations between labor and capital inside the capitalist factory proceeded." The 1905 associations refer to the *rabochie tovarishchestva* recommended in a proposal by the engineering professor F. V. Fomin. See Kats and Milonov, *1905 god: Professional'noe dvizhenie*, pp. 319–21.

41. Mitel'man et al., *Istoriia Putilovskogo zavoda*, p. 183. *NPRR*, pp. 8, 193–94.

ready wanted to do. The Shidlovskii elections themselves completed this work by bringing the idea and reality of deputies into factories whose workers had been slower to organize. But the idea of elected representatives had preceded the Commission, having grown out of the strike movement and having acquired popularity through the agitation connected with it.

The idea also outlived the Shidlovskii Commission. The basis of its continued life resided in the factory-level organizations that began to appear after mid-February as a direct institutionalization of the strike movement and of the first free election of workers' representatives. They were known by different names, such as "starostas' council," "deputies' commission," or "plant committee" (*sovet starost* or *starostata, komissiia vybornykh, zavodskii komitet*). Sometimes they had no name at all, being simply a small group of leaders to whom workers could turn with grievances, those who helped shape the workers' energies during strikes. The Bolshevik weaver Iakov Mikhailov later wrote that "after the Shidlovskii Commission, which never met, workers' deputies [at the New Spinnery] kept their places, and the workers turned to them for the resolution of conflicts, [but] the management did not recognize these deputies and they constantly found themselves 'between the hammer and the anvil.'"[42] As the strike movement receded in the spring and early summer, these leadership groupings fell victim to the same letdown and consequent passivity among workers that in the past had accounted for the disappearance of factory leadership following strikes. The police, of course, did their part, by arresting a number of the Shidlovskii electors[43] and by assisting jittery employers in keeping the factory population under almost constant surveillance.

It appears, therefore, that most of the Shidlovskii electors and factory leadership groupings receded back into the work force, re-emerging during strikes and demonstrations, only to disappear again after the temporary backing provided by the solidarity of a struggle had faded. A case in point was Andrei Konovalov, an elector from the Baltic Shipyard who was arrested after the collapse of the Commission, went underground after his release, but continued to reappear briefly at his old shop to hand out leaflets. Another example was Ivan Simonov, an electrician at the Train Car Construction Works, whose activities will be discussed below.[44] Those electors who stayed at their jobs by remaining politically inactive were probably not easily forgot-

42. *Pervaia russkaia revoliutsiia v Peterburge 1905 g.*, vol. 1, p. 123.

43. A record of 13 such arrests may be found in TsGAOR, deloproizvodstvo VII, 1905, delo 934, ll. 7–8, but there were probably many more.

44. Kuznetsov, Livshits, and Pliasunov, *Baltiiskii sudostroitel'nyi 1856–1917*, p. 311.

ten, since they had taken a great risk by becoming deputies in the first place. But the embryonic factory committees did not reemerge in any force until October.[45]

Only at a few factories where workers had convinced the management during the January and February strikes that there was greater risk in trying to remove their deputies than in leaving them in place or where management policy encouraged them did some kind of leadership groups remain. Both of these conditions were met at the Nevsky Works, which had provided some of the most active and popular electors to the Commission's metalworkers group. Ten of the original 12 Shidlovskii electors were reelected to an elders' council or *starostata* of 20 deputies and 20 alternates on March 19. Plant director Hippius apparently viewed his active involvement with the body as a means of avoiding open conflict with his work force, but he also had to grant it concessions in order to insure its authority among workers. As a result, the deputies played a more active and aggressive role than the 1903 Law on *Starosty* envisaged, securing abolition of the plant's blacklist, organizing aid to striking workers at other factories, and winning a number of smaller concessions from the Nevsky management.[46]

Even in January and February a pattern was set among factory workers that determined the form and process of later organizing efforts. The strike movement had not only provided the occasion for organizing; the absence by and large of trade unionist or political traditions among workers meant that strikes determined the shape and nature of working-class organization as well. The absence of an organized labor movement, the illegality of combination, and the structure of capitalist social relations within the factory system meant that the dominant experience of cohesion and organized effectiveness in 1905, especially during the first months, was still felt in the immediate work environment. The Assembly of Russian Workers did not change this pattern despite its focusing solidarity in neighborhood locals. On the contrary, the Assembly rose to the leadership of the city's workers as a whole, and in the process furthered strike organization at individual factories and merged its authority with that of the Putilov Plant

45. Piskarev, "Vospominaniia," p. 102. Shuster argues that the factory committees were most characteristic of the spring and summer and were responsible for sustaining a militant posture among workers despite the downturn in the strike movement. But evidence of formally constituted factory committees at any but one or two of the larger plants during this period is difficult to find. *Peterburgskie rabochie*, pp. 116–19.

46. Paialin, *Zavod imeni Lenina*, pp. 137–39. Nikolaev, "Iz revoliutsionnogo proshlogo," pp. 72–73. Tsytsarin, "Vospominaniia metallista," pp. 39–40. LGIA, fond 1239, op. 1, d. 103, ll. 23–25, 36–40.

strikers. The great hope invested in the Assembly and the revival of its locals stemmed from its functioning as an extension and an amplification of, rather than an alternative to, factory-level solidarity. The network of locals and the general strike of January promised to end the isolation and relative impotence of separate strikes and protests by building onto factory solidarity a superstructure of leadership and authority that would bring the strength of the many to aid the weakness of the few. The Shidlovskii elections renewed and advanced this development by transmitting the practice of the better-organized workers to those less well-organized, ensuring that every medium and large factory in the city at least produced a group of spokesmen, however diffident and inexperienced. A start had been made. Factory-level solidarity expressed in strikes, meetings, protests, and demonstrations thus continued to be the building blocks of the labor movement.

WORKING-CLASS LEADERSHIP

As with factory organization, so with the parallel problem of working-class leadership, the events of January and February made it possible both to draw together the experience of the past and to reshape it. The sources of leadership were threefold: first was the Assembly and the idea of an independent movement of radical reform it represented; second were the revolutionary parties, especially the party of the working class, both in rhetoric and in actual deed, the Social Democrats; finally there were the left liberals, similar to the Assembly adherents in political orientation, who, even though more remote from the labor movement, were an important influence among the large numbers of workers who increasingly felt themselves to be a part of the broader liberation movement. These varied sources of worker leadership will be discussed in this and the following section.

Estimates of the political makeup of the Shidlovskii electors have set the proportion of Assembly adherents at about 65 to 75 percent.[47]

47. *Iskra*, no. 92 (Mar. 10, 1905), and Kol'tsov, "Rabochie v 1905–1907," p. 198, estimated that 40 percent of the electors were "politically radically inclined," 30–35 percent were "Economists," and 20 percent "organized Social Democrats." The writer Tan (V. G. Bogoraz), who attended all the electors' meetings, estimated that 180 of the 400 were "Gaponists," while 80 were Social Democrats and another 80 "Economists (i.e., standing exclusively for economic demands)"; the rest were "indistinguishable". Kniazeva and Inozemtsev, "K istorii rabochikh vyborov," p. 201. Both the *Iskra* and the Tan estimates are summarized in Schwarz, *The Revolution of 1905*, p. 113, where the author quite reasonably supposes that the "Economists" probably also included many workers formerly connected with the Assembly. The conservatively inclined "workerists" identi-

This conclusion is not surprising in light of the popularity of the demand to reopen the 11 Assembly locals, the familiarity with Assembly leaders and activists at many factories, and the age restriction on electors imposed by Shidlovskii's election rules (discussed below). Unfortunately, very little is known about this large group of factory leaders, although the character and fate of one such worker leader has been recorded in a very revealing sketch by the organizer Somov:

> The undoubted leader of the Putilov Plant deputies was the fitter K., 40–45 years old, very intelligent, and very well read in his time, especially in belles lettres and literary criticism. He was thoroughly informed on issues of Russian socio-political literature (*publitsistika*) and was himself the writer of very sad and beautiful poetry. He was an excellent orator, speaking a thoroughly literary language, and was a particularly fine reciter. He gathered people around him, usually in a tavern, on the streets, or especially at his home, and either spoke or gave them a dramatic reading. His home was constantly crowded with people, and he eagerly invited us [i.e., Mensheviks, intellectuals] there, usually adding at the same time that he had already said everything and knew that he already "bored" his listeners; therefore new people had to take his place. In fact, a fresh audience could always be found at his house, hungrily devouring the speaker's words and treating the host with great respect. K. himself had at one time been exiled from one of the central provinces and had worked at the Putilov Plant for about three years. He had belonged to the Zubatovist society from the beginning and even after everything did not break his ties with it, right down to the present. . . . Generally, K. was undoubtedly a talented sort, but had too little initiative and was insufficiently active. When he was pushed, he temporarily took an interest and displayed a rather wide-ranging activism, but then quickly tired of it and, as always, drank. After the campaign around the Shidlovskii Commission, he abandoned all public concerns and, it seems, even left Petersburg.[48]

Although K. may not have been typical of factory leaders who looked to the Assembly, the fact that such a person did so does say something about the range of the organization's appeal. At the very least, K. challenges the stereotype of Assembly enthusiasts as politi-

---

fied among the Assembly's inner circle during the discussions of December 1904 indicate that "Economist" sentiment (in Tan's sense) in the Assembly was significant. For the purpose of the estimate made here, all "Economists" have been counted as adherents of the Assembly.

48. Somov, "Iz istorii," pp. 47–48. The identity of K., if we may trust Somov's description, is probably Aleksei Kondrat'ev, the only Putilov fitter whose name begins with "K" among the Shidlovskii electors (from the Shidlovskii File).

cally backward. K. not only invited socialists to his home, he had apparently had a brush with the law, possibly as a former revolutionary himself. His adherence to the Assembly should probably be compared with that of the Karelinists and others who came to support Gapon because his organization addressed itself to the needs of the masses of workers rather than to the cultivation of small numbers of cadre workers, whether or not K. had "been through the party school." Whatever the exact case, K. was clearly a developed worker-intellectual, and his adherence to the mass factory movement would seem to have been based on a relatively sophisticated understanding of society and politics rather on belief in the Tsar. Although he may have become caught up in the apocalyptic utopianism that developed in the Assembly meetings just prior to January 9, he would have been capable of a soberer view. In these qualities, he perfectly symbolized the lasting place that should be assigned Gaponism in the development of the Russian labor movement: a variety of labor reformism, pilloried by the Social Democrats as "Economism" and "trade-unionism," if not out-and-out government provocation, but not lacking a radical and, in the context of Russia in 1905, even revolutionary, political content.

But Gapon, the liberals, and even Economists were relative newcomers to the labor movement compared to the revolutionary socialists, whose presence among Petersburg workers had lasted over three decades and whose Sisyphean labors had earned them a respected place among a large number of Petersburg workers, even if not the majority and even if most of those prepared to respect them would normally have avoided direct contact with them. The same studies that gave high estimates of the number of Assembly adherents among the Shidlovskii electors also set the proportion of Social Democrats among them at 20 percent. This would seem to be excessively high if the small number of organized socialist adherents among factory workers and the relative weakness of both Social Democratic factions over the previous two years are considered.[49] However, if the definition is not confined to the active membership of then-existing organizations, but includes former members, like the Karelinists, who still considered themselves socialists, or others who followed the lead of socialist spokespersons, the figure is probably not excessive. In addition, there were three general circumstances that, though not con-

49. The sixteen Social Democrats I have been able to identify among the Shidlovskii electors should not be considered definitive, since most of the SD electors probably did not come to public notice and, if arrested, did not necessarily reveal their political affiliations. Shidlovskii File.

firming the 20 percent estimate, would also argue against rejecting it out of hand.

The first is the mood of disillusionment and distrust of the government and traditional authority that prevailed among workers after January 9. This mood has often been remarked upon, both by contemporary observers and by later historians, many of whom have interpreted it as a new and widespread embrace of Social Democratic and revolutionary politics by workers. Recruitment of workers to Social Democratic organizations and factory circles unquestionably increased after the January Days. Worker membership in Bolshevik circles rose from 145 in January to 732 in March in four out of six city districts where the faction had organizations. The Mensheviks, who began the year with a larger following, claimed 1,200 to 1,300 organized workers by April.[50] These figures are modest indeed given the many years of sacrifice and hard work by the Social Democrats and the dramatic deflation of Tsarist authority among workers after January 9.

Thus, although recruitment to the revolutionary parties increased as a result of Bloody Sunday, the impact on most workers was limited to a willingness to listen to their speakers and read their leaflets and did not entail a wholesale turn to organized socialism. Yet even this much change made it possible for the existing socialists to exercise more influence in the factories and made it more likely that former socialists would involve themselves once more in the labor movement.

The second circumstance that made the Social Democrats more acceptable in this period was the decision by both factions to tailor their tactics to those put forth in the independent workers' petitions. Rather than oppose the popular will as they had done in January, and would do again later in the year, the socialists abandoned their initial impulse to call for a boycott of the Commission and instead took part in the campaign. As a result they enjoyed unprecedented exposure and influence among workers. Their agitators were able to intervene

---

50. Bondarevskaia, *Peterburgskii komitet RSDRP v revoliutsii 1905–1907 gg.*, pp. 79–80. Lane, *The Roots of Russian Communism*, pp. 72–74. Both estimates are based on party sources, the minutes of the (Bolshevik) Third Party Congress, and *Iskra*, no. 97, respectively. The recruitment of workers to the Socialist Revolutionary Party probably also increased after Bloody Sunday, but information about the SRs in St. Petersburg is too sparse and contradictory to support a specific statement. See Hildermeier, *Die Sozialrevolutionäre Partei Russlands*, pp. 117–19, 215, 257–58, 299. In recognition of this likelihood, the term "socialists" is used in this discussion and elsewhere to mean "SDs and probably also SRs."

openly at factory elections as well as at the electors' meetings and at a number of secret meetings with workers held to discuss the campaign.[51] The Social Democratic initiative around the Shidlovskii campaign came in the midst of a renewal of party energies, which were rapidly recovering from the extreme low ebb of 1904. This upswing and the considerable energy and courage of party agitators in making factory contacts and speaking at meetings were not lost on the workers, who respected those who sacrificed and risked themselves in the workers' cause.

Finally, the stormy events of January and February created a situation that demanded factory leadership, and this in itself improved the stock of the organized socialists considerably. In the long years of underground propaganda and circle work, a considerable number of worker socialists had been produced, and although many of them had since become inactive, the dramatic upsurge of labor militancy in early 1905 brought many "out of the woodwork" as strike leaders, Shidlovskii electors, or spokesmen for their shops and work groups. There was no other comparably trained, nonsocialist group from which such leaders could have been drawn, and this probably made for a larger proportion of socialists among leaders than among rank-and-file workers. For instance, Nikifor Titov, a Shidlovskii elector from the Russian Spinnery and an old participant in socialist workers' circles, had joined the Assembly in 1904, but later returned to Social Democratic ranks, probably after January 9. Iakov Mikhailov, a weaver and active Social Democrat since the 1890's, had already suffered several arrests, imprisonment, and exile, and had just completed a four-year period of military service at the end of 1904. In January 1905, Mikhailov was working as a postman in Petersburg, having apparently failed to renew his ties to the party. After Bloody Sunday he secured factory work, and he went on to play an active role in the labor movement for the rest of the year (although he seems not to have taken up party work again until the fall). On the other hand some former socialists had changed their minds in the meantime and took a moderate stance in 1905: Anton Zakharov, for example, an elector from the James Beck Spinnery and a circle member at the Maxwell Mills during the stormy events of December 1898, not only declined to return to the party, he even voted against it and against the views of most other

51. Kniazeva and Inozemtsev, "K istorii rabochikh vyborov," pp. 178–79; and TsGAOR, os. otd. 1905, d. 4, ch. 1, t. III, ll. 30–31, 53–54, where two such secret meetings are reported in police memoranda.

electors when he joined the minority that favored proceeding with the election of Shidlovskii deputies despite the agreed-upon boycott of this stage of the plan.[52]

The clearest example of a political conversion to Social Democracy stemming from the events of January is offered by Ivan Petrovich Simonov, a thirty-year-old electrical technician from the Train Car Construction Works, which he represented as a Shidlovskii elector and later as a Soviet deputy. Simonov had been a government supporter before January, but after joining the Assembly he became a militant labor leader in his district, and gradually moved into the orbit of the RSDRP, which he eventually joined. He was apparently a gifted speaker and leader who found his voice during the January and February events and in the process discovered the importance of the information, support, and cooperation the party could provide. Somov described him as "an energetic and intelligent worker, . . . who had almost never in his life read a thing, and was not generally a lover of reading, but [possessed] a splendid temperament and was unusually active." During the January Days he began to distinguish himself as a speaker at the Putilov Embankment, a meeting place of workers of the southern part of Narva district (the area called "beyond the Moscow Gate," *za Moskovskoi zastavoi*), where he "enjoyed immense influence." Once elected a Shidlovskii deputy, he took an active role in both worker and deputy meetings, coordinating the exchange of information and petition demands among factories and between deputies and workers. Both during the Shidlovskii campaign and for months afterward, he skillfully avoided arrest even though he made frequent public appearances. In the course of this activity Simonov drew closer and closer to the Social Democrats and later finally joined the party. His case is a clear example of the gains possible from supporting and encouraging talented independents. As Somov later wrote, Simonov "acted in accord with the Social Democratic district organization, but all the time [he himself] remained the heart of the movement."[53]

Converts from the ranks of the formerly indifferent or even from former opponents of the socialists were not very frequent, especially

52. Titov: Perazich, "Tekstil'shchiki v komissii," p. 50. Mikhailov and Zakharov: Ia. Mikhailov, *Iz zhizni rabochego. Vospominaniia chlena soveta rabochikh deputatov 1905 g.*, pp. 46–57. Zakharov: Kochergin, "90–e gody na fabrike 'Rabochii' (b. Maksvel')," p. 196.

53. Somov, "Iz istorii," pp. 48–49. *NPRR*, p. 706. TsGAOR, Osob. otd., 1905, d. 4, ch. 1, t. II, ll. 136–37.

converts as capable and energetic as Simonov, but their persuasiveness in reconciling ordinary workers to socialist presence and influence must have been considerable.

There were also a number of identifiable socialist worker leaders whose activism in 1905 represented a continuing commitment from earlier years. Vasilii Tsytsarin, a Bolshevik lathe operator and Shidlovskii elector from Nevsky Ship and Machine Works, was a popular and influential factory leader and a loyal party cadre. He had opposed the Assembly, was arrested in June 1905 for inciting Nevsky workers to violence against the police, and served as a delegate to the Bolshevik Tammerfors Conference in December. The historian of the Nevsky Works, N. P. Paialin, called him one of the three main "movers" (*tolkachi*) at the plant, together with the Menshevik Efrem Gudkov and the Liberationist Ivan Makeev. Semen Nikolaev, another Shidlovskii elector from Nevsky Ship, recalled Tsytsarin's popularity and "length of political experience" and noted the prominent role he played at the electors' meetings.[54] The Nevsky Works had a number of experienced and sophisticated leaders besides Tsytsarin, but at some plants either the absence of competition or the superior stature of one individual elevated a single leader to the status of chief or *vozhak* of the entire work force. Such a figure was Nikolai Klopov, Bolshevik foreman, factory deputy, and leader of the January strike at the Sestroretsk Armaments Works (located in the Finnish Gulf suburb of Sestroretsk). Unfortunately, very little is known about him except that he had been an adherent of the People's Will and the Petersburg Union of Struggle in earlier years, and was still regarded by the police as "extremely dangerous," all the more so because he had "immense authority among the workers."[55]

Another such figure was Petr Aleksandrovich Zlydnev, the Menshevik leader of the Obukhov workers from his first appearance at the plant in 1903 through his arrest as a member of the Soviet's Presidium and Executive Committee in December 1905. Zlydnev was probably the single most eminent and influential Petersburg factory leader to emerge in the revolutionary year. Although best known for his role in the Soviet and at the trial of its leaders, he had been the dominant political presence at the Obukhov Plant long before Bloody Sunday

54. *Revoliutsionnoe dvizhenie v Rossii vesnoi i letom 1905 goda*, p. 282. Paialin, *Zavod imeni Lenina*, p. 128; and in *Bor'ba klassov*, 7–8 (1935), p. 89. Nikolaev, "Iz revoliutsionnogo proshlogo," pp. 70–72.

55. Tarasov, "Bol'shevistskaia organizatsiia i Sestroretskie rabochie v 1905 godu," p. 105. *NPRR*, p. 142.

(as even the Stalin-period historian of the plant grudgingly admits), and he served as a Shidlovskii deputy and leader at the election meetings.[56] At Zlydnev's premature death in 1914, Leon Trotsky wrote a pithy and insightful tribute to his former friend and colleague. He recalled that Zlydnev's work as a machinist earned him high regard from the Obukhov management, but that

> he was valued even more by the Obukhov workers. In him there was something strong, internally dependable, quietly persistent. Seeing him and listening to him, workers felt that Petr Aleksandrovich did not go to extremes but also did not give way under pressure. And in politics he had a keen eye. He gauged people perfectly, evaluated circumstances with a flair and, being a realist to the bone, did not suffer from hasty judgment. He liked to listen more than to talk and, listening, he knew how to distinguish the verbal husk from the factual kernel. He did not have the agitator's fieriness, but he could speak marvelously in his own way: there was even a Ukrainian humor in his [speaking] style, but disciplined by rationality and completely free of southern dilettantism.

But Zlydnev's stature as a leader went beyond the factory milieu, as his preeminence in the Soviet later bore out.

> Between workers and intellectuals, even those holding one and the same point of view, there will long remain a kind of psychological distance, for which no organizational ties will prove adequate—a result of differences of social origin, lodged in the unconscious. In the case of Zlydnev, this distance was not at all noticeable. Petr Aleksandrovich wrote with grammatical errors—only in exile did he fully master the secrets of etymology and syntax—but he felt himself not only on an equal footing with any "leading intellectuals": his quiet conviction, his realistic insight, and the inner force of his personality—unnoticed by himself—inspired in many a feeling of his superiority over them.[57]

This self-possession in the presence of intellectuals was not lost on workers, whose conflict over simultaneously needing and admiring the intelligentsia while distrusting and keeping a distance from them, so accurately indicated by Trotsky, has been referred to earlier. The whole topic will be discussed again, but it can be observed here that if a worker leader like Zlydnev had the ability to cut through this particular knot, there is little wonder that he may have been perceived

56. Rozanov, *Obukhovtsy*, p. 161. "Sudebnaia rech' P.A. Zlydneva," *KL*, 5(38) (1930), pp. 35–46. Kolokol'nikov, "Otryvki iz vospominanii 1905–1907 gg.," pp. 215–16. *1905: SRD*.

57. L. D. Trotskii, *Sochineniia* (M.-L., 1926), vol. 8, pp. 198–200.

by workers (and others) to have possessed a certain unfathomable superiority.

Given the presence at the outset of the 1905 Revolution of leaders and models such as these, it may well be the case that as many as 20 percent of the Shidlovskii electors considered themselves Social Democrats. But it should also be clear that the concept of who was a socialist was somewhat elastic, and that party membership or, even more, sympathy toward a particular party, could vary greatly. For example, young, fresh recruits to party ranks presented a completely different political prospect to the revolutionaries than did active or re-activated party veterans. At some factories, the weakness of socialist influence early in 1905 was due not so much to the absence of socialists as to their youth and inexperience.

Such was the case at the Putilov Works, for instance. After January 9, Assembly loyalists continued to dominate the plant's leadership, and Social Democratic circle participants at the 13,000-strong enterprise numbered only about 50. Although the socialists proposed candidates for the Shidlovskii elections, not one of the 26 electors chosen at Putilov can be identified as a Social Democrat, so that it may be said that non-party types and Assembly loyalists carried the day. In this context, it should be remembered that the Shidlovskii rules required that electors be at least 25 years old, and most socialist circle members were younger than that. The Gaponist leaders, on the other hand, tended to be older workers, which also meant that they were better-known and had longer terms of service at the plant. In addition, most of the Social Democratic circle workers seem to have been new to party work—even those who were old enough to qualify as electors—and were therefore reluctant or ill-qualified to stand for election. These conditions were not unique to the Putilov Works but could be found in varying degrees at many other Petersburg factories.[58] The Menshevik organizer Somov, who worked with the Putilov party organization during the Shidlovskii campaign, noted that because of the small influence exercised by Social Democratic workers, they could find only one actual party member to stand for election; they were therefore forced to propose other circle members or sympathizers (not yet party members), sometimes without their knowledge. Somov related that the whole undertaking was so doubtful that he

58. Among compositors, for instance, the age qualification and "political unreliability" were cited as reasons for the failure of organized revolutionaries to take part in the Shidlovskii elections. *ILSRPP*, p. 113.

met with some of the candidates only on the eve of the elections "in order to subject their [political] 'consciousness' to a preliminary 'examination.'"[59]

In other cases, resistance to socialists was insurmountable, but appeal could be made to workers on the basis of a more fundamental currency. Somov also worked among the much less experienced workers of the huge Russian-American Rubber Factory (6,000 hands), where the confused dynamics following January 9 had witnessed, among other things, the emergence of widespread Black Hundreds agitation. The work force was of a "low cultural level," with only about 600–700 skilled workers. The workers had struck in January, however, and the announcement of the Shidlovskii Commission had again stirred its more socially and politically conscious elements into action. Somov entered the scene after an early election had produced a set of electors from among the older, more conservative workers. However, as a result of the militant stance being taken at other factories, some of the more critical elements were beginning to have doubts about these electors. Exploiting these doubts, the handful of Social Democratic workers at the factory brought their young agitator to one of the factory meetings. "But the assemblage had only to see before it a person with the seditious physiognomy of a *kursistka* [female student], and it melted away by more than three-fourths: all the old and influential workers immediately sought salvation from sedition in flight."[60] Somov himself then held a series of lengthy conversations with the deputies, whom he persuaded to circulate a petition before sending it on to Shidlovskii. "In the course of our general interviews the electors made their demands broader and broader, and willingly joined in with the general demands of the period, although they approved [the call for] a constituent assembly out of politeness rather than internal conviction." He continued:

> By and large, however, the thinking of the workers progressed so powerfully that even these backward representatives of backward workers more than vindicated my hopes. I had the opportunity to see them at the general electors' assembly at the Countess Panina House, and it turned out that my rubber worker electors lent themselves to the general fighting mood and revealed such consciousness and understanding of the meaning of all Shidlovskii's ventures, that I simply did not recognize them.[61]

59. Somov, "Iz istorii," pp. 46–47.
60. *Ibid.*, p. 50.
61. *Ibid.*, pp. 50–52.

Generalizing from this experience, Somov concluded that though "only the most insignificant percentage [of the Shidlovskii electors] was organized Social Democrats," nonetheless "the ideological [*ideinoe*] influence of Social Democracy was . . . decisive, and agitation among the electors was very intensively and successfully conducted by it."[62] Although this claim may be questioned in light of the earlier worker petitions and the role of the left-liberal lawyers, there can be little doubt that Social Democrats contributed materially to the outcome of the campaign and that their agitation was of far greater importance for them and for most Petersburg workers than was their success in providing electors. Somov's emphasis on *organized* Social Democrats is noteworthy in that it helps to explain his low estimate of party representation among the electors and expresses the organizer's preference for trained, experienced, and reliable cadres.

In the end, however, emphasis should probably be placed on the broader "ideological" influence of the socialists on the masses of workers now awakened to political alternatives by the collapse of Tsarist authority. Because the number of veteran socialist worker leaders was inadequate to the demand for them at the more militant factories, and because most of the new recruits were unsuited to leadership, it seems most accurate to stress the socialists' impact on the broad ranks of workers, who were previously untouched by or indifferent to them. The distrust in which the government appeared to hold the factory population and the government's own "lawlessness" during the January Days reduced the sharp distinction ordinary workers had customarily made between themselves and the revolutionaries. Although socialist opposition to the Assembly had been quite unpopular, it is evident that the short-term effect of the workers' involvement with the organization had been more suffering. In the same period, party orators at the factory gates became a more frequent and familiar occurrence, and their leaflets and newspapers were now read and discussed more widely and openly.

For all the exposure to working-class audiences that Social Democrats had gained during the Shidlovskii campaign, none of their leaders could match the popularity and influence of the left-liberal lawyer Georgii Stepanovich Nosar'. He later became the president of the Petersburg Soviet of Workers' Deputies, but he made his debut in labor politics during the same earlier period when some workers were finding their way to socialism, while the majority, to one degree or an-

62. *Ibid.*, p. 52.

other, still hoped to reconstitute the citywide solidarity and promise of reform represented by the Assembly.

Nosar' was the son of an educated peasant of Poltava province who was connected with the People's Will and exiled to Siberia for his part in peasant disorders. After attending secondary school in Pereiaslav, where the family settled after exile, he entered the law faculty of Petersburg University. In 1899 he was himself arrested and exiled for three years under police surveillance after playing a prominent part in student reform initiatives. Somehow he managed while in exile to persuade the authorities to permit him to take his examinations and to give him credit for courses he could not attend. Receiving his diploma, he went to work as legal counsel for the Kharkov-Nikolaev Railroad, defending the road at times against its own workers, while maintaining connections with liberal oppositionist circles. Nosar' was reportedly a very skillful and successful lawyer. He took no active part in the January Days, but had in the meantime returned to Petersburg and established his own contacts among workers.[63]

Sometime after January 9 several weavers from the Nikol'sk Factory on the Vyborg Side (one of the Cheshire mills) sought out Nosar' for legal advice on securing strike pay from the management. His efforts on their behalf were successful, and as a result he gained great popularity at the factory as well as considerable influence over its strike committee. When the Shidlovskii Commission was announced, the Cheshire workers from Nikol'sk were the first to submit a petition to the Senator requesting the reopening of the 11 locals, and Nosar' was undoubtedly a supporter of this initiative, if not its instigator.[64] Nosar' and Margulies both played important initiatory and facilitating roles in making public the deeply felt needs and intensely popular sentiments expressed in the petitions. The influence Nosar' exerted

63. *Bol'shaia sovetskaia entsiklopediia* (M., 1934), vol. 60, p. 227. Sverchkov, *G. S. Nosar'-Khrustalev (opyt politicheskoi biografii)*, pp. 5–7.

64. Perazich, "Tekstil'shchiki," pp. 51–52. TsGIA, fond 1205, op. XVI t., 1905, d. 1, l. 134. There is a little confusion about the earliest petition to reach Shidlovskii. The one listed here as *listok* 134 of the Shidlovskii Commission archive was dated February 1, 1905 (the earliest petition found there), and emanated from the Nikol'sk workers, who were under the influence of Nosar'. That much is certain. The police documents on the arrest of Margulies describe him as telling the nine workers he met with on February 1 about an earlier delegation and petition to Shidlovskii from "four workers of the Petersburg district" (Okun', ed., *Putilovets*, pp. 98–99). The petition collection in the Shidlovskii archive is not necessarily complete, but neither is Margulies's reference to the Petersburg district necessarily accurate. But even if it could be established that four workers from the Petersburg district preceded the Nosar'-inspired Cheshire workers, the interpretation of the situation given here would not be materially altered.

on workers resulted not from awakening them to these feelings and giving them political shape, as Gapon and the Assembly had done, but from combining issues that most clearly expressed what the greatest number of Petersburg workers felt at the time, limiting his thinking and outlook to these issues, and giving them clear, public, and forceful expression. The lawyer Nosar' was not so much the *political leader* of the Petersburg workers as he was their *public advocate*.

Of course, Nosar' did have a political outlook of his own which, though concealed to the superficial observer by his advocacy of the workers' cause, was actually confirmed in the kind of leadership he provided. Nosar' is usually characterized as a "left Liberationist" liberal, and whether or not he was actually a member of the Union of Liberation, his participation in the Shidlovskii campaign and the perspective he brought to this participation certainly bear out this characterization. About half of the petitions to Shidlovskii he inspired advocated the admission of nonworkers to the Commission if elected by the workers. This was insisted upon by Margulies and doubtlessly also by Nosar', but it also appealed to the need felt by many workers for the advice and aid of educated persons in dealing with public affairs. Indeed, it would have been perfectly reasonable for the workers to demand the right to legal counsel in the Commission. One of the police documents on Margulies describes him as advocating just that; but the other one imputes to him the demand that outsiders serve as deputies rather than legal counsel, and the petitions themselves demanded the same. As Margulies put it, "intelligentsia representatives . . . will know how to represent the interests of workers in the commission and to defend them there from the capitalists better than the workers themselves."[65] This conviction, doubtless shared by Nosar' and other liberal professionals sympathetic to labor, reflected a faith in the power of educated society to do for the lower classes what they seemingly could not do for themselves.

Yet it is also true that Nosar' went further than most labor liberals in accommodating himself to the needs of the workers and in exposing himself to the danger of arrest. In November 1905 he even joined the Menshevik faction—although he later denied it. In an apologia published in 1918, he described his political credo in the following terms:

> Due to personal experience as a representative of labor and the unconscious promptings of intuition, I felt that the Russian liberation move-

65. Kniazeva and Inozemtsev, "K istorii rabochikh vyborov," p. 180.

ment would take the form of a labor movement or it would not take place in Russia at all. But I did not join the noisy current of Marxism, although the movement to Marxism and the proletariat was the most modish intelligentsia illness at the time, much like an influenza. The Marxism of the economic draftsmen, [which had] everything from ideology to religion and art inclusively emerging vertically from the stomach, sickened my nature by its schematism, its obvious simplification, and its distortion of all of life's complexity.[66]

He went on to deny ever joining the Social Democrats, and listed the persons who had held the greatest personal attraction for him: N. K. Mikhailovskii, P. A. Kropotkin, Adjutant General P. A. Vannovskii, I. I. Mechnikov, Jean Jaurès, and V. D. Burtsev. As an émigré from 1907 to 1915, Nosar' fancied himself a syndicalist and led a small group of his own. In 1917 he tried to join the Petrograd Soviet, but was rejected by the now far more radical body. He then returned to the Ukraine, where he soon emerged as head of an "Independent Pereiaslav Republic." During the Civil War he supported Hetman Skoropadskii, then Petliura. In 1918 he was shot by the Cheka.[67]

In February 1905, however, Nosar' gained entry to the labor movement and established his popularity among workers as a non-party "friend of labor." Given this and his apparently sincere sympathy for workers, he must have seemed like a second Gapon to many workers. Nosar' was certainly aware of the nostalgia for the Assembly, if not for the priest, whose independent line and preeminent authority among workers he now sought to emulate. In a letter to Shidlovskii, Nosar' asked that the 11 locals be reopened on his personal authority.[68] When this failed and the demand to admit nonworkers as deputies met with resistance from many workers and was ignored in Shidlovskii's election rules, Nosar' persuaded a Nikol'sk elector, the weaver Petr Khrustalev, to allow him to take his place at the elector meetings, and the lawyer Nosar' was reborn as the bogus labor deputy "Khrustalev-Nosar'." In this persona, Nosar' presided over the seven-branch electors' meeting on February 16, but when he appeared at the textile branch gathering on the 18th, his identity was publicly unmasked by one of the workers who favored the immediate election of deputies. Nosar' quickly confirmed his real identity when questioned by the policeman present

66. *Iz nedavnogo proshlogo* (Percislav, 1918), quoted in Sverchkov, *G. S. Nosar'-Khrustalev*, pp. 10–11. Schwarz, *The Revolution of 1905*, p. 173.

67. Sverchkov, *G. S. Nosar'-Khrustalev*, pp. 33, 45–50. V. Kantorovich, "Khrustalev-Nosar'," *Byloe*, 4 (32), 1925, pp. 117–53.

68. Schwarz, *The Revolution of 1905*, p. 92. Nevskii, "Vybory," pp. 89–90.

and was arrested. The electors leaped from their seats, shouting "We don't need elections!" and "Down with the autocracy!," and the meeting hall emptied except for the few *tekstil'shchiki* who still held out for elections. As a result of this incident, Nosar' became a cause célèbre throughout the capital and a hero of liberal educated society.[69]

Nosar' enjoyed tremendous popularity among workers in 1905. As chairman of the seven-branch meeting on February 16 he visited the simultaneous meeting of the metalworker electors to coordinate the activities of the two groups, and he met with a warm reception and perfect agreement among them.[70] After the Shidlovskii debacle he kept his ties with textile workers and in early October represented them at a meeting of union leaders in Moscow (later dubbed the First All-Russian Conference of Trade Unions).[71] Nosar' also drew close to the Petersburg printing workers and first appeared in the Soviet as one of their representatives. He became Soviet chairman because of his popularity and renown, but also because he seemed to stand above, or aside from, the rivalries of the revolutionary parties.

Unfortunately, for all the contact Nosar' had with workers, not enough is known about it to be able to describe or explain his popularity in more precise terms. It does seem clear that he communicated to workers the kind of sincere and nonpartisan dedication to their cause that had made Gapon so popular, and in that respect the liberal lawyer *was* the true successor of the erratic priest. But the differences between the two figures are equally important. Nosar' was both politically more adept and less ambiguous in his opposition to the autocracy than Gapon. Like the priest, he had the ability and the inclination to manipulate existing institutions in order to achieve both individual and class gains for the workers. But unlike Gapon he was not attached to the old order and felt freer to stand openly for its overthrow. As a result, Nosar' was less inhibited in working with revolutionaries, and

69. Perazich, "Tekstil'shchiki," pp. 56–57. Sverchkov, *G. S. Nosar'-Khrustalev*, p. 8.
70. Nikolaev, "Iz revoliutsionnogo proshlogo," p. 71.
71. Perazich, "Tekstil'shchiki," p. 60. Schwarz, "The Liberationists and the Trade Union Movement," in *The Revolution of 1905*, pp. 315–19. Kolokol'nikov and Rapoport, *1905–1907 gg. v professional'nom dvizhenii*, pp. 47–49, 168–70. The popularity of Nosar' with workers seemed to be matched by his unpopularity with other intelligentsia labor leaders: the trade unionist and academic V. V. Sviatlovskii, in an interview with Iu. Milonov, later claimed that Nosar' sought but was refused admission to the Central Bureau of Trade Unions, which, even though dominated by Mensheviks, found him "not to be [their] kind of person." TsGAOR, fond 6935, op. 2, d. 101b, l. 2. The author is grateful to Jonathan Sanders for supplying this information. See also Trotskii, *Sochineniia* (cited in n. 57 above), vol. 8, pp. 190–97.

he seems to have become increasingly involved with them, eventually joining one of their factions. All of these traits of his personality paralleled the mood and inclinations of workers after January 9, and they help explain his great popularity among them. He represented the workers' own impatience for labor reform as well as their newly found and still diffident openness to revolutionary politics. Nosar' symbolized the link between the labor movement and the non-party radical intelligentsia, and therefore the wider antigovernment coalition; even more, he epitomized for workers the power of educated society to aid them in their own struggles, without ulterior motive.

WORKERS AND THE INTELLIGENTSIA

In all the foregoing examples of working-class leadership, there seem to be undercurrents of patterned assumptions about workers, the intelligentsia, and the nature of their interrelationships. Although a complete roadmap cannot be drawn until more is known about the terrain, it would be appropriate to bring together the small parts of the picture encountered thus far.

First of all, in the weeks following Bloody Sunday a significant shift took place in many workers' attitudes toward the socialists in their midst: they suddenly began to be viewed in a far more positive light, as if the danger previously thought to be risked in associating with them had been forgotten. The smith Aleksei Buzinov recalled this change of heart at his plant, the Nevsky Ship and Machine Works, in the following terms:

> If earlier no one [even] saw them [i.e., the socialists working at the plant], or perhaps did not want to notice them in order to keep out of trouble, now everyone suddenly knew that these were smart, well-informed people. Many dug around in their past, memories began to come to light, and it turned out that someone here and there, somehow or other, had been in contact with socialists. Then too the general upheaval brought all the socialists from among the workers to the notice of the factory. Now they were paid court to, actually, even fawned over. But they were all our own—factory workers, our kind of people, not ones to hold grudges. From their side I do not recall a single reproach, personal or otherwise, for earlier threats or insults. In the workers' attitudes toward them, it began to be recognized that the socialists were the leaders of the labor movement. They were paid heed to, they were looked after in a special way, with a kind of crude but touching good-heartedness.[72]

72. Buzinov, *Za nevskoi zastavoi*, p. 49.

Buzinov perceptively observed that the emergence of socialist leaders in the factories was less a matter of accepting something entirely new than a complex interaction of new circumstances and feelings giving life to slumbering memories. All along, it seems, workers in some sense knew that the factory socialists were among the most intelligent and best-informed workers—i.e., worker intellectuals—yet political repression had been strangely aided by psychological repression, and now that the one had broken down, the other too was giving way.

Actually, the workers sought the help not only of the socialists, but of better-educated people generally, and they turned to the intelligentsia, irrespective of party. In a continuation of the passage above in which the observations about socialists were made, Buzinov recalled the dramatic political transformation that his fellow workers underwent after January 9, as they began to read newspapers aloud in the shops and eagerly awaited the latest political leaflet. Work became a secondary concern, a mere means to sustain life, not its main focus. A thirst for knowledge and self-improvement, always the concern of a minority of the skilled workers, now became an obsession of a much larger number of workers, as if the January 9 massacre had been due to something the workers themselves had lacked, something they were now determined to learn. This thrust toward self-help resulted in a great multiplication of organizations among workers, *kassy* for different purposes, brotherhoods, and study circles for self-education and self-improvement. Painfully aware of their own ignorance and feeling the need for assistance with these projects, workers' circles sought the help of the intelligentsia, socialist and otherwise. They delegated members to hunt out these invaluable counselors and teachers, as if in search of the legendary Firebird, as Buzinov put it. Some took time off work to conduct these searches, and members of one group even tried to hire a student tutor with money they raised among themselves.[73]

What was the larger assumption being expressed in seeking out not only revolutionaries, but other kinds of educated advisers as well? What forgotten memory had been stirred to life in this case? If it was only a matter of finding tutors, the search for trained and knowledgeable assistance could be easily understood. Yet something more seems to have been involved. Semen Nikolaev, who was quoted earlier bearing witness to the talent and popularity of plant leader Tsytsarin, was himself a Shidlovskii elector, and he attributed his selection to his attendance at the evening classes of the Kornilov School, so that "I stood

73. *Ibid.*, pp. 47–49, 51–52.

out from the mass [of workers] by my intellectual development." Although Nikolaev's judgment about the exact reason for his selection may be questioned, he points to a phenomenon in the factories that is fairly well documented and not difficult to understand: just as high status and regard were accorded to elites of knowledge and talent in Russian society generally, so in the factory status was granted and leaders chosen with very similar standards. This deference to the educated was in fact so widespread and unquestioning among Russian workers as to suggest that they accepted the intelligentsia and intelligentsia values more extensively and more exclusively as the embodiment of modern, urban ideals than did workers in countries farther west. The intelligentsia constituted one of the prime normative models of personal fulfillment acknowledged by Russian workers, especially that stratum of skilled, literate, and well-paid workers that has been prominently mentioned in this study.[74]

The example of the Putilov fitter K., described above by Somov, shows that this attraction to the intelligentsia could even involve a merging of life-styles between the factory elite and the urban intelligentsia. K.'s literary language and literary pretensions, his reading habits, his talent at recitation, his salon and the spirit of enlightenment he cultivated there, and his unenthusiastic but dutiful performance of political responsibilities could easily have been the pastimes of a cultivated *intelligent* of the leisured classes or the liberal professions. It is curious that workers could feel the kind of trust and even reverence that Somov describes for a figure who seemed so much unlike the ordinary worker, so much the intelligentsia dandy. Somehow, Russian workers had not only a place for this hybrid personality, but a respected place. Perhaps only in Russia was the marriage of literature and politics so well developed, and one wonders whether a figure such as K. would have commanded as much status in a British or a German factory.

These observations should be seen in the context of the considerable evidence compiled by Allan Wildman to document what he calls a "chronic tension between the *intelligenty* and the workers."[75] His contention forms the other pole of possibility in what was clearly a highly

74. What is being referred to here is an admiration for the power of knowledge and learning to do good for man and society, not an admiration for the formal culture of the educated classes. The latter was also found among Russian workers, but it was not unique to them. See, for example, Robert Michels, *Political Parties. A Sociological Study of the Oligarchical Tendencies of Modern Democracy* (New York, 1959 [1915]), p. 64.

75. Wildman, *The Making of a Workers' Revolution*, esp. pp. 89–117.

variable relationship. Wildman's evidence is limited to the period of Economism and the *Iskra* attack upon it, and is confined to worker-intellectuals and committed labor activists who came directly into conflict with intelligentsia revolutionaries over the leadership of workers' organizations. By 1905, not only was Economism long since defeated, both in the Russian underground and abroad, but the intelligentsia as a whole had gained new prominence in the nationwide antiwar and antigovernment opposition, and the labor movement had struck new roots in previously inactive groups and strata of workers. As a result, 1905 was on the whole a period of rapprochement between workers and intelligentsia under the assumed umbrella of an all-class, all-party opposition to the autocracy. Yet, there is a lasting validity to Wildman's stress on the tension in the relationship of workers and intelligentsia, as was confirmed after 1905 and during the period of reaction after 1907 in the widespread belief among workers that they had been "betrayed" by the intelligentsia.

But aside from such gross shifts of emphasis from period to period, the relationship also varied from case to case depending upon the bond of trust established between individual *intelligenty* or worker-*intelligenty* and a given group of workers. Hence, Nosar', Somov, and the fitter K. enjoyed such trust, whereas the lawyer Finkel' (whom Gapon had brought to the inner circle's meetings to argue the merits of a public demonstration) and many of the Social Democratic orators who spoke against the Tsar at the Assembly meetings did not. Buzinov's description of the change of heart his workmates underwent after January 9 with respect to worker socialists shows just how labile and emotional these judgments could be. At the same time, these examples also show that the exact political choices available and other immediate political circumstances were probably of greater moment than any standing prejudice for or against *intelligenty* per se. But the point remains that Petersburg workers at no time displayed universal sympathy or antipathy toward members of the intelligentsia or toward those workers who were clearly connected with them and their organizations.

All of this suggests that long before 1905 Petersburg workers had learned to mediate their relationship with the intelligentsia through their own worker intelligentsia. It does seem to be the case that workers in factories with greater numbers or proportions of worker intellectuals accepted political intellectuals from outside the factory more easily, whereas those without them accepted them less easily or not at all. Evidence of the former situation, however, comes from those large metal plants where the overall political and intellectual level was higher, and it is difficult to specify and make precise the linking role of the worker intellectuals in a setting where so many other factors were at play. Nevertheless, the examples of the fitter K. and Semen Nikolaev's admiring references to Tsytsarin, his factory's leading Bolshevik worker, indicate that a cordial and tolerant relationship normally existed between the socialist and non-socialist worker intellectuals, and this alliance certainly did help to "legitimize" socialist intellectuals from outside the factory who came, let us say, to address a worker meeting.

Liberal intellectuals were also accepted by factory workers, both as part of an antigovernment opposition whose components were not carefully distinguished by them, or when they spoke about the workers' own needs. Nosar' was the prime example of trust and deference applied to a member of the liberal intelligentsia, and this was possible because Nosar' himself closed the distance by aiding a group of workers. It was a rarer occurrence for workers to seek out intelligentsia help, but this too began to change after January 9, not only on an individual basis and for practical ends, as with Buzinov's workmates seeking tutors and organizers, but on the larger plane of political alliance-making.

Except for worker intellectuals and the relative handful of other workers who were familiar with revolutionary politics, most workers did not distinguish very clearly between and among political parties and beliefs, but lumped together socialists with liberals and other oppositionists. As a result, workers in 1905 thought of the antigovernment movement as more unitary, and they were more open to leadership by the liberal/democratic intelligentsia, than at any other period before or since. The popularity of a figure like Nosar' would have been unthinkable in 1917 and for some time before that.

The experience of 1905 would advance the political education of many Russian workers immeasurably, but at the beginning of the year the majority of factory workers active in Petersburg appear to have had fairly unstructured political views, and should therefore have been as open to liberal and democratic leadership as to socialist. This attitude appears to have been held by most workers until well into the fall of 1905. Gapon's vaguely trade-unionist reformism was no barrier to his leadership and popularity; why should Nosar' have been different? The irony of this situation is that the socialists, both Populist and Marxist, had themselves, in years past, stressed many of the political demands and tactics that both workers and liberals in 1905 would find quite compatible with an all-inclusive left bloc rather than exclusively with a specific socialist party. It is instructive to recall that the Social Democrats' own program-minimum stood for the overthrow of autocracy, a democratic republic, civil rights, an elected legislature, and the eight-hour day. Workers first heard of the primacy of political struggle over economic from socialist mentors, and they were encouraged to participate in public demonstrations from the same quarter. By 1905 the Union of Liberation, and later the Kadets, stood for all these things as well, and it is understandable that political novices combined these programmatic resemblances with the patent need for unity in the opposition and viewed it as whole rather than fragmented.[76]

The socialists began to gain the upper hand among workers in early 1905, chiefly because they sent organizers and agitators to the factories, while the liberals did not. But the socialists were still prime targets for arrest, and they remained wedded to their clandestine networks, so they were unable to satisfy the workers' desire to link up with something bigger and more public. The openness and publicness of the liberal/democratic opposition therefore remained one of its main attractions for Petersburg workers. This will become clearer as the events of the rest of the year unfold. Given the workers' enthusiasm for self-organization and public protest, the government lost an especially pregnant opportunity to drive a wedge between workers and socialists by granting freedom of assembly and organization early in 1905. But to compound the error, it also continued to bottle up workers in their factories and to enforce the suppression of even factory-level assembly and organization. This repressive strategy did not eliminate the urge to organize, but drove it with redoubled force into the two available channels, clandestine workplace organization and an ongoing effort, long after the suppression of the Shidlovskii electors, to emulate and join in with the public protest of educated society.

Why then did the liberals not capitalize on their advantages and bring the workers under their sway? As we saw in Chapter 3, Struve was encouraging this from the pages of *Liberation*. Why did they not send organizers to the factories? Aside from a lack of agitators, there may have been other problems, endemic to the non-socialist intelligentsia. In this regard, the initiatives of Petersburg's Union of Engineers in linking their struggle with that of the factory workers are instructive.

76. The Social Democratic minimum program in effect in 1905 is available in *Vtoroi s"ezd RSDRP. Iiul'-avgust 1903 goda. Protokoly*, pp. 418–24.

It will be recalled that one of the four political intiatives resolved upon by the Union of Liberation in the fall of 1904 was the formation of unions of professional groups. The engineers and technicians of the capital were the first to respond to the call. At a banquet on December 5, 1904, the All-Russian Union of Engineers and Technicians of All Specialties became the first of a number of professional unions to be formed. The moving spirit was Leonid Ivanovich Lutugin, Professor of Geology at the St. Petersburg Mining Institute and a long-time civic activist. Lutugin and others had prepared a banquet resolution that carried unanimously and became the union's first statement of aims. It called for civil liberties and a legislature in which "society" participated—by which was clearly meant "educated society, not the masses." The moderate resolution carefully avoided mention of a constituent assembly or the "four-tail" suffrage formula. The strategy was to cement an alliance of the engineers with influential factory owners and government figures, many of whom attended the banquet. Yet the resolution's authors seem to have sensed the unique position of engineers *between* labor and capital, both in factories and in society, when they wrote that the reforms called for were meant to achieve "stability in economic policy and the protection of labor." Like most of the liberal intelligentsia and the Union of Liberation as a whole, the engineers were most interested in mobilizing their own kind and in preserving an alliance with the more moderate wing of reform, be they landowners or factory owners. And like most of the rest of the liberal intelligentsia as well, the engineers cast themselves in the role of educated protectors of the workers.[77]

Following the momentous events of January 1905, the leaders of the Engineers' Union did not change their basic attitude toward workers. They produced a new resolution that enunciated the same political positions as the banquet resolution but gave more attention to the importance of labor and, notably, to the importance of engineers as their closest allies and spokesmen. Again they demanded political liberties, but this time in the name of the working class as well: "Our industrial workers totally lack the legal means to defend their interests and, in particular, lack the possibility to organize themselves for this purpose into unions. . . . We, and especially those of us who by our positions stand close to the workers, consider it our responsibility to attest that the idea of political freedom has been known in the work-

77. Sanders, "The Union of Unions: Political, Economic, Civil, and Human Rights Organizations in the 1905 Russian Revolution," ch. 3, pp. 49–53.

ers' milieu for a long time."[78] After January 9 the size and complexity of the liberation movement had increased immensely, and it should not be surprising that the engineers, like most of the rest of the liberal opposition, found it difficult to adjust to a situation that had suddenly challenged it either to lead the workers or to surrender leadership to those who could. The engineers were neither organized nor necessarily motivated, no matter how close some of them stood to workers, to carry this out. Nevertheless, their actions in the next few weeks seem to have been dictated by the same genuine and deeply felt sympathy for workers that animated most of educated society following the slaughter of the innocents on Bloody Sunday.

Some time in the fourth week of January, the leaders of the Engineers' Union agreed with representatives of the Imperial Russian Technical Society to conduct joint hearings on the labor problem. From this new collaboration, the Union derived a distinct advantage: the Society's auditorium was offered to it on a regular basis for its meetings, thereby placing it under the patronage of a quasi-governmental agency and freeing it from having to justify each gathering to the police. These joint arrangements for hearings on labor coincided with the announcement of the Shidlovskii Commission, which stirred up great controversy in oppositionist circles, and the first of several popular and well-attended sessions of the joint hearings turned into a tumultuous forum that debated the merits of the new labor commission.

At the session of February 11, a confrontation occurred that forced the Engineers' Union to retreat from whatever ideas it may have had about leading the labor movement. The meeting was attended by over 1,000 persons, including 300 workers, most of them, according to one source, Shidlovskii electors.[79] All major viewpoints were represented, including the Social Democratic. A number of opinions on the Shidlovskii Commission were voiced from various quarters, the bulk of them favoring boycott as a sign of noncooperation with the government. Then the Bolshevik S. I. Gusev put forth for adoption by the meeting the Petersburg Committee's resolution on the Commission, which called for participation in the elections but refusal to participate in the Commission itself. This caused a scandal in the meeting when an SR and other opponents of the Social Democrats spoke against the resolution, although in truth more against its authors.

78. *Pravo*, no. 4 (Jan. 30, 1905), cols. 266, 268.
79. *Iskra*, no. 89 (Feb. 24, 1905), p. 6.

V. I. Kovalevskii, the Technical Society official who chaired the meeting, sought to escape from this impasse by ruling that he did not have the power to bring the resolution to a vote. He was advised that he need not be bound by the Society's rules if he would but adjourn the official meeting and continue as a popular meeting, which might entertain the resolution. This was done, although sharp attacks on the Bolshevik resolution and apparently on the propriety of the workers' presence as well continued to be made. Then one of the workers, apparently also a socialist speaking in support of the Bolshevik resolution, addressed what many of his fellow workers must have felt to be the broader underlying issue:

> Here you are all the time howling about solidarity, about unity, spilling crocodile tears, but when the workers themselves come to you and want to speak their minds on everything that pains them, everything for which the working class has spilled its blood, you throw them out on their ear. You protest against the tutelage [*opeka*] of Tsarism and say that Russian society has grown up. Yes, it has grown up, but it has also outgrown those limits within which you intend to squeeze it. Neither Tsarism's tutelage, nor yours, nor anyone's is wanted. We demand the rights to think for ourselves, to look after our own needs, and [you may] rest assured that we are not five-year-old kids and that we will make our lives as good as possible under existing capitalist conditions![80]

The Liberationist A. I. Novikov hastened to rebut this statement, accusing the speaker and the Social Democrats generally of creating divisiveness between workers and the intelligentsia. Before a vote was taken, however, Professor Lutugin spoke against voting on the grounds that the other partner to the meeting, the Engineers' Union, would suffer the consequences at the hands of the police. Kovalevskii then adjourned the meeting.[81]

The episode well illustrates several aspects of worker-intelligentsia relations in 1905. First, as in the confrontations with workers during the banquet campaign, the engineers' reception of the workers at the February 11 meeting was colored by the presence of socialists. "Workerphilia" became mixed up with resentment of the revolutionary party activists and the threat they posed to the liberals' legal tactics. This confusion and resentment are understandable, since

80. *Vpered*, no. 9 (Feb. 23, 1905), p. 13.
81. *Ibid.*, p. 14. *Iskra*, no. 89 (Feb. 24, 1905), p. 6. There are discrepancies between these two accounts, and the exact sequence and development of the meeting is open to interpretation. Cf., for example, Sanders, "The Union of Unions," ch. 5, pp. 17–20, who sees Lutugin as the cause of the dissension.

the socialists probably did intend to challenge the engineers' bid for leadership of the factory population. But the episode also illustrates that Petersburg workers in 1905 were very protective of the *autonomy* of their labor movement—more than at any previous time and, in important respects, more than in later periods as well. How this affected the revolutionary parties will become abundantly clear as this account moves through the year. The engineers' superior airs, implied by the accusation of intelligentsia *opeka*, would seem even more objectionable to workers after the experience of the Assembly, the January strike, and the reaction to Bloody Sunday.

In sum, either by overreacting to the proposed Bolshevik resolution or by failing to understand the actual popularity among workers of participation in the Shidlovskii elections, the engineers did turn a deaf ear to workers' deeply felt needs. However close they *felt* to workers, whatever their subjective attitudes, their behavior at the February 11 meeting proved to be a revealing comment on where their true interests might lie. For if the objection to adopting the resolution was its association with a revolutionary party rather than its substance, a parallel resolution with the same position under the Union's own sponsorship could have been drafted and voted upon. Instead, the Union leadership drew back from such action lest it lose its convenient meeting arrangements. In the end, the situation was defined not by the interests shared by factory engineers and workers, but by what *divided* them, the semi-privileged position that engineers, as educated professionals, occupied in Russian society.

Beyond the establishment of the Union and the February 11 meeting, there appears to have been no serious attempt to implement the engineers' idea that their middle position in factories could be used to protect and defend workers. In the single known case where factory engineers as a group appeared to intervene on behalf of workers, a close examination indicates that in the factory, as in the meeting hall, the engineers made use of labor protest as a vehicle to define their own interests, organize themselves, and put forth their own demands. In March 1905 the engineers at the Izhorsk Works, one of the Naval Ministry's giant shipbuilding plants, produced a detailed commentary on a list of workers' demands presented earlier. The engineers served as foremen and section chiefs in the plant, and in those positions they were the first to receive workers' complaints, yet they did not possess the authority to solve the problems they were constantly faced with. Their attempt to deal systematically with this situation resulted in the commentary, a cold and sober analysis of each demand, along with recommendations about which could be met at no cost to the plant and warnings about which were most likely to produce continued unrest if ignored. They also asked to be consulted regularly by higher management on all decisions affecting labor-management relations and the technical equipping of the shops.[82] That is, the engineers were conditioning their opening to labor on the compatibility of any projected reforms with a streamlined and more efficient factory order, the vision of which they were willing to share with management in exchange for a share of power in the new order. Thus although the engineers' document, which was ignored by the Izhorsk management, eased the way to meeting some of the workers' demands, its fundamental thrust was not a passion for justice toward labor but a passion for plant rationalization.

One can better understand the engineers' lack of success among workers compared to the popularity of a figure like Nosar' by recalling that Nosar' had no stake in the factory order except the defense of workers' rights. The engineers claimed that their close proximity to factory labor gave them a special insight and mandate to involve themselves with workers politically. Yet the outcome of such involvement at the Izhorsk Works indicates that their close proximity to workers may have been more of a handicap than an advantage. Factory engineers had a definite place and viewpoint by virtue of being a part of the factory order, and this interfered with a clear perception of the workers' own place and viewpoint.

Moreover, Nosar' acted and was perceived to be acting as an individual, whereas the enginers acted as an interest group. Whatever the workers' attitude toward the intelligentsia as a whole, Nosar' could be thought of as an exception or as representing the intelligentsia's more selfless values. Individual engineers may have acted similarly on behalf of workers and won their confidence (although I have found no record of this). In the case of the Izhorsk engineers, they did not do so but instead voiced their own interest in greater authority through greater efficiency. In thus viewing a situation of overall change and improvement from the angle of their own particular interests, they behaved no worse or no better than other intelligentsia professionals, and other social groups generally.

The relations of the engineers with workers appear to have been determined by those qualities they shared with the rest of the intelli-

82. M. M. Mikhailov, "1905 god na Izhorskom zavode (Okonchanie)," pp. 189–92, 208–10.

gentsia, and the special qualifications they claimed to have in dealing with workers may have been more a hindrance than a help. Outside the factories, the engineers behaved very much like the rest of the liberal and democratic intelligentsia, combining an abstract commitment to greater freedom for all and aid to the lower classes with a clear preference for a tutelary relationship with "the people" and an overweening sense of superiority and entitlement to lead the entire opposition movement. Yet, as more professional groups were organized, the manner in which the liberal and democratic intelligentsia dealt with the workers' revolution assumed decisive importance in determining the political outcome of the assault on the autocracy. The beginnings made in January and February did not bode well for an outcome favorable to the liberals.

Nevertheless, Nosar' was popular not for his personal qualities alone, and his popularity cannot be properly understood without recognizing the political symbolism involved—a helping hand to workers extended by educated society, an offer of alliance in a common fight against the old order. In other words, what seems to have appealed to workers was the traditional commitment of the educated classes to the people's welfare, their sense of noblesse oblige toward the lower classes, rather than either socialism, on the one hand, or the parallel interests of new professional groups, on the other. Whether or not the workers' trust and affection for Nosar' was misplaced, its very existence indicates that the great majority of Petersburg workers were still open to accepting aid, alliance, and leadership from the liberal/democratic intelligentsia. If the liberals failed to develop and sustain this alliance and this leadership in 1905, the antipathy of workers toward them should not be counted among the most important causes, even though workers could be quite aware and resentful of intelligentsia condescension to them, as we have seen.[83] Instead, the causes should probably be sought in the plans and tactics of the liberals themselves.

CONCLUSION: THE FIRST PHASE OF PROTEST

It is perhaps appropriate to draw together and summarize the meaning of the events that had been unfolding in St. Petersburg since

83. Only the socialists or monarchists could hope to produce a rival to Nosar' for leadership and popularity in 1905, but neither did so. The interrelationship of leadership, popularity, and politics demands much closer scrutiny than it has received. Soviet

late 1904. The upsurge of mass political activity and consciousness in 1905 was the joint product of the inexperienced protest by an incipient labor movement and the quest of intelligentsia elites for a mass following. Neither one nor the other can alone bear the burden of explanation for the explosion of protest and politics that began in January 1905. The novelty and the potency of this upheaval consisted in the *combination* of two powerful movements: the one rootless, novel, but massive, urban-based, and potentially more consistent and disciplined than any popular movement of protest yet faced by the autocracy; the other rooted in the professions, the culture of educated society, and the tradition of civic idealism of Russia's intelligentsia, now at the height of its ideological influence and numerical preponderance as an organized and unified movement in the cities, projecting itself as a rival political elite to that of the government and the court.

The blending of these two currents to form a new revolutionary opposition in 1905 assimilated the underground work of the revolutionary parties among industrial workers since the 1870's into a broader fusion of social forces that drew into the struggle strata, trades, and categories of workers far beyond those yet reached by the revolutionaries operating on their own.

Contrary to the claims of many Soviet accounts, this new labor movement was not under the direct influence of the Social Democratic Party or its Bolshevik faction, and although it owed a great deal to SD agitation and organizing efforts, it was the product of many other influences as well. The example of the political springtime, inspired and organized by the liberal intelligentsia, had a great impact on the workers of the capital. The links between workers and the socialist and nonsocialist intelligentsia remained important throughout 1905 in St. Petersburg, as the political physiognomy of the workers' two most popular leaders indicates: the priest and labor reformer Georgii Gapon and the left-Liberationist lawyer Khrustalev-Nosar'.

More important than the direct impact of individuals or party doc-

---

historians of the period and of labor normally ignore Nosar', apparently because he represented a "backward" political tendency among workers ("bourgeois democracy"), but this formula hardly explains his popularity, and one suspects that attempting a better explanation would bring up issues they have not been willing to discuss. Nosar' seems to have been popular among many strata of workers, not only those that might be considered less politically developed. Although it was the less developed textile workers who first brought Nosar' to public notice, it need only be remembered that in the fall he was elected president of the Petersburg Soviet, 60 percent of whose deputies were metalworkers.

trines, Russian workers in 1905 displayed an exceptional and rapid assimilation of the political meaning of their labor protests. Contrary to the labor strategies of the Liberationist Struve or of the Mensheviks and Bolsheviks,[84] Russian workers would neither confine their protests to factory issues nor horde up their energies for the "knockout punch" against the autocracy. Instead, a great and relentless strike fever seized factory workers after January 9, powered as much by moral outrage as by a sense of material deprivation. This outrage was for most workers more aptly expressed as political slogans—"Down with Autocracy!," "Constituent Assembly!"—and radical economic demands—"Eight-hour day!" "Inviolability of factory deputies!"—than as lists of measured factory demands that might have been met by their employers. The rational political insight that the interest of workers in the factory setting was linked to the weakening or overthrow of autocratic power was thus imbedded in a more widely felt and more "spontaneous" outrage at the years of oppression at the workplace, finally released as a result of January 9th and of the leadership, encouragement, and example of the intelligentsia, liberal and revolutionary. Much political growth among the Petersburg workers in 1905 involved the merger of this rational insight with this anger and indignation; the naming and therefore the comprehension of a rage that was otherwise incomprehensible, simultaneously confined by and yet overflowing the factory walls.

84. On Bolshevik impatience with the "spontaneous" strike movement in early 1905, see Chapter 4, note 61.

CHAPTER SIX

The Unity and Diversity of the Opposition, March-September 1905

———— ◆•◆ ————

THE LIBERALS TAKE THE LEAD

The class and ideological divergences between educated society and the lower classes were too obvious and potent an issue for the embattled government not to have sought to use them to its political advantage in combatting the opposition. On February 18 and 19, about the time the Shidlovskii Commission was losing its political viability, the Tsar published a three-part declaration of intentions that set the political tone for the next half year. The first part was a general manifesto responding to the January events, which condemned the attempts of a criminal movement to destroy the state order and called for a strengthening of punitive measures and the support of "right-thinking" persons. The second was an imperial *ukaz* to the Senate that granted the right to petition the Tsar on matters of "public well-being and state needs." The third was a rescript to Interior Minister Bulygin proclaiming a body of representatives "elected from the population" for the preliminary examination of legislative proposals, i.e., a consultative assembly.[1]

The three measures codified for the conditions of 1905 the more general carrot-and-stick approach that the regime had always applied: the "criminal leaders" of disorders were put on warning, and the police, the extreme Right, and those subjects whose interests suffered from the continuation of protest (such as employers and property owners) were reassured of the regime's backing. Moderate and

---

1. *Krizis samoderzhaviia*, pp. 183–84. For the text of the three measures, see *Sputnik izbiratelia na 1906 god. Osvoboditel'noe dvizhenie i sovremennye ego formy*, pp. 239–42.

conservative liberals were given a legal outlet for their energies, and some of the activities they were already engaged in were retroactively sanctioned; this small concession by the government seemed to promise that petitions to the throne might even achieve something. Finally, the promise of a consultative assembly signaled the government's acknowledgment that change in the organization of the state power was needed and that it was willing to take the initiative in reforming itself, thus assuaging the more moderate sections of the opposition and shifting the terms of the national debate away from the contest of power between government and opposition to focus instead on the kinds of reforms needed.

Seen in this light, the government's February initiatives, which barely began to address the demands now being raised on all sides by the opposition, proved to be sufficient to keep the lid on for another six months, while the government worked to resolve the war in the Far East. The result was a relative stabilization in relations with the opposition, an equilibrium that even managed to withstand two further crushing military defeats. The Battle of Mukden in February demonstrated the impossibility of a land victory, discouraged the last of those still hopeful of a Russian victory, and strengthened the press campaign to sue for an immediate peace. The spectacular destruction of the Baltic Fleet in the Tsushima Straits on May 14 finally led even the regime to begin secret peace explorations, though it continued to speak publicly of its intention to fight on.[2]

Throughout these military debacles, despite continuing, militant, and increasingly better-organized protest, the opposition did not improve its overall unity and did not mount a decisive attack on the autocracy. On the contrary, with better organization and sharper self-definition came greater differentiation among both liberals and workers, and greater divergence between them. Despite the Potemkin mutiny and other more or less isolated military revolts over the spring and summer, the loyalty of the armed forces to the throne was on the whole unshaken. Ironically, a reinvigoration of the opposition, a renewed attack on the autocracy, and the most serious military revolts came in the fall of 1905, after the Peace of Portsmouth had ended the war with Japan.[3]

The evolution of the opposition over the middle portion of 1905 was mainly the result of its own internal needs, initiatives, and con-

2. Pavlovich, "Vneshnaia politika," pp. 28–29.

3. On the loyalty of the army and the military mutinies, see Bushnell, *Mutiny amid Repression. Russian Soldiers in the Revolution of 1905–1906.*

flicts, and it is this process that forms the subject of this chapter. Although an active and militant labor movement burgeoned in other areas of the Empire over the summer (e.g., in Lodz and Ivanovo-Voznesensk), in St. Petersburg labor entered a period of virtual dormancy (see Tables 18 and 19, below). The liberal/democratic opposition of the professions and educated society, on the other hand, entered a new period of efflorescence, organizing professional and political unions, sharpening zemstvo opposition, sparring publicly with the government, and forming ties with all parts of society, even dabbling in labor organizing. Benefiting from the government's wariness after the great strikes and protests of January and February, the liberals were able to seize on the *ukaz* of February 18 as the legal basis for a wide variety of public oppositional activities, from meetings and the publication of oppositionist news and statements to the formation of protopolitical organizations.

Most of the major developments in the evolution of the liberal/democratic movement took place in the period from March through September.[4] Although the liberals had never been firmly unified, the Union of Liberation had fostered the *hope* of drawing together rural and urban, zemstvo and intelligentsia, moderate and radical tendencies into a single party, and this hope still enjoyed considerable vitality in March. By September, however, the movement had divided over the nature of the legislature—generally known as the Bulygin Duma—into a moderate wing led by P. N. Miliukov and others favoring participation through what became (in October) the Constitutional Democratic Party and a radical wing led by the Union of Unions, favoring boycott and solidarity with the labor movement and revolutionary parties.[5] This divergence of principle and politics was a sign of the movement's very success, in the sense that more precise programs and separate organizational existences meant clearer commitment and more effective political action. Political maturation had made it pos-

4. Unfortunately, this is also the most neglected period in the secondary literature, which as a rule concentrates either on the period before 1905 or on that from October 1905 onward. Chermenskii, *Burzhuaziia i tsarizm v pervoi russkoi revoliutsii*, gives the fullest recent treatment, albeit hostile. Briefer accounts appear in Emmons, *The Formation of Political Parties*, esp. chs. 1 and 2, and Galai, *The Liberation Movement in Russia, 1900–1905*, pp. 243–73. Sanders, "The Union of Unions," has proven to be the richest and most informative single study describing relations between left liberals and labor, but it offers no comprehensive interpretation of the entire liberal movement. The zemstvo wing of the liberals is trenchantly examined in Roberta Manning, *The Crisis of the Old Order in Russia. Government and Gentry.*

5. Galai, *The Liberation Movement*, pp. 243–45. Martynov, "Istoriia konstitutsionno-demokraticheskoi partii," pp. 6–7.

sible to leave behind the marriage of convenience that the Union of Liberation had always been to some degree.

Although both zemstvo and professional organizations edged leftward in program, a key episode in the late spring brought out their divergent styles and political proclivities. Like the Union of Unions, the zemstvo activists were committed to a constituent assembly and "four-tail" suffrage. Yet, in a futile attempt to preserve the integrity of the zemstvo movement, they took special care to stem the defection of a group of Slavophile liberals by making them welcome at the Third Zemstvo Congress (May 24–26), even though the Slavophiles were in fundamental disagreement with the constitutionalists. The joint gathering, dubbed the "coalition congress" because of this effort, then voted to send sixteen representatives to meet with the Tsar, in an attempt to bridge the gap between the ruler and the representatives of society. Duly observing the traditional polite signs of deference, the deputation presented a petition calling for the convocation of popular representatives to decide, jointly with the Tsar, the questions of war and peace and a new state order.[6] As a political gesture the audience with the Tsar signaled to observers not only a somewhat audacious dramatization of their political views, but also an assumption that the future political arrangements they envisioned would be compatible with the monarchy and with the Tsar-subject relationship.

This gesture of the *zemtsy* not only did not prevent the defection of the Slavophiles, it antagonized the democratic wing of the Liberationist alliance, which in the wake of the Tsushima disaster was disposed to isolate and discredit the monarchy, not support and cooperate with it. This antagonistic reaction strengthened the hand of those on the Left who were already prepared to jettison the moderates for the sake of liberal/democratic unity and firmer ties with the mass movement. Within the newly organized Union of Unions a number of socialist participants sponsored radical resolutions such as that endorsed in the wake of the Tsushima defeat calling on "all the Russian people, societies, and organizations" to convene a constituent assembly "in revolutionary fashion" (*iavochnym poriadkom*, as a *fait accompli*, in disregard of the law).[7] The presence of such anger and militancy undoubtedly helped provoke the withdrawal of the Zemstvo Constitutionalists and the Academic Union from the Union of Unions after its first congress; the *zemtsy* never returned and henceforth confined

6. Emmons, *The Formation of Political Parties*, pp. 98–102. Galai, *The Liberation Movement*, p. 252.

7. Galai, *The Liberation Movement*, p. 253.

their activities to politically temperate, mostly zemstvo, circles. Thus, disagreements over strategy, tone, and style, rather than program, fed divisiveness among the liberals. One of the key problems at issue was whether and *how* the liberals should seek to win the mass movement to their side. The same issue underlay the Union of Union's later rejection of participation in a consultative duma.

These resolutions and debates were accomplished at a number of congresses and gatherings held over the spring and summer, mostly in St. Petersburg. From March through September, the Union of Liberation met three times, zemstvo representatives four times, and the Union of Unions three times; in between or overlapping with these larger gatherings were congresses of smaller and constituent groups such as the Engineers' Union, the Zemstvo Constitutionalists, and the Peasants' Union.[8] The bustle of this activity alone helped restore to the intelligentsia of the capital its sense of being the center of the antigovernment opposition. The declarations and proceedings of these gatherings were openly published, and meetings of the professional unions were held in defiance of regulations restricting public association—activities that always drew the attention and admiration of the citizenry. Many newspapers made their own campaigns for a free press by carrying precisely such news, pushing at the limits of censorship.

The impression that the opposition was centered in the intelligentsia was reinforced for workers by the overall lack of focused oppositional activities in their own ranks after February and by the lack of publicity about the mostly local or clandestine activity that was taking place. Under these circumstances many workers continued to rely on intelligentsia models and examples for their own activities. Hence the awakening of large numbers of Petersburg workers to political protest then and throughout 1905 occurred in a cultural mold defined and nurtured by the intelligentsia, and the combination of intelligentsia culture and oppositional politics was nowhere stronger than in Petersburg. One of the unique features of the revolution that labor underwent in 1905 is to be found in the fact that the civic rituals of assemblage and elections, of oratory and debate, of public statements of principle and resolve, largely practiced by and identified with the liberal intelligentsia, entered deeply into the particular class consciousness that was developing among St. Petersburg's workers.

8. For a partial list of these congresses, see D. W. Treadgold, *Lenin and His Rivals* (New York, 1955), pp. 286–87.

Since the liberals projected their movement or party as a universal, all-class formation, they were increasingly compelled to face the need to capture a mass following. We have seen in Chapter 3 that Petr Struve, just prior to January 9, found the low cultural level of workers a barrier to political participation and proposed a joint Liberationist and Social Democratic effort to educate and organize workers into reformist labor unions. In that statement and in others subsequent to January 9, Struve also expressed a reluctance to see the liberal movement compete directly with the socialists for the allegiance of the workers, an unspoken acknowledgment of the claim the socialists had already staked out in the factories. However, he did not write again at length about workers for several months, turning his attention instead to the problem of attracting the peasantry.[9]

Then, in May, the editor of *Liberation* turned again to the workers in a lengthy reply to a correspondent who had complained in the previous issue that the Liberationists too easily and opportunistically aped the extreme positions of the revolutionary parties, asking how they could hold to their own principles while still attracting a mass following.[10] Forced to confront the problem of a now mobilized working class, and chastened by several months during which the socialists had evinced practically no interest in joint political ventures with the Liberationists, Struve finally admitted, in effect, that the Liberationists were in direct competition with the socialist parties for the allegiance of the "popular masses." He argued that the "revolutionism" of the latter would precipitate clashes with the state in which the workers, and therefore their socialist leadership, would suffer defeat, whereupon the Liberationists' program would prove more attractive to the mass of workers due to its practicality and lack of doctrinal demands they did not understand. Previously convinced that the workers' low cultural level and lack of education made them ill-prepared for political participation, Struve now discovered that they had "a healthy instinct for reality and a sure sense of the possible."[11]

In addressing the question of why the "revolutionism" of the socialist parties was nevertheless winning a mass following while the lib-

9. E.g., *Osvobozhdenie*, no. 67 (Mar. 5/18, 1905), pp. 281–82, no. 68 (Apr. 2/15, 1905), pp. 294–95. Struve's original statement on workers, "Nasushchnaia zadacha vremeni," appeared in *Osvobozhdenie*, no. 63 (Jan. 7/20, 1905).

10. U-v, "Kak ne poteriat' sebia?," *Osvobozhdenie*, no. 69–70 (May 7/20, 1905), pp. 333–34. "U-v" has been identified as S. A. Kotliarevskii: Emmons, *The Formation of Political Parties*, pp. 37, 410, n. 49.

11. "Kak naiti sebia?," *Osvobozhdenie*, no. 71 (May 18/31, 1905), p. 337.

erals were not, Struve asserted that the liberals were making no effort and losing out by default. The key element in this failure Struve found to be the liberals' neglect of the student youth, a key link with the mass movement, whom he claimed always to have "possessed 'great moral resources'" and to have constituted a "specific, actual political force which must not be ignored." He thought the reasons for the liberals' almost complete estrangement from students were many and complex, but he put particular emphasis on its results: "We, as a political party or as a political tendency, have done and do nothing or almost nothing to influence the student youth. Therefore, among other results, the problem of influence on the popular masses, in its practical aspect, runs up against the absence of sufficient agitational and propagandist 'personnel.'"[12]

Struve had hit on a problem of fundamental importance in the alignment of forces in the 1905 Revolution, a shortcoming in the implementation of liberal/democratic politics that was never remedied, but seemingly only forgotten about. The attractiveness of the socialist parties to that part of "student youth" that was politically active in 1905 was overwhelming, and constituted one of the revolutionaries' great secret resources in the conquest of the masses. For without the orators and other agitators willing to take the risks of carrying a political message out to the street corners and to the factory gates, a political party in 1905 had to count on the public coming to its writings and meetings of its own accord. Such a passive approach limited a party's influence to the narrow arena of activity the law and the state would permit. The liberal/democratic intelligentsia, for all the impact of its public stances and the eminence of its leaders and spokespersons, remained on the whole a band of generals without sergeants.

The failure to recruit students did not mean the liberal/democratic movement lacked its advocates among workers. Certain working-class unions were recruited into the Union of Unions, and new initiatives were taken by the Engineers' Union to give leadership to the factory population, as will be seen below. Moreover, the liberal/democratic intelligentsia, despite suffering from the limitations outlined by Struve, which made them an unequal competitor with the socialist parties in the "struggle for the popular masses," nevertheless continued to enjoy the admiration and respect of the lower classes, including many workers. The continuing prestige among workers of the leaders of Russia's modernizing sector may even be said to have benefited to a certain

12. *Ibid.*, p. 340.

extent from the lack of close contact. If the liberals had no presence in the factories, they could not be held to account for the travails of the labor movement, as were the socialists. If familiarity breeds contempt, distance preserves illusions.

THE FACTORY MOVEMENT IN THE SPRING AND SUMMER

After the excitement and drama of January and February, the strike movement in Petersburg and throughout the Empire fell to a somewhat lower level during the ensuing half-year and only reached massive proportions again with the political and general strikes of October, November, and December. The seven-month period from March through September accounted for little more than one-quarter of all strikers in 1905, whether in St. Petersburg or the Empire as a whole (see Tables 18 and 19).

Nonetheless, strikes remained endemic and occurred at historically unprecedented levels throughout the spring and summer of 1905. The number of strikers in Russia in every *month* except September exceeded all strikers for any given *year* from 1895 to 1904 (except 1903), and the relative magnitudes for Petersburg would have been comparable.[13] The awakening of the great mass of factory workers to the need for improvement of their material conditions and the status of their rights within the workplace continued to provide the most important source of energy and inspiration to the entire opposition movement. The events of the first two months of the year had brought forth factory leadership and strikes which attained districtwide and even citywide proportions without yielding to most workers any lasting or satisfying results. In the period that followed, the strike movement sought to widen and improve the means of struggle as well as to raise anew the still largely unmet demands.

In addition, the upsurge of protest among practically all other classes and national groups throughout Russia after January 9 promoted and sustained the revolt among workers, especially in St. Petersburg. Military defeats at the hands of Japan and Russia's eventual disengagement from the costly and humiliating war in the Far East fueled the whole antigovernment opposition; major strikes, demonstrations, and shootings erupted in other provinces over the spring

13. *Stachki 1905*, p. 6, and *Stachki 1895–1904*, Appendix, p. 17. Comparative figures for Petersburg are not available.

TABLE 18
Man-Days Lost in St. Petersburg Province from Strikes

Month	Man-days lost		Month	Man-days lost	
	No.	Pct.		No.	Pct.
January	942,441	20.3%	July	454,780	9.8%
February	601,980	13.0	August	108,891	2.3
March	158,123	3.4	September	9,678	0.2
April	80,247	1.7	October	506,385	10.9
May	143,531	3.1	November	774,034	16.7
June	302,727	6.9	December	555,000	12.0

SOURCE: *VPR*, p. 514; V. Leont'ev, "Stachki 1905 goda v S.-Peterburge," p. 54 (for December only).

TABLE 19
Number of Strikers in Russia in 1905, by Month

Month	Strikers in Russia		Month	Strikers in Russia	
	No.	Pct.		No.	Pct.
January	414,438	15.3%	July	150,059	5.5%
February	291,210	10.7	August	78,343	2.9
March	72,472	2.7	September	36,629	1.4
April	80,568	3.0	October	481,364	17.8
May	219,990	8.1	November	323,349	11.9
June	142,641	5.3	December	418,215	15.4

SOURCE: *Stachki 1905*, p. 6.

and summer; naval and military mutinies marked the incipient disintegration of Tsarist authority in the ranks of its own institutions; and the Petersburg workers themselves demonstrated against the war and struck on the occasion of the call-up of military reservists from the factories in mid-June. Meetings, demonstrations, industrial organization, and, of course, strikes were still for the most part illegal, and the continuing presence of troops and police in factory districts to enforce these bans, even though they may have contributed to a superficial orderliness, simultaneously embodied and dramatized the government repression that everyone spoke against and helped to school a whole new generation of strikers to the need for political liberties and a constitutional order. As a result, political protest, already awakened by the Assembly's struggle and the Shidlovskii campaign, continued to be voiced in strikes normally confined to industrial issues, combining overt political demands with those applicable to workers alone and providing them with allies and sympathizers within the broader nationwide opposition movement.

The most immediate catalysts and beneficiaries of politicized labor protest, however, were the parties of the extreme left, especially the Social Democrats. While these parties directly recruited only a small portion of the workers exposed to their ideas, their agitational influence spread outward to a much greater number. Building on their gains during January and February, revolutionaries began to exercise a degree of leadership in factory struggles never before witnessed. Following the first widespread contacts between party agitators and factory workers during the Shidlovskii campaign, socialist leaflets, newspapers, and orators became an increasingly frequent and familiar part of factory strikes and protests. By midsummer this agitational initiative met with a new enthusiasm for mass meetings, now often held on the factory premises in defiance of the police and the management. Speakers from the revolutionary parties were not only accepted at these meetings but were even demanded and listened to attentively. Ever larger numbers of workers became acquainted with socialist slogans, programs, and ideas in this manner, and a new tradition of mass meetings and political oratory was set.

But this greater sympathy and willingness to listen was a relative change, not a wholesale shift. The suspicion with which many workers had viewed revolutionaries for the many years preceding 1905 was never entirely overcome. Working-class fortunes were not seen as closely linked with those of the revolutionary parties by more than several hundred workers in a city teeming with tens of thousands of factory workers.[14] Although this represented an increase over the period before January 9, and although oppositionist sentiment among workers was on the upswing in these months, the political conclusions drawn by most workers continued to be heterogeneous. All the revolutionary parties had greatly strengthened their following among workers, but none of them spoke for the workers as a whole. In addition, sympathy for revolutionary politics was only one reaction to the continuing upheaval among workers. The wellspring of anger and

14. Party membership figures cannot be established with precision. Martov estimated that the Mensheviks had 1,200 to 1,300 organized workers in Petersburg in the first half of 1905, and the Bolsheviks several hundred; by October the two organizations were about equal in strength (he did not venture another figure). *Istoriia rossiiskoi sotsial-demokratii*, p. 125. Compare Nevskii, *Rabochee dvizhenie v ianvarskie dni 1905 goda*, pp. 159–60, which gives an estimated worker membership for *both* factions at the end of the spring of only 800–1,000.

the awakened determination to improve their lot continued to follow channels more immediately available to factory workers: impromptu strikes and guerrilla tactics within the factory, labor demonstrations in the form of funerals and memorial services for fallen comrades, and defensive responses to unemployment, lockouts, and the ever-present police surveillance.

With the downturn in strike activity following the end of the Shidlovskii campaign, frustration and discontent with the factory order was sometimes directed against individual management personnel. Demands for the dismissal of unpopular foremen and overseers were often accomplished by direct action: workers would seize the offender, put him in a sack, and cart him out of the factory. By March 18 the Factory Inspectorate had recorded more than twenty cases of such "sackings" in St. Petersburg, and a large number probably went unrecorded. The problem was apparently so severe that the Ministry of Finance formed a commission on violence against management personnel to hear workers' complaints and adjudicate disputes. Factory managements responded by threatening to dismiss the workers involved, but the hated overseer frequently had to leave anyway because of the continuing threat of physical harm. The virtue of this direct-action tactic was that it simultaneously shamed the person sacked and deprived him of his authority among the other workers, thereby insuring some change in the situation, even if he remained in the factory afterward. In addition, the lesson was not lost on other management bullies: after two "sackings" at the Putilov Works, for instance, the other foremen reportedly became much more polite toward workers.[15]

The strikes that did take place in the spring and summer frequently required more than the usual in-plant grievances to get started, although economic demands continued to be raised and dissatisfaction over the failure to win them continued to heat up the ongoing struggle with factory managements. Now that it was clear that strikes cost the participants needed wages and did not normally produce material gains, however, it took more than the acknowledgment of common factory grievances to bring workers out. Shorter strikes connected with some moral or political issue consequently became more characteristic of the period after February.

15. Shuster, *Peterburgskie rabochie*, pp. 119–20. Mitel'man et al., *Istoriia Putilovskogo zavoda*, p. 206. On the Finance Ministry's commission, see LGIA, fond 1239, op. 1, d. 103, ll. 36–40.

In early April, for instance, Putilov workers struck in connection with the death and burial of three workers involved in an industrial accident. The management responded by closing the plant for two weeks to weed out the "troublemakers." Funerals were one of the few occasions when workers could gather legally and publicly in large numbers, and it is not surprising that burial services often provided the occasion for demonstrations of factory solidarity. About a week before the Putilov funeral demonstration, a young worker was killed by a foreman at the Paul textile mill in the Schlüsselburg suburb. His funeral was attended by thousands of workers, who were addressed by speakers from the revolutionary parties and left undisturbed by the police watching from outside the cemetery walls. Although denunciations of the autocracy and calls for armed uprising were heard, the greatest impression was made by the Menshevik speaker K. M. Ermolaev, who talked about the misery of the textile worker's life. The demonstration was so moving and invigorating that workers returned to the cemetery on the two following Sundays, ostensibly to lay wreaths and continue mourning, but actually to recapture the solidarity and militant resolve of the first gathering. Workers returning from one of these repeat performances on April 3 encountered army troops guarding the Paul mills. Their spirits high from the demonstration and from singing revolutionary songs on the trek back, the workers attacked the troops with stones, bricks, and even firearms. The fighting went on until late that night. Revolutionary leaflets were found among some of those arrested, and reports of frequent antigovernment meetings in the neighborhood apparently convinced the police that the riot was inspired by revolutionaries.[16]

Notwithstanding the continuation of such militancy, it proved impossible just a month later for the Social Democrats to bring the Petersburg workers out on strike in observance of the international workingmen's holiday on May 1. Partly this was because the strike was called for May 2 (May 1 fell on a Sunday) and partly because the Bolsheviks and Mensheviks disagreed on the format of the demonstrations. Yet both factions had made extensive agitational preparations during the last days of April; meetings were held at several factories around the city, and the Mensheviks alone issued some 100,000 copies of eight different leaflets. Drawing on what they took to be a ground-

16. *RDVL*, pp. 256–58. Kolokol'nikov, "Otryvki iz vospominanii 1905–1907 gg.," p. 219. Two other funeral demonstrations in this period are recounted in TsGAOR, fond 124, op. 43, d. 1744, l. 5, and d. 1745, 1905, l. 1.

swell of popular support since January 9, the Bolsheviks called for a two-day strike and for meetings and celebrations on May Day to review revolutionary forces and discuss armed uprising, although they opposed street demonstrations. Their rivals shared the view that it was time to demonstrate labor solidarity in preparation for an uprising but not to start an actual uprising. The Mensheviks nevertheless pushed closer to the edge by calling for street demonstrations, armed to defend against police attacks, though not directed at an uprising or even at obvious political objectives such as the Winter Palace. The results of these preparations, as even Social Democratic writers have admitted, were a "terrible disappointment." Only four large factories struck on May 2 (Nevsky Ship and Machine, Paul, Lessner, and St. Petersburg Metal); the Train Car Construction workers also struck on May 2 and 3, but in connection with a dispute already in progress.[17]

From among those trades that normally worked on Sundays, port hands, bakers (from about 20 to 30 shops), and some printers struck on May 1. The bakers' strike illustrates the mute anger and militancy possible among even such newcomers to the strike movement as these central city artisans: the participants raised no fresh demands but simply reiterated their standing desire for Sundays off, breaking windows at some shops and putting kerosene in the dough at others.[18]

Despite the weak response in terms of strike activity, a number of meetings and street demonstrations did take place throughout the city on May 1. Workers met in the woods, in cemeteries, and in other secluded places, but also, in some cases, on factory premises. In addition, participants gathered in the streets at several points in the city, but they were easily dispersed by soldiers and police. Only on Vasilevsky Island did marchers offer some resistance, beating up two policemen and continuing on their way until they were forced to retreat by a detachment of Cossacks. On the whole, the Social Democrats' May Day strategy may be said to have succeeded insofar as a number of meetings were held, yet the day witnessed no serious disorders. However, party organizers experienced the day as a signal failure: only 4,500 workers took part throughout the entire city, hardly a "review of the revolutionary army."[19] In both factions, esti-

17. Shuster, *Peterburgskie rabochie*, pp. 122–24. Shidlovskii, "Pervomaiskii den' 1905 g. v Peterburge i okrestnostiakh," pp. 168–71. *RDVL*, pp. 268–69.

18. B. Ivanov, *Professional'noe dvizhenie rabochikh khlebo-pekarno-konditerskogo proizvodstva Petrograda i gubernii (s 1903–1917 g.)*, pp. 26–27.

19. *RDVL*, p. 270. Shidlovskii, "Pervomaiskii den'," pp. 175–82. TsGAOR, fond 124, op. 43, d. 1747, 1905, l. 1.

mates of their successes since January had led organizers to believe that they were rapidly conquering the mass workers movement, and it was shattering and demoralizing to receive so sharp a lesson in just how deceived they had been. According to S. I. Somov, a witness and participant in the Petersburg events, not only did the "worker masses" fail to appear, not even all workers organized by the party demonstrated; fully half of those who came into the streets were not even workers, but rather students and organizers. This forced the members, Somov wrote, "to undergo a radical review of all their 'party values.'" He found that worker members were not only disappointed, but even angry at the party's failure, a feeling not far removed from that of ordinary workers:

> The mass of Petersburg workers, who listen sympathetically to the Social Democratic orators and willingly read Social Democratic leaflets, have looked on the party as on something very good, self-sacrificing, and caring toward workers (*rabocheliubivyi*), but [they] have regarded it not as their very own workers' cause, but as [something] alien, of the intelligentsia. They have been extremely interested in party slogans, have very often approved of them, but have not felt it necessary at all to take part in putting them into effect. The workers were sincerely convinced that the party would do something great and good for them on May 1st, and rode around town by the hundreds on the roofs of horse trams to admire the battle that the Social Democratic Party would give the autocracy, it hardly occurring to them that the course and outcome of the battle depended on their active participation in it. When the May Day battle did not take place due to the absence of an army in the field, the workers laughed at the party, which betrayed their hopes, and at their own gullibility.[20]

The Social Democrats responded to this setback in different ways. Menshevik-oriented workers concluded that the party's failure had been to leave uncorrected the predominance of intelligentsia influence and the lack of democracy in party life. This conclusion emerged in a series of meetings among oppositional workers that took place after the May Day fiasco. The leading workers of the party attended, and regular party work nearly came to a halt while the causes of the crisis were explored. In a reprise of the disputes of the Economist era, these workers told Somov, "We want to be masters in our workers' party, we do not want to carry out only the technical functions in it.

20. Somov, "Iz istorii sotsialdemokraticheskogo dvizheniia v Peterburge v 1905 godu," pp. 171–72.

It's time to bring an end to playing godparent, which has become such an established practice in the party that intellectuals easily make a career in it. The only way out of the shameful position the party has placed itself in is its reorganization on democratic principles. The elective principle must be made the basis of all party organizations from top to bottom."[21]

Somov and the bulk of the Menshevik leadership, unwilling and unable to turn back the clock to the era of *Rabochee delo* and *Rabochaia mysl'*, then deftly drew the conclusion that to increase the workers' sense of participation in the party, the party itself must increase its participation in legal workers' organizations, in "the workers' legal economic struggle," that it must not only actively participate in existing trade unions and the like, "but also take the initiative in creating such organizations."[22]

The Bolsheviks eventually came around to this position as well, but only after dealing with the legacy of Lenin's *What Is to Be Done?*— the fear that too unguarded an approach to trade unions would risk lapsing into "Economism." So, although the approach of the local Bolshevik organizers was often more flexible, the faction took the position that Bolsheviks should work only in unions (and other labor organizations) that were formally subordinated to the party. (Although Lenin's own attitude to trade unions in 1905 was much more flexible, he did not press it on his followers in Russia.)[23] This wariness of "Economism" was not totally unwarranted, since there were Mensheviks and others who, believing that the alienation of workers from the party was due to the party's "long-standing contempt for the economic struggle," concluded that the purpose of unions was to address this struggle and that the party should recruit workers by participating in unions in this spirit.[24]

The weak showing on May 1 and the strikes and public demonstrations during the spring months were complemented by the "sackings," the political funerals, and other initiatives at the factory level aimed at making gains without resorting to strikes. Taken together, they sustained a fighting mood and linked the militancy of January

21. *Ibid.*, pp. 172–73, 174.

22. *Iskra*, no. 100 (May 15/28, 1905), translated and quoted by Schwarz, *The Revolution of 1905*, pp. 152–53.

23. *Ibid.*, pp. 153–66.

24. Hoover Institution Archives, Nicolaevsky Collection, Box 109, Folder 58, "Letter from Petersburg," pp. 16–19, attributed to the Menshevik trade union organizer and historian Viktor Grinevich (M. G. Kogan).

with that of the fall. At a number of factories, the workers began to bring lawsuits against managements to win pay for time lost during strikes, suits that were frequently won when it could be shown that they had been forced to quit work by strikers from other factories or by factory closings at the behest of management. Suits were also brought against managements for violations of the 1897 law on the length of the workday, and against failures to pay the two-weeks' severance pay to dismissed workers required by law. Workers had of course sued their employers for years, but the scale on which such litigation was now being pursued and the sympathy workers now enjoyed in the judgments rendered were new.[25]

In a more militant vein, workers at a number of metal plants early in May renewed attempts first begun in January to institute eight- and nine-hour workdays at the workers' initiative (*iavochnym poriadkom*), only now on a more extensive scale. Some encouragement to this new campaign was undoubtedly provided by the initiatives taken in response to the January strikes and the exigencies of the war by several government departments (railroads, artillery, navy) in granting the workers of their factories nine-hour days. Begun in February, the measure affected some 42,000 workers in the Petersburg area by mid-May, at which time the workers at several metalworking plants sought to win similarly shortened workdays. At the Train Car Construction Plant and at four metal factories on the Vyborg Side, attempts to win an eight-hour day actually resulted in strikes; at other factories, workers instituted eight- and nine-hour days by simply quitting work early. The most determined and successful effort was made by workers at the Izhorsk Works in the nearby town of Kolpino. Certain shops of this naval equipment plant had been left on 11- and 12-hour schedules while the rest of the plant was put on a nine-hour day. On May 19, the workers of the excluded shops instituted their own shorter workday, which they sustained for more than a month before the management finally acceded to the demand.[26]

The attempt by workers to take control of the most basic material circumstances in their lives apparent in the lawsuits and the shorter-workday campaigns also included a new form of interfactory cooperation: in mid-June apartment renters among workers of the Schlüssel-

25. Shuster, *Peterburgskie rabochie*, p. 125. For the experiences of a Petersburg labor lawyer just prior to 1905, see Berenshtam, *Za pravo!*

26. Shuster, *Peterburgskie rabochie*, pp. 125–26. Smolin, "Bor'ba peterburgskikh rabochikh za 8-chasovoi rabochii den' v gody pervoi russkoi revoliutsii," pp. 117–20.

burg suburb refused to pay a 20-percent rent increase imposed in
May and instead called for a 20-percent reduction, withheld their
rent, and organized against evictions. The resistance began at the initiative of the *starosta* council at the Obukhov Plant, and the councils at
Neva Ship and Machine and at the Aleksandrovsk Works soon joined
forces with the *obukhovtsy*. "Apartment commissions" were formed at
each plant, and a joint Apartment Boycott Commission took charge of
ensuring that housing vacated by evictions remained empty and that
the impounded property of evictees was not inventoried and auc-
tioned. By July the courts were jammed with lawsuits brought by landlords seeking overdue rent, and the combined pressure persuaded
some of them to reduce rents and to accept payment by installments.[27]

It is noteworthy that the rent strike was initiated and organized by
the factory committees at two or three of the most politically developed metal plants in the city, but that it was not repeated elsewhere,
even though unemployment and renters' hardships were widespread.
This points up the key role factory committees could play with respect
not only to industrial and political issues, but to the consumer needs
of workers as well. The problem was that the committees at most factories did not preserve an unbroken and continuous existence throughout the spring and summer months. Aside from the Nevsky, Obukhov,
and a few other plants where strikes, more flexible management, and
a high level of political awareness and militancy ensured that the authority of the workers' representatives would continue to be recognized, factory committees for the most part dropped from view after
February, although the memory of their activities and the need for
protection and representation remained strong. Remnants of the
committees survived at some metal plants or revived at times during
strikes, but elsewhere, especially in the textile factories, they appear to
have waned with the strike movement itself.[28] (Printers preserved
their own unique form of shop and district representation, which is
discussed below.) For most workers, factory representation was a
fairly new experience, and it is noteworthy that both the Nevsky and
the Obukhov plants had histories of elected deputies and worker
leadership that preceded January 9th. At most factories, therefore,
the waning of the strike movement had made possible the reassertion
of managerial and police authority. Only when this traditional pattern

27. *Ibid.*, pp. 126–27. *RDVL*, pp. 283–84.
28. Kolokol'nikov, "Kak voznik v Peterburge soiuz rabochikh po metallu," p. 24.
Kolokol'nikov, "Otryvki iz vospominanii," p. 215.

was again widely disrupted in the mass strikes of the fall would aggressive factory leadership reemerge on a large scale.[29]

While this kind of strike-substitutionism was taking place in the capital, the strike movement was again gaining ground throughout the country as a whole. On May 12 an immense strike broke out among the textile workers and artisans of Ivanovo-Voznesensk in Vladimir province. Although the strike, which lasted about two months, ended in defeat for the workers, they showed great solidarity and discipline, establishing a unified strike committee and holding together despite extreme hardship and repeated attacks by police and army units. On June 3 mounted and foot soldiers disrupted one of the regular strike meetings, provoking resistance, killing 28 workers in the process, and wounding many others. Five days later Cossacks fired into a crowd of demonstrators in Lodz (Petrokow province), killing 18 and wounding 20. The strike under way there among factory workers since the middle of May became general when, as a result of the shootings, all stores and offices closed. Barricades were erected in several quarters of the city; shots were exchanged between armed workers and troops, killing dozens; and arson and pogroms broke out in the midst of the violence and disorder. In Odessa, strikes begun in May flared up again on June 14 after the arrest of an assembly of workers' deputies. Strikers circulated through the city, closing down other factories and clashing with troops. Early the next morning the battleship *Potemkin*, in the hands of mutineers, put in to Odessa harbor. The attention drawn by the dramatic mutiny took the focus off the local strikes, but it inspired and energized the antigovernment opposition throughout the country. Partly as a result of the events in Ivanovo-Voznesensk, Lodz, and Odessa, strikes and violence spread to dozens of other towns in the same or adjoining provinces, e.g., Kostroma, Belostok, Warsaw, Ekaterinoslav, Nikolaev, Kharkov, and Tiflis.[30]

Although the *Potemkin* mutiny has captured the most notoriety and attention, the strikes and urban disorders in the Central Industrial Region, Poland, and the south affected workers more directly. The

29. V. I. Nevskii has argued that the survival of factory committees after the passing of the Shidlovskii Commission was more extensive than that described in this account, although his evidence does not go beyond what has been examined here. *Sovety i vooru-zhennoe vostanie v 1905 godu*, pp. 12–13. Shuster, *Peterburgskie rabochie*, pp. 116–19, makes the same claim, although in a more qualified manner.

30. Kol'tsov, "Rabochie v 1905–1907 gg.," pp. 216–24. Anweiler, *The Soviets*, pp. 40–43. Volkovicher, "Iiun'skie dni v Lodzi."

strikers raised predominantly economic demands, and many were quite wary of political involvement, but the inevitable and violent intervention of the authorities ensured that political lessons could be drawn from the experience, even if political tactics were not yet employed. In Petersburg, where workers had been clubbed, shot at, and denied material and legal improvements for months, the strikes to the south and west now raised new hopes of a nationwide strike movement.

But the events that actually stirred the capital's workers into motion again were of more political import. In mid-May, news of the crushing defeat of the Russian fleet at the hands of the Japanese spread in revolutionary Russia. The outcome of the Tsushima battle had a more direct and immediate impact in Petersburg, since the sailors of the defeated fleet had been stationed in Kronstadt and Petersburg, where they left many friends and relatives behind. Thus, a resolution of Petersburg workers, referring to the defeat, proclaimed, "9,000 more *residents* (*zhiteli*) killed in a naval battle! . . . Will there ever be an end to this criminal war, to these bloody sacrifices? . . . Deep resentment and indignation overflow our hearts, and we advance the call, Down with the criminal government, Down with the criminal war, We demand peace!"[31]

In the middle of June the government announced a call-up of reserves from the factories of Petersburg. A Bolshevik leaflet declared: "Comrades! A mobilization has been announced. Mobilization not for the war with Japan, since on August 5 the plenipotentiaries will gather to conclude a peace, but for the struggle with the internal enemy, with us, comrades!" Citing the recent events in Lodz, Warsaw, and Odessa, and the *Potemkin* mutiny, as evidence that the regime's "final moment is near," the leaflet went on to urge Petersburg workers to rejoin the common struggle. "Comrades! In order to break down and weaken the government, we cannot allow the creation of new troop cadres. We will fight against the mobilization, all refusing, as a man, to be on summons! Let this not be single instance[s] or isolated occurrence[s], but a planned, well-considered struggle of the whole proletariat. Only then will our refusal, comrades, frighten the government, only then will it deliver the death blow to the military might of the Tsar and his stooges."

The leaflet went on to call for a strike as well: "With this strike our

31. Emphasis added. *RDVL*, p. 272. The resolution was reprinted from the newspaper *Sotsial Demokrat*, no. 7 (June 10, 1905), pp. 12–15; its origins were not otherwise specified, although the text makes it clear that the authors were Social Democrats and "conscious workers."

refusal to enter the ranks of the army will acquire an even more ominous meaning in the struggle between the people and Tsarism and will be the first step toward its complete destruction."[32]

Beginning some weeks earlier, mass protest meetings and gatherings in response to the Tsushima disaster had been held at the Baltic, Obukhov, Putilov, and Nevsky plants. With the announcement of mobilization, workers at several of these plants went on strike, principally as a protest against the war and mobilization but, as usual, this sentiment was underpinned and reinforced by the continuing desire to improve or protect their economic position. At the Nevsky Plant workers struck on June 16, demanding a report on their donations to the Red Cross (presumably war-related) and income guarantees for the families of those called to the colors; next day, these demands were embellished with expressions of solidarity with the *Potemkin* mutineers and a protest against the war and the mobilization. At the Putilov Works, a strike broke out on June 20 in protest of the dismissal of 180 smiths two days earlier, although aroused antiwar sentiment undoubtedly also contributed to the mood; later, demands for a nine-hour day, elected deputies, and a 20 percent wage raise were added. On June 21, Laferm tobacco workers struck with identical demands. On June 20 the Obukhov workers, thousands of whom had earlier signed an antiwar resolution, struck in solidarity with the sailors of the *Potemkin*. Several other factories on the Schlüsselburg Road also struck, including one freight car shop of the Aleksandrovsk Machine Works, where the workers carted out a foreman in a sack. Even in distant Sestroretsk, workers of the Artillery Department's armaments plant greeted the mobilization on June 15 with heavy absenteeism, informal street demonstrations, and a boisterous gathering, 200 strong, to see off the reservists at the railroad station.[33] Partly as a result of these events, more Petersburg workers struck in June than in any month since February, and July totals exceeded those of June.

On July 9 enormous strikes and demonstrations were held in the city to mark the first half year since Bloody Sunday. The day fell on a Saturday, when many factories normally scheduled shortened work days, and this probably helped swell the numbers of strikers. Yet the turnout would have been large in any case, since no event could rival January 9th in calling forth from Petersburg workers a sense of personal involvement and tragic loss. This sense of personal involvement

32. *RDVL*, pp. 276–77.

33. Thirteen electors were arrested for their part in the campaign. TsGAOR, delopr. VII, 1905, d. 934, ll. 7–8.

contrasted strikingly with the lack of involvement the workers had shown on the May Day holiday. The determination of workers to mark the day was so pronounced and widespread that some managers simply closed their factories in order to avoid conflicts. Both factions of the Social Democrats wisely joined forces with the Socialist Revolutionaries in supporting the proposed memorial with preparatory agitation, meetings, and leaflets. In all, upwards of 35,000 workers struck on July 9th, while many others took off part of the day to attend one of the ten or more requiem services for the Sunday victims held in various parts of the city. The one-day demonstration strike provided the momentum for raising and renewing economic demands at individual factories, and at least 25,000 workers struck again on Monday, July 11.[34]

Like the January 9 demonstration itself, the public observance of the passage of half a year appeared to look backward in time and to steep itself in traditionally sanctified sentiment and sorrow for past suffering. In actuality, it represented a new step for workers in affirming and identifying the shape of their most recent history, in inventing their own tradition, and in redefining their relationship to social and political authority. In creating their own holiday, they also took the time for it from that claimed by their factory owners and managers, much as they would later fashion weapons for their collective self-defense from materials appropriated at the workplace. The July 9 observances not only invested past suffering with moral authority, they employed that authority as a weapon in the struggle with employers and the government.

This moral authority extended well beyond the city's boundaries, as the Sestroretsk armaments workers demonstrated. Though located some 20 kilometers from Petersburg, they joined the July 9 solemnities by forming a huge procession and marching through the surrounding countryside—dotted with the dachas of their social superi-

34. *RDVL*, pp. 274–83. Shuster, *Peterburgskie rabochie*, pp. 131–33. Kolokol'nikov, "Otryvki," pp. 216–17. *RDVL*, pp. 289–98. Shuster, *Peterburgskie rabochie*, pp. 133–35. Estimates of the number of strikers on July 9 vary widely. A bulletin of the Bolshevik Petersburg Committee claimed 60,000, while the Bolshevik newspaper *Proletarii* ventured 100,000. The last figure is probably too high, and the bulletin's method of calculation is patently inaccurate. Yet Shuster's figure of 35,000, though based on the City Governor's figures, may be too low. The City Governor's list of factories striking on July 9 (*RDVL*, pp. 291–95)—probably the same list Shuster used—omits smaller shops and factories as well as all nonindustrial enterprises. Still another estimate, based partly on Factory Inspectorate figures, puts the number of participants at about 50,000. Smolin, "Pervaia russkaia revoliutsiia," p. 304.

ors—bearing banners reading "Proletarians of All Countries, Unite!" and "Eternal Remembrance to the Fighters for Freedom." Coming to a local health resort, they found preparations under way for a ball and concert to be held the same evening. The demonstrators later returned and, confronting the assembled guests, demanded that the festivities be canceled in view of the solemn occasion. Troops sent to guard the ball did not prevent the communication of this demand and, without further incident, the orchestra refused to play and the guests departed.[35]

For all the solidarity generated on occasions such as July 9, the goal and direction of the factory movement remained uncertain during the spring and summer. The moods and attitudes of workers are more difficult to fathom in this period because the written record of 1905 has stressed the months immediately preceding and immediately following and has all but forgotten the seemingly uneventful time between. Nevertheless, it is evident that by summer the factory movement had come to be broadly politicized and committed to the general aims of the multiclass opposition, though still lacking a single, coherent program and strategy or a single organization and leadership. The anger of these workers still ran high, but its transformation into effective political expression had apparently lost ground since February, when a certain unity of purpose and organizational resolve had been attained. The factory population remained a militant but a malleable entity.

However, it would be erroneous to assume from this that these workers were simply adrift. The all-class democratic vision shared with the liberal opposition and expressed in demands and statements made earlier in the year was certainly still influential. The Sestroretsk demonstration on July 9 illustrated both the strength of the workers' assumption that their concerns could find support among other elements of society and the validity of that assumption. Yet, such expressions of political solidarity across class lines were rarer in the spring and summer than in the months immediately preceding and following. The greater isolation of workers in the factories and neighborhoods in this period probably did more to instill a sense of the need for self-sufficiency and better factory organization than to teach the benefits of cross-class solidarity. Nevertheless, the double emphasis of an outreaching, civic, "united front" orientation and a preoccupation with the day-to-day factory issues remained characteristic of the labor

35. *RDVL*, pp. 301–2.

movement, but a new organizational expression of the two elements would not emerge until the fall.

In the meantime, inspired by the élan and initiative of the factory population, new groups of workers from smaller factories and workshops began to stir in these same spring and summer months. In the new conditions of government weakness and public initiative prevailing since January, they began to press for labor organizations in their trades and industries. Simultaneously, renewed efforts by left liberals and the revolutionary parties to harness the energy of the labor movement aided and encouraged the new organizing initiatives.

THE STRUGGLE FOR UNIONIZATION

The small shops and factories of the city were much less prone to strike than the large factories, many of them resorting to that tactic, if at all, only in the great strike of October. Nevertheless, as a result of the January and February strikes a number of them began to seek improved working conditions by other means, and this gave rise to several initiatives during the spring and summer to form trade and labor unions using both legal and illegal methods. The workers at the larger plants, especially metalworkers, remained by and large uninvolved in these unionization efforts. The workers most active in forming unions in 1905 were those with a prior history of self-help association (e.g., mutual-aid or funeral funds) or those whose individual enterprises were too small or disunited to form a viable base for mobilization and strike action and who were forced to seek structures linking a number of enterprises in the same trade.[36] The need to look beyond the walls of individual enterprises was furthered by the paternalism and close personal relations between workers and owners characteristic of smaller factories and shops, which made it much more difficult to concert efforts within their walls. This is not to say that these workers necessarily viewed unionization as an alternative to the strikes and political protests of the workers in large-scale enterprises. On the contrary, for most, unionization was carried out as a result and in imitation of the militancy of workers at the big plants. The textile workers both struck at a high rate and formed unions in 1905, and they constituted

36. Trades with preexisting forms of labor organization did not necessarily produce the strongest or earliest unions in 1905. For instance, Petersburg's retail clerks had had a network of semilegal *kruzhki* before 1905, yet they did not form a union until September, and did not strike as a group until October. Ivanova and Shelokhaev, "Torgovye sluzhashchie v revoliutsii 1905–1907 gg.," pp. 173, 179, 185.

an exceptional case among industries with large plants. Others were swept up for the first time in the October General Strike. Many of them shared the same oppositionist political feelings that were gripping the working class and urban society as a whole, and "union" for them was often little more than their own variant of a factory committee, deputies' council, or political grouping, i.e., an organization that could mobilize their own segment of the work force for both industrial and civic struggle.

The earliest efforts to form unions had been made among a number of artisan and white-collar occupations as early as January 1905, although some of them had organized proto-union mutual-aid funds before that date. Small groups from trades such as watchmaking, tailoring, printing, and shoemaking began meeting secretly as early as January and February to discuss the unionization of their trades. Would-be organizers from retail clerks (*prikazchiki*), pharmacists, and office workers (*kontorshchiki*) followed suit. The illegality of association and of public meetings continued in force, so that these pioneer unionists experienced enormous difficulties in the form of arrests and harassment. The results of these early efforts were meager, and actual unions in these trades had in most cases to await the freer conditions of the fall months. When they approached the authorities for aid, the craftsmen were sometimes referred to their respective Artisanal Boards, which in turn referred them back to the police; the effect was to hamper and frustrate the formation of unions, to reinforce the reliance of artisans and white-collar elements on industrial workers and their methods of struggle, and to strengthen their support of the fight for general political rights. Most of the unions actually founded before the fall remained small organizing nuclei with no mass membership. Even in the fall, when dozens of unions claiming to represent thousands of members were founded during barely two months of the "Days of Liberty," the great majority of them remained ephemeral affairs which perished in the government crackdown in December. Hence, to speak of unions in 1905 is to speak mainly of a *struggle* to establish them rather than of substantial and lasting organizations.[37]

Among the few exceptions to this general situation the most impor-

37. Sviatlovskii, *Professional'noe dvizhenie v Rossii*, pp. 105–13. Grinevich, "Ocherk razvitiia professional'nogo dvizheniia v g. S.-Peterburge," pp. 116–19; and *Professional'noe dvizhenie rabochikh v Rossii*, pp. 32–35. Antoshkin, *Professional'noe dvizhenie v Rossii. Posobie dlia samoobrazovaniia i kursov po professional'nomu dvizheniiu*, pp. 78–81. Shalaeva and Leiberov, "Profsoiuzy Peterburga v 1905 godu," pp. 20–22. Bonnell, *Roots of Rebellion*, pp. 122–38.

tant (and the single most successful trade union founded in 1905 or later) was the St. Petersburg Union of Printing Trade Workers (*Soiuz rabochikh pechatnogo dela*).[38] Prior to 1905 printing workers had been more active with self-help organizations, agitation among themselves on working conditions, and bargaining attempts than any other trade, and the initiation of talks with printshop owners to establish standard wage rates in the trade in January 1905 marked a kind of culmination of this involvement. In no other trade had worker-management relations advanced to the point of face-to-face negotiations on a citywide basis. Unfortunately, little more came of these talks than the creation of a group of elected worker representatives. They acquired the right to hold meetings among themselves and with larger groups of printers under the auspices of the Society of Printers (*Russkoe Obshchestvo Deiatelei Pechatnogo Dela*), a professional organization whose members included publishers, editors, owners, and workers in the printing trades. From the beginning of 1905 printers were in a different position from that of other trades, as they never lacked indirect government sanction as a body and a place to meet. When a wage rates agreement favorable to the owners was adopted in February, the printing deputies called a strike in support of their own rates schedule. The printers were undoubtedly seeking to benefit from the lessons of the January Days, when many other categories of workers seemed to leap ahead of them in dramatic job actions. But due to internal differences and disagreements, the strike call was heeded by workers from only part of the printing establishments, and in late March the employers' version of the rates was accepted at most shops. In response to this situation the wage-rate deputies decided to form a union of printing workers.

At a meeting of 300 delegates from St. Petersburg's printing, lithography, bookbinding, and letter-casting shops on April 3, a committee of six was elected to draft a union constitution. By late June the bylaws had been written, adopted, and submitted to the City Governor for approval. In the meantime, the new union began to function despite its as-yet unofficial status. In mid-August, the delegates empowered the union to collect dues, and quarters for the union's offices were rented.[39]

38. For a brief account of the structure and subculture of the printing trades prior to 1905, see Appendix 2. A detailed history of the industry in the postreform era may be found in Steinberg, "Consciousness and Conflict in a Russian Industry. The Printers of St. Petersburg and Moscow, 1855–1905."

39. *ILSRPP*, pp. 108–14, 133–50. Severianin, "Soiuz rabochikh pechatnogo dela." Steinberg, "Consciousness and Conflict," pp. 610–54.

Throughout the spring and summer months, the leaders of the printers' union were able to maintain contact with the rank-and-file printing workers and thus avoid the isolation and the kind of paper existence that was the fate of most other unionizing efforts in Petersburg. This was made possible by the establishment in May of a high-quality union publication (*Pechatnyi Vestnik*) and by the shared experience of the wage-rates campaign. In addition, the organizers made use, during the formation of the union, of district assemblies (*raionnye sobraniia*) of printers, which were little more than weekly gatherings of the most active workers and unionists, but which very effectively linked the union leadership with local neighborhoods and shops. As the union took shape, this informal representation was given organized and consistent form in a union provision that "authorized representatives" (*upolnomochennye*) be chosen to maintain ties between a shop's workers and the union center, representing them in the union's bureau and carrying its instructions back to them. The representative was chosen from among the "deputies" (*vybornye*), one of whom was elected for every 30 workers in a shop. The deputies functioned as shop stewards or factory committeemen, the spokesmen and representatives of the workers before management. Because the union never distinguished between members and nonmembers, it enjoyed the solidarity of a closed shop in the printing industry without the drawback of compelling union membership to keep one's job. Before the summer was out the printers' union had forged solid ties with its constituents in the shops and put control of the union in their hands. This network of shop-based representation made the printers' organization a model of democratic unionism and made printing the best-organized trade in the city. By the end of 1905 the printers had become the embodiment of much that the labor movement stood for, and the union assumed a leading role in the October General Strike and in the Soviet of Workers' Deputies.[40]

Almost simultaneously with the organization of the printers union, the Liberationists' long-term plan to form unions of professionals took another step forward with the establishment of a union federation combining professionals, special-interest political groups, and

40. *ILSRPP*, pp. 171–73. Grinevich, "Ocherk razvitiia," pp. 214–15. Grinevich, *Professional'noe dvizhenie*, pp. 30–32. The leading role printers played in Petersburg aligned them with their fellow craftsmen in Europe and the United States, where printers were the first trade to form national and international unions and have often been exemplary trade unionists. See S. M. Lipset, M. Trow, and J. Coleman, *Union Democracy* (New York, 1962 [orig. ed. 1956]), pp. 27–34.

several workers' unions. The Union of Unions held its founding congress in Moscow on May 8 and 9, when a common platform was adopted by some fourteen organizations, including unions of lawyers, writers, and engineers; pressure groups, also called "unions," for the defense of Jewish and womens' rights; and labor unions of railroad workers, teachers, pharmacists, and office workers and bookkeepers. Such a diverse group had of necessity to remain party neutral as an organization, although individual members of parties were free to participate in both unions and federation. No political platform was adopted at first so as to exclude no person or organization willing to fight "for political liberation of Russia on the basis of democratism."[41]

A second congress of the Union of Unions was called for May 24–25 in order to make a concerted response to the Tsushima disaster. Their mood already heightened, the delegates received a further shock when the government leaked news of the content of the Duma project announced in February: it was to be a consultative assembly, elected by limited suffrage, and would not be accompanied by the grant of broad civil and political liberties. Practically the entire opposition was sharply disappointed, from the constitutionalists leftward.[42] Until that point, it had been possible to hope that, despite the parameters of the February Rescript, reason, patriotism, and the pressure of the now mass opposition might persuade the government to make a more generous beginning. The government, now intensely embarrassed by the defeat and already fearful of the growth of the opposition, apparently decided that public knowledge of the Duma settlement might serve the regime better than the prolongation of these hopes. In this they succeeded brilliantly, at least in the short run. While the zemstvo men moved to shore up their solidarity with their most conservative elements by setting up the "coalition congress," the Union of Unions moved decidedly to the left. This divided the opposition significantly for the first time, and as the year wore on the division only widened.

At the second congress, the delegates passed a resolution addressed to "all Russian people, societies, and organizations," deliberately con-

41. Leikina-Svirskaia, *Russkaia intelligentsiia v 1900–1917 godakh*, pp. 221–22. On the establishment of the Union of Unions, see Sanders, "The Union of Unions," ch. 8; Chermenskii, *Burzhuaziia i tsarizm*, pp. 97–100; Trotskii, *Iz istorii odnogo goda. II. Intelligentsiia*, pp. 56–58; Cherevanin, "Dvizhenie intelligentsii," pp. 170–83; Kirpichnikov, "L. I. Lutugin i Soiuz Soiuzov"; Sverchkov, "Soiuz Soiuzov"; Galai, *The Liberation Movement*, pp. 245–50.

42. Galai, *The Liberation Movement*, p. 254. Sanders, "The Union of Unions," ch. 8, pp. 20–23.

trasting themselves with the zemstvo men's appeal to the Tsar, and calling for the convocation of a constituent assembly, by revolutionary means, that would put an end to both the war and the existing regime. The president of the congress and author of the resolution, Professor Pavel N. Miliukov, also called on the assemblage to act on their political convictions in any way they wanted: "*All means are now legitimate*, against the terrible threat which exists by the very continuance of the present government."[43] The congress went on record in favor of consultation with the revolutionary parties with an eye to adopting common tactics, and it instructed its Central Bureau to draft a policy on the Bulygin Duma reflecting the delegates' negative attitude, and to draw up plans for a constituent assembly.[44] The Union of Union's trend toward increasingly radical means of struggle continued, fueled by increasing government harassment of the intelligentsia unions and their publications, by external events such as the Potemkin Mutiny in June, and by continuing disappointment in the government's attitude toward the liberal opposition and its meager reform plans.

It was not surprising, therefore, that at the third congress of the professional union federation, held July 1–3, the delegates voted by a two-to-one margin to protest the Bulygin Duma, to forbid any of its members from participating in it or even in the elections to it, and to agitate against participation by others. Another parting of the ways took place: Miliukov, again presiding, had by this time come to favor participation in the Bulygin Duma, but his popularity and eloquence failed to carry the day. About a month later he left the union federation, and although he still hoped to draw the left liberals into the Constitutional Democratic Party and into elections to the Bulygin Duma, he did so henceforth from outside the Union of Unions.[45]

Needless to say, this leftward movement of the intelligentsia unions was accompanied by many expressions of sympathy and solidarity with the workers' movement. In its first published program, issued in March, the Union of Liberation had included a demand for the eight-hour working day, and several of the professional unions adopted similar expressions of solidarity with the labor movement. The Engineers' Union, apparently undaunted by its earlier failure to achieve rapport with the labor movement on the Shidlovskii Commission,[46] continued to regard itself as the spokesman for industrial workers. At

43. Quoted in Sanders, "The Union of Unions," ch. 8, p. 25.
44. *Ibid.*, p. 29. Martynov, "Istoriia," pp. 8–9.
45. Sanders, "The Union of Unions," ch. 8, pp. 58–62.
46. See Chapter 5 above.

its first all-Russian congress in mid-May, the Engineers' Union adopted a detailed and thoughtful program of labor demands, including not only freedom to strike, the eight-hour day, and a comprehensive state insurance program, but also workers' control over the implementation of legislation affecting them, paid maternity leave, and women doctors in those branches of industry employing women. The program also called for the convening of an all-Russian congress of workers, for support of the May Day holiday, and for temporary alliances between the Engineers' Union and any revolutionary party willing to accept a democratic, constitutional system and the defense of labor through legislation. This willingness to work with revolutionaries was underlined by the election of the Bolshevik engineer G. M. Krzhizhanovskii to the union's bureau. In addition, many intelligentsia unions collected money and rendered material aid to the labor movement throughout the year. Engineers at the congress pledged not to participate in the compilation of blacklists of "undesirable" workers, and this would have helped align engineers with the workers if they had heeded it.[47]

However solicitous of workers' needs these policies were, the principal aim of the Engineers' Union remained the political mobilization of the profession. That is perhaps the reason why neither the engineers nor any other intelligentsia union became directly involved in organizing workers, why the Union of Unions as a whole confined its support of labor to gestures undertaken at a distance. It may also be the case that the Social Democratic members of the intelligentsia unions worked to keep their unions from coming into direct competition with the socialists in labor organizing, since SD influence in the Union of Unions was on the rise.[48]

There was also a lot of talk, at the engineers' first congress and earlier, of a strike action by one profession or another, or by all profes-

47. Sanders, "The Union of Unions," ch. 5, pp. 32–42; ch. 8, p. 57.
48. Miliukov claimed that the SDs dominated the Petersburg branch of the Union of Unions in the fall. *Vospominaniia (1859–1917)*, vol. 1, p. 342 (or, in English translation, *Political Memoirs, 1905–1917*, p. 77). Certainly, the Union of Unions was a more hospitable setting for the SDs after it officially condemned the Bulygin Duma at its Third Congress in early July, and their influence in the organization undoubtedly increased, as did that of all leftists in the intelligentsia federation. Whether this amounted to domination or not cannot be established without further research. Miliukov's memoirs, after all, are notoriously unreliable—he claimed that he missed the Union of Union's Third Congress, for example, whereas he not only attended, but served as its chairman! Miliukov, *Vospominaniia*, vol. 1, p. 292. See Sanders, "The Union of Unions," ch. 8, pp. 58–59, note 171.

sions at once in a general strike. These ambitious plans did not materialize until railroad, printing, metal, and other industrial workers
initiated what became the October General Strike, although the Union
of Unions and several of its member unions aided the process by discussing and broadcasting the idea. One perhaps unanticipated result
of this talk and the congress resolutions it produced, however, was
that the police and the government formed the erroneous impression
that the intelligentsia of the Union of Liberation and the Union of
Unions were responsible for the major oppositional events of 1905—
such as the October Strike and the creation of the Soviet of Workers'
Deputies.[49] Hence, it is important to examine the result of these strike
resolutions among the intelligentsia unionists when they first occurred
in the spring and summer.

In every case examined, these proposals, brought to the floor of a
congress or meeting in the course of general discussions, were either
defeated on the spot or passed but rendered ineffective by the manner of their implementation. For instance, when a strike of engineers
was proposed at the union's May congress, it was referred for discussion to the local level. At the first lawyers' congress in March, a proposal for a demonstration strike of lawyers was harshly criticized from
the floor and finally defeated; a statement of principle condemned
the use of the strike as "a systematic means of struggle." At the First
All-Russian Congress of Writers and Journalists in April, the Social
Democrats proposed (passive) support of a general strike on May Day,
but the congress passed a union program that ruled out divisive social
issues, and the Marxists left to establish their own separate union. In
June, the Petersburg members of the Union of Medical Personnel
(physicians and *fel'dshery*), generally a radical and very dedicated
group, declined to participate in a general strike, probably because
they felt the public would be better served if medical services continued to be provided. In other instances resistance to striking seemed
to be directed more at socialist influence than strike action as such, but
whatever the reason, a pattern of radical rhetoric and moderate be-

49. The belief was firm enough to provoke the arrest and month-long detention of
a number of Union of Union leaders on August 7, including Miliukov, although he
later surmised that the authorities immediately realized their error. (*Vospominaniia*,
vol. 1, p. 301.) Yet the police continued to view the Union of Unions as the archinstigator
of revolution well into the fall. For one among numerous examples, see TsGAOR, fond
102, VII delopr., 1904, delo 2, ch. 73, ll. 265–660b. Sanders has repeatedly documented and rebutted these frequently expressed police suspicions. See also Schwarz,
"The Myth of the 'Liberationist' Origin of the Petersburg Soviet of Workers' Deputies,"
The Revolution of 1905, pp. 331–34.

havior appeared to characterize the intelligentsia unionists as a whole.

Talk of strike action by intelligentsia unions was powerfully renewed at the Union of Union's post-Tsushima Second Congress in late May, when the union voted to advocate the overthrow of autocracy by any means possible, and the most feasible means was understood to be the organization of a general strike. Yet, even in the greater urgency of the moment, the idea of an intelligentsia-led strike apparently still provoked much doubt. After "heated debate," a motion to authorize the organization's central bureau to organize a general political strike carried, four unions to three, but *six* other unions abstained. In light of this division, the implementation of the resolution was sensibly limited to polling each union about its position on a strike.[50]

The one Union of Unions component whose workers struck in the summer of 1905 was the Union of Railroad Workers and Employees, although the union itself was not the organizer of the strikes. The union had been formed by the white-collar employees (*sluzhashchie*) of the offices and depots rather than the blue-collar element of the yards and shops, who stood behind most of the strikes. Although the latter began joining in greater numbers in the second half of the year, the politically more moderate employees dominated the leadership from the beginning. The first president of the union, V. N. Pereverzev, has been described as a "non-party democrat" and a "semi-Kadet, semi-SR."[51] The union was organized in Moscow in April, after railroad workers had been involved in strikes for several months. For this union, strikes were not something to be discussed and planned ahead, but an endemic reality that continued on one or more lines throughout the spring and summer.[52] The association of the railroad workers with the Union of Unions was clearly due to the ascendency of the white-collar element, although the mixed composition of the union pulled it in two directions: that of intelligentsia-style oppositionism and that of the rough and tumble of the industrial strike movement.[53]

50. Sanders, "The Union of Unions," ch. 5, pp. 40, 61–63, 90–91; ch. 8, pp. 26–27, 56–57. Galai, *The Liberation Movement*, p. 248. TsGAOR, fond 518, op. 1, d. 8, l. 4.

51. Reichman, *Railwaymen and Revolution. Russia, 1905*, pp. 164, 175, 181, 184–85. Pushkareva, *Zheleznodorozhniki Rossii v burzhuazno-demokraticheskikh revoliutsiiakh*, pp. 119–20.

52. Reichman, *Railwaymen and Revolution*, pp. 181–85. Rostov, *Zheleznodorozhniki v revoliutsionnom dvizhenii 1905 g.*, pp. 43–62.

53. Railroad Union representatives apparently had reservations about their participation in the intelligentsia federation from the beginning; they attended only its first two congresses, and in the fall the union aligned itself with the Petersburg Soviet of

Before October, however, the railroad union did not have a very strong presence in Petersburg, and although shop and station workers struck along with other metal and factory workers, none of the lines servicing the capital was shut down.

There is much less information on the other semiproletarian groups that belonged to the Union of Unions. Very little is known, for instance, about the pharmacists' union in Petersburg, which got started in April, but remained a small group that sought organization as professionals rather than as workers. After a protracted strike began in September, the union assumed a working-class orientation, and in October it joined the Soviet.[54] The Union of Office Workers and Bookkeepers was from the outset a moderate, well-organized group that eschewed strike action in favor of the maximum exploitation of existing legal or semilegal means. It was aided and influenced in its organization by Liberationists such as Sergei Prokopovich, and its association with the Union of Unions was therefore understandable, although its members also became radicalized in the fall and joined the Soviet.[55]

The association of some of the earliest and most viable unions with the Liberationists and the Union of Unions (office workers and bookkeepers, pharmacists, railroad employees, printers) not only represents the greatest success the liberals achieved in drawing wage labor into the folds of their all-class political alliance, it also suggests a greater compatibility on the part of these categories of workers with Liberationist politics than was present among factory workers. What truth is there to this? On the whole, such compatibility as there was would seem to have been more social and cultural than political. All these groups were either white-collar workers, who were closer to the intelligentsia in consciousness and self-image than was the factory population, or were closely identified with the values of the intelligentsia, as in the case of the printers, who were normally led by the highly literate compositors. In terms of social geography as well, these categories of workers were located for the most part in the center of the city, i.e., the area where the influence of educated society was greatest, and their awareness of intelligentsia hegemony was sharper

---

Workers' Deputies. V. Romanov, "Dvizhenie sredi sluzhashchikh i rabochikh russkikh zheleznykh dorog v 1905 g.," *Obrazovanie*, no. 6 (1907), p. 29, and no. 7 (1907), p. 71.

54. Sanders, "The Union of Unions," ch. 4, pp. 106–7; ch. 9, pp. 24–33.

55. Antoshkin, *Ocherk dvizheniia sluzhashchikh v Rossii (So vtoroi poloviny XIX veka)*, p. 38. Kats and Milonov, *1905 god: Professional'noe dvizhenie*, pp. 42, 62–63.

and clearer than among factory workers. Hence, it was relatively easy for these workers to identify at the outset with the cause led by eminent representatives of the educated elite. Nevertheless, as the year wore on, they cast their fate increasingly with the labor movement of the factory population, swelling the new socialist-oriented opposition and drawing with them some of the more radical professionals of the Union of Unions, many of whose erstwhile liberal allies had meanwhile moved toward compromise with the regime.

On the whole, Petersburg factory workers showed less interest in unions and made less progress in organizing them in 1905 than their high level of strike and protest activity might lead one to expect. This was partly due to the self-sufficiency of the factory. Unlike craftsmen and white-collar workers, the factory proletariat was able in many cases to meet, to strike, and sometimes even to win concessions from employers without going beyond the factory premises. Since January 1905 the workers of practically every large and medium-size factory in the city had joined the struggle directly with their managements; they perceived strikes as the means of winning demands, and questions of organization revolved for the most part around the means to promote and sustain strikes within their factories—factory deputies, meetings, demonstrations. As mentioned earlier, unionization was an immediate need principally for those workers in small factories, shops, and offices who could not bring pressure to bear on employers without combining and meeting outside the place of work.[56]

In addition, the factory workers' closest and most influential political allies—the Social Democrats—deeply distrusted the moderate revisionist implications of trade unionism and, before October, usually did not promote the growth of organizations that might compete with their own party organizing in the factories. To be sure, the development of a mass movement after January 9 and the reappraisal of party fortunes following the May Day failure in Petersburg did lead both Social Democratic factions to look more favorably on unions and to take a greater hand in labor organizations outside Social Democratic control. In this effort to assume leadership of the working class, the Mensheviks generally showed greater sympathy and rendered more willing aid to fledgling unions than their rivals, and they eventually produced a number of leading SD trade unionists.[57]

56. Antoshkin, *Professional'noe dvizhenie*, pp. 77–85.
57. Schwarz, *The Revolution of 1905*, pp. 143–66.

During the greater part of 1905 the most consistent proponents of unionism in Petersburg were men of a left-liberal persuasion such as Petr Struve, editor of *Liberation*, who in early January had recommended that Union of Liberation members help organize a legal trade union movement;[58] S. N. Prokopovich, the labor specialist, former "Economist," and left Liberationist;[59] and self-appointed tribunes of labor like the lawyers Margulies and Nosar'. Nosar', who also aided the printers' union, preserved his ties with the textile workers on the Vyborg Side, and in the spring held a series of meetings with them directed at forming a union; later, in early October, he represented them at the First All-Russian Conference of Trade Unions in Moscow.[60]

Hence it was the Liberationists who first approached the largest and most militant group of factory workers, those of the metal trades, with proposals to form a union. According to the Menshevik unionist Kolokol'nikov, "a group of left Liberationists" spread the idea of a single "general labor union" quite widely among Petersburg factory workers during the early spring. Each factory was to form an autonomous union, and the resulting unions would be federated at the district, city, and national levels. Decisions of the whole organization were not to be binding on the member unions, and the organization was to be non-party (*bespartiinaia*). In response to this idea, Prokopovich delivered a lecture on trade unions at the Smolensk evening school in the Schlüsselburg district at the end of March in which he criticized the idea of "one big union" as impractical and proposed in its place a "Union of Labor Unions," a more conventional federation of trade groupings, which would, presumably, take its place alongside the intelligentsia's Union of Unions.[61]

The closest this agitation came to producing results was the encouragement it gave the workers and deputies from the large metal plants of the Schlüsselburg district to form factory unions. In May a meeting of representatives of the Nevsky, Obukhov, Aleksandrovsk, and Putilov plants was held in the cafeteria of the Nevsky Ship and Ma-

58. See *ibid.*, p. 149, and Chapter 3 above.

59. Kolokol'nikov and Rapoport, *1905–1907 gg. v professional'nom dvizhenii. I i II vserossiiskie konferentsii professional'nykh soiuzov*, pp. 168–69. Prokopovich expounded his well-informed views on the need for a broad, nonpolitical trade-union movement in Russia in the pamphlet *Soiuzy rabochikh i ihk zadachi* and the book *K rabochemu voprosu v Rossii.*

60. Kolokol'nikov and Rapoport, *1905–1907 gg.*, pp. 169–70.

61. *Ibid.*, pp. 23–26. Kolokol'nikov, "Otryvki iz vospominanii," p. 218. Schwarz, "The Liberationists and the Trade Union Movement," *The Revolution of 1905*, pp. 315–19.

chine Works. As a result, a "factory mutual-aid union" (*zavodskii soiuz vzaimopomoshchi*) was organized at Nevsky and membership registration and dues collection were begun. Despite its modest title, the union was quite militant, extending its competence to all problems affecting workers, including strike leadership, and reserving the right to take political stands. Apparently the meeting produced no comparable organizations at the other plants. The strikes of June and July interrupted the growth and consolidation of the Nevsky union, and the issue was debated again in August among Nevsky workers. A difference of opinion arose at this time between the Social Democrats, who favored organizing a regular trade union, and the moderates, led by the Liberationist *starosta* Makeev, who defended the kind of factory union suggested earlier by the left Liberationists. Surviving evidence does not make it possible to form a clear idea of the exact nature of the disagreement, but the draft constitution that resulted indicates that a kind of compromise was struck since it provided for a union of metalworkers not confined to the Nevsky plant, but made the factory the basic unit of organization in union governance. In late September the Obukhov workers prepared the draft constitution of a "trade organization," indicating that the idea of a metalworkers' union was still in the air, but for some reason very slow in getting started. Again these plans were put aside with the revival of mass strikes in October. The Soviet of Workers' Deputies further delayed the organization of unions among metal and other factory workers by itself fulfilling some of the functions of a union. As a result, the Petersburg Union of Metalworkers was not founded until the spring of 1906, although unions among wood, leather, and textile workers made a start in November of 1905.[62]

Hence, although the Liberationists first pressed the cause, no union of metalworkers was actually organized as a direct result of their efforts. The basis for even the limited success at the Nevsky Ship and Machine Works, as discussed in the previous chapter, was the ingrained "factory patriotism" of the large metal plants and the prestige

62. Grinevich, "Ocherk razvitiia," pp. 225–26. *Idem*, "Pis'mo iz Peterburga," Hoover Institution Archives, no. 109, box 5, pp. 14–15. Paialin, *Zavod imeni Lenina*, pp. 139–40. Kolokol'nikov, "Kak voznik," p. 27. Kats and Milonov, *1905*, p. 38. *Russkaia gazeta*, Sept. 25, 1905. For the text of the Nevsky union's constitution, see *Russkaia gazeta*, Oct. 2, 3, 1905, or Kats and Milonov, *1905*, pp. 224–26. Bonnell, *Roots of Rebellion*, pp. 145–46. An outline of the kinds of issues to be dealt with by the proposed "trade union of skilled metallurgical industry workers" may be found in LGIA, F. 1267, op. 1, d. 1054, ll. 15–16.

and authority of the Nevsky Works' *starosta* council. It was this group's nearly unique influence and stature with both management and workers, rather than the appeal of Liberationist propaganda, that made it possible to organize a factory union. Soon after the Shidlovskii campaign the council had established its competence to represent the factory's workers before the management and had won a number of concessions. The notion of a factory union represented only the next step in formalizing and consolidating the council's authority. One of its members later wrote that "the *starosta* council, by the very nature of its work, had much in common with a trade union."[63] The idea of a union came and went at Nevsky Ship in 1905, but the more fundamental social reality supporting it was the widespread acceptance and popularity of a group of elected factory deputies and the greater suitability of this arrangement to Russian conditions.

The tendency of organizational cohesiveness among metalworkers to coincide with the boundaries of the individual factory was also evident in two attempts to found Zubatov-style unions (i.e., ostensibly independent, but actually enjoying government sanction) among Petersburg workers in 1905. One of them was the "Mutual-Aid Society of Machine Workers," begun in October 1904 by M. A. Ushakov as a counterbalance to Gapon's Assembly. He had founded the first but unsuccessful Zubatovist union in Petersburg in 1902, had later joined the Assembly, but had been expelled at the end of 1903. Keeping pace with the new mood among workers after January 9, Ushakov began to move leftward, adapting to the now expanded prospects for labor reform: he now tried to promote the mutual-aid society as an all-Russian metalworkers' union. He also called for a national federation of trade unions and arbitration boards and later supported worker participation in the Duma and legislation granting freedom to strike, assemble, and unionize. Ushakov's aim was still to deprive the revolutionaries of working-class support by offering a legal alternative, but the events of 1905 forced (or permitted) him to assume the stance of an independent trade-union reformist. The extent of his influence on workers is not precisely known, but because he stood aside from the great strikes and the Soviet of Workers' Deputies (and because his reputation as a Zubatovist was never forgotten) it is not likely to have been large. His strongest support both before and during 1905 was to be found among the 3,000 workers of the Government Stationers, where he worked as a foundryman. In this respect, Ushakov's

63. Tsytsarin, "Vospominaniia metallista," p. 39.

mutual-aid society and various organizing experiments in 1905 can be viewed as attempts to project outward the influence and personal magnetism he exercised at his own place of work. On the whole, these efforts were not very successful, especially after the establishment of a metalworkers' union in 1906, although a remnant of Ushakov's organization survived until the reaction under Stolypin.[64]

The "St. Petersburg General Labor Union," founded among the workers of the Siemens-Halske Electro-Technical Works in April 1905, was yet another organizing effort aimed at an entire occupation or class, which nevertheless drew its cohesiveness from the social and political arrangements of a single factory. The union's inspirer and leader was the young metalworker's assistant Vasilii Smesov (born 1883), who, despite his youth, had already been exposed to socialist politics and had been arrested for participation in a strike. Although he apparently made some arrangement with the police at that time, Smesov also seems to have evolved into a genuine trade-union reformist. In addition, he enjoyed the advantage of not being a known Zubatovist, and when he returned to work at Siemens-Halske in early 1905 he was able to gather around him a group of workers of moderate views and to argue with the factory's socialists on the basis of principle and political philosophy. Partly because the union was amenable to direct control by the ranks (resembling, in this respect, a factory committee), Smesov had to give ground and, like Ushakov, was himself drawn to the left. In May 1905 the union leadership was forced by the workers to support a strike at the plant, despite Smesov's preference for mediation and his opposition to strikes; moreover, the Siemens workers struck again in July, October, and December. By the end of the year, the union's original commitment to mutual aid, mediation, and cultural activities had receded to the background, and its newspaper *Rabochii Vestnik* (*The Workers' Herald*) was purveying the language and sentiments of class struggle. In 1906 the union led two strikes, and Smesov himself was arrested in connection with one of them and spent a month in prison. The Smesov union thus went the way of other government labor organizations, whose very commitment to the viewpoint of ordinary, "apolitical" workers had ended by subverting their original conservative inspiration.[65]

64. Vasil'ev, "Ushakovshchina." Semenov-Bulkin, *Soiuz metallistov i departament politsii*, pp. 29–36. Bulkin puts the peak membership of the mutual-aid society at 500, drawn mostly from workers at the Government Stationers and other factories of the near periphery, but he also hints at the existence of "rather many ideological supporters" in other districts. *Soiuz Metallistov*, p. 29.

65. Semenov-Bulkin, "Smesovshchina"; *idem, Soiuz metallistov*, pp. 36–46.

Smesov's St. Petersburg General Labor Union began as an organization of the Siemens workers and ended as much the same thing. A membership tabulation for the first eight months of 1906 showed that 297 out of 393 workers who joined in that period (76 percent) worked at Siemens; almost all the rest came from neighboring plants on Vasilevsky Island.[66] Though the membership of the union in 1905 may have been somewhat larger, there is nothing to indicate that its composition was more diverse. Soon after 1906 the Smesov organization was absorbed by the Vasilevsky Island branch of the new Petersburg Metalworkers' Union.

It is perhaps inevitable that the leftward-moving Zubatovists and the left-liberal labor activists in search of a following should cross paths. This occurred at a public meeting held in late May or early June of 1905 in the City Duma devoted to the creation of a Society of Labor (*Obshchestvo truda*). The meeting was organized by a collaborator of Ushakov's, sanctioned by the police, and chaired by the ever-present Nosar'. About 250 workers attended, and the meeting probably stimulated considerable interest throughout laboring Petersburg, since it promised to draw together local factory groups and union initiatives in different parts of the city. Even the Social Democrats, normally contemptuous of reformist and government-sanctioned labor activities, took part in the meeting.[67]

This survey of unionization in Petersburg prior to the fall of 1905 has shown that "union" was a very elastic term. Not only was it used to describe completely different social realities—even just among workers, leaving aside the intelligentsia unions—but the different parties to the unionizing effort saw different things in the same unions, and even the same people in the same organizations intended different things at different times of the year. The major problem faced by both intelligentsia unions and labor unions was their lack of sanction in law and the illegality of even the activities necessary to organize a union. In this sense, real unionization began only in 1906, after a law granting limited rights of combination was passed on March 4. Although the new rights were so highly circumscribed that the young

66. Semenov-Bulkin, "Smesovshchina," p. 164.
67. Kolokol'nikov, "Kak voznik," p. 26. *Idem*, "Otryvki iz vospominanii," pp. 218–24. Tsytsarin, "Vospominaniia metallista," p. 39. Vasil'ev, "Ushakovshchina," pp. 246–47, where the date of the meeting was given as July. However, Vasil'ev's documentation is scanty, and he makes no claim to personal participation, as could Kolokol'nikov, whose dating has been used here. Unfortunately, only scant information on the meeting and its impact was found.

Russian trade-union movement remained weak and stunted, a legal framework had at least been established. In 1905, however, it was the illegality of union activity that guided the shape of events among unionizers. Most organizing initiatives begun before October came to very little due to the impossibility for most workers of meeting and organizing publicly. The intelligentsia professionals were generally better connected and found ways of circumventing restrictions—as with the engineers, who were legally sheltered by the Imperial Russian Technical Society. Those workers who enjoyed somewhat protected conditions, like the printers, were similarly able to make much better progress, although they enjoyed other advantages as well.

But the absence of civil liberties in 1905 also radicalized all unionizing efforts, so that even groups like the office workers and bookkeepers, which began with a strong disposition to work "through channels," had by the fall joined the newly formed Soviet of Workers' Deputies. The "radicalism" animating the would-be unionists was the plainly logical view that all workers had a greater stake in achieving the general conditions of freedom necessary to create viable, stable public organizations before organizing to win concessions at the workplace. In this manner, interest in unionization engendered political protest; economic improvement awaited political reform. This meant for many backing the general, nonpartisan aims of the Liberationist opposition: elections, a constitution, civil liberties. Professor Miliukov, soon to be chosen leader of the Union of Unions, carried this logic one step further by asserting in late April that party platforms and politics inside the intelligentsia unions were premature, that the unions' whole purpose was to draw people together on the basis of the widest possible opposition to Russia's lack of freedom. Even though he also viewed unions as transitional organizations on the way toward political parties, he argued that too early a division along party lines not only was illogical before the freedoms existed even to form parties, but would also drive people out of the unions.[68]

Although this reasoning was aimed chiefly at the machinations of the revolutionary parties in the intelligentsia unions, it was also widely applied in the workers' unions, where many took official positions as "non-party" (*bespartiinye*) organizations. However, these restrictions did not prevent Social Democrats and others from working inside the non-party unions while also forming party unions of their own.[69]

68. "'Partii' ili 'soiuzy,'" *God bor'by. Publitsisticheskaia khronika, 1905–1906* (SPb., 1907), pp. 34–41, first published in *Syn otechestva*, no. 55 (Apr. 21, 1905).

69. For example, the Bolsheviks participated in the Railroad Union while simulta-

More frequently and successfully, the socialists became indispensable union leaders and spokespersons, thereby bringing their politics to bear on union affairs unofficially. Examples of this are furnished by the Mensheviks Sverchkov (with the office workers and bookkeepers), Grinevich-Kogan (among the metalworkers), and Somov (on the Central Bureau of Trade Unions), and by the Bolsheviks Boldyreva (in the Textile Workers Union) and Leont'ev-Kints (among the retail clerks).[70]

For most would-be unionists from the unskilled, artisan, service, clerical, and slower-moving factory population, however, a center of ferment and a style of political protest was much nearer at hand than the Liberationists and the Union of Unionists: the strike movement of workers from the large plants and factories surrounding the city center. The most effective blow of the opposition in 1905 was possible once a great cross section of the working population realized that one had to change the political order before lasting gains on the job could be made, and that the general strike was the most effective means of attacking the political order directly. In this manner, unionization helped engender the general strikes of the fall by posing questions that could lead workers to this conclusion. But the interaction between striking and unionization was reciprocal: yes, many would-be unionizers eventually saw the prior need for political reform and demonstrated this by joining the general strike; but in addition, initially less active groups of workers, witnessing the strikes and militancy of the large factory population, awoke to the potential power of organized workers (for the first time in many cases) and, thinking they could win some workplace concessions by entering the fray, also came by this route to the idea of forming unions. The printers are the clearest example of the first alternative, and the *prikazchiki*[71] of the second; but the reciprocity of striking and organization was imbedded within each case as well.

The starting point in this process of mutual interaction that first drew together the working class of the city on such a broad basis was the large metalworking and textile factories, especially the former. The explosion of this population in January had begun the mass strike movement, and the same workers were its mainstay through the

neously attempting to form unions subordinate to themselves among smaller groups of railroad workers. See Reichman, *Railwaymen and Revolution*, esp. pp. 171–75.

70. Kats and Milonov, *1905*, pp. 38, 42, 43, 74. Glickman, *Russian Factory Women*, p. 197. Ivanova and Shelokhaev, "Torgovye sluzhashchie," pp. 191–92.

71. See above, pp. 413–17.

end of the year. When it was defeated in December, the government and the employers rolled back not only the whole working class, but the entire revolution. Given the militancy and the élan of these self-sufficient bastions of protest, there is little reason to speculate about why no trade union of metalworkers was formed in 1905. "Unions" were in that year indebted to and frequently also derivative of another, broader struggle, and metalworkers more than practically any other trade viewed themselves as occupying the very center of that broader struggle.

THE SEPTEMBER DAYS

Although strikes in Petersburg continued at a fairly high level throughout July, there were fewer in August and the fewest of the year in September. This was due in part to a number of lockouts and partial layoffs announced in July and afterward in response to a shortage of production contracts. But the layoffs were also an attempt to crush the strike movement once and for all. The greatest of these befell the Putilov workers, who were idled for two months and suffered extreme hardships, despite the generous contributions of fellow workers at other factories and the organization of free soup kitchens and food distribution. The Putilov management claimed that the concessions it had made to the workers as the result of earlier strikes had strained the company's finances to the breaking point, and that it had no choice but to close the plant. This argument was repeated by Finance Minister Kokovtsov in a report to Governor-General Trepov (since May also deputy interior minister). But it was also true that the management used the closing as an occasion to weed out political troublemakers when rehiring began; as a result, over 3,000 former employees were eliminated.[72]

And yet, despite the decline of strike activity and the added discouragement of lockouts, unemployment, and hunger, the workers' movement in the late summer of 1905 did not simply return to where it began. Although its principal weapon, strike activity at the big plants, was temporarily dormant, the momentum of the preceding months was carried forward along other channels. Among the trades and occupations that now joined the strike movement and kept it simmering were those not earlier motivated by the militancy of the large metal plants. Strikes among these workers, although slower to get

---

72. *RDVL*, pp. 304–7. Mitel'man et al., *Istoriia Putilovskogo zavoda*, pp. 220–28.

started, were nevertheless not dependent on simultaneous strikes among other workers. Dockers at various port and harbor facilities of the city struck repeatedly throughout the period from June through September. Those at the Kronstadt Commercial Port, although they raised almost exclusively economic demands, were the most persistent and militant. This was due in part to the fact that news of the war and of events elsewhere in the Empire was both more accessible and more disturbing due to the proximity of naval and military garrisons on the island. But construction workers and dockers at the New Port in the city also struck several times. Besides dockers, the summer months witnessed strikes by sawmill and brickyard workers, slaughterhouse workers, waiters, spinning assistants, pharmacists, and mail carriers. Of course, strikes continued at metal plants, especially in the Schlüsselburg and Vyborg districts, but at a reduced level, and lockouts continued to occur.[73]

A strike of pharmacy employees (*farmatsevty*, or simply "pharmacists"), which began on September 6 and spread to all the apothecaries of the city within a few days, is of particular interest because it was called and led by the new union of pharmacists. Moreover, the strikers only gradually won their demands against the isolated pharmacy owners, who gave in one at a time, and the strike consequently stretched out into October. The union negotiated with owners, conducted mass meetings that helped to hold the strikers together, and advanced demands for shorter work shifts, higher wages, more paid time off for illness and vacations, and health insurance.[74] The pharmacists' strike was one of the threads connecting the spring and summer union organizing with the widespread entry into the strike movement in October of many nonindustrial occupations, unionized or not, and it showed that some of these groups came out in force in the fall not only because of the renewal of mass strikes by the factory proletariat, but also because of the growth of their own thinking, struggle, and organizing.

Meanwhile, the fighting mood of the factory population was also maintained and expressed in an increasing number of mass meetings and gatherings (*massovki, skhodki*) held at many of the larger metal plants. Meetings held on the factory premises were normal during strikes and periods of political unrest. Now, in the relatively quiet

73. Dorovatovskii and Zlotin, "Khronika rabochego i professional'nogo dvizheniia v Peterburge v 1905 g.," pp. 220–25. *RDVL*, p. 300. *VPSO*, pp. 21–24.

74. *Russkaia gazeta*, Sept. 8, 10, 11, 25, Oct. 7, 1905. Dorovatovskii and Zlotin, "Khronika," pp. 223–24. Also, see note 54 above.

months of August and September, they continued to be held with some regularity. They were held chiefly to protest the narrow rights and limited franchise of the Bulygin Duma (officially announced on August 6) but also to continue the ferment generated by unmet factory demands, government and managerial repression, and an increasing acceptance in the factory districts of the political demands held in common by the liberal and socialist oppositions: the end of autocracy, civil and political rights, and a constituent assembly elected by "four-tail" suffrage. Speakers from the revolutionary parties became not only an accepted but an expected and welcome part of these meetings, where they contributed to the élan by incisive commentary on the political situation and by their agitation in favor of "revolutionary self-government" and "armed uprising."[75] In most cases, the revolutionary orators were the central focus of the meetings, and the constant danger of arrest compelled the factory audiences to guard and protect the speaker. This lent the meetings the character of demonstrations for the very right to hold such gatherings, which both enhanced the political messages of the speakers and created a mood of wariness and defiance. A dilemma was thus posed for the police and factory managements: the gatherings were illegal and disrupted managerial authority, yet if they were attacked and dispersed, the workers acquired yet another occasion to defy the legal order and disrupt the factory routine. When the management of the Obukhov Works threatened to take measures if a mid-September political *skhodka* was repeated, both the workers and the Bolshevik orators responded by holding another one on the very next day: when a police detachment then attempted to arrest the speaker, the workers drove it off with a hail of cobblestones. The encounter clearly raised the temperature of the crowd, and the meeting later broke up with the audience echoing the speaker's closing slogan, "Down with the Autoc-

75. "Revolutionary self-government" and "armed uprising" were the tactical positions of the Mensheviks and Bolsheviks, respectively, during the summer and early fall of 1905 and were discussed and debated in the factory meetings. The positions were not mutually exclusive, but turned around the question of which should come first. Lenin and the Bolsheviks thought that a revolutionary government should be formed after a victorious uprising and from the forces that made it. The Mensheviks viewed the uprising as growing out of the heightened consciousness and organization of masses of workers, possible only through self-governing, nonparty organs such as unions, soviets, agitation committees, and even a workers' congress. Schapiro, *The Communist Party of the Soviet Union*, p. 67. Schwarz, *The Revolution of 1905*, pp. 131–34, 168–71, 230–35. Woytinsky, *Gody pobed i porazhenii*, vol. 1, pp. 138–42. Dan, *The Origins of Bolshevism*, pp. 364–66.

racy!" and spilling out onto Schlüsselburg Road singing the "Workers' Marseillaise," while the police withdrew to the city.[76]

The excitement and satisfaction of conquering an island of freedom under the very noses of the authorities dramatized and amplified the political message of the factory meetings, but the thirst for meetings and oratory among Petersburg workers outstripped their ability to organize them. As the professional intelligentsia had come to regard their congresses as "Russian parliaments," so on a less imposing scale the capital's workers, in the eighth and ninth months of their own kind of civic agitation, used political meetings to probe the meaning of this upheaval and of their part in it. Surviving evidence indicates that most of the factory meetings were held in the large metal plants of the suburbs and outlying districts, where workers more often had the experience and self-confidence to take control of their factories. But the absence of factory meetings in other quarters of the city did not mean that the need and desire for public political ritual were absent. On the contrary, the hunger for public assemblage among workers was now urgently pressing against the limits imposed by the existing laws.

In late August a key law was changed, making possible legal public meetings in Petersburg and several other cities on a scale never before seen and initiating a new chapter in the political development of the working class. On August 27 the government issued new temporary regulations on universities, restoring to the higher schools the autonomy abolished by Alexander III in 1884. The key provisions put the university buildings in the hands of the self-governing bodies of the students and faculty and made the university off-limits to the police and government authorities. Socialists dominated the student leadership, and the debate that followed the restoration of autonomy revolved around whether the students should continue the strike begun in February 1905 or return to school in order to open the universities and put their now inviolable facilities at the service of the revolution. The latter position, supported by the Social Democratic students, carried the day, so that sometime after mid-September, increasing numbers of workers and other nonstudents began to attend the political meetings held daily in Russia's newly liberated lecture halls, including, in St. Petersburg, those of the University, the Technological Institute, the Lesgaft Courses, the Military-Medical Academy, and other schools.

76. *RDVL*, pp. 303–4, 876, note 98. *VPSO*, pp. 23–25, 29–30, 33. Shuster, *Peterburgskie rabochie*, p. 139.

Lectures and other university business were conducted during the day, and in the evening the lecture halls and auditoriums were opened to the public. The students especially welcomed workers, whom they perceived as both the most active agent and as the deserving benefactor of the revolutionary struggle. Workers flocked to the higher schools, both because of their mystique as centers of knowledge, and because of the clearly felt need, expressed in the factory *skhodki*, to discern their part in the great events of the day. Before long the workers took over the evening meetings, even asking students not to attend so that their places might be filled by the swelling numbers of participants from the factory population. This request was complied with at most of the higher schools, and significant numbers of workers joined the university crowds; the factory *skhodka* was merged with "white-collar" protest, as political activists, mainly orators from the revolutionary parties, addressed audiences of workers and urban, educated elements.[77] There is no evidence of liberals addressing these meetings, although one might reasonably expect them to have done so. It cannot be determined whether, for instance, they were excluded from the rostrum by the socialist student leadership or whether perhaps they voluntarily deferred to speakers from the revolutionary parties, who normally had fewer opportunities to speak publicly than the liberals, even in 1905.

Students in the higher schools of Russia played a unique and important, possibly decisive, part in the development of the revolution, especially those most active and committed, who adhered to the revolutionary parties. This was particularly important in Petersburg, which had more institutions of higher learning than any other city in Russia. Besides the university and the other schools named above, there were the institutes for mining, forestry, and civil engineering; the newer Polytechnical Institute; the Women's Medical Institute; the Academy of the Arts; the Theological Academy; and the musical con-

77. Woytinsky, *Gody pobed*, pp. 41–60. A. E. Ivanov, "Demokraticheskoe studenchestvo v 1905–1907 gg.," pp. 181–89. D. [D'iakonov], *1905 i 1906 god v Peterburgskom Universitete. Skhodki i mitingi (khronika). Sovet starost (ocherk)*, pp. 21–24. W. H. E. Johnson, *Russia's Educational Heritage* (Pittsburgh, 1950), pp. 180–81. Keep, *The Rise of Social Democracy in Russia*, pp. 216–18. Gusiatnikov, *Revoliutsionnoe studencheskoe dvizhenie v Rossii, 1899–1907*, esp. pp. 150–63. Erman, *Intelligentsiia v pervoi russkoi revoliutsii*, pp. 146–50.

78. Erman, *Intelligentsiia v pervoi russkoi revoliutsii*, p. 58. The term "university students" should be understood to stand for the broader category of students in all "higher educational institutions" (*vysshie uchebnye zavedeniia* or "VUZy"), including all those institutions listed in the text, not just the university.

servatory. In January and February an estimated 99 percent of university students had gone on strike in protest of the Bloody Sunday massacre.[78] In Petersburg, this included all the schools aside from the Theological Academy and the military schools. Since workers had begun to attend student meetings at that point, the September meetings were not entirely unprecedented.[79]

The political collaboration of students and workers in Petersburg went back more than a generation to the Populist circles of the 1870's. As the moral intensity of the intelligentsia always found its sharpest expression in its younger members, the commitment of students to the Left survived the years of reaction and came to be reflected, just prior to 1905, in an increase of student strikes and protests and in large numbers of students enrolled in the ranks of the revolutionary parties. The newer protests, like those of the professional groups, combined broad political concerns and issues affecting students alone, and this continued into 1905.[80] The Socialist Revolutionaries reported heavy student recruitment from their organized beginning in 1900, and at the end of 1904 the Social Democrats had student groups with 100 members at 14 VUZy (higher educational institutions) in Petersburg, while 500 other students took part in SD circles. After January 9, student recruitment accelerated so that, for instance, in the fall the Bolshevik student organization at Petersburg University alone had 104 members.[81]

Wladimir Woytinsky, a Bolshevik agitator and one of the student leaders at Petersburg University who worked to make these meetings possible, later wrote that "never and nowhere have I seen popular assemblies where such enthusiasm reigned, where the flame of idealism burned so brightly, as at our September meetings." He observed no demagoguery and very little interparty polemicizing at the meetings, even though both Social Democratic factions, the Socialist Revolutionaries, and even a few anarchists shared the platform, and even though controversial topics such as party programs and attitudes toward the Bulygin Duma were discussed. This was probably due to the efforts of the speakers themselves, who responded to the workers' sense of solidarity, and who would have avoided party polemics because they

79. D. [D'iakonov], *1905 i 1906 god*, p. 8. A. E. Ivanov, "Demokraticheskoe," p. 178.

80. Such in-house issues at Petersburg University were chronicled: D. [D'iakonov], *1905 i 1906 god*.

81. Hildermeier, *Die Sozialrevolutionäre Partei Russlands*, p. 117. *Tret'ii s"ezd RSDRP*, p. 561. Gusiatnikov, *Revoliutsionnoe*, p. 166.

knew that they usually annoyed a proletarian audience. It was as if the entire history of intelligentsia-worker propaganda circles was being rapidly reenacted at these meetings, including didactic lectures on related topics such as the Western trade-union movement and the history of revolutionary struggle in Russia. The enthusiasm and swelling numbers of workers in attendance invite comparisons with the meetings of the Assembly during the week preceding January 9, but the resemblance was a superficial one. Not only were the fall meetings almost completely in the hands of the leftist parties, but a different mood also seemed to prevail among the workers. Woytinsky recalled witnessing a young worker begin to address one of the September meetings in plaintive tones about the misery and suffering of factory life, much in the spirit of the Assembly workers' oratory; only now he was listened to coldly by the other workers and finally told to step down and let others who knew more speak.[82]

The composition of the large meetings at the University by early October was almost completely proletarian, according to Woytinsky, with "factory workers from the periphery" of the city predominant. The factory population of the outer districts had again come to the city center to register their existence to educated society and to appropriate some of its power and influence—only now the workers were being courted, with open doors, available auditoriums, and orators clamoring to address them.

Along with the mass meetings went a whole series of other meetings of smaller and more specialized groups—students, intelligentsia, and workers of separate trades and occupations—both in the higher schools and outside them. During the first half of September, for instance, the *Russian Gazette* reported meetings of the Union of Retail Clerks (*prikazchiki*), of typesetters, of barbers, of clubs of women *intelligenty*, and of countless groups of students. The grant of autonomy to the higher schools and the flurry of student activity that ensued seem to have stimulated a new wave of organizing and civic optimism, and the meetings announced in the newspapers were probably only a sampling of the number that actually took place. Moreover, during the first half of September only the students held their meetings in the University and higher schools, since those institutions had not yet opened their doors to the public. The others met in public halls such as the *Solianoi Gorodok* and the Countess Panina House, indicating that the government had begun to relax its usual ban on public meetings.

82. Woytinsky, *Gody pobed*, pp. 60–63.

Following the official announcement of the Bulygin Duma on August 6, a special conference under Count D. M. Sol'skii had been appointed to work out the legislation necessary to implement the elections. Among the topics it addressed was the question of public election meetings, and it eventually produced regulations issued as the imperial *ukaz* of October 12, 1905, specifying the conditions under which political meetings could take place. Yet the legislation was prepared by the middle of September, and a more relaxed regimen of public meetings was applied, at least in the capital, even earlier.[83]

As further evidence of a new policy, the government also began to appear more responsive to the part of the work force not employed in factories. Around September 9 the State Senate issued a legal clarification (*raz"iasnenie*) that banned work on Sundays and holidays in artisan enterprises. The same day the government finally gave permission for an All-Russian Congress of Mutual Aid Societies to be held, which the Kharkov Artisans' Mutual Aid Society had been organizing for three years. (The Congress, which met in Moscow on October 6 and 7, came to be known as the First All-Russian Conference of Trade Unions, an attempt to form a national federation of unions before the existence of a legal framework for it.)[84] On or about September 12 the City Governor's office gave the office workers' and bookkeepers' union permission to hold district meetings as long as it complied with several conditions. In response, workers from a number of nonfactory trade groups turned to the city government for assistance. Striking pharmacists asked the City Duma to mediate their dispute with the owners, and after some consultation it did intervene. Chimney sweeps, horse tram conductors, the Union of Retail Clerks, and probably several other groups also approached the government with petitions and requests for assistance and advice. As in February, the proffered hand of government paternalism was quickly seized.[85]

In the second half of September the clamor and excitement increased with the opening of the higher schools to public political meetings. The militancy of workers was therefore actually on the upswing just prior to October, whereas the government was apparently acting on the belief that the end of the war and the end of the summer strikes would bring a degree of docility among workers sufficient to

83. The text of the *ukaz* may be found in *Sputnik izbiratelia za 1906 god*, pp. 271–74. *Krizis samoderzhaviia v Rossii. 1895–1917*, pp. 215–16, 218–19.

84. *Russkaia gazeta*, Sept. 24, 1905. Ainzaft, *Pervyi etap professional'nogo dvizheniia v Rossii (1905–1907 gg.)*, vol. 1, pp. 244–48.

85. *Russkaia gazeta*, Sept. 6, 9, 11, 13, 16, 17, 20, 1905.

harness the labor movement through a policy of concessions. The government now initiated a number of measures intended to mollify factory workers and artisans and to assure them that the government had not lost sight of their interests. Around September 20 the Justice Ministry made public a circular instructing its representatives to cease criminal prosecution of strikers pending legislative review of the question of the punishability of strikes. A few days later a commission of the War Ministry, reporting on conditions among workers at its several Petersburg plants, recommended introduction of an eight-hour day, a minimum wage, and other reforms favoring the workers. Toward the end of September the head of the Mining Institute, where a dispute had erupted between the students and professors over the use of the buildings for public meetings, turned to Finance Minister Kokovtsov for support. Kokovtsov replied that "he had nothing against setting up meetings in the building of the Mining Institute." Since by the end of September the character of these meetings had been clearly established, this was tantamount to saying that the Finance Minister (within whose competence both the Factory Inspectorate and the well-being of Russian industry fell) was prepared to tolerate regular, public assemblies of workers, addressed by revolutionary agitators. Kokovtsov may have been misquoted, or the statement may have been a lapse, but it was not entirely out of keeping with the general tone of the period. Even the police and hard-line officials like Petersburg Governor-General Trepov were aligned for the time being with the new mood: sometime during the first week of October, Trepov agreed to a petition of the Obukhov workers for the release from prison of some of their arrested fellow workers.[86]

These small concessions, if noticed, produced no apparent response among the factory workers, who in any event had been better able to find or capture meeting space than most of the artisans, office workers, and the casual and unskilled laborers. In the absence of evidence, it may be asked what the workers could have been expecting from a government that, in its recent election law, still excluded them from political participation? Whether the government might eventually have cajoled workers onto the path of moderate reform and legal change, however, remains a moot question. The events that would bring new confrontation between the government and the opposition movement were already under way during the same days and weeks when the authorities were seeking to translate the struggle

86. *Ibid.*, Sept. 21, 25, Oct. 1, 7, 1905.

from political into economic and legalistic terms. The strikes and demonstrations in Moscow that would eventually ignite the nation-wide general strike of October began in the third week of September among the printing workers. Simultaneously, in Petersburg, talks opened between representatives of railroad workers and the Ministry of Communication over pension funds. There began a contrapuntal relationship between the labor movements in the two capitals. The railroad representatives received permission from the government to meet first by themselves, and they used the opportunity to upgrade the status of the meeting by renaming themselves the "First All-Russian Congress of Railroad Employee Delegates." Apparently in the spirit of its new policy on public meetings, the government let the change stand, and the delegates continued to meet. Meanwhile, the strike in Moscow had led to clashes with the police, bloodshed, and heightened anger among workers, and a "soviet" of workers' representatives had been formed to direct the strike among the printers (and in November, among Moscow factory workers generally). Railroad workers, who had called for a general strike as early as July, and had hailed the delegates' congress in Petersburg as their first public, nationwide leadership, were moved to action by these events. Reacting to a rumor that the Petersburg delegates had been arrested, workers on the Moscow-Kazan line struck on October 6; the following day the Central Bureau of the Railroad Union summoned all other lines in the country to a general strike, which in fact materialized within a few days.[87]

News of these events was difficult to obtain in the newspapers, and the workers of Petersburg turned naturally to their University meetings for full and up-to-date information. The meetings thus became public forums at which the general strike and the whole strategy of the working class were debated and analyzed. In this way the meetings served as the medium through which Petersburg workers renewed their militancy and restored their will to strike. The genesis of the October General Strike in Petersburg is a subject that belongs to the next chapter. Suffice it to say that once the prospect of a renewed and large-scale strike movement arose during the first week of October, the meetings increased in size and purposefulness, and they continued to be held every evening through October 15, when troops

---

87. Kol'tsov, "Rabochie v 1905–1907," pp. 229–32. Keep, *The Rise of Social Democracy*, pp. 178–79, 219–21. Rostov, *Zheleznodorozhniki v revoliutsionnom dvizhenii 1905 g.*, pp. 64–68. Woytinsky, *Gody pobed*, p. 132. Anweiler, *The Soviets*, pp. 39, 43–44, 47–48. Reichman, *Railwaymen and Revolution*, pp. 186–98.

were finally used to close the higher schools to public meetings. The day before, Trepov had marked the end of the government's conciliatory labor policy in Petersburg with his famous order to the police and troops in the city: "Don't spare the cartridges, and don't fire blank volleys."[88] By that time the whole country, including Petersburg, was in the grip of a general strike, the Petersburg Soviet of Workers' Deputies was in the process of formation, and the government's reponse was wavering between a severe, violent repression and a constitutional charter, which it granted a few days later.

Why, it may be wondered, did the government hesitate so long before closing down the meetings that contributed so handily and materially to the enlargement and solidarity of the strike movement? Woytinsky posed the same question and cited four factors that caused the government to hesitate before adopting repressive measures: (1) the pressure of the world opinion, in that Petersburg was the location of foreign embassies and the home base of most foreign correspondents; (2) the immobilization of government hard-liners by the pressure of "a spineless, eternally vacillating, capricious autocrat"; (3) the memory of Bloody Sunday and the consequent reluctance to be again in the position of shooting down unarmed workers; and (4) uncertainty about the reliability of the troops.[89] Yet these explanations can be applied to the entire period following January 9, not just September and October, and they do not account for the constant and routine use of police and troops against strikes, demonstrations, and meetings among workers throughout the spring and summer of 1905. If the government sent troops to close the Shidlovskii electors' meetings on February 18 but did not close the University meetings in September, more was at stake in the fall than fear of another atrocity and Russia's image abroad.

A move against the University meetings would have brought the government into open conflict not only with workers, but with students as well, and with the urban, liberal opposition generally. It would have violated the August 27 decree on university autonomy and cemented an alliance of the labor movement and a much broader and more influential political opposition consisting of everyone concerned with the extension of civil liberties and the rule of law. In this respect the University meetings were one of the most ingenious and consequential political tactics Petersburg workers availed themselves

88. *Russkaia gazeta*, Oct. 22, 1905. Woytinsky, *Gody pobed*, pp. 97–98, 102–10.
89. Woytinsky, *Gody pobed*, pp. 96–97.

of in 1905. First, they brought workers under the protective mantle of the opposition movement of educated society without compromising labor's own political independence, and they reconcentrated workers' determination and ability to participate in the strike movements of the fall. Second, the renewal of the strikes in Moscow, which began almost simultaneously with the mass meetings of workers in Petersburg, meant that the government was under additional pressure to respect the inviolability of the meetings lest it promote the spread of strikes beyond Moscow. Even though the meetings were known to be discussing a renewal of working-class action, and even armed uprising, subversive talk was apparently preferable to revolutionary action. Although some strikes began in Petersburg during the first week of October, the meetings still went untouched, and they remained so until well after the strikes became general around October 12. The policy of concessions to labor could be seen to be failing by the end of September, and yet the government persisted. Just when control was slipping from its hands, it had to feign perfect control.

CHAPTER SEVEN

The First Revolution in October

—◆•◆•◆—

THE LIBERALS IN LATE SUMMER

Although the government faced an increasingly numerous and unified opposition from January 9 through October 17, a close examination of the state of affairs within the opposition reveals simultaneous divisions and disagreements on every hand. In the revolutionary camp the well-known cleavages between Mensheviks and Bolsheviks and between Marxists and Populists continued in force. The divisions in the liberal camp that were brought into the open by the petition and deputation to the throne on June 6 became even more pronounced in the second half of the summer.

Among the liberals and democrats, four major groups could be discerned at this time. On the right were those favoring a minimally reformed and modified monarchy, although the group also included cautious constitutionalists. These urban and rural moderates, nominally headed by D. N. Shipov, sought to strike a balance between a reformed autocracy, obtained with a minimum of disturbance to public order, and the careful containment of the chaotic forces of the popular upheaval, whose potential for violence and tyranny these men probably feared more than they did the autocracy's. At midsummer, this group was the strongest supporter of the Bulygin Duma as the appropriate next stage of Russian political development. However, after the liberal deputation to the Tsar, the group dropped from prominent participation in events, emerging again only in September and October, when it formed the nucleus of the Octobrist Party.[1]

1. The four positions outlined here have been distilled from the studies listed in notes 4 and 41 of Chapter 6 and from Miliukov, *Vospominaniia*; V. V. Leontovich, *Istoriia*

A second group, the left liberals, remained unswayed by offers of a consultative assembly and held to the aim of achieving a constituent assembly elected by universal, equal, secret, and direct ballot. This group favored the advent of a parliamentary and constitutional order, but refused for the time being to confine its opposition to parliamentary methods of struggle. Instead, it sought to unify the opposition to autocracy by building alliances with the revolutionary left and by encouraging the emergence and organization of the mass movement. Its chief tactic was the simultaneous mobilization of the intelligentsia and the working class through the unionization of occupational groups, and its main organizational instrument was the Union of Unions. Many of its most prominent members were socialists by conviction, both Marxist and Populist, but normally of a more moderate cut than those of the organized socialist parties. Wholly representative of the group were such leftists of the Petersburg "Big Group" that had formerly dominated the Union of Liberation as Elena Kuskova, Sergei Prokopovich, Nikolai Annenskii, and Aleksei Peshekhonov. These intelligentsia political leaders favored a lawful, nonviolent strategy and open political work and organizing; they might aptly be dubbed "constitutional socialists." By applying an "industrial" rather than a parliamentary model of politics, the left liberals also contributed to the outbreak and strength of the great strikes of fall 1905.

Third were those like Paul Miliukov, who favored precisely the parliamentary tactics rejected by the leftists. Their programmatic aims were very often as radical as those of the left liberals, but they confined themselves to moderate tactics in their pursuit. Miliukov had broken with the Union of Unions over this issue after its Third Congress in early July. His principal political associates then became members of the Union of Zemstvo Constitutionalists and their moderate intelligentsia allies, who had expressed their distaste for Union of Unions politics even earlier by their absence from the second and third congresses of the union federation. Members of some of the moderate unions, especially the professors, apparently shared this outlook but hesitated between the *zemtsy* and the intelligentsia unionists. The group as a whole believed either that the Bulygin Duma offered a better means of achieving liberal goals than a prolongation of extraparliamentary opposition; or that supporting those liberals who favored the Bulygin Duma as an end in itself was potentially more fruitful in the long run than an alliance with the socialists and

---

liberalizma v Rossii, 1762–1914, trans. I. Ilovaiskaia (Paris, 1980); and articles in *Osvobozhdenie* and *Pravo*.

the mass movement; or both. Unlike the left liberals, they felt that the time had come to form a political party, to stand for elections, and to further the revolution by parliamentary means. Accordingly, by the late summer the group's principal political aim was the formation of a Constitutional Democratic Party (Kadets).

The distinctness of these three groups was by no means as clear to the participants as this presentation might imply, however. The rapidly changing political situation, inexperience, and hopes for a single opposition party prolonged and delayed political self-definition among liberals in 1905. This was particularly true of the fourth and largest group of liberals, made up of those left over from the other three groups, i.e., the great bulk of the delegates of the zemstvo, municipal, and professional congresses, who, though concerned and mobilized, had less pronounced and definite views. Miliukov had indicated in April just how extensive this lag in political development was when he wrote that unions were a convenient and temporary means of mobilizing people of differing political views, but that the basis of actual political unity in them was very thin and that the further political development of the liberal movement would expose sharp differences over program, priorities, and tactics. (He wisely refrained from predicting just how soon that would take place.) The unions could serve as vehicles for bringing out and debating these differences, but the aim must be the formation of politically more homogeneous groups, i.e., political parties. In this view the unions were but an antechamber to real political life. Miliukov thus unwittingly foretold his later break with the intelligentsia unions, but he also indicated how relatively late and historically retarded the Russian liberals were in sorting out political differences among themselves, compared to the Right and the Left.[2]

This may serve to remind the historical observer of the political inexperience of most of the liberals in 1905 and of the misfortune of any political group in making its public debut amidst a revolution. It may also help to explain the unsteady swings in tactics, organization, and opinion among zemstvo and professional activists in 1905, from one congress to another, from one month to another. By comparison, the Mensheviks and Bolsheviks were pillars of sobriety and stability even though they themselves were at times hard put to adapt to the rapid and unexpected unfolding of events.

Zemstvo representatives, for instance, meeting at their Fourth Con-

2. Miliukov, "'Partii' ili 'soiuzy'," *Syn otechestva* (Apr. 21, 1905), reprinted in *God bor'by*, pp. 34–41.

gress (July 6–8), veered away from the conciliatory line taken a month earlier in their delegation to the Tsar. The Bulygin Duma project, now approved by the Committee of Ministers but not yet issued as a law, was rejected by the delegates. Instead, they adopted a detailed plan for converting the autocracy into a constitutional monarchy drafted by Moscow University law professor S. A. Muromtsev and on its basis urged delegates to campaign against the government's proposal in their home provinces. The Congress also issued an appeal directly to the people, pointing out that the Bulygin Duma excluded them from participation and urging them to begin discussing it in a peaceful manner. These measures matched and reflected a remarkable groundswell of local activity by zemstvo men in the summer of 1905, seeking to draw the rural and even the peasant population into political education and participation. This activity and the positions taken by the July Congress were apparently influenced not only by the rebuff of the June petition to the Tsar, but by the first appearance of rural protest and organization by Third Element groups (i.e., rural professionals) and by the peasants themselves.[3] Hence, although the *zemtsy* had already expressed their disinclination to left-liberal politics and to the Union of Unions, they themselves continued to be drawn to the left.

By the time of the Fifth Zemstvo Congress (September 12–15) the government had ended the war in the Far East, enacted the Bulygin Duma into law, and announced the temporary regulations restoring university autonomy. As the oppositional element most likely to respond to government concessions, the *zemtsy* could have been expected to move once more to the right. Although such a trend did materialize, it was met with and overbalanced by new initiatives on the part of the Zemstvo Constitutionalists, the more progressive part of the *zemtsy*, who were now actively working to draw the zemstvo movement into a liberal political party and had organized the September congress largely for that purpose. They succeeded in winning support at the congress for participation in the Bulygin Duma for the purpose of transforming it from within into an assembly more representative of the population (*narodnoe predstavitel'stvo*). The formation of local electoral committees was approved, as were autonomy for Poland, the right of workers to strike, and—most interestingly of all for a body of landowners—a peasant land fund formed in part from expropriated private land, albeit justly compensated.[4]

A rightward trend among the liberals, although still involving a

3. Manning, *The Crisis of the Old Order*, pp. 114–23.
4. *Ibid.*, pp. 133–36. Emmons, *The Formation of Political Parties*, pp. 33–34, 40–41.

minority, began to assume a distinct identity at the Fifth Congress. A group of leaders that would later found the Octobrist Party, led by Aleksandr Guchkov and including Dmitrii Shipov, Count Petr Geiden, and others, offered stiff resistance to a proposal that would have committed the body to a sweeping program of cultural autonomy and administrative decentralization for the non-Russian nationalities of the Empire. These moderates also blocked approval of several other program points proposed by the constitutionalists and restricted the mandate of the local electoral committees to prevent them from advocating the election of specific candidates.[5]

A gathering designed to help form a single liberal party thus succeeded in refining disagreements between the Shipov and Miliukov varieties of liberalism and in providing the occasion for the consolidation of a *second* party grouping. The process of "sorting out" liberal views and programs clarified differences but also fragmented the movement's meager forces.

Fundamental disagreements of political strategy continued to dog the left liberals as well. Although the Union of Unions voted in early July to boycott the Bulygin Duma, sentiment was by no means unanimous. The delegate vote was 41 for, 21 against the boycott motion, but the vote by union was nine for, three against, and four abstaining. The vote by unions, counting abstentions, showed that the number of those with some degree of reservation or opposition to the boycott very nearly matched the number favoring it. However, the wording of the resolution makes it difficult to gauge the exact sentiment toward the Bulygin Duma very precisely. It committed the federation not only to opposing the Bulygin Duma, but to opposing every representative body not based on the "four-tail" elective principle; it forbade individual Union of Unions members not only from participating in the Bulygin Duma but even from taking part in election campaigns; and it obliged members to agitate actively for boycott at election meetings. Given these provisions, it is likely that much of the opposition and abstention did not represent support for the Bulygin Duma, but disagreement with the extremism of one or more provisions. On the other hand, the motion was opposed by the leader of the Union of Unions, Miliukov, who did favor participation, and it is likely that a significant number of delegates agreed with his strategy.[6]

About one month later, on August 7, Miliukov and a group of

5. Emmons, pp. 104–7. Manning, *The Crisis of the Old Order*, pp. 134–37.

6. Sanders, "The Union of Unions," ch. 8, p. 61, where the resolution is quoted and the vote described from diverse sources. See also Cherevanin, "Dvizhenie intelligentsii," pp. 184–85.

Union of Unions leaders were arrested at an informal gathering called to discuss the same divisive issue. The official enactment of the Bulygin Duma into law on the previous day apparently provided the authorities with the occasion to lop off what they perceived to be a radical and dangerous leadership group, since the government was still acting on its exaggerated belief that the Union of Unions was the lynchpin of the entire revolutionary movement.[7]

During the month or so when the Petersburg leaders were imprisoned, the Moscow branch of the Union of Unions functioned as the federation's central leadership. A more favorable attitude toward participation in the Bulygin Duma apparently prevailed among intelligentsia professionals in the second capital, and this strengthened the other pole of opinion within the organization. At a meeting of the Moscow local bureau on September 8, attended by delegates from a variety of unions as well as the Menshevik and SR parties, a majority voted against the boycott and in favor of organized participation in elections in Moscow and Moscow province. An election commission was established to conduct agitation in the name of the Moscow Bureau of the Union of Unions.[8] On September 14 a joint meeting of the Moscow local and Petersburg central bureaus took place to plan the next congress of the organization. Here again, powerful sentiment for participation in the Bulygin Duma was expressed, although the apparent absence of the strongest proponents of boycott from this meeting may have contributed to this showing. A reconsideration of the whole question of participation in the forthcoming Bulygin elections and Duma was postponed until the Fourth Union of Unions Congress, set for October 20–23.[9]

Since the Third Congress in July, opinion inside the separate intelligentsia unions seems to have been slowly moving in Miliukov's direction, in both Moscow and St. Petersburg. For instance, delegates of the Union of Lawyers had voted for the strong boycott resolution at the July Congress, but at the union's own Second Congress (October 5–6) an "immense majority" voted to participate in the new consultative body in order to carry the revolution inside the Duma.[10]

7. Ironically, an article by the liberal leader opposing the boycott of the Bulygin Duma happened to appear the very same day. Miliukov, *Vospominaniia*, vol. 1, pp. 300–302 (*Political Memoirs*, pp. 41–43).

8. Sanders, "The Union of Unions," ch. 9, pp. 34–36.

9. *Ibid.*, pp. 36–37 and n. 120. Chart 1 shows stronger support for a boycott, however, than is claimed in the text.

10. Cherevanin, "Dvizhenie intelligentsii," p. 185. This was a congress of the entire union, many of whose members came from Petersburg, and the fact that it was held in Moscow should not have affected the vote.

At the end of the summer, therefore, the liberals were arrayed in at least three groups, politically more conscious and better organized than nine months earlier, but no better unified. The divisions among them were not unusual or excessive, considering the social diversity they encompassed, ranging from moderate landowners to radical retail clerks, from industrialists and city fathers in search of reasonable reform to neo-Populist "Third Element" physicians and Social Democratic teachers. But most of the leaders of the liberal organizations, conscious of their numerical inferiority and isolation in the country as a whole, still hoped and worked for a unified movement. Miliukov in particular became a specialist at stressing a moderate and reasonable course to the radical democrats of the Union of Unions and radical democracy to the moderates of the zemstvo congresses, presumably seeking to maintain communication between divergent political and social components of the original Union of Liberation and to embody its promise of unity in a new party that would be both constitutionalist and democratic. Given the diverse trends *within* as well as between each liberal faction, however, the recapture of this unity in a single party would probably not be complete or immediate. Unification and political self-definition were working at cross-purposes, and there were clear signs that more than one party would emerge from the debates over program and strategy.

THE OCTOBER GENERAL STRIKE IN PETERSBURG

By the early days of October, it was clear that the government's hope of preventing the revival of the strike movement in the capital was fading. On Sunday, October 2, a crowd of several thousand mourners—students, workers, and intellectuals, "all of thinking Petersburg," as the *Russian Gazette* put it—followed the body of Prince S. N. Trubetskoi, the liberal rector of Moscow University, through the streets to the train that would bear him home. Because it was more of a political demonstration than a funeral procession, many workers and ordinary citizens joined the crowd, and its great size and mixed-class composition can be attributed in part to a growing need, felt by all strata of the population, to demonstrate opposition to the regime. The demonstration also resulted from the newly formed opposition of the university meetings, which, in creating a new community of discourse, had also created a new community of protest. Hence the procession in honor of the liberal rector was also marked by red flags, revolutionary songs, and skirmishes with the police and Cossacks. Once the crowd reached the Nikolaev Railroad Terminal in the center of the city, the police tried to disperse it, but they were powerless to prevent some 2,000 persons from heading up Nevsky Prospect, pausing at Kazan Square, a traditional site of demonstrations, and then proceeding on to Admiralty Square. There the crowd removed hats, knelt, and sang a hymn in memory of the victims of the January massacre. Still followed and harassed by the police, the demonstrators then crossed the river and entered the sanctuary of the university buildings.[11]

The procession perfectly symbolized the all-class unity of the antigovernment opposition, so recently reaffirmed in the university meetings. It was not necessarily love or respect for the distinctly moderate liberal rector that brought the workers out, but Trubetskoi's *acceptability* as a symbol of the opposition and the opportunity to demonstrate against the government again. Funerals had provided workers with occasions to meet and demonstrate in their factory districts earlier in 1905, and they may have felt the solemnity of the occasion would similarly deter the police and Cossacks from their usual violent treatment of demonstrators. As a symbolic display of all-class unity, the Trubetskoi demonstration was the political equivalent of the Bauman funeral demonstration in Moscow later in the month, although with the shoe on the other foot: Nikolai Bauman was a Bolshevik professional who fell victim to a black hundreds attacker October 18. His funeral two days later, far from emphasizing Bauman's party, provided the occasion for a huge procession to the cemetery and a demonstration against monarchic extremism that similarly linked workers, students, and members of educated Society.[12]

On the same day, 3,000 dockers at the barge basin of the St. Petersburg's New Port struck for higher wages, shorter hours, and more control over hiring, firing, and piecework rates.[13] That evening, at the behest of the Petersburg printers' union, over 3,000 printing workers gathered at the Countess Panina House to hear an appeal for support from a representative of striking Moscow printers. News of the Moscow strikes and street violence had been agitating Petersburg printers for several days. "Looking at the sea of heads, the excited faces, and the burning eyes of printing workers, who had assembled at the summons of their own union organ, [the union's] Bureau mem-

11. *VPSO*, pp. 344–45. *Russkaia Gazeta*, Oct. 3, 1905. *Novoe vremia*, Oct. 6, 1905.
12. Engelstein, *Moscow, 1905. Working-Class Organization and Political Conflict*, p. 141, estimates 100,000 in attendance.
13. Dorovatovskii and Zlotin, "Khronika," p. 225.

bers were convinced that the first Petersburg trade union was a force
and that the time for decisive action had come."[14] The Moscow delegate requested a sympathy strike and material assistance; the meeting
responded by taking up a collection and voting a three-day strike
without demands.

The strike turned out to be a model of solidarity and discipline. On
Monday, October 3, most typesetting work stopped, a dozen or more
Petersburg newspapers ceased publication, and a large percentage of
workers in the associated crafts joined the compositors. Even workers
at the Government Stationers and other state printing enterprises
participated. Troops sent to disperse a crowd of government printers,
who had gathered in the courtyard of their plant, fired on them, killing two and wounding 21. Although most shops raised no demands,
the lithographers formed their own strike committee, formulated demands, and began to organize their own union. On October 5, a second mass meeting of printing workers reaffirmed the decision to resume work on the 6th, and this was accomplished with perfect order.
Because the printers' union was legally sanctioned, the meetings were
held with government permission and in the presence of the Assistant
Inspector of Typographies. In addition, the strike was aided by a
number of sympathetic typography owners, who simply closed their
shops.

Nevertheless, the strike was a triumph of craft and industrial solidarity. For the first time, printers successfully applied the tactics of
factory workers by striking as entire shops, by forcing nonstrikers to
quit work, and by demonstrating in the streets. This created an impression of militancy that did not go unnoticed by the factory workers
themselves, who took encouragement in their own strike movements
and offered support to the printers. Several representatives of factory
workers appeared at the printers' second mass meeting to announce
the outbreak of strikes or promise solidarity among their constituents.
The union-led three-day printers' strike thus marked the entry of that
trade into the mainstream of the Petersburg movement of factory labor and removed the stigma of their feeble strike performance earlier
in the year. Union recruitment among printers in October increased
sixfold over that of the previous month, and the union's influence and
prestige within the liberation movement generally also rose.[15]

    14. *ILSRPP*, p. 185. Grinevich, "Ocherk razvitiia," pp. 228–29.
    15. *ILSRPP*, pp. 185–88. Dorovatovskii and Zlotin, "Khronika," pp. 225–26. *Novoe
vremia*, Oct. 6, 7, 1905. *VPSO*, pp. 342–43.

While the printers' strike was still in progress, more strikes broke out in the most volatile and militant of the city's industrial districts, the Schlüsselburg suburb. Shortly before noon on October 4, a dispute erupted among workers of two shops at the Nevsky Ship and Machine Works when a locomotive drove into the yard to move some loaded cars. The origins of the dispute are obscure, but workers threw stones and metal objects at the locomotive, which quickly drove away, and then brought the rest of the factory out on strike. The strikers headed down the Schlüsselburg Road, singing the "Marseillaise," and soon turned out the workers of most of the other plants and factories of the district. Windows were broken and the gates forced at the Paul cotton mill, and the management of the neighboring Spassk and Petrov mills wisely closed for lunch early, before a similar fate befell their factories. Strike agitation was clearly favored by the noontime hour, when workers were idled. Demonstrators stopped the steam tram by stoning it, then greeted the prompt arrival of the police and Cossacks with rocks and revolver shots. Several persons were killed and wounded. Barricades were built and liquor stores raided. In the evening some 30 street lamps were broken, and reinforced detachments of police patrolled the district throughout the night.[16]

The political impact of these strikes and disorders was greater than those of the Obukhov Defense of 1901, which they resembled in some respects. Occurring in the context of the printers' strike, the crowded and popular university meetings, the railroad pension congress (discussed in the previous chapter), and the strikes and violence in Moscow, the Schlüsselburg disorders evoked for the authorities the prospect of unified, simultaneous, and citywide insurgency. A Justice Ministry report of October 5 called the strikes "in all probability the beginning of a general strike in Petersburg's industrial enterprises."[17] The strikers, for their part, took a more modest view. The day after the first outburst occurred, with the strikes continuing but civil order restored, they issued the following demands over the signature of

16. Paialin, *Zavod imeni Lenina*, pp. 160–63. *VPSO*, pp. 347–49, 388–89. *Novoe vremia*, Oct. 6, 7, 1905. An occasion for the attack on the locomotive may have been provided by plant director Hippius's threat to dismiss workers in two separate shops who had requested the removal of two supervisors. LGIA, fond 1239, op. 1, d. 103, ll. 101–4.

17. *VPSO*, p. 347. Only one account claims that these strikes were the result of advanced planning, but it lacks substantiation: A. Shestakov, "Vseobshchaia oktiabr'skaia stachka 1905 goda," p. 278. Compare the more detailed and better documented account of Paialin (previous note), which avoids such a claim.

the "Workers Strike Committee beyond the Nevsky Gate" (*za Nevskoi zastavoi*, i.e., Schlüsselburg district):[18]

Comrade Men and Women Workers:

We demand from the owners:

1. A 9-hour work day: this means that no owner has the right to force his workers to work more than 9 hours.
2. A 20-percent addition to wages so that piece-rate workers do not lose from the reduction of the work day.
3. For unskilled workers not less than 1 ruble per day.
4. A 50-percent reduction in house rent. We make this demand on the landlords. They are stripping us naked. We say to them that from today on we will pay only half of what we have been paying. Let those who pay 20 rubles pay 10, those who pay 4 rubles, 2, and so forth.

We demand from the government:

1. Freedom of workers' meetings and assemblies. Russian educated society, in the person of students and zemstvo activists, enjoy these rights and we need them even more.
2. That the police not interfere in our strike.
3. That no one be arrested for the strike.
4. All just workers' demands are extremely modest.
5. We declare that we intend to conduct our strike peacefully if the police and troops do not use violence against us.

The same day the Obukhov workers, who had resisted participating in the events of October 4, joined the strike and issued their own demands, which went beyond those of the Strike Committee by requiring full civil liberties, popular participation in the State Duma, the release of political prisoners, and an eight-hour day. The *obukhovtsy* also decided to strike only until October 10, and set this term from the outset in the manner of the printers' strike. Actually, this decision combined militancy with necessity since the absence of orders had already forced the Obukhov management, at the end of September, to announce the dismissal of some workers and a four-day workweek for the rest. It was therefore not surprising that the management approved the workers' decision to strike for four days, and that the strikers raised the demand that "all machine production orders, both state and private, be filled exclusively in Russia, and in no manner

18. *VPSO*, p. 350.

abroad." Even at the highly politicized Obukhov Plant, strike sentiment was fueled by economic hardship.[19]

Most of the Schlüsselburg district strikes ended on October 6 without touching off a general strike, even though two other factories in
other parts of the city struck at the same time.[20] Strikes did not become
general in Petersburg until about October 13. The strikes of printers
and of Schlüsselburg workers were therefore more of a storm warning than the storm itself. Still, the demands they raised illustrated several important links between the October strikes and the preceding
period. The overall modesty of the Strike Committee's demands reflected the caution and lowered expectations produced by the reduced level of strikes, the layoffs, and the lockouts of August and September. The demands for participation in State Duma elections and
for civil liberties reflected the two major themes of recent worker
meetings, both in the factories and in the higher schools. The demand
for lower rents showed that the summer apartment strike had not
been forgotten and that the economic squeeze on worker-renters
had even increased in that the amount of the reduction demanded
had risen. Finally, the emergence of a districtwide strike committee
carried forward into organized form both the practice of striking in
district and neighborhood cohorts and the cooperation of factory
committees during the apartment strike and the unionization drive.
Despite the rapid resort to violence, the strikes put forth moderate,
almost perfunctory, "economic" demands, indicating that although
such demands may have lost some of their power to mobilize strikers
by months of fruitless repetition in previous struggles, they were still
needed and wanted in the factories. But the strikes also displayed a
more explicit political thrust against the government than anything
that had been seen for several months.

While these events were reawakening strike fever by day, the university meetings were furthering the same end by night. On October 5, in
the middle of the printers' and Schlüsselburg workers' strikes, the

19. *VPSO*, pp. 349–50. *Russkaia gazeta*, Oct. 1, 1905. The delay and predetermined
length of the strike at the Obukhov Plant were probably due to the influence of the
Social Democrats, both factions of which sought to avoid a premature dissipation of
proletarian energy at this point. See the account of the Obukhov strike in *Proletarii*,
no. 24 (Oct. 25, 1905), in *VPSO*, p. 389, which, however, claimed this influence exclusively for the Bolsheviks, distorted the nature of the *obukhovtsy's* strike demands, and
failed to mention the management's complicity in the strike.

20. *VPSO*, pp. 348–49. *Novoe vremia*, Oct. 8, 1905.

largest meetings to date took place in the main hall of Petersburg University. Some 12,000 persons, of whom about 7,000 were reportedly workers, gathered to hear news of the strikes and were treated to the usual fare of political commentary, debate, and oratory. The Schlüsselburg strikers passed out proclamations signed by the Strike Committee that had authored the demands. Meeting participants heard news of the events of October 4 on the Schlüsselburg Road and of the shootings at the Government Stationers.[21]

With the spread of strikes to Petersburg, the character of the higher school meetings changed. While the mass political meetings grew in size and solidarity, individual trade and occupational groups began increasingly to make use of the smaller meeting rooms in the school buildings to organize and prepare to strike. Even during the mass meeting of October 5, pharmacists met separately in an adjoining room. With the outbreak of railroad strikes in the Moscow area on October 6 and 7, the imminence of a nationwide strike quickened the interest of all Petersburg workers, and in particular those of the capital's railroad lines. On October 8, 500 to 600 representatives of Petersburg's railroad workers gathered in the cafeteria of the Military Medical Academy where they discussed economic grievances and the need to strengthen the union. Other groups, such as workers of the Franco-Russian Plant, also met at the Academy and at other schools the same night. On October 9 there were meetings of secondary-school teachers, shop clerks, jewelers, and, again, railroad workers. (Jewelry shop employees had been on strike since October 4 and were finally meeting to draw up their demands.)

The renewal of strikes and the greater ease with which meetings could be organized were encouraging the emergence of protest from a number of groups whose discontent had not hitherto been heard. Physicians of the city's hospitals submitted a number of demands on their working conditions to the Municipal Board, backing them up with the threat of a strike. A Union of Foremen and Technicians met on October 8, protested the assignment of "police duties" to foremen (*mastera*), and heard a report on the dismissal of a senior foreman from the St. Petersburg Pipe Plant for belonging to the union. In an apparent attempt to benefit from the widespread sympathy for workers then current, the Union assembly, after discussing the report, "voted to express its profound distress at the rude mockery of the worker's person (*lichnost' rabotnika*)," thereby downplaying the distinc-

21. *VPSO*, pp. 349, 674, n. 162. *Novoe vremia*, Oct. 7, 1905.

tion between foreman and worker by using a term, *rabotnik*, that could apply to both.[22] The city's master barbers, some 5,000 strong, renewed demands for a shorter workday and a weekly day of rest, demands first raised in the spring but ignored by most owners. Even janitors (*dvorniki*), normally considered a conservative lot with close ties to the police, had formed a Society of Janitors and Porters and put forth demands for the improvement of their material and living conditions.[23]

Meanwhile, the mass political meetings of workers held nightly in the higher schools also changed in character. "Their mood became more businesslike and concentrated; telegrams were read, reports were made from the audience; a new discussion procedure was observed—by trades, separate plants, and districts."[24] The Schlüsselburg strikes in Petersburg and the railroad strikes in Moscow had put a general strike on the agenda, and the workers were beginning to organize it in the university meetings. The same topic dominated a mass meeting at the Military Medical Academy on October 8, yet "*all* the orators of *all* the parties spoke out *against* a strike," an eyewitness reported.[25] The parties had decided that the next agenda item was not a strike, but an *uprising* and that the meetings would be used to educate the workers to that point of view, to move them beyond "anarchistic strikism" to a political *coup*.

The revolutionary parties had been concerned for a number of months about the often fruitless and therefore pointless dissipation of energy in the normally unplanned and uncoordinated strike movement. But because such strikes were popular among workers, because they dramatized the continuing conflict to all concerned, and most of all because the revolutionaries were powerless to prevent them, they usually went along with them and soft-pedaled criticism. In addition, strikes had not been as numerous in recent months as they had been earlier in the year. But now that they had a larger audience among workers and a nationwide strike was taking shape, the revolutionaries made their disagreements explicit. On October 6, for instance, a Bolshevik-led meeting of 600 workers in the Narva district passed a set of resolutions which warmly saluted the Moscow and Petersburg workers, not for their strikes but for their defense of the right to assemble, and warned against aiding the government's aim of re-

22. *Novoe vremia*, Oct. 10, 1905. It is assumed that the newspaper paraphrased accurately the language of the resolution.
23. *Ibid.*, Oct. 9, 10, 12, 1905. *Russkaia gazeta*, Oct. 9, 12, 1905.
24. Woytinsky, *Gody pobed*, p. 92.
25. *Ibid.*

pression of workers by giving way "to premature outbursts of discontent." Apparently pressured by the meeting to mention the general strike, the authors of the resolutions wrote, clumsily and with obvious unwillingness, that along with propaganda for an armed uprising there should be spread "the idea of the need to prepare for the introduction of a general political strike"; but they added that "an immediate political strike in the Narva district was untimely and capable of harming the interests of the [politically] conscious proletariat."[26] The Mensheviks and Socialist Revolutionaries shared the Bolsheviks' hopes that the rising labor militancy of early October would lead to a decisive political breakthrough, and they therefore also shared their negative response to the workers' growing enthusiasm for yet another wave of inadequately led and poorly organized strikes that might dissipate interest in an uprising. All three groups continued to oppose an immediate general strike in meetings held on October 9, 10, and 11.[27]

As the general strike spread outward from Moscow along the railroad lines, sweeping in factories and towns along the way, the workers of the nation's capital strongly felt the urge to strike but remained at work and debated the issues in meetings, divided against their would-be leaders. For the time being, no pro-strike leadership or unifying force arose to take their place. Petersburg railroad workers were insufficiently unified to provide that force, although they were moving toward action under the dual impact of the Moscow strikes and the local political ferment.

The presence of the All-Russian Railroad Delegates' Congress in the capital (the renamed railroad pension fund talks) both aided and hindered this movement, as may be judged from the October 8 meeting of several hundred local representatives of the white-collar employees and some line workers of the four principal Petersburg railroads, the Nikolaev, the Baltic, the Petersburg-Warsaw, and the Moscow-Vindavo-Rybinsk. Members of the Delegates' Congress were also present, and one of them, the lawyer Govorov, was chosen president of the meeting. Although representatives described the economic oppression and lack of rights and dignified treatment to which railroad employees were subjected, their anger seemed well-contained. This was due, in all likelihood, to the moderateness of the white-collar employees and Congress delegates, who outnumbered and over-

26. *VPSO*, p. 390. On the evolution of Bolshevik attitudes toward the strike movement, see Schwarz, *The Russian Revolution of 1905*, pp. 130–38.

27. Woytinsky, *Gody pobed*, pp. 93–94.

whelmed the blue-collar element. Without even expressing solidarity with the Moscow railroad strikers, the meeting called only for the drafting of a list of demands and increased enrollment in the union. Once enough employees were union members, the meeting decided, the union would present its demands to the government; only at that time, should the need be felt, would the union resort to a general strike.[28] Hence, another possible source of general strike leadership in Petersburg refused the role, and mounting pro-strike sentiment still lacked a rallying center.

On Monday, October 10, the Obukhov strikers returned to work. Meanwhile, all rail traffic out of Moscow ceased that same day, and the Nikolaev Railroad, connecting Petersburg with Moscow, moved closer to a strike. In the early evening of October 11, Nikolaev road switchmen struck in protest against the cruelty of station chief Podgorichani-Petrovich, who had beaten one of the switchmen a few days earlier, and all traffic stopped the next day.[29]

That same evening, October 11, another meeting of the railroad employees was held, this time at the University. The contrast with the earlier meeting was noticeable and significant. It was held in the largest auditorium, yet still overflowed into the corridors, the other rooms and halls being filled with other groups of workers and students. The police estimated the whole crowd at about 10,000, of which the railroaders must have accounted for several thousand. The meeting was nominally announced to report the railroad delegate's progress in talks with the government, but the mood of the meeting was more extreme than it had been three days earlier, and there was soon only one topic of discussion on the floor: the coming strike. There was little question of the desirability of an immediate strike, and discussion centered around the question of its form. Two distinct choices were posed, a three-day walkout in sympathy with the Moscow railroad strikers, which would raise no independent demands, and a strike with demands, which would last until all the demands were met. Unable to reach an agreement, the railroaders nevertheless did not permit this to turn them from their purpose; they ended the meeting by resolving on an immediate strike, while leaving its exact form to the strike bureau of each individual railroad to determine.[30]

28. *Ibid.*, p. 133. *Novoe vremia*, Oct. 9, 1905. For a comprehensive account of the beginning of the all-Russian railroad strike, see Reichman, *Railwaymen and Revolution*, pp. 196–208.

29. *VPSO*, pp. 291–92. *Novoe vremia*, Oct. 11, 1905.

30. *Ibid.*, Oct. 12, 1905. *VPSO*, p. 355.

The reversal of mood among the railroad workers was attributable not only to the upswing in pro-strike sentiment among Petersburg workers generally, but to the composition of the meeting as well, which included a preponderance of line, shop, and depot workers, now mobilized by the approach of the Moscow strike and the switch-men's walkout at the Nikolaev terminal. The militancy and impatience for action of the blue-collar element among workers of the Petersburg rail net were thus of prime importance in tilting them, and with them all of working Petersburg, toward a general strike. The day after the meeting, October 12, the four major lines serving the capital ceased to operate.[31]

Thus the railroad workers of Petersburg, after much debate and hesitation, decided to strike, and it is difficult, perhaps pointless, to seek to specify a precise cause or agency. Did the Congress of Railroad Delegates begin the strike in Petersburg? It appears that they only provided the forum in which the large concentrations of shop and de-pot workers (Petersburg *metallisty*, in fact) brought their considerable militancy to bear. Yet, the congress also drew the attention of the pub-lic and thereby dramatized the railroad strike from its beginning, and its lengthy deliberations may be said to have provided an incubation time during which the idea of a general strike germinated among other workers and strata of the Petersburg population.

The opposition of the revolutionary parties to a general strike con-tinued throughout these days, but their ranks began to waver. The Mensheviks were the first to give way, partly because their point of view gave more credence and importance to the "spontaneous" ini-tiative of the masses than did that of the Bolsheviks. On October 10, the Petersburg Group of the Mensheviks decided to accede to the popular urgings for a general strike and, at the same time, to call for the election of a "Workers' Committee" to direct the strike. The next day some 50 agitators went among the city's factories, asking workers to decide on the question of the strike and to elect deputies to the Workers' Committee on the same basis as the Shidlovskii elections, one representative for every 500 workers.[32] The Menshevik agitators were warmly received in the factory districts, but they contributed little to the precipitation of the general strike, whose participants were

31. *Novoe vremia*, Oct. 13, 1905. Krugliakov, "Pravitel'stvo i zheleznodorozhnye zabastovki v Peterburge v 1905 godu," pp. 69–71. Pushkareva, *Zheleznodorozhniki*, pp. 152, 153.

32. Kozovlev [S. S. Zborovskii], "Kak voznik Sovet," pp. 41–42.

taking their cue from the railroad workers and were already on strike or going into action on October 12.

The Bolsheviks continued to oppose the strike throughout the 11th and 12th. Yet the Bolsheviks were in close contact with mass sentiment through their agitators in the public meetings, and their resolute opposition to the strike had begun to create dissension and defections in their own ranks. Wladimir Woytinsky, a Bolshevik agitator and popular speaker at the university meetings, recalled addressing an audience of Vyborg district workers at the Military Medical Academy on October 11. Anticipating that he would have to take a position on the strike, he sent a runner to the Petersburg Committee for instructions on its latest position, which, given the situation, might be expected to change momentarily. Meanwhile, he began a speech on strikes in general and, without taking a position, turned the floor over to speakers from the audience, all of whom enthusiastically urged an immediate strike. Then Woytinsky, as a party representative, was asked to take a position and, having still received no instructions, half involuntarily began: "Comrades! What can I add to what has already been said? *Hail to the general strike!*" As he spoke, a message from the Petersburg Committee arrived on the stage, over two hours after it had been sent for. When he had finished, Woytinsky received the note and read: "Directive to agitators—Clarify the pros and cons of striking. [Signed] PC of the RSDRP."

The next day, October 12, the agitators still had no clear instructions from the Committee. Solomon Schwarz, who, like Woytinsky, was a student and Bolshevik agitator at the time, recalled that his Petersburg district agitators decided among themselves to speak that day under the slogan "Hail to *organizing* a strike," a formula which, in practice, sounded very much like support for the strike itself. On the evening of the 12th, the Petersburg Committee finally decided to throw its support behind what was, by that time, all but an accomplished fact. The first Bolshevik leaflet calling for a general strike appeared on the morning of October 13.[33]

It was thus the railroad workers, now backed by most of the other railroads of the country, that provided the initial rallying point for the general strike in Petersburg. The only other major group of workers

33. Schwarz, *The Russian Revolution of 1905*, pp. 139–41 and n. 16. Woytinsky, *Gody pobed*, pp. 95–96. Schwarz's dating of the first Bolshevik leaflet favoring a strike has been preferred to the varied and indefinite dating given in Soviet sources, because Schwarz's is definite and was recalled from his direct participation in the events.

to strike on the 12th was from the factories and plants of the Schlüssel-burg district. But by October 11, the railroad strike in other cities had already begun to create a crisis atmosphere in the capital, threatening to cut off goods and services and thereby adding another reason why thousands more workers might as well decide to strike. On that day the prices of meat and other consumer goods began to rise due to the shortage of deliveries from Moscow, and the post office stopped accepting parcels and letters following the curtailment of service on the Nikolaev Railroad. Passengers holding tickets on trains no longer running were fuming against the railroad administration, which was refusing for the time being to refund their fares. Suburban residents in the city anxiously arranged transportation home before all lines closed.[34]

On October 13 work in a much larger portion of the city's industries and offices ceased. Large parts of the industrial work force in the Vyborg, Petersburg, and Moscow districts went on strike, dominated as usual by Petersburg's two largest industries, metalworking and cotton textiles. Simultaneously, printers, pharmacists, watchmakers, clerks, horse tram operators, and white-collar employees from an import warehouse, an insurance company, and the Provincial Zemstvo Board quit work. Small groups of strikers appeared in several districts, forcibly closing shops and businesses. Late that night workers clashed with an army patrol. The *Russian Word* reported tersely: "From the morning on today, the mood of Petersburg has been strained to the highest degree. *Gostinyi Dvor* and the markets are boarded up, business in many commercial establishments has ceased. On Vasilevsky Island and the Petersburg Side Cossacks and military patrols are everywhere. Those at work today will join the strike tomorrow."[35] One of the electricity stations ceased to function. Reinforced military and police units occupied the post office and telegraph. Residents mobbed the remaining stores to stockpile goods, as if under siege. The city's workers were going on strike, but their action drew in or affected so many other parts of the population that it produced the impression of a vast civil disturbance gripping the entire city.

The government's response to these events was immediate. On October 14 Petersburg Governor-General Trepov issued a barely dis-

34. *Novoe vremia*, Oct. 12, 13, 1905. Shuster, *Peterburgskie rabochie*, p. 147. Dorovatovskii and Zlotin, "Khronika," p. 227.

35. Dorovatovskii and Zlotin, "Khronika," p. 227. *VPSO*, pp. 357–59. Smolin, "Pervaia russkaia revoliutsiia," p. 315. Obninskii, *Polgoda russkoi revoliutsii*, pp. 31–32. *Novoe vremia*, Oct. 14, 1905.

guised threat to shoot the strikers on sight. In an order published in the *Government Herald* and subsequently posted all over the city, he referred to the "rumors of supposedly impending mass disorders," which he asked the population not to believe since "measures for the protection of person and property in the capital have been taken." Then he came to the real point of the order: "If, however, attempts to create disorders arise anywhere, they will be terminated at the very outset and serious developments will consequently not obtain. I have ordered the troops and police to suppress any such attempt immediately and in the most decisive manner [and] upon a show of resistance to this on the part of the crowd—not to fire blank volleys and not to spare cartridges."[36] Trepov ended by noting that the residents of the capital should consider themselves warned of the possible consequences of joining "disorderly crowds."

The same day, October 14, more workers of all types joined the strike. Several of the metalworking giants outside the Schlüsselburg district—the Baltic Shipyard, the Putilov Works, the Franco-Russian Plant—as well as a number of large and medium-size metal and textile factories were struck. Apparently self-appointed agitators again appeared in the streets, seeking to close shops and stores. More pharmacists, tram operators, insurance employees, printers, and railroad workers walked out, and they were joined by some bank employees, secondary-school students, and actors. The next day, more of the same groups joined the strike, including 60 telephone operators, over 200 State Bank employees, and even 30 school pupils, aged ten to fourteen.[37] The general strike, discussed for at least two weeks and begun October 12, was fully realized on the 14th.

Not every shop and factory in the city had closed. Some of the very large establishments, such as the Russian-American Rubber Factory, the Mechanized Shoe Factory, and the St. Petersburg Pipe Plant, continued to operate right through the middle of October (although the first two struck later in the month), and small and medium factories probably struck in smaller proportions than the large. Indeed, the monthly figures for man-days lost to strikes among factory workers in Petersburg province (see Table 18, Chapter 6) show that October ranked behind January, February, November, and December and only slightly ahead of July. Considered along with other evidence, this indicates that strikes were shorter in October, but also that fewer in-

36. *VPSO*, p. 354.
37. *Ibid.*, pp. 358–67. Obninskii, *Polgoda*, p. 32.

dustrial establishments struck than in the massive work stoppages earlier in the year. It would be reasonable to conclude that discouragement, wage losses, dismissals, and lockouts during nine months of striking had dulled the fighting edge of the factory proletariat, but that would constitute only part of the truth. During the same period workers at the most militant and active plants had also learned that in order to win and enforce concessions against their employers, they had to secure political changes: minimally, the rights to speak, organize, meet, and strike freely; optimally, the overthrow of autocracy and its replacement with a democratic political order. Short of a political breakthrough, strikes for factory-related grievances would continue either to fail or to produce concessions that could be diminished or retracted later.

Not surprisingly, therefore, workers at a number of the politically more radical or experienced plants now struck for purely political reasons and for limited terms. Workers at the Obukhov, Putilov, Baltic, and Franco-Russian works, all walking out on October 13 and 14, declared sympathy strikes or raised only political demands, and they fixed the end of their strikes in advance for Monday, October 17.[38] These decisions corresponded with and in part reflected adherence to the policies of the revolutionary parties, which had sought for years to turn strikes in a political direction, and more recently had come to oppose strikes in favor of husbanding energies for a political *coup*. This was most clearly reflected in the strike resolution of 2,000 Obukhov workers (written by Bolsheviks) calling for the organization of an armed uprising under the leadership of the RSDRP and asking workers to refrain from "individual clashes with the police and troops, since we must enter into a decisive battle when this is to our advantage and not to that of our enemy."[39] This conception of political priorities during the October strike was of course characteristic of the radical workers, and it was opposed not only by workers who opposed strikes of any kind but also by those who favored fighting for job- and factory-related demands alone. Within the population of the factories, both views found their greatest support among the less skilled, lower paid, and less educated workers—i.e., those who were both less developed politically and harder hit by strikes. However, the experience of the fall strikes showed that this group was normally willing to subordinate itself to worker leaders favoring political strikes—when they

38. *VPSO*, pp. 352–53, 359.
39. *Ibid.*, p. 356.

were present in the factory—and to combine "economic" and political demands.

The unique feature of the October strike, which made it truly "general," was the participation of many categories of white-collar, artisan, and service workers alongside the factory proletariat. The sequence of events on October 12–15 shows that most of these workers did not wait to be called out by the striking factory proletariat, but came out on their own, taking as their cue the strike of Petersburg railroaders, but also drawing on their own greater state of readiness, made possible by the government's easing of restrictions on public meetings. These workers not only brought the strike into the center of the city from the beginning; they also ensured that the strike affected every Petersburg resident, in many cases directly and materially. By denying the urban public newspapers, tram service, food, medicine, banking, and even some government services, the artisan and white-collar elements did more to halt everyday life and to dramatize the strike, especially to wealthier citizens, than did the factory workers, confined as they normally were to their industrial suburbs and neighborhoods. These new protesters—most of them were striking for the first time in the year—along with railroad, telegraph, gas, electricity, and telephone strikers, created a total and crippling shutdown in the nerve center of the Empire. The government, which had weathered many purely proletarian strikes and could have weathered one more, had to back down this time.

Yet the same non–factory workers whose participation was so crucial to the political impact of the October strike expressed, in their public statements, mainly grievances of an "economic" nature. An unstated sympathy with the anti-government movement probably lurked beneath the surface in many cases, but the fact remains that the bulk of artisanal, office, and service workers did not put forth political demands even in the fall of 1905. Exceptions to this general rule occurred among printing workers, who aligned themselves with the Bolshevik position on the strike at a meeting on October 14; State Bank employees, who struck to join "the popular struggle for the rights of man and citizen," and to show solidarity with the "demands of the country on the immediate liquidation of the old order"; and some of the city's tailors, for whom political demands predominated over "economic" ones for a while in October.[40] In all other known

40. *ILSRPP*, pp. 197–98. *VPSO*, pp. 363–64. Gruzdev, *Trud i bor'ba shveinikov v Peterburge 1905–1916 gg.*, p. 30. There were probably also a number of smaller groups of artisans participating in the October strike whose close personal ties and shared work

cases, job- and factory-related demands and grievances seem to have been uppermost in the minds of these strikers. Of course, the conditions and attitudes prevailing in 1905 tended to draw all worker protest into the strike movement, after which it became, ipso facto, politically subversive, no matter what was originally intended. For instance, artisan trades and occupations such as shoemaking, tailoring, and skilled woodworking, whose main organizing efforts before October had been directed toward forming a union, participated in the October strike to further the same aims that their unionization efforts had failed to achieve.[41] And, from the standpoint of the government (and much of educated society), the October strikers fell into an already polarized pattern of expectations, established earlier by the nine-month struggle of the factory proletariat, which had conditioned the government to read in any strike a protest against its policies and its very existence.

The manner in which the October strike came about in Petersburg and other large cities emphasized motives common to all the protesters rather than the specific needs of the strike's separate components. The great upsurge of civic passion, the outpouring of political rhetoric, the rallying of all the classes and groups of the Empire in common opposition to the brutal and authoritarian regime—all cast a patriotic and political luster over the October days, subtly reshaping motives and irresistibly inviting participation by all parts of the population.

In Petersburg especially, the whole upheaval had taken on prodigious rhetorical dimensions. Since the outbreak of the general strike on October 12, the numbers attending meetings in the higher schools had grown enormously. Crowds at the University alone were estimated at 10,000 on October 11; at 20,000 on October 12; 30,000 on the 13th; and 50,000 on the 14th, including the overflow that went to the Art Academy.[42] Since September these meetings had been domi-

---

cultures served to intensify both social cohesiveness and political commitment, although the same conditions also isolated them and kept them from influencing significantly the mass labor movement—e.g., the Petersburg knitters discussed by V. Perazich, "Soiuz viazal'shchikov (1902–1907 gg.)," *Materialy po istorii professional'nogo dvizheniia v Peterburge za 1905–1907 gg.* (L., 1926), pp. 179–91.

41. Dorovatovskii and Zlotin, "Khronika," pp. 227–28. Pnin, "Iz istorii . . . torgovykh sluzhashchikh v Peterburge," pp. 276, 282–84. Gordon, "Iz zhizni rabochikh . . . na gorodskikh zheleznykh dorogakh," p. 95. Shatilova, "Peterburgskie kozhevniki," p. 68. Gruzdev, *Trud i bor'ba shveinikov,* pp. 30, 46–48. Ainzaft, *Istoriia rabochego . . . dvizheniia derevoobdelochnikov,* pp. 104–5.

42. *VPSO,* pp. 355, 357, 361. *Russkaia gazeta,* Oct. 13, 1905.

nated by the factory proletariat, but with the revival of strikes and demonstrations in October, wider circles of workers and the urban educated opposition were mobilized and began to swell the crowds in the lecture halls and auditoriums. There the activists from these non-factory groups rehearsed the general strike with factory workers from the outer districts, absorbing the latter's revolutionary oratory and their seriousness, ardor, and solidarity. All workers, factory and non-factory alike, were equally barred from meeting among themselves to concert their strike and unionizing plans. Hence the meetings pre-pared the workers of the city center (white-collar, artisan, and service employees) not only to strike among themselves, but to strike at the same time as the factory workers of the periphery. The workers of the center followed and drew inspiration from the factory workers, but thanks to the university meetings they were also able, even prior to the strike in some cases, to delineate the aims and needs of their own particular trades.

With the outbreak of the general strike, the meetings not only grew in size, they became politically and psychologically indispensable as the strikers themselves came in search of the information and the re-affirmation of unity and commitment necessary to every strike. The university meetings became a kind of general assembly of the strike, albeit lacking a leadership that was either unified or responsible to the strikers. The principal Bolshevik strategy was to transform the gen-eral strike into an armed uprising, but there was, overall, very little support for this among the workers. Woytinsky reported that in the mass meetings before the strike began, workers readily acclaimed the need for an armed uprising when this was invoked by revolutionary orators, though all they really wanted was a general strike.[43] Once the strike was under way, a lot more talk was heard at the meetings about the need to acquire arms, and money was regularly collected to pur-chase them. Large-scale, bloody clashes between government forces and the citizenries of Kharkov, Ekaterinoslav, and a number of other towns contributed to fears and hopes in Petersburg that the hour of a nationwide uprising was at hand. As early as October 12, one speaker at the University appointed a time and place for the distribution of tickets that could later be exchanged for weapons. Meeting-goers were instructed to forge weapons in the metal shops, to take them from police and soldiers, and to steal them from gunshops and arse-nals. On October 15, Bolshevik orators called on the workers to ap-

43. Woytinsky, *Gody pobed*, p. 94.

pear the next day at the University with their weapons, while Trepov's troops waited outside the meeting to close it and all further public meetings in the higher schools.[44]

Apparently, several hundred workers did assemble the next day along the University Embankment, concealing weapons such as knives, brass knuckles, and small revolvers. Cossacks guarded the buildings, and foot and mounted patrols could be seen throughout the city. The disparity of forces proved to be too much for the young agitators, who were unwilling to take the certain death of countless workers on their consciences; Woytinsky and two companions spent all afternoon quietly persuading the assembled workers to go home peacefully, arguing that their weapons and numbers were still inadequate. Only on the next day were the Bolshevik agitators finally told by a representative of the Petersburg Committee that, aside from a few dozen revolvers already distributed, there were and would be no weapons. The shipment expected had been seized at the border; the government had taken all rifled weapons from gunshops and locked them up in the Peter-Paul Fortress, leaving only shotguns; and the military units that might have joined an insurrection had been deprived of their weapons.[45]

THE SOVIET OF WORKERS' DEPUTIES

Since October 10, the Petersburg Mensheviks had been forming a Workers' Committee that was intended to direct the strike throughout the city and to turn the whole movement toward an uprising. The effort was an immediate and brilliant success. By October 13, the first meeting of the "Petersburg General Workers' Committee" (*Obshchii Rabochii Komitet Peterburga*) was held in the Technological Institute. The gathering of some 40 workers' deputies was chaired by the Menshevik S. S. Zborovskii. Over the next nine days, the group met seven more times. Attendance was uneven, but by the third meeting on October 15, 226 deputies from 96 factories, five trade unions, and the railroad strikers' committee gathered. With the experience of the Shidlovskii Commission behind them and a leaderless general strike before them, Petersburg workers participated actively and enthusiastically in the election of their own deputies. On October 17, the

44. *VPSO*, pp. 353, 358, 360, 361, 363, 364, 365. Shestakov, "Vseobshchaia oktiabr'skaia stachka," pp. 307–14. Woytinsky, *Gody pobed*, p. 153. Trotsky, *1905*, pp. 94–96.
45. Woytinsky, *Gody pobed*, pp. 150–55, 160–63.

body was renamed the St. Petersburg Soviet of Workers' Deputies and an Executive Committee was constituted of two representatives elected from each of seven city districts, plus spokesmen without voting rights from the three revolutionary parties and, later, from trade unions. Workers were to elect one deputy for every 500 workers, but no further restrictions were placed on deputy selection, and even this rule was not strictly observed or enforced. By mid-November the Soviet consisted of 562 deputies from 147 factories, 34 shops, and 16 trade unions.[46]

The political character of the Soviet was from the beginning an object of controversy and contention. It was, of course, always a formation of the Left, an organ of extreme democracy. Many of the elected deputies were Social Democrats and Socialist Revolutionaries, and several of them sat on the Soviet's Executive Committee. Precise figures are unavailable, but impressionistic evidence indicates that a significantly higher proportion of members and close sympathizers of revolutionary organizations served as Soviet deputies than had served as Shidlovskii electors, an impression consistent with the greater acceptability of revolutionaries among workers in the fall and with the increases in party recruitment. In addition, formal representatives of the SRs and the two SD factions were invited to join the Executive Committee in an advisory capacity, without a vote.

Although the idea of a workers' council originated independently in several quarters about the same time, the Mensheviks were chiefly responsible for organizing it, and Social Democratic influence was dominant throughout its brief history.[47] The Mensheviks opposed turning the Soviet into a direct instrument of party policy, but regarded it as an organ of "revolutionary self-government," that is, a vehicle for expanding and advancing the aims of the revolution, accessible to workers of all factions and especially to those belonging to no party at all. This allowed it to function as an excellent arena for

46. Kozovlev, "Kak voznik Sovet," pp. 41–43; Nosar', "Istoriia Soveta Rabochikh Deputatov," pp. 146–47. Evgenii, "Peterburgskii Sovet Rabochikh Deputatov," pp. 4–5. *1905: SRD*, pp. 5–20. Knuniants, "Pervyi sovet rabochikh deputatov," pp. 217–19.

47. For claims that the Soviet originated among the Mensheviks, see Evgenii, "Peterburgskii Sovet," and Woytinsky, *Gody pobed*, pp. 138–41; among the Liberationists, Schwarz, *The Russian Revolution of 1905*, pp. 331–34; among Nosar' and the Petersburg printers, Nosar', "Istoriia Soveta," p. 61; with Trotsky, "Pis'mo L. Trotskogo v Istpart," in Sverchkov, *Na zare revoliutsii*, p. 6. Even the anarchist Voline (V. M. Eichenbaum), in a highly questionable account, claimed that he and Nosar' originated the Soviet in January 1905: Voline, *The Unknown Revolution, 1917–1921*, trans. H. Cantine and F. Perlman (Detroit and Chicago, 1974; orig. ed. 1947), pp. 98–101.

recruitment into the party. The Mensheviks therefore strove to keep the Soviet free from identification with any one party or faction, and they succeeded largely because the policy was heartily endorsed by the majority of deputies.

Bolshevik leadership in Petersburg opposed this arrangement at first, feeling that the Soviet should accept Social Democratic leadership or risk falling under the control of nonrevolutionary elements. Within two weeks of the Soviet's founding, the Bolsheviks organized a number of initiatives ranging from a call for the body to accept the Social Democratic program (the position taken by a joint council of Bolsheviks and Mensheviks) to a threat that the Bolsheviks would leave the Soviet unless the Social Democratic program and leadership were accepted. The milder of these proposals even won support among workers at some factories, but when the Bolsheviks tried to discuss it in the Soviet itself (on October 29), their effort was rebuffed in short order by a majority of deputies. Even Bolshevik ranks were divided by the issue, and some of them openly sided with the Menshevik approach to the problem.[48] The Bolsheviks remained in the Soviet, and did not raise the question of formal affiliation in it again. The Socialist Revolutionaries were the weakest of the three major formations, and they rankled under Social Democratic ascendancy in the Soviet but never sought to win sole and exclusive dominance for themselves. The Soviet therefore never officially moved into the orbit of Russian Social Democracy or into that of any other political group.

The Soviet's party-neutral status (*bespartiinost'*) reflected the deepest wishes of the worker deputies themselves. Not only did the Soviet never adopt a single party's program, it never embodied its aims in an official program of any kind. Instead, its lack of commitment to any established party became one of its defining characteristics, and the choice (on October 14) of Khrustalev-Nosar' as chairman of the Soviet effectively symbolized and embodied this neutrality. Nosar' apparently still represented to most workers the general aims of the revolution, their link to the nationwide liberation movement, and his later conversion to Menshevism did not seem to affect this reputation. Given his popularity and his role as a kind of intelligentsia tribune to the workers, and given the Soviet's party-neutrality, it seems peculiar that no closer ties were forged with the intelligentsia union movement. Re-

48. Anweiler, *The Soviets*, pp. 67–69, 76–77. Schwarz, *The Russian Revolution of 1905*, pp. 178–84. Woytinsky, *Gody pobed*, pp. 192–94. Sverchkov, *Na zare revoliutsii*, pp. 6–7. *1905: SRD*, p. 21.

quests by both the Union of Unions and the Engineers' Union to join the Soviet were rejected, although semiproletarian affiliates of the liberal federation, like the unions of bookkeepers and office workers, of railroad workers, and of pharmacists, were admitted.[49] In all probability, the political opposition of the Social Democrats, exercised through the Executive Committee, explains the exclusion. This ruling most likely did not reflect the wishes of the rank-and-file worker deputies, who were party-neutral, and their failure to reverse the decision from the floor of the assembly probably indicates a lack of close familiarity and direct contacts with liberal activists rather than hostility. Despite this rebuff, the radical rump of the intelligentsia union movement continued to render close political, financial, and material support to the Soviet and to cooperate closely on projects of joint interest.

Official postures and programs aside, however, the Soviet did assume the outlines of a political identity from the preponderant influence of Social Democrats among its leaders and by virtue of its assumption of leadership of the general strike when the hopes, illusions, and energies of both workers and the whole Russian opposition were at their height. This identity resolved itself into two broad and overlapping areas of activity: strike leadership, and the mediation of relations between the working class and state power. The politics of the Soviet took shape at the height of expectations—widely current in oppositionist circles since the outbreak of the railroad strike in Moscow—that the collapse or overthrow of the Tsarist regime was imminent. Organized on the eve of the closing of the higher schools to public meetings, the Soviet fell heir to the élan and illusions of those meetings, including the notion that the "preparation of an armed uprising" was on the agenda of the day. Notwithstanding the fact that insurrections are not best organized in open, deliberative bodies such as the Soviet, it did continue to regard "armed uprising" as a near and desirable aim. The Soviet did not itself arm the workers, but it encouraged them to arm and to organize themselves. At the same time, the bulk of the Soviet's efforts was directed toward legitimizing itself as a nonviolent force on the left of the national opposition, striving simultaneously to establish a new legality based on its exercise of direct democracy and to extend its power and authority among workers and the city and national population as a whole. The difficulty of these tasks was increased by the fact that the period of the Soviet's in-

49. Sanders, "The Union of Unions," ch. 10, p. 32.

fluence coincided with the gradual recuperation of state power and authority.

The early days of the Soviet's activities were totally absorbed by the whirl and tension of events as the general strike movement continued to build. From the outset the Soviet announced its intention to direct strikes through a system that locked together factory-level committees with a citywide centralized leadership. Calling for the election of deputies at every factory and plant, one of the first proclamations of the body stated:

> The assembly of factory deputies will comprise the factory or plant Committee. The assembly of the deputies of all factories and plants will comprise the General Labor Committee of Petersburg. This Committee, uniting our movement, will give it organization, unity, power. It will be the representative of the needs of Petersburg workers before the rest of society. It will determine what we are to do during a strike and will indicate when to end it. Organize, comrades! Hurry and elect your deputies.[50]

Punctuating this call with a historic grandeur that would continue to characterize the Soviet's rhetoric, the statement concluded: "Decisive events in Russia will be accomplished in the coming days. They will determine for many years the fate of the working class, and we must face these events in complete readiness, united by our General Labor Committee, under the glorious red banner of the proletariat of all countries and working peoples."

The first measures of the Soviet were relatively modest. They defied Trepov's order closing the higher schools and asked workers to attend meetings in them on October 15. The efforts of individual strikers to close stores and shops were backed by a Soviet order demanding their closing, arranging limited hours for foodstores, and threatening violence to kiosks and news vendors who continued to sell newspapers. Workers were exhorted forcibly to encourage nonstrikers to quit work and especially to aid shop clerks in closing stores still in operation. On October 15 most workers in textile, glass, and tobacco factories, as well as most brewers and confectioners, still had not struck. Trepov had threatened all store owners with exile from Petersburg if they closed without police permission. On October 17, the Soviet extended its order to close to all commercial and industrial enterprises, threatening them all with physical destruction should the order be ig-

50. *1905: SRD*, p. 6. *Izvestiia SRD*, p. 7.

nored. These efforts only served to align the Soviet with a movement already in full swing, however, and the threats of violence were, in most cases, probably not carried out. By October 17, for instance, most textile factories were on strike.[51]

More controversial was a measure introduced at the October 14 session to petition the Petersburg City Duma to provide meeting places for the Soviet, to appropriate money for the unemployed, to regulate the prices of consumer goods, and to cease payment of city funds for the maintenance of the police, the gendarmes, and other military commands. Many deputies objected to the idea of approaching the Duma when it was initially proposed, since they did not believe a petition would be accepted and apparently felt the Soviet would be left in an awkward position. The measure's sponsors argued that the revolution had already moved several other city dumas to the left and that the Soviet should exploit the agitational possibilites of the moment, when it was attracting the attention of both educated society and its working masses. The measure passed, and the next day two more demands were added, requiring the immediate withdrawal of troops guarding the waterworks, under threat of turning off the water supply, and demanding that the Duma

> distribute from the people's resources at its disposal money needed for the arming of the Petersburg proletariat and students who had come over to the side of the proletariat, [all] struggling for the people's freedom.
>
> The leadership of this part of the popular revolutionary army must be in the hands of the proletariat itself.
>
> The money should be given to the General Labor Soviet.[52]

On Sunday, October 16, fourteen members of the Soviet appeared as a delegation at a special session of the Duma called for the purpose of meeting them. Advocates of the measure had not mistaken its agitational value. The Union of Unions supported the Soviet's demands and sent its own delegation to the Duma; students and professors of the Technological Institute each followed suit. All of these delegations were barred at the door of the Duma building by the police, who admitted only recognized delegates from the Soviet, the Union of

51. *1905: SRD*, pp. 6–9. Nosar', "Istoriia soveta," pp. 72–74. Nosar' claimed that *all* textile factories closed by the 16th. This cannot be verified with precise information and seems to be an exaggeration; besides, the 16th was a Sunday, when textile and most other factories closed anyway.

52. Nosar', "Istoriia Soveta," p. 67.

Unions, and the professors. The students' delegation and all curious onlookers were detained, and the threat of arrest hung heavily in the air for everyone involved in the event. The appearance of the workers' deputies before the city fathers made for a novel and memorable confrontation and called forth feelings not entirely anticipated in the Soviet's resolutions. The Bolshevik leader and delegation member Bogdan M. Knuniants noted that it produced

> a rather curious picture. In these solemn surroundings, among these *burzhui* [slang for "bourgeois"] in frock coats, aristocrats and bureaucrats with their decorations, there suddenly appeared 14 persons "right off the streets," dressed in terrible taste. . . . Many of us were completely hoarse from speeches at meetings, and the "moral" fathers very likely thought with horror that we had lost our voices from drunkenness. In addition, we were all in coats and galoshes and were irritated by our long wait and encounter with the police.

Nevertheless, the delegation was accorded a polite hearing, received private assurances from Duma members that they would "do everything" for the workers, and were given safe passage past the police on their way out. The Soviet never returned to the Duma, and the Duma members, for all their promises, never met the major demands of the Soviet.[53]

On Monday, October 17, the strike reached its high-water mark. The Soviet voted to continue the strike, maintaining that a premature return to work in the capital might slow the growth of the national movement and that "the present strike can deliver the decisive blow to the tottering autocracy." The deputies went on to strengthen and expand their activities by again threatening to enforce their shutdown order to factory and store owners with property damage, by arranging for the organization of district branches of the Soviet, by beginning the organization of a strike fund, and by recommending that workers not pay rent or bills during the strike.

Though the Soviet was clearly still being carried by the momentum of the strike, there was already evidence that its existence was making a difference. Workers at all but one of the large metal plants that had

---

53. *Ibid.*, pp. 66–71. *1905: SRD*, pp. 7, 9. Rubin [Knuniants] in *Obrazovanie*, no. 5 (1906), pp. 132, 135. Morgan, "The St. Petersburg Soviet of Workers' Deputies," pp. 56–59, 61–65. The Duma did make good on at least one demand: 11,000 rubles collected over the summer to aid workers locked out at the Putilov Plant were later handed over to Soviet deputies by Duma members. V. I. Perafort, "Na Putilovskom zavode," in *Vospomananiia Soveta*, p. 50.

declared political strikes until the 17th continued their strikes past that date. At the Nevsky and Obukhov works, mass meetings of 7,000 and 10,000, respectively, were held on the 17th, opening a new period of mass factory meetings. They were stimulated by the expansive mood of the strikers and, in part, necessitated by the closing of the higher schools to political meetings on the night of October 15. The meetings drew together not only the workers from the metalworking giants where they were held, but workers from neighboring factories as well. The format of the meetings was much the same as those held in the higher schools, with exhortations to prepare for an assault on the autocracy.[54] Yet the revival of factory meetings was also furthered and facilitated by the dual emphasis of the Soviet, which conceived of itself as an extension of factory-level activity and deliberation while it dignified and amplified local proceedings with the assurance that they formed an organic part of a larger whole, led and supervised by a central authority that the workers themselves controlled. Beginning at the large metal plants, then gradually spreading to smaller enterprises and other industries, the factory meeting became the principal means by which the deputies, who organized and led them, communicated the Soviet's decisions to the workers and received instructions and a sense of the factory mood from them.

OCTOBER 18

For several days, however, activity in the factories was outmatched by the excitement of activity in the streets. Ever since the outbreak of strikes in Moscow, which had resulted in violent clashes and shootings, a fear was afoot that the bloody confrontation of January might be repeated in the capital. The violence occasioned by the Schlüsselburg and printers' strikes confirmed this fear. Even though calmness and order were restored afterward, the exhortations to armed uprising at the mass meetings, and the preparations for it, kept the urban public on edge. General Trepov's order "not to spare cartridges" and his forcible closing of the higher schools, which gave him a pretext to awe the Petersburg citizenry by parading his troops around the city, brought anxiety to a high pitch, creating a mood of impending disaster.

Many workers were apparently ready for a fight. Several hundred with small arms assembled in front of the University on October 16 in answer to the Bolshevik agitators' call. Others gathered and cached

54. *1905: SRD*, pp. 10–11. *VPSO*, pp. 373–74.

arms in response to the more frequently heard summons to *prepare*
for an uprising if not to stage one. Woytinsky later claimed—though
without adequate explanation—that workers were not frightened by
Trepov's threats because they believed that, in a showdown, the soldiers would not shoot at them. Woytinsky went on to argue that the
intelligentsia and the bourgeoisie were certain that the troops would
fire on the workers, and they were consequently far more fearful than
the workers of a bloody outcome to the now seemingly unavoidable
confrontation.[55] Yet it is unlikely that workers did not, by and large,
share this fear. Several hundred—perhaps even a few thousand—
workers were apparently prepared for an armed confrontation with
the government (the exact numbers cannot be established), but the
vast majority would probably have opposed an uprising at this time.
Of course, almost as great a majority favored the results of an uprising, the overthrow of the autocracy being closely associated with
liberation as workers and citizens. But there seems to have been relatively little support among most workers for serving as the instruments of an uprising. This was undoubtedly based on a sound conviction that they were outgunned and that the soldiers, as in January,
would not hesitate to shoot them down. While workers were more accustomed to the sight of armed police and soldiers than their bourgeois allies, and while they did not voice their misgivings as openly
and freely, neither were they ready to risk everything against such uneven odds. It follows that Trepov's show of strength had some of its
desired effect on workers and that workers shared some of the awful
tension and anxiety that gripped other parts of the population.

As it turned out, the government backed down first. On October 17
it announced that it would grant civil liberties, an extension of the
franchise to parts of the population previously excluded from forthcoming elections to the State Duma, and a guarantee that the Duma's
consent would be necessary to make future legislation effective.[56] With
the publication of the October Manifesto, a new era in Russia's constitutional history was opened and the struggle between state and society
was given a new framework. The Manifesto supplied the government
with the moral basis to initiate an attack on the forces of the revolution, but it also gave the many parties, unions, and organizations of

55. Woytinsky, *Gody pobed*, pp. 146–47.
56. The text of the October Manifesto may be found in *Polnoe sobranie zakonov
Rossiiskoi imperii. Sobranie tret'e*, vol. 25, cols. 754–55, or in *Sputnik izbiratelia na 1906*,
pp. 274–75. The English text is contained in B. Dmytryshyn, *Imperial Russia. A Source
Book, 1700–1917* (New York, 1967), pp. 314–15.

the opposition legal sanction to expand and intensify their activities. The defeat of the revolution was prepared, and the "Days of Freedom" were opened.

Public reaction to the October Manifesto did not affect Petersburg until the 18th. A hint at the direction events would probably have taken had it not been for the distraction and political reorientation brought by the Manifesto occurred on the evening of October 17 when a crowd of 200 textile workers surrounded two policemen and a Cossack patrol and stoned them until the arrival of more Cossacks put the workers to flight.[57] Later, in another part of town, nervous army troops fired into the Technological Institute, claiming that a bomb had been thrown at them from within. Much of the same tinderbox tension, mixed with jubilation, hope, and disbelief, characterized the demonstrations, processions, and public meetings that burst forth on October 18.

From about mid-morning, the streets began to fill with people as news of the new freedoms rapidly spread about town. They met at familiar places—the University, public squares, and large intersections—and held impromptu meetings, which were enveloped in a flood of oratory reflecting all shades of opinion, but principally that of the Left. Workers and students, the city's most practiced demonstrators, made up a large part of the crowds. They sang revolutionary songs and carried red flags, although other demonstrators bore the national colors, and social diversity in the street scene was noticeable. Many demonstrators felt it was an occasion to celebrate Russia's liberation, whereas others viewed it as a vindication of the justice and potency of the monarchy and therefore a cause for patriotic posturings. The Left, including the newly formed Constitutional Democratic Party, the political and trade unions, and a great many rank-and-file workers as well as the revolutionary parties, reacted with instinctual distrust and anxious vigilance about the future. For most of the October 18 demonstrators, however, the news of the Manifesto was too fresh and sudden for them to have sorted out their feelings, and they moved about the streets in a mood that mingled joy, disbelief, wariness, and continuing anxiety. Because of this, the Left was able to use its superior organization and experience with street politics to set its mark upon the day.

In the morning crowds formed and roamed the streets in search of

57. *VPSO*, p. 371. Nosar', "Istoriia Soveta," p. 79. *Izvestiia SRD*, no. 3 (Oct. 20, 1905), p. 26.

speakers. Around noon, several of these walking audiences gathered on the square in front of Kazan Cathedral; after hearing several speeches it was dispersed by Cossacks. Much of this now enlarged crowd went across the river to the University grounds, where the buildings had been forced earlier in the day and this key sanctuary "recaptured" by the liberation movement. From the balcony of the main building a number of speakers addressed the gigantic audience below. Among them was Leon Trotsky, one of the Social Democrats' most brilliant orators and a leading figure in the Soviet. He later recreated his speech in his history of 1905:

> Citizens! Now that we have got the ruling clique with its back to the wall, they promise us freedom. They promise us electoral rights and legislative power. Who promises these things? Nicholas the Second. Does he promise them of his own good will? Or with a pure heart? Nobody could say that for him. . . . It is this tireless hangman on the throne whom we have forced to promise us freedom. What a great triumph! But do not be too quick to celebrate victory; victory is not yet complete. . . . Look around, citizens; has anything changed since yesterday? Have the gates of our prisons been opened? The Peter and Paul Fortress still dominates the city, doesn't it? Don't you still hear groans and the gnashing of teeth from behind its accursed walls? Have our brothers returned to their homes from the Siberian deserts? "Amnesty! Amnesty! Amnesty!" comes the shout from below. . . . But citizens, is an amnesty all? Today they will let out hundreds of political fighters, tomorrow they will seize thousands of others. Isn't the order to spare no bullets hanging by the side of the manifesto about our freedom? . . . Isn't Trepov, the hangman, master of Petersburg? "Down with Trepov!" came the answering shout. Yes, down with Trepov! But is he the only one? Are there no villains in the bureaucracy's reserves to take his place? Trepov rules over us with the help of the army. The guardsmen covered in the blood of January 9 are his support and his strength. It is they whom he orders not to spare bullets against your breasts and heads. We cannot, we do not want to, we must not live at gunpoint. Citizens! Let our demand be the withdrawal of troops from Petersburg! Let no single soldier remain within a radius of 25 *versts* from the capital! The free citizens themselves will maintain order. No one shall suffer from violence and arbitrary rule. The people will take everyone under their protection. "Out with the troops! All troops to leave Petersburg!"[58]

Trotsky's demands were picked up by other speakers, and a large meeting inside the University later approved the following list, which

58. Trotsky, *1905*, pp. 113–17. *VPSO*, pp. 374–77. Woytinsky, *Gody pobed*, pp. 165–69.

represents the clearest programmatic meaning given to the day's events by any group or party:[59]

1. Complete political amnesty.
2. Abolition of the death penalty.
3. Creation of a people's militia.
4. Dismissal of Trepov.
5. Removal of troops from Petersburg.

Yet these oratorical fireworks and the astute political demands they elicited from the crowd did not imply a firm resolve, since they were approved by a passing and unorganized assemblage whose thoughts and feelings about the new freedoms had not yet crystallized. Contrary to the fearful stereotyping of the police reports, this was not a revolutionary crowd. The Soviet leader Knuniants seems closer to the truth in surmising: "This was not a militant crowd, capable of stopping at nothing, a crowd which the smallest obstacle would kindle the more and drive to accomplish high heroic deeds. On the contrary, our demonstrators were in a good-hearted holiday mood, and they were incapable of anything militant."[60] But holiday mood or not, it was also a nervous crowd. The often penetrating Woytinsky, witnessing the demonstrators fleeing Kazan Square at the mention of approaching Cossacks, wrote: "the crowd was inclined to panic: the man in the street, even though he rejoiced in the Manifesto, even though he was ready to believe the Tsar's word, all the same expected that following the announcement of freedom some kind of catastrophe had to take place—either a mass shooting, or a Jewish pogrom, or something else of that sort. . . ."

This nervousness mixed with hope for improvement, this light-heartedness in the face of disaster, imposed restraints on crowd dynamics and gave the demonstrators an aspect of gentleness that was not contradicted by the militant phrases of the speechmakers. For all the tension and talk of weapons and an uprising in the preceding three weeks, practically no violence was initiated by the crowd on October 18. Around 8 P.M. some 2,000 workers and students on the Vyborg Side, when ordered by the officer of a half-troop of Cossacks to disperse, replied with shouts and a hail of stones. The Cossacks opened fire, wounding three demonstrators. That was the only clear-cut case of violence initiated by a crowd recorded in police documents for either October 18 or 19.[61]

59. Woytinsky, *Gody pobed*, p. 169.
60. Knuniants, "Pervyi sovet," p. 259.
61. *VPSO*, p. 381. The only act of individual terror discovered on October 18 oc-

All other reported bloodshed was initiated and perpetrated by jittery and overzealous soldiers or provoked by right-wing demonstrators. In the morning a crowd listening to a speaker on Zabalkanskii Prospect was sabered by a cavalry detachment. Among the wounded was history professor Evgenii Tarle. In the same neighborhood later that day, demonstrators were fired on from the Semenovskii Regiment's barracks. One agitator, standing on a lamppost distributing leaflets, was killed outright by a shot apparently aimed at him, and four others were wounded, including a seven-year-old boy. On Nevsky Prospect at about the same time a large crowd on its way from the University to demonstrate for the release of prisoners encountered a large demonstration of extreme patriots, bearing national flags and religious banners. Some fighting occurred, and at least two were wounded by gunfire. The right-wing crowd ranged about the city until nightfall, attacking students and *intelligenty*. Several other instances of troops firing on demonstrators occurred until late into the evening of the 18th. The City Governor's office put the toll for the day at five killed and twelve wounded, although the exact figure was undoubtedly higher since some of the killed and injured were probably removed and cared for privately, as occurred after the January shootings, to spare the victims or relatives the attention of the authorities.[62]

The grandest demonstration of the day took place after the University crowd, intent on enforcing its demand for amnesty, headed back through the center of town on its way to the Preliminary Detention Prison ("*predvarilka*"). In search of leaders, the crowd first visited the Soviet of Workers' Deputies, then in afternoon session in the building of the Rozhdestvensk Courses. The Soviet chose Knuniants, Nosar', and Trotsky to lead the crowd and passed a resolution calling for the arming of the proletariat, the continuation of the strike, and a constituent assembly, as well as political amnesty and the withdrawal

curred when a student named Smirnov slashed the cheek of Major General Shmakov near the Tsarskoe Selo Railroad Terminal. The student was then so badly cut up by nearby soldiers that he was sent to the hospital in danger of his life. Oksman, "Iz bumag D. F. Trepova," p. 460.

62. Oksman, "Iz bumag D. F. Trepova," p. 459. *VPSO*, pp. 374–75, 382. *Izvestiia SRD*, no. 3 (Oct. 20), p. 27. Sverchkov, *Na zare revoliutsii*, p. 111. Woytinsky, *Gody pobed*, p. 169. Reporting the clash on Nevsky Prospect, the police did not indicate who initiated the violence and mentioned shooting only from the "crowd of revolutionaries." The police report is unreliable here since it concealed the political coloration of the right-wing demonstrators and failed to mention their later excesses (*VPSO*, p. 375). Sverchkov claimed that the patriotic demonstration was "hastily organized by the police from the tradesmen of the Haymarket," but he seemed uncertain of its exact origins.

of troops from the city. Then the deputies distributed themselves in the crowd to help preserve order, and the whole company set off. The *troika* of leaders seemed to have the crowd's safety prominently in mind, for instead of leading it directly to the prison, which was surrounded by troops, it toured once more around the city, gathering more demonstrators along the way. At one point, the leaders were approached by a delegation from the Union of Engineers, which assured them that an amnesty order had already been signed, that political prisoners would be freed the next day, but that troops at the prison had orders to shoot. The leaders then dispersed the demonstration, promising to organize another should the amnesty not materialize within a few days. In fact, a limited amnesty was granted on October 22.[63]

After the tremendous anxiety and expenditure of energy on October 18, disappointment at not having achieved anything tangible was keenly felt the next day. No street demonstrations or meetings took place, and the "rejoicing woven with fear" gave way to "hopeless despondency." The higher schools, forcibly reopened by demonstrators on the 18th, were again closed to public meetings. Although it could not be helped, the Soviet had in a sense failed a hopeful public, and the urban crowd would not rise again to place itself so trustingly in the hands of the workers' deputies. News of bloody pogroms all over Russia in the wake of the October Manifesto began to reach the capital. The isolation of the Soviet and the revolutionary movement had begun, although this would become apparent to participants only gradually.[64]

THE SOVIET BETWEEN WORKER AND TSAR

In working-class districts, another mood prevailed. The strike was still in full swing, and the events of October 18, which could only be read as encouragement, expanded support for political demands. Workers at a few factories returned to work on the 19th, but others

63. Woytinsky, *Gody pobed,* pp. 169–71. Sverchkov, *Na zare revoliutsii,* pp. 109–11, maintains that the delegation of engineers later proved to be self-appointed. Cf. Nosar', "Istoriia Soveta," pp. 83–84, who first reported this information, but went on to defend the *troika*'s decision to disband the demonstration rather than have it flee at the first sight of Cossacks. Nosar' too felt the October 18 crowd was too skittish and fearful to carry off anything as ambitious as another storming of the Bastille.

64. Woytinsky, *Gody pobed,* p. 175. *Izvestiia SRD,* no. 3 (Oct. 20), p. 26. On the pogroms, see Maevskii, "Obshchaia kartina dvizheniia," pp. 96–104.

struck anew or for the first time. Frightened by the activities of the 18th, managers at a number of plants had voluntarily closed down. Strikers remained active in the streets, agitating for wider support and asserting their control of factory neighborhoods in familiar ways. A crowd of striking barbers moved about the central districts, closing more shops in their trade. Putilov workers from the vessel shop seized their foreman, carried him out of the plant on a hospital stretcher, and dumped him in the road. Factory meetings continued to encourage workers to arm themselves, even to seize arms from policemen and soldiers if need be. A revealing development in the revolutionary process at the factory level unfolded at the Baltic Shipyards on the morning of October 19. The plant director walked into the machine shop while workers were holding a political meeting to ask why they were not working and what they wanted. "Instead of an answer to my question," he wrote, "there followed a series of insulting phrases together with the declaration that they, the skilled workers [*masterovye*], did not acknowledge me as plant director and proposed to manage things themselves [*upravliat'sia sami soboi*]." This promise was apparently not carried out, and it may have represented little more than a passing flash of anger. Wittingly or unwittingly, however, it gave expression to the logical next step in a struggle that did not seem to admit of compromise and signaled the factory workers' increasingly developed sense of their own power. This assertion of worker self-confidence also expressed the political solidarity workers felt with other oppositionist elements in society, and it is not accidental that it emerged at the height of the October strike and at a moment when public support of the factory movement was most pronounced.[65]

The position of the Soviet after October 18 both reflected this factory-level militancy and sought to go beyond it. At the session of October 19, Chairman Nosar', reporting for the Executive Committee, recommended ending the general strike in Petersburg on October 21 at noon. The reasoning of the leaders was that the strike had given people a victory by forcing the regime to back down, but that it was still necessary "to arm ourselves for the final struggle for the calling of a Constituent Assembly." A parallel recommendation and argument, delivered by Trotsky for the Social Democrats' Federated Council,[66]

65. *VPSO*, pp. 377–78, 381–82, 385. Woytinsky, *Gody pobed*, p. 176.

66. The Social Democratic Federated Council (*Federativnyi ob"edinennyi sovet*) was formed around October 17 to plan and coordinate the activities of Petersburg's Mensheviks and Bolsheviks in the areas of oral and written agitation "and all other public actions of the proletariat," which apparently included strategy and tactics in the Soviet.

set as the aim of further efforts the achievement of a democratic republic and explicitly called for an "even grander and more impressive attack on the staggering monarchy, which can be conclusively swept away only by a victorious popular uprising." The Executive Committee's proposal was passed by an "immense majority" of the deputies, and "unanimous solidarity" with the Council's resolution was expressed.[67]

The reasoning of the Soviet leaders was clear, confident, and inventive. The strike in Petersburg would end piecemeal and of its own accord within a few days anyway, as it had already begun to do elsewhere in Russia. By voting to end it voluntarily and simultaneously, the deputies sought to convert what usually proved to be a straggly and demoralizing experience into an assertion of discipline and an affirmation of their control over the factory movement. Beyond that, the decision contained a message from the leaders to the factory ranks that strikes alone, even a general strike, would not bring down the autocracy, and that other means were required. Belief in the irresistible power of the strike was endemic at the factory level, a perhaps unavoidable consequence of political inexperience, the relative novelty of mass strikes, and the drama of unity and sacrifice for collective gains that strikes always call forth. In this respect, the near unanimity with which the factory deputies voted to end the strike marked their recognition that citywide unity and the authority of the Soviet outweighed the claims of factory and district sentiment. As it was, the railroad workers resisted the Soviet's decision and decided to continue their strike beyond the 21st, while the pharmacists had to be persuaded not to end their strike a day early as they intended. At the last minute the Soviet specifically exempted from its ruling those workers who were conducting "economic" strikes and desired to continue until specific concessions were won.[68]

The commitment to armed uprising was dictated by the logic of the Soviet's revolutionary leadership and the continuing forward momentum among workers produced by the general strike and the Manifesto of October 17. The leaders from the parties were committed to it, and since the Soviet could never be reconciled with the autocracy, it

---

Izvestiia SRD, no. 2 (Oct. 18), p. 12. Schwarz claimed that the council was also intended to pave the way for a unification congress of the two factions. *The Russian Revolution of 1905*, pp. 182, 235–38.

67. *1905: SRD*, pp. 13–14.

68. *Ibid.*, pp. 14, 16–17.

would perish unless it acted against the regime that would destroy it. This emphasis on the continuing imminence of an ultimate resolution of political tensions was also an agitational tactic to encourage workers to continue to prepare for an uprising and to keep all the revolutionary forces at the fighting ready. None of the revolutionary parties really felt conditions were ripe for an uprising in the fall of 1905. Even Lenin, who began calling for an armed uprising right after January 9 and whose Bolshevik followers raised the question at every new turn of events throughout 1905, wrote on October 13 in response to an urgent query from the Petersburg Committee: "The time of the uprising? Who would take it on himself to specify it? I would personally willingly delay it till spring and until the return of the Manchurian army; I am inclined to think that it is to our advantage to delay it. But we'll not be asked in any event."[69] Nevertheless, preparation for the event was in itself a source of power because it contributed to the "ripening" of conditions. The problem was that calling for an uprising was not in itself sufficient to keep workers in a combative mood. A strike would do this, but it would end by exhausting and demoralizing workers and therefore defeat the purpose of sustaining and enlarging militancy. In addressing itself to this problem, the Soviet was resourceful and inventive, but it was never able to surmount its ultimate dependence on the energy and initiative of the factory movement.

With respect to street demonstrations, the Soviet made two attempts to renew them, albeit warily and without determination. On October 19, while the Soviet was in session, it sent three representatives to Kazan Square to offer leadership to any new gathering that might appear there. Apparently none did, and the three representatives were arrested and roughed up by the police. A delegation sent to Count Witte succeeded in securing the release of the arrestees.[70] The next day, the Executive Committee proposed a procession of mourning for the victims of the October 18 events. While the proposed demonstration met with unanimous approval, lively objections were made to the Executive Committee's plan to inform Witte that the demonstration would take place and to demand the removal of troops and police from the streets, with the proviso that the Soviet itself

---

69. Quoted in Bondarevskaia, *Peterburgskii komitet RSDRP*, p. 127, from Lenin, *Polnoe sobranie sochinenii*, vol. 47, p. 100. The respect accorded to the guiding role of spontaneous forces by the author of "What Is to Be Done?" in this passage is striking, yet there is no reason to question the Bolshevik leader's usually sober and penetrating assessment of political prospects in this instance.

70. *1905: SRD*, pp. 14–15.

would maintain order. Some maintained that the Soviet should not approach a representative of the government that had done the shooting, but the deputies agreed to the measure once it became clear that no principle was being risked. Preparations for the demonstration went forward in the factory districts. On October 22, one day before the planned event, Governor-General Trepov officially prohibited it in a public announcement, threatening dire consequences should his order be disobeyed. A delegation from the City Duma appeared at the Soviet the same day to warn that Trepov planned to arm and unleash gangs of right-wing terrorists to provoke situations that would give his troops a pretext to shoot at the demonstrators. The delegation pleaded with the Soviet deputies to spare the citizenry this mortal danger. The deputies then voted to cancel the demonstration. As it turned out, they had overreacted. The next morning, the papers carried an announcement from Trepov rescinding his previous order and giving permission for the funeral demonstration, providing that it followed a predesignated route. The Bolsheviks were so put out by this misjudgment and lost opportunity that they tried at factory meetings to secure motions censuring the Soviet leadership. Since the demand for the removal of troops had not been met, a demonstration under Trepov's conditions would still have risked violence. Trotsky, probably by now the chief architect of the Soviet's policy, later maintained that the Soviet "canceled the funeral procession so as not to provoke a clash without first trying to make use of the confused and hesitant 'new regime' [i.e., the apparently reformed monarchy during the "Days of Freedom"] for widespread agitational and organizational work among the masses."[71]

A more modest, but also more successful, project was undertaken on October 19 when the Soviet resolved that "only those newspapers can be published whose editors ignore the censorship committee, do not send their issues to the censor, and generally behave as does the Deputies' Soviet in publishing its newspaper." Owners refusing to comply were threatened with a continuation of the strike by compositors, confiscation and destruction of their publications, and even destruction of machinery and equipment. Printing workers complying with the order by striking would be rendered aid by the Soviet, and those who refused to comply would be ostracized ("boycotted").[72]

71. *Ibid.*, pp. 16, 19–20. Woytinsky, *Gody pobed*, pp. 189–92. Dan, *The Origins of Bolshevism*, p. 345. Trotsky, *1905*, pp. 126–30, 265.

72. *1905: SRD*, p. 14.

The initiative for this project had come from the union of printing workers, and it had fairly solid rank-and-file support. The union had conceived of the idea during the first printers' strike (October 3–5), and a number of newspaper editors, during the general strike, had agreed to comply. But the editors had begun to waver after the apparent guarantees of the October Manifesto were announced, and only the efforts and determination of the printing workers, with the backing of the Soviet, ensured the establishment of the first in-country free press in Russian history. The measure was so effective that the printing workers' union decided, on October 30, to extend it to book and journal publication as well. The new freedom resulted in the founding of a plethora of new journals and newspapers, including the first open and domestically published revolutionary organs such as the Bolshevik *New Life* (*Novaia zhizn'*) and the Menshevik *Beginnings* (*Nachalo*). Even the most conservative publishers were forced to comply with the Soviet's order, but once they did, the printing workers, for their part, printed every variety of opinion except black hundreds' literature calling for violence.[73]

Before the second week of its existence, the Soviet had begun to form a sense of its power and authority. Its delegations had been received and treated respectfully by some of the highest officials of the city and the country. Its sanction and leadership of the amnesty demonstration were sought and recognized by masses of citizens on October 18. Even General Trepov had backed down at the prospect of another Soviet-led demonstration. When its deputies ran afoul of the law, a fairly frequent occurrence, a word from the Soviet leadership usually sufficed to secure their release. It frequently intervened in conflicts between employers and workers, and in this area too found acceptance of its overriding authority in labor questions, if not always compliance with its wishes. In addition to the exploitation of legal channels, the Soviet exercised a "right of seizure" (*zakhvatnoe pravo*) in order to attain its ends. The Soviet's newspaper *Izvestiia Soveta Rabochikh Deputatov*, besides circumventing the government censors, was also printed by illegal means. Armed bands of workers would take over a typography for a few hours and stand guard while revolutionary printers did their work. Workers were encouraged to form armed squads (*druzhiny* or *desiatki*) in their factories for self-defense and, it

73. *Ibid.*, p. 18. Simanovskii, "Proletariat i svoboda pechati," pp. 217–41. *ILSRPP*, pp. 204–8. Trotsky, *1905*, pp. 140–56. *Izvestiia SRD*, no. 5 (Nov. 3), p. 42. Grinevich, "Ocherk razvitiia," pp. 233–35.

was understood, for an eventual uprising.[74] The most important and consequential application of the right of seizure, however, was the organization of a campaign to win the eight-hour workday by encouraging workers to put it into practice on their own initiative.

The campaign began, as earlier in the year, among the workers themselves and at the end of a strike. On October 24 workers of the Nevsky Ship and Machine Works, after a poll of the shops, announced to the management that they would work only eight hours beginning that same day. Workers at the nearby Aleksandrovsk Machine Works also shortened their day on the 24th to meet and formulate demands that they presented to the director of shops the next day. Two days later, Aleksandrovsk workers voted by secret ballot to institute an eight-hour day on their own. Somewhat more decorously, workers at the Obukhov Plant, the third metalworking giant of the Schlüsselburg district, requested permission to work eight instead of the usual nine hours, assuring the management that the skilled workers would try to keep production at the same level. But the next day, October 27, a meeting of the skilled workers decided to institute the eight-hour day themselves, without awaiting a reply from the Naval Ministry, where their request had been sent.[75] During the same week workers in other districts of the city also initiated their own eight-hour schedules: at the St. Petersburg Metal, Nobel, and Lessner machine and metalworking plants in the Vyborg district; the Siemens and Halske electrical works on Vasilevsky Island; the Nevsky Spinnery in the Rozhdestvensk district; and at the Aivaz Machine-Building Works in the Alexander Nevsky district. At many other factories, workers made plans to begin eight-hour days on Monday, October 31, or the next day.[76]

Petersburg workers had attempted to win the eight-hour day on their own before in 1905, but those efforts had usually collapsed after a few days. Some had achieved a nine-hour compromise (ten hours and more having been standard before 1905), and workers at railroad and naval installations had been granted nine-hour days by their respective ministries during the first half of the year, as noted earlier. Now the movement revived with a new vigor. It bore a resemblance to earlier efforts in that it occurred predominantly at large metal and machine plants, arose in the wake of a strike, and embodied conflict-

74. Simanovskii, "Kak pechatalis'," pp. 281–92. *Vospominaniia Soveta*, pp. 21–22, 45. *1905: SRD*, pp. 15, 18, 22, 24, 25.
75. *VPSO*, pp. 387, 392–94.
76. *Istoriia Soveta*, p. 102. *1905: SRD*, p. 22.

ing sentiments among the returning strikers. After the October General Strike, however, the mood among workers was buoyant and highly expectant rather than defeated and depressed as after previous strikes. The partial victory of October 17, the government's cautious attitude, and the hopefulness of the "Days of Liberty" contributed to this, but the collective strength and fighting readiness of the Soviet made the real difference, because its authority directly affected the terms of the struggle at the factory level. Even the workers of the Nevsky Works, probably the factory work force most capable of militant and independent action in all the city, claimed Soviet sanction for the initiation of the eight-hour day on October 24. At other plants, Soviet deputies led and organized the campaign. Although the Nevsky workers were in error in thinking, as they claimed, that the Soviet had called for establishment of the shortened workday as early as October 19, their reference to it illustrates the reinforcement the existence of the Soviet lent to struggles at even the most militant plants.[77]

The Soviet was thus true to the aims the factory movement had put forth as early as the Shidlovskii campaign of February, but the inadequacy of democratic representation alone to a workers' authority engaged in a polarized power struggle was now apparent, and it became increasingly plain that the Soviet lacked a capacity for disciplined action and tight maneuver due to its coalition leadership and strict control by the deputies. Much of the ardor and determination of the demonstrations, resolutions, and oratory after October 17 was carried back to the factories after work resumed on the 21st, and some of the democratic frenzy of the streets captivated and increasingly dominated the factory population.

The advent of the Soviet of Workers' Deputies meant that Petersburg workers emerged from the October strike more united and better organized than ever before. Workers resumed their struggle for their rights in the workplace with a new energy drawn from the partial victory of October 17 and from the assurance that the new labor authority would strengthen their efforts to an unprecedented degree. The Soviet raised to a new level the workers' sense of personal dignity and collective potency, and it won the loyalty and respect of a great portion of the factory population. Yet the Soviet's actual power was quite problematic. It was clear that the government would move against the Soviet as soon as it felt the political situation would bear it.

77. *VPSO*, p. 387.

Being unprepared for armed struggle, the Soviet could prolong its existence only by altering the political situation and forestalling the government's attack. Its authority among workers was not based primarily on its ability to organize them as a fighting force, and an attempt to seize state power would probably have overreached the Soviet's mandate. The Soviet consequently never sought seriously to do this. On the other hand, the deputies took perhaps too much satisfaction in the moral superiority of their democratic politics and gave too little thought to how they might preserve these politics, i.e., how they might survive as an organization. As a democratic body, the Soviet stood close to factory-level opinion and faithfully reflected the enthusiasms of the rank and file. Although survival dictated that the workers "prepare for an armed uprising" with efficiency and dispatch, the Soviet's leaders acceded to factory-level enthusiasm for mass activity aimed at the improvement of working conditions. The latter course of action strengthened the Soviet's political position in the short run by mobilizing large numbers of workers and keeping activity in the factory districts at a high pitch. But it also produced other results that seriously impaired the Soviet's ability to defend itself.

CHAPTER EIGHT

The November Strike and the
Eight-Hour Day

POPULAR RESPONSE TO THE MANIFESTO

During most of the last week of October, while work resumed and the eight-hour agitation took hold in factory districts, the Soviet did not meet. When it gathered again on October 29, it faced a heavy agenda, and the session sat until 2 A.M. In the course of the usual reports from individual factories, the eight-hour issue came to the fore, and a great number of deputies were apprised for the first time of just how far the movement had gone. Loud applause greeted the reports, and an irresistible urge arose to give the eight-hour campaign the force of a Soviet decree. In the course of the ensuing debate, one deputy pointed out that the Petersburg proletariat could not single-handedly win the eight-hour day, but added that his factory would implement any ruling favoring it. Deputies from the Putilov Works and two other metal plants supported the idea, but pleaded that conditions at their factories would make it impossible to put it into practice in the immediate future. The *putilovtsy* were still suffering the effects of the summer lockout, and they stood under the threat of another one in case of further disorders. According to witnesses, one lone voice from the back of the hall shouted, "We haven't finished with absolutism, and you begin a struggle with the capitalists." The voice went unheeded and unseconded as the meeting moved on to pass the following resolution:

> The Soviet of Workers' Deputies hails those comrades who have introduced the eight-hour workday at their factories by revolutionary means.
> The Soviet of Workers' Deputies thinks that the introduction of the

eight-hour workday everywhere requires a corresponding raise of wage rates so that wages remain at least at their former level. The Soviet of Workers' Deputies unanimously decrees that all remaining factories and plants of Petersburg introduce the eight-hour workday by revolutionary means beginning October 31. The mutual support of workers of all districts will guarantee the successful execution of the Soviet's decree.

Thus without prior discussion and consideration by the Executive Committee, and as the result of stormy and enthusiastic acclaim from the floor during a particularly busy and hectic session, the Soviet committed the workers of Petersburg to an undertaking that would focus a major portion of their energy on the factory struggle and away from the key political issue of the Soviet's own survival.[1]

On the first two days of the Soviet-led campaign, a number of plants and factories joined the ranks of those already imposing eight-hour days on their managements. Among them, large and medium metal and machine plants still predominated, but port workers, some textile workers, and a scattering of shop clerks and workers in small wood and glassmaking shops were also included. The response to the Soviet's decree was far from overwhelming, and it is unlikely that the movement would have grown significantly had other events not intervened. The practical arrangements necessary for the kind of long-term struggle that an eight-hour campaign would require could not be made at most factories on such short notice. Nosar' pointed out that French workers had spent a year and a half preparing to implement the eight-hour day, whereas Petersburg workers were given a day and a half![2] Those workers who had joined the campaign by November 1 were politically motivated, interested primarily in keeping the pressure on their employers and exercising immediate and direct

1. *1905: SRD*, pp. 22–23. Nosar', "Istoriia Soveta," pp. 102–3. B. Petrov-Radin, "Bor'ba za vos'michasovoi rabochii den'," p. 249. Woytinsky, *Gody pobed*, pp. 216–18. The SR leader Victor Chernov claimed that at this meeting he spoke against the eight-hour day and in favor of sending deputations to start new soviets all over Russia instead. He recalled that his ideas were listened to by a considerable part of the meeting, especially the Social Democratic intelligentsia, although he did not know why. But he was unable to finish his speech due to the arrival of Vera Zasulich and Leo Deutsch, who drew away the attention of the meeting. Chernov, *Pered burei. Vospominaniia*, p. 252. Although Chernov's speech made for more than one lone voice that spoke against the campaign, the fact that it was not reported or recalled in any of the above sources and that the audience was so easily distracted seems to confirm the unpopularity of the view at that time.

2. Nosar', "Istoriia Soveta," pp. 104–5.

control over an important aspect of the factory routine, if only for a time. Their approach had more in common with the desire of the Baltic Shipyard machine workers to take over the plant than with the sober efforts of eight-hour reformers in countries where workers already enjoyed civil liberties and freedom of action. Moreover, far from all Petersburg workers were so motivated as yet.

One reason for this is that they had not all yet elected deputies or recognized the authority of the Soviet: 281 deputies had attended the session of October 29, and although that was a large group for October, it represented only half the number counted in mid-November. In small workshops and in industries outside of metalworking, it normally took longer for the Soviet's message and authority to spread and root itself. This did not mean, however, that workers in enterprises of this type and scale were supine or passive during the second half of October. On the contrary, evidence points to continuing—even increasing—militancy among a great number and variety of workers, both within and without the Soviet. Workers of the Mechanized Shoe Factory, who had failed to strike earlier in the month, suddenly walked out on October 29 in support of a single dismissed worker. Two days later the factory's 2,100 workers, although known for their political backwardness, produced a list of 25 demands that included freedom of assembly and the withdrawal of troops from the factory, along with demands concerned with the more immediate conditions of work. In some plants a struggle between slower-moving workers and radical workers was evident. On October 29, the Soviet received a report that ten workers at the Nail Plant on Vasilevsky Island had been dismissed in apparent response to a workers' petition to rid the plant of agitators. The deputies commissioned a delegation to try to get the dismissed workers rehired and to spread the Soviet's influence at the plant. A remarkable transformation then ensued, although it was probably not due alone to the delegation's influence: the 1,700 workers of the Nail Plant struck on November 1 for an eight-hour day, and they remained on strike through mid-November.[3]

A number of workers had continued or initiated strikes for "economic" demands after the end of the general strike. One estimate put the number of such strikers at 7,000 on October 24, and at about twice that number one week later, so that worker militancy not directed primarily at the overthrow of the autocracy was increasing during the last week of October. During the same week a number of

3. *1905: SRD*, pp. 20, 21–22. *VPSO*, pp. 394–96. *VPR*, p. 352.

union organizing efforts resumed after the interruption of the October strike, indicating a similar return to bread-and-butter issues. A union of tailors and fur workers began to enroll members, and the first mass organizing meetings were held for textile workers, lithographers, shoemakers, seamstresses, bakers, draftsmen, and orchestra musicians.[4]

Together with these long-standing concerns, a new development added to workers' sense of urgency and desire for organization during the same period: the advent of a movement of gangs of the extreme patriotic Right—popularly known as "black hundreds"—which were conducting a campaign of terror throughout Russia, directed against groups they held responsible for the revolution—intellectuals, workers, students, and non-Russian nationalities, especially Jews. Their bloody and barbaric pogroms broke out all over Russia on October 18 and raged for about one month, killing 3,500 to 4,000, wounding over 10,000, and destroying tens of millions of rubles' worth of property.[5] A black hundreds crowd had appeared in Petersburg on October 18 and clashed with demonstrators celebrating their new freedom. Although they never mounted a major pogrom in the capital, black hundreds gangs continued to frighten the greater part of the citizenry by their sporadic beatings of intellectuals and workers. Rumors of their plans to murder revolutionary leaders and agitators circulated freely. Moreover, black hundreds groups began to emerge in a number of factories, where right-wing workers had always been present but had never been as organized or menacing as now. They reported to the police on the activities of the revolutionary workers, terrorized individual activists, and sought to galvanize worker opinion against the Left.[6] Overall, though, their effect was probably to galvanize worker opinion in Petersburg against the threat of the radical Right, and they provided the principal reason for the arming of the workers.

The formless anxiety of the whole liberation movement probably helped to exaggerate somewhat the black hundreds danger in Petersburg, and the widely held belief that they were instruments of gov-

4. Dorovatovskii and Zlotin, "Khronika," pp. 229–31.

5. Maevskii, "Obshchaia kartina," pp. 103–4. Heinz-Dietrich Löwe, *Antisemitismus und reaktionäre Utopie. Russischer Konservatismus im Kampf gegen den Wandel vom Staat und Gesellschaft, 1890–1917* (Hamburg, 1978), pp. 87–98.

6. Glukhochenkov, "Iz raboty chernoi sotni v 1905–1907 gg.," pp. 148–51. *Pervaia russkaia revoliutsiia v Peterburge 1905 g.*, vol. 2, pp. 58–60. Nosar', "Istoriia Soveta," p. 93. Woytinsky, *Gody pobed*, pp. 218–19.

ernment policy, never convincingly dispelled, certainly added to the fear of them. It will be recalled that a large part of the reason the Soviet canceled the mourning demonstration planned for October 23 was the fear on the part of the deputies and a large part of the public that the black hundreds in Petersburg were under Trepov's control and that he was prepared to unleash them on the mourners.

Whereas fear of the pogromists paralyzed most of the public, it moved the workers to arm themselves in self-defense. During the week of October 24 new rumors circulated that the long-expected pogrom would take place on Sunday, October 30. The Soviet had already supplied its members with sidearms for individual protection against right-wing terrorists and had encouraged workers to acquire arms. Now workers themselves collected money for weapons and, this proving far from adequate, began producing their own weapons in the metal shops—knives, pikes, bludgeons, and so forth. Workers at some plants were even able to supply such weapons to those at others, where the material or opportunity to make them was lacking. Armed squads were organized at a number of factories, and in some districts they were used to patrol the streets at night. This activity reached a high pitch on October 29, when some of these homemade weapons were displayed at the Soviet meeting and a report on the self-defense efforts under way was given. No pogrom took place the next day, and this was widely believed to be the result of the armed preparedness of the Soviet and the factory workers, a belief that even police director A. A. Lopukhin confided to Witte.[7]

During the same tense and hectic week, a revolt broke out among the soldiers and sailors of the Kronstadt military garrison, an island some twenty miles from Petersburg and headquarters of the Baltic Fleet. Already an unruly and unstable garrison early in 1905, Kronstadt had witnessed food riots in the summer. The October Manifesto encouraged the island's servicemen to hope for a rapid improvement in their lot, despite the warnings of the naval authorities that it did not apply to them. On October 23 a large demonstration of Kronstadt sailors had decided to petition the Tsar to grant them civil liberties, shorter terms of service, and unrestricted access to liquor, "since sailors," the petition added, "are not children under their parents' care." Another meeting was set for a week later, and the enlivened spirits of

7. Woytinsky, *Gody pobed*, pp. 219–21. *VPR*, pp. 346–47. Nosar', "Istoriia Soveta," pp. 94–95. Sverchkov, *Na zare revoliutsii*, pp. 121–22. *Vospominaniia Soveta*, pp. 49–50, 54, 60, 83, 87, 88, 93–94.

the servicemen led to an outbreak of rowdyism and disorders. On October 26, members of an infantry company were arrested after presenting their commander with a list of demands. As they were being taken to military prison, a crowd of rowdy soldiers and sailors tried to free them and the guards opened fire. This shooting touched off the revolt. More sailors and some artillerymen joined the crowd from their barracks, some bringing their weapons with them. The crowd first attacked and pillaged the military buildings, but after it broke into the state liquor stores, some of the apparently drunken rioters burned and looted civilian homes and stores. Some of the troops called out to quell the riot refused to fight fellow servicemen, and others joined the rioters. Military units had to be brought from the capital the next day to restore order. The authorities treated the revolt as a matter of military discipline and prepared to subject some 1,200 arrestees to field courts-martial, which entailed possible summary death sentences.[8]

News of the draconian punishment hanging over the Kronstadt rioters reached Petersburg on October 29. Despite the preoccupation of the Soviet and the revolutionary parties with the black hundreds and the implementation of the eight-hour day, they planned a strong supportive response to the first significant breach of military discipline in the Petersburg area. On the first two days of the new workweek, October 31 and November 1, meetings at a dozen or so of the most highly politicized metal plants passed resolutions protesting the pending death sentences, calling for worker support of the soldiers and sailors, and either threatening a strike or promising support for whatever form of protest the Soviet or Social Democratic Party decided upon. Although the resolutions seemed to express an elemental response among workers to the Kronstadt events, and although many workers could easily sympathize with the position of the rioters because of the similarity it bore to their own, the fact that the response emerged on such short notice and almost always called for a strike or some other form of protest indicates a degree of systematic agitation on the part of the Soviet and the revolutionary parties.[9]

8. Bushnell, *Mutiny amid Repression*, pp. 82–85. Maevskii, "Obshchaia kartina," pp. 110–11. Zharnovetskii, "Kronshtadtskie vosstaniia v 1905–1906 gg.," p. 56. *1905: SRD*, pp. 27–30. Samples of the kinds of demands raised by the Kronstadt mutineers are available in Woytinsky, *Gody pobed*, pp. 229–30, and in Vvedenskii, "Noiabr'skaia zabastovka," p. 203.

9. *1905: SRD*, p. 30. *Izvestiia SRD*, no. 5 (Nov. 3), pp. 39–42.

THE NOVEMBER GENERAL STRIKE

The Soviet session of November 1 devoted its entire agenda to two items: the October 28 declaration of martial law in Poland, against which some of the factory meetings had also protested, and the Kronstadt events. After brief and modest speeches by two Polish delegates, a long description of the situation among the Kronstadt soldiers and sailors was given by an eyewitness. Then the 12 plants and one district where protest resolutions had been passed read their resolutions to the deputies. A roll call of 13 other factories, districts, and unions present showed that nine of them were ready to strike, including most of the railroaders, the printers, the office workers, the Foremen and Technicians' Union, and the Moscow, Petersburg, and Vyborg districts. The unions of retail clerks, pharmacists, and tailors reported they would not strike; the watchmakers, that they could not say until they had discussed the question. The entire Soviet then held "a long and detailed discussion," at the end of which the body adopted the following Executive Committee resolution:

> The Soviet of Workers' Deputies summons the revolutionary proletariat of Petersburg, by means of a general political strike, the formidable power [*groznaia sila*] of which has already been proven, and by means of general protest meetings, to demonstrate its fraternal solidarity with the revolutionary soldiers of Kronstadt and the revolutionary proletariat of Poland. Tomorrow, November 2, at 12:00 noon, the workers of Petersburg will stop work with the slogans:
> 1. Down with the field courts!
> 2. Down with the death penalty!
> 3. Down with martial law in Poland and in all Russia![10]

With the support of some of the more revolutionary metal plants, therefore, the Soviet leaders succeeded in calling the Petersburg workers out on a second general political strike only 11 days after the first one ended. This was possible at this time because of the militancy still felt by workers in a variety of industries and work situations and because of the highly malleable nature of that militancy, expressed in the eight-hour-day movement, sharpened by the black hundreds danger, and further manifested in the willingness to form alliances with the angriest and most recent victims of Tsarist oppression in the continuing struggle against autocracy and the factory order. The Soviet

10. *1905: SRD*, pp. 24–32.

had reached the peak of its authority and influence, and it probably acted none too soon from the point of view of mobilizing the greatest number of workers. Its aim, by striking in support of the Kronstadt mutineers, was to unite discontent in the armed forces with the workers' movement, thereby "disarming the autocracy and arming the revolution." A special summons to the "Soldiers of the Petersburg Garrison" was appended to the strike resolution, and it called for cooperation in saving "our brother sailors who are threatened by death." Soviet meetings during the strike also urged workers to leaflet and agitate among the soldiers.

The Polish issue was secondary in this concern, but it had the effect (1) of broadening the meaning of the strike beyond the purely local issue, and (2) of stressing the Soviet's efforts to reach out to other dissident groups for mutual support.[11]

The response to the strike call was overwhelming. On November 2, the police counted 112,493 workers from 112 factories on strike. The list included most of the giant and many of the large metal plants, some of the large textile factories, many printing shops, and a sprinkling of shoe, munitions, tobacco, and other factories. The Factory Inspectorate found 119,232 workers from 526 factories on strike on November 3, indicating that a large number of small factories and shops joined the strike as it progressed.[12] Although these two sets of figures are not necessarily comparable, it is true that many workshops and small factories did strike in November, some for the first time in the year.[13] In November, 773,034 man-days were lost to strikes in Petersburg, the second-highest total for any month in 1905 and 53 percent more than were lost in October.[14] Many of the striking factories in trades other than metal, as well as some smaller metal works, elected deputies to the Soviet for the first time, which accounts for the increase in the size of the body in November. Among these were the

---

11. *Ibid.*, p. 32. Nosar', "Istoriia Soveta," p. 196. Woytinsky, *Gody pobed*, pp. 232–33. The Executive Committee resisted an attempt by the Socialist Revolutionaries to make the strike a protest against the imposition of martial law in Saratov, Simbirsk, and Tambov provinces as well, and the addition of "and in all Russia" to the protest covering Poland was probably a concession to that interest. Woytinsky, *Gody pobed*, pp. 236–37.

12. *VPR*, pp. 360–61. Dorovatovskii and Zlotin, "Khronika," p. 232. Factory Inspectorate figures generally omitted workshops with 15 or fewer workers, but police estimates were even more slanted toward large enterprises.

13. Vvedenskii, "Noiabr'skaia zabastovka," p. 209.

14. *VPR*, p. 514, or see above, Chapter 6, Tables 18 and 19.

15. Nosar', "Istoriia Soveta," pp. 112–13. *Spisok 1903*.

Schaff (*Shaf*) machine factory (26 workers), the Meier carpentry shop (23 workers), and the Olof underwear factory (55 workers).[15]

How can this gigantic turnout be explained? Contemporary historians and memoirists have left the impression that the whole of the Petersburg proletariat moved with the thinking of its leading elements and struck essentially for the reasons given in the Soviet's strike resolution.[16] But this does not consider the broad range of political experience and sophistication among workers, and it does not explain how the vast bulk of them, not versed in revolutionary politics, came to join a political strike.

By the fall of the year revolutionary workers at most of the larger metal plants had benefited markedly from widespread disillusionment with the government and had apparently won broader recognition, and possibly even the respect accorded any group whose vision, rejected earlier, is later confirmed by events. Whatever the cause, the firm and practically unchallenged leadership of revolutionary workers, usually Social Democrats, seems to have been established in many of the larger metal plants by the beginning of the November strike. This applied not only to the metal plants of two districts in particular, Schlüsselburg (Nevsky, Obukhov, and Aleksandrovsk) and Vyborg (St. Petersburg Metal, Lessner, Phoenix, and others), but also to the Baltic Shipyard, the Franco-Russian Plant, and a number of smaller and lesser known metal works such as the Geisler Electrical Machine Plant in the Petersburg district and the Possel' Horseshoe Factory on Vasilevsky Island.[17] The deputies from metal plants like these made up the Soviet's most enthusiastic, constant, and articulate supporters, and the body was in many ways the general expression of the revolutionary *praxis* of the large metal plants. In mid-November deputies from metal plants, large and small, accounted for 62 percent of the Soviet's deputies (as shown in the accompanying tabulation), and in early November they probably formed an even larger proportion.[18]

The political process at factories in other industries, and even at some metal plants, had taken different forms. The tendency among them to follow the example and lead to the most active and militant workers in a district, observable earlier in the year, was still seen in the

16. For instance, Trotsky, *1905*, pp. 166–68; Nosar', "Istoriia Soveta," pp. 106–10; and Vvedenskii, "Noiabr'skaia zabastovka," pp. 204–7; Woytinsky, *Gody pobed*, pp. 231–33.

17. See, e.g., the memoirs of former Soviet deputies in *Vospominaniia Soveta*, pp. 58–88 *passim*.

18. Nosar', "Istoriia Soveta," p. 147.

Industry/occupation	No.	Pct.	Industry/occupation	No.	Pct.
Metalworking	351	62%	Chemicals	9	2
Textiles	47	10	Lighting	7	<1
Printing and Paper	32	6	Glass	3	0.5
Woodworking	23	4	Clothing	2	<0.4
Tobacco and Candy	20	4	Watches and Jewelry	2	<0.4
Rubber, Shoes, Leather	15	3	Commercial Employees	12	<2
Explosives	11	2	Office Workers and		
Communications (railroad, horse tram, ferry, postal and telegraph workers)	11	2	Pharmacists	7	<1
			Total	562	100%

fall. Only now, much of the authority of the most militant and effective worker leaders had become embodied in the Soviet, and all the deputies returned to the factory districts invested with the aura of that authority. The network of deputies gave the Soviet a familiar face in factory neighborhoods and made it the fulfillment of what Petersburg's new mass labor movement had been seeking since the demise of the Assembly. In addition, the availability of meeting places and especially the gigantic factory meetings during the Days of Freedom enabled militants in all types of factories to broaden and deepen their influence among workers and for the factory population to develop a better-informed understanding of their political participation.

The greater number and variety of November strikers would not have been possible, however, had the workers in the less politicized factories and workshops not viewed the strike as more or less relevant to their immediate working situations. As was noted, the number of "economic" strikes was increasing during the two weeks preceding the November strike, and the Soviet's strike call coincided with this rising tide and enlarged it by providing the kind of disruptive ambience that transformed passive resentment into active protest.

An occurrence at the Putilov Works on October 31 offers an example of the continuing power of immediate, in-plant concerns to ignite workers where more remote and political issues might fail. The Putilov case would seem to be an exception since it was a large metal plant with a great deal of political experience, but it was the exception that proved the rule. Speakers were explaining to a large meeting of workers the Soviet's decree on the self-initiated eight-hour day in an effort to overcome the opposition that the deputies had warned of. Before a decision was reached, someone raised the question of the pending dismissal of 800 *putilovtsy* for the forceful "sacking" of two hated plant foremen on October 18. The workers became very agitated by this issue and decided to strike unless the 800 dismissals were canceled. Two days later, they made good on the threat.[19] Thus, though their deputies claimed that the Putilov workers were too exhausted to show enthusiasm for an eight-hour-day campaign, they proved ready to strike to save the jobs of fellow workers. Their behavior is suggestive of preferences and priorities applied by other workers in other instances in 1905 and, for that reason, bears closer examination.

Somehow, the reality and immediacy of the threat to fellow workers provoked greater militancy and self-sacrifice than the prospect of another political fight of uncertain outcome. This choice suggests not only a willingness to respond to the emergency of an immediate threat to 800 real people, but also possibly a certain realism about the attainability of the eight-hour day by factory action alone. The proposed campaign may have been seen as a kind of "demonstration," i.e., important, but not as urgent as the defense of those threatened with dismissal. Yet both issues affected on-the-job, factory concerns, and both also involved a struggle for control of the workplace in which workers were taking the situation into their own hands and asserting their rights. Hence, both issues were intensely "political," and the Putilov workers' decision was perhaps less a comment on the ultimate worth of the eight-hour day than on its attainability at this particular time. Their responsiveness to the need of those threatened with dismissal held an urgency of its own that had nothing to do with the worthiness of the other issue.

It therefore seems that, however much Petersburg workers sympathized with the Kronstadt mutineers, they also had issues in mind closer to their work lives. Such was likely the case at most of the factories whose workers had not yet elected deputies to the Soviet—the bulk of the November strikers—and even at some factories with deputies, as the Putilov case shows. Unmet demands from past strikes, standing grievances as well as grievances newly arisen—all found an outlet in the cause of the Kronstadt mutineers and the Polish workers. The sparseness of information makes it impossible to illustrate this in detail, but one example will help to reconstruct the general situation. K. I. Monker, assistant manager of the Nevsky Thread Factory (1,700 workers) in the Rozhdestvensk district, left a brief account of the November strike at the factory in his diary:[20]

> November 2: . . . Our workers held a meeting in the cafeteria at 8:00 P.M. at which they passed a resolution to strike tomorrow at 9:00 in the

19. *VPR*, pp. 358, 360, 856, n. 89.
20. "Dnevnik . . . Monkera," pp. 218–19.

morning in support of the general political strike. However, this resolution was subsequently changed. Delegates were elected. . . .

November 3: The factory began to operate at full capacity. At 10:00 in the morning nine delegates elected at the meeting the previous day arrived to present themselves to Mister Riddell [the manager]. Returning to the shops, the delegates began to persuade the workers to strike out of sympathy with the general strike taking place in the city, which is aimed at forcing the government to do away with the death sentences passed on the insurrectionary Kronstadt sailors. After lunch no one returned to the factory. For a while the workers gathered in the court and interfered with the boilermakers raising steam. . . .

November 4: The factory stood idle the whole day. General strike of all factories and plants of the city. Everything peaceful. No disorders. A meeting of our workers at 12:00 in the cafeteria. Order of the day: an eight-hour workday. Pregnant women want to receive wages for two months before birth and four months after [apparently while on leave].

The cotton spinners struck until the afternoon of November 7, and Monker mentioned no further demands or grievances. But on November 8:

The bleachers, through their delegate, an office worker in the bleaching department, handed Stuart [the foreman] the following demands:

1. Install a ventilator on the second floor, in the bleaching shop.
2. Supply the linkers with overalls.
3. A supplement of 10 kopecks per day for all workers of the bleaching department.

Monker's dry and laconic account fails to convey the excitement that must have accompanied the strike; it was the first time since February that the whole factory had struck. The bleachers' petition was more typical of the kind of struggle that had been waged in the meantime: one shop or department at a time; small demands normally applying only to that shop; and, usually, no strike. Two weeks before the bleachers, it was the polishers; before them, the dyers. This pattern of striking illustrates the more pronounced separation of tasks and functions in the large textile mills as compared to the metal plants, where the functional and administrative divisions were looser and permitted greater communication among workers of the separate shops. Every part of Monker's factory must have had unmet demands and outstanding grievances, but none of them seemed able to unite the whole factory at once. This compartmentalization of group experience and therefore of protest did not make the textile workers impervious to political strikes; on the contrary, a political strike may have been the one kind capable of drawing them all together at once. Monker's account leaves little doubt that the thread workers did strike for the sake of the Kronstadt sailors. Yet it seems perfectly understandable that these servants of an industry that worked the longest hours for the lowest pay should have discussed at their strike meeting not the army and the insurrection, but a shorter workday and better treatment for the working mothers. Their participation in the general strike does seem to have galvanized protest at the factory. For the rest of November, complaints were raised by a greater number of departments, and the polishers struck in support of a list of demands somewhat broader than usual. In December, the whole factory once more joined a political strike.[21]

For the first two days of the general strike, November 2 and 3, spirits were high, and the Soviet on those days busied itself with the work of broadening and strengthening the strike. The deputies proposed mass meetings of strikers, which would visit non-striking factories and attempt to close them, threatening destruction of machinery if necessary. Two groups received special attention, postal workers and coachmen. Since the post office was heavily guarded by troops, the Soviet decided to try to bring the employees out by approaching the union-organizing group among the postal workers. Coachmen had ceased to operate in working-class neighborhoods for fear of violence, but they were still at work in the center of the city. A suggestion that threats and violence be used against the coachmen was rejected in favor of agitation and persuasion only; the black hundreds were apparently strong among them, and the application of force might drive the whole group to oppose the strike.

A discussion of the position of army troops produced a resolution not only to increase efforts to reach them with written leaflets, "but also to develop the broadest possible oral agitation; let every worker with a relative, godparent, or others in the barracks go and talk to them; wherever possible, send deputies there, invite [the soldiers] to meetings, and so forth." Reports were given of meetings among soldiers of three separate units, one in direct defiance of an officer's orders. Trotsky, who had spoken at a private meeting where some 40 liberal army officers had been present, told the deputies that the officers had felt bound to permit agitation among the troops and not to shoot at the people and that one speaker had defined their duty as the defense of "the order created by the Manifesto of October 17 against

21. *Ibid.*, pp. 219–22, and n. 33.

a possible revolution from above." When the Soviet leader had sec-
onded these sentiments to the officers and added that it was also the
officers' duty "to help the proletariat arm itself to defend its rights,"
they had applauded him. "This shows," Trotsky concluded cautiously
to the deputies, "that even among the guards officers things are not
going so well for Tsarist absolutism."[22]

Actually, the rebellion in military ranks, though extensive and serious, came late to Russia in 1905, was mixed in complex ways with
continuing loyalty to the autocracy, and remained surprisingly little
affected by the revolution among civilians, even though the October
Manifesto was its principal catalyst.[23] Military troops in Petersburg
were certainly no exception to this rule; if anything, their constant de-
ployment against revolutionary disorders in and around the capital
since January contributed to a pro-government posture. By one calculation, the entire St. Petersburg Military District witnessed 18 mutinies between October 18 and the end of 1905, about 8.5 percent of
the total for the period throughout European Russia and Siberia, a
seemingly low incidence, given the heightened political activism of
the St. Petersburg area among the urban population. As elsewhere
in Russia, most of these mutinies (11) came in November, and this
was certainly promoted by the existence of the Soviet, which stressed
the importance of links with the lower ranks of the military more
than any other political organization in the capital. Yet, on balance,
this stress and the defense of the Kronstadt mutineers accomplished
little toward converting the Petersburg military garrison to revolution.
Troops from St. Petersburg proved to be some of the most accomplished and reliable in putting down the disorders of December 1905,
including the Moscow Uprising and punitive expeditions in the Baltic
region.[24]

On November 4 the Soviet's Executive Committee recommended
to the deputies that the strike be terminated on Monday, November 7.

22. *1905: SRD*, pp. 32–39.
23. Bushnell, *Mutiny amid Repression*, esp. pp. 86–105.
24. *Ibid.*, pp. 91, 92, 116, 141. Akhun and Petrov, *Bol'sheviki i armiia v 1905–1917
gg. Voennaia organizatsiia pri Peterburgskom komitete RSDRP (b.) i revoliutsionnoe dvizhenie v
voiskakh Peterburga*, pp. 17–23, 31–32. The three revolutionary parties, though their
members served in the ranks, and though committed in program to organizing military
personnel, did not actually form organizations to accomplish this until late 1905 and
1906, i.e., after the great wave of mutinies in November and December. Akhun and
Petrov, pp. 10, 14, 29, 33. Bushnell, *Mutiny amid Repression*, pp. 58–60, 154–56. For a
lengthier discussion of this topic, see chapter 4 of Bushnell, "Mutineers and Revolutionaries: Military Revolution in Russia, 1905–1907."

The Committee had divided nine to six on the measure, and the representatives of the revolutionary parties (who lacked voting rights)
had all opposed it. In the long debate that ensued in the full Soviet,
proponents of the measure argued that the strike mood at a number
of factories was declining, and that only a firm assurance that the
strike was not open-ended would make it possible for their workers to
continue another few days and for the Soviet to preserve its authority
among them. Their opponents argued with greater plausibility that
the Soviet would lose even more authority if it ended the strike before the government had given any sign of meeting its demands, and
that the Soviet had a greater duty to the stronger elements of the
strike, those that favored sacrifice for the sake of winning concessions
on the questions of the threatened death sentences and the Polish
situation. Moreover, there were signs that the strike might spread beyond the capital: a telegram from the Moscow railroaders had expressed their willingness to follow the lead of the Petersburg Soviet,
and the Soviet had initiated efforts to broadcast its strike call to other
cities. There was thus reason to believe, on November 4, that the
strike was still expanding. The opponents of termination won the day,
and the body voted not to set a date for the end of the strike.[25]

But by the next day, the balance of forces within and without the
Soviet had shifted. Despite some signs that the strike might yet spread
beyond Petersburg, such as a telegram announcing a strike in solidarity with the Soviet's demands among railroad workers in Rybinsk
and the appearance in the Soviet of a peasant delegate with similar
expressions of solidarity from his militant constituents, the Executive
Committee and the majority of speakers now voted to terminate the
strike at noon on November 7. News that the Petersburg railroad
workers would return at that time helped to sway opinion, and the
government had announced its intention not to try the Kronstadt mutineers in field courts martial, thus removing the threat of death sentences and providing the strikers with a partial victory.[26] Nevertheless,
a canvass of factory-level opinion among the deputies showed that
workers at 92 out of 147 factories polled (63 percent) were ready to
continue striking for an indefinite period; that those at 25 others were
preparing to return to work on November 7; and that workers at only
three factories had returned voluntarily. A gap had opened up be-

25. Bushnell, *Mutiny amid Repression*, pp. 36, 41–2. Nosar' "Istoriia Soveta,"
pp. 119–21.
26. *1905: SRD*, pp. 43–45. Trotsky, *1905*, p. 170.

tween the course of action produced at the factory level by the very momentum of the strike and that which Soviet leaders felt wisdom dictated.

Before a vote was taken, Trotsky rose to speak for the Executive Committee. His speech so succinctly summed up the juncture of tactic and strategy at this crucial moment, and this moment was so representative of the Soviet's overall dilemma, that it is worth summarizing at some length. Referring to the government's abandonment of field courts martial, he pointed out that even had that not been conceded the Soviet would have had to call on workers to end the strike. The strike had achieved its aim by showing support to the growing unrest among soldiers and by demonstrating the discipline of the Petersburg workers; what more should the deputies expect of it?

> Certain comrades are demanding that the strike should continue until the Kronstadt sailors have been placed under trial by jury and martial law in Poland has been lifted. In other words, until the fall of the present government, for Tsarism will move all its forces against our strike, comrades, we have got to face that fact. If we consider that the purpose of our action is the overthrow of the autocracy, then—I agree with the comrades—we would have to fight to the finish. But our tactics are not at all based on that model. Our actions are a series of consecutive battles [*riad postupatel'nykh bitv*]. Their purpose is to disorganize the government and to win new friends, including the army. In discussing whether or not we should continue the strike, we are in substance discussing whether to retain the demonstrative nature of the strike or to turn it into a decisive struggle, that is, to continue it to the point of total victory or defeat. Taking this latter point of view, we would have to regard a premature termination of the strike as a sign of our indecisiveness. But that is not at all the case. We are not afraid of battles or defeats. Our defeats are but steps to our victory. But for each battle we seek the most favorable conditions. I ask you: to whose advantage is it to put off the decisive clash, ours or the government's? Ours, comrades! For tomorrow we shall be stronger than we are today.[27]

The speaker then reminded his audience that the conditions favoring the spread of the revolutionary word through meetings and a free

27. Nosar', "Istoriia Soveta," p. 121. Trotsky's speech appeared in at least three published versions, each containing the same essential content. The briefest is in the Soviet's minutes for November 5 (*1905: SRD*, pp. 45–47, or *Izvestiia SRD*, no. 7 [Nov. 7], pp. 63–64); a somewhat fuller variant was given by Nosar' in "Istoriia Soveta," pp. 122–24; the fullest version appears in Trotsky, *1905*, pp. 171–74. The passages quoted here have been taken from the last-named source, but where conflicts with the other texts have occurred, that of Nosar' has been preferred.

press were created only a short time before and that the fullest use of these conditions for agitation and organization among the proletariat had yet to be made. How long would this take? "We must extend the period of preparation of the masses for decisive action, perhaps by a month or two, in order then to act as an army which is as united and organized as absolutely possible." Yet Trotsky was actually uncertain when the "decisive struggle" would come. A few lines later he reminded his listeners of the electoral campaign set for spring 1906, which "must bring the entire revolutionary proletariat to its feet." The campaign, he speculated, "will, in all probability, end with the proletariat blowing up the whole government."

Yet, militant posturing aside, the speech offered a realistic assessment of the Soviet's position and an insight into the strategic thinking of its leadership from that point on. The revolutionary politics of the Soviet was on new and uncharted terrain with but one certainty to guide itself: the government was determined to end the Soviet's existence as soon as the political situation permitted. The task adopted by the Soviet's leadership was therefore to heighten the insurrectionary mood and organize a revolutionary army as expeditiously as it could without provoking the government to move against it before it was prepared to defend itself.

The notion of "consecutive battles" was simultaneously a confession of the Soviet's present weakness and an appeal to overcome that weakness. It was a restatement of previous Soviet assertions that *it* would choose the time of the "decisive struggle," and not allow either the government or its own impatient supporters to move it to precipitate action. It also contained lessons drawn from the November strike itself, which, despite the cautious and limited wording of the strike resolution and the appeal to the soldiers, was certainly intended to elicit as great a response as possible from both the Petersburg Garrison and workers elsewhere in Russia.

The November strike's failure to provoke either another nationwide strike or a strategic breakthrough in "disarming the autocracy" dictated a tactical retreat to cut losses and remain in readiness for the next opportunity to lead or swell a mass rising. There was, of course, no direct evidence in Trotsky's speech of disappointment in the achievements of the November strike. Yet the sense he conveyed of being ready for sharp and precipitate turns in the revolutionary struggle and his repeated stress on the imminence and certainty of a "decisive struggle" could be read as expressing anxiety over the outcome of the entire endeavor.

On November 5, with 63 percent of the factories polled willing to continue the strike, the Soviet leadership decided that the workers had achieved as much as they could for the present in the struggle with the autocracy and that the continuing militancy in the factories was a good hedge against either a general retreat by the workers or too early an attack on the Soviet by the government. But the militancy of the factories was not so easily deactivated to be stored up for future use or turned to politically more expedient activities. Although the deputies were persuaded to end the strike on November 7, many of their constituents felt deprived of a victory, not in the struggle with the autocracy, but in the struggle with their employers.

THE EIGHT-HOUR-DAY CAMPAIGN

The great majority of strikers returned to work at noon on November 7, in compliance with the Soviet's resolution. But the insurgency that had been gathering throughout the previous month and especially during the past week now rushed to fill the only vessel provided for it by the Soviet: the eight-hour-day campaign begun on October 29 and interrupted by the political strike on November 2. The linkage of the eight-hour issue with back-to-work sentiments was as irresistible as ever. Workers at the factories that had already begun to work eight hours a day on their own simply picked up where they had left off, and they were now joined by many others whose militancy had been brought to a head by the November strike. Together, they made up the most loyal and militant supporters of the Soviet: all the large and many small and medium metal plants, most of the cotton textile factories, and some woodworking, tobacco, glass, and vodka enterprises.[28] These workers demonstrated their greater militancy by respecting the Soviet's decree on the end of the strike despite their willingness to strike longer; but by the same token, they became the most determined eight-hour campaigners.

The employers immediately responded to this continuing turmoil with mass dismissals and lockouts. Although this tactic had been applied earlier in 1905 at individual factories, it was now resorted to on a gigantic scale. As early as November 5, workers at three factories had already been completely dismissed, and those at ten others had been threatened with the same fate. Prior to that, employers had treated strikers with greater caution. During the October strike, many of

28. *VPR*, pp. 382–84.

them had given their workers half, and a few even full, pay for the days of strike. Even the management of the Nevsky Thread Factory had voluntarily closed for two days at half-pay during the height of the street demonstrations. This cautious accommodation continued during the first days of the eight-hour-day campaign, before November 2. Owners and managers had not on the whole sought sanctions against workers who departed after only eight hours, and some of them had stated their intentions to continue paying wages at prevailing piece rates, and for those employed at time rates according to the amount of time actually worked.[29]

But with the renewal of the eight-hour-day campaign on November 7, factory owners felt it was time to close ranks and take a firm line with their workers. On or about November 8, representatives of 72 metalworking plants in the Petersburg area met and issued a statement in which they threatened to close their plants unless the workers gave up the campaign. The statement advanced arguments encountered earlier in the year, such as that Russian workers actually worked fewer hours per year than West European workers owing to the greater number of holidays observed in Russia. A similar statement soon issued from a meeting of 19 textile manufacturers.[30] More important than the statements was the dispatch with which the industrialists put their threats into practice. By November 10, some 19,000 workers were idled, mostly from lockouts; on November 13, the Soviet claimed that some 100,000 had been thrown out of work.[31] The accuracy of this last figure cannot be precisely verified, but an estimate indicates that it was somewhat exaggerated. An analysis of the situations at 61 factories reported in the press for November 9–11 and representing about 80,000 workers shows that only 18 factories (30 percent) had experienced lockouts by November 11. If the Soviet's estimate were accurate, the number of locked-out workers would have had to increase over fourfold during the two days before its estimate was made. That would seem improbable, especially since only one of the two days was a workday.[32]

29. Nosar', "Istoriia Soveta," pp. 121, 127–28. "Dnevnik . . . Monkera," p. 217.

30. Petrov-Radin, "Bor'ba za vos'michasovoi rabochii den'," pp. 252–53. Woytinsky claimed that glass manufacturers took a similar stand. *Gody pobed*, p. 262.

31. Dorovatovskii and Zlotin, "Khronika," p. 234. *1905: SRD*, pp. 62, 67. Petrov-Radin, "Bor'ba," p. 254.

32. The estimate assumes an equal number of workers in the locked-out factories as in the others. The analysis of the 61 factories was made by the author from rather uneven and inconsistent reports in *Novaia zhizn'* and *Syn otechestva*, reprinted in *VPR*, pp. 380–86 and 388–89.

Nevertheless, the number of idled workers was large and unprecedented, and the Soviet's exaggeration is understandable in light of its alarm at the political implications of the lockouts and the counterrevolutionary offensive that accompanied them. During the week following the return to work, police and troops moved back into factory neighborhoods and began to intervene more actively. At least one bloody clash occurred with armed workers, and in a separate incident workers had their weapons taken from them. The large factory meetings, which were central to the workers' political life and to the communications networks of both the Soviet and the revolutionary parties, became more difficult to hold. Earlier, managers had willingly provided meeting space on the factory premises; now many of them refused, and there were troops on hand to enforce their wishes. Delegations of workers and Soviet deputies, seeking to mediate disputes at state enterprises, were turned away by government ministers or received only as private individuals. The Soviet itself was prevented by the police from meeting on November 10, and although this was due to a technical irregularity in connection with government regulations governing meetings, it provoked gloomy forebodings.[33]

In the face of this mounting attack, the most revolutionary workers fought on with courage and determination. Of the 61 factories surveyed, workers at 24 had returned to work on terms set by their employers, but in at least six of these cases they worked under protest and looked forward to renewed struggle at an early date. Workers at the Baranovskii Machine Plant resolved on November 7 that "In view of the exhaustion of our strength by the political strike, we have decided to work 10 hours temporarily, but with the intention of preparing for the forthcoming struggle with the autocratic regime for the political rights of laborers and for the eight-hour workday. We are not folding our arms, but have unanimously decided, at the first summons of the Soviet of Workers' Deputies, to join battle again and deliver the final blow to the hated police regime. . . ."

At least four of the 61 factories remained on strike, and five others were conducting eight-hour-day campaigns with some success. A few managers agreed to an eight-hour regime on the condition that it eventually be adopted in other factories. A larger number of others had compromised with their workers by granting some reduction of the workday short of the eight-hour demand. Most printers, for in-

33. Nosar', "Istoriia Soveta," pp. 129, 132–33. *1905: SRD*, pp. 49, 59, 65. Paialin, *Zavod imeni Lenina*, pp. 174–77.

stance, accepted a nine-hour day when this was offered by the owners. But some workers stood on principle: When workers at the Geisler Electrical Machine Plant were offered a nine-hour day, only 19 out of a reported 500 workers voted for it in preference to eight hours. "The rest agreed to [accept] dismissal in case the demand was not satisfied. The director promised to think it over." Workers at the Bekmen Distillery and the Kirchner Bindery took a similar position. Weavers at the Cheshire Factory on Rezvyi Island also refused an offer of a nine-hour day and continued their strike because the manager denied their demands.[34]

Despite this continuing militancy by some of the Soviet's most ardent supporters—and perhaps partly because of it—surprise, confusion, and near-paralysis overtook the deputies during the week of November 7. Expecting that workers would move from the partial victory of the November strike to preparation for the next in a series of battles that would encroach on the power of the autocracy, the Soviet found instead that its own power was being encroached upon and that it was powerless to turn the tide. The eight-hour-day campaign was a losing cause from the viewpoint of preserving unity of action and directing energies toward the struggle with the political regime. It was atomizing the factory movement led by the Soviet into a series of separate struggles with individual employers in which the collective strength of the Soviet could not be brought directly to bear. In directing attention toward the factory regime rather than the political regime, the eight-hour-day campaign tilted worker militancy toward "economic" issues since it posed immediately the question of wage and production levels. Yet, as we have seen, it also had a powerful political resonance, organically bound up with the domination of workers by capitalists; as a result, no one in the Soviet, least of all the Social Democrats, seemed to think of the campaign as anything but a continuation of the political struggle—until it was too late. The most loyal, energetic, and militant deputies were also the inspirers and leaders of the eight-hour-day campaign, and there was no base of support within the body from which to oppose that dominant bloc.

Aside from the "lone voices" of opposition, the Soviet's leaders perceived some of these problems even before the November strike had ended. At the session of November 6, the Executive Committee recommended to the body that "in light of the present economic crisis,

34. *VPR*, pp. 380–84. There were actually about 350, not 500, workers at the Geisler Plant.

the introduction of the eight-hour day presents certain difficulties, [so that the Executive Committee] does not think it possible to raise the demand for its immediate realization." It went on to recommend the formation of trade unions as better suited to oversee the introduction of the eight-hour workday. A long and heated debate then followed in which the proponents of a direct and immediate campaign were still very numerous. A compromise resolution was finally passed, which avoided insistence on universal introduction of the eight-hour day in favor of a recommendation that workers "apply every effort to the most rapid creation of unions and an all-Russian congress of trade organizations" and that they "immediately and simultaneously achieve [any] shortening of working time possible, aiming at the conquest in the near future (*stremias' k skoreishemu zavoevaniiu*) of the eight-hour workday by the organized proletariat."[35] Yet the compromise was only apparent, since the real choice to be made was between postponing any campaign for shorter hours or not; reservations about trade unions and the difference between "immediate" and "in the near future" would be lost in practice. In effect, therefore, the proponents of the eight-hour-day campaign were given the go-ahead.

The main problem, however, was not that the Executive Committee lost control of the resolution but that few if any of the Soviet leaders viewed the eight-hour day "by revolutionary means" as at all divergent from the central political thrust of the working class. Both Social Democratic factions fully cooperated in the campaign, even leading the way in the factory districts. The Bolshevik *Novaia zhizn'* had written of the campaign soon after it was resolved upon in the Soviet on October 29 that it was "a fact which should be noted in the annals of not only the Russian, but even the worldwide labor movement. Only a proletariat which is organized and conscious of its power is in a position to advance and carry out the demand for an eight-hour workday." Even after the lockouts had cut short the campaign, the Menshevik *Nachalo* insisted that the idea had not been abandoned nor the proletariat defeated, but that it would take up the struggle again at the first convenient moment.[36]

This faith in the limitless strength and potential of the proletariat, or at least the willingness to believe that militant support of an eight-hour day was tantamount to attaining it, was apparently just as strong

35. *1905: SRD*, pp. 52–54. Nosar', "Istoriia Soveta," pp. 129–31; Petrov-Radin, "Bor'ba," pp. 253–54.
36. Petrov-Radin, "Bor'ba," pp. 249–50, 258–64.

after the November strike as before. Had not the workers just terminated the largest and best-organized political strike of the year from a position of strength? A resumption of the eight-hour-day campaign seemed an appropriate sequel to this triumph. Few doubted that the proletariat would win the demand, and only the form of the victory was in question. Unfortunately, this self-confidence was accompanied by an underestimation of the government's own continuing strength. When a printers' union representative suggested that organization and detailed study of conditions in different branches of production should precede a call for introduction of the eight-hour day, a member of the Executive Committee replied that workers were ready to take on the capitalists because "the autocracy has already died off, and all that's needed is to drive the last nail into its coffin. . . ."[37]

The Soviet's leaders were thus ill-prepared to react swiftly to the new challenges that arose during the week of November 7. The Executive Committee met three times, but it seemed unable to take hold of a situation that was rapidly turning into a rout. Finally, on November 11, convinced that the lockouts were overtaking the invincible determination of the eight-hour campaigners, the committee called a temporary halt to "agitation for the immediate introduction of the eight-hour workday by revolutionary means."[38]

The Soviet did not meet again in full session until November 12. The unity of purpose apparent six days earlier now gave way to open dissension, confusion, and indecision. Most of the session was devoted to the problem of lockouts, and it was filled with a sense of impending defeat. Speakers from most factories felt the challenges from employers and the government should be met with renewed militancy and determination to continue to fight for eight hours of work. A few called for a reevaluation of the measure's feasibility. "The most numerous group of speakers found that the Soviet had made a mistake in rousing the masses to a struggle which requires not only enthusiasm, but the solidarity and organization of the whole proletariat in even greater measure." The stress of the moment even sharpened disagreements over the level of commitment among different factories and deputies. The Bolshevik woman deputy from the Maxwell textile factory, A. G. Egorova-Boldyreva, addressed herself to the Putilov workers: "You accustom your wives to eat and sleep well (*sladko est' i miagko spat'*) and it's therefore frightening for you to be without wages,

37. *1905: SRD*, pp. 52–53.
38. *Ibid.*, p. 56.

but we are not afraid of that, we are ready to die to win eight hours of work, we will fight to the finish! Victory or death! Long live the eight-hour workday!"[39] Again and again, the speakers raised the question of what action to take. The deputies from the Nevsky Ship and Machine Works proposed a two- or three-day general strike to force the re-opening of the locked-out factories. No action was taken, however, and the session served mainly to make the deputies aware of the desperateness of the situation they were facing. The most that can be said of the Nevsky deputies' suggestion is that it helped to define the problem as one of how to defend against lockouts rather than how to continue the eight-hour-day campaign.[40]

The session of November 13 was freer of histrionics and recriminations. An Executive Committee resolution calling for an end to the eight-hour-day campaign and for agitation and organization on an all-Russian basis was finally passed with only six dissenting votes. Because struggles were still in progress in some factories, provisions were made for them to continue and for their workers to be aided by those of other factories; the universal eight-hour day was to "remain a task of our struggle" in the future. The proposal of a new general strike to fight lockouts was taken up again. A poll of district representatives found nearly all of them in favor of the measure; the printers' union, the railroaders, and some of the other unions were also ready to strike. Sobriety prevailed, however, and some of the deputies went on to express the need for a rest from more strikes, while others felt the authority of the Soviet would suffer should this strike not achieve its intended aim. The continuing dedication to struggle, as well as the desperation of many workers were well conveyed by the deputy from Narva district: "We all await the instructions of the Soviet; if a strike is resolved, the men of Narva will take part. We have 30,000 workers. In order to weaken the government we have decided to abstain from vodka for three months. Anyone caught drunk will be fined 3 rubles. . . . Join us, comrades." In the next two weeks at least ten factories took similar measures.[41] The deputies were asked to arrange wage deductions at their factories for unemployment relief to locked-out workers. At the end of the session, an Executive Committee resolution incorporating the strike demand was passed unani-

39. Nosar', "Istoriia Soveta," p. 134. *1905: SRD*, p. 59.

40. *1905: SRD*, pp. 58–61.

41. *Ibid.*, pp. 65–66. VPR, pp. 399–400, 418, 422. Shuster, *Peterburgskie rabochie*, pp. 191–92.

mously; but the strike call was made to the whole Russian proletariat and postponed to the indefinite future, pending the coordination of action with other cities and groups. Fuming against the joint provocation of the government and the "reactionary bourgeoisie," and demanding the reopening of the factories, the resolution was above all a cry for help from a body that now understood the limits of its power and felt its enemies drawing near:[42]

> Citizens! More than 100,000 workers have been thrown onto the pavement in Petersburg and other cities.
>
> The S.W.D. declares that the cause of freedom is in danger. . . . The workers must exert and are exerting every effort to unite the whole struggle—the all-Russian proletariat, the revolutionary peasantry, the army, and the fleet, which have already risen up heroically for freedom.
>
> The Petersburg proletariat proposes to all workers and all strata of the people and society to support the dismissed workers by every means, material, moral, and political.

LIBERAL SUPPORT AND DISSENT

Among the liberals, the fall events, far from bringing a noticeably greater measure of unity, had etched more deeply the divisions already apparent at the end of the summer, and this in turn affected the political prospects of labor and the rest of the opposition.[43] The founding congress of the Constitutional Democratic Party (October 12–18) coincided with the publication of the October Manifesto. The announcement of a new and more generous electoral law and Duma—even though suspiciously vague and imprecise—confirmed the commitment of the Kadets to electoral politics, especially given their earlier resolution to participate in the more weakly empowered Bulygin Duma. The Manifesto had increased the powers of the projected legislative body and expanded the electorate, and it promised to institutionalize these rights and the rules governing the legislature in law, i.e., to grant something resembling a constitution. Hence the Manifesto vindicated the Kadets' militancy to the Right and set definite limits to the Left's hopes for political reform, and it should have aided the Kadets in drawing less well-organized groups and individuals to their party, especially during the tense and uncertain "Days of Liberty" that followed the announcement of the Manifesto. Yet as during the late

42. *1905: SRD*, pp. 62–68.
43. See above, pp. 304–10.

summer, the divisions within the liberal movement became increasingly more pronounced and the separate camps better organized. Although many did move toward the Kadets, a new constitutionalist party formed to their right, and attitudes toward the mass movement continued to divide those to the left. The events of the fall rearranged the conditions of disunity, but they did not improve them, and they certainly did not increase the possibility of realizing the Kadets' ambition of reunifying the entire antigovernment opposition under its leadership—at least not in the short run.[44]

The one faction of the liberals that never sought to exercise such leadership moved decisively out of the revolutionary opposition altogether in the fall. The ranks of the moderate *zemtsy* who had begun to separate themselves from Miliukov and the Zemstvo Constitutionalists by supporting Shipov and Guchkov at the September Zemstvo Congress had in the meantime grown, and they responded to October 17 and the rise in popular violence that followed, including a sharp increase of peasant land seizures, by inclining even more openly and enthusiastically toward compromise with the monarchy and toward moderating the positions taken by the congress. They concluded that the revolutionary stance of the *zemtsy* should stop, that October 17 had brought the process of reform far enough, and that the effort of the government to restore order in the country must now be supported. This powerful revival of moderate liberal opinion found expression in the Union of October 17, or "Octobrists," a new party begun by Guchkov and Shipov in late October and early November, as a moderate constitutionalist alternative to the Kadets.[45]

At the Sixth Zemstvo Congress, held in Moscow on November 6–13, the Octobrists pressed a more aggressive campaign to oppose or modify the stance of the Kadet-led majority on a number of questions, including its demands for constituent functions in the new Duma, for abolition of the death penalty, and for autonomy for Poland. An Octobrist "Appeal," issued during the Congress, made the October Manifesto the basis of a new political order in which "the Russian people had become politically free, the state had become a state ruled by law, and the regime had become a constitutional mon-

44. Galai, *The Liberation Movement in Russia*, chs. 11, 12. Donald Treadgold, *Lenin and His Rivals* (New York, 1955), chs. 6, 10. Martynov, "Istoriia K.D. Partii," pp. 11–15. William G. Rosenberg, "Kadets and the Politics of Ambivalence, 1905–1917," *Essays on Russian Liberalism*, ed. Charles Timberlake (Columbia, Mo., 1972), pp. 139–41.

45. Emmons, *The Formation of Political Parties*, pp. 107–9.

archy."[46] Even the Kadets, apparently responding to the new post-October mood, moderated their demands at this congress by withholding the introduction of their now fully drafted agrarian and labor programs and by stressing the positive possible outcome of the October Manifesto.

Although the Octobrists' position received less than 15 percent of the Congress's support, the tide had begun to turn against the Kadets in zemstvo circles. The gap between the Kadet-dominated zemstvo congresses and provincial gentry opinion began to widen after October 17. Over the winter of 1905–6, Kadet policies and sympathizers came under attack by the provincial gentry, now aroused against the revolution and its spokesmen in their own midst by the peasant riots and seizures, which had reached alarming proportions in the fall.[47] The great majority of zemstvo assemblies throughout the country repudiated the positions taken by the November Zemstvo Congress, and began moving rapidly to the right, even beyond the Octobrists.[48]

The Kadet attempt to knit together zemstvo constitutionalism with intelligentsia and popular revolution on the basis of a commitment to radical parliamentary reform naturally suffered a severe blow from these developments. Kadet prospects on the Left were no more sanguine. The rejection of the October Manifesto by the labor movement nationwide and the consolidation of the Petersburg Left in and around the Soviet made the prospect of liberal-socialist collaboration even more distant.

But the Kadets had their own reasons for finding unity with the Left more remote in the fall. While the bulk of the Kadets welcomed the October General Strike as a true expression of national unity and a justifiable display of nonviolent force against a recalcitrant government, their reaction to the November strike was quite negative. An unsigned editorial in the unofficial Kadet journal *Pravo* condemned the second strike as unwarranted and compared it unfavorably with the October strike, which it deemed "victorious" because of its unanimity and success and despite the pogroms and bloodshed that followed. The lack of such broad support in the November strike, however, meant that it not only made no gain for the revolution but risked provoking the government and the Right and interfering with

46. *Ibid.*, pp. 109 and 110–12, where the Octobrists' political program is described. The full program may be found in *Sputnik izbiratelia*, pp. 175–81.

47. Teodor Shanin, *Russia, 1905–7. Revolution as a Moment of Truth* (New Haven, Conn., 1986), pp. 93–95. Harcave, *First Blood*, pp. 216–17.

48. Manning, *The Crisis of the Old Order*, pp. 184, 187–202 *passim*.

the upcoming Duma elections and with the growth of democracy generally.[49] Such criticism of the Soviet and the socialists was expanded upon in another unsigned editorial disapproving of the eight-hour-day campaign and the attempt to bring land seized by peasants under the authority of the Peasants' Union, policies that were attributed to SD and SR leadership, respectively. These policies, in the author's opinion, were only adding to the disunity and disagreement among the forces of the opposition, weakening it at a moment when "the decisive hour is drawing near."[50] The author of both these articles was very likely the right Kadet Vladimir Hessen (Gessen), editor of *Pravo*, or one of his like-minded colleagues. These statements, although possibly not reflecting the attitudes of all Kadets, clearly marked, by virtue of their open and public nature at a time when the opposition was under attack by the government and the "decisive hour" near, a parting of ways between an important faction of the Kadets and the now socialist-led Soviet and Union of Unions.

A few days after the appearance of the second article, Miliukov made known his own reactions to the November strikes and the politics of the Soviet. The liberal leader had long paid lip service to the need to organize the mass movement but had never done much about it. Even Struve had at least discussed the problem earlier in the year.[51] Miliukov later wrote in his memoirs that the liberals had been "cut off from [the] process" by which the revolution had spread to the masses after January 9 and that he had not been well informed about developments among the leaders of the socialist parties.[52] In his introductory speech at the founding congress of the Kadet Party in October, Miliukov spoke of a friendliness to the Left that he felt should characterize the party's attitude, but now that he was involved in clarifying the position of the new party he was understandably less interested in possible cross-party alliances and more concerned with the possible divisiveness of socialist ideas among the Kadets themselves.

> Our party will never defend these interests [of agrarians and industrialists, narrowly conceived] at the cost of the interests of the toiling classes. Between us and our—we would like to say not opponents, but associates on the Left there also exists a certain boundary, but it has a different character than that which we maintain on the Right. We do

49. "Vtoraia zabastovka," *Pravo*, 44 (Nov. 13, 1905), cols. 3582–84.
50. "Smuta," *Pravo*, 47 (Nov. 27, 1905), cols. 3779–82.
51. See above, pp. 132–33, 257–59.
52. Miliukov, *Political Memoirs*, p. 35 (*Vospominaniia*, vol. 1, p. 293).

not join in with their demands for a democratic republic and socialization of the means of production. Some of us do not support these watchwords because they regard them as generally unacceptable, others, because they regard them as standing beyond the bounds of practical politics. As long as it is possible to move toward a common goal together despite this difference of motives, both groups will act as a single whole; any attempt to emphasize the demands just mentioned and to bring them into the program will result in immediate schism. We do not doubt, however, that in our midst there is sufficient political farsightedness and reasonability to avoid this schism at the present moment.[53]

It should have been clear from his past political pronouncements that Miliukov counted himself among those who found the goals of the Left impracticable, not disagreeable.

This speech preceded the October Manifesto by a few days. Afterward, Miliukov apparently avoided open criticism of the Left, but in late November he broke his silence. Outwardly addressing an appeal to the revolutionary movement as if still in solidarity with its aims, he delivered a stern warning about the dire results likely to follow from its disruptive tactics. Perhaps aware of his lack of complete credibility before a left liberal and socialist readership, and apparently stung by some of the taunts he had received from that quarter, Miliukov alternated between urgent appeals on the need to win over the masses to the moderate opposition and pointed counterthrusts against the socialist parties. Both reveal a continuing attempt to woo the left intelligentsia to the Kadet Party, to enlist their aid in conquering the rural vote for the liberals.[54]

Miliukov frankly described the task at hand as a struggle between the government and the revolutionary forces for the support of the vast majority of what he regarded as the ignorant and impressionable public in the middle:

In the gap between the government and its organs on the one hand, and the active, struggling groups on the other, lies a broad territory of more or less passive social elements. At heightened political moments like the present an extraordinarily great amount depends on the mood of this middle, normally silent mass. Sometimes everything depends on this mood, and it is worth giving expression to this mood in the sharpest terms in order that, as if by magic, the political scenery of the next mo-

53. Miliukov, *God bor'by*, p. 100.

54. Miliukov, "Osnovnye zadachi momenta," *God bor'by*, pp. 163–69, reprinted from *Svobodnyi narod*, no. 1 (Dec. 1, 1905).

ment be changed. [For] from them, from these depths, issue pogroms and agrarian conflagrations; from them can issue a Thermidorian Reaction or a Napoleonic plebiscite. To them, to these depths, one must go, one must get to know them in order to have the right to prophesy the future of the Russian Revolution; there one must sow ideas and symbols in order, one way or another, to influence this future.[55]

The government understands the need, Miliukov continued, and has canceled redemption payments and instigated pogroms in the countryside. It is not too late for the "Russian opposition and the revolutionary liberation movement" (as he carefully addressed his appeal) to make a difference, but another political strike at this time would set back the effort. "We will be staking the success of the movement on the play of a card and will risk losing sight of its main aim if we count on the sharpening of class antagonisms."

Because it was clear that he was rounding on the socialist parties at this point, Miliukov interestingly allowed that Petersburg, "where the struggle of literary circles has in excessive measure concealed the struggle of political parties," might constitute an exception to his strictures. That is, he seemed to indicate, the impact of another strike on the Petersburg population might not drive large parts of it into the arms of the counterrevolution because of more widespread political support for the strikers, a more developed sense of common purpose between liberals and socialists. No, his remarks were intended to apply to "the depths of Russia" where a "centuries-long silence" had given way to "the sharpest and most antagonistic political mood," where the situation was more polarized as a result, and where his warnings should have the greatest weight.[56] Yet it was also true that events in Petersburg would affect and be affected by the mood in the provinces, that Miliukov was addressing the unaffiliated left intelligentsia throughout Russia, including Petersburg, and that his article was a veiled attack on the policy of the Soviet and the socialist parties.

As if to remove any lingering doubt, Miliukov ended the article by openly mocking the Social Democrats and Socialist Revolutionaries. Replying to those who had demanded to know whether he stood "with the people or with the government," he stated: "Yes, we are for the revolution, as long as it serves the aims of political liberation and social reform. . . . Yes, we are with the people, but we refuse the pretensions of those who alone wish to speak in the name of the people

55. *Ibid.*, p. 166.
56. *Ibid.*, p. 166–67.

and limit the concept of the people to the bookish concept of a 'conscious proletariat.'" He asserted that trade unions among workers were replacing "purely party groupings." Moreover, the SRs' agrarian program was outdated and theoretically weak, and their support of land confiscations presented a serious danger to the entire liberation movement.[57]

Miliukov thus pleaded an archetypal liberal case for reason, moderation, and social peace, and against extremism from the government and the Right or from the revolutionaries, whose policies fed off one another and were leading to the ruin of true democracy, i.e., social reform under parliamentary rule. Although the specific arguments and issues he raised indicate that he was addressing primarily the unaffiliated left intelligentsia, the article was also a broader appeal to all desiring reform in the Russian Empire, a call to reconstitute the earlier broad unity of the constitutional and democratic opposition in the ranks of the Kadet Party. He also recognized that a somewhat different situation prevailed in St. Petersburg, almost as if the unity of the pre-October national opposition lingered there more substantially than elsewhere in the country, implying that the opposition there would have to make allowances for its skewed perception in order to recognize the validity of what he was pointing out.

From the viewpoint of the labor movement in St. Petersburg, however, its differences with the Kadets and moderate liberals became clearer and more pronounced after October 17 than they had been before. The new liberal party's approval of the October Manifesto and disapproval of the November general strike scarcely moved them closer to most workers. Miliukov's disparagement of the socialist parties came at a time when workers of the capital, made more vulnerable by the defeats suffered in November, acknowledged socialist leadership more unequivocally and in greater numbers than ever before, and his words would probably only have confirmed their trust of the socialists and distrust of the Kadets.

The Union of Unions meanwhile persisted in its policy of mobilizing the forces of the opposition through the organization of intelligentsia and worker unions. In response to the October Manifesto, its leaders issued a defiant condemnation of martial law and the absence of civil liberties, restating their commitment to a constituent assembly elected by four-tail suffrage and resolving to "remain at their posts"

57. *Ibid.*, pp. 167–68.

until such an assembly was granted.[58] However, their role as the foremost tribune of left democracy in 1905 was now increasingly preempted by the labor and revolutionary upsurge called forth by the October Strike and by the St. Petersburg Soviet of Workers' Deputies.

Nevertheless, the Union of Unions supported and encouraged the Soviet in every conceivable way. Urged by its members and concerned as always to show solidarity with the labor movement, the federation's Central Bureau voted as early as October 11 to join the general strike. By October 14 all the member unions either had struck or had voted to strike. Moreover, in October the intelligentsia unions asked their members for three days' pay each, raising some 12,500 rubles for the Soviet in short order. In the earliest days of its existence, the Soviet also acted jointly with the Union of Unions. The delegation to the City Duma, for instance, was joined by a delegation from the intelligentsia unionists, and when the higher schools were closed to public meetings on October 15, the unionists secured meeting space for the Soviet at the Free Economic Society.[59]

Union of Unions leaders also sought on several other occasions to cooperate with and even gain representation in the Soviet, but they were refused outright. "The minutes of the [Union of Unions'] central bureau," Jonathan Sanders reports from archival sources, "contained repeated references and reports about proposed joint discussions and activities with the Soviet. On 6 November the Central Committee (TsK) decided to ask the Soviet to accept two TsK representatives with 'consultative voices,' [and] as late as 4 December at a meeting of the TsK the representative of a group of lawyers spoke about the need to have a permanent delegate in the Soviet." The Engineers' Union was also refused membership in the Soviet.[60] These refusals were probably due to the opposition of the socialist parties, since the willingness of the deputies to associate with and even be led by left liberals was clear from the election of Nosar' as president of the Soviet and from the Soviet's early cooperation with the Union of Unions, i.e., before socialist influence inside the Soviet was consolidated.

Despite the Soviet's rejection of a formal association, however, the Union of Unions maintained fairly close informal ties with the Soviet's

58. *Syn otechestva*, Oct. 22, 1905, p. 3. Quoted by Sanders, "The Union of Unions," ch. 10, pp. 35–36.

59. Sanders, "The Union of Unions," ch. 10, pp. 30–32.

60. *Ibid.*, p. 32 and n. 140. Anne D. Morgan maintains that the Engineers' Union was admitted to the Soviet, but the claim is inadequately documented and inconsistent with her own reasoning: "The St. Petersburg Soviet of Workers' Deputies," pp. 80, 94.

leaders. For instance, the following trade unions belonging to the Union of Unions also joined the Soviet: the pharmacists, railroad workers, retail clerks, and office workers/bookkeepers. The leaders of these unions even sat on the Executive Committee of the Soviet as full voting members. In addition, representatives of these and other unions worked with socialist party representatives, Nosar', and left liberals such as Sergei Prokopovich, V. V. Sviatlovskii, and A. A. Evdokimov at the First All-Russian Trade Union Conference and in the Petersburg Central Bureau of Trade Unions, a group founded in St. Petersburg in October 1905.[61]

In the fall, therefore, there was at least some basis for the notion entertained by the police that the Union of Unions was the prime cause of revolutionary unrest in the capital, even though the belief was still exaggerated, oversimplified, and much too conspiratorial to account for the reality of the situation. In the first place, the differences between the views of the Union of Unions' Central Bureau and those of its membership grew wider in the fall. The "Big Group" of Petersburg's radical intelligentsia leaders had dominated the Central Bureau throughout the year, but their views spoke for an increasingly narrower part of the union federation after October 17. Thus, despite enthusiastic votes of support of the November political strike by the Union of Unions as a whole, several member unions did not observe the vote, and among the unions that did the portion of the membership that actually struck was far from unanimous. A meeting of the union bureaus on November 2 voted overwhelmingly to support the strike called the day before by the Soviet, with teachers' and academics' unions the only exceptions. But after the union leaders had consulted with their respective memberships, there was much less support among them than the vote of the leaders had indicated. For instance, only a part of the engineers and technicians supported the November strike, and a number of them resigned from the union over the issue. Others, like teachers, medical personnel, and even some lawyers, felt their responsibilities to the public outweighed their responsibility to the labor movement. Most of the railroads operating out of the capital supported the strike, but railroad union leaders re-

61. Kats and Milonov, *1905 god. Professional'noe dvizhenie*, pp. 67, 69, 72. Kolokol'nikov and Rapoport, *1905–1907 gg. v professional'nom dvizhenii*, pp. 31–32, 125–29, 135–37. Grinevich, "Ocherk razvitiia," pp. 245–52. V. Sviatlovskii, "Iz istorii S.-Peterburgskogo Tsentral'nogo Biuro Professional'nykh rabochikh soiuzov," *Trud tekhnika*, no. 1–2, Jan. 27, 1907, cols. 5–18. See also an interview with Sviatlovskii in TsGAOR, fond 6935, op. 2, d. 101b, ll. 1–15.

fused to use their authority to make the strike national, partly because of fatigue among their workers, but also because in November the unity of purpose the railroad workers had achieved in October had been lost to the pursuit of local and economic issues.[62]

In addition, true to Miliukov's April assessment,[63] the Union of Unions had continued to harbor a number of more specific political programs and groupings. The "Days of Liberty" had made it possible to meet and publish openly for the first time, and besides facilitating the founding of the Kadet Party, they gave rise to a number of new party groupings, mainly to the left of the Kadets. During the very months of the Union of Unions' continuing loyal support of the Soviet, a great many of the same left liberals and non-party socialists were in the process of shifting from unity on the basis of professional affiliation, developing better articulated political programs, and positioning themselves to participate in the parliamentary politics of the approaching Duma period. Their efforts led to the establishment of such new splinter parties as the Freethinkers, the Radicals, the *Bezzaglavtsy*, and, later, the Popular Socialist Party.[64]

The events of the fall had therefore accelerated the process of political self-definition among the liberals, preparing them for participation in the elections to the State Duma promised in the October Manifesto. In the process, however, the earlier hopes of the Kadets and the left liberals to join forces with each other and with the mass movement became more remote. For despite the efforts of the Union of Unions loyalists to support and cooperate with the Soviet, the socialist leadership of the latter prevented the formation of a larger left bloc, as the intelligentsia unionists apparently desired. The Union of Unions spoke for too small a part of the liberal alliance to have tempted the Soviet or the revolutionary parties, which by the fall had developed much better relations of their own with the mass movement and seemed disinclined to risk them with the liberals, whom they distrusted in any event. Workers themselves have left no evidence of repudiating the intelligentsia unionists at this point, but neither is there evidence of workers opposing the Soviet's rebuff of the Union of

62. Sanders, "The Union of Unions," ch. 11, pp. 24–25, 52–55. Pushkareva, *Zheleznodorozhniki*, pp. 185–86. Sanders is the only published source of information on the participation of individual unions, but it is not complete, and complete information on all the unions may not have survived.

63. See above, p. 306.

64. Emmons, *The Formation of Political Parties*, pp. 78–88, 201–3. N. D. Erofeev, *Narodnye sotsialisty v pervoi russkoi revoliutsii* (M., 1979), especially pp. 54–86.

Unions' bid to join it. Perhaps the earlier need for intelligentsia assistance was being filled, for the time being, by the Soviet and the socialist parties. Perhaps the workers and their deputies took the Union of Unions at its word and counted on its support without regarding formal membership in the Soviet as necessary to sustain the alliance, which it seems not to have been. Because this precluded the formation of a strong leftist bloc, the drift of individual unions and members toward the Kadet center seems to have ensued among some, while other Union of Unions members emulated Kadet strategy by forming their own party groupings with an eye toward the Duma elections.

It appears that the Kadets expected most of their electoral support to come from urban middle strata and the rural masses, apparently assuming, as Struve had earlier in the year, that urban workers were in the hands of the socialists. This fundamental assumption was somewhat complicated by the fact that in the fall Miliukov continued his approach of applying moderate tactics yet holding to a radical program, though most of his energy was apparently devoted to defending Kadet policies before the *zemtsy* and the government. Would those who remained in the Union of Unions and those who joined the new splinter parties not eventually have to vote with or for the Kadets in any case? The polarization of the political situation after October 17 must have increasingly disturbed him because of the threat it posed to prospects for moderate, peaceful reform. Although he did not speak out about it until December 1, the approaching confrontation between the government and the revolutionary movement must have restrained him from linking the Kadets too closely with either side.

The liberals' inability to offer a unified leadership to the entire revolutionary opposition therefore persisted, even at the very height of the liberation movement in the fall of 1905. They either tried to unite the movement with too narrow a base, or they overlooked it altogether.

SOVIET DEPUTIES AND THE FACTORY POPULATION

Although the government intended to dismember the workers' authority as its supporters feared, it was proceeding cautiously. Although the Soviet continued to organize for another all-Russian general strike, it was forced by the lockouts to coordinate its plans with those of other groups and areas of the country, and it ceased to be as great an immediate threat, and therefore as great a force, as it had once been. After November 13 it was incapable of calling another strike of Petersburg workers without risking certain defeat and a further increase in the ranks of the unemployed. Yet the Soviet's ability to call the majority of the workers out on strike, when all was said and done, had been the only real basis of its power and authority in the eyes of the government. It did not lose this authority immediately after November 13, and it was still a force to be reckoned with; but the workers had suffered a defeat under its leadership, and a haunting sense of powerlessness now affected the Executive Committee and the inner circles of the Soviet.[65]

In the factories, a mood of discouragement was slower to take hold. Concentration on the political fortunes of the whole movement was not as intensive there as in the Soviet, and a number of other considerations made for a different outlook.

Support of the Soviet among the factory population had been truly popular, but it had never been unanimous or monolithic. Opposition to its authority and leadership of some kind or degree appeared from an early date at all types and sizes of enterprises. One of the most penetrating published accounts of events at any factory during October and November describes great dissension and turmoil among the workers of the Train Car Construction Plant (4,000 workers), the largest and most militant work force in the region known popularly as *za Moskovskoi zastavoi* ("beyond the Moscow gates," the area south of Spassk district). Although workers at the plant struck on October 13 and promptly elected deputies to the Soviet, workers from some of the more conservative shops began to return to work on the 17th, and the deputies had to bring them out on strike again with force and persuasion. Around October 20, a back-to-work movement was organized by the same deputies with the cooperation of management personnel, who admitted them to the otherwise locked plant. Defense of the Soviet's strike policy fell to A. V. Burov (a Social Democrat) and Ivan Azarov, whose authority and influence among the workers was great enough to allow them to break into the meeting and to turn it around, although they were nearly beaten by the more conservative workers in the process. The Train Car workers elected Dmitrii Synkov, an older, moderate worker, president of the plant's deputies, but when they also decided to institute an eight-hour day "by revolutionary means," Synkov resigned his office. Again in November, the workers struck at the behest of the Soviet but began returning to work only

65. Woytinsky, *Gody pobed*, pp. 266–67.

two days later; the whole plant did not resume operations until November 7. A management diarist noted that the majority of the workers did not sympathize with the November strike. At this point, and perhaps earlier as well, it appears that a minority of the work force aligned itself with the deputies and the Soviet, then persuaded or forced the rest of the workers to go along. This group decided to resume the eight-hour campaign on November 8, but it was unable to implement the decision because the workers were now threatened with mass dismissals.[66]

Similar resistance to strikes and Soviet policies was encountered at other plants and factories. Aleksei Piskarev, deputy from the Ozoling Machine Plant (150 workers), contrasted strike participation in October with that in November, when workers struck unwillingly, and he noted that only a small part of the workers conducted an eight-hour campaign. Even at the more militant Possel' Horseshoe Works (500 workers) on Vasilevsky Island, which struck in each of the last three months of 1905 and campaigned for an eight-hour day until a lockout closed the plant, strike opposition was not absent. Determined resistance to the October strike was led by "disappointed Gaponists," according to Possel' deputy G. A. Borozdin, a Social Democrat and member of one of the most active and influential revolutionary circles in the district. At the Svirskii Furniture Factory (116 workers) in Alexander Nevsky district, strike opposition centered among the older workers while its 25-year-old deputy, N. A. Kuznetsov, drew support from the younger and more radical element. The older workers reluctantly went along with the Soviet-directed policies, and they were undoubtedly mollified when the management agreed to grant an eight-hour day. But when the Svirskii workers were locked out in late November, the older, conservative element turned on Kuznetsov, claiming he had lied to and betrayed them, and they tried to throw him out a window. In some plants and industries, the pro-Soviet element was a distinct minority and was unable to surmount ingrained conservatism. The Osipov Leather Works (750 workers) was made up of about 70 percent unskilled workers, illiterate peasants exclusively from Pskov province; the rest were saddlemakers and other kinds of skilled leather workers. With management complicity, the unskilled workers met separately from the skilled and elected a conservative deputy, who never attended the Soviet or took part in its work. The

66. Livshits, "Bor'ba za 8-chasovoi rabochii den' v Peterburge v 1905 godu," pp. 116–30. *VPR*, p. 381.

next day, the saddlemakers elected as their deputy S. V. Adashev, a former Gaponist who had joined the Bolsheviks shortly before the October strike. Adashev participated in the Soviet both before and after its arrest and later headed the leather workers' union, but he seems to have had little influence among the majority of workers at his own plant.[67]

The picture that emerges is not so very different from that already suggested by events at the Train Car Plant: a small group of Soviet loyalists leading a much larger group of passive, moderate, and even conservative workers with varying degrees of success. The group of activists could be very small indeed. V. F. Semenov, alternate deputy at the Phoenix Machine Construction Works, one of the more militant plants in the Vyborg district, reported that there were only 16 or 17 Soviet activists among the 400 or so Phoenix workers. Nevertheless, they were sufficient to provide an effective communications network around the plant, whose workers displayed great militancy and unity to the very end of the year.

Another consideration that has been applied to the labor movement in the fall was the cumulative psychological exhaustion of workers who had been striking all year long. Insofar as Russian workers as a whole were drained at the end of 1905, those in Petersburg should have been among the most seriously affected, having been engaged in strikes since early January. But how important was this fatigue at all in accounting for the political attitudes and behavior of workers anywhere toward the end of the year? Even the Putilov workers, who had come through a two-month lockout and who resisted organizing an eight-hour-day campaign, struck again in November to protect the jobs of protesting fellow workers. Was it stress or a differing view of what was worth striking for that stood behind workers' apparent fatigue? Exhaustion did not prevent them from responding to the arrest of the Soviet with yet another massive strike in December. Indeed, before that momentous event the continuing energy and commitment of workers was most notable.[68]

Despite the lockouts and the defeat of the eight-hour campaign, workers continued on the whole to display defiance toward their employers and the authorities and devotion to their deputies and the Soviet. During this period, the number of factory and union deputies in

67. These observations come from the memoirs of Soviet deputies in *Vospominaniia Soveta*: Ozoling, p. 29; Possel', pp. 59–61; Svirskii, pp. 91–98; Osipov, pp. 104–7.

68. *Ibid.*, pp. 37, 84–85. Woytinsky, *Gody pobed*, p. 268. Paialin, *Zavod imeni Lenina*, p. 178. Shuster, *Peterburgskie rabochie*, pp. 183–92, 204.

the Soviet rose to an all-time high. Many deputies noted a rapid growth in political awareness and a disciplined adherence to the decisions of the Soviet among their workers, even at those factories where opposition was also reported. Although strikes became less numerous after November 13, workers at some factories, such as the Nail Plant and the Mechanized Shoe Factory, remained on strike throughout, and those at many others continued to press for shorter hours or other concessions without striking. In addition, a whole series of non–factory workers struck during the second half of November, including local participants in a nationwide post and telegraph strike. Factory meetings, although now less frequent and massive, resumed the defiant and demonstration-like character they had before October 17. The large number of workers who had to return to work under the conditions in force before a strike or an eight-hour campaign were not necessarily broken by the experience. Perhaps they had learned to view strikes as a "series of consecutive battles," no one of which was likely to be decisive. They resisted the attempts of management to dismiss their deputies or factory revolutionaries during the rehiring process, and they willingly contributed from their wages to aid locked-out fellow workers at other factories. In short, although most factory workers were not in a position to strike again immediately, their commitment to the strike movement and to the aims of the Soviet remained at a high level. From this point of view, the Soviet's policy after November 13 of gathering allies for another big strike or "decisive struggle" was certainly in step with the factory mood.[69]

What accounted for this continuing militancy and loyalty to the Soviet, tenuous and conditional though it was? The many positive reasons for it—the embodiment in the Soviet of the workers' quest for a citywide body of representatives, its incorporation of factory and district mass meetings, its merging of respected factory leadership with that of the revolutionary parties, its forthright stand against both the government and employers, and its strike leadership—have all been mentioned. The most general negative reasons were inertia and the lack of a viable alternative, or in light of the evidence of opposition to strikes and to Soviet policy, the lack of a *moderate* alternative. A great number of trade unions were formed throughout November, but for reasons that will subsequently be made clear they were a moderate but not a viable alternative. Industrial unions and other all-inclusive

69. Dorovatovskii and Zlotin, "Khronika," pp. 236–45. *VPR*, pp. 296–97, 399–400, 404–6, 409, 412–14, 420–23. *Vospominaniia Soveta*, pp. 21, 85, 86–87, 108, 117. Paialin, *Zavod imeni Lenina*, pp. 177–80. Shuster, *Peterburgskie rabochie*, pp. 196–98.

schemes of labor association, such as those of Smesov and Ushakov, enjoyed too little popularity to be considered alternatives to the Soviet. The same can be said of an initiative to reopen the 11 locals of Gapon's Assembly in November.[70] The limited interest shown in the spring and summer in left-Liberationist factory unions was either absorbed by the Soviet or fell victim to a lack of interest in unions sufficient to overcome the practical obstacles to forming one, especially where factory-level solidarity and deputies already existed.[71] Nosar' himself became a leader of the Soviet and a captive of Social Democratic policy, and the Union of Unions became a completely loyal supporter of the deputies' body, hardly the voice of moderation. The alliance of in-factory leaders and the revolutionary intelligentsia that the Soviet represented was difficult to compete with, and no organization even came close to doing so.

For the most part, therefore, workers with moderate and conservative instincts could either support the Soviet or go without protection and organization in their factory struggles. Those that chose the latter course in the fall of 1905 became inactive and dropped from view; but in the many enterprises where factory struggles continued, a large degree of support and sympathy for the Soviet also continued. Moreover, the government's and employers' open attack on the labor movement after November 7 put workers in even greater need of the one organization that provided collective strength and a unified purpose. Although the Petersburg labor movement was objectively weakened and thrown on the defensive around mid-November, most workers who remained in the struggle reacted by rallying to the Soviet rather than by abandoning it. (An increased recruitment of workers to revolutionary parties and circles toward the end of the year may also be attributed to the same embattled mood.)[72]

Black hundreds agitation and organization in and around the factories undoubtedly contributed to and benefited from antistrike sentiment among workers, but the extent of their influence is difficult to gauge. References to black hundreds groups and individuals in

70. *1905: SRD*, p. 57. Sablinsky, *The Road to Bloody Sunday*, pp. 300–308.
71. Kolokol'nikov and Rapoport, *1905–1907 gg. v professional'nom dvizhenii*, pp. 26–33.
72. Shuster, *Peterburgskie rabochie*, pp. 168–69. Lane, *The Roots of Russian Communism*, pp. 75–77. Increased worker recruitment may not apply to the Socialist Revolutionaries, or not in the same measure as it did to the Social Democrats. At least no mention of increased SR worker recruitment in Petersburg is made in works where one might expect to find it.

contemporary and historical writings have usually been too casual and imprecise to distinguish between conservative, antistrike opinion, which had always been present in the factories, and of genuine black hundreds sentiment, stemming from organizations that had arisen only in 1905, such as the Union of the Russian People and the Society for Active Struggle with Revolution and Anarchy. The overall strength of organized black hundreds activity among factory workers has apparently never been analyzed. It is clear, however, that both organized and unorganized "black hundreds" agitation and activity in the factory milieu are mentioned much more frequently in the fall than earlier. Given the wide range of educational and cultural development among factory workers, often in the same enterprise, there can be little doubt that the emergence or reemergence at this time of conservative and reactionary sentiment both reflected and amplified discontent with Soviet and revolutionary policies.[73] Yet it is equally clear that the organized black hundreds, aside from presenting a constant threat and an occasional immediate danger of physical violence, did not have a significant impact on Petersburg labor politics in 1905. Although they had organized groups at some factories, their concentration on political vigilantism and their lack of a labor program left them without appeal to the vast majority of workers, even among those who opposed strikes. Their victimization of revolutionaries and workers, and the Soviet's efforts to organize and arm workers against them, effectively set them outside the labor movement. The violent and aggressive tactics of the black hundreds and their identification with a nationwide attack on the revolution created exaggerated imaginings of the menace they actually presented. As was mentioned earlier, fear of the "black hundreds danger" probably did more to strengthen the Soviet's consensus among workers than reactionary heckling and violence did to break it down. Lacking a moderate alternative in the factory, most workers chose to link their fate to that of the Soviet-led revolution and the dictates of class struggle rather than return to the authoritarian monarchism of either Witte and the industrialists or the pogromists.

    73. References to black hundreds in and around the factories may be found in *Vospominaniia Soveta*, pp. 52, 83, 96, 107; Glukhochenkov, "Iz raboty chernoi sotni," pp. 148–50; Peskovoi, "Na zavode Rechkina v 1905 g.," pp. 179, 191; Vinogradov, "Iz istorii 1905 goda na Metallicheskom zavode," pp. 45–47; and Paialin, *Zavod imeni Lenina*, pp. 173, 175. The worker E. A. Rizgolet claimed that the two largest organized groups among workers at the Train Car Plant were Mensheviks and black hundreds belonging to the Union of the Russian People. *Pervaia russkaia revoliutsiia*, vol. 2, p. 88.

Yet the Soviet was too much a creation of the factory struggle not to have addressed itself quite attentively—at least at some factories—to workers' more mundane and material needs. The Soviet deputies in a number of cases also assumed the duties of the factory deputies who had preceded them. Besides carrying the Soviet's decisions to the factories for approval, they drafted strike demands and voiced the grievances of the factory work force to the management. As early as the week of October 24, for instance, the Train Car Plant deputies drew up a set of demands including full pay for the October strike, the re-hiring of all workers dismissed since the May strikes, and the use of a sum of donated money for a workers' library and an aid fund. Instead of adding a demand for an eight-hour day, the deputies appealed to the workers to implement it on their own initiative. A meeting at the St. Petersburg Metal Plant on October 27 voted to support a Bolshevik-sponsored directive to the Soviet that it accept the Social Democratic program as its own since "we workers need to unite solidly in one party in order to fight tirelessly in its ranks for our interests. Otherwise, the bourgeois parties will seize in their hands all the fruits of victory achieved by us." This appeal to working-class interest fitted perfectly well with the theme of the previous speaker: higher wages, abolition of overtime work, and the eight-hour day. Attention to in-plant, "economic" demands went hand in hand with the broader political aims of the Soviet as two sides of the same struggle.[74]

At these plants and in many others, the key issue linking the two sides was the eight-hour day. To workers, the eight-hour demand was very nearly the epitome of all their efforts in 1905, a direct material improvement in their everyday circumstances, the reclaiming of a part of their lives from imprisonment in the factory. The courage and perseverance with which they fought for it attested to the vividness of their hopes and the sharpened sense of justice which the demand evoked. A letter from a worker announcing a self-initiated nine-and-a-half-hour day at his textile dyeing factory described the terrible enervation produced by the extremes of heat and dampness and dye-contaminated air during the usual eleven hours of work. In concluding, he voiced a kind of reasonable extremism that a great many workers felt about a shorter workday: ". . . we do not have the strength to prolong this gradual exhaustion of both the physical and

74. Livshits, "Bor'ba za 8-chasovoi rabochii den'," p. 123. Vinogradov, "Iz istorii 1905 goda na Metallicheskom zavode," pp. 40–42. See also Kuznetsov, Livshits, and Pliasunov, *Baltiiskii sudostroitel'nyi*, p. 325.

moral aspects of the human individual. We will fight to the last drop of blood."[75] The strength of such sentiment undoubtedly helped to bind the moderate and less politically developed strata of the factory population to the Soviet. The eight-hour day served to unify the revival of economic demands after the end of the October strike and the new wave of deputy elections that accompanied it.

The identification of Soviet deputies with the in-plant, "economic" needs of workers was enhanced by the resurrection of factory committees during the "Days of Liberty." The activities of the factory committees in the fall were probably limited by the small numbers of Soviet activists on hand, their efforts being confined in most cases to handling demands and grievances in addition to their Soviet responsibilities. In some factories the committees took on broader duties. At the Train Car Construction Plant the factory committee distributed money to the families of imprisoned and needy workers, arranged lectures and readings, and expanded the factory library. Despite the fluctuations of the broader movement and a chronic struggle at the factory between workers who wanted the committee to make in-plant issues a top priority and those who felt "that economic questions can in no way be posed at a time when a struggle for political rights is under way," the committee's efforts to meet the workers' direct material and educational needs went forward energetically and without interruption from October 19 until the end of the year.[76]

On the whole, however, such attention to the mundane requirements of the factory population was not typical of the Soviet deputies' activity. There is not much evidence of deputies elected in the fall who served in the factory and not in the Soviet, although it is distinctly possible that this was not untypical among more conservative workers such as those at the Osipov Leather Works. The inability and unwillingness of Soviet leaders to reorient their activities to fill essentially trade union functions became clear on November 6 and afterward when the Executive Committee called for organization along industrial lines to facilitate the eight-hour-day campaign, while itself remaining a body of factory deputies. The Soviet appealed to the most revolutionary elements in the factories to the end, but it also won the allegiance of more moderate workers by its support of a shorter workday, defense against the black hundreds, and efforts to aid locked-out workers. Although it never advocated strikes over in-plant issues, the

75. Quoted by Petrov-Radin, "Bor'ba," p. 254.
76. Peskovoi, "Na zavode Rechkina," pp. 188–89, 191.

Soviet supported "economic" strikes initiated by the workers because it not only understood but personified the link between "economic" and political struggle. Most of all, the Soviet enjoyed the sympathy and respect of workers of diverse views and levels of political sophistication because they regarded it, with whatever reservations, as their own creation.

UNIONIZATION DURING THE "DAYS OF LIBERTY"

As large and diverse as the November strike was among factory workers, it did not draw together the same alliance of forces that had made for the strength and impact of the October Days. Most of the white-collar workers and retail clerks did not strike in November. The horse-tram and most stores continued to function; post and telegraph service and horse-cabs in the center of the city operated as normal. Equally as important, political support of the strike was not as widespread and unreserved as in October. The Union of Unions leaders recommended that the separate unions join the November strike, but, as we have seen, the response left no doubt that most members declined to do so. Large parts of the intelligentsia reacted negatively to the Kronstadt mutiny, viewing it as more of a drunken pogrom than as a movement of liberation, and they were disinclined to come to the sailors' aid. Liberal spokesmen even sided with the government in opposing the strike as an attempt to draw the army into politics, and they found the Polish issue an inappropriate reason to strike because it pleaded a particular cause in contrast to the transnational demands of the October strike. Those liberals who did protest the situation were careful to dissociate themselves from the Soviet's protest.[77] As encouraging as the November turnout was, it amounted to an almost purely proletarian effort; the isolation of the Soviet and the labor Left had become an unavoidable fact.

The Soviet's leadership did not admit to regrets or second thoughts about this isolation from the liberals. In his speech of November 5, Trotsky was mindful of the hostility of the bourgeoisie and the waning sympathy of the intelligentsia, but instead of warning of the Soviet's isolation he told the deputies, "Remember that at the moment of decision we must count only on ourselves."[78] The resolution of No-

77. Nosar', "Istoriia Soveta," pp. 115–16. Woytinsky, *Gody pobed*, pp. 231–32, 246, 250–61. Martynov, "Istoriia K. D. Partii," pp. 13–14, 18–19.
78. Trotsky, *1905*, p. 173. Nosar', "Istoriia Soveta," p. 124.

vember 13, despite its appeal to "all strata of society" to aid the lockout victims, continued this line of thinking with respect to possible
liberal allies by anticipating alliances in a future strike with the proletariat elsewhere in Russia, the revolutionary peasantry, the army,
and the fleet. To this end, delegates were dispatched to other cities
and industrial areas to make contact with their workers. They traveled
to Moscow, in the Central Industrial Region, and along the Volga,
establishing ties with the All-Russian Peasants' Union, the Postal-
Telegraph Union, and other groups. In Moscow, their appearance
helped to revive the workers' soviet of that city. This work was considerably facilitated by the efforts of provincial labor organizations and
soviets (of which some 40–50 formed in other cities in 1905) to contact the Petersburg Soviet. By mid-November word of its exploits had
reached the remotest stretches of the Empire, and fraternal greetings,
expressions of solidarity, and proposals of joint action poured in to
the Soviet at the capital. The Kharkov Mutual Aid Society's idea of an
all-Russian congress of trade unions was expanded in the fall to include soviets, strike committees, and revolutionary parties. (Although
scheduled for November 15, the press of events forced its postpone-
ment to December, and it never met.) A delegate from the Jewish Social Democratic Bund was admitted to the Soviet to help coordinate
activities with the northwest frontier area. Delegates from workers in
Revel', from Finnish army troops, from the Peasants' Union, and from
the Polish Socialist Party appeared at Soviet sessions. Just at the time
of the Soviet's greatest weakness, when it began to search in earnest
for allies elsewhere in the country, all of revolutionary Russia was turning to it for leadership. This mutual effort lent substance to the belief
that the workers' movement was not a receding but a rising tide.[79]

   In Petersburg itself, the Soviet also supported newly organizing
groups of workers. On November 15 post and telegraph workers in
several cities struck; two days later, part of those in Petersburg followed suit. On November 19, the Soviet took the hesitant postal strike
under its protection, granting the strikers 2,000 rubles, encouraging
them not to send government telegrams, and calling for a boycott of
postal trains by the public generally and the railroad workers in particular. The Executive Committee sent speakers to the strikers' meetings, found them meeting places, and printed the Postal-Telegraph
Union's proclamations. Nosar' claimed that "it can be maintained

79. Nosar', "Istoriia Soveta," pp. 137–39. N. N. Glebov-Putilovskii, "Agitatsiia za
sovety po Rossii," *Vospominaniia Soveta*, pp. 129–32. Anweiler, *The Soviets*, pp. 47,
259–60. *1905: SRD*, pp. 69, 73.

without exaggeration that without the participation of the Soviet, the postal-telegraph strike in Petersburg would have miscarried."[80]

During the same period the Soviet devoted greater energy and attention to organizing unions generally, rendering them some of the same aid it extended to the postal workers. Unions in some 40 different Petersburg trades and industries were begun in 1905, the vast bulk of them after the end of October. Except for those unions with some semblance of an organized membership before the fall (such as printers, pharmacists, and retail clerks), most of the new activity was little more than organizing initiatives; it was not a period of union organizing as much as it was one of union agitation. Small nuclei of union enthusiasts met, drafted a constitution, and called a mass meeting of their trade. Most of this activity did not pass beyond that stage before the government repression of the labor movement all but ended union activities in December. Union organizing was further hampered by the absence of skilled and knowledgeable organizers. M. G. Kogan, the eminent Petersburg Menshevik unionist, complained of the kinds of agitators he had to work with:

> Many was the time when one was forced to argue with "agitators" who, disregarding both the composition of a meeting and the order of the day, appeared at trade union gatherings with speeches on "the armed uprising," "the provisional government," and so forth. Seeing everything from the viewpoint of "utilization" [i.e., of worker enthusiasm to further the revolution] and without pondering the tasks of building an organization, these comrades often involuntarily wrecked meetings of trade unions.[81]

In this regard, Soviet assistance to the union movement may have been something of a mixed blessing.

In the fall of 1905, as earlier, the desire for unionization enjoyed its greatest popularity among artisans (such as tailors, shoemakers, watchmakers, and bakers) and service workers (barbers, painters, gardeners, floor polishers, chimney sweeps, waiters, cooks, and tavern workers). Union-organizing initiatives even arose among such normally conservative or politically undeveloped groups as domestic servants, janitors, coachmen, and policemen. This has led Kogan and others to associate unionization with nonfactory labor and with "the

---

80. Dorovatovskii and Zlotin, "Khronika," p. 238. Nosar', "Istoriia Soveta," p. 140. *1905: SRD*, pp. 69–71. Bazilevich, *Ocherki po istorii professional'nogo dvizheniia rabotnikov sviazi 1905–1906*, pp. 328–30.

81. Grinevich [M. G. Kogan], "Ocherk razvitiia," p. 238.

backward, less cultivated state of workers, the unskilled. This circumstance," he continued, "explains the fact, strange at first glance, that
Petersburg artisans and unskilled workers organized trade unions
earliest of all, factory workers, only at a later period." In 1905 factory workers were totally engrossed in political struggle, according to
this view.[82]

Though there is some truth in this contrast, it also oversimplifies
matters considerably. First, it is wrongheaded to separate political and
economic struggles so radically. In 1905 workers tended to associate
rather than dissociate them in their strikes and demands. The Soviet
found it not only desirable but necessary to encourage the formation
of trade unions and to include their representatives in its ranks. The
unionization drive of the fall arose from and in close connection with
the October strike, the Days of Freedom, and the advent of the Soviet.
The union organizers, if not political men, were deeply affected by the
mood of political renewal that surrounded them, and they wrote it into
their union charters. The constitution of the Union of Journeymen
Plumbers, for instance, read: "This union sets as its task the organization and defense of the proletariat in order to form a single laboring
family in pursuit of one and the same goal: the discovery for the Russian worker of the rights of man and citizen and a yearning for
the final victory of living, human labor over a heartless capitalism."
Even Kogan noted that the unions formed in the fall set themselves
broad demands as well as narrower, immediate ones; the former
amounted "for the most part to a copy of the minimum program of the
RSDRP."[83] The unionization movement in 1905 was therefore part
and parcel of the liberation movement and of the revolution.

Second, factory workers *did* take part in the union agitation in
1905. Organizational meetings were held not only by workers in
tradition-bound and politically less-developed industries in the fall or
earlier (e.g., among woodworkers, leather workers, and rubber workers), but by metal and textile workers as well. There was certainly
enough in-plant dissatisfaction not adequately attended to by the Soviet deputies to have fueled a large-scale union movement in even the
most "political" factories. Soviet politics rather than trade union politics came to dominate the factory work force in 1905 not because

82. *Ibid.*, pp. 236–41. Dorovatovskii and Zlotin, "Khronika," pp. 229–47 *passim.*
Shuster, *Peterburgskie rabochie*, pp. 183–88. Woytinsky, *Gody pobed*, pp. 199–213. Ainzaft, *Pervyi etap professional'nogo dvizheniia v Rossii (1905–1907 gg.)*, pp. 53–56. Antoshkin, *Professional'noe dvizhenie*, pp. 78–82.

83. Ainzaft, *Pervyi etap*, p. 49. Grinevich, "Ocherk razvitiia," p. 240.

trade union concerns were alien to factory workers, but because the Soviet represented a truer continuation of the more defiant and politicized patterns of struggle developed before and during 1905, involving strikes, deputies, factory patriotism, district solidarity, factory meetings, a citywide labor authority. These patterns made it possible to politicize factory workers more rapidly and thoroughly than other workers, and by the fall this superior political development had become a point of pride among them, sustaining their devotion to the Soviet. The lessons of the eight-hour-day struggle showed, moreover, that it had become politically imperative for workers to organize along trade and industrial lines. It was wholly characteristic of the Petersburg labor movement to have backed into this conclusion after first having attempted to win a hearing by a more direct and political route. With the revival and wider development of trade and labor unions under semilegal circumstances in 1906 and 1907, factory workers formed and participated in them along with other categories of workers.

Finally, the easy distinction between the organizing preferences of factory and artisanal workers leaves out of account the indebtedness of the union agitation to the strike movement. Most of the factory workers who sought to form unions had been on strike earlier in November and now turned to union organization as a means of strengthening their position against their managers. Some of the service workers—domestic servants, chimney sweeps, coachmen, and floor polishers—struck for the first time after the end of the November strike. Others went on from union agitation to join the December political strike, including office workers in insurance firms and a publishing house, gold and silver craftsmen, gardeners, waiters, and tavern workers. Many of the union-organizing meetings produced lists of immediate demands, lending them the aspect of strike meetings, even though the workers in question did not necessarily strike. All demands so drafted were "economic" in nature, affecting working conditions, although the eight-hour day occupied a prominent place. Why should gardeners or employees of the Petersburg City Administration not also work eight hours?[84] In short, even though most of these union nuclei did not belong to the Soviet and would not necessarily have respected its decrees, by their actions and demands they counted themselves within a broader movement over which the Soviet still had immense authority. By the last week of November it appeared very much as though this movement, and with it the potential impact of a new Soviet-led strike, would continue to grow.

84. Dorovatovskii and Zlotin, "Khronika," pp. 235–46 *passim.*

THE LAST DAYS OF THE SOVIET OF
WORKERS' DEPUTIES

These new sources of support must be weighed against the waning strength of the factory movement after the end of the November strike in assessing the position of the Soviet and the labor movement on the eve of their demise. The ambiguity of the situation was undoubtedly sufficient to give the government pause in considering when to move against the Soviet. On the one hand, the continuing defiance and militancy in the factory districts and the mobilization of much of the nonfactory work force promised that any significant infringement of the Soviet's authority would be met by another upheaval. On the other hand, further delay would permit the alliances with other parts of the country a chance to mature, making more likely an all-Russian response to a blow against the Petersburg Soviet. If the Soviet could be provoked into calling a strike at an early date, however, its strength and duration would be limited, and it would provide the occasion for a harsh repression. These considerations seemed to inform the government's decision to arrest Chairman Nosar' on November 26, less than two weeks after the Soviet's retreat from the eight-hour-day campaign.

At the full session of the Soviet, already scheduled for the next day, the majority of speakers maintained that the workers should not allow themselves to be drawn into battle before they were ready. "The arrest of individuals cannot paralyze the course of the revolution once the masses have come on the scene. The best support for comrade Khrustalev is to continue the cause to which he gave all his energy." Without haste or panic, therefore, the Soviet issued its terse response to the arrest: "On November 26 the chairman of the Soviet of Workers' Deputies, Comrade Khrustalev-Nosar', was taken into custody by the Tsarist government. The Soviet is temporarily electing a new chairman and continuing to prepare for an armed uprising."[85]

The Soviet's response to the arrest had been debated at the Executive Committee meeting on November 26. The Socialist Revolutionary leader Chernov had spoken in favor of replying to government repressive measures with acts of terror. Others apparently raised the possibility of transforming the Soviet into an underground organization. But the Committee decided to continue to pursue Trotsky's policy, first publicly enunciated in his speech of November 5, of "con-

85. *1905: SRD*, p. 73.

tinuing to prepare for an armed uprising." Describing that meeting, Trotsky later wrote:

> To abandon the public arena after Khrustalev's arrest was something the Soviet could not do: a freely elected parliament of the working class, it owed its strength precisely to the public character of its activities. To dissolve its organization would have meant deliberately giving an opening to the enemy. Only one solution remained: to continue along the same path as before, heading towards a conflict. . . . During the brief period that remained before the opening of military operations, the Soviet had to establish the closest possible liaison with other towns, with the peasants' union, the railwaymen's union, the Postal and Telegraph Union, and the army.

The sense of an imminent clash, the determination to live or die as an open and public body, and the continuing work of "preparation"— all in fact characterized the Soviet's last days. Mention of "the opening of military operations" was disingenuous, however, insofar as it indicated that the Soviet was prepared for armed conflict. Apart from encouraging workers to arm and organize themselves, the Soviet had not planned and still did not seriously plan to engage in "military operations." The Petersburg Soviet of 1905, unlike its more famous successor in 1917, did not take on itself the organization of an armed uprising. The essence of its revolutionary policy, under Trotsky's guidance, was to prepare for an uprising politically, through agitation and organization, but not to organize the practical means to accomplish it.[86]

Workers at a number of factories were ready to strike in response to the arrest of Nosar', but the call for restraint and Soviet discipline prevailed. The labor movement thereby avoided a premature fight with the government as it had intended, but it also signaled to its opponents and to its supporters throughout the country that the first important political attack on it would go unchallenged. Despite the promise of a bigger struggle to come, the Soviet now sensed its weakness and vulnerability precisely when it was seeking to draw together all its resources and support to meet the approaching events. "The mood of Soviet members every day became more and more indecisive and sluggish," one deputy later observed. "Party quarrels and fractional disagreements began." The choice of a new leadership on November 27 produced a heated debate because the presidium elected

86. Zvezdin, "Poslednye dni Soveta (26 noiabria–3 dekabria)," pp. 174–76. Trotsky, *1905*, pp. 220–21. Dan, *The Origins of Bolshevism*, pp. 305–6.

to replace Nosar' consisted only of Menshevik Social Democrats—
Trotsky, P. A. Zlydnev (leader of the Obukhov workers), and D. F.
Sverchkov (a leader of office workers). The choice offended the SRs
and it violated the Soviet's principle of non-party leadership, but the
deputies nonetheless voted their approval of the new leaders.[87]

The crisis atmosphere also drew the Soviet closer to its allies and
produced one last creative response to the government. On December 2 the Soviet issued a "Financial Manifesto" jointly with the Peasants' Union, the Polish Socialist Party, the Socialist Revolutionaries,
and the Social Democrats. The document described an impending
government bankruptcy, the result of stagnating industry, a flight of
foreign capital, and the misuse of public funds; only a new government could save the country from financial ruin. "It is necessary to cut
the government off from the last source of its existence: financial
revenue. This is necessary not only for the country's political and economic liberation, but also, more particularly, in order to restore the
financial equilibrium of the state." The Manifesto called on the citizenry to refuse the government taxes and redemption payments, to
withdraw deposits from savings banks, and to demand wages in hard
currency. Given the Soviet's unwillingness to respond to growing government repression with a new strike, the Financial Manifesto was an
ingenious attempt to continue the struggle on terms not favorable to
the government. Besides linking together a variety of revolutionary
allies, it opened a new avenue of support that moderate urban groups
still sympathetic to the workers and the Soviet might easily enter; participation required only a small, individual, and completely legal effort,
the collective effect of which could, nevertheless, devastate the government. The financial boycott was all but lost sight of in the press of
events, but some 94 million rubles were withdrawn from savings
banks in December 1905, compared to a 4 million ruble surplus in deposits during the same month in 1904.[88]

The government was among those most aware of the potential danger of the Manifesto. On the same day it appeared, issues of the four
liberal and four socialist newspapers that printed it were seized and
their publication temporarily suspended. The action was also consistent with a harder line the government had been taking since the
latter part of November. Martial law had been declared in the city of
Kiev and in Lifland, Chernigov, and Penza provinces to cope with

87. *Vospominaniia Soveta*, pp. 46, 90. *1905: SRD*, p. 74. Zvezdin, "Poslednye dni Soveta," 172–73, 177–78.
88. Zvezdin, "Poslednye dni Soveta," pp. 183, 187–94. Trotsky, *1905*, pp. 225–27.
1905: SRD, pp. 80–82. *Izvestiia SRD*, no. 8 (n.d.), pp. 81–82.

peasant disorders. New press regulations issued on November 24 abolished preliminary discussion of "issues of state importance." The emergency powers of governors and other local officials were strengthened. On December 1, the Tsar received delegations from the Union of the Russian People and other extreme right-wing groups and blessed them with the title of "true sons of Russia." On December 2, a Senate *ukaz* outlawed strikes among railroad, telephone, and postal and telegraph workers, but it was written in such a way as to include all strikers within its provisions, which threatened violators with up to four years' imprisonment.[89]

On December 3 the government arrested the Soviet. A full session was planned for 7 P.M. in the building of the Free Economic Society, and the Executive Committee had gathered at 4. Toward the end of the Committee's meeting, word arrived that soldiers and police were coming to arrest the body. Deputies and a number of outsiders—the press, party agitators, petitioners, and guests—had already begun to gather in another chamber, but the Executive Committee decided not to disperse either its own or the larger session. Several members familiar with the Soviet's day-to-day business were asked to leave the meeting to avoid arrest, but before they were able to make their exit, the building was surrounded. Trotsky announced the impending arrests to the deputies, asking them to offer no resistance and not to give their names to the police. The Executive Committee then resumed its meeting, even delaying the arresting officers while it destroyed some papers and concluded its proceedings in an orderly manner. In all, 260 persons were seized, including 37 members of the Executive Committee.[90]

Workers responded to the Soviet's arrest by immediately electing new deputies, who, along with those that had escaped arrest, formed a "Second Soviet" under the leadership of Parvus (A. I. Helphand), Trotsky's political collaborator and author of the Financial Manifesto. The Second Soviet, which never had the same authority as the first, succeeded in holding one full meeting (on December 12) and five Executive Committee sessions before its leaders were arrested on January 2, 1906.[91]

The arrest of the Petersburg Soviet on December 3 provoked a new

89. Zvezdin, "Poslednye dni Soveta," pp. 194–95. Trotsky, *1905*, pp. 227–28. Obninskii, *Novyi stroi. Chast' pervaia. Manifesty 17 oktiabria 1905 g.–8 iiulia 1906 g.*, p. 56.

90. Zvezdin, "Poslednye dni Soveta," pp. 198–99. Obninskii, *Polgoda*, p. 102. Trotsky, *1905*, pp. 231–33. A list of arrestees appears in *1905: SRD*, pp. 136–53.

91. *1905: SRD*, pp. 85–95, 153–58. VPR, pp. 461–63. *Vospominaniia Soveta*, pp. 47, 83, 88, 107, 123.

nationwide political strike, beginning in Moscow on December 7, followed by Petersburg, Minsk, and Taganrog on the 8th, and by 29 other towns during the next week. The Moscow strike escalated into an armed insurrection of major proportions; smaller uprisings broke out in Nizhnii Novgorod, Kharkov, and Rostov; the Baltic provinces were gripped simultaneously by peasant violence and by urban strikes; and discontent among the soldiers of the demoralized Manchurian army produced insubordination and disorders in several Siberian towns. In many areas the events of the year reached their climax in December. But the strikes and uprisings were not coordinated, and they did not have the same impact as the October General Strike. Other areas seemed to have already passed the peak of their energies and commitment.[92]

Petersburg was such an area. At the Executive Committee session of December 3, a representative of the Social Democratic Federated Council had urged that the Soviet call a general strike at the earliest possible moment in response to the new strike law and the closing of the eight newspapers. The reaction to this proposal was mixed, reflecting an uneven mood in the city's factories and districts and political differences within the Executive Committee. Among the speakers reported in the minutes, opinions were about evenly divided: some supported the Social Democrats' proposal, one of the Bolsheviks among them adding that the strike should be linked to street demonstrations, and the Vasilevsky district deputy urged that it be turned toward an uprising. Others felt Petersburg should await the action of other workers such as the railroaders, whose congress was to meet on December 5. Trotsky wanted Petersburg's strike call to follow those of other towns. Still others, especially factory and district deputies, favored a longer or even an indefinite delay. The Vyborg district spokesman was ready to see the Soviet arrested rather than have it act prematurely. Finally, the SR and railroad representatives felt that the only appropriate response to the government's recent actions was to proceed from a strike to an armed uprising, but they found that the Soviet was not ready for an uprising any more than it was a week earlier when the deputies had warned themselves about not giving way to government provocation.[93]

The Executive Committee did not reach a decision before its arrest.

92. Keep, *The Rise of Social Democracy*, pp. 242–64. *Ocherki istorii SSSR. Pervaia russkaia burzhuazno-demokraticheskaia revoliutsiia 1905–1907 gg.*, pp. 183–214. Trotsky, *1905*, p. 235.

93. *1905: SRD*, pp. 82–85. Trotsky, *1905*, p. 235.

The disunity and apparent lack of strike enthusiasm in some of the factory districts would not have made for a resolute decision in any case. The extent to which the recommendations and reports of readiness were predicated on the assumption that the workers had to be prepared for more than a strike—whether that be street demonstrations or an uprising—is not clear from the abbreviated minutes of that last session. Certainly the Socialist Revolutionary speaker must have voiced an assumption shared by more of those present than his supporter from the railroad workers. The disappointment at not being prepared at this crucial moment for the "decisive struggle" that the Soviet had spoken of so frequently must have been overwhelming. The leaders were reduced to their last gambit. "We knew," wrote Sverchkov, "that our arrest would serve as the best public summons of the whole working class to insurrection."[94] No one can gainsay that it did, and the Soviet's leaders went to prison with a sense of self-sacrifice as well as with some disappointment. Only the insurrection took place in Moscow, not in the capital.

Petersburg workers began their strike on December 8 and it quickly peaked on the next day. The City Governor's office estimated that about 111,000 workers in 200 factories struck on December 9, while the Factory Inspectorate reported the same day some 92,000 on strike. These estimates are subject to the usual exceptions and qualifications, but less so than in October and November. Railroaders in the Petersburg area did not strike in the same numbers and with as great an effect as earlier, and there is little evidence that retail clerks struck at all. This was to a small degree offset by the participation of some of the newly unionized groups. But the continued operation of postal services (the postal-telegraph strike having just ended), most stores, and most railroad lines meant that the December strike was not as "general" as earlier strikes and did not have as great a political impact. Most of all, the mood of the strikers fell off more quickly than previously. Although nearly three-quarters of the strikers reported by the Factory Inspectorate were still on strike on Monday, December 12, only half of them were striking on the 14th. The full session of the Second Soviet on December 12 heard reports of waning strike enthusiasm, new lockouts, and back-to-work sentiment from almost all districts and unions, including the usually militant printers and workers of the Schlüsselburg district. Exhortations to support the Moscow insurgents and a resolution to "continue the strike and enter imme-

94. Sverchkov, *Na zare revoliutsii*, p. 162.

diately into *open struggle*" did not change the fundamental impressions that the Petersburg workers were losing the strike four days after it began.[95]

Attention in December was focused on events in Moscow, and the leading city of proletarian struggle in 1905 was not to be the scene of its closing events. Some historians have been quick to conclude that the fatigue of the most militant and active workers was by December far advanced.[96] More important was the exhaustion of political options. The government had initiated a major repression directed at the labor and revolutionary movements. State-owned factories had been among the first to threaten and initiate lockouts during and after the November strike; police and soldiers had been given a freer hand in factory districts; the liberal and revolutionary press had been attacked and subjected to new censorship regulations; and workers could now be imprisoned for striking. Since November 26 the leading organ of the Petersburg labor movement had been under open attack, and now its most militant leaders and deputies had been arrested. The Soviet's arrest not only removed important strike leaders, it deprived workers of a sense of continuity in their struggle and robbed them of an important element of their collective courage. If the Soviet could be arrested, what could happen to them? Now they were to move on to an uprising, but how could there be an uprising without the Soviet? Precisely those elements among the workers who were most convinced that the December strike should escalate to political action were the most downcast and discouraged by the situation facing them.

By December 17 the Moscow uprising was all but defeated, and only 19,000 workers remained on strike in Petersburg. Lockouts had been renewed and factory meetings banned. There was no chance of renewing the struggle in the near future, but the severity of the government's repression now also rolled back most of the gains made by labor and the opposition during the Days of Freedom. Revolutionaries and armed workers' squads were arrested or put to flight; union offices were searched, closed, and in some cases their leaders were arrested; newspapers and journals were seized and banned and their offices, printing facilities, and even some booksellers were raided and

95. *VPR*, pp. 465–77. Dorovatovskii and Zlotin, "Khronika," pp. 245–46. Push-kareva, *Zheleznodorozhniki*, pp. 205–6. Shuster, *Peterburgskie rabochie*, pp. 200–224. *1905: SRD*, pp. 87–89.

96. For example, Kol'tsov, "Rabochie v 1905–1907 gg.," p. 241. Shuster, *Peterburgskie rabochie*, p. 204.

closed. A similar crackdown took place in other towns, and military punitive expeditions with the right of summary execution were dispatched to the provinces and border areas, which they "pacified" with fire and sword.[97] The defeat of the December strikes and uprisings had brought the triumph of reaction.

97. Dorovatovskii and Zlotin, "Khronika," p. 247. Obninskii, *Polgoda*, pp. 102–8, 136–318. Ainzaft, *Pervyi etap*, pp. 57–58. Smolin, "Pervaia russkaia revoliutsiia v Peterburge," pp. 363–64. Maevskii, "Obshchaia kartina," pp. 174–76.

Conclusion

From the first citywide strike in 1896 to the arrest of the Soviet of Workers' Deputies in December 1905, the workers of Petersburg created a labor movement of unprecedented size, militancy, and self-conscious solidarity. Although this study has made the issue of worker autonomy a *leitmotif*, I have not tried to claim that the workers built a labor movement unaided. Indeed, workers found no inconsistency in the notion that they could aspire to the utmost autonomy and at the same time seek and accept outside help. From the very start their efforts were prompted and guided by revolutionary organizers, above all, by Social Democratic activists. Those tireless and dedicated men and women were at the side of the workers, literally or figuratively, in practically every major strike or demonstration from 1896 onward. Although the SDs cannot be said to have *led* the working class in this period (in the same sense that they did in 1917), they played the most important role of all the political parties in steering and shaping the newly radicalized workers.

The socialists were also influenced by the labor movement, whose mass mobilization in 1905 provided them with a real and full-scale object of contemplation and planning for the first time, rescuing them from the debilitating sectarian wrangling characteristic of their previous history and vindicating their years of sacrifice and effort. The revolutionary parties emerged from the 1905 Revolution with wider contacts among workers than ever before and with a firmer and more realistic grasp of their entire political project.

Yet, because most existing literature on the subject asserts or as-

sumes too direct and simple a relationship between the work of the
SDs and the labor upsurge of 1905, it has been important to stress
that the workers did not owe the advent of this militancy and the formation of their political views to the SDs alone (or even to all socialists
alone). The popularity of the Assembly of Russian Workers showed
that great masses of the capital's workers, independently of the socialists and even against their advice, accepted Gapon's organization
as the labor organization that many now understood they needed.
Most of the marchers and petitioners of January 9 had joined the Assembly after it took a stand in defense of the dismissed workers, and
this explains its popularity better than Gapon's personal magnetism,
which is more easily understood as an amplifying and dramatizing
factor in a more fundamental process of labor mobilization and political awakening.[1] The January strike in Petersburg gave way to a year-
long convulsion of strikes and demonstrations and an even more
extended period of labor revolt that lasted through 1907. These developments ended by bringing the labor movement much closer to
the organized revolutionary parties than ever before, but this certainly did not mean that the revolutionaries were in control of the labor movement or that their ascendency was ubiquitous, uncontested,
or inevitable. On the contrary, careful examination of the Petersburg
labor movement in 1904 and 1905 has shown that the political consciousness of Russian workers assumed a configuration more eclectic,
independent, and complex than that desired or assumed to exist by
the SDs. Workers seemed to accept or reject socialist advice less out
of loyalty or opposition to an ideology or leader than out of a perception that such advice conformed to or contradicted their own ideas
and aims.

Much less obvious than the enthusiasm for the Assembly or even
their mixed feelings toward the socialists was the workers' openness to
and solidarity with the liberal and democratic opposition, the groups
whose protests in late 1904 had provided the original example and
stimulus to the workers' independent political action. The directness,
publicness, and close proximity of the liberals' demonstrations seem
to have been particularly appealing to workers, since they cut through
the knot of legally sanctioned injustices that the workers felt so keenly.
To workers these early protests, accomplished by the most prominent
figures of educated society, certainly seemed more substantial and

1. For further details, see Surh, "Petersburg's First Mass Labor Organization,"
pp. 436–41.

influential than their own fledgling efforts. It is therefore not at all surprising that the public debut of the mass labor movement in Petersburg was staged in more or less open emulation of the zemstvo and intelligentsia demonstrations of the fall of 1904.

The Assembly experience in fact reawakened a previously dormant capacity among Petersburg workers for bold, open, and disarmingly selfless mass action and solidarity. Although both political and economic demands and strikes arose, it was often impossible to distinguish between them. As in previous years, the distinction was blurred by the implicitly political thrust of all factory confrontations under the restrictive conditions of Tsarist legality. But in 1905 another element was added—an anger, indignation, and thirst for moral rectification that put a political glow into practically every strike or work action. Few strikers seemed to believe that higher wages or a shorter workday would make up for the indignities and injustices they suffered; most seemed to feel that the moment for total redress was at hand. Those workers who did make significant "economic" gains such as the *putilovtsy* before the summer lockout, did not stop striking or expanding their demands. Petersburg workers repeatedly threw aside their "rational" self-interest in favor of sweeping gestures of solidarity such as striking to protect a small number of threatened workers in their own factory or striking in sympathy with a strike in a neighboring factory. In 1905 workers often seemed to be bearing moral witness to their sufferings more than organizing goal-directed strategies to win specific demands.

In keeping with this attitude, and despite the early display of labor unity in the January 9 petition march, the workers' political views were much more heterogeneous and inchoate than they seemed at first. In order to find their political bearings after the demise of the Assembly, Petersburg workers turned to more familiar models and leaders. Some looked to the revolutionary parties, but most were apparently still not prepared to tread so separate and specific a political path, at least at first, though various degrees of respect and admiration for the socialists were common among them. Instead, the first instinct of most workers seems to have been to form an independent labor movement, accepting the aid of socialists and liberals alike, and to join their protest efforts to those of the apparently united political opposition. A clear distinction between strategies of reform and strategies of revolution was not yet a significant factor in their thinking.

In the course of the year, these attitudes and feelings became reshaped to a degree. On the one hand, the apparent unity of the opposition began to evaporate by the fall; as the liberals resolved themselves into separate and more carefully defined factions, the number of them open to alliance with the labor movement and the revolutionary parties diminished considerably. On the other hand, the Petersburg Soviet drew workers into a closer relationship with the revolutionary parties in a manner that seemed to combine autonomy and respect with close assistance. Intelligentsia leaders from the socialist parties came to exercise day-to-day control of the Soviet through their ascendancy in its Executive Committee, yet the Soviet's ardent commitment to the radically democratic role the deputies assumed in the Soviet and in their factories gave them considerable control over the party leaders and over the Soviet's policies. At the same time, the vagueness and generality of the Soviet's political program made it more of an offshoot of the multiclass democratic opposition than the instrument of a single political party, as some of the socialists wanted to regard it. In this light, the important questions may have been not why the Soviet's deputies failed to lead an armed uprising but whether they had ever abandoned the hope and desire for a unified oppositional movement, and how solid and permanent their alliance with the revolutionary parties was at the end of 1905.

The workers' greater willingness by the fall to follow socialist leaders, both in the Soviet and out of it, may indicate that they had overcome some of their distrust not only of socialists, but also of intellectuals or students, from whom most of the socialist organizers and agitators were drawn. This may have meant that by the fall they were correspondingly more open to closer relations with the liberal and democratic intelligentsia as well. On the other hand, their greater openness to the socialists may have implied that they had come to share the latter's animus toward the liberal and democratic movements. Perhaps they even began to distinguish between liberals and democrats. Unfortunately, it is not possible to engage in more than informed speculation, but the changes in these relations were almost certainly subtle and mixed; they were also possibly quite transient.

The workers' adherence to the broad democratic opposition had a rough ideological counterpart in their passionate affirmation of autonomy, *glasnost'*, and democratic form in their own undertakings. The Soviet of Workers' Deputies was the clearest illustration of this commitment to grass-roots control, open and democratically regulated meetings, and party neutrality. The strong and loyal support of the Soviet in the factories suggests that an internalization or at least an implantation of this new democratic "culture" had taken place among

Petersburg workers by the fall of 1905. The liberals' activity in 1904 appears to have precipitated a parallel civic enthusiasm and initiative among workers, drawing out of them an interest in broad democratic values that stemmed from the experience of their own earlier strikes and protests and from the encouragement some of them had received from clandestine socialist groups to engage in open political struggle. For years the socialists had worked to persuade workers to strike, to celebrate the May Day holiday with strikes and public demonstrations, and to join the public protests of students and intelligentsia. It is a small irony of labor politics in this period that when the moment of political blossoming finally arrived in 1905, this stress on the openness of political life probably led workers to view the liberals, who made a principle of the publicness of politics, with greater sympathy than the still-clandestine socialists. The first large-scale affirmation of an in-cipient democratic political culture appeared in the worker petitions to the Shidlovskii Commission and in the ensuing campaign. A similar preoccupation with the right to meet publicly, to debate issues, and to elect representatives continued to animate the workers' strikes and demonstrations throughout the year, becoming intertwined with the material needs and demands they fought for.

One of the key links between these civic and political concerns and the struggle over factory grievances was the issue of workers' depu-ties. The idea of elected deputies arose originally from the struggle between workers and their employers, and it appeared again among the workers' demands of January 1905, in which such deputies were viewed as joint regulators with management of production and labor supply. In February the idea of workers' representatives before man-agement was combined with that of representatives before the gov-ernment, which increased the authority and strengthened the political function of deputies.

The institution of elected deputies in 1905 received its most fre-quent and extensive development at the large metalworking plants, which were also the sites of the most pronounced "factory patriotism" and contained the largest contingents of revolutionary workers or circle participants. The giant machine-building plants, shipyards, and armaments works of the capital witnessed the largest and most fre-quent mass meetings, and they elected the lion's share of Soviet depu-ties. The metalworkers made up the Soviet's most loyal and energetic supporters. It was as if the skilled metalworkers' pride in the control of their work had been translated into pride in the control of their deputies and of their political circumstances generally. All these characteristics made metalworkers the vanguard of the Petersburg (and Russian) labor movement. The same qualities probably contributed to their swing to Bolshevism, in Petersburg and elsewhere, in later years.[2] But throughout most of 1905 they nurtured a political outlook that viewed the labor movement as one part of the broad anti-autocratic coalition. The aims of the strike movement were apparently still felt by most workers to be compatible with those of the intelligentsia and zemstvo opposition, even though a number of workers were now learning that this was not necessarily the case. Although it is not clear exactly when large numbers of workers began to question this assumption, their disillusionment may have begun with the decisions of the *zemtsy* and a large portion of the intelligentsia to participate in the Bulygin Duma or in the State Duma. Flagging liberal support for the labor movement in November, including even open disapproval of the November strike, added to the workers' growing sense of isolation from, even "desertion" by, educated society.[3]

In political terms, 1905 witnessed the failure of the liberal-democratic opposition to win, or for the most part even seriously to bid for, the support of the labor movement. The socialists' cultivation of worker support was not seriously challenged. From their rise to prominence in late 1904 onward, the right and center of the liberal coalition, aided by such unity-conscious pragmatists as Miliukov, failed to seek a popular following by organizational means. Instead, they apparently counted on winning a popular electoral following, based on their political program and on a sense of their eminence and entitlement to lead the nation. Neither the Bulygin Duma nor the State Duma gave very much importance to workers as a voting bloc, so the calculation of short-term advantage reinforced rather than contra-

2. Haimson, "The Problem of Social Stability," pt. 1; Hogan, "Labor and Management," chap. 11; Smith, *Red Petrograd*.

3. I have found only indirect evidence of this change of attitude. For instance, in his speech to the Soviet arguing for an end to the November strike, Trotsky reminded the deputies that "in decisive action we must count only on ourselves. The liberal bourgeoisie is already beginning to treat us with distrust and even hostility. The democratic intelligentsia is vacillating." Nosar', "Istoriia Soveta," p. 124, or Trotsky, *1905*, p. 173. The failure of Petersburg workers and their electors to vote for kadet candidates during the elections to the First Duma is another indirect indication that workers turned away from the liberals after the fall (although the workers' curias of Moscow, Kostroma, and Vladimir provinces did elect Kadets). Moreover, among all the workers' curias, the rate of nonparticipation in First Duma elections was highest among Petersburg's eligible factories (54 percent), suggesting a high rate of loyalty to the boycott tactic initiated by the revolutionary parties. Emmons, *The Formation of Political Parties*, pp. 290–91 (note that figures printed there contain an error).

dicted the inability and unwillingness of liberals of the Kadet persuasion to make a special effort to bring labor into their political fold.

This was perhaps a sound calculation, for even those socialists and left liberals of the Union of Unions who did make an effort to reach workers—because they lacked firm organizational backing—proved unable to form lasting or effective political ties. Due principally to their illegality during most of 1905, unions of factory and artisanal workers were slow to form and difficult to sustain, and most of those that did organize resisted joining the coalition of political and professional unions. Individual organizing initiatives undertaken by Liberationists such as Prokopovich, Nosar', and Margulies met with enough success to indicate that a larger and more concerted effort might have won considerable numbers of workers to a left reform party such as the Kadets. But the liberals lacked the personnel for such an effort—a student following in particular. The Union of Unions accomplished a great deal in organizing the ranks of the professional and politically unaffiliated intelligentsia, but this promising formation was unable to merge with the movement of factory and other industrial workers.

Hence the broad and inclusive political alliance suggested by the preferences of the majority of workers and their deputies in 1905 was not to be. In any event, the free and open conditions on which it might have been built and sustained were swept away by a resurgent autocracy in a matter of days in December. In the years that followed, the prospect of a unified antigovernment alliance became even more remote than it was at the end of 1905. Petersburg's workers were never again presented with the possibility of even a loose coalition of liberals, democrats, and socialists, since the liberals moved increasingly rightward and the socialists continued to be dominated by opponents of collaboration with "bourgeois" parties.

By reducing further the already small worker representation in the Dumas and by supplementing its meager labor legislation with large doses of repression, the government itself remained the chief obstacle to open and democratic labor politics. The small legal labor movement permitted after 1905 mocked rather than recreated the autonomy and sense of liberation first felt in 1905, and that experience was henceforth recaptured only in conditions of illegality, during strikes and disorders. Partly as a result of this narrower field of choice, the workers' political fate became increasingly linked with that of the clandestine revolutionary parties, and the memory of the radical democracy so enthusiastically nurtured and practiced in 1905 eventually became fused with the older tradition of intelligentsia socialism. The now politically aroused working class apparently experienced the slightly more relaxed conditions of the Duma period as *more* confining and intolerable than earlier conditions, and, still unreconciled to the autocracy, workers became increasingly willing to contest their position from the viewpoint of organized socialism.

The exigencies of war and revolution later distorted the memory of the actual alignment of preferences and priorities among workers in 1905, and since the direct democracy of the first Soviet was not expedient to the consolidation of Bolshevik state power, it was the name and not the substance that was incorporated into the new state. The ideal of the Soviet may therefore be thought of as utopian in that the conditions in which it arose were unsuited to its realization. Nevertheless, utopias inspire and uplift social movements, as this one certainly did. It is well worth recalling that the ideal of worker self-rule achieved one of its first and finest incarnations among the workers of St. Petersburg.

Reference Matter

The Industrial Crisis and
St. Petersburg Labor

————————— •••• —————————

Although the causes and general economic effects of the industrial crisis of 1899–1904 have been closely analyzed, its effect on the labor movement, presumed to have been profound, has not been differentiated by industry or geographical area or very extensively studied at all.[1] Soviet historians have treated the crisis as a decisive step in the country's transition from the capitalist stage of development to the imperialist, monopoly-capitalist stage, and even as the opening of the revolutionary era that brought the downfall of autocracy and capitalism.[2] Yet even the labor historians have dwelt more on the changes that the crisis produced in machine technology, in the degree of concentration and monopolization, and in the linkages between industrial and banking capital than on its immediate effects upon the working class.[3] Yet 3,000 firms closed from 1900 to 1903, and 90,000 workers were idled in the Ukrainian iron and steel industry alone. The effect of the crisis on different industries varied a great deal. It was felt first in textile manufacturing and later, but more heavily, in the metal industry. It affected the everyday life of working Russia,

1. V. Mukoseev, "Promyshlennyi pod"em ili promyshlennyi krizis," *Obrazovanie* (1907), nos. 8 (pp. 25–48), 9 (pp. 44–73), 10 (pp. 1–23). A. Piletskii, "Ekonomicheskii krizis i ego okonchanie," *Obrazovanie*, no. 4 (1906), otd. II, pp. 29–53. Balabanov, "Promyshlennost' v Rossii v nachale XX veka." Khromov, *Ekonomicheskoe razvitie Rossii v XIX–XX vekakh, 1800–1917*, pp. 307–13.

2. S. I. Potolov, "Proletariat Peterburga na rubezhe XIX–XX vv.," in *Istoriia rabochikh Leningrada*, p. 231. A. M. Solov'eva in *Rabochii klass Rossii. Ot zarozhdeniia do nachala XX v.*, ed. M. S. Volin, Iu. I. Kir'ianov, et al. (M., 1983), p. 180. A. P. Korelin in Bovykin et al., eds., *Rabochii klass v pervoi rossiiskoi revoliutsii 1905–1907 gg.*, p. 31.

3. For example, see Bovykin et al., eds., *Rabochii klass*, p. 383, n. 26.

APPENDIX TABLE 1

Production in Key Industries, 1896–1904

(millions of rubles; cotton and sugar in ooo tons)

Ind.	1896	1897	1898	1899	1900	1901	1902	1903	1904
Fu	66.7	79.3	103.6	146.8	178.0	133.3	117.6	126.0	175.9
FM	118.0	139.3	164.9	178.0	218.8	188.8	161.5	148.5	173.2
AP	69.2	76.3	72.0	67.8	63.6	76.6	73.7	74.9	67.3
Si	22.1	25.8	26.7	27.3	27.7	24.9	24.9	27.9	26.5
MW	228.7	268.6	313.4	307.6	297.0	337.2	313.3	339.0	354.0
LH	49.7	55.5	55.0	54.2	53.4	63.5	60.4	58.6	60.0
Gl	51.9	60.8	61.1	61.2	61.0	77.0	74.9	77.5	73.0
Wo	90.2	91.0	91.6	94.8	92.3	105.7	108.9	112.5	133.9
Ct	153.0	152.3	157.5	179.5	187.5	183.7	194.6	198.9	209.7
Su	564.5	534.3	544.5	562.7	673.4	661.5	758.1	893.1	903.3
WW	63.8	70.8	72.2	73.8	73.8	79.6	78.7	87.8	85.9
CD	37.1	39.1	39.1	38.9	40.4	50.3	54.5	52.9	52.4
Pa	32.6	33.6	35.9	38.1	40.4	41.6	42.7	43.8	45.0
Rubles total	830.0	940.1	1,035.5	1,088.5	1,146.4	1,178.5	1,111.1	1,149.4	1,247.1

Key: Fu = fuel; FM = ferrous metallurgy; AP = animal products; Si = silk; MW = metalworking; LH = linen, hemp, jute; Gl = glass; Wo = woolens; Ct = cotton; Su = sugar; WW = woodworking; CD = basic chemicals and dyes; Pa = paper.
SOURCE: S. G. Strumilin, *Ocherki ekonomicheskoi istorii Rossii i SSSR* (M., 1966), p. 449. Attributed to [V. E.] Varzar and [L. B.] Kafengauz, [no title, but probably] *Svod statisticheskikh dannykh po fabrichno-zavodskoi promyshlennosti s 1887 po 1926 g.* (M.-L., 1929–30).

and it left bankruptcies, unemployment, and even death by starvation in its wake.[4]

However, it appears that St. Petersburg escaped its worst effects. Its dominant industries—cotton textiles, metalworking, and chemicals— were not the hardest hit. Instead, it was fuel production and the ferrous metal industry (iron and steel manufacture) that took the brunt of the downturn, not machine building and hot metalworking, Petersburg's specialties.[5] (See Appendix Table 1.) The Petersburg metal industry was also helped by the fact that it was so largely based on production at state plants or private ones working under government contracts, mainly for weapons and railroad equipment. This linkage

4. Martov, *Razvitie krupnoi promyshlennosti i rabochee dvizhenie v Rossii*, pp. 175–99. Tugan–Baranovskii, *Russkaia fabrika*, pp. 275–78. Portal, "The Industrialization of Russia," p. 844. Von Laue, *Sergei Witte and the Industrialization of Russia*, p. 213. Strumilin, "Promyshlennye krizisy v Rossii (1847–1907)," pp. 446–50. Iakovlev, *Ekonomicheskie krizisy*, pp. 250–308 (see especially the table on p. 449).

5. Livshits, *Razmeshchenie promyshlennosti v dorevoliutsionnoi Rossii*, pp. 204–6, 245–47. Petersburg accounted for most of the 33.6 percent of Russian machine building attributed to the Northwest Region. *Ibid.*, p. 205, n.

cushioned the capital's machine builders and their workers from the shocks of the market. Orders for rails and rolling stock alone may have delayed the effects of the crisis on the whole industry for a year or more: in 1902 Petersburg produced more locomotives than it had in an average year in the 1890's, the decade of Russia's railroad boom. Then by 1904, increased weapons contracts flowing from the needs of the war with Japan helped the metal industry make an earlier recovery than most other industries. Metalworkers in Petersburg therefore benefited more from government contracts and as a result suffered less from the industrial crisis than their counterparts in other areas.[6]

Data from 17 large metalworking enterprises in Petersburg for 1901 and 1904 show an increase in both wages and factory size over the three years that was *greater*, on a yearly average, than the increase from 1891 to 1901. The number of workers in the 17 plants rose from 22,000 in 1891 to 47,000 in 1901 to 56,000 in 1904; average annual wages increased from 359 to 431 to 471 rubles and included all categories of workers.[7] These averages, because they include the recovery year of 1904, may conceal downturns in the intervening years. For instance, the Putilov Works (12,300 workers in 1901) cut back its work force by 23 percent in 1902, and the same year production declined 45 percent compared to 1899–1900.[8] Still, strike activity among metalworkers of the capital remained at a low ebb despite the explosion of vast strike movements in south Russia in 1903 and strikes by over 14,000 Petersburg textile workers the same year. In fact, the city's metalworkers did not strike again until 1905.

On balance, then, it appears that the crisis, though a major contributory cause of labor militancy in some areas, cannot be said to have had this effect in St. Petersburg.[9] In the absence of detailed

6. Strumilin, "Promyshlennye krizisy," p. 450. Portal, "Industrialization," p. 831. Bulkin, *Na zare profdvizheniia*, pp. 25, 30–31. Hogan stresses the different growth rates and results of the crisis on different sectors within the Petersburg metal industry, but points out that back orders for rolling stock kept engine and freight car manufacturers occupied until 1907: "Labor and Management," p. 104.

7. Bulkin, *Na zare profdvizheniia*, table facing p. 52.

8. Iakovlev, *Ekonomicheskie krizisy*, p. 272.

9. A. M. Pankratova has made an intriguingly consistent argument for a direct connection between the 1899–1904 crisis and the 1905 Revolution by stressing the role of the southern strikes. The Ukrainian ferrous metal industry, including coal and iron ore mining, and the Baku oil drilling and processing operations were among the most heavily hit by the crisis, and this contributed to a number of large strikes over a wide area in the years from 1902 through 1904. But to argue, as Pankratova does (albeit with some qualifications), that the 1905 Revolution *began* in Rostov and Baku rather than in

knowledge of changes in earnings and working conditions over this relatively short period, we can only conclude that the impact of the crisis on Petersburg workers was tempered by the lingering momentum of the 1890's boom. While the explosion of labor militancy in 1905 probably owed something to the stored-up resentment at setbacks suffered in the previous half-decade, it was also due to other kinds of causes, as should be quite clear from the account of it given in this work.

Petersburg and Moscow requires a more careful and thorough reassessment of a much wider network of events than she undertakes, although she certainly succeeds in highlighting the importance of the events in the south: "Rabochii klass i rabochee dvizhenie nakanune revoliutsii 1905 goda," pp. 449–51, 466–72, 490–504.

The Petersburg Printers

The printing workers of the capital were exceptional in several respects. Their culture, organization, and strike dynamics were different from those found among the workers in the two major industries of Petersburg, metalworking and textiles, and yet they were also atypical of the group they most closely resembled, highly urbanized craft workers in small shops. "Printers" were actually a congeries of several separate trades and skill levels, including compositors (or typesetters, *naborshchiki*), press workers of various types and skill levels, lithographers, bookbinders, letter founders, zincographers, and stereotypers, each of these involving further gradation and types of skills. They worked predominantly in small and medium shops all over the city, although half of them were located in Kazan, Spassk, and Moscow districts. In 1900 the city census reported 15,387 printing workers in Petersburg, representing somewhat more than twice the number recorded in 1881; by 1905 one estimate put the number of printers at 16,000–17,000.[1] While this made for a growth rate somewhat greater than that of the city as a whole during the quarter century before 1905, in absolute numbers of workers, printers ranked in

1. Once again, in this study's usage, "small" means fewer than 100 workers. The Factory Inspectorate's figure of 71 for the average size of a printing establishment would in actuality be somewhat lower due to the Inspectorate's omission of shops with fewer than 16 workers. The work *Istoriia Leningradskogo soiuza rabochikh poligraficheskogo proizvodstva. Kniga pervaia, 1904–1907. Kollektivnyi trud*, written by some of the printers' leaders in 1905, is the source for most of the information given here. A thoroughgoing account of the culture and structure of the printing industry prior to 1905 may be found in Steinberg, "Consciousness and Conflict."

the middle range of the city's industries (see Chapter 1, Table 3). Moreover, the expansion did not for the most part affect the size of existing shops, but was accounted for by the establishment of new ones.

As in metal shops, printing establishments consisted of a wide and steeply graded range of skills. Monthly wages ranged from 12 to 80 rubles. At the top of the scale were compositors (*naborshchiki*), "the most literate, developed, discontented, and sometimes even reckless element in printing institutions." They made up about a third of all printing workers and predominated in many print shops. Compositors had more control over their work than other printers, coming and going more or less as they pleased, and they enjoyed more respect from workers and management alike, all of whom addressed them as "*Vy*" and "*Gospodin*" (the formal "you" and "Mister"). Many compositors stemmed from classes considered "better" than the proletariat, but it was their high salaries and literacy, the respect accorded them, and their relative independence from management that gave them a pronounced sense of superiority to other printers and, indeed, to most other workers.[2]

Naturally, some varieties of typesetting work paid better than others so that compositors were themselves economically stratified. But cutting across economic distinctions among compositors was a social and psychological type whose values revealed something about the class character of Russian typographical work as a whole. He was called an "aristocrat" (*aristokrat*) and has been described as always well-dressed, wearing starched collars and working in his own overalls; as sporting artfully coiffured hair and riding a bicycle to work in the summer; as frequenting theaters and balls, visiting the races, sporting events, and clubs; and as "generally maintaining a 'high tone.'"[3] It seems clear that at least one part of the compositors in St. Petersburg used their superior status among printers as a warrant for claiming membership in polite society, integrating thereby the upper ranks of the printing trades with the middle classes. But a variety of values and personal styles prevailed among the capital's compositors as well, and it was their high degree of individuation that requires emphasis rather than their orientation toward or away from the working class. Newspaper setters, for instance, were the best paid of the group, but their work-

2. *ILSRPP*, pp. 11, 13. It may even be said without exaggeration that the compositors felt themselves to be a labor elite, a trait apparently common to the trade wherever it has been practiced. Lipset, Trow, and Coleman, *Union Democracy* (cited in Chap. 6, n. 40), p. 27.

3. *ILSRPP*, pp. 14–15.

ing conditions were also very oppressive. Together with their constant awareness of social and political developments from reading the copy they set, their own working conditions made them more sharply sensitive to society's "burning questions" and more active in proposing solutions than any other section of printers; not surprisingly, they became the pacesetters for the political awakening of printers in 1905. At the same time, compositors could be footloose, changing jobs frequently or simply leaving the city for another locale or on extended vacations. Some joined acting companies and lived the bohemian life, although they usually returned to Petersburg in the fall.[4]

Other categories of printers shared two things with compositors: work in small shops and groups, and elaborate internal stratification by skill level and wage. Printshop workers, aside from compositors, consisted of masters and journeymen printers, pressmen, inkers, examiners, and several other specialties, and their wages ranged from about 12 to 60 rubles per month. Bookbinders were divided into 16 different specialties, earning from 15 to 50 rubles. Letter founders consisted of founders, engravers, justifiers, finishers, and five types of assistants, and they were paid 20 to 50 rubles. The smaller numbers of zincographers and stereotypers were similarly stratified and remunerated. Some of these craftsmen and assistants worked in larger shops, combining several stages or processes of the business; others worked in separate shops devoted to their specialty.

This segmentation and particularism of shop, specialty, and wage level was compounded by a spirit of exclusiveness, probably drawn from the example of the compositors, but true of every trade and specialization. Skilled workers avoided the unskilled, educated the uneducated, sober printers the drinkers, Germans the Russians, and city dwellers the rural types. This exclusiveness was most pronounced among compositors, who maintained a kind of sectarianism of specialty. The compositors of particular newspapers, whose work demanded close mutual reliance and interdependence, long hours, and few days off, developed a tight corporate spirit, which was furthered by their higher pay and more developed social conciousness. Table setters (*tablichniki*) habitually worked in closed associations or "companies" (*kompanii*), which functioned like producers' artels, receiving a collective wage and dividing it among the members according to the numbers of hours worked, levying their own fines for absenteeism, and dismissing undesirable members. By closing their ranks to out-

4. *Ibid.*, pp. 18–19, 33–34.

siders, the companies applied the strategy common to most craft workers of keeping their labor scarce and therefore their wages high— an arrangement apparently accepted by the majority of the shops. With their elected *starosty*, self-government, and protective exclusivity, the table setters' companies were probably the closest thing to trade unionism practiced by any group of printers or workers prior to 1905, although the newspaper setters also maintained a high degree of self-rule and independence.[5]

The exclusivity of printers probably contributed to slowing their combination as a trade group, although the illegality of unions before 1905 was, of course, the primary barrier. Still, printers were one of the earliest professions to form legal mutual-aid funds (*kassy vzaimopomoshchi*) and were their steadiest and most enthusiastic participants down to 1905. Around 1900, some 4,000–5,000 Petersburg printers, or about a fifth of the work force, participated in such funds.[6] However, these funds apparently did not overcome the exclusiveness prevailing among printers or contribute much to the formation of a class solidarity that could have counterposed itself to owners and managers. On the contrary, the small shop structure of a great part of the printing trades produced the illusion of a mutuality of interests between workers and owners, since the latter often worked with, swore at, and even drank with their employees. Many owners had friends and contemporaries among their workers and felt close to their interests, and they often even participated in mutual-aid funds or contributed to them.[7] The paternalism of the printshops had a strong admixture of fraternalism.

This paternalism was reflected in the political development of Petersburg printers. For most of their history, owners and workers

5. *Ibid.*, pp. 43–47, 18, 28–32.

6. Severianin, "Soiuz rabochikh pechatnogo dela," p. 53, assumes a greater number of printers to have been in the capital than the figure given above. *ILSRPP*, pp. 87–88, plays down the role of the funds in drawing together significant numbers of workers and providing an early example of solidarity around trade-union issues. For a more positive view, see Prokopovich, *K rabochemu voprosu v Rossii*, pp. 1–44. Ainzaft, "Byli li kassy vzaimopomoshchi odnim iz istokov rossiiskogo professional'nogo dvizheniia?," gives a summary and critique of the lively polemical literature of the period addressed to the question posed in the title of his article. He found that among the variety of organizations described by the term "mutual-aid funds," those of printers and shop clerks were better qualified to be considered sources of later unions because they displayed a consistently voluntary character and a greater degree of self-government. Ainzaft, "Byli," p. 84.

7. *ILSRPP*, pp. 34–35.

alike gave credence to the notion that the printing trades were a seamless profession, without class divisions. The All-Russian Congress of Printers (*Deiateli Pechatnogo Dela*), which met in March 1895, was a case in point. Although the Congress was organized by owners and the Imperial Russian Technical Society, and although very few of the 300 participants were workers, it passed resolutions favoring the abolition of Sunday work, better training of apprentices, and state medical insurance, calling the latter "an important and pressing matter." Although the resolutions had very few results, worker leaders from among the printers also hewed to a nonantagonistic approach. Printers had published a number of journals addressed to workers before 1905, but the first to win a large readership was *The Compositor* (*Naborshchik*), which first appeared in 1902. Although two-thirds of every issue was devoted to airing the problems and complaints of printing workers, the journal's editorial line favored cooperation with the owners in worker-management relations. Of course, a legal publication in Tsarist Russia such as *Naborshchik* could hardly have preached antagonism toward management openly, and the journal undoubtedly did help to mobilize printers' social consciousness during the years of growing unrest before 1905. In fact, however, there seems to have been no more revolutionary activity among printers than there was among most other factory or artisanal workers—that is to say, very little, when the number of workers in Petersburg is taken into account. The revolutionary parties concentrated their efforts at larger establishments and, notwithstanding the existence of a half-dozen or so circles of revolutionary printers in the city, political hegemony in the industry as a whole appears to have been held by moderates.[8]

Not that the fuel for more militant politics was absent. With the exception of some typographies, large parts of all shops consisted of workers paid subsistence wages or less. Even among compositors, conditions of work were far from ideal. Most book setters earned considerably less than the other categories, and many of them worked under labor contractors (*pauki*, literally, spiders) who paid their crews 2 to 4 kopecks less per 1,000 letters than they received. All compositors normally worked longer hours at the same rate when managers ordered it, even newspaper setters, most of whom also normally worked Sundays, nights, and holidays during rushes. Nor did all compositors lead the life of *aristokraty*, whose upwardly directed social values were counterbalanced by the downcast life-style of another type of

8. *Ibid.*, pp. 17, 78, 81–83, 99–100. Severianin, "Soiuz," p. 53.

naborshchik, the "Italians" (*ital'iantsy*). These often skilled and capable workers had no regular place of residence, but slept in the printshops, in flophouses, or in the open. They were drinkers and *byvshie liudi* ("ex-people," has-beens). The owners exploited their condition, which was due in some cases to mental or emotional unbalance, by underpaying them and allowing them to drink in the shop, to sleep there, and to work the hours they desired. Such exploitation was particularly prevalent in very small shops, known as "commodes" and "traps" (*komody, lovushki*). The smaller *kompanii*, when in need of extra hands, also hired them at lower rates than members received.[9]

The rapid turnover, frequently lowered wage rates, labor-contracting arrangements, and alleged social pathology among printers resulted in part from the surplus of printers in the capital and the apparently increasing use by owners of half-trained workers (*nedouchki*) and apprentices in place of fully trained and highly paid personnel. Printing was one of the few trades that showed an increase in the use of child labor from 1881 to 1900. A discussion of measures to regulate wage rates among printers began in 1884 and was mentioned at the printers' congress in 1895, but it seems to have gathered steam only after 1902, when bolder expressions of discontent were being heard throughout society; a 1903 strike of Moscow printers set a militant example. Under the impact of the political springtime in 1904, and undoubtedly encouraged by a successful strike among Petersburg letter founders, compositors began drafting a new wage rates proposal.[10]

Nevertheless, the strike of January 1905 had found printers divided. Compositors had by and large boycotted the Assembly, counting instead on obtaining improvements within the confines of the profession. Their social and cultural sophistication meant they would probably have been familiar with the intelligentsia's condemnation of the "police union"; and this, rather than explicit political disagreements, precluded association with the more naive and less developed type of worker that swelled the Assembly's meetings. A few compositors did attend the tumultuous meetings of January, and one of them even read the wage rates proposal at a January 8 meeting of one of the locals, but on the whole they resisted and remained alien to the spirit of mass recruitment and enthusiasm fostered by the Assembly.

9. *ILSRPP*, pp. 15–16, 24–31. *Pechatnyi vestnik*, no. 4 (July 24, 1905), pp. 4–5. For a vivid description of the seamier side of the trade, see the memoirs of the Petersburg printer Bol'shakov in TsGAOR, fond 6864, d. 60, ll. 1–9.

10. *ILSRPP*, pp. 46, 102–4.

To be sure, some printing workers responded to the appeals of striking factory workers, when the latter called them out on January 7.

> But the compositors felt somewhat discouraged when the factory workers who came to the printshops to shut them down (*snimat' s raboty*) could not explain right off the whole point of the strike, but directed [the printers] to the appropriate section of the Gaponist Assembly; "Everything will be explained there tomorrow." "What do we have in common with the Gaponist section?" the compositors asked. "We don't have representatives there."[11]

The compositors' leadership of the printing trades was being put to the test, and their narrow craft pride and exclusiveness did not prevail in all the cases. In addition, some of those printers in allied trades, such as bookbinders, lithographers, and pressmen, did take part in the Assembly. Indeed, several of Gapon's Social Democratic lieutenants, most notably Karelin, Usanov, and Kharitonov, were from the printing trades. Not surprisingly, some compositors felt their self-assurance shaken: "There's a general strike in Petersburg, we're being shut down, but where are our typographical organizations? Why do they know nothing and do not participate in the movement? Why have we, who for a number of years have had several of our own institutions, our own journal, turned up in the rear of the movement?"[12]

So printers did take part in the January strike, albeit reluctantly in some cases and not, for the most part, by rallying to the Assembly or Gapon. Indeed, the orientation away from the Assembly of many printers, especially their compositor leaders, makes this group's participation in the strike one of the best illustrations available of the infectious force of the January events as a social and political movement quite aside from the Gapon enthusiasm. Nevertheless, printer participation was far from complete.

The City File lists 93 printshops, binderies, letter foundries, and lithographies that struck in 1905.[13] Of these, 55 were located in the central districts of Admiralty, Kazan, Kolomensk, Liteiny, and Spassk, and 38 were located in the seven other districts (none was listed for the suburbs). In January, only 20 of the centrally located printing trades shops, or 36 percent, struck; in the outer districts, by contrast, striking

11. *Ibid.*, pp. 33, 103, 106.
12. *Ibid.*, p. 106.
13. This figure represents 69 percent of the typographies and lithographies listed by the Factory Inspectorate in Petersburg province, a very high participation rate. *Statistika neschastnykh sluchaev . . . za 1904*, pp. 16–21.

shops numbered 24, or 68 percent. Thus a substantially greater proportion of the shops in the outer districts, which were on the whole larger, were swept along by the January events, and this would seem to be in keeping with the weaker participation of the central districts generally in the January strike and the stronger strike sentiment generated in the peripheral districts by workers from the larger firms in, above all, metalworking and textiles.

By February, when they struck against the wage rates settlement imposed on them, the printing workers began to behave more like the factory work force. They were also accorded representation on the Shidlovskii Commission, and the 45 electors they chose, as in other trades, helped to define a set of leaders in the shops of the trade, balancing the citywide and industrywide focus of the wage rate representatives with the flexibility and hands-on concreteness of shop-floor leaders. The printers proved to be quick studies of the labor revolt rising around them, and in their further organizing, strikes, and protests they were able to combine the inspiration and lessons of their artisanal past with those of the militant factory tradition. This was an advantage no other Petersburg workers from the craft tradition enjoyed, and it certainly helps explain the much greater success of the printers at union organizing in 1905.

Bibliography

———————◆•◆•◆———————

Below I list the abbreviations used in the footnotes with the corresponding forms under which full citations can be found in the pages that follow. The Bibliography proper is divided into two sections, the first listing archival sources, and the second published sources in both Russian and Western languages together. At the end I append a list of newspapers and journals.

ILSRPP
> *Istoriia Leningradskogo soiuza rabochikh poligraficheskogo proizvodstva*

Izvestiia SRD
> *Izvestiia Soveta Rabochikh Deputatov. S.-Peterburg, 17-go oktiabria—14-go dekabria 1905 goda*

KL
> *Krasnaia letopis'*

LGIA
> *Leningradskii Gosudarstvennyi Istoricheskii Arkhiv*

NPRR
> *Nachalo pervoi russkoi revoliutsii*

ODR
> *Obshchestvennoe dvizhenie v Rossii v nachale XX-go veka*

Peterburg, 1881
> *S.-Peterburg po perepisi 15 dekabria 1881 goda*

Peterburg, 1890
> *S.-Peterburg po perepisi 15 dekabria 1890 goda*

Peterburg, 1900
> *S.-Peterburg po perepisi 15 dekabria 1900 goda*

RDR
    Rabochee dvizhenie v Rossii v XIX veke

RDVL
    Revoliutsionnoe dvizhenie v Rossii vesnoi i letom 1905 goda

Spisok 1903
    Spisok fabrik i zavodov evropeiskoi Rossii

Stachki 1895–1904
    V. E. Varzar, *Statisticheskie svedeniia o stachkakh rabochikh na fabrikakh i zavodakh za desiatiletie 1895–1904 gg.*

Stachki 1905
    Varzar, *Statistika stachek rabochikh na fabrikakh i zavodakh za 1905 god*

TsGAOR
    Tsentral'nyi Gosudarstvennyi Arkhiv Oktiabr'skoi Revoliutsii

TsGIA
    Tsentral'nyi Gosudarstvennyi Istoricheskii Arkhiv

1905: SRD
    1905 god v Peterburge. Vypusk II: Sovet Rabochikh Deputatov. Sbornik materialov

Vospominaniia Soveta
    1905. Vospominaniia chlenov SPb Soveta Rabochikh Deputatov

VPR
    Vysshii pod"em revoliutsii 1905–1907 gg.

VPSO
    Vserossiiskaia politicheskaia stachka v oktiabre 1905 goda

UNPUBLISHED ARCHIVAL SOURCES

Leningradskii Gosudarstvennyi Istoricheskii Arkhiv [LGIA]. Leningrad.
    Fond 223, S.-Peterburgskaia Remeslennaia Uprava. Opis' 1, dela 5415, 5419, 5426.
    Fond 569, Kantseliariia S.-Peterburgskogo Gradonachal'nika. Opis' 18, delo 204.
    Fond 792, Petrogradskaia Gorodskaia Duma. Opis' 1, dela 8618, 9139, 9453.
    Fond 1173, Petrogradskii Trubochnyi Zavod. Opis' 1, dela 3960, 7205, 7224.
    Fond 1229, Fabrichnaia Inspektsiia Petrogradskoi Gubernii. Opis' 1, delo 13.
    Fond 1239, Pravlenie Obshchestva Nevskogo Sudostroitel'nogo i Mekhanicheskogo Zavoda. Opis' 1, delo 103.
    Fond 1267, Obukhovskii Staleliteinyi Zavod. Opis' 1, dela 1047, 1054; op. 12, d. 54; op. 17, d. 1526.

Fond 1295, Aktsionernoe Obshchestvo "Kompaniia Sampsonievskoi Bumagopriadil'noi i Tkatskoi Manufaktury." Opis' 1, dela 51, 56.

Fond 1458, Ekspeditsiia Zagotovleniia Gosudarstvennykh Bumag. Opis' 2, dela 787, 822, 888.

Fond 2075, Kantseliariia Peterburgskogo General-Gubernatora. Opis' 2, delo 1; op. 4, d. 1a, 1b; op. 5, d. 1, 6, 42; op. 6, d. 101, 353, 358.

Tsentral'nyi Gosudarstvennyi Arkhiv Oktiabr'skoi Revoliutsii [TsGAOR]. Moscow.

Fond 102, Departament Politsii.
—Deloproizvodstvo VII, 1904, delo 2, chast' 73;
—Deloproizvodstvo VII, 1905, dela 934, 1683, 3931; opis' 43, d. 6239;
—Opis' 168, ed. khr. 39, 1905;
—Osobyi otdel, 1905, delo 4, chast' 1, toma 1–3; d. 2540, t. 2; opis' 5, d. 1800.

Fond 124, Ministerstvo Iustitsii. Opis' 43, dela 1741, 1744, 1745, 1747.

Fond 518, Soiuz soiuzov. Opis' 1, dela 6, 8, 11, 13, 15, 16, 18, 22.

Komissiia VTsSPS po izucheniiu istorii professional'nogo dvizheniia (Istprof VTsSPS): Fond 6860, delo 37; f. 6864, d. 60; f. 6866, ed. khr. 2, 71.

Tsentral'nyi Gosudarstvennyi Istoricheskii Arkhiv [TsGIA]. Leningrad.

Fond 150, Petrogradskoe Obshchestvo Zavodchikov i Fabrikantov. Opis' 1, delo No. 646.

Fond 1205, Osobaia Komissiia dlia vyiasneniia prichin nedovol'stva rabochikh Peterburga i ego prigorodov i izyskaniia mer k ustraneniiu ikh v budushchem ("komissiia Shidlovskogo"). Opis' XVIt., 1905, dela 1, 2.

Hoover Institution Archives. Nicolaevsky Collection. Stanford, California.
No. 16, Box 2, N. T[rotskii], "Bulyginskaia Duma i Nashi Zadachi."
No. 91, Box 1, Pis'ma iz Rossii v "Iskru" 1905 g.; Pis'mo Iu. Larina.
No. 109, Box 5, Pis'mo iz Peterburga.

PUBLISHED SOURCES

In the bibliographical entries that follow, the letters "L.," "M.," "P.," and "SPb." stand for, respectively, Leningrad, Moscow, Petrograd, and St. Petersburg.

Ainzaft, S. "Byli li kassy vzaimopomoshchi odnim iz istokov rossiiskogo professional'nogo dvizheniia?" In *Materialy po istorii professional'nogo dvizheniia v Rossii*, sb. 2 (M., 1924), pp. 75–101.

———. *Istoriia rabochego i professional'nogo dvizheniia derevoobdelochnikov do revoliutsii 1917 goda*. M., 1928.

———. *Pervyi etap professional'nogo dvizheniia v Rossii (1905–1907 gg.)* M.-Gomel', 1924.

————. *Zubatovshchina i gaponovshchina*. M., 1922; 4th ed., M., 1925.

Akademiia nauk SSSR. Fundamental'naia biblioteka obshchestvennykh nauk. *Istoriia SSSR. Ukazatel' sovetskoi literatury za 1917–1952 gg. Istoriia SSSR v period kapitalisma (1861–1917)*. Ed. K. R. Simon. Vol. 2. M., 1958.

Akhun, M. I., and M. Lur'e. "Ot vseobshchei politicheskoi stachki k vooruzhennomu vosstaniiu (Khronika revoliutsionnykh sobytii sentiabria–dekabria 1905 g.)." *Istoricheskie zapiski*, no. 11 (M., 1941), pp. 3–56.

Akhun, M. I., and V. A. Petrov. *Bol'sheviki i armiia v 1905–1917 gg. Voennaia organizatsiia pri Peterburgskom Komitete RSDRP (b.) i revoliutsionnoe dvizhenie v voiskakh Peterburga*. L., 1929.

Anan'ich, B. V., R. Sh. Ganelin, V. S. Diakin, et al. *Krizis samoderzhaviia v Rossii 1895–1917*. L., 1984.

Andronov, F. "Iz istorii professional'nogo dvizheniia izvozchikov v Peterburge." *Materialy po istorii professional'nogo dvizheniia v Rossii*, sb. 3 (M., 1925), pp. 111–15.

Antoshkin, D. *Ocherk dvizheniia sluzhashchikh v Rossii (So vtoroi poloviny XIX veka)*. M., 1921.

————. *Professional'noe dvizhenie v Rossii. Posobie dlia samoobrazovaniia i kursov po professional'nomu dvizheniiu*. 3d ed. M., 1925.

Anweiler, Oskar. *The Soviets: The Russian Workers, Peasants, and Soldiers Councils, 1905–1921*. Trans. Ruth Hein. New York, 1974; orig. German ed. 1958.

Arkhiv istorii truda v Rossii. 12 nos. (P. and L., 1921–25). The last three nos. were issued under the title *Trud v Rossii*.

Babakhan, N. *Sovety 1905 g.* M., 1923.

Bakhtiarov, A. *Briukho Peterburga. Obshchestvenno-fiziologicheskie ocherki*. SPb., 1888.

————. *Otpetye liudi. Ocherki iz zhizni pogibshikh liudei*. SPb., 1903.

————. *Proletariat i ulichnye tipy Peterburga. Bytovye ocherki*. SPb., 1895.

Balabanov, M. "Promyshlennost' v Rossii v nachale XX veka." *ODR*, I, 58–87.

Bater, James H. "Between Old and New: St. Petersburg in the Late Imperial Era." In Michael Hamm, ed., *The City in Late Imperial Russia* (Bloomington, Ind., 1986), pp. 42–78.

————. "The Journey to Work in St. Petersburg, 1860–1914." *Journal of Transport History*, 2, no. 4 (Sept. 1974), 214–33.

————. *St. Petersburg. Industrialization and Change*. London, 1976.

Bazilevich, K. V. *Ocherki po istorii professional'nogo dvizheniia rabotnikov sviazi 1905–1906 gg.* M., 1925.

Berenshtam, Vladimir. *Za pravo!* 2d ed. SPb., 1905.

Bernshtein-Kogan, S. *Chislennost', sostav i polozhenie peterburgskikh rabochikh. Opyt statisticheskogo issledovaniia*. SPb., 1910.

Blek, A. L. "Usloviia truda rabochikh na peterburgskikh zavodakh po dannym 1901 goda (Baltiiskii i drugie desiat' zavodov)." *Arkhiv istorii truda v Rossii*, kn. 2 (P., 1921), pp. 65–85.

Bondarevskaia, T. P. *Peterburgskii komitet RSDRP v revoliutsii 1905–1907 gg.* L., 1975.

Bonnell, Victoria E. *Roots of Rebellion. Workers' Politics and Organizations in St. Petersburg and Moscow, 1900–1914.* Berkeley, Calif., 1983.

Bortnik, M. "V 1901–1904 na Peterburgskom Trubochnom Zavode." *Krasnaia letopis'*, 1 (28) (1929), pp. 182–219.

Bovykin, V. I., S. V. Tiutiukin, et al. *Rabochii klass v pervoi rossiiskoi revoliutsii 1905–1907 gg.* M., 1981.

Brody, David. *Steelworkers in America. The Non-union Era.* Cambridge, Mass., 1960.

Brower, Daniel R. "Labor Violence in Russia in the Late Nineteenth Century." *Slavic Review*, 41, no. 3 (Fall 1982), pp. 417–53.

Buiko, A. M. *Put' rabochego. Zapiski starogo bol'shevika.* M., 1934.

Bukhbinder, N. A., ed. "K istorii 'Sobraniia russkikh fabrichno-zavodskikh rabochikh g. S.-Peterburga'." *Krasnaia letopis'*, no. 1 (1922), pp. 288–329.

Bulkin, F. A. *Na zare profdvizheniia. Istoriia Peterburgskogo soiuza metallistov 1906–1914.* L.-M., 1924.

Bushnell, John. "Mutineers and Revolutionaries: Military Revolution in Russia, 1905–1907." Ph.D. diss., Indiana Univ., 1977.

———. *Mutiny amid Repression. Russian Soldiers in the Revolution of 1905–1906.* Bloomington, Ind., 1985.

Buzinov, Aleksei. *Za nevskoi zastavoi. Zapiski rabochego.* M.-L., 1930.

Chaadaeva, O., ed. *Pervoe maia v tsarskoi Rossii. 1890–1916 gg. Sbornik dokumentov.* N. p., 1939.

Cherevanin, N. "Dvizhenie intelligentsii." *ODR*, II, pt. 2, pp. 146–202.

Chermenskii, E. D. *Burzhuaziia i tsarizm v pervoi russkoi revoliutsii.* 2d ed. M., 1970.

Chernov, V. M. *Pered burei. Vospominaniia.* New York, 1953.

Confino, Michael. "On Intellectuals and Intellectual Traditions in 18th and 19th Century Russia." *Daedalus*, no. 101–2 (1972), pp. 117–50.

D. [D'iakonov]. *1905 i 1906 god v Peterburgskom Universitete. Skhodki i mitingi (khronika). Sovet starost (ocherk).* SPb., 1907.

Dan, Theodore. *The Origins of Bolshevism.* Trans. J. Carmichael. London, 1964.

Deutsch, Leo [L. G. Deich]. *Der Pope Gapon und seine Rolle in der russischen Revolution.* Berlin, 1910.

"Dnevnik upravliaiushchego Nevskoi Nitochnoi Fabriki K. I. Monkera za 1905–1906 gody." *Voprosy grazhdanskoi istorii*, I (L., 1935), pp. 197–256.

Dorovatovskii, N. S. *Peterburg i ego zhizn'.* SPb., 1914.

Dorovatovskii, P., and V. Zlotin, "Khronika rabochego i professional'nogo dvizheniia v Peterburge v 1905 g." *Materialy po istorii professional'nogo dvizheniia v Peterburge za 1905–1907 gg.* (L., 1926), pp. 208–47.

Emmons, Terence. *The Formation of Political Parties and the First National Elections in Russia.* Cambridge, Mass., 1983.

————. "Russia's Banquet Campaign." *California Slavic Studies*, 10 (1977), pp. 45–86.

————. "The Statutes of the Union of Liberation." *Russian Review*, 33, no. 1 (Jan. 1974), pp. 80–85.

Engelstein, Laura. "Moscow in the 1905 Revolution: A Study in Class Conflict and Political Organization." Ph.D. diss., Stanford Univ., 1976.

————. *Moscow, 1905. Working-Class Organization and Political Conflict.* Stanford, Calif., 1982.

Eremeev, I. E., ed. *Gorod S.-Peterburg s tochki zreniia meditsinskoi politsii. Sostavlenno po rasporiazheniiu S.-Peterburgskogo Gradonachal'nika general-maiora N. V. Kleigel'sa vrachami Peterburgskoi stolichnoi politsii.* SPb., 1897.

Erman, L. K. *Intelligentsiia v pervoi russkoi revoliutsii.* M., 1966.

Evgenii [E. Maevskii]. "Peterburgskii Sovet Rabochikh Deputatov (Ocherk vozniknoveniia]." *Otkliki sovremennosti*, no. 5 (1906), pp. 1–11.

Filippov, Aleksei. "Stranichki minuvshego. I: Neskol'ko slov o Gapone." *Novyi zhurnal dlia vsekh*, no. 6 (June 1913), cols. 105–22.

Fischer, George. *Russian Liberalism. From Gentry to Intelligentsia.* Cambridge, Mass., 1958.

Fotiev, A. "Pochtovo-telegrafnaia zabastovka v 1905 g." *Materialy po istorii professional'nogo dvizheniia v Peterburge za 1905–1907 gg.* (L., 1926), pp. 82–94.

Frankel, Jonathan. "Economism: A Heresy Exploited." *Slavic Review*, 22, no. 2 (1963), pp. 263–84.

Freeze, G. L. "A National Liberation Movement and the Shift in Russian Liberalism, 1901–1903." *Slavic Review*, 28, no. 1 (Mar. 1969), pp. 81–91.

Galai, Shmuel. "The Impact of the War on the Russian Liberals in 1904–5." *Government and Opposition*, 1, no. 1 (Nov. 1965), pp. 85–109.

————. *The Liberation Movement in Russia, 1900–1905.* Cambridge, Eng., 1973.

————. "The Role of the Union of Unions in the Revolution of 1905." *Jahrbücher für Geschichte Osteuropas*, 24, no. 4 (1976), pp. 512–25.

Ganelin, R. Sh. "Kanun 'Krovavogo Voskresen'ia' (Tsarskie vlasti 6–8 ianvaria 1905 goda)." *Voprosy istorii*, no. 1 (1980), pp. 32–43.

Gapon, Georgii. *Istoriia moei zhizni.* Ed. A. A. Shilov. L., 1925.

————. *The Story of My Life.* London, 1906.

Gavrilov, A. "Vospominaniia starogo obukhovtsa," *Krasnaia letopis'*, 4 (19) (1926), pp. 58–67.

Gerschenkron, Alexander. *Economic Backwardness in Historical Perspective.* Cambridge, Mass., 1962.

Glickman, Rose L. *Russian Factory Women. Workplace and Society, 1880–1914.* Berkeley, Calif., 1984.

Glukhochenkov, I. "Iz raboty chernoi sotni v 1905–1907 gg." *Krasnaia letopis'*, 4 (15) (1925), pp. 148–51.

Gordon, Maks. "Iz zhizni rabochikh i sluzhashchikh na gorodskikh zheleznykh dorogakh Petrograda." *Arkhiv istorii truda v Rossii* (P., 1923), kn. 8, pp. 79–103; kn. 9, pp. 133–46.

————. "Iz zhizni rabochikh i sluzhashchikh na petrogradskikh vodopro-vodakh." *Arkhiv istorii truda v Rossii* (P., 1923), kn. 10, pp. 75–93.

Gorin, P. *Ocherki po istorii Sovetov Rabochikh deputatov v 1905 godu*. M., 1925.

Gor'kii, A. M. "Pop Gapon. Ocherk." *Arkhiv A. M. Gor'kogo*, vol. 6 (M., 1957), pp. 14–24.

Grigor'evskii, M. [M. G. Lunts]. *Politseiskii sotsializm v Rossii (Zubatovshchina)*. SPb., 1906.

Grinevich, V. [M. G. Kogan]. "Ocherk razvitiia professional'nogo dvizheniia v g. S.-Peterburge." *Obrazovanie*, 1906, no. 8, pp. 209–26; no. 9, pp. 226–55; no. 10, pp. 109–28.

————. *Professional'noe dvizhenie rabochikh v Rossii*. SPb., 1908.

Gruzdev, S. I. *Trud i bor'ba shveinikov v Peterburge 1905–1916 gg. Istoricheskii ocherk*. L., 1929.

Gurevich, L. *Deviatoe ianvaria*. Kharkov, 1926.

————. "Narodnoe dvizhenie v Peterburge 9-go ianvaria 1905 g." *Byloe*, 1 (Jan. 1906), pp. 195–223.

Gusiatnikov, P. S. *Revoliutsionnoe studencheskoe dvizhenie v Rossii 1899–1907*. M., 1971.

Haimson, Leopold H. "The Problem of Social Stability in Urban Russia, 1905–1917." *Slavic Review*, 23, no. 4 (Dec. 1964), pp. 619–42; 24, no. 1 (Mar. 1965), pp. 1–22.

————. *The Russian Marxists and the Origins of Bolshevism*. Cambridge, Mass., 1955.

Harcave, Sidney. *First Blood. The Russian Revolution of 1905*. New York, 1964.

Harding, Neil, ed. *Marxism in Russia. Key Documents, 1879–1906*. Cambridge, Eng., 1983.

Hildermeier, M. *Die Sozialrevolutionäre Partei Russlands. Agrarsozialismus und Modernisierung im Zarenreich (1900–1914)*. Cologne and Vienna, 1978.

Hobsbawm, E. J. *Labouring Men*. New York, 1967.

————. *Workers: Worlds of Labor*. New York, 1984.

Hogan, Heather J. "Industrial Rationalization and the Roots of Labor Mili-tance in the St. Petersburg Metalworking Industry, 1901–1914." *Russian Review*, 42, no. 4 (Apr. 1983), pp. 163–90.

————. "Labor and Management in Conflict: The St. Petersburg Metal Work-ing Industry, 1900–1914." Ph.D. diss., Univ. of Michigan, 1981.

————. "The Origins of the Scientific Management Movement in Russia." Unpublished paper. January 1983.

Iakovlev, A. F. *Ekonomicheskie krizisy v Rossii*. M., 1955.

Iakub, R., and S. Ia. Rapoport, eds. *Sistematicheskii ukazatel' literatury po profes-sional'nomu dvizheniiu v Rossii*. Vyp. 1. M., 1923.

Iatsunskii, V. K. "Rol' Peterburga v promyshlennom razvitii dorevoliutsionnoi Rossii." *Voprosy istorii*, no. 9 (Sept. 1954), pp. 95–103.

Istoriia Leningradskogo soiuza rabochikh poligraficheskogo proizvodstva. Kniga per-vaia. 1904–1907. Kollektivnyi trud. L., 1925.

Istoriia rabochego klassa Leningrada. Vypusk II. (Iz istorii rabochego klassa Peterburga-Petrograda.) Ed. V. A. Ovsiankin. L., 1963.

Istoriia rabochikh Leningrada. Tom pervyi. 1703–fevral' 1917. L., 1972.

Iukhneva, N. V. *Etnicheskii sostav i etnosotsial'naia struktura naseleniia Peterburga. Vtoraia polovina XIX–nachalo XX veka. Statisticheskii analiz.* L., 1984.

———. "Iz istorii stachechnogo dvizheniia peterburgskikh rabochikh posle Obukhovskoi Oborony (stachka rabochikh nevskoi zastavy v mae 1901 goda)." *Uchenye zapiski L G U. Seriia istoricheskikh nauk,* vyp. 32 (1959), pp. 201–16.

———. "Nakanune Obukhovskoi oborony (Pervomaiskaia stachka v Peterburge v 1901 godu)." *Vestnik leningradskogo universiteta,* 16, no. 2 (L., 1961), pp. 57–67.

Ivanov, A. E. "Demokraticheskoe studenchestvo v 1905–1907 gg." *Istoricheskie zapiski,* no. 107 (1982), pp. 171–225.

Ivanov, B. *Professional'noe dvizhenie rabochikh khlebo-pekarno-konditerskogo proizvodstva Petrograda i gubernii (s 1903–1917 g.).* M., 1920.

Ivanov, L. M. "Boikot Bulyginskoi Dumy i stachka v oktiabre 1905 g. (K voprosu o rasstanovke boriushchikhsia sil)." *Istoricheskie zapiski,* no. 83 (1983), pp. 137–58.

———. "Proletariat i samoderzhavie: nekotorye voprosy ideologicheskogo vozdeistviia tsarizma na rabochikh." *Proletariat Rossii na puti k oktiabriu 1917 goda (oblik, bor'ba, gegemoniia). Materialy k nauchnoi sessii po istorii proletariata, posviashchennoi 50-letiiu Velikogo Oktiabria. 14–17 noiabria 1967 goda. Chast' 1* (Odessa, 1967), pp. 92–106.

———. "Samoderzhavie, burzhuaziia i rabochie (k voprosu ob ideologicheskom vliianii na proletariat)." *Voprosy istorii,* no. 1 (1971), pp. 81–96.

Ivanov, N. "Maiskaia zabastovka 1901 goda na fabrike Cheshera (Vospominaniia)." *Krasnaia letopis',* 3 (14) (1925), pp. 255–56.

Ivanova, N. A., and V. V. Shelokhaev. "Torgovye sluzhashchie v revoliutsii 1905–1907 gg." *Istoricheskie zapiski,* no. 101 (1978), pp. 160–216.

Izvestiia Soveta Rabochikh Deputatov. S.-Peterburg, 17-go oktiabria–14-go dekabria 1905 goda. Preface and notes by D. Sverchkov. L., 1925.

Johnson, Robert E. *Peasant and Proletarian. The Working Class of Moscow in the Late Nineteenth Century.* New Brunswick, N.J., 1979.

Jones, G. Stedman. "Class Struggle and the Industrial Revolution." *Languages of Class. Studies in English Working Class History, 1832–1932,* pp. 25–75. Cambridge, Eng., 1983.

Kanatchikov, S. I. *Iz istoriia moego bytiia.* M., 1932. English trans.: *A Radical Worker in Tsarist Russia. The Autobiography of Semen Ivanovich Kanatchikov.* Ed. and trans. Reginald E. Zelnik. Stanford, Calif., 1986.

Karapinka, Orysia. "The Idea of the City in Russian Letters from Pushkin to Tolstoy." Ph.D. diss., Univ. of California, 1971.

Karelin, A. E. "Deviatoe ianvaria i Gapon. Vospominaniia (Zapisano so slov A. E. Karelina)." *Krasnaia letopis',* no. 1 (1922), pp. 106–16.

Karelina, V. "Na zare rabochego dvizheniia v S.-Peterburge (Vospominaniia V. M. Karelinoi)." *Krasnaia letopis',* no. 4 (1922), pp. 12–20.

————. "Rabotnitsy v Gaponovskikh obshchestvakh." In P. F. Kudelli, ed., *Rabotnitsa v 1905 g. v S.-Peterburge. Sbornik statei i vospominanii* (M., 1926), pp. 14–26.

Kats, A., and Iu. Milonov. *1905 god. Professional'noe dvizhenie.* M.-L., 1926. [In series *1905. Materialy i dokumenty,* ed. M. N. Pokrovskii. At head of title: Komissiia TsIK SSSR po organizatsii prazdnovaniia 20-letiia revoliutsii 1905 g. i Istpart TsK VKP (b).]

Keep, J. L. H. *The Rise of Social Democracy in Russia.* Oxford, 1963.

Khromov, P. A. *Ekonomicheskoe razvitie Rossii v XIX–XX vekakh, 1800–1917.* N.p., 1950.

Kir'ianov, Iu. I. *Perekhod k massovoi politicheskoi bor'be. Rabochii klass nakanune pervoi rossiiskoi revoliutsii.* M., 1987.

————. *Zhiznennyi uroven' rabochikh Rossii (konets XIX–nachalo XX v.).* M., 1979.

————, and P. V. Pronina. *Polozheniie proletariata Rossii. Ukazatel' literatury.* 2 vols. M., 1972.

Kirpichnikov, S. D. "L. I. Lutugin i Soiuz Soiuzov." *Byloe,* 6 (34) (1925), pp. 134–46.

Klaas, G. K. *Moi pervye shagi na revoliutsionnom puti. Iz vospominanii o rabochem dvizhenii v Peterburge i Pribaltiiskom krae v 1904–1905 gg.* L., 1926.

Kniazeva, M., and M. Inozemtsev. "K istorii rabochikh vyborov v Komissiiu Shidlovskogo." *Istoriia proletariata SSSR,* 2 (22) (1935), pp. 161–202.

Knuniants, B. M. "Pervyi sovet rabochikh deputatov." *Izbrannye proizvedeniia 1903–1911 gg.,* pp. 202–321. Erevan, 1958. This long article was reprinted, with alterations and annotations, from B. Rubin [Knuniants]. "Pervyi sovet rabochikh deputatov." *Obrazovanie,* 1906, no. 5, pp. 115–44; no. 6, pp. 85–118.

Kobiakov, R. "Gapon i Okhrannoe otdelenie do 1905 goda." *Byloe,* no. 1 (29) (1925), pp. 28–45.

Kochergin, K. I. "90-e gody na fabrike 'Rabochii' (b. Maksvel')." *Krasnaia letopis',* 1931, no. 4 (43), pp. 101–19; nos. 5–6 (44–45), pp. 194–209.

Koenker, Diane. *Moscow Workers and the 1917 Revolution.* Princeton, N.J., 1981.

[Kolokol'nikov, P.] "Kak voznik v Peterburge soiuz rabochikh po metallu." *Materialy ob ekonomicheskom polozhenii i professional'noi organizatsii Peterburgskikh rabochikh po metallu,* pp. 22–32, SPb., 1909.

Kolokol'nikov, P. "Otryvki iz vospominanii 1905–1907 gg." *Materialy po istorii professional'nogo dvizheniia v Rossii,* sb. 2 (M., 1924), pp. 211–24.

————, and S. Rapoport. *1905–1907 gg. v professional'nom dvizhenii. I i II Vserossiiskie konferentsii professional'nykh soiuzov.* M., 1925.

Kol'tsov, D. "Rabochie v 1905–1907 gg." *ODR,* II, pt. 1, 185–341.

————. "Rabochie v 1890–1904 gg." *ODR,* I, 183–229.

Kommunisticheskaia Akademiia. Biblioteka. *Pervaia russkaia revoliutsiia. Ukazatel' literatury.* Ed. G. K. Derman. M., 1930.

Korablev, Iu. I., ed. *Revoliutsiia 1905–1907 godov v Rossii.* M., 1975.

Korelin, A. P. "Russkii 'politseiskii sotsializm' (Zubatovshchina)." *Voprosy istorii,* no. 10 (Oct. 1968), pp. 41–58.

Korol'chuk, E., and E. Sokolova, *Khronika revoliutsionnogo rabochego dvizheniia v Peterburge. Tom 1 (1870–1904 gg.).* L., 1940.

Kozovlev, A. [S. S. Zborovskii]. "Kak voznik Sovet." *Istoriia Soveta Rabochikh Deputatov g. S.-Peterburga,* pp. 22–44. SPb., 1906.

Krivosheina, E. *Peterburgskii sovet rabochikh deputatov v 1905 godu.* M., 1926.

Krizis samoderzhaviia v Rossii 1895–1917. L., 1984.

Krugliakov, V. "Pravitel'stvo i zheleznodorozhnye zabastovki v Peterburge v 1905 godu." *Krasnaia letopis',* 2 (13) (1925), pp. 64–89.

———. "Zabastovka sredi zheleznodorozhnikov v nachale 1905 goda v Peterburge." *Krasnaia letopis',* 1 (12) (1925), pp. 57–66.

Krupskaia, N. *Memories of Lenin.* Trans. E. Verney. New York, 1930.

Kruze, E. E., and D. G. Kutsentov. "Naselenie Peterburga." *Ocherki istorii Leningrada,* III (L., 1956), pp. 104–46.

Kutsentov, D. G. "Naselenie Peterburga. Polozhenie peterburgskikh rabochikh." *Ocherki istorii Leningrada,* II (L., 1957), 170–228.

———. "Peterburgskii proletariat v 90-kh godakh XIX veka (Chislennost', sostav i ekonomicheskoe polozhenie rabochikh)." *Istoriia rabochego klassa Leningrada,* vyp. II (L., 1963), pp. 19–48.

Kuznetsov, K. A., L. Z. Livshits, and V. I. Pliasunov. *Baltiiskii sudostroitel'nyi 1856–1917. Ocherk istorii Baltiiskogo sudostroitel'nogo zavoda imeni S. Ordzhonikidze,* I (L., 1970).

Kuznetsova, L[idiia] S[ergeevna]. *Stachechnaia bor'ba peterburgskogo proletariata v 1905 g.* L., 1955.

Lane, David. *The Roots of Russian Communism. A Social and Historical Study of Russian Social Democracy, 1898–1907.* Assen, 1969.

Laverychev, V. Ia. *Tsarizm i rabochii vopros v Rossii (1861–1917 gg.).* M., 1972.

———. "Obshchaia tendentsiia razvitiia burzhuazno-liberal'nogo dvizheniia v Rossii v kontse XIX–nachale XX veka." *Istoriia SSSR,* no. 3 (1976), pp. 46–65.

———. "O popytkakh vozdeistviia rossiiskoi liberal'noi burzhuazii na rabochii klass v 1905–1907 gg." In *Pervaia russkaia revoliutsiia—general'naia repetitsiia velikogo Oktiabria* (Tbilisi, 1977), pp. 214–30.

Leikina-Svirskaia, V. P. *Intelligentsiia v Rossii vo vtoroi polovine XIX veka.* M., 1971.

———. *Russkaia intelligentsiia v 1900–1917 godakh.* M., 1981.

Leont'ev, V. "Stachki 1905 goda v S.-Peterburge." *Russkoe bogatstvo,* no. 6 (1907), pp. 53–57.

Leontief, Wassily [Vasilii Leont'ev]. *Die Baumwollindustrie in St. Petersburg und ihre Arbeiter.* Munich, 1906.

Livshits, R. S. *Razmeshchenie promyshlennosti v dorevoliutsionnoi Rossii.* M., 1955.

Livshits, S. "Bor'ba za 8-chasovoi rabochii den' v Peterburge v 1905 godu." *Krasnaia letopis',* no. 4 (15) (1925), pp. 116–35.

Lunev, V., and V. Shilov. *Nevskii raion.* L., 1966.

L'vovich, A. "Trebovaniia rabochikh Baltiiskogo i drugikh morskikh zavodov v ianvarskie dni 1905 goda." *Arkhiv istorii truda v Rossii*, kn. 4 (1) (P., 1922), pp. 85–96.

Luxemburg, Rosa. *The Mass Strike, the Political Party and the Trade Unions.* Trans. Patrick Lavin. Columbo, Ceylon, 1964; orig. ed. 1906.

Maevskii, E. "Obshchaia kartina dvizheniia." *ODR*, II, pt. 1, pp. 35–184.

Malia, Martin E. "What Is the Intelligentsia?" *Daedalus*, 89, no. 3 (Summer 1960), pp. 441–58.

Mandel'berg, V. *Iz perezhitogo.* Davos, Switz., 1910.

Manning, Roberta. *The Crisis of the Old Order in Russia. Government and Gentry.* Princeton, N.J., 1982.

Martov, L. [Iu. O.]. *Istoriia rossiiskoi sotsial-demokratii.* 3d ed. P.-M., 1923.

———. "Razvitie promyshlennosti i rabochee dvizhenie s 1893 do 1903 g." In *Istoriia Rossii v XIX veke* (n.p., n.d. [but SPb.: Granat, 1907–11]), vol. 8, pp. 67–156. Published separately as *Razvitie krupnoi promyshlennosti i rabochee dvizhenie v Rossii.* P. & M., 1923.

Martynov, A. "Istoriia Konstitutsionno-Demokraticheskoi Partii." *ODR*, III, pp. 1–85.

Marx, Karl. *The Eighteenth Brumaire of Louis Bonaparte.* New York, n.d.

Materialy po istorii professional'nogo dvizheniia v Peterburge za 1905–1907 gg. L., 1926.

Materialy po istorii professional'nogo dvizheniia v Rossii. 5 vols. M., 1924–27. [At head of title: Komissiia po izucheniiu istorii professional'nogo dvizheniia v Rossii. Istprof VTsSPS.]

McDaniel, Tim. *Autocracy, Capitalism, and Revolution in Russia.* Berkeley, Calif., 1988.

McKinsey, Pamela S. "From City Workers to Peasantry: The Beginning of the Russian Movement 'To the People.'" *Slavic Review*, 38, no. 4 (Dec. 1979), pp. 629–49.

Melancon, Michael. "The Socialist Revolutionaries from 1902 to 1907: Peasant and Workers' Party," *Russian History*, 12, no. 1 (1985), pp. 2–47.

Mikhailov, Iakov. *Iz zhizni rabochego. Vospominaniia chlena Soveta Rabochikh Deputatov. 1905 g.* L., 1925.

Mikhailov, M. M. "1905 god na Izhorskom zavode (Okonchanie)." *Krasnaia letopis'*, 3 (48) (1932), pp. 189–210.

Miliukov, P. N. *God bor'by. Publitsisticheskaia khronika, 1905–1906.* SPb., 1907.

———. *Vospominaniia (1859–1917).* 2 vols. New York, 1955. English version: *Political Memoirs, 1905–1917.* Trans. Carl Goldberg. Ann Arbor, Mich., 1967.

Mitel'man, M., B. Glebov, and A. Ul'ianskii. *Istoriia Putilovskogo zavoda, 1801–1917.* 3d ed. M., 1961.

Morgan, Anne. "The St. Petersburg Soviet of Workers' Deputies. A Study of Labor Organization in the 1905 Russian Revolution." Ph.D. diss., Indiana Univ., 1979.

Nachalo pervoi russkoi revoliutsii. Ianvar'-mart 1905 goda. Edited by N. S. Trusova et al. M., 1955. [A volume in the series *Revoliutsiia 1905–1907 gg. v Rossii. Dokumenty i materialy.*]

Neuberger, Joan. "Crime and Culture: Hooliganism in St. Petersburg, 1900–1914." Ph.D. diss., Stanford Univ., 1985.

Nevskii, V. I. "Peterburgskaia sotsial-demokraticheskaia organizatsiia v ianvare 1905 goda." *Krasnaia letopis'*, 1 (12) (1925), pp. 145–56.

————. *Rabochee dvizhenie v ianvarskie dni 1905 goda.* M., 1930.

————. *Sovety i vooruzhennoe vosstanie v 1905 godu.* M., 1931.

————. "Vybory v komissiiu senatora Shidlovskogo (1905 g.)." *Arkhiv istorii truda v Rossii*, kn. 3 (1922), pp. 78–90.

Nikitin, I. *Pervye rabochie soiuzy i sotsialdemocraticheskie organizatsii v Rossii (70–80 gg. XIX veka).* M., 1952.

Nikolaev, S. A. "Iz revoliutsionnogo proshlogo Nevskogo sudostroitel'nogo i mekhanicheskogo zavoda." *Krasnaia letopis'*, 1 (12) (1925), pp. 67–74.

Nikol'skii, D. P. "Shlissel'burgskii prigorodnyi uchastok v sanitarnom otnoshenii." *Vestnik obshchestvennoi gigieny, sudebnoi i prakticheskoi meditsiny* (Aug. 1901), pp. 1136–70.

Norton, Barbara T. "E. D. Kuskova: A Political Biography of a Russian Democrat. Part 1 (1869–1905)." Ph.D. diss., Pennsylvania State University, 1981.

Nosar', Georgii S. [Khrustalev-Nosar']. "Istoriia Soveta Rabochikh Deputatov (do 26-go noiabria 1905 g.)." In *Istoriia Soveta Rabochikh Deputatov g. S.-Peterburga* (SPb., 1906), pp. 45–169.

"O piatom gode (Iz stenogrammy torzhestvennogo plenuma 22 dekabria 1930 g. . . . posviashchennogo 25-letnemu iubeleiu Soveta 1905 goda)." *Krasnaia letopis'*, 1 (40) (1931), pp. 121–32.

Obninskii, Viktor. *Novyi stroi. Chast' pervaia. Manifesty 17 oktiabria 1905 g.–8 iiulia 1906 g.* M., 1909.

————. *Polgoda russkoi revoliutsii. Sbornik materialov k istorii russkoi revoliutsii (oktiabr' 1905–aprel' 1906 gg.).* Vol. 1. M., 1906.

Obshchestvennoe dvizhenie v Rossii v nachale XX-go veka. Ed. L. Martov, P. Maslov, and A. Potresov. 4 vols. SPb., 1909–14.

Ocherki istorii Leningrada. Ed. B. M. Kochakov et al. Vol. I: *Period feodalizma (1703–1861 gg.).* M.-L., 1955. Vol. II: *Period kapitalizma. Vtoraia polovina XIX veka.* M.-L., 1957. Vol. III: *Period imperializma i burzhuazno-demokraticheskikh revoliutsii. 1895–1917 gg.* M.-L., 1956.

Ocherki istorii SSSR. Pervaia russkaia burzhuazno-demokraticheskaia revoliutsiia 1905–1907 gg. Ed. A. M. Pankratova and G. D. Kostomarov. M., 1955.

Oksman, Iu. "Iz bumag D. F. Trepova." *Krasnyi arkhiv*, no. 4–5 (11–12) (1925), pp. 448–66.

Okun', S. B., ed. *Putilovets v trekh revoliutsiiakh. Sbornik materialov po istorii Putilovskogo zavoda.* M.-L., 1933.

Onufriev, Evgenii. *Za nevskoi zastavoi (Vospominaniia starogo bol'shevika).* M., 1968.

Ot podpol'nogo kruzhka k proletarskoi diktature. Vyp. 3. Tysiacha deviat'sot piatyi god. M.-L., 1930.

Bibliography 441

Ozerov, I. Kh. *Politika po rabochemu voprosu v Rossii za poslednie gody*. SPb., 1906.
Paialin, N. "Shlissel'burgskii trakt (Nevskaia zastava)." *Bor'ba klassov*, no. 11 (1934), pp. 51–57.
——. *Zavod imeni Lenina 1857–1918*. M.-L., 1933.
Pankratova, A. M. *Fabzavkomy Rossii v bor'be za sotsialisticheskuiu fabriku*. M., 1923.
——. "Rabochii klass i rabochee dvizhenie nakanune revoliutsii 1905 goda." In M. N. Pokrovskii, ed., *1905. Istoriia revoliutsionnogo dvizheniia v otdel'nykh ocherkakh* (M.-L., 1926), vol. 1, pp. 393–504.
——, ed. *Ocherki istorii proletariata SSSR. Proletariat tsarskoi Rossii*. M., 1931.
Pavlov, Ivan. "Iz vospominanii o 'Rabochem soiuze' i sviashchennike Gapone." *Minuvshie gody*, nos. 3, 4 (Mar., Apr. 1908), pp. 22–57, 75–107.
Pavlovich, M. "Vneshnaia politika i russko-iaponskaia voina." *ODR*, II, pt. 1, pp. 1–32.
Pazhitnov, K. A. *Polozhenie rabochego klassa v Rossii*. 3d ed. Vol. II. L., 1924.
——. *Problema remeslennykh tsekhov v zakonodatel'stve russkogo absoliutizma*. M., 1952.
Pearl, Deborah L. "Revolutionaries and Workers: A Study of Revolutionary Propaganda Among Russian Workers, 1880–1892." Ph.D. diss., Univ. of California, Berkeley, 1984.
Perazich, V. "Tekstil'shchiki v komissii Shidlovskogo." *Krasnaia letopis'*, 6 (39) (1930), pp. 40–64.
Persits, M. M. *Ateizm russkogo rabochego (1870–1905 gg.)*. M., 1965.
Pervaia russkaia revoliutsiia v Peterburge 1905 g. Edited by Ts. Zelikson-Bobrovskaia. 2 vols. L.-M., 1925.
Peskovoi, I. "Na zavode Rechkina v 1905 g.," *Krasnaia letopis'*, no. 3 (14) (1925), pp. 179–92.
Peterburgskie bol'sheviki v period pod"ema pervoi russkoi revolutsii 1905–1907 gg. Sbornik dokumentov i materialov. L., 1955.
Petrov, N. P. "Deviatoe ianvaria (Vospominaniia uchastnika)." *Izvestiia*, Jan. 22, 1922.
——. "Zapiski o Gapone rabochego N. P. Petrova." *Vsemirnyi vestnik*, no. 1 (1907), pp. 35–53.
Petrov-Radin, B. [B. M. Knuniants]. "Bor'ba za vos'michasovoi rabochii den'." In *Istoriia Soveta Rabochikh Deputatov g. S.-Peterburga* (SPb., 1906), pp. 242–64.
Piskarev, A. "Vospominaniia chlena Peterburgskogo soveta rabochikh deputatov 1905 g." *Krasnaia letopis'*, 4 (15) (1925), pp. 102–15.
Plekhanov, G. V. "Sviashchennik G. Gapon." *Sochineniia*, vol. 13 (M.-L., 1926), pp. 198–203.
Pnin, K. "Iz istorii professional'nogo dvizheniia torgovykh sluzhashchikh v Peterburge." *Materialy po istorii professional'nogo dvizheniia v Rossii*, sb. III (M., 1925), pp. 274–92.
Pogozhev, A. V. *Uchet, chislennost' i sostav rabochikh v Rossii. Materialy po statistike truda*. SPb., 1906.

Pollard, Allan. "The Russian Intelligentsia: The Mind of Russia." *California Slavic Studies*, no. 3 (1964), pp. 1–32.

Portal, Roger. "The Industrialization of Russia." *Cambridge Economic History of Europe*, vol. 6, pt. 2 (Cambridge, Eng., 1966), pp. 801–72.

Pospielovsky, Dmitry. *Russian Police Trade-Unionism. Experiment or Provocation?* London, 1971.

Presniakov, A. "1905 god." *Byloe*, 4 (32) (1925), pp. 3–35.

Prokopovich, S. N. *K rabochemu voprosu v Rossii.* SPb., 1905.

————. "Oktiabr'skaia zabastovka." *Bez zaglaviia*, no. 1 (24 Jan., 1906), pp. 17–27.

————. *Soiuzy rabochikh i ikh zadachi.* SPb., 1905.

Pushkareva, I. M. *Zheleznodorozhniki Rossii v burzhuazno-demokraticheskikh revoliutsiiakh.* M., 1975.

Putilovtsy v 1905 godu. Ed. B. Pozern. L., 1931. [Memoirs.]

"Rabochee dvizhenie na zavodakh Peterburga v mae 1901 g." *Krasnyi arkhiv*, 3 (76) (1936), pp. 49–66.

Rabochee dvizhenie v Rossii v 1901–1904 gg. Sbornik dokumentov. Edited by L. M. Ivanov. L., 1975.

Rabochee dvizhenie v Rossii v XIX veke. Sbornik dokumentov i materialov. Edited by A. M. Pankratova, L. M. Ivanov, et al. 4 vols. M.-L., 1950–63.

Raeff, Marc. *The Origins of the Russian Intelligentsia. The 18th Century Nobility.* New York, 1966.

Rashin, A. G. *Formirovanie rabochego klassa Rossii. Istoriko-ekonomicheskie ocherki.* M., 1958.

————. *Naselenie Rossii za 100 let (1811–1913 gg.).* M., 1956.

Reichman, Henry. *Railwaymen and Revolution. Russia, 1905.* Berkeley, Calif., 1987.

————. "Russian Railwaymen and the Revolution of 1905." Ph.D. diss., Univ. of California, Berkeley, 1977.

Revoliutsionnoe dvizhenie v Rossii vesnoi i letom 1905 goda. Aprel'-sentiabr'. Chast' pervaia. Edited by N. S. Trusova et al. M., 1957. [A volume in the series *Revoliutsiia 1905–1907 gg. v Rossii. Dokumenty i materialy.*]

Revoliutsiia 1905–1907 gg. v Rossii. Dokumenty i materialy. Edited by A. M. Pankratova et al. M. or M.-L., 1955–63. A multivolume collection of documents, of which four volumes are relevant to Petersburg in 1905: *Nachalo pervoi russkoi revoliutsii; Revoliutsionnoe dvizhenie v Rossii vesnoi i letom 1905 goda*, Part 1; *Vserossiiskaia politicheskaia stachka v oktiabre 1905 goda*, Part 1; *Vysshii pod"em revoliutsii 1905–1907 gg. Vooruzhennye vosstaniia*, Part 1.

Riasanovsky, Nicholas V. "Notes on the Emergence and Nature of the Russian Intelligentsia." In T. G. Stavrou, ed., *Art and Culture in Nineteenth-Century Russia* (Bloomington, Ind., 1983), pp. 3–25.

Rieber, Alfred J. *Merchants and Entrepreneurs in Imperial Russia.* Chapel Hill, N.C., 1983.

Romanov, B. "K kharakteristike Gapona (nekotorye dannye o zabastovke na Putilovskom zavode v 1905 g.)." *Krasnaia letopis'*, no. 2 (13) (1925), pp. 37–48.

———, ed. *Rabochii vopros v komissii V. N. Kokovtsova v 1905 g.* M., 1926.

Rostov, N. *Zheleznodorozhniki v revoliutsionnom dvizhenii 1905 g.* M.-L., 1926.

Rozanov, M. D. "'Obukhovskaia oborona' (Iz istorii Obukhovskogo zavoda— 1901 g.)." *Istoriia proletariata SSSR*, 2 (22) (1935), pp. 68–112.

———. *Obukhovtsy.* L., 1938.

Rubel', A. N. "Zhilishcha bednago naseleniia g. S.-Peterburga." *Vestnik obshchestvennoi gigieny, sudebnoi i prakticheskoi meditsiny* (Apr. 1899), pp. 424–45.

Rubin, B. [B. M. Knuniants]. "Pervyi sovet rabochikh deputatov." *Obrazovanie* (1906), no. 5, pp. 115–44; no. 6, pp. 85–118.

R-v, B. [B. Romanov]. "Ianvarskaia zabastovka 1905 g. v Peterburge (Materialy dlia kalendaria)." *Krasnaia letopis'*, 6 (33) (1929), pp. 25–44.

Sablinsky, Walter. "The Road to Bloody Sunday. Father Gapon, His Labor Organization, and the Massacre of Bloody Sunday." Ph.D. diss., Univ. of California, Berkeley, 1968.

———. *The Road to Bloody Sunday. Father Gapon and the St. Petersburg Massacre of 1905.* Princeton, N.J., 1976.

Sanders, Jonathan. "Lessons from the Periphery: Saratov, January 1905," *Slavic Review*, 46, no. 2 (Summer 1987), pp. 229–44.

———. "The Union of Unions: Political, Economic, Civil, and Human Rights Organizations in the 1905 Revolution." Ph.D. diss., Columbia University, 1983.

S[ankt]-Peterburg po peripisi 15-go dekabria 1881 goda. Chast' II. Vypusk 1. SPb., 1883–84.

S.-Peterburg po perepisi 15 dekabria 1890 goda. Chast' I. Vypusk 1. SPb., 1891. Chast' I. Vypusk 2. SPb., 1892.

S.-Peterburg po perepisi 15 dekabria 1900 goda. Vypusk 1. SPb., 1903. Vypusk 2. SPb., 1903.

S.-Peterburgskaia stolichnaia politsiia i Gradonachal'stvo. Kratkii istoricheskii ocherk. SPb., 1903.

Sbornik materialov po istorii Soiuza stroitelei. 1906 6/V 1926. L., 1926.

Schapiro, Leonard. *The Communist Party of the Soviet Union.* New York, 1960.

Schneiderman, Jeremiah. *Sergei Zubatov and Revolutionary Marxism. The Struggle for the Working Class in Tsarist Russia.* Ithaca, N.Y., 1976.

———. "The Tsarist Government and the Labor Movement, 1898–1903; the Zubatovshchina." Ph.D. diss., Univ. of California, Berkeley, 1966.

Schwarz, Solomon M. *The Russian Revolution of 1905. The Workers' Movement and the Formation of Bolshevism and Menshevism.* Chicago, 1967.

Semanov, S. N. *Krovavoe voskresen'e.* L., 1965.

———. *Peterburgskie rabochie nakanune pervoi russkoi revoliutsii.* M.-L., 1966.

Semenov-Bulkin, F. "Smesovshchina." *Trud v Rossii*, no. 1 (1925), pp. 153–70.

———. *Soiuz metallistov i departament politsii.* L., 1926.

Severianin, Petr. "Soiuz rabochikh pechatnogo dela." *Bez zaglaviia*, no. 14 (1906), pp. 52–62.

Sh., T. I. "K istorii peterburgskoi stachki tekstil'shchikov v 1896 g." *Krasnaia letopis'*, no. 2 (41) (1931), pp. 94–107.

Shalaeva, E. I., and I. P. Leiberov. "Profsoiuzy Peterburga v 1905 godu." *Voprosy istorii*, Oct. 1955, pp. 18–30.

Shapovalov, A. S. *Na puti k marksizmu (Po doroge k marksizmu). Zapiski rabochego revoliutsionera. V trekh chastiakh.* L., 1925.

Shatilova, T. *Ocherk istorii Leningradskogo soiuza khimikov 1905–1918.* L., 1927.

———. "Peterburgskie kozhevniki v 1905–1907 gg." *Krasnaia letopis'*, no. 5 (38) (1930), pp. 65–84.

Shatsillo, K. F. "Formirovanie programmy zemskogo liberalizma i ee bankrotstvo nakanune pervoi russkoi revoliutsii (1901–1904 gg.)." *Istoricheskie zapiski*, no. 97 (1976), pp. 74–98.

———. "Novoe o 'Soiuze Osvobozhdeniia'." *Istoriia SSSR*, no. 4 (1975), pp. 132–45.

———. "O sostave russkogo liberalizma nakanune revoliutsii 1905–1907 godov." *Istoriia SSSR*, no. 1 (1980), pp. 62–74.

———. *Russkii liberalizm nakanune revoliutsii 1905–1907 gg. Organizatsiia. Programmy. Taktika.* M., 1985.

Shcheglov, I. "Stachki i organizatsiia soiuza stroitelei v 1906 g." In *Materialy po istorii professional'nogo dvizheniia v Peterburge za 1905–1907 gg.* (L., 1926), pp. 172–78.

Shestakov, A. "Vseobshchaia oktiabr'skaia stachka 1905 goda." In M. N. Pokrovskii, ed., *1905. Istoriia revoliutsionnogo dvizheniia v otdel'nykh ocherkakh* (M.-L., 1925), II, pp. 264–352.

Shidlovskii, G. "Pervomaiskii den' 1905 g. v Peterburge i okrestnostiakh." *Krasnaia letopis'*, no. 2 (13) (1925), pp. 168–85.

Shilov, A. A. "K dokumental'noi istorii 'Petitsii' 9-go ianvaria 1905 g." *Krasnaia letopis'*, no 2 (13) (1925), pp. 19–36.

Shorter, Edward, and Charles Tilly. *Strikes in France, 1830–1968.* Cambridge, Eng., 1974.

Shotman, A. V. *Zapiski starogo bol'shevika.* 3d ed. L., 1963.

Shuster, U. A. *Peterburgskie rabochie v 1905–1907 gg.* L., 1976.

Simanovskii, A. "Kak pechatalis' 'Izvestiia Soveta Rabochikh Deputatov.'" In *Istoriia Soveta Rabochikh Deputatov g. S.-Peterburga* (SPb., 1906), pp. 281–92.

———. "Proletariat i svoboda pechati." In *Istoriia Soveta Rabochikh Deputatov g. S.-Peterburga* (SPb., 1906), pp. 217–41.

Simbirskii, N. *Pravda o Gapone i 9-m ianvare.* SPb., 1906.

Smith, S. A. *Red Petrograd. Revolution in the Factories, 1917–1918.* Cambridge, Eng., 1983.

———. "Craft Consciousness, Class Consciousness: Petrograd, 1917." *History Workshop Journal*, no. 11 (1981), pp. 33–56.

Smolin, I. S. "Bor'ba peterburgskikh rabochikh za 8-chasovoi rabochii den' v gody pervoi russkoi revoliutsii." *Istoriia rabochego klassa Leningrada*, II (L., 1963), pp. 113–31.

———. "Pervaia russkaia revoliutsiia v Peterburge." *Ocherki istorii Leningrada*, III (L., 1956), pp. 223–409.

Somov, S. I. "Iz istorii sotsialdemokraticheskogo dvizheniia v Peterburge v 1905 godu." *Byloe*, 4 (16) (Apr. 1907), pp. 22–55; 5 (17) (May 1907), pp. 152–78.

Spisok fabrik i zavodov evropeiskoi Rossii. SPb., 1903. [At head of title: Ministerstvo Finansov.]

Spisok fabrik i zavodov Rossii 1910 g. Po offitsial'nym dannym fabrichnago, podatnogo i gornago nadzora. M., SPb., Warsaw, n.d. [At head of title: Ministerstvo Finansov i Ministerstvo Torgovli i Promyshlennosti.]

Sputnik izbiratelia na 1906 god. Osvoboditel'noe dvizhenie i sovremennyia ego formy. SPb., [1906?].

Statistika neschastnykh sluchaev s rabochimi v promyshlennykh zavedeniiakh podchinennykh nadzoru fabrichnoi inspektsii za 1904 god. SPb., 1907. [At head of title: Ministerstvo Torgovli i Promyshlennosti. Otdel promyshlennosti.]

Steinberg, Mark D. "Consciousness and Conflict in a Russian Industry. The Printers of St. Petersburg and Moscow, 1885–1905." Ph.D. diss., Univ. of California, Berkeley, 1987.

Stolpianskii, P. N. *Zhizn' i byt peterburgskoi fabriki za 210 let ee sushchestvovaniia 1704–1914 gg.* L., 1925.

Strumilin, S. G. "Promyshlennye krizisy v Rossii (1847–1907)." In *Ocherki ekonomicheskoi istorii Rossii i SSSR* (M., 1966), pp. 414–58.

Sulimov. "Vospominaniia obukhovtsa (1900–1903 gg.)." *Proletarskaia revoliutsiia*, no. 12 (1922), pp. 145–69.

Surh, Gerald D. "Workers in 1905: Strikes, Workplace Democracy, and Revolution." Ph.D. diss., Univ. of California, Berkeley, 1979.

———. "Petersburg's First Mass Labor Organization: The Assembly of Russian Workers and Father Gapon." *Russian Review*, 40, no. 3 (July 1981), pp. 241–62; 40, no. 4 (Oct. 1981), pp. 412–41.

Suslova, F. M. "Peterburgskie stachki 1895–1896 godov i ikh vliianie na razvitie massovogo rabochego dvizheniia," *Istoriia rabochego klassa Leningrada*, II (L., 1963), pp. 49–91.

Sverchkov, D. F. *G. S. Nosar'-Khrustalev (opyt politicheskoi biografii).* L., 1925.

———. *Na zare revoliutsii.* M., 1921.

———. "Soiuz soiuzov." *Krasnaia letopis'*, no. 3 (14) (1925), pp. 149–62.

Sveshnikov, N. *Peterburgskie Viazemskie trushchoby i ihk obitateli. Original'nyi ocherk s natury.* SPb., 1900.

Sviatlovskii, V. V. *Professional'noe dvizhenie v Rossii.* SPb., 1907.

———. "Iz istorii S.-Peterburgskogo Tsentral'nogo Biuro Professional'nykh rabochikh soiuzov." *Trud Tekhnika*, no. 1–2 (27 Jan. 1907), cols. 5–18.

Syromiatnikova, M. "Rabochee dvizhenie na zavodakh Peterburga v mae 1901 g." *Krasnyi arkhiv*, 3 (76) (1936), pp. 49–66.

Taimi, A. P. *Stranitsy perezhitogo.* 3d ed. Petrozavodsk, 1955.

Takhtarev, K. M. *Rabochee dvizhenie v Peterburge (1893–1901 gg.). Po lychnym vospominaniiam i zametkam.* 4th ed., L., 1924.

Tarasov, V. "Bol'shevistskaia organizatsiia i Sestroretskie rabochie v 1905 godu." *Krasnaia letopis',* no. 1 (16) (1926), pp. 105–30.

Thompson, E. P. *The Making of the English Working Class.* New York, 1963.

Timofeev, P. *Chem zhivet zavodskii rabochii.* SPb., 1906.

———. "Ocherki zavodskoi zhizni," *Russkoe bogatstvo,* nos. 9, 10 (1905).

———. "Zavodskie budni (Iz zapisok rabochego)," *Russkoe bogatstvo,* nos. 8, 9 (1903).

Tret'ii s"ezd RSDRP. Aprel'-mai 1905 goda. Protokoly. M., 1959.

Trotskii, N. [L. D.] *Iz istorii odnogo goda. II. Intelligentsiia.* SPb., n.d. [1906].

———. *Politicheskie siluety,* vol. 8 of *Sochineniia.* M.-L., 1926. [Sketches of Nosar' and P. A. Zlydnev, pp. 190–208.]

Trotsky, Leon. *1905.* Trans. Anya Bostock. New York, 1972.

Trud v Rossii. See *Arkhiv istorii truda v Rossii.*

Tsytsarin, V. "Vospominaniia metallista." *Vestnik truda,* no. 12 (61) (Dec. 1925), pp. 34–40.

Tugan-Baranovskii, M. *Russkaia Fabrika.* 6th ed. M.-L., 1934.

1905 god v Peterburge. Vypusk I: Sotsialdemokraticheskie listovki. Edited by S. N. Valk, F. G. Matasova, K. K. Sokolova, and V. N. Fedorova. L., 1925. [At head of title: Otdel Leningradskogo Gubernskogo Komiteta RKP (b) po izucheniiu istorii Oktiabr'skoi revoliutsii i RKP (b) i komissiia Leningradskogo Gubernskogo Ispolnitel'nogo Komiteta Sovetov Rabochikh, Krest'ianskikh i Krasnoarmeiskikh Deputatov po organizatsii prazdnovaniia 20 letiia revoliutsii 1905 goda.]

1905 god v Peterburge. Vypusk II: Sovet Rabochikh Deputatov. Sbornik materialov. Edited by N. I. Sidorov. L., 1925. [At head of title: Otdel Leningradskogo Komiteta RKP (b) po izucheniiu istorii Oktiabr'skoi revoliutsii i RKP (b). . . .]

1905. Istoriia revoliutsionnogo dvizheniia v otdel'nykh ocherkakh. Ed. M. N. Pokrovskogo. 3 vols. M., 1925–27. [At head of title: Komissiia TsIK SSSR po organizatsii prazdnovaniia 20-letiia revoliutsii 1905 g. i Istpart TsK VKP (b).]

1905. Vospominaniia chlenov SPB Soveta Rabochikh Deputatov. Ed. P. F. Kudelli and G. L. Shidlovskii. L., 1926. [At head of title: Otdel Leningradskogo Gubernskogo Komiteta RKP (b) po izucheniiu istorii Oktiabr'skoi revoliutsii i RKP (b). . . .]

Ushakov, A. V. *Revoliutsionnoe dvizhenie demokraticheskoi intelligentsii v Rossii 1895–1904.* M., 1976.

Valk, S. N. "Obshchestvennoe dvizhenie v Peterburge v 90-kh i nachala 900-kh godov." In *Ocherki istorii Leningrada.* (M.-L., 1956), III, pp. 147–222.

Varnashev, N. M. "Ot nachala do kontsa s gaponovskoi organizatsiei (Vospominaniia)." In V. I. Nevskii, ed., *Istoriko-revoliutsionnyi sbornik* (L. 1924), I, pp. 177–208.

Varzar, V. E. *Statistika stachek rabochikh na fabrikakh i zavodakh za 1905 god.* SPb., 1908. [At head of title: Ministerstvo Torgovli i Promyshlennosti. Otdel promyshlennosti.]

————. *Statisticheskie svedeniia o stachkakh rabochikh na fabrikakh i zavodakh za desiatiletie 1895–1904 goda.* SPb., 1905. [At head of title: Ministerstvo Torgovli i Promyshlennosti. Otdel promyshlennosti.]

Vasil'ev, P. "Ushakovshchina." *Trud v Rossii,* no. 1 (1925), pp. 143–52.

Verner, Andrew M. "Nicholas II and the Role of the Autocrat." Ph.D. diss., Columbia Univ., 1983.

Vinogradov, V. P. "Iz istorii 1905 goda na Metallicheskom zavode." In *O revoliutsionnom proshlom peterburgskogo Metallicheskogo zavoda (1886–1905) Sbornik* (L., 1926), pp. 33–51.

Volkovicher, I. "Iiun'skie dni v Lodzi." In M. N. Pokrovskii, ed., *1905. Istoriia revoliutsionnogo dvizheniia v otdel'nykh ocherkakh* (M.-L., 1925), vol. II, pp. 168–79.

Von Laue, T. H. "Russian Labor Between Field and Factory, 1892–1903." *California Slavic Studies,* no. 3 (1964), pp. 33–65.

————. *Sergei Witte and the Industrialization of Russia.* New York and London, 1963.

Vserossiiskaia politicheskaia stachka v oktiabre 1905 goda. Chast' pervaia. Edited by L. M. Ivanov et al. M.-L., 1955. [A volume in the series *Revoliutsiia 1905–1907 gg. v Rossii. Dokumenty i materialy.*]

Vtoroi s"ezd RSDRP. Iiul'-avgust 1903 goda. Protokoly. M., 1959.

Vvedenskii, S. [D. M. Sverchkov]. "Noiabr'skaia zabastovka." In *Istoriia Soveta Rabochikh Deputatov g. S.-Peterburga* (SPb., 1906), pp. 201–16.

Vysshii pod"em revoliutsii 1905–1907 gg. Vooruzhennye vosstaniia noiabr'-dekabr' 1905 goda. Chast' pervaia. Edited by A. L. Sidorov et al. M., 1955. [A volume in the series *Revoliutsiia 1905–1907 gg. v Rossii. Dokumenty i materialy.*]

Walkin, Jacob. *The Rise of Democracy in Pre-Revolutionary Russia. Political and Social Institutions Under the Last Three Czars.* London, 1963.

Ward, Benjamin. "Wild Socialism in Russia: The Origins." *California Slavic Studies,* no. 3 (1964), pp. 127–48.

Wildman, Allan K. *The Making of a Workers' Revolution. Russian Social Democracy, 1891–1903.* Chicago, 1967.

Woytinsky, W. [V. Voitinskii]. *Gody pobed i porazhenii. Kniga pervaia: 1905-yi god.* Berlin, Petersburg, Moscow, 1923.

Zelnik, Reginald E. *Labor and Society in Tsarist Russia. The Factory Workers of St. Petersburg, 1855–1870.* Stanford, Calif., 1971.

————. "The Peasant and the Factory." In Wayne S. Vucinich, ed., *The Peasant in Nineteenth Century Russia* (Stanford, Calif., 1968), pp. 158–90.

————. "Populists and Workers. The First Encounter between Populist Students and Industrial Workers in St. Petersburg, 1871–74." *Soviet Studies,* 24, no. 2 (Oct. 1972), pp. 251–69.

————. "Russian Bebels: An Introduction to the Memoirs of the Russian

Workers Semen Kanatchikov and Matvei Fisher." *Russian Review*, 35, no. 3 (July 1976), pp. 249–89; 35, no. 4 (Oct. 1976), pp. 417–47.

———. "Russian Workers and the Revolutionary Movement." *Journal of Social History* (Winter 1972–73), pp. 214–36.

Zharnovetskii, K. "Kronshtadtskie vosstaniia v 1905–1906 gg." *Krasnaia letopis'*, 3 (14) (1925), pp. 48–102.

Zlydnev, P. A. "Sudebnaia rech' P. A. Zlydneva." *Krasnaia letopis'*, 5 (38) (1930), pp. 35–46.

Zubatov, S. V. "Zubatovshchina." *Byloe*, no. 4 (26) (1917), pp. 157–78.

Zvezdin, V. "Poslednie dni Soveta (26 noiabria–3 dekabria)." In *Istoriia Soveta Rabochikh Deputatov g. S.-Peterburga* (SPb., 1906), pp. 170–200.

NEWSPAPERS AND JOURNALS
(1905 unless otherwise stated)

Golos izvozchika, 1906
Iskra, 1900–1905
Izvestiia Soveta Rabochikh Deputatov
Listok bulochnikov i konditerov, 1906
Nachalo
Novoe vremia, 1904–6
Osvobozhdenie, 1904–5
Pechatnyi vestnik, 1905–6

Pravo
Proletarii
Rabochii golos
Rabochii po metallu, 1906
Revoliutsionnaia Rossiia
Russkaia gazeta
Severnyi golos
Syn Otechestva
Vpered

Index

Library of Congress Cataloging-in-Publication Data

Surh, Gerald Dennis.
  1905 in St. Petersburg : labor, society, and revolution / Gerald
D. Surh.
    p.   cm.
    Bibliography: p.
    Includes index.
    ISBN 0–8047–1499–1 (alk. paper) :
    1. Labor and laboring classes—Russian S.F.S.R.—Leningrad—
Political activity—History—20th century.   2. Strikes and
lockouts—Russian S.F.S.R.—Leningrad—History—20th century.
3. Soviet Union—History—Revolution of 1905.   I. Title.
HD8530.L52S87   1989   88–38696
322'.2'0947453—dc 19   CIP